UNIVERSITY OF NEBRASKA PRESS • LINCOLN AND LONDON

INDIAN SLAVERY in COLONIAL AMERICA

Edited and with an introduction

by Alan Gallay

Chapter 2, "Indian Slavery in Colonial New England," by Margaret Ellen Newell © 2009 Margaret Ellen Newell.

Chapter 3, "A Little Flesh We Offer You: The Origins of Indian Slavery in New France," by Brett Rushforth, originally appeared in *William and Mary Quarterly* 60, no. 4: 777–808.

Chapter 4, "South Carolina's Entrance into the Indian Slave Trade," by Alan Gallay, is adapted from Alan Gallay, *The Indian Slave Trade: The Rise of the English Empire in the American South*. New Haven CT: Yale University Press, 2002. Copyright © 2002 by Yale University Press. Used by permission of the publisher.

Chapter 9, "'We Betray Our Own Nation': Indian Slavery and Multi-ethnic Communities in the Southwest Borderlands," is adapted from "'Lest We Go in Search of Relief to Our Lands and Our Nation': Customary Justice and Colonial Law in the New Mexico Borderlands, 1680–1821," by James Brooks, in *The Many Legalities of Early America*, edited by Bruce H. Mann and Christopher L. Tomlins. Published for the Omohundro Institute of Early American History and Culture. Copyright © 2001 by the University of North Carolina Press. Used by permission of the publisher.

Indian slavery in colonial America / edited and with an introduction by Alan Gallay.
p.   cm.
Includes bibliographical references and index.
ISBN 978-0-8032-2200-7 (cloth : alk. paper)
1. Indian slaves—United States—History. 2. Indian slaves—North America—History. 3. Slavery—United States—History—Colonial period, ca. 1600–1775. 4. Slavery—North America—History—17th century. 5. Slavery—North America—History—18th century. 6. Slave trade—United States—History. 7. Slave trade—North America—History. 8. Indians, Treatment of—United States—History. 9. Indians, Treatment of—North America—History. I. Gallay, Alan.
E98.S6153 2009
973.04'97—dc22
2009026124

Set in Quadraat and Quadraat Sans by Bob Reitz.
Designed by R. W. Boeche.

Contents

Maps

Introduction
Indian Slavery in Historical Context
Alan Gallay

In 1702 Pierre Le Moyne d'Iberville, attempting to establish the new French colony of Louisiana, tried to broker a peace between the two most powerful peoples in the region, the Choctaws and the Chickasaws. Although over 700 miles away, the English in South Carolina had destabilized the entire Lower Mississippi Valley by setting in motion a trade in Indian slaves. Along the Mississippi River, and extending west as far as Texas, south to the Gulf of Mexico, and east into the interior of the Southeast, native peoples turned on one another—sometimes old enemies, but frequently people with whom they'd had no quarrel, perhaps had not even known—and captured them for transportation overland to Charles Town, South Carolina, for export to transatlantic ports. With no settlers or soldiers within 700 miles, the English had exerted formidable influence in the region from which they benefited profitably. The money accrued from Indian slaves taken in the Old Southwest, as well as from thousands of victims in Florida, the Carolinas, and elsewhere, was used to capitalize what became a hugely successful plantation regime in the mainland English colonies.

For the infant French colony to succeed, the French had to end English influence in the region—to separate the English from their chief ally, the Chickasaws. At a meeting with the Chickasaws, Iberville lectured and scolded them: the English had exploited the Chickasaws for their own purposes by setting them to slave upon the Choctaws. For the previous eight to ten years, at English "instigation," the Chickasaws had "taken more than 500 prisoners and killed more than 1,800 Chaquetas. Those prisoners were sold; but taking those prisoners," Iberville reminded the Chickasaws, "cost you more than 800 men, slain on various war parties, who would be living at this moment if it had not been for the English." All the English cared about, Iberville assured the Chickasaws, were "blood and slaves." He derided Chickasaw ignorance of that fact that their own captives were sold by their enemies to the English, who sent them into slavery in the West Indies. The "ultimate plan of the Englishman," he warned, "after weakening you by means of wars, is to come and seize you in your villages and then send you to be sold somewhere else, in faraway countries from which you can never return, as the English have treated others, you know."[1]

The spread of Indian slavery that accompanied European settlement of North America had tremendous impact on native peoples, not just the enslaved, as Iberville noted, but on the slavers too. Slavery itself existed in Native America before European arrival, but the scale altered considerably when Europeans organized an international slave trade in American Indian slaves that led to the decimation of entire groups and depopulation of large areas. The surviving native peoples underwent dramatic political, cultural, and economic changes. Those not killed in raids faced the worst fate: lifelong misery as slaves.

The Study of Indian Slavery

When Almon Wheeler Lauber published *Indian Slavery in Colonial Times within the Present Limits of the United States* (1913), the scholarly community treated it as an interesting aside, but hardly worth additional study despite Lauber marshaling an impressive array of evidence pointing to the ubiquity of Indian enslavement by European colonists.[2] Perhaps this occurred for teleological reasons: African slavery became the prevalent form of labor in the United States, so how important could Indian slavery have been? Perhaps, too, examination of Indian slavery would have forced scholars away from the dominant paradigms of Native American history—the loss of land from Euro-American encroachment, the societal and cultural up-heaval experienced by native peoples, and the resistance of Indians to the "civilizing" offers of the United States.

As the essays in this volume make clear, Indian slavery was not peripheral in the history of Native America, but central to the story. Indian slavery and slaving adds new context and elaboration to a host of larger narratives—the loss of land and autonomy by native groups, the entry of native peoples into the international market economy, and the evolution of native polities and social systems. Study of the wide-scale enslavement of Native Americans also beckons us to reconsider the nature, forms, and impact of European colonialism, empire-building, and capitalistic devel-opment in the Atlantic world.

Over the last sixty years great strides have been made in the study of transatlantic slavery. Data collecting and methodological sophistica-tion have increased our knowledge of the character and breadth of the internal slave trade in Africa and the external slave trade to the Americas. Diaspora studies are revealing the nature of the cultural transformation of Africans in the Americas, the varieties of slave experience, and the re-ligious, communal, and familial impact of slavery on both the enslaved and their masters.[3] Study of Indian enslavement provides new context for understanding the enslavement of Africans in Africa and the Americas, and the evolution of race and racism as historical concepts and ideologies in the Atlantic world. Too often racialization of Native Americans and Africans is analyzed separately and sequentially. The European construc-tion of indigenous Americans as "others"—savage heathens inhabiting a dangerous wilderness that threatened the souls and bodies of Euro-Americans—is usually deemed too different from the creation of Africans as others to warrant comparison. Yet both Indians and Africans were depicted as savage heathens, with comparative reference made to their skin color, nudity, and other characteristics allegedly denoting racial inferiority and barbarism. Since Indians and Africans presumably were encountered in different ways—the first in their own villages and on the "warpath," the Africans as chattel slaves mostly laboring on plantations, there seemed little need for comparison beyond a few superficialities that both were viewed

3

by Europeans as inferiors. But when we consider that so many natives were kept as slaves, sharing the same condition with the vast majority of Africans in America, we must reexamine racialization in early America. Although Africans and Indians for the most part *were* viewed differently, they received similar treatment, often were described with similar labels, and frequently were lumped together by law.

Of course Africans and Native Americans were vastly different peoples. Likewise there was great cultural diversity within Native America and Africa. In our modern world, when viewing the past, many expect Africans and Native Americans to have thought and acted in racialized ways. We express surprise that Africans did not unite against European slave traders in Africa, and that Indians did not ban together against European settlers—almost as if enslavement or defeat were their own fault. Not only were the differences too great, and the enmities too strong, for peoples in Africa or the Americas to unite as one, but the very same can be said of Europeans, who, despite their shared identity as Christians, would not and could not unite together against Africans or Native Americans. The competition between Europeans took precedence over unity—they had no reason to unite against Africans or Native Americans. Similarly, enmities and alliances among Africans and American Indians often held precedence in their lives and precluded unity of each against Europeans—cultural differences also may have been too much to overcome. Race as a concept possessed by early modern peoples was ambiguous, though more fully realized and important to Europeans than to Africans and Native Americans. Africans, Americans, and Europeans recognized difference in each other, culturally and physically—but these differences, even when they became obsessions, did not forge unity strong enough to overcome the disagreements and hostilities that existed within their own larger cultural grouping. Nationalism, ethnicity, and religious and tribal affiliations greatly shaped self-identity and hostilities toward others. This is not to say that racism and racial identification were of no importance, only that a multitude of factors and experiences forged the imaginative lives and behaviors of individuals and groups in the first centuries of European colonialism.

Although early modern peoples did not unite along presumed

racial lines, racism did play a central role in the European enslavement of American Indians and African peoples. Racism took many forms; at its worst it identified particular peoples as inferior and deserving of enslavement. Racist feelings and thoughts were subject to an array of contingencies, however, that forestalled it becoming an ideology until late in the colonial period. Thus we must consider racism as but one factor in the processes by which people became slaves. Large historical forces and local contingencies shaped both the slave trades and the practice of slavery. The cross-oceanic immigration of millions of people, the international transport and exchange of goods, ideas, technologies, and microbes, and the organization of European empires and private interests to exploit Africa and the Americas—all these played considerable roles in making slavery the preeminent economic institution of the early modern Atlantic world. Yet even these forces do not reveal the entire story of slaving. The capture and sale of an American Indian in northern New England differed from the capture and sale of a person in Texas, or Hispaniola, or the Gold Coast, making generalization about slave trading as difficult to hazard as generalization about Europeans, Africans, and American Indians.

A remarkable variety of experiences distinguished slaving by region and colony, while the life of a slave differed not only by location, but the nature of work, the size of the labor force, and the temperament and power of the owner. The slaves themselves also differed one from the other. The experience of those born into slavery, at least psychologically, varied considerably from those born into freedom. But the realities of slavery also varied considerably. Slaves in Spanish colonies possessed legal rights denied them in British and Dutch colonies.[4] Physical treatment tended to be extremely brutal in the West Indies compared to in New England. In all cases slavery meant a denial of freedom, but degrees of autonomy and privilege in slavery did not necessarily mean more or less contentment. An artisanal slave living in better physical circumstances than a plantation slave could have been just as apt to run away or rebel. We can generalize that the overwhelming majority of slaves wished they were free, but sharing a condition as slaves did not necessarily create unity in the slave quarters. Competition and resentments fostered hostility. Ethnicity divided slaves, whether Angolans from Bantu people in South Carolina, or in Boston, where southern Indian slaves ran away and committed crimes together, though infrequently alongside New England Indians or African slaves.[5] Analysis of the diversity of the slave experience, the many slave trades, the processes of enslavement, and the variety in character, circumstance, and purpose by which people became slavers or captives, masters or slaves, increases our understanding of the multitude of ways that humanity survived and perpetuated oppression within slavery, and the historical forces they all contended with in the early modern world.

The study of Indian slavery opens pathways to further address slavery's meaning for individuals and these historical forces. It offers vantage points for exploring the meaning, substance, and form of Indian-European relations in virtually every colony, the varied responses to colonialism among native peoples, and new ways for examining the relations that existed between and within native groups. We can then compare the practice of Indian slavery from one region to the next as a way of assessing differences and similarities among peoples and colonies. Wherever Indian slavery occurred on a significant scale the institution had tremendous impact. This compels us to rethink colonies' and regions' histories. Imperial and proprietary directives, and colonial laws, barred or limited Indian enslavement, yet the porousness of these laws calls into question colonists' assertions that they lived under the "rule of law." The widespread and illicit abuse of Indian labor provides a lens for examining the insouciance and weakness of imperial governments' control over their colonies. Empires have been measured by the degree of authority they wielded over colonists, whose resistance to trade laws, taxes, and religious and social policies is viewed almost as a "market adjustment" inevitable from the great distance between the imperial center and the colonial periphery. Perhaps it is time to consider an alternative paradigm of colonies largely controlling their own destinies, and making adjustments only to keep the imperial center from interfering with local control. Certainly colonists' drive to control indigenous labor displays tension between center and periphery. The Spanish government, in particular, contested colonial policies in regard to native labor, sometimes successfully, sometimes not, although its policies changed over time and varied in different geographic regions of the empire; the British rarely asserted themselves—whether from lack of power or concern is only a secondary issue—British colonists largely constructed their own Indian policies, including those concerning labor. In both instances, Spanish and British colonists and local officials largely succeeded at instituting economic systems from which they profited greatly by indigenous labor.

Indian slavery and slaving also forces us to reexamine the internal histories of native peoples. For some indigenous peoples, we know little beyond their victimization as slaves or their activities as slavers. For many Indians, their engagement in slaving, or their victimization, was the critical moment in their history. Using North America above Mexico as an example, the powerful native confederacies of the American South—Choctaws, Chickasaws, Cherokees and Creeks—all formed largely as a result of slaving. The histories of the Comanches, Apaches, Utes, and other southwestern peoples were indubitably shaped by slaving. Indian slavery adds clarity to the "Middle Ground" in the Great Lakes region, the sexual dynamics of European and native diplomacy in Texas, and the crumbling of the Spanish missions in Florida. In New England, seventeen Indian slaves comprised a key component of the ship's cargo that opened Massachusetts' trade with the Caribbean. Indian slavery was an important part of the story of the key event in seventeenth-century New England history, King Philip's War, and no less of a significant moral and political figure than Roger Williams, de facto leader of Rhode Island, at several points in his life had to make crucial moral and political decisions regarding the enslavement of Indians. Indian slavery played a critical role in fomenting Bacon's Rebellion in Virginia—the watershed event in Virginia's colonial history—and directly led to the pan-Indian Yamasee War, which not only almost wiped out South Carolina, but is arguably the most important event in South Carolina history before the American Civil War.

Slavery in Historical Perspective

To understand the practice and significance of Indian slavery, we must contextualize slavery itself. Slavery was a common institution in human history and remained so in the early modern world. But there is a huge

privileges based on birth, and ethnic divisions between themselves and "others" that denoted superiority of the one and inferiority of the other. In the "natural" order, bloodlines defined a person's place in society, and though in some indigenous cultures there was a rough equality among members, equality itself was an irrelevant concept. Kinship, ethnicity, tribal affiliations, and gender defined the social order.

To say that slavery was common and widely perceived as the natural condition for a portion of humanity is not to excuse its practice, nor dismiss its impact upon its victims. Instead, it helps us contextualize and understand how slavery became the most important economic institution of European colonialism in the Atlantic world. Europeans did not introduce slavery to the New World, but they did introduce a large internal and external slave trade, creating societies based on the exploitation of human labor. The results were catastrophic for its victims and for entire societies, while also of the first importance in the creation of the "modern" world. Slave trading and New World slavery fueled the building of European empires, and the rise of capitalism and industrialization.[16] The mass enslavement of peoples, while generating much of the wealth and superstructure of the modern world, also contributed to, and initiated, many of its problems—displacement and diaspora, ideologies of race and racism, colonialism and imperialism, environmental degradation, and impoverishment of indigenous peoples. Until we solve the problems that are the legacy of slavery and colonialism, study of these institutions remains relevant.

We must, however, not de-historicize the past through presentism. There are those, for instance, who wish to ignore or hide the fact that the enslavement of Africans in Africa, at least during the first centuries of the international slave trade, almost entirely was conducted by Africans and not Europeans. The fear of discussing and publicizing this "complicity" arises from the belief that slavery was solely a crime committed by whites upon blacks (or Europeans upon Africans), and that showing non-European participation in slaving undermines the historical critique of European imperialism and colonialism as fostering a racism whose intent was the subjugation of nonwhite peoples. But the facts do not undermine the critique. As noted earlier, Africans, like Europeans and Native Americans, had no reason to form racial solidarity with people along lines of skin color. The active participation of Africans in the slave trade as slavers, and the ownership of Africans by Africans, does not alter the fact that Europeans made their form of slavery one based on race: almost entirely, only non-Europeans would be enslaved (though certainly some Europeans considered the propriety of enslaving poor Europeans, and many European servants were treated as slaves within the New World plantation complex).[17] The historical matrix that created race-based slavery arose from a confluence of forces in which the factor of race was, at least at the onset of New World colonization, difficult to distinguish from other sources of hostility toward "others." To unravel the racialization of Africans by Europeans, we must consider more broadly *who* became slaves in the early modern Atlantic world.

Today most people are under the mistaken assumption that "slave" and "African" were synonymous in the early modern world, and that the enslavement of non-Africans only occurred, if at all, peripherally. Europeans, it is presumed, were not enslaved. Yet from the 1530s through the 1780s, over one million Europeans were held as slaves in North Africa, and hundreds of thousands more were kept in bondage under the Ottomans in eastern Europe and Asia.[18] In the mid-seventeenth century, more English were held as slaves in Africa than Africans were kept as slaves in English colonies.[19] Slavery was not the peculiar condition of any particular people in the early modern world, but in the Western world would become generally associated with Africans, and over time, particularly in the eighteenth and nineteenth centuries, an ideology of racism developed to justify African enslavement. This later development should not obscure the foundations of New World slavery as a widespread and ubiquitous institution of the Atlantic world that victimized Europeans and Native Americans, as well as Africans.

Slavery and New World Colonialism

European mass enslavement of non-Europeans in the New World began with Columbus's arrival in Hispaniola. By 1493, Columbus had initiated a trade in indigenous American slaves, which the Spanish extended over the next two decades in their conquests of Puerto Rico, Jamaica, and Cuba. The quest for slave labor even led the Spanish to places they had no intention of settling. Juan Ponce de Leon invaded the Bahamas to procure natives for enslavement elsewhere. By the time Ponce de Leon reached Florida in 1513, on another slaving foray, word had preceded him of Spanish intentions and, for the first time, New World native peoples greeted the Europeans with violence upon initial contact.[20]

The story of Spain's entry into the New World is often presented as an epic drama of courage and discovery, with unfortunate consequences for the native population owing to disease, ignorance, and misunderstanding. An alternative version emphasizes the greed, xenophobia, and racism of the European invaders who maliciously abused indigenous peoples and spread a swath of destruction through the Americas. Spanish overseas expansion indeed was characterized by ignorance and cruelty, and native peoples were victimized intentionally and unintentionally. It would be a mistake, however, to single out the Spanish as more malevolent than other Europeans in the New World, for the colonizing experiences of all the Europeans—Spanish, Portuguese, French, Dutch, English, Danes, and Swedes, among others—displayed a great deal of malevolence, greed, racism, and xenophobia. Each European empire developed its own policies and practices that distinguished one from the other, but the forms of colonialism within these empires varied by time and place, and from a host of contingencies.

The Spanish were not inalterably or invariably cruel in their conquests of America. The administration of colonies and their interactions with native peoples displayed immense variance. In New Mexico, for instance, Spain constructed an array of policies that treated native peoples differently, one group from the next.[21] Similar variance can be seen in the other European empires. Demography, geography, relative military power, and an array of economic, political, and social conditions forced Europeans to adapt to each locale they settled, and to each group of people they encountered.

With all of the variation within colonialism there were important similarities. Colonialism revolved around the exploitation of natural resources.[22] Europeans developed the New World's rich agricultural lands to produce staple crops for use at home and for sale abroad. They also undertook intensive mining to extract precious metals. Governments, private companies, and individuals sought wealth through an array of other extractive industries, notably forestry, fishing, trapping, and dye making. To achieve their ends of maximizing profits, the Europeans required large numbers of laborers. Those in a position to exploit New World resources sought not only a sufficiently large work force to undertake heavy labor, often under inhospitable and dangerous conditions, but workers who could be driven extraordinarily hard. Especially in the sixteenth and seventeenth centuries, on the sugar plantations of Brazil and the West Indies, and in the American mines, laborers were worked to death, providing profits great enough to allow masters easy purchase of replacements.

African slave labor filled many needs, but America's indigenous peoples also were forced to work as slaves, or through coercive labor levies. Unable to procure large numbers of indigenous laborers, the Europeans turned to poor Europeans: indentured servants, criminals, political prisoners, and prisoners of war.[23] Many of the bonded servants expected freedom on fulfillment of their terms of service, but masters often worked them to death. Racism undoubtedly played a role in the abuse of non-European laborers, but the poor treatment of European workers displays the preeminence of profit in the plantation complex—masters grossly exploited whomever they could. Distant from the laws, institutions, and social controls of the mother countries that regulated master-worker relations, New World masters acted with impunity as sovereigns over their work force. Treatment of European workers in the New World, later in the colonial period, improved as imperial and local governments took stronger measures to protect laborers; simultaneously, English colonial governments codified brutal treatment of slaves, while in the Iberian empires many laws were enacted to protect slaves.

One is tempted to say that most slaves were treated no better than animals, but in fact animals often received better treatment—an observation made by many contemporaries. Not until the mid-eighteenth century did growing numbers of New World masters perceive their slaves in more paternalistic ways—they continued to exploit their workers for profit, but as the price of replacements rose they considered that improved treatment might lead to greater profits. Masters also saw that natural increase among slaves improved their property holdings and enlarged the legacy they could provide their children. Profits guided masters' behavior in almost all cases—at least until pangs of conscience and guilt infiltrated the great house. What seems so remarkable in retrospect is how long it took for Euro-American masters to conceive of the basic humanity of those they owned.

The story of New World colonialism is a story where slavery occupies a central place. Without slavery most colonies would have remained small outposts. Without slavery the Europeans might not have built empires in the New World—certainly they would have taken very different forms. New England, indeed, succeeded without slavery as its primary labor source, but the region's economic success owed to its participation in an Atlantic-world economy that hinged on slave-produced goods. New Englanders actively engaged in the international slave trade, processed slave-produced sugar into rum, and supplied slave colonies with food and lumber. In the French empire, slavery was not the central form of labor in New France. But the value of Canada to France was inconsiderable compared to the slave-based sugar islands of the West Indies. Spain, too, settled areas where slavery was relatively unimportant—but many of these peripheral regions were colonized primarily to protect more important areas of the empire, where the Spanish used slavery and other forms of forced labor to produce the commodities that maintained the empire. Slavery came later to many of these long-established central areas of the empire, when the demographic collapse of the indigenous population made the importation of slave labor feasible to develop local plantation economies. The Spanish empire in the Americas could have persisted without slavery, but not without tribute labor.

Without slavery the movement of European peoples to the New World would have been hindered. Slave-produced goods from the Americas took up most of the cargo space on the transit to Europe. For the return voyage, manufactured goods occupied comparatively less space, which led ship owners to offer relatively inexpensive passage—otherwise they would have had to carry more ballast. Just as important, the opportunity to own slaves and produce staple crops, or to work in related trades, provided a major incentive for Europeans to move to the Americas. In summary, without slavery, many colonies would have withered on the vine. The European powers would have made little attempt to develop New World empires. The limited economic opportunities would have deterred migration, except for those seeking land for mere subsistence. Conceivably, immigration to the New World would have been characterized by trickles.

The use of slaves in colonizing the Americas was logical in the colonial mind. As already noted, the precedents for employing slave labor were there for all to see. Slaves could be obtained by purchase or capture. Purchase implied a legal right to own the slave—the onus was on the slaves to prove their right to freedom. Laws protecting Africans from European enslavement were almost entirely nonexistent, and those that protected Native Americans often were disregarded. Those who felt the need to justify bondage beyond their legal ownership declared the enslaved inferior or deserving of punishment. Inferiority was stamped as a badge on people who were different on ethnic grounds, or possessors of other perceived cultural, racial, or physical traits that designated them as deserving of subordination. These designations, however, often occurred after the fact of enslavement. The basic rationale employed by Europeans, Africans, and Native Americans: slavery was the just desserts of war captives. All considered that sparing the captives' life entitled the captor to keep the individual as a slave. Slavery, then, was a by-product of war. The Europeans, however, did not capture Africans in war. They rationalized that other Africans had done so, and they had then purchased legitimate slaves. As with enslavement of Native Americans, whether made captive by themselves or others, Europeans conveniently ignored the long-held belief in Europe that slaves should be made of only those taken in a "just war"—whereas the overwhelming majority of first-generation slaves in European colonies were taken captive in wars conducted primarily to obtain slaves.[24]

The Europeans could have enslaved their European war captives—and indeed, occasionally they shipped these captives to labor in the New World, or imprisoned at hard labor enemy captives taken in the Americas. But Europeans largely focused their efforts on non-Europeans. Racism and availability identified who should be enslaved. They deemed Africans and Americans "savages," and most importantly, "heathens"—non-Christians deserving no better fate than slavery. (European slave owners conveniently disregarded that their African slaves might be Christians or Muslims when they arrived in the Americas, and instead focused on other aspects of their alleged inferiority.) There existed less division among Europeans concerning the irredeemability of Africans, than Native Americans. Although the Portuguese missionized Africans in Kongo and Angola, for the most part, in the first centuries of colonialism, European missionization efforts were far greater among Native Americans than Africans. The Spanish, famously, created missions and hoped to Christianize their charges by degrees, a tactic followed by other Catholic powers. Protestants displayed much less interest in converting Indians, and when they did so seemed more interested in completely transforming them into Europeans. They tried to alter their dress and gender roles, instill in them European notions of property, and completely discard all vestiges of Indianness.[25] There were, of course, dissenting views on what to do with Indians. Some Europeans thought that native societies should be left alone. Other Europeans abandoned their own societies to become Indians. Whatever good will or hopes some Europeans held toward Native Americans, those who wished to prevent the exploitation of their labor rarely had the power or will to prevent abusive treatment by others.

European Enslavement of Native Americans and Africans in the New World

European empire building in the New World began with the "discovery" of gold in Hispaniola, but the conquest of Mexico with its stores and mines of gold committed the empire to expansion. Instead of providing a new passage to the Indies and access to Asia's exotic goods, the newly discovered Americas were found to possess their own valuable commodities. The search for precious metals led to spectacular success with the silver mines of Peru, but also to disastrous failures. The quest for gold and silver led the Spanish and other Europeans to seek nonexistent treasure cities like Cibolla in the American Southwest and El Dorado in South America. Several large Spanish expeditions entered Florida, each an unmitigated disaster—all hoping to repeat the success of Mexico and Peru. The most famous of these was Hernan De Soto's entrada (1539–1542) of over 600 that traversed the greater part of the American Southeast (while Coronado simultaneously looked for Cibolla in a lengthy foray that extended from California to Kansas). A veteran from the conquest of Peru, De Soto had views of Native Americans that were made evident in his preparations to wrest riches from America: he brought the iron implements necessary to secure coffles of slaves. But it was the broader spectrum of De Soto's treatment of Native Americans, in the context of his seemingly pointless wandering, that proved a scandal in Spain. Except for a store of pearls, no riches were located. Spanish sovereignty had not been placed over an inch of new land, but worse, an outcry arose over the expedition's alienation of native peoples, one after the other, by sadism and violence that included murder, rape, maiming, and enslavement. The conquistadors horrified not only the natives, but many in Spain, as the conquistadors had not distinguished between friendly and hostile Indians, turning on those who welcomed them with friendship and hospitality. The De Soto entrada led to a reassessment of goals and methods in Spanish overseas expansion. Calls for reform in the treatment of native peoples, led by the priest Bartolomé de Las Casas, received support from King Philip II, who put an end to the age of the conquistador. In future Spanish expeditions, the king demanded that the cross accompany the sword, and religious were sent to America to bring the heathen to Christianity. Colonization of new lands, for the glory of Christ and Spain, rather than self-aggrandizement of private interests, was *supposed* to guide the extension of Spain's New World empire. To that end, enslavement of native peoples was prohibited. Later in his life Las Casas rued that he had not called for prohibitions of African slavery as well, despite his early support of it as a substitute for American slavery.[26]

Despite the ban, Spanish colonials continued to enslave native peoples, sometimes outright, but often by creating new categories of unfree labor that varied from place to place dependent upon local circumstances. When the Spanish had power to demand workers from dependent native peoples—a form of tribute often called *encomienda*—they forced Indians to labor in rotation for specific periods of time.[27] At its worst the *encomienda* made the indigenous peoples into de facto slaves who worked in the mines and in the fields, producing crops for trade and in support of the military, the religious, the government, and private individuals. They built forts, roads, and housing. The Spanish archives are filled with letters and petitions from Indians and their supporters (especially sympathetic priests) protesting forced labor. The inability of the mother country to prevent abuses of Indians was common in all the European empires. Local government officials and colonists could not resist the money to be made from buying and selling Indians and their labor.

The colonizers' demands for labor could not be entirely met by indigenous people, particularly after European-introduced epidemic diseases produced a catastrophic demographic decline in the American Indian population in densely populated areas, such as Mexico and coastal Peru. The development of the most valuable of all American crops, sugar, led to a shift at the end of the sixteenth century from mining to plantations as the key to wealth for large numbers of Europeans in the Americas, particularly where the indigenous population had greatly declined. Sugar became the defining crop of colonialism—the linchpin around which the Portuguese, French, Spanish, English, Dutch, and Danes built their New World empires. Sugar cultivation created an insatiable demand for workers in the Caribbean, where the indigenous population had been decimated from disease, warfare, and enslavement, and in Brazil, which developed the largest of all plantation complexes. The obvious source for new laborers lay in West Africa because of the available supply and its propinquity to the American colonies.

Contrary to popular perceptions of slavery, African labor did not entirely replace the labor of Native Americans, who continued to comprise the bulk of the workforce in many colonies, and a significant proportion in some places where African slavery flourished. Yet a mythology arose in the Western world to explain the ostensible replacement of Native American with

African labor. Natives, the story goes, were physically inferior to Africans and could not perform the difficult physical tasks of plantation slavery. Moreover, familiarity with the terrain allowed Indians greater ease to escape than Africans. Indians also succumbed to disease, and presumably were too proud to wear chains and tolerate ownership by another, and thus withered and died. Africans, on the other hand, presumably were used to the demands of agriculture in hot countries and made natural slaves, as in their homelands they lived in societies where "big men" forced them into subservience. The most racist version of this scenario posited that Africans preferred being slaves.

It is true that Native Americans died in large numbers from European-borne diseases, and native peoples could more easily escape enslavement than Africans in places where they had familiarity with the terrain. But Native Americans often were transported as slaves to distant colonies, and long-term exposure to Europeans reduced susceptibility to disease. Not that either of these factors mattered much to sixteenth- and seventeenth-century slavers and slaveholders, as they rarely considered that any slave would last an extended number of years, and merely hoped to earn as great a profit as they could during the slave's expected short-term life. Only in places where there were limited opportunities for replacement laborers, or among slaveholders who possessed only one or a few slaves, and thus lived on the margin of profitability, can we expect to see concern for preservation of human chattel—at least until the value of slaves rose so high that even with replacements available masters sought to preserve their valuable bondpeople.

American Indians continued to be enslaved through the centuries of colonialism because there were profits to be made from their labor. Masters were skilled at forcing the belligerent and non-cooperative to work—whether the workers were Indian, African, or European. For instance, gender conventions among many native peoples proscribed that women, not men, should perform the bulk of agricultural labor; this did not prevent slaveholders from successfully forcing native men to work in the fields. Neither was there anything peculiar in the inherent or cultural make-up of Africans to make them a desirable alternative as slaves—the

African slave trade became the central form of labor in the European empires because of the *availability* of Africans for enslavement. There were not enough available American Indians, nor poor Europeans to fill labor demands.

After the widespread enslavement of American Indians in Latin America in the sixteenth century, Spanish colonials had turned to various forms of forced labor to evade the imperial prohibition on American Indian slavery. In this second stage of enslavement of Native Americans, other European powers established colonies, and they too enslaved American Indians through the remainder of the colonial era. The essays in this volume focus on the second stage in much of the area of the future United States.

The Indian Slave Trade in North America

It is appropriate here to offer a few observations comparing the European trade in Native American slaves in North America with the simultaneous trade of Africans in Africa. In both, the indigenous peoples largely were responsible for the capture of victims for sale to the Europeans. A significant difference: in Africa, a large intra-continental slave trade preceded the arrival of Europeans, which had no parallel in the Americas. For centuries this trade conveyed Africans from sub-Saharan Africa to North Africa. Moreover, in West Africa, which became the main supplier of Africans to the European Atlantic colonies, slaves were a major form of property—the victims of warfare and slave raiding. Many highly organized African societies possessed a surplus of slaves, which they traded to obtain European goods.[28] In contrast, although American Indians kept slaves, slavery was not a significant part of the economy in most American societies.

The character of the slave trade with Europeans in Africa and North America depended on geography, demography, and the extent of European military power. In Africa, the Europeans maintained their presence through isolated coastal forts. Outside of Portuguese Kongo and Angola, few Europeans settled in the slave-trading areas, in part because of fear of malaria, but also because of the strength of African polities that made colonization difficult. The European coastal forts did not have to protect vulnerable colonists and they also exerted minimal power in the larger region. They primarily functioned as way stations for slaves before their exportation, while providing a modicum of security for the Europeans against other Europeans. The forts' survival and ability to trade generally depended on the good will of local African rulers, who charged a variety of taxes to the Europeans competing for the trade.[29]

In the Americas, the Europeans could employ their substantial military power to capture and enslave Indians in the West Indies—the Europeans could easily scour many of these islands for victims. On the American mainland, however, European military power was more limited and thus frequently dependent on native allies. This was especially true north of Mexico, where virtually all the European colonies relied on natives for defense and the conduct of military operations. In Peru and elsewhere in South America, the Europeans possessed a clear advantage in weaponry. Steel swords, in particular, did much damage in combat, and natives lacked the weaponry to counter. Bolstered by Native American alliances, the Spanish had relatively quick success in subduing large centralized native polities in Mexico and Peru.[30] European military technology also gave them superiority at sea where they could employ large ships outfitted with cannon to transport slaves throughout the Atlantic world. They also constructed substantial coastal forts in the Americas to protect against invaders by sea, and to provide refuge against land-based forces.[31] But the Native American slave trade was not conducted, for the most part, at these coastal forts. Moreover, these forts provided little to no protection for inland settlements. Indigenous invaders could destroy towns, farms, and plantations, and usually ignored heavily populated coastal areas. Inland forts almost always were constructed of wood and provided only limited security. They could be burned or circumvented by raiders. Mainland colonies thus required native allies to secure far-flung settlements against hostile natives and Europeans. To conduct offensive operations, the Europeans ordinarily enlisted native troops familiar with the terrain, who moved more easily than Europeans in pursuit of enemies, and generally were more skilled at the type of strategies and tactics necessary for success in the inland continent. Not until the French and Indian War (1754–1761), termed in Europe the Seven Years' War (1757–1763), did the Europeans possess significant numbers of troops and experience in the area of the future United States to successfully conduct large-scale military expeditions on their own against powerful native groups, though there were a few exceptions before this time period.

North of Mexico, the Europeans generally lacked the necessary personnel and military capability to procure Indian slaves away from the coast. The Europeans also faced American Indian peoples highly skilled in the bow and arrow as an effective weapon in the terrain of the eastern woodlands. For Europeans to succeed militarily in the inland continent, they required native allies, who almost always comprised the bulk of soldiers—whether the purpose was to obtain slaves or otherwise.[32] Even then, capture of natives was difficult. Native women and children fled before European troops, finding refuge in well-hidden and difficult-to-access havens; native armies adeptly ambushed European forays into their country. (The English had more success going against Spanish mission Indians in Florida because the Indians lived in more confined environments—but even then native guides and soldiers were the key to success for the invaders.) Europeans thus relied upon native allies to do their bidding, which was also cost-effective given the expense of moving European and colonial soldiers long distances. Even under joint operations it was not unusual for Europeans to accede to native directives, strategies, and tactics; the Europeans recognized native military superiority, but also natives often refused to fight under European direction. This underwent some alteration in the eighteenth century, as Europeans became more skilled, or thought they were, in the warfare necessary for the inland continent, but natives still persisted in refusing to fight under conditions they judged disadvantageous and frequently abandoned invasions. Whether in New Mexico or Texas, along the Mississippi or in Florida, New England or Iroquoia, the capture of indigenous people for sale to the Europeans largely was conduced by native peoples, and less frequently by European armies where natives comprised the more significant military contingent.

The motives of native slavers varied. Through slaving, American Indians gained European alliance and access to a network of slaving allies. Additionally, they received weaponry and other highly valued trade goods.

Refusal to join in the slaving left a group vulnerable to attacks by the slaving allies of the Europeans. Simply put, in places where slaving reached frenzied proportions, natives had to choose between becoming slavers or being enslaved themselves. It was not unusual for groups engaging in slaving to become victimized themselves, and for victimized groups to become slavers. Slaving broke old friendships and increased the numbers of one's enemies, even as it propagated opportunities for new alliances.

Slaving was not always a matter of survival and a way to secure a group against enemies. Some slavers' primary motive lay in the desire to obtain European trade goods—and they not only went against enemies, but against distant people they did not know. Arguably these raiders could have been dependent on European goods, and slaving might have been the only way—or at least the easiest way—to obtain slaves, but many natives undertook slaving before dependency had occurred. Many native peoples desired European trade goods, and not just weaponry, but labor-saving tools such as metal knives, axes, and pots, as well as woolen blankets and clothing.

Securing alliances, gaining trade goods, and defending against the danger of their own enslavement were three major reasons why natives became slavers, but the essays in this volume explore other reasons as well, reasons whose roots lie within indigenous societies. As we have seen, the capture and enslavement of humans was not new to most indigenous peoples. The purpose of these forays was not to obtain slaves, but part of a larger cultural matrix that involved achieving revenge against enemies. Indians' personal and group motives often took precedence over European market conditions as factors when Indians agreed to become slavers for Europeans, but likely there was a combination of these and other motives.

There were many paths to enslavement. Capture in raids was but one path. Within European colonies, where natives lived under difficult circumstances, they could be enslaved through a variety of means. Mission Indians in Florida, the Southwest, and elsewhere in the Spanish empire often were forced to work against their will with little or no monetary compensation. In New England, courts forced Native Americans found guilty of minor crimes into a lifetime of servitude. Natives could also be enslaved for debt, or reclassified as Africans and enslaved in places where

Indian slavery had become illegal. It was not unusual for "friendly" Indians to be kidnapped and sold into slavery.

Many of the Indian slaves captured in North America were shipped to the West Indies to work as agricultural laborers. Others remained in North America and were employed in any number of tasks. In urban areas like Boston and Portsmouth, Indian slaves were domestic servants, unskilled laborers, and trained as artisans—ownership extended across a broad spectrum of society from ministers to merchants, from rope makers to sailors.[33] On the Spanish missions, natives generally worked in the fields, as carriers, and on construction projects. In New Mexico, the Spanish also created *genizaros* modeled on the Turkish Janissaries—soldier-slaves given land for their families, but whose status remained as slaves.[34] With labor the key to wealth in the New World, slaves, bonded servants, and the working poor could be put to any number of tasks for commercial, subsistence, and military purposes.

The Europeans in North America above Mexico were more apt to consider the morality of enslaving free Indians, and to keeping Indians as slaves, than to consider the propriety of enslaving Africans. Certainly in the seventeenth century few colonials, particularly in the plantation and mining economies, gave much thought to enslavement of Africans. Virtually all Africans in the colonies were slaves, so that colonists thought slavery a natural condition for Africans. But Native Americans lived in and outside colonial settlements as free people—to enslave them meant to transform their status from free to unfree. Many Europeans thought it reprehensible to withdraw freedom from an individual except as punishment for crime or as the just desserts of war captives. Even among the slavers there was division between those who believed only enemy Indians should be enslaved, and those who considered all Indians as potential slaves. Encountering free natives led many to feel pangs of conscience over the enslavement of some, or to oppose their enslavement outright. Some hoped to missionize and Europeanize Indians, and ultimately to assimilate them into their society. But by the early eighteenth century, many Euro-Americans had given up hopes of assimilating native peoples. Increasingly colonists thought Indians irredeemable savages, and it was also clear that most natives did not want to assimilate, especially under European terms. Concurrently Europeans began considering the assimilation of African slaves, not to the end of providing freedom, but to "civilize" them to their condition as slaves through Christianization.[35] Although some Europeans truly worried over the fate of African souls, and of their own souls for not providing their charges with the opportunity of achieving salvation, they hoped that Christianization would make their slaves more manageable and less dangerous.[36] Perhaps it was no coincidence that the Christianization of African bondpeople became popular as imports from Africa reached a crescendo in the second and third quarters of the eighteenth century, partly as a response to the growing threat of rebelliousness in the slave quarters that led to the burning of plantations, the poisoning of masters, and outright rebellions in South Carolina and New York, as well as suspected conspiracies in other colonies. By the mid-eighteenth century, the import of hundreds of thousands of Africans, and the natural increase of enslaved Africans led Euro-Americans to conceive of slavery as nearly synonymous with African peoples.[37] Simultaneously the number of Native American slaves declined. Florida, New England, Virginia, and other coastal areas had lost much of their native population, largely through warfare, disease, enslavement, and outright removal.

The capture of native peoples declined east of the Mississippi when most Indians refused to participate in large-scale slaving. In the American South, the recently formed Indian confederacies, which included both the victims of slaving and the slavers themselves, saw how slaving had weakened them and refused to undertake wars to obtain slaves. They obtained European trade goods through hunting animals rather than humans, and also forged diplomatic strategies of not growing too close to any European power by doing their bidding—instead they played the Europeans against one another.[38] They used their formidable military power as a wedge to get European goods in the form of presents to insure their "good behavior." The growing imperial competition between France and Britain, particularly in the North, also precluded wars to obtain slaves, as the Europeans feared alienating native peoples who could then support the other side. Moreover, the Iroquois tended to incorporate captives into their society as replacements for those lost during the long and devastating "Iroquois

Wars."[39] Many of the Iroquois' Algonkian neighbors were too diffuse and perhaps disorganized to undertake slaving on a grand scale. After decades of warfare, they, too, desired peace. Indian slavery persisted north of the Ohio River, and natives were captured and sold from the St. Lawrence Seaway through the Missouri country, but there were fewer expeditions to obtain slaves. Overall, as slave raiding declined east of the Mississippi, it increased in the Southwest, as Spanish traders out of Texas and New Mexico, and French traders operating from New Orleans into the Missouri country, employed natives to go slaving.

The essays in this book vary in intent. Some explore the development of Indian slavery in specific colonial contexts, while others assess the impact and varieties of bondage upon particular groups of natives. None profess to be definitive studies of any particular group, place, or issue involving Indian slavery—but all contribute to our understanding of slavery's importance in the early modern Atlantic world.

The focus of this collection is on the seventeenth and eighteenth centuries. The enslavement of Native Americans did not end in the eighteenth century—not until the American Civil War did the U.S. government institute a program to eradicate Indian slavery in Utah and Colorado, and enslavement continued in California well into the 1870s.[40] In the East, American Indians labored as slaves on plantations from Virginia to Texas throughout the antebellum period. Indian slavery also flourished in the nineteenth-century Pacific Northwest, particularly among aboriginal peoples. One of the most famous Native Americans of the nineteenth century, Sacajawea, was a slave. Coverage of nineteenth-century Indian slavery, in general, however, has been excluded from this volume—it would make the book unwieldy while introducing an array of issues that would overcomplicate our initial attempts to come to terms with the evolving character of Indian slavery alongside of the establishment of colonial societies in North America above Mexico.

This collection also has a geographic "tilt" to the southeast and southwest in the coverage of Indian slavery. In part this results from more archival research and scholarship having been produced on these regions.

James F. Brooks, *Captives and Cousins: Slavery, Kinship, and Community in the Southwest Borderlands* (2002), and Alan Gallay, *The Indian Slave Trade: The Rise of the English Empire in the American South, 1670–1717* (2002), provided a foundation for scholars to undertake specialized studies of Indian slavery in these regions, some of which are presented in this book. Forthcoming books by two authors with essays in this volume—one on Indian slavery in New England, by Margaret Newell, and one on New France, by Brett Rushforth—should pave the way for expansion of studies in those areas. Likewise we can expect more work in the coming years on Indian slavery in the trans-Mississippian region, as new books by Carl Ekberg and Kathleen Du Val have laid the groundwork.[41] This volume only peripherally treats the colonies of New Netherland/New York and Pennsylvania, as they have yet to attract scholars to undertake sustained work in the primary sources—though we know that Indian slavery and an Indian slave trade were present in the Mid-Atlantic colonies.

With so much left to uncover on Indian slavery in early America, it is still too early to take full measure of its entire significance. With each new study we are learning so much more about the life experiences of individuals and groups, the centrality of slaves and slaving in various places, and the relationship of Indian slavery to the overall development of colonial America. The challenge for future scholars lies not only in digging deeper and in new areas, which will be valuable in and of itself, but the erasing of the binary paradigms by which many practitioners of historical study and the public understand early America. The European-versus-African and European-versus-Indian tropes used to compartmentalize colonial America have cast a distorting veneer upon the past. A nuanced reckoning of Indian slavery will not only help us understand the material, political, economic, social, and diplomatic foundations of early America, it will provide new ways for understanding how Americans envisioned their past, present, and future.

Notes

1. The author gratefully thanks Kenneth J. Andrien and Carolina Coleman for their helpful comments on this essay. Richebourg Gaillard McWilliams, trans. and ed., *Iberville's Gulf Journals* (University of Alabama Press, 1981), 172.

2. Almon Wheeler Lauber, *Indian Slavery in Colonial Times within the Present Limits of the United States* (1913; repr., Williamstown MA: Corner House, 1979).

3. The best bibliographies on slavery are Joseph C. Miller, *Slavery and Slaving in World History: A Bibliography, 1900–1991*, 2nd ed. (Armonk NY: M. E. Sharpe, 1999) and *Slavery and Slaving in World History: A Bibliography, Vol. 2, 1992–96* (Armonk NY: M. E. Sharpe, 1999).

4. For the history of slave law in the Americas, see Alan Watson, *Slave Law in the Americas* (Athens: University of Georgia Press, 1989); Thomas D. Morris, *Southern Slavery and the Law, 1610–1860* (Chapel Hill: University of North Carolina Press, 1986); Lauren Benton, *Law and Colonial Cultures: Legal Regimes in World History, 1400–1900* (New York: Cambridge University Press, 2001); Hugh Thomas, *The Slave Trade* (New York: Simon & Schuster, 1997); John H. Elliott, *Empires of the Atlantic World: Britain and Spain in America, 1492–1830* (New Haven: Yale University Press, 2006).

5. There is a huge and growing literature on the African diaspora and the impact of ethnicity among Africans in the Americas. Some good places to start include Linda M. Heywood, ed., *Central Africans and Cultural Transformations in the American Diaspora* (Cambridge: Cambridge University Press, 2002); James H. Sweet, *Recreating Africa: Culture, Kinship, and Religion in the African-Portuguese World, 1441–1770* (Chapel Hill: University of North Carolina Press, 2006); Gwendolyn Midlo Hall, *Slavery and African Ethnicities in America: Restoring the Links* (Chapel Hill: University of North Carolina Press, 2005); Paul E. Lovejoy and David V. Trotman, eds., *Trans-Atlantic Dimensions of Ethnicity in the African Diaspora* (London: Continuum, 2003); Walter C. Rucker, *The River Flows On: Black Resistance, Culture, and Identity Formation in Early America* (Baton Rouge: Louisiana University Press, 2006). For discussion of ethnicity and its relationship to rebellion in South Carolina, see Mark M. Smith, ed., *Stono: Documenting and Interpreting a Southern Slave Revolt* (Columbia: University of South Carolina Press, 2005). On Southern Indian slaves in Boston, see Alan Gallay, *The Indian Slave Trade: The Rise of the English Empire in the American South, 1670–1717* (New Haven: Yale University Press, 2002).

6. Defining "slave" and coming to term with the great variety of slave systems in human history often has been of more concern to anthropologists than historians. For an introduction to the difficulties and problems, see James L. Watson, ed., *Asian and African Systems of Slavery* (Berkeley: University of California Press, 2000) and Claude Meillassoux, *Anthropology of Slavery: The Womb of Iron and Gold*, trans. Alide Dasnois (Chicago: University of Chicago Press, 1991).

7. Orlando Patterson, *Slavery and Social Death: A Comparative Study* (Cambridge: Harvard University Press, 1982).

8. On Roman slavery, see Keith R. Bradley, *Slaves and Masters in the Roman Empire: A Study in Social Control* (New York: Oxford University Press, 1984); Keith Hopkins, *Conquerors and Slaves* (New York: Cambridge University Press, 1978); Thomas Wiedemann, *Greek and Roman Slavery* (Baltimore: Johns Hopkins University Press, 1981).

9. For Viking slavery in Iceland, see Carl O. Williams, *Thraldom in Ancient Iceland* (Chicago: University of Chicago Press, 1937); Barry Cunliff, *Facing the Ocean: The Atlantic and Its Peoples 8000 BC–AD 1500* (Oxford: Oxford University Press, 2001); but also see Ruth Mazo Karras, *Slavery and Society in Medieval Scandinavia* (New Haven: Yale University Press, 1988).

10. For slavery in the Ottoman Empire, see Bernard Lewis, *Race and Slavery in the Middle East* (New York: Oxford University Press, 1990); Ehud R. Toledano, *Slavery and Abolition in the Ottoman Middle East* (Seattle: University of Washington Press, 1998); Daniel Goffman, *The Ottoman Empire and Early Modern Europe* (Cambridge: Cambridge University Press, 2002); Colin Imber, *The Ottoman Empire, 1300–1650: The Structure of Power* (New York: Palgrave Macmillan, 2002);

Cemal Kafadar, *Between Two Worlds: The Construction of the Ottoman State* (Berkeley: University of California Press, 1995).

11. On the history of African slavery in Portugal before expansion to the Americas, see A. C. de C. M. Saunders, *A Social History of Black Slaves and Freedmen in Portugal, 1441–1555* (Cambridge: Cambridge University Press, 1982). For the linkage between sugar production and slavery, particularly among the Iberian powers in both old and new world settings, see the important collection of essays in Stuart B. Schwartz, ed., *Tropical Babylons: Sugar and the Making of the Atlantic World, 1450–1680* (Chapel Hill: University of North Carolina Press, 2004). Other important works examining the first stages of European slavery of Africans include Charles Verlinden, *The Beginnings of Modern Colonialism: Eleven Essays with an Introduction* (Ithaca: Cornell University Press, 1970); Robin Blackburn, *The Making of New World Slavery: From the Baroque to the Modern, 1492–1800* (London: Verso, 1997); Patrick Manning, *Slavery and African Life: Occidental, Oriental and African Slave Trades* (Cambridge: Cambridge University Press, 1990.

12. Paul E. Lovejoy, *Transformations in Slavery: A History of Slavery in Africa*, 2nd ed. (New York: Cambridge University Press, 2000); John Thornton, *Africa and Africans in the Making of the Atlantic World*, 2nd ed. (New York: Cambridge University Press, 1998); Joseph C. Miller, *Way of Death: Merchant Capitalism and the Angolan Slave Trade, 1730–1830* (Madison: University of Wisconsin Press, 1988); Stuart B. Schwartz, *Sugar Plantations in the Formation of Brazilian Society: Bahia 1550–1835* (Cambridge: Cambridge University Press, 1985); Herbert S. Klein, *African Slavery in Latin America and the Caribbean* (New York: Oxford University Press, 1986); Herbert S. Klein, *The Atlantic Slave Trade* (New York: Cambridge University Press, 1999); David Eltis, *The Rise of African Slavery in the Americas* (New York: Cambridge University Press, 2000); Barbara Solow, ed., *Slavery and the Rise of the Atlantic System* (New York: Cambridge University Press, 1991); Philip D. Curtin, *The Rise and Fall of the Plantation Complex*, 2nd ed. (New York: Cambridge University Press, 1999); Robert C. Davis, *Christian Slaves, Muslim Masters: White Slavery in the Mediterranean, the Barbary Coast, and Italy, 1500–1800* (New York: Palgrave Macmillan, 2003).

13. Inga Clendinnen speculates on the Aztec use of slaves for both labor and ritualistic purposes in *Aztecs* (New York: Cambridge University Press, 1991). See also Michael E. Smith, *Aztecs* (Cambridge: Blackwell Publishers, 1996). On Aztec conquests and tribute, see Ross Hassig, *Aztec Warfare: Imperial Expansion and Political Control* (Norman: University of Oklahoma Press, 1988) and *Trade, Tribute, and Transportation: The Sixteenth-Century Political Economy of the Valley of Mexico* (Norman: University of Oklahoma Press, 1985).

14. Leland Donald, *Aboriginal Slavery on the Northwest Coast of North America* (Berkeley: University of California Press, 1997).

15. James F. Brooks, *Captives and Cousins: Slavery, Kinship, and Community in the Southwest Borderlands* (Chapel Hill: University of North Carolina Press, 2002), 31–35, 45–46.

16. The classic work on the economic significance of slavery and the international slave trade to the economic development of the Western world is Eric Williams, *Capitalism and Slavery* (Chapel Hill: University of North Carolina Press, 1944, reprint 1994). For a collection of essays discussing Williams's thesis, see Barbara L. Solow and Stanley L. Engerman, eds., *British Capitalism and Caribbean Slavery: The Legacy of Eric Williams* (Cambridge: Cambridge University Press, 1987), but also see Russell R. Menard, "Reckoning with Williams: Capitalism and Slavery and the Reconstruction of Early American History," *Callaloo* 20 no. 4 (1997), 791–99; Kenneth Morgan, *Slavery, Atlantic Trade and the British Economy, 1660–1800* (Cambridge: Cambridge University Press, 2000) and Eltis, *Rise of African Slavery*. Williams's critique of the

importance of European imperialism to the modern world should be supplemented and compared with Immanuel Wallerstein, *The Modern World System: Capitalistic Agriculture and the Origins of the European World Economy in the Sixteenth Century* (New York: Academic Press, 1974) and Eric R. Wolf, *Europe and the People Without History* (Berkeley: University of California Press, 1982).

17. See, for instance, Edmund S. Morgan, *American Slavery, American Freedom: The Ordeal of Colonial Virginia* (New York: W. W. Norton, 1975).

18. For an excellent history of Europeans held as slaves in North Africa, see Davis, *Christian Slaves, Muslim Masters*. Narratives of English enslavement can be found in Daniel J. Vitkus, ed., *Piracy, Slavery, and Redemption* (New York: Columbia University Press, 2001).

19. Linda Colley, *Captives: The Story of Britain's Pursuit of Empire and How Its Soldiers and Civilians Were Held Captive by the Dream of Global Supremacy, 1600–1850* (New York: Pantheon Books, 2002).

20. Recent books on the early stages of Spanish conquest include Hugh Thomas, *Rivers of Gold: The Rise of the Spanish Empire, from Columbus to Magellan* (New York: Random House, 2004); Henry Kamen, *Empire: How Spain Became a World Power, 1492–1763* (New York: HarperCollins, 2003); Elliott, *Empires of the Atlantic World*. For a provocative comparison of Spain and other European powers taking possession of land in the Americas, see Patricia Seed, *Ceremonies of Possession in Europe's Conquest of the New World* (Cambridge: Cambridge University Press, 1995).

21. The literature on the variability of Spanish policies is immense, but some key examples are Edward H. Spicer, *Cycles of Conquest: The Impact of Spain, Mexico, and the United States on the Indians of the Southwest, 1533–1960* (Tucson: University of Arizona Press, 1962); Inga Clendinnen, *Ambivalent Conquests: Maya and Spaniard in Yucatan, 1517–1570* (Cambridge: Cambridge University Press, 1987); Eugene H. Korth, *Spanish Policy in Colonial Chile: The Struggle for Social Justice, 1535–1700* (Stanford: Stanford University Press, 1968); Alexander Marchant, *From Barter to Slavery: The Economic Relations of Portuguese and Indians in the Settlement of Brazil, 1500–1580* (Baltimore: Johns Hopkins University Press, 1942); John Hemming, *Red Gold: The Conquest of the Brazilian Indians* (Cambridge: Harvard University Press, 1978); Barbara Ganson, *The Guaraní under Spanish Rule in the Río de la Plata* (Stanford: Stanford University Press, 2003); James Saeger, *The Chaco Mission Frontier: The Guaycuruan Experience* (Tucson: University of Arizona Press, 2000); Silvio Zavala, *New Viewpoints on the Spanish Colonization of America* (Philadelphia: University of Pennsylvania Press, 1943); Ramon Gutierrez, *When Jesus Came the Corn Mothers Went Away: Marriage, Sexuality, and Power in New Mexico, 1500–1846* (Stanford: Stanford University Press, 1991); David Weber and Jane Rausch, eds., *Where Cultures Meet: Frontiers in Latin American History* (Wilmington DE: SR Books, 1994).

22. For an excellent discussion of sixteenth-century Spanish views of natural resources in the Americas, see James Lockhart, "Trunk Lines and Feeder Lines: The Spanish Reaction to American Resources," in Kenneth J. Andrien and Rolena Adorno, eds., *Transatlantic Encounters: Europeans and Andeans in the Sixteenth Century* (Berkeley: University of California Press, 1991), 90–120. For English perceptions, somewhat formed by Spanish experience, see Peter C. Mancall, *Hakluyt's Promise: An Elizabethan's Obsession for an English America* (New Haven: Yale University Press, 2007).

23. Pieter Cornelis Spierenburg, *The Prison Experience: Disciplinary Institutions and Their Inmates in Early Modern Europe* (New Brunswick: Rutgers University Press, 1991); Eltis, *Rise of African Slavery*; Hilary Beckles, *White Servitude and Black Slavery in Barbados, 1627–1715* (Knoxville: University of Tennessee Press, 1989); Peter Wilson Coldham, *Emigrants in Chains: A Social History of*

Forced Emigration to the Americas of Felons, Destitute Children, Political and Religious Non-Conformists, Vagabonds, Beggars and other Undesirables, 1607–1776 (Baltimore: Genealogical Publishing Co., 1992); David W. Galenson, *Traders, Planters, and Slaves: Market Behavior in Early English America* (Cambridge: Cambridge University Press, 1986) and *White Servitude in Colonial America: An Economic Analysis* (Cambridge: Cambridge University Press, 1982).

24. There are many works that explore the development of the rationales and justifications for African enslavement. A good starting place is David Brion Davis, *The Problem of Slavery in Western Culture* (Ithaca: Cornell University Press, 1966) and *Slavery and Human Progress* (New York: Oxford University Press, 1984). See also Winthrop D. Jordan, *White over Black: American Attitudes toward the Negro, 1550–1812* (Chapel Hill: University of North Carolina Press, 1968); and Elliott, *Empires of the Atlantic World*.

25. James Axtell, *The Invasion Within: The Contest of Cultures in Colonial North America* (New York: Oxford University Press, 1985).

26. There are numerous studies of the De Soto entrada. The best place to start is Charles Hudson, *Knights of Spain, Warriors of the Sun: Hernando De Soto and the South's Ancient Chiefdoms* (Athens: University of Georgia Press, 1997). For the evolution and change in Spanish "reform" of their American empire, see Lewis Hanke, *The Spanish Struggle for Justice in the Conquest of America* (Philadelphia: University of Pennsylvania Press, 1949); Korth, *Spanish Policy in Colonial Chile*. For Las Casas, see Bartolomé de Las Casas, *An Account, Much Abbreviated, of the Destruction of the Indies with Related Texts*, ed. with an introduction by Franklin W. Knight, trans. Andrew Hurley (Indianapolis: Hackett Publishing Company, 2003); Juan Friede and Benjamin Keen, eds., *Bartolomé de Las Casas in History: Toward an Understanding of the Man and his Work* (DeKalb: Northern Illinois University Press, 1971); David M. Traboulay, *Columbus and Las Casas: The Conquest and Christianization of America, 1492–1566* (Lanham MD: University Press of America, 1994); Ralph H. Vigil, "The Expedition of Hernando De Soto and the Spanish Struggle for Justice," in Patricia Galloway, ed., *The Hernando de Soto Expedition: History, Historiography, and "Discovery" in the Southeast* (Lincoln: University of Nebraska Press, 1997).

27. For the use of slave and other forms of forced native labor by the Spanish in their New World empires, see Lolita Gutiérrez Brockington, *The Leverage of Labor: Managing the Cortés Haciendas in Tehunantepec, 1588–1688* (Durham: Duke University Press, 1989); Jeffrey A. Cole, *The Potosí Mita: Compulsory Indian Labor in the Andes* (Stanford: Stanford University Press, 1985); Linda A. Newson, *Life and Death in Early Colonial Ecuador* (Norman: University of Oklahoma Press, 1995); William L. Sherman, *Forced Native Labor in Sixteenth-Century Central America* (Lincoln: University of Nebraska Press, 1979); Juan A. Villamarin and Judith E. Villamarin, *Indian Labor in Mainland Spanish America* (Newark: University of Delaware, 1975). For other works that specifically explore the encomieda, see Charles Gibson, *The Aztecs under Spanish Rule: A History of the Indians of the Valley of Mexico* (Stanford: Stanford University Press, 1964); Lesley Byrd Simpson, *The Encomienda in New Spain: The Beginnings of Spanish Mexico* (Berkeley: University of California Press, 1966); Troy S. Floyd, *The Columbus Dynasty in the Caribbean, 1492–1566* (Albuquerque: University of New Mexico Press, 1973).

28. The best overview is Thornton, *Africa and Africans*.

29. Thornton, *Africa and Africans* and John K. Thornton, *Warfare in Atlantic Africa, 1500–1800* (London: Routledge, 1999); Robert Harms, *The Diligent: A Voyage Through the Worlds of the Slave Trade* (New York: Basic Books, 2003); Robin Law, *Ouidah: The Social History of a West African Slaving Port, 1727–1892* (Athens: Ohio University Press, 2004).

30. For a first-rate assessment of the military dynamics and the role of technology in Spanish conquest, see John F. Guilmartin Jr., "The Cutting Edge: An Analysis of the Spanish

Invasion and Overthrow of the Inca Empire, 1532–1539," in Andrien and Adorno, *Transatlantic Encounters*, 40–69.

31. Geoffrey Parker, *The Military Revolution: Military Innovation and the Rise of the West, 1500–1800* (Cambridge: Cambridge University Press, 1988) and "The Artillery Fortress as an Engine of Overseas Expansion, 1480–1750," in *Success is Never Final: Empire, War and Faith in Early Modern Europe* (New York: Basic Books, 2002). For forts in North America, see the many entries in Alan Gallay, ed., *The Colonial Wars of North America, 1512–1763: An Encyclopedia* (New York: Garland, 1996).

32. Gallay, *Indian Slave Trade*.

33. Gallay, *Indian Slave trade*, chapter 11.

34. Brooks, *Captives and Cousins*.

35. A very good starting point for the dynamics of Christianization of Africans is Sylvia R. Frey and Betty Wood, *Come Shouting to Zion: African American Protestantism in the American South and British Caribbean to 1830* (Chapel Hill: University of North Carolina Press, 1998). But also see Jon Sensbach, *Rebecca's Revival: Creating Black Christianity in the Atlantic World* (Cambridge: Harvard University Press, 2005).

36. The classic study of masters' use of Christianity to bolster their own power within the slave system—and to salve their conscience—is Eugene D. Genovese, *Roll, Jordan, Roll: The World the Slaves Made* (New York: Pantheon, 1974). For the origins of this process in the eighteenth century, see Alan Gallay, *The Formation of a Planter Elite: Jonathan Bryan and the Southern Colonial Frontier* (Athens: University of Georgia Press, 1989). These should be supplemented with Albert J. Raboteau, *Slave Religion: The "Invisible Institution" in the Antebellum South* (New York: Oxford University Press, 1978).

37. On the evolution of African slavery in the mainland English colonies, see Peter H. Wood, *Black Majority: Negroes in Colonial South Carolina from 1670 through the Stono Rebellion* (New York: Norton, 1974); Ira Berlin, *Many Thousands Gone: The First Two Centuries of Slavery in North America* (Cambridge: Harvard University Press, 1998) and *Generations of Captivity: A History of African American Slaves* (Cambridge: Harvard University Press, 2003).

38. For a superb discussion of the Indian trade, see Kathryn E. Holland Braund, *Deerskins and Duffels: The Creek Indian Trade with Anglo-America, 1685–1815* (Lincoln: University of Nebraska Press, 1993).

39. On Iroquois incorporation of captives, see Daniel K. Richter, *The Ordeal of the Longhouse: The Peoples of the Iroquois League in the Era of European Colonization* (Chapel Hill: University of North Carolina Press, 1992).

40. L. R. Bailey, *Indian Slave Trade in the Southwest: A Study of Slave-Trading and the Taking of Captives* (Los Angeles: Westernlore Press, 1966); Sondra Jones, *The Trial of Don Pedro León Luján: The Attack Against Slavery and Mexican Traders in Utah* (Salt Lake City: University of Utah Press, 2002).

41. Carl J. Ekberg, *Stealing Indian Women: Native Slavery in the Illinois Country* (Urbana: University of Illinois Press, 2007); Kathleen DuVal, *The Native Ground: Indians and Colonists in the Heart of the Continent* (Philadelphia: University of Pennsylvania Press, 2006).

1. Indian Slavery in Colonial New England
Margaret Ellen Newell

In August of 1744, Dr. Alexander Hamilton, an Annapolis physician, passed through the southern Connecticut town of Norwalk. There he and his African slave, Dromo, aroused considerable attention. Hamilton noted that "the children were frightened att my negroe, for here negroe slaves are not so much in use . . . their servants being chiefly bound or indentured Indians."[1] Dr. Hamilton's observations highlight the fact that Native Americans formed an important part of New England's culture of slavery.[2] Throughout New England before 1700, and in some sub-regions thereafter—like the Norwalk of Hamilton's visit—Native American servitude was the dominant form of nonwhite labor. New England armies, courts, and magistrates enslaved more than 1,300 Indian men, women and children in the seventeenth century alone, and bound hundreds of others into finite terms of servitude in the eighteenth century. New Englanders also imported Indian slaves from other parts of North America (notably the Carolinas) and from the Caribbean. Some remained to labor in white households and fields, while the colonists exported hundreds of others in a tragic diaspora to Europe, the Mediterranean, the Wine Islands, and the Caribbean.

Despite this reality, we still know more about the handful of white captives among the Indians than we do about the thousands of Native Americans who served European masters.[3] There are several reasons why the history of Indian slaves and servants in New England remains obscure. Standard scholarly accounts of the region's labor economy generally stress

the colonists' tendency to rely on wage laborers, neighbors, white indentured servants, and their own large families for workers. In other words,
the supposition is that the New England colonists simply did not need
slave labor. While it is true that Indian slavery was not the dominant form
of labor in New England, forced Indian labor augmented white labor in
important ways. Two related myths—that Indians made poor servants,
and that Native Americans were exterminated or pushed out of southern
New England in the aftermath of King Philip's War in 1675–1676—have
further muddied their history.

Indian servitude as practiced in New England also presents
some conceptual challenges to traditional definitions of slavery in North
America. The precise legal status of Indian workers is sometimes hard
to determine. Indians in colonial New England could find themselves in
any of a number of forms of involuntary servitude and slavery. "Slavery"
and "servitude" were poorly defined terms in British America for much of
the seventeenth century, and New England was no exception. Contracts,
writs, and bills of sale often used them interchangeably. The legal codes
that defined slave status in the southern and Caribbean colonies beginning in the 1630s and 1640s came much later in New England, and were
less extensive. Some of the Indians I study were slaves, and some were
indentured servants. Some Indians voluntarily worked as day laborers
or contracted their labor to English masters for periods of time, and it is
often difficult to distinguish these more voluntary servants from those
who faced various forms of coercion. Chattel slavery and freedom were
at opposite ends of a broad spectrum, and many Indians occupied points
along that spectrum in varying degrees of unfreedom.

The ad hoc nature of Indian slavery and servitude in New England
did not soften its effects for its victims. Moreover, once enmeshed in relations of servitude, Native Americans who were putatively free, or bound
for finite terms, might find themselves in a state of de facto enslavement.
Owners frequently sought to convert Indian workers into de jure slaves;
enslavement persisted even after Indian slavery was officially outlawed.
And although, unlike slavery, servitude was not legally a permanent or
heritable state, some Indian families experienced a kind of serial servitude

that bound successive generations. Some masters asserted ownership over the children of Indian servants, seeking to transform them into slaves. Thus the experiences of Indians help illustrate the variety of systems of bondage in Early America and invite comparisons with other societies.

Indian slavery was not a frontier phenomenon in New England, unlike other regions of colonial America. Nor was it short-lived. As an institution, it flourished for nearly two centuries in some of the most densely populated areas of British North America. While a number of scholars have argued persuasively that the New England colonists arrived with (or quickly developed) a strong racialist attitude about Indian and African difference and inferiority, equally compelling evidence points to a more complex, evolving set of views regarding the Indians' nature and humanity.[4] Historian David Eltis contends that what made American slavery unique in historical terms was that European settlers drew a rigid line between "insiders"—people like themselves who could never be enslaved—and nonwhite, mostly African "outsiders" who could be subjected to enslavement.[5] But one of the unique features of Indian relations in southern New England is that the colonists and the Crown gradually asserted sovereignty over the native inhabitants during the seventeenth century, ironically transforming them into subjects with collective rights in land and other privileges that Africans did not enjoy. One of these privileges, commonly embodied in law after 1700, was a prohibition of Indian enslavement. In other words, the Indians of southern New England became legal insiders. Yet despite laws explicitly designed to protect Indians, forced servitude continued into the eighteenth century, and new forms of coercion augmented the traditional enslavement of prisoners of war that characterized the seventeenth century.

Even before the English planted colonies in New England, capture and enslavement of Indians marked the earliest contact between English projectors and the native inhabitants. Explorers frequently kidnapped Indians in the early 1600s for several reasons, including as proof of contact, and as a means of acquiring interpreters and guides for future expeditions. Captain George Waymouth, who visited the region in 1605, took four Abenakis to

London at the behest of Sir Fernando Gorges, the backer of the Sagada-hoc plantation in Maine. Gorges commissioned other kidnappings that he hoped would facilitate colonizing the New England coast, including the capture of a Martha's Vineyard sachem, Epenow. Parading captives as symbols of England's power and maritime empire, and exemplars of exoti-cism, became a feature of court life for the next century. Before turning him over to Gorges, Epenow's kidnappers displayed him as a physical marvel in London taverns and coffeehouses.[6] While most of these kidnappings were putatively strategic, some adventurers aimed at capturing slaves for profit. A member of John Smith's 1614 expedition to New England, Thomas Hunt, captured twenty-seven Pawtuxet and Nauset Indians on Cape Cod and "carried them with him to Maligo [Malaga] and there sold those silly Salvages for Rials of eight."[7]

Some of the captives died of disease or their wounds, others were recaptured by English rivals, and still others remained in slavery in Europe, but a few managed to return to New England, often as members of English-sponsored expeditions. Epenow escaped and rejoined his people, while Misquantum, or Squanto (who was kidnapped twice), played a more complex role, serving as crucial interpreter and go-between first for Gorges' lieutenants, and subsequently for the Pilgrims at Plymouth. As historian Neal Salisbury points out, these kidnappings drove some prospective English allies and trading partners into the arms of the French and generated suspicion and enmity among others.[8]

Enslavement of Indians in New England entered a new phase during the Pequot War of 1636–1637. The combined forces of Massachusetts, Connecticut, and Plymouth colonies, and their Niantic, Narragansett, and Mohegan Indian allies, defeated and decimated the Pequots, killing approximately 700, or nearly one out of four. The victors also divided the "bootie" of war, including Pequot territory, wampum, household goods—and captives. English and Indian forces executed many (mostly male) prisoners and divided the rest of the survivors, most of them noncombatants, as the war's human spoils. Victorious generals Israel Stoughton and Samuel Davenport remitted approximately 250 native captives to Connecticut and Massachusetts authorities in June and July of 1637 to "be disposed aboute in the townes" as household servants.[9] Not all of the captives remained in New England, however; of the prisoners brought to Boston, Governor John Winthrop noted that seventeen "male children" composed part of the cargo on the trading ship that initiated Massachusetts Bay Colony's much-desired trade with the Atlantic and Caribbean islands—a trade that became crucial to the colony's economic future.[10]

Was the wartime enslavement of Indians inevitable? In New Spain, questions about the humanity of Native Americans and the morality of enslaving them prompted extensive public debate and commanded the attention of both church and state.[11] These debates prompted a royal prohibition of Indian slavery in 1542, although the reality of *encomienda*, tribute demands, and forced labor drafts for mining and other operations approximated slavery for many of the native inhabitants of Spanish America. In contrast, the relative absence of public discourse or reference to precedent regarding the adoption of Indian slavery during the Pequot War in New England is striking, especially in the context of the Puritans' attention to matters of law. Many New Englanders would become involved in the transatlantic slave trade by the late seventeenth century, but they played an even more active role in the enslavement of Indians, and thus directly confronted moral and legal imperatives.

On the one hand, several cultural and legal forces worked against a policy of enslavement in New England. Even though the missionary efforts of the New England colonists proved notoriously ineffective, evangelization of the natives formed a core justification for Puritan colonial ventures and territorial claims. Massachusetts authorities codified this sense of a higher purpose in the colony's seal, which sported an Indian who begged "Please come and help me." Even those colonists who emphasized the Indians' savagery and lack of civilized accoutrements did not initially advocate enslavement. For example, John Winthrop invoked the doctrine of *vacuum domicilium*—the notion that Indians did not work and improve the soil—to justify the appropriation of Indian lands, not their persons. Whereas many civil and religious authorities in Spain justified Indian slavery by arguing that indigenous peoples represented a lower order of life in the Aristotelian schema and were therefore naturally suited to slave status, most ministers and officials in New England affirmed the Indians' essential humanity. Roger Williams contrasted some aspects of Indian spirituality and culture favorably with that of the colonists, noting, "Boast not proud English, of thy birth & blood, / Thy brother Indian is by birth as Good. / Of one blood God made Him, and Thee & All."[12] Royal policy and local law reinforced this recognition. In 1665 King Charles II defined the Native Americans as coequal subjects of the crown, and reminded New Englanders that the biblical category of "'children of men' comprehends Indians as well as English."[13]

Early legal codes in the region also protected individuals against some forms of enslavement. Massachusetts Bay's 1641 code, Body of Liberties, permitted enslavement only of captives taken in a just war. The code's 1647 revision, Laws and Liberties, drew on both Mosaic and English common law traditions to define kidnapping, or "man-stealing," as a capital crime. Authorities invoked this statute on several occasions in the 1600s to free both Africans and Indians whom they adjudged to be kidnapped and wrongfully enslaved.[14]

At the same time, law and practice regarding the treatment of captured soldiers and noncombatants during wartime in seventeenth-century Europe offered conflicting guidance. European policy makers were moving toward a notion of international law concerning warfare, embodied in Hugo Grotius's The Law of War and Peace (1625, 1631). Still, contemporaries identified many exceptions when it was permissible to attack civilians and sequester captives, although the New England colonists did not refer to these exceptions in authorizing enslavement of the Pequot captives. The Christian tradition of the just, defensive war, which the Puritans invoked in their conflict with the Pequots, allowed the enslavement of non-Christian captives; Grotius regarded enslavement as a merciful alternative to execution. In addition, English precedents existed for condemning criminals and prisoners of war to a set term of enforced service sometimes referred to as "slavery." Enslavement was a lesser punishment than death for capital crimes such as murder or treason. New England authorities and military leaders frequently identified Pequots as "murderers of English," and did not grant them the protective status of soldiers of a sovereign nation.

Against the backdrop of the English Civil War, the enslavement of "traitors" and the abuse of military prisoners and civilians intensified in ways that may have influenced New Englanders. Parliament dispatched Scots prisoners of war to serve as indentured servants in New England in the 1640s and 1650s, and some royalist sympathizers were sent to the Caribbean as "slaves." Local authorities sentenced English settlers accused of treason to "slavery" in early Barbados and Bermuda.[15] For whites, however, slavery in these circumstances was neither a permanent nor a heritable status. It was more akin to indentured servitude: after serving their terms, the condemned could expect to resume the same rights and privileges of any English citizen. Moreover, English "slaves" were men, while the majority of the natives enslaved by the colonists during the Pequot War were noncombatant women and children, and these native captives faced a vastly different situation. In the case of the Pequot captives, some had set terms of service, but others apparently served for life. Runaway Pequots appear in court records more than ten years after the war's end. The citizens of Hingham, Massachusetts, testified in 1676 to the long presence in their community of "Indian Servants part of them being Captives and part of them apprentices for years: some of which were bought with money and some given to ye Petitioners."[16] New England Indians who were exported to Bermuda, Providence Island or other plantations became chattel slaves with no provision for release.

From the beginning of the conflict, New England governments used the promise of plunder as a means of recruiting and paying troops, and plunder included captives. Richard Davenport noted, "Conetecut men have had their equall share in women and treys (Indian household goods/ wampum)."[17] Commanders like Israel Stoughton viewed the right to claim Indian women and children as part of their due. Having dispatched 202 survivors from the "swamp battle" of 1637 to Winthrop in Boston, he informed the governor that "ther is one . . . that is the fairest and largest that I saw amongst them to whome I have given a coate to cloath her: It is my desire to have her for a servant. . . . There is a little Squa that Steward Calacot desireth . . . Lifetennant Davenport allso desireth one, to witt a tall one that hath 3 stroakes upon her stummach thus-///+."[18] One can only speculate as to whether soldiers demanded these captives as sexual partners as well as household servants. At least one high-status female captive assumed that her fate would include rape, and a runaway Pequot girl reported to Roger Williams that she had been sexually assaulted by fellow servants and then beaten by her master.[19] Overall, there is little evidence that New Englanders engaged in the kind of trade in women and children as prospective wives and sexual partners that James Brooks and Juliana Barr have identified in the Southwest.[20] Rather, the goal was to acquire women and children—and men and boys—as household servants.

A few colonial leaders privately questioned the colonies' policy of enslavement of captives, both on moral and strategic grounds. Roger Williams of Rhode Island, who had been exiled from Massachusetts for his religious views but served as a crucial go-between in maintaining the colonists' alliance with the Narragansett Indians, expressed moral and legal discomfort with Indian slavery. In a series of letters to Massachusetts governor John Winthrop, Williams raised troubling questions about the fate of Pequot captives. Williams carefully kept his criticisms private. His interpretation of Mosaic law led him to conclude that identifiable Indian "murderers . . . deserved Death," but he condemned the massacre of women and children.[21] The Old Testament provided equivocal guidance on what to do with the survivors. "Sir concerning captives (pardon my wonted boldnes)," he wrote in July 1637, "the scripture is full of mysterie and the old Testament of Tipes." Yahweh had certainly ordered the Israelites to make a "perpetuall warr" and exterminate the Amalekites, but Williams saw this as an exceptional event. The enslavement of women and children in particular seemed to violate the teachings of 2 Kings 14:5–6 by visiting the sins of the fathers upon innocent relatives. Two weeks later, however, through moral gymnastics, Williams transformed the enslavement of noncombatants into a justifiable means of punishing male warriors; in other words, "the Enemie may lawfully be weakned and despoild of all Comfort of wife and Children, etc." Still, out of strategic considerations, he urged Winthrop to qualify the policy of enslavement, and to substitute a tributary system or a finite period of servitude followed by freedom "after a due time of trayning up to labour, and restraint."[22]

Ultimately neither moral nor legal considerations checked the colonists' move toward Indian slavery. Even ministers closely concerned with evangelization of Native Americans seldom went on the record against Indian slavery in the seventeenth century. Indeed, many clergymen themselves owned Indian slaves. Writing to John Winthrop in 1637, the Rev. Hugh Peter noted that "Mr. Endecot and my selfe . . . have heard of a dividence of women and children in the bay and would bee glad of a share viz. a yong woman or girle and a boy." Peter proceeded to outline a plan for shipping additional "boyes" to Bermuda, a plan that Winthrop later tried to carry out.[23] Forty years later, missionary John Eliot, viewing the havoc that kidnapping wrought on his communities of praying Indians, did criticize the practice as inimical to both the colonies' safety and their purported religious errand. "To sell souls for money seemeth to me a dangerous merchandise," he wrote; "All men of reading condemn the Spaniard for cruelty upon this point." But Eliot was no Bartolomé de Las Casas; his public writings largely avoided the subject, and he and other missionaries generally reserved their concern for praying Indians. Daniel Gookin, a Massachusetts magistrate who oversaw several Indian communities during the second half of the seventeenth century, sought to protect his charges from enslavement but himself engaged in the capture, sale, and transport of numerous Indians during King Philip's War. Similarly, despite his reservations, Roger Williams aided the Bay Colony in the distribution and sale of Pequot Indian captives, negotiated the return of runaways from the Indian protectors to whom they had fled, and generally facilitated the enslavement policy. Indeed, in 1676 the citizens of Providence asked him to preside over the division of profits from the sale of captives, which he did.

One group of New Englanders attempted to create a debate over Indian slavery—the Indians themselves. In the aftermath of the Pequot War, Native American and Euro-American concepts of slavery clashed dramatically. As allies of the English colonists, the Narragansetts, Niantics, and Mohegans shared in the division of the war's human spoils. Williams served as a chief negotiator during these proceedings.[24] Initially Williams reported to John Winthrop that Miantonomo, the Narragansett sachem, "liked well" the United Colonies' plan for the Pequot captives—"that they should live with the English and themselves as Slaves." The victorious Indians even acceded to the transport of some captives to England and to the execution of some male warriors. Yet negotiations foundered over the treatment of noncombatants and those who had surrendered peacefully, especially women and children.[25] The Narragansetts proposed that they "be not enslaved, like those which are taken in warr: but (as they say is their generall Custome) be vsed kindly, haue howses and goods and fields given them."[26] In other words, the Narragansetts defined captivity and slavery differently than did the English. They balked at the notion of condemning captives to chattel slavery and potential export to the Caribbean. Ayanemo, the Niantic sachem, also wrangled with Bay authorities over the fate of Pequot refugees and tried to forestall attempts to round them up. The Mohegan sachem, Uncas, resolved some of these issues through the marketplace; in addition to his share of the captives, he purchased Indians from English traders in order to augment his own community.[27]

Anthropologist Kathleen Bragdon points out that although their culture stressed reciprocity and communalism, the Algonkians of coastal southern New England understood hierarchy. New England Indians lived in societies characterized by social inequality, and status differences were becoming more pronounced in the decades immediately before and after English colonization.[28] Roger Williams noted the presence among the Narragansetts of "obscure and meane persons . . . [that] have no name."[29] But there is little evidence that the Indians of southern New England regularly sought captives for labor, torture, or adoption in the ways that other groups like the Iroquois, the Eastern Indians, or the Mississippians did. Even Uncas, the Mohegan leader whose regional power depended on his close ties with Connecticut and who coveted his share of Pequot captives, sought to place himself at the top of a network of tributary relationships with Pequot survivors, not to control completely their labor and persons.

Authorities in Massachusetts and Connecticut put enormous pressure on their former allies to accept the slave status of Pequot captives among the English and to return runaways. The gap between local tribes' desire to assimilate Indian refugees and the colonists' desire to isolate and subjugate them continued to cause friction through the succeeding decades. Massachusetts inserted a "fugitive slave" clause into a 1638 treaty with the Narragansetts, and the Commissioners of the United Colonies—the military alliance formed by Massachusetts, Plymouth, Connecticut, and New Haven—further resolved in 1646 to "damadge seise & bring away any of the plantation of Indians that shall entertaine, p[ro]tect or rescue" Indians accused of crimes against the English. If any harbored runaways, both the fugitives and their Narragansett and Niantic protectors would be bound "either to serue or to be shipped out & exchanged for Negroes."[30] The exchangeability of Indians and African slaves appeared as a motif in other correspondence relating to Indian captives in the 1640s and 1650s.

If Indian enslavement sparked little moral, legal, or political debate and discussion among the English colonists, contemporaries were perfectly clear about its utility. Colonial governments and interested individuals offered a number of material, strategic, and social justifications for the policy of enslavement over the course of the seventeenth century. Foremost among these rationales, particularly during the critical 1630s, when enslavement first became widespread, was the overwhelming need for labor both in New England and in affiliated Caribbean plantations. One has only to skim the *Winthrop Papers* and other contemporary correspondence to uncover scores of complaints regarding the lack of servants and the impossibility of keeping bondsmen and women. In a New World environment characterized by abundant land and paucity of labor, many colonists recognized "that our servants will still desire freedome to plant for themselves, and not stay but for verie great wages."[31] The hiring of Indian workers was already so prevalent by 1636 that the Massachusetts General Court stepped in to regulate the practice. In this context, Indian slaves represented a crucial source of workers. By the 1640s, Winthrop was fielding requests from the governor of Bermuda for Indian slaves, and other New Englanders were urging a war against the Narragansetts for the "gaynefull pilladge" of securing Indian workers.[32] Binding Indians offered a solution to labor shortages and a means of punishing, controlling, and/ or acculturating local native populations.

In addition to enslavement during warfare, seventeenth-century colonial governments and courts occasionally condemned individual Indians to terms of service or "perpetuall slaverie" for a variety of infractions, ranging from sheltering enemy Indians, debt, and theft, to assault, drunkenness, and "insolent carryage." By the 1650s, Indians appeared with greater frequency before English courts, as colonial governments asserted their legal jurisdiction over larger territories and the native groups and individuals that inhabited them. The assemblies of all four New England colonies passed increasing amounts of legislation aimed at controlling Indian behavior, whether it be access to firearms and boats, alcohol consumption, land usage rights, and freedom of movement, which meant that more Indians found themselves standing accused of crimes against English colonists in court. Some of these laws explicitly gave plaintiffs or officials the right to seize Indians' persons. The Connecticut General Court ordered in 1650 that Indians who committed crimes against English settlers and failed to make restitution could be seized "either to serve [the victim] or to be shipped out."[33] Ten years later Connecticut authorities received permission from the United Colonies to seize four Narragansett Indians accused of robbing colonists and to sell them to Barbados.[34] The General Assembly of Rhode Island decreed in 1659 that any Indian convicted of theft or property damage who failed to "pay and discharge all the damages, costs, and restitutions by law due" could "be sould as a slave to any forraigne country of the English subjects."[35] The Assembly recommended sale as a particularly appropriate penalty in cases where the defendants showed "insolency," suggesting that binding Indians also might serve as a means of social control. Plymouth officials passed a similar law in 1673, which permitted creditors to bind debtor Indians into terms of service.[36] Criminal sentences occasionally involved servitude as well. Plymouth's General Court condemned an "Indian, called Hoken, that hath bin a notoriouse theife," in absentia, and ordered in 1674 that if captured he be sold to Barbados "to free the collonie from soe ill a member."[37]

Cases of Indian enslavement for debt or criminality were rare before 1675. In part this was because colonial courts held limited effective jurisdiction over many Native Americans. Also, as members of intact tribes with significant assets in land and varying degrees of independence, native defendants had resources to draw upon to pay fines, and often sachems or white patrons to represent them in court. Despite the Plymouth and Rhode Island laws that singled out Native Americans for punishment by servitude, overall Indians appeared no more likely to receive such sentences than other groups in colonial society, at least at first. In several instances, seventeenth-century Suffolk County courts occasionally ordered that white thieves, debtors, and unruly servants be sold so that the profits could be used to make restitution to their victims and their communities. There is some evidence of ethnic discrimination in that criminal sentences against Indians in Suffolk more frequently permitted—even ordered—the sale of individuals "to Barbados" or other plantations outside of New England.[38]

King Philip's War, 1675–1676, transformed the practice of Indian slavery in several ways. This brutal conflict pitted the New England colonists and their Mohegan, Pequot, and Christian Indian allies against the Wampanoags, Narragansetts, Nipmucs, and other groups. Its extent and destruction eclipsed earlier conflicts in the region. Twenty-five hundred colonists lost their lives, dozens of others were made captive, and nearly one of seven towns in New England was destroyed. For Native Americans, the outcome was even more devastating, as an already declining population of approximately 11,000 in southern New England experienced an estimated 5,000 casualties.

During King Philip's War, the colonists built on strategies of enslavement developed during the Pequot War, with disastrous results for Native American communities. Colonial declarations of war in 1675–1676 ordered enslavement of captives, in the context of a just, defensive war against a foreign aggressor. At the same time, in an apparent contradiction, they also accused the Indians of having "rebelled and revolted from their obediences"—in other words, of committing treason.[39] The charge of treason had consequences, since "rebel" Indians did not enjoy the legal immunity of soldiers in a sovereign army, and could be punished for the civil crimes of treason, assault, and murder.[40] Indeed, field commanders, war councils, and, later, local courts executed male captives on these grounds. But for most captives the outcome was the same regardless of whether they were charged with murder, treason, or waging an unjust war.

Plymouth, Massachusetts, and Connecticut officials held public auctions of hundreds of captives at a time, as did the towns of Portsmouth and Providence in Rhode Island. Colonial governments assigned groups of captives to individuals as rewards for wartime service, and as a form of monetary restitution to war-battered English towns. Once again, the colonies treated control of captives as part of soldiers' recompense, and once again the majority of captives were noncombatant women and children. Lieutenant Jonathan Fairbanks, a member of Gibbs's Company, encountered some children in a wigwam near Rehoboth, "amonst thim a young girle of about ten or twelve years of age whome yr petitioner upon Mr. Gibbs promiss that she should be his own, tooke her up upon his horse."[41]

Captors and purchasers of these enslaved Indians exported many hundreds of them to the Wine Islands, Spain, England, and Jamaica, in a painful diaspora. Indeed, Plymouth passed Orders in Council requiring that owners sell or send abroad all male captives above the age of fourteen. Plymouth Colony authorities shipped 178 captives aboard a single vessel bound for Cadiz in October 1675.[42] Captain Richard Waldron seized 200 Pennacook and Wampanoag Indians who had come to his Maine outpost under a flag of truce and offers of amnesty, and shipped at least some of them to the Azores.[43] Boston merchant Samuel Shrimpton informed his wife Elizabeth in July 1676, "I bought 9 [captives] the other day to send to Jamaica but I thinke to keep 3 of them upon ye Island." Shrimpton subsequently purchased sixteen more Indian men, women, and children.[44] In November 1675, Massachusetts General Court offered a group of nine Indian women whose husbands had been captured and condemned by English forces a painful choice: to follow their husbands and bring their children into slavery abroad, or to accept permanent separation. One, "Sara the Wife of Great David with one child at her back," agreed to go "if to king charles his Country to ye English." Sara apparently knew enough about the potential fate of Indian captives abroad to prefer servitude in England to the Caribbean.[45] Those Indians who remained in the Northeast still might find themselves living in white households hundreds of miles from home and kin. Since kin ties formed an important part of Native American ethnic identity, such separations represented a severe cultural blow.

Unlike in the Pequot War, during King Philip's War neutrality or previous loyalty to the English offered southern New England Indians little protection against enslavement. Wartime hysteria led the United Colonies to intern many Christian Indians in camps on Deer Island and Long Island, for the Indians' protection from angry vigilantes as well as for the colonists' security. Ill-supplied and removed from their sources of subsistence, the interned Indians suffered terrible deprivation. In addition they formed an attractive target for kidnappers, who raided the coastal encampments at Deer Island and Long Island, indiscriminately seizing dozens of "friend" Indians for sale and export. Others abducted Indians—some of whom, ironically, were already servants, slaves, or dependents of white masters—from farms and wigwams along the Rhode Island, Massachusetts, and Maine coasts. Massachusetts also authorized its agents to forcibly draft Indians from the camps as guides, seaman, soldiers, and manual laborers.

Even families of those Indians who fought alongside English forces were vulnerable to capture and sale in the absence of male relatives. For example, in March 1679, friends of John Sassamon—the pro-English Indian interpreter and spy whose supposed murder by one of Philip's associates served as the United Colonies' pretext for beginning King Philip's War—complained that Sassamon's sister had been "claimed as his servant" by one John Burge. The commissioners recommended that Burge receive compensation in exchange for her freedom, "halfe out of the Indian Stocke as due to Sassamon for service; and the other halfe by her frinds."[46] In June of 1675, Plymouth's Council of War ordered that Indian children under English jurisdiction be removed from their families and forcibly apprenticed to white families. In the summer of 1676, Daniel Gookin bound fifty mostly Nipmuc Indian children ranging in age from three to sixteen into servitude to age twenty-four.[47] Some were war orphans, but others had living parents; siblings were divided to different masters and sent far from kin.

The sheer scale of enslavement and dislocation during King Philip's War prompted some local and provincial authorities to try and regulate the practice. The colonists' security concerns led some to question the wisdom of enslaving Indians, since many worried about the threat of a potentially hostile captive servant population. In response, Massachusetts,

47

Connecticut, and Rhode Island moved to bring captive Indians under more direct government control. At the onset of the conflict, Massachusetts and Plymouth passed Orders in Council against keeping adult Indian servants, although both permitted children under the age of twelve for boys and fifteen for girls to remain. Individual towns imposed their own temporary restrictions on enslavement. The inhabitants of Portsmouth, Rhode Island, banned the introduction of any new Indian slaves and servants into their community in March 1675, and Providence authorities did the same, briefly, in 1676. The Rhode Island General Assembly forbade enslavement *except* for debt in March 1676; captive Indians and any noncombatants who surrendered were to be treated instead as indentured servants and, ideally, sold out of the area. Other laws followed that encouraged inhabitants to export their Indian slaves.

A few officials attempted to stem some of the worst abuses. Missionary John Eliot and Indian guardian Daniel Gookin, as well as Indian leaders, had begged colonial governments for help in protecting their charges from indiscriminate kidnappings, and the courts did invoke the 1648 man-stealing law on a couple of occasions to discourage enslavement. A Massachusetts court indicted Samuel Fuller and John Gorham in November of 1675 "for kidnapping Indians and selling them as slaves at Fyal" in the Azores Islands, and Boston merchants William Waldron and Henry Lawton faced a grand jury in 1677 for kidnapping and shipping seventeen Maine Indians to the Azores.[48] Although juries acquitted Waldron and only fined Lawton, the Court of Assistants did seize part of the proceeds of Waldron's venture and sent agents to redeem some of the captives he had betrayed and shipped to the Azores in 1677. Amazingly, several of these Indians managed to return to New England.[49] Other new laws passed in Plymouth and Rhode Island in 1676–1677 prohibited the extension of existing Indian indentures past contracted limits, the contracting of new indentures without permission of a justice, and the exportation of Indians outside of the region without the approval of local magistrates.[50]

But although colonial authorities and courts finally intervened in the last quarter of the seventeenth century to regulate the conditions of Indian servitude and slavery, their actions hardly amounted to a prohibition of an already entrenched system. Most of the wartime laws limiting Indian slavery were short-lived and unenforceable, and apparently had little effect on the movement of Indian slaves and servants. In fact, once the immediate danger of Indian attack had subsided in a particular area, individuals and communities immediately protested the restrictions and sought exemption from the new laws on the grounds that removing the Indians would cause severe economic hardship. Owners bombarded Plymouth officials with petitions requesting to keep their Indian servants. The same Rhode Island towns that earlier had banned the presence of bound Indians within their borders held public auctions of captives and distributed the profits at town meetings in the summer and autumn of 1676. Roger Williams himself presided over such a "Distribucion" in Providence in October 1676.[51] Plymouth officials also passed legislation confirming the ownership rights of colonists who already held Indians in perpetuity, even as they tried to limit new cases of enslavement. The most significant law regarding Indian slavery—Rhode Island's outright ban—offered only the barest protections for victims, since its sliding age-scale permitted binding children for up to thirty years—effectively a lifetime for some.

Still, the cessation of conflict meant that the capture and ongoing enslavement of local Indians in southern New England had ended. More fundamentally, now, through conquest and treaty the colonial governments—particularly the powerful Massachusetts Bay—had come to view all the Indians of southern New England as subject peoples answerable to English courts and laws. They now extended to all Native Americans the relationship that the colonists had previously established with scattered communities of Christian Indians. The colonies' legal hegemony was a double-edged sword, however, since as subjects or tributaries, the Indians had recourse to some of the privileges of citizenship—notably the petition and the courts. Some captives and their relatives, as well as some Indian leaders, effectively used petitions, lawsuits, and other strategies to protest wrongful enslavement and to redeem some of its victims.

In adjusting to this new world of postwar Indian relations, the colonists first turned to sources outside the region for a continuing supply of Indian slaves. Despite these changes, native slavery and involuntary servitude persisted and even flourished into the eighteenth century. Initially New Englanders evaded the new barriers to enslaving local Indians by importing natives. Unlike the shattered Indian societies of southern New England, native tribes in northern New England—and the Indians from southern New England who took refuge with them—remained quasi-sovereign, independent entities, having emerged from King Philip's War with their regional power enhanced.[52] Warfare on the northeastern frontier raged for several more years, and resumed again in earnest in 1689. Massachusetts passed several acts at the onset of King William's War in 1689, 1694, and again in 1704–1707 that used the taking and selling of Indian captives—especially women and children—as a means of recruiting and paying troops.[53] Despite exceptions such as Richard Waldron's seizure of hundreds of Indians in 1676, however, pressure from New York and from imperial authorities who feared alienating potential Indian allies, as well as the northern Indians' ability to take English hostages in retaliation, all protected the northern Indians from the scale of enslavement that had afflicted the Indians of southern New England.[54]

Another potential source of Indian slaves came from the southeast. From the beginnings of settlement in the early 1670s English settlers in the Carolinas had been enslaving local Indians. Growing English markets for captives spurred Anglo-Indian wars against the Westos in 1680, the Yaddos in 1704, and the Yamasees in 1715. These conflicts, augmented by chronic English slaving raids on Indian missions in Spanish Florida, fed an exploding Indian slave trade in Charles Town, one that exported captives throughout the British empire—including to New England.[55]

The growing numbers of so-called "Eastern," "Spanish," and "Carolina" Indians (all of whom New Englanders perceived as being more warlike and less acculturated than the local natives) began to worry authorities in the eighteenth century. As part of a 1709 law entitled "An Act to Encourage the Importation of White Servants," the Massachusetts General Court subjected the Indian slave trade to the same taxes as the trade in enslaved Africans. Later that year, authorities added a requirement that importers provide some proof that Indians had been legally enslaved in the plantation that exported them. Rhode Island passed similar laws, but the taxes apparently failed to discourage importers, because both assemblies, joined by Connecticut, eventually mandated the immediate re-exportation of any Eastern, Spanish and Carolina Indians brought into the area on pain of a £50 fine. The Rhode Island re-export law cited the "divers conspiracies, insurrections, rapes, thefts and other execrable crimes, [which] have been lately perpetrated . . . by Indian slaves" from other regions as a reason ordering the new restrictions. Both colonies granted numerous exemptions to individual owners permitting them to keep their "Carolina Indians," however, and other importers simply ignored the law.[56] Newspaper advertisements in the decade after the 1712 law went into effect indicate that Carolina and Spanish Indians continued to be bought and sold in Boston through the early 1720s, and held as slaves decades thereafter.

Aside from importing Indians from other regions, however, New Englanders in the eighteenth century had found new vehicles—legislation and the courts—through which to control the labor of many local Indians. With slavery officially outlawed, the colonists instead turned to the court-sanctioned sentencing of Native Americans to long periods of involuntary servitude. The sale of Indians for debt or in restitution for criminal penalties and legal fees, the legal and illegal extension of indentures, and the forcible apprenticeship of children, all became more prevalent in the eighteenth century. A number of legal changes facilitated this turn to what I call "judicial enslavement."[57]

Following King Philip's War, Massachusetts forcibly resettled most of the decimated population of "friend" Indians (except those already bound into labor) into designated enclaves—four towns in the seventeenth century, and four more after Massachusetts annexed Plymouth and Martha's Vineyard, both of which had sizable native populations, in 1691.[58] Rhode Island and Connecticut did not conduct a resettlement on this scale, but both colonies drew sharp boundaries between English settlements and the now shrunken Indian town and tribal land claims, essentially creating reservations in the Narragansett country and Sakonnet in Rhode Island and in southeastern and northern Connecticut. Indians residing in the designated towns or reservations enjoyed rights that might include shared rights to land, lease incomes, and protection from enslavement.

Southern New England Indians continued to pursue traditional subsistence economies well into the eighteenth century, but their already decimated land resources declined steadily through sale and appropriation. The dwindling land base meant that natives depended on English markets and storekeepers for a variety of necessities: food, clothing, medical care. Some Indians resisted resettlement, and continued to live in or near English towns, where they worked as day laborers or servants, along with Indians bound to colonists during the wars. Such individuals occupied a precarious position both economically and politically, however, since they lacked even the minimal legal and economic protections that tribal membership afforded.

Meanwhile the growth of the English population and the expansion of settlement brought colonists and Indians into frequent contact. Proximity to English settlers increased the potential for charges of trespass, destruction of property by livestock, contention over the ownership of resources or goods, damages, assault, and other encounters. Increased access to alcohol contributed both to the loss of native assets and to drunken assaults and conflicts.[59] As a result, Indians began to appear more frequently before colonial courts immediately following King Philip's War, and this pattern continued throughout the eighteenth century. Many defendants now lacked the resources to pay their fines and debts, or else they shared rights in collective resources that could not be liquidated. By the late seventeenth century, many of the sachem-patrons who had protected earlier generations of Indians in New England courts had died and the changing leadership structure and material base of Indian communities meant that that few would-be successors could claim a similar legitimacy, power, and independence. This left Indian defendants in civil and criminal cases vulnerable to being sentenced to long terms of involuntary servitude.

Legal changes that ostensibly had nothing to with native affairs made the situation worse. All the New England colonies passed legislation between 1670 and 1700 that increased the damages that defendants could claim in cases of theft to double or triple the value of the goods stolen, plus restitution. (The Plymouth law was an exception in that it singled out Indians for a harsher fourfold restitution penalty.) Courts charged higher legal fees and costs in the eighteenth century, which were folded into the defendants' fines and thus could translate into additional years of service for Indians sold into service. Martha's Vineyard's 1672 legal code included a provision aimed at protecting the inhabitants from the evils of debtors' prison—but the law provided that in lieu of prison the debtor's "Person shall be sold for Satisfaction." To make matters worse for Native Americans, court officials tended to value Indian labor at a lower rate than that of prevailing wage rates for Europeans, which meant that an Indian would have to serve a longer term to pay off the debt. At the same time, the sentencing of Euro-Americans to servitude became more rare, and most of these cases involved Irish or members of other outsider groups.[60]

In some areas the shift to judicial enslavement was dramatic. Of the twenty-two Indians convicted of trespass, theft, or assault in Martha's Vineyard between 1675 and 1687, only two received sentences involving servitude—one twelve days, one two years.[61] In January 1688 alone, however, the Dukes County Court convicted thirteen Indians of "killing Cattle and Shepe," or "Eatting of mottin [mutton] that was stolen"; each judgment included a rider providing that if the defendant failed to pay the fines and costs assessed, he or she should be sold into service for periods ranging from three months to seven years. Those who received sentences of over two years could be sold "in any part of ye kings dominyons."[62] The court bound eight more Indians to terms of six months to thirty years in 1689–1690 for offenses that included stealing a handkerchief. Sometimes victorious plaintiffs assumed control of the Indians' labor, as in the case of Mathew Mayhew, who sold two Indians convicted of stealing about £8 from him in 1693 to a buyer in Southold, Long Island, for seven-year terms.[63] Other plaintiffs chose to receive their restitution in cash, so Martha's Vineyard instituted a regular public "Vandue" or auction of Indian convicts. Similarly, in Bristol County, Massachusetts, Indian defendants abruptly began to receive terms of servitude from the court of general sessions there in 1705.[64] The Newport, Rhode Island, Supreme Court condemned at least fifteen Indian men, women, and children to terms of service between 1704 and 1725.[65]

In other parts of New England, Indians accused of debt or petty crime might never come before a jury. As part of the postwar reorganization of Indian communities, Massachusetts and later Rhode Island and Connecticut created a multi-tiered system of adjudication for cases involving reservation Indians. Massachusetts authorities accepted the authority of Indian-run "courts" for mediation of disputes within a tribe or community, although Indian plaintiffs sometimes chose to appeal or resolve their differences in English courts. In criminal cases, or any civil case involving a white plaintiff or defendant, however, Indians had to appear before white authorities. In establishing Indian towns or reservations, colonial governments appointed justices of the peace—sometimes called "overseers," "guardians" or "trustees"—to supervise legal affairs. In counties near reservations, the justices held court, took evidence, rendered decisions, and decided whether cases were serious enough to merit hearing in Superior Court or courts of oyer and terminer. This process meant that many civil and criminal cases involving Indians never went to juries, except on appeal.[66] Apart from these provisions affecting Indians alone, justices of the peace throughout New England were authorized to hold court in their homes and decide civil cases worth less than forty shillings, and criminal misdemeanor cases, regardless of the defendant's race.

Unlike sessions or common pleas courts, the justices' court papers were considered the private property of the men who held the office, so very few of these records survive, making it difficult to determine how many Indians they sentenced to servitude. Some judges, such as Benjamin Church of Bristol, were sincere advocates for Native Americans. Even Church, however, bound Indians into service, and other justices and local officials evidently abused their authority to entrap Indians for profit. William Woddell and Thomas Thornton of Rhode Island were among several constables and justices who appeared frequently as signatories on Indian indentures and bills of sale. Woddell operated an Indian servant and slave clearinghouse, and Thornton's activities in illegally binding Indians to labor became so outrageous that several whites in Portsmouth petitioned the Assembly at Newport to intervene.[67] Justice John Prentiss of New London, Connecticut, also traded in Indian labor even as he presided over cases involving Indians, as did his neighbor, Joshua Hempstead.

Meanwhile, other New England natives, though technically free and not defendants at court, were becoming enmeshed in cycles of dependence with merchants, local landowners, and ships' captains that could lead to long-term servitude. Daniel Vickers notes that whaling vessels operating in Cape Cod, Martha's Vineyard, and Nantucket relied almost exclusively on Indian labor, and he estimates that nearly three-quarters of the Indian whalers in Nantucket by the mid-1730s turned over their entire earnings to white masters after every voyage.[68] What began as debt peonage could lead to even more serious forms of servitude for members of an extended family. Gideon Hawley, a Congregationalist missionary among the Mashpee Indians at Plymouth, explained that many Indian men became debt peons in the whaling industry and worked until death, injury, or old age left them incapable, with nothing but debt to show for their labor. As a result, "there is scarcely an Indian Boy among us not indented to an English Master . . . the true reason of it is, their neighbours find means to involve the Indians so deeply in debt as they are obliged to make over ye boys, if they have any, for security till payment."[69]

As Hawley noted, many creditors intentionally encouraged Indians to pledge their credit for food, liquor, or funeral costs. Once in debt it was almost impossible for Native Americans to clear their commitments. In some cases these relationships resembled the kinds of relatively benign ongoing book-debt relations that many white New Englanders maintained with neighbors and storekeepers, with constant exchanges and credits for goods and labor that the Indians provided. In other cases, however, creditors coerced Indian debtors to contract their own labor or the labor of their children for terms of months and years. In 1703, "Jefrey Indian" of Stonington, Connecticut, effectively mortgaged his five-year-old daughter Ann to serve Daniel Mason for twelve years in order to clear debts incurred during his wife's illness and funeral.[70]

Indian communities actively protested judicial enslavement. Simon Popmoney, George Wapuck, and other Mashpee Indian leaders petitioned in the Massachusetts General Court in 1700. They complained, "Thro Ignorance of the Law, weaknes, foolishnes, & Inconsideration some of us that are Elder, & severall of our Children have run in to the English mens Debts, and not being able, nor perhaps careful to pay att the time appointed; our Self & our poor Children, are frequently made Servants for an unreasonable time." The petitioners delicately accused white plaintiffs of abusing debt proceedings to control Indian labor.[71] In the end, Massachusetts adopted the Indians' suggestions for amelioration in an "Act for Preventing Abuses to the Indians" passed later that year. The law acknowledged "the Executions and oppression which some of the English exercise towards the Indians by drawing them to consent to covenant or bind themselves or Children apprentices or Servants for an unreasonable term on pretence of or to make Satisfaction for some small debt contracted or damage done to them."[72] Each indenture would require the approbation of two or more justices of the peace, who reviewed the contracts and ensured that they followed the proper form. Contracts were to be finite in term, specific about the master's obligations, and signed by the Indian in question. Indians already bound into suspect indentures could petition local justices to review their cases.

Still, this law and others like it subsequently adopted in Connecticut and Rhode Island seem to have had little impact on the sentencing of Indians to servitude for debt and criminal activity. The colonies passed more legislation in the 1720s and 1730s; finally Massachusetts and Connecticut forbade extending credit to Indians or bringing suits against Indians for any debt above ten shillings. But abuses persisted. Minister Gideon Hawley made the lament quoted earlier about the universality of debt and forced indenture of children among the Mashpee Indians in 1760. He also blamed judges and sentencing practices in part for the problem, and urged the Massachusetts Council to recommend that Indians receive only corporal punishment rather than fines and fees for civil and petty criminal offenses. The efficacy of laws against illegal extension of indentures depended on the integrity of the justices who oversaw them and their personal interest in Indian labor, which varied.

Once indentured, whether voluntarily or involuntarily, Indians encountered many abuses. They could find themselves bought and sold, separated from families, and taken from the region. Running away, stealing from one's master, engaging in a sexual relationship, bearing a child, and

a host of other violations could double or triple a servant's time obligations. Owners of white and African servants throughout British America
had employed all of these methods to extend periods of service since the
early seventeenth century. But by the eighteenth century colonial governments had taken steps to protect English servants from the worst abuses.[73]
Moreover, in general white servitude was a stage in life rather than a lifetime
state. Indians, once enmeshed in apprenticeship or servitude, found it difficult to escape the status for long, if at all. Interestingly, the first Indians
sentenced to servitude by civil courts in Bristol County, Massachusetts,
were already servants. Under such conditions, an indentured servant—
especially a woman or a child—could easily become a de facto slave. Joshua
Hempstead of Connecticut memorialized "old Rachel formerly a Servt to
Capt. John Prenttis" in his diary in 1746: "I Supose She was near 80 years
of age. She was a Captive taken in the Narhaganset war in 1675." In other
words Rachel, a child captive who should have served only a set term,
spent her entire life in service to the Prentiss family.[74] Another example
was "Phebee an Indian Maid or Girle," who petitioned Bristol authorities
for her freedom in 1701. Phebee's owner, James Smith, had put her out to
service to another master, John Burt. But when she reached her majority,
which signaled the end of her obligation to Burt, Smith claimed her as
"his slave for life" on the grounds that her parents had been his servants,
and demanded that she be returned to him. In the end the court ordered
Phebee to work as Burt's indentured servant for an additional four years,
with Smith to receive her yearly wages."[75] The case of Phebee was by no
means unique, as other litigation over the extension of indentures and
the sale of servants into conditions of slavery attested. Another servant,
Sarah Chauqum of Rhode Island, confronted a similar situation in 1733,
when her master sold her as a slave to Edward Robinson of New London,
Connecticut. Sarah won her freedom by establishing her Indian ancestry
to the court's satisfaction—her mother resided in the Narragansett Indian
reservation town South Kingstown.[76] The outright kidnapping or removal
of Indian children for sale as slaves in other colonies was prevalent enough
to be the target of special legislation.

One of the things that distinguished chattel slavery from servitude was its heritability. In the case of Indian indentured servants, it is difficult to determine the extent to which children automatically followed in their parents' footsteps, but at least some did. Eighteenth-century probate inventories and advertisements for the sale of servants and slaves sometimes listed Indian women and their children together—indirect evidence that those children were following the status of their mothers. Occasionally wills revealed the assumption that Indians were slaves for life, as in the case of Daniel Coggeshall of Kingstown, Rhode Island, who left "my Indian woman and her sucking child Jeffery" to his wife and children "during the term of their natural lives." And whereas probate administrators and newspaper advertisements often noted the time remaining on the contracts of white servants, they omitted such information in entries for Indians.[77] In the face of numerous complaints that white masters were unlawfully selling or extending the contracts of apprenticed Indian children just before the children came of age, Plymouth colony merely required that colonists interested in purchasing the children of enslaved captives obtain the court's permission first. Massachusetts passed similar legislation three times in the eighteenth century, imposing heavy fines on those who sent Indian children "across the sea," suggesting that the practice continued.[78]

At minimum such children probably served as forced "apprentices" until adulthood. Indentures of Indian children increasingly differed from those of their white counterparts over the course of the eighteenth century. Typically Indian contracts began to omit the masters' obligations and lacked some of the usual provisions regarding training for a trade and education. Fewer parents appeared as signatories; instead, local justices commonly bound out such children, and parents' presence or absence as advocates for their children could be crucial in determining indenture provisions. The death of a parent might mean slippage into enslavement. In 1723 David Green of Jamestown, Rhode Island, bound "Hannah being a Girl half Indian and Half Negro" as an indentured servant to another master when her mother, his servant, died. Hannah was one and a half. The indenture refers to her as a "servant or slave," but tellingly her indented master George Mumford was to return Hannah to Green upon completion of the indenture twenty years later, which suggests that Green planned to claim her labor for life.[79]

During this same period, the New England colonies were defining the legal parameters of the institution of slavery in ways that had enormous consequences for Indian servants. Between 1685 and 1720, colonial governments passed a spate of legislation regarding people of color, analogous to the Black Codes of the Chesapeake and other slave societies. The New England laws specifically included Indian slaves and servants in their strictures, which ranged from restrictions on travel and assembly, to urban curfews for "Indian, negro, or mulatto servants and slaves." New England officials also created separate penalties and processes, including summary courts without juries, for "Indians, negroes, mulattoes, slaves or others" who stole or disposed of stolen goods. Blacks and Indians seem to have received harsher punishments and more frequent corporal punishment than whites for identical crimes in the eighteenth century. And, as judicial enslavement became more common in cases involving Indians, it became less common for Europeans. Courts in all three colonies—Massachusetts, Connecticut, and Rhode Island—condemned a handful of white defendants—usually servants and often identifiable as Irish or members of "outsider" groups—to servitude in the eighteenth century, but cases involving Indians outnumbered these scattered examples. Whites were also more likely to be offered other court-mandated solutions for working off their debt short of servitude.

These racialized laws had their own circular effect, especially as the number of African slaves in New England increased in the eighteenth century. Color became associated with slavery, and slavery with color, and in the process the very "Indianness" of many Indian servants came under attack. Court documents fostered ethnic slippage by designating Indian servants as mixed-race or black, often over their objections.[80] Racial designations had enormous significance, as the case of Sarah Chauqum illustrates. Enslaving Indians in Rhode Island was technically illegal, but her master listed her as a "mollato" in the bill of sale to Edward Robinson. Sarah won her freedom by asserting her Narragansett Indian identity, but not all Indians were able to avoid passing from servitude to slavery.

Moreover, by the 1720s some New England Indians and their offspring *were* mixed-race, and this trend increased during succeeding decades. The demographic catastrophes wrought by war and enslavement left many tribes facing extremely skewed sex ratios, so Indian women found partners among free, servant, and enslaved African populations. In particular, female servants often married the African and mixed-race men, free and slave, whom they worked and socialized with in their free time. Choosing a black partner could have serious ramifications, as in the case of Patience Boston, an Indian servant from Cape Cod. Bound into "apprenticeship" to a white household by her father at age three, Patience was a self-described "mischievous and rebellious servant." She completed her term of service at age twenty-one, "happy that I had no Body to Command me." But when she married an African servant or slave (the precise status of her husband, a whaleman, is unclear) she became "bound for life" to her husband's master.[81]

By the mid eighteenth century, bound Indian workers could be found throughout the region; they became especially concentrated in cities such as Boston, Providence, and New London, as well as the countryside of Narragansett, Cape Cod/Plymouth, Martha's Vineyard, southeastern Connecticut, Nantucket, and Maine. Not all Indians became slaves or involuntary servants; some farmed common lands, raised livestock, hunted, traded, worked as day laborers, contracted their own labor as laborers or seamen, and produced finished goods for sale. Yet the first reliable census of a New England colony, the Rhode Island census of 1774, attests to the prevalence of Indian servitude on the eve of Revolution. At that time, 35.5 percent of all Indians in Rhode Island lived with white families; the proportion grows to over 50 percent if one excludes free Indians living in the largest Indian town, Charlestown.[82]

The enslavement of Indians had important consequences for both the Native American community and for New England society as a whole. Black and Indian workers helped construct the New England economy, at a terrible cost. Forced servitude and enslavement profoundly affected fertility, mortality, child rearing, kin networks, gender roles, and other aspects of native life. Time spent in English homes influenced Indian dress, religion, language acquisition, and a host of other practices. The history of Indian slavery in New England also illustrates the complex relationship among law, behavior, and the creation of racial identity in multiethnic colonial societies. New England was a legalistic society, yet it was slow to create a body of law regarding slavery, and the existing law was unevenly enforced. By 1700, even as the importation of African slaves began to increase dramatically and slave codes became more prevalent, the colonial governments instituted the first of many legal protections designed to prevent Indian enslavement and long-term servitude. At least some New Englanders came to perceive moral wrong in the enslavement of Indians, and free Indians occupied an intermediate status in an emerging racial caste system. Yet, even as Native Americans and their allies used the legal means at their disposal to protest enslavement and forced servitude, these efforts succeeded only in a few individual cases. In practice English colonists continued to coerce Indian labor regardless of the law. Meanwhile those Indians enmeshed in slavery and servitude—the unfree margin of an already subaltern group—found their status eroded further by mid-century as many became classified as Africans, which stripped them of protections that Indians enjoyed in law. As historian Thomas Doughton notes, servitude, not just slavery, was becoming racialized in eighteenth-century New England in ways that negatively affected indigenous peoples. The ad hoc nature of Indian slavery in eighteenth-century New England made it a less visible part of this "society with slaves," but may help explain why ultimately it was so hard to abolish.

Notes

1. Carl Bridenbaugh, ed., *Gentleman's Progress: The Itinerarium of Dr. Alexander Hamilton, 1744* (Chapel Hill NC: University of North Carolina Press, 1948), 167–68. My thanks to Geoffrey Plank, who drew my attention to this quotation.

2. Ira Berlin distinguishes between "slave societies" where slavery was a dominant form of labor, and "societies with slaves," where slavery shared the stage with other systems. Ira Berlin, *Many Thousands Gone: The First Two Centuries of Slavery in North America* (Cambridge MA: Harvard University Press, 1998), 8–9.

3. For white captives, see James Axtell, *The Invasion Within: The Contest of Cultures in Colonial North America* (New York: Oxford University Press, 1985), especially chapter 13, and John Demos, *The Unredeemed Captive: A Family Story of Early New England* (New York: Alfred A. Knopf, 1994). Almon Lauber published a volume on Indian slavery in the Americas in 1913 that included a discussion of Indian slavery in New England, but only recently have scholars turned their attention to the subject, and then mostly in the context of the immediate aftermath of the Pequot War and King Philip's War. See Almon Wheeler Lauber, *Indian Slavery*

in *Colonial Times within the Present Limits of the United States* (1913; repr., Williamstown MA: Corner House, 1979); Jill Lepore, *The Name of War: King Philip's War and the Origins of American Identity* (New York: Alfred A. Knopf, 1998). Scholars who have examined Indian servitude and slavery in a broader context include David J. Silverman, "The Impact of Indentured Servitude on Southern New England Indian Society and Culture, 1680–1810," *New England Quarterly* 74 (2001), and *Faith and Boundaries: Colonists, Christianity, and Community among the Wampanoag Indians of Martha's Vineyard, 1600–1871* (New York: Cambridge University Press, 2005); Ann Marie Plane, *Colonial Intimacies: Indian Marriage in Early New England* (Ithaca NY: Cornell University Press, 2000); Yasuhide Kawashima, "Indian Servitude in the Northeast," in Wilcomb E. Washburn, ed., *Handbook of North American Indians*, Vol. 4, History of Indian-White Relations (Washington DC: Smithsonian Institution, 1988); John Sainsbury, "Indian Labor in Early Rhode Island," *New England Quarterly* 47 (1975) 378–93; Joshua Micah Marshall, "'A Melancholy People': Anglo-Indian Relations in Early Warwick, Rhode Island, 1642–1675," *New England Quarterly* 68 (1995): 402–28.

4. See, for example, the essays by John Wood Sweet and Robin Blackburn in the "Constructing Race" symposium, *William and Mary Quarterly* 54 (1997). Joyce E. Chaplin, *Subject Matter: Technology, the Body, and Science on the Anglo-American Frontier, 1500–1676* (Cambridge MA: Harvard University Press, 2001), argues that notions of Indian inferiority developed over time.

5. David Eltis, *The Rise of African Slavery in the Americas* (Cambridge: Cambridge University Press, 1998).

6. Ronald Takaki is one of several scholars who speculate that Epenow inspired William Shakespeare to create the character Caliban in *The Tempest*. Ronald T. Takaki, "The Tempest in the Wilderness: The Racialization of Savagery," *Journal of American History* 79 (December 1992), 892–912.

7. Smith expressed dismay at the "trechery" of Hunt's actions. Philip L. Barbour, ed., *The Complete Works of Captain John Smith*, 3 vols. (Chapel Hill NC, 1986), 2:401. Gorges later recorded that "the Friers of those parts took the rest from them, and kept them to be instructed in the Christian faith." Neal Salisbury, *Manitou and Providence: Indians, Europeans, and the making of New England, 1500–1643* (New York: Oxford University Press, 1982), 107, and "Squanto: Last of the Patuxets," in David G. Sweet and Gary B. Nash, eds., *Struggle and Survival in Colonial America* (Berkeley: University of California Press, 1981).

8. Salisbury, *Manitou*, 90–96.

9. Israel Stoughton to John Winthrop, [c. June 28, 1637]; John Winthrop to William Bradford, July 28, 1637, both in *Winthrop Papers*, 6 vols. (Boston: Massachusetts Historical Society, 1929–) [hereafter *WP*], 3:435–36, 456–58.

10. John Winthrop, *Winthrop's Journal: "History of New England"*, 2 vols., ed. James K. Hosmer (New York: Charles Scribner's Sons, 1908), 1:227.

11. See Anthony Pagden, *The Fall of Natural Man: the American Indian and the Origins of Comparative Ethnology* (New York: Cambridge University Press, 1982).

12. Roger Williams, *A Key into the Language of America*, ed. John J. Teunissen and Evelyn J. Hinz (Detroit MI: Wayne State University Press, 1973), 133.

13. See the "Response of the Royal Commissioners," May 1665, Nathaniel Shurtleff, ed., *Records of the Governor and Company of the Massachusetts Bay in New England*, 4 vols. (Boston, 1854), 4:213 [hereafter *Mass. Recs.*].

14. In a case that inspired the 1647 statute, the Massachusetts General Court eagerly prosecuted the case of two Africans whom the court deemed "fraudulently & iniuriously taken & brought from Gynny" by Captain Smith of the ship *Rainbow*. The court ordered them freed and returned to their homes in Africa. *Mass. Recs.*, 3:49, 58, 84.

15. On Scots prisoners of war in New England, see Stephen Innes, *Labor in a New Land: Economy and Society in Seventeenth-Century Springfield* (Princeton NJ: Princeton University Press, 1983), 9–10, 58, 86, 109.

16. For the runaway Pequot girl, see Richard Morris to John Coggeshall [May 1647], in *WP*, 4:164–65; "Petition of the Inhabitants of Hingham to the Council," December 21, 1676, Miscellaneous Bound Photostats, Massachusetts Historical Society.

17. Richard Davenport to Hugh Peter, *WP*, 3:452–54.

18. Israel Stoughton to John Winthrop, [ca. June 28, 1637], *WP*, 3:435–36.

19. See, for example, John Winthrop to William Bradford, July 28, 1637, *WP*, 3:456–58.

20. James F. Brooks, *Captives and Cousins: Slavery, Kinship, and Community in the Southwest Borderlands* (Chapel Hill: University of North Carolina Press for the Institute for Early American History and Culture, 2002); Juliana Barr, "From Captives to Slaves: Commodifying Women in the Borderlands," *Journal of American History* 92 (2005).

21. Roger Williams to John Winthrop, July 15, 1637, in *WP*, 3:451.

22. Roger Williams to John Winthrop, July 15, 1637, *WP*, 3:451, 459; Williams to Winthrop, July 31, 1637, *WP*, 4:17.

23. Hugh Peter to John Winthrop, July 15, 1637, *WP*, 3:450.

24. In the Tripartite Treaty of 1638, the United Colonies assigned approximately eighty captives to the Narragansetts, twenty to Ninigret, the Niantic sachem, and one hundred to the Mohegans—a post-contact client tribe of Connecticut that had numbered approximately fifty before the Pequot War. Harry M. Ward, *The United Colonies of New England* (New York: Vantage Press, 1961), 29–38.

25. Francis Jennings notes that the Narragansetts also deplored the English practice of killing noncombatants in battle, which violated their customs of warfare. See Francis Jennings, *The Invasion of America: Indians, Colonialism, and the Cant of Conquest* (Chapel Hill: University of North Carolina Press for the Institute for Early American History and Culture, 1975), 223, and Patrick Malone, *The Skulking Way of War: Technology and Tactics among the New England Indians* (Baltimore: Johns Hopkins University Press, 1993), 29–30, 102–103.

26. Williams to Winthrop, [ca. June 21, 1637], *WP*, 3:433–34.

27. Roger Williams to John Winthrop, [Sept. 1638?], *WP*, 6:57.

28. Kathleen J. Bragdon, *Native People of Southern New England, 1500–1650* (Norman: University of Oklahoma Press, 1996), 99–100. Other works that explore the experience of Indian and white captives among Indian captors include Daniel K. Richter, "War and Culture: The Iroquois Experience," *William and Mary Quarterly*, 40 (1983), 528–99.

29. Williams, *Key*, 96.

30. *Acts of the Commissioners of the United Colonies of New England*, July 15, 1646, in *Records of the Colony of New Plymouth*, 12 vols. (Boston, 1856–1861) [hereafter cited as *RCNP*] 9:70.

31. Emmanuel Downing to John Winthrop, ca. August 1645, *WP*, 4:38.

32. For a request that Winthrop send some Indians to labor in Bermuda's nascent "Shuger workes," see William Berkeley to John Winthrop, June 12 and 25, 1648. Emanuel Downing recommended that the New England colonies seek Indian captives in order to exchange them for enslaved Africans; Emanuel Downing to John Winthrop, [c. August 1645]. Both in *WP*, 5:38, 229, 232.

33. *The Public Records of the Colony of Connecticut, 1636–1776*, 15 vols. (1850; repr. New York: AMS Press, 1968), 1:532.

34. Lauber, *Indian Slavery*, 206.

35. *Records of the Colony of Rhode Island and Providence Plantations*, John Russell Bartlett, ed., 10 vols. (Providence RI, 1856–1865) [hereafter RI *Recs.*], 1:414–15.

36. *RCNP*, 11:234.

37. *RCNP*, 5:151–52; James P. Ronda, "Red and White at the Bench: Indians and the Law in Plymouth Colony, 1620–1691," *Essex Institute Historical Collections*, vol. 110 (1974), 200–215, quotation from 211.

38. *Records of the Suffolk County Court, 1671–1680*, Samuel Eliot Morison, ed., 2 vols. (Boston: Colonial Society of Massachusetts, 1933), 1:548–49.

39. *RCNP*, 5:173; Governor Leverett's Certificate, September 12, 1676, Miscellaneous Bound Documents, Massachusetts Historical Society, Boston.

40. For a similar argument, see James D. Drake, *King Philip's War: Civil War in New England, 1675–1676* (Amherst MA: University of Massachusetts Press, 1999), 112–14.

41. April 19, 1676, Petition of Jonathan Fairbanks, Photostats, Massachusetts Historical Society, Boston.

42. *RCNP*, 5:173–74.

43. See Colin G. Calloway, *The Western Abenakis of Vermont, 1600–1800* (Norman: University of Oklahoma Press, 1990), 81.

44. Samuel Shrimpton to Elizabeth Shrimpton, July 8, 1676, Miscellaneous Bound Documents, Massachusetts Historical Society, Boston.

45. "The names of 9:Women wth 6: children great & Small Examined By the Committee of the Genrll Court this 5 Nov:1675 in Boston," Massachusetts Archives Collection [hereafter *MAC*], vol. 30, 184a, Massachusetts State Archives, Boston.

46. *RCNP* 10:366. For a discussion of this incident in the context of Indian marital relations, see Plane, *Colonial Intimacies*.

47. Daniel Gookin, "Indian Children Put to Service, August 10, 1676," *New England Historical and Genealogical Register* 8 (1854), 270–73.

48. *Records of the Court of Assistants of the Colony of the Massachusetts Bay, 1630–1692*, John Noble, ed., 3 vols.(Boston: Published by the County of Suffolk, 1901), 1:86, 88.

49. See, for example, "Petition of William Ahaton," *MAC* 30:176, 207a; "Petition of Waban, Samuel Tomputawin, and other Indians of Natick and Punkapaugh," *MAC* 30:229; "Petition from Joseph and William Wannukkow," September 5, 1676 and "Petition from severall Indians belonginge to Naticke and Punkapaugo," [November 1676], Photostats, Massachusetts Historical Society; "Indictment for kidnapping Indians," November 2, 1675, Miscellaneous Bound Documents, Massachusetts Historical Society; "Petition of Bernard Trott to the Governor, Councill and Assembly," *MAC* 31:1.

50. *The Early Records of the Town of Portsmouth*, Clarence S. Brigham, ed. (Providence RI, 1901), 187–88; Lepore, *Name of War*, 170.

51. *The Early Records of the Town of Providence, Vol. XV, Being the Providence Town Papers, Vol. I, 1639–April 1682* (Providence RI, 1899), 151–54.

52. Jenny Hale Pulsipher, *Subjects unto the Same King: Indians, English, and the Contest for Authority in Colonial New England* (Philadelphia: University of Pennsylvania Press, 2005), 236–37.

53. *The Acts and Resolves, Public and Private, of the Province of the Massachusetts-Bay*, 21 vols. (Boston: Wright and Potter, 1869–1922) [hereafter *Mass. Acts and Resolves*], 1:176, 530, 558, 594, 600.

54. See, for example, "Petition from Peter Freeman, Indean of Narraganset," May 1685, *Mass. Recs.*, 5:477; "Petition from Jno. Paine to the Governors of Connecticut, Massachusetts, Plymouth, and the Commissioners of the United Colonies," October 1676, Photostats, Massachusetts Historical Society; Daniel Gookin, "Certificate for John Nemasittwas," Nov. 20, 1676, Photostats, Massachusetts Historical Society.

55. Gary B. Nash, *Red, White, and Black: The Peoples of Early North America* (Englewood Cliffs NJ: Prentice-Hall, 1992), 131–33, 136–37; Alan Gallay, *The Indian Slave Trade: The Rise of the English Empire in the American South, 1670–1717* (New Haven: Yale University Press 2002).

56. *Mass. Acts and Resolves*, 1:634, 696; RI *Recs.*, 3:482–83, 4:131, 185–86.

57. Daniel Vickers has also used this term, although he focuses on debt peonage. See Vickers, "The First Indian Whalemen of Nantucket," *William and Mary Quarterly* 40 (1983), 560–83.

58. Daniel Mandell, *Behind the Frontier: Indians in Eighteenth-Century Eastern Massachusetts* (Lincoln: University of Nebraska Press, 1996), 29; Jean M. O'Brien, *Dispossession by Degrees: Indian Land and Identity in Natick, Massachusetts, 1650–1790* (New York: Cambridge University Press, 1998), 65–71; Order in Council, March 19, 1689/90.

59. For more on the effects of alcohol consumption on New England's Native Americans, see Peter Mancall, *Deadly Medicine: Indians and Alcohol in Early America* (Ithaca NY: Cornell University Press, 1995).

60. *Records of the Suffolk County Court, 1671–1680*, David Konig, ed., 2 vols. (Boston: Colonial Society of Massachusetts, 1983), 1:89, 113, 258, 259, 521, 557; 2:869, 1015, 1016, 1157.

61. William Southmound v. Sassimmmin an Indian; Joseph Daggett v. Zackery Wonhosoott, May 26, 1685, Dukes County Quarterly Court of Sessions, Vol. I, 1675–1716, Dukes County Court House, Edgartown, Massachusetts.

62. "Spetiall Court at Edgartown January ye 14th [16]87/8," Dukes County Quarterly Court of Sessions.

63. "Declaration against James Covell and Keoiape [Keipe] two indian youths," September 11, 1693, Dukes County Quarterly Court of Sessions; Charles Banks, "unpublished notes re: Indian slavery," Banks Manuscripts, Box 174a, folder 24, Martha's Vineyard Historical Society, Edgartown, Massachusetts.

64. See the case of Ebeneezer Commoson and Isaac Solomon, Bristol [Massachusetts] Court of General Sessions, Vol. 2, Jan 19, 1704/5, 71–72, Supreme Judicial Court, Massachusetts State Archives, Boston, Massachusetts.

65. [Newport] *Rhode Island General Court of Trials, 1671–1730*, transcribed by Jane Fletcher Fiske (Boxford MA: self-published, 1998), 221.

66. See James P. Ronda, "Red and White at the Bench: Indians and the Law in Plymouth Colony, 1620–1691," *Essex Institute Historical Collections*, 110 (1974), 214; Yasuhide Kawashima, "Jurisdiction of the Colonial Courts over the Indians in Massachusetts, 1689–1763," *New England Quarterly* 42 (1969), 532–50, especially 542–44.

67. "Petition for release of Grigory an Indian from indenture," October 1732, Petitions to the Rhode Island General Assembly, Vol. 2, 1728–1733, item 69, Rhode Island State Archives, Providence, Rhode Island.

68. Daniel Vickers, "The First Whalemen of Nantucket," in Colin Calloway, ed., *After King Philip's War: Presence and Persistence in Indian New England* (Hanover NH: University Press of New England, 1997), 90–113, 105–6.

69. Gideon Hawley to Andrew Oliver, Dec. 9, 1760, Gideon Hawley Papers, Congregational Society, Boston, Massachusetts.

70. See writ in the case of Mason v. Fish, May 28, 1716, New London County Court Files, Native Americans, Box 1, Folder 9, Connecticut State Archives, Hartford, Connecticut.

71. "Petition to the Governor of Massachusetts from Simon Popmoney . . . on behalf of their neighbors asking to protect the Younger Indians," MAC 30:456.

72. MAC 30:460.

73. For abuses of Euro-American and African servants in the American context, see Edmund Morgan, *American Slavery, American Freedom: The Ordeal of Colonial Virginia* (New York: W. W. Norton, 1975), and Kenneth Morgan, *Slavery and Servitude in Colonial North America* (New York: New York University Press, 2001).

74. "Diary of Joshua Hempstead, 1711–1758," *New London County Historical Society, Collections,* Vol. I (Providence RI: Published by the Society, 1901), 465.

75. "Petition of Phebee an Indian Maid," July 8, 1701, Bristol County Court of General Sessions of the Peace Record Book, 1697–1702, Massachusetts State Archives.

76. Sarah [Chauqum] v. Robinson, September 1724, Newport Supreme Court Record Book, Vol. B, 1725–1741, and Washington, South Kingstown Justices' Court, July 1733 prosecution bond, Rhode Island Judicial Records Center, Pawtucket, Rhode Island. In earlier documents Sarah appears as "Sarah Mollatto."

77. Sainsbury, "Indian Labor in Early Rhode Island," 386; Jane Fletcher Fiske, *Gleanings from Newport Court Files, 1659–1783* (Boxford MA, 1999), #658; *Boston News-Letter,* March 3–10, 1718.

78. *RCNP* 5:223, 253; *Mass. Acts and Resolves,* 1:436; 2:104, 364.

79. Indenture, December 10, 1723, Shepley Papers, vol. 15, document 19, Rhode Island Historical Society, Providence, Rhode Island. For a detailed comparative study of Rhode Island indentures across racial lines, see John E. Murray and Ruth Wallis Herndon, "Markets for Children in Early America: A Political Economy of Pauper Apprenticeship," *Journal of Economic History* 62 (June 2002), 356–82, and Ruth Wallis Herdon and Ella Wilcox Sekatau, "Colonizing the Children: Indian Youngsters in Servitude in Early Rhode Island," in Colin G. Calloway and Neal Salisbury, eds., *Reinterpreting New England Indians and the Colonial Experience* (Boston: Colonial Society of Massachusetts, 2004), 137–62.

80. Ruth Wallis Herndon and Ella Wilcox Sekatau also note the increasing tendency of Rhode Island officials to designate Narragansett Indian people as "Negro" or "Black," although they locate the shift in the latter half of the eighteenth century, especially in the post-Revolutionary period. See their "The Right to a Name: The Narragansett People and Rhode Island Officials in the Revolutionary Era," in Calloway, ed., *After King Philip's War,* 114–43.

81. Patience was sold and resold several times after being tried for infanticide and acquitted; she was finally convicted in 1738 of killing the grandchildren of her then master, a minister in Falmouth, Maine. See Samuel and Joseph Moody, *A Faithful Narrative of the Wicked Life and Remarkable Conversion of Patience Boston* (Boston, 1738), in Daniel A. Cohen, *Pillars of Salt, Monuments of Grace: New England Crime Literature and the Origins of American Popular Culture, 1674–1860* (New York: Oxford University Press, 1993), 72–74.

82. Sainsbury, "Indian Labor," 379, 392–93.

2. "They shalbe slaves for their lives"
Indian Slavery in Colonial Virginia
C. S. Everett

During the seventeenth and eighteenth centuries, Virginians enslaved perhaps thousands of American Indians. Heretofore generally unnoticed or
ignored by scholars, the trafficking in humans ran not simply into, but
through and out of the Old Dominion. This domestic slave trade preceded
the mass importation of Africans in the late seventeenth and early eighteenth
centuries. Moreover, this trade is part of Virginia's broad history, affecting
and affected by other events, policies, and practices. Indeed, rather than
being merely incidental to African slavery, Indian slavery was ubiquitous,
and probably a central component of Virginia's storied past.[1]

Historians, researchers, and scholars have written more frequently
about Virginia than any other early English North American colony.[2] Despite the rich historiography, historians—with a few prominent exceptions—have scarcely noticed that American Indian heritage and history
are integral facets of the colony's past. In simplest terms, Virginia's colonial history is Captain John Smith and Pocahontas, Jamestown, tobacco
agriculture, the birthplace of African slavery in English North America,
Bacon's Rebellion, majestic plantations, George Washington, Yorktown,
and the young Thomas Jefferson. Indians figure little in the grand narrative, except for initially obstructing westward-sweeping colonists and
committing the massacre of 1622. For most of the twentieth century, Indian
history has been written and told almost wholly from the perspective of

cultural anthropologists, who even now hold sway over representing the region's Indian history.[3]

As far as conveying and even preserving cultural knowledge, describing aboriginal medicine and religion, outlining syncretism, adaptation, and explaining ethnic identity and persistence, anthropology as a discipline has done a great service in terms of what scholars and laypersons alike know of Virginia Indians. Nevertheless there has been little progress toward integrating Indian history into the warp and weft of the general historical fabric; Indians are still largely segregated from "Virginia" history. As this essay will indicate, though, Indians and their history—which includes slavery—are very much part of that broader history.

There are several historians who have noted the existence of Indian slavery in Virginia. Almon Wheeler Lauber's treatment (from 1913) is perhaps the first and oldest, if not the best known, and provides a very general overview.[4] However, the few scholars to write subsequently on the subject have limited themselves to Lauber's work and conclusions. According to Lauber, Indian slavery in Virginia was largely insignificant, relatively sporadic, and practiced only from the late 1670s into the early eighteenth century, being technically legal only from 1681 to 1705. One historian, J. Leitch Wright, however, has gone beyond Lauber in perceiving Indian slavery's greater significance. Although Wright did not focus exclusively on Virginia, he made a good case for Indian slavery having a longer lifespan and argued that it was a more widespread practice than was indicated by Lauber. Moreover, Wright breached the critically important subjects of interracial and intercultural mingling.[5] Virginia anthropologists have downplayed this mingling in an effort to counteract an earlier generation's refusal to acknowledge the persistence of Indian identity due to African admixture. Some earlier scholars—and others—considered the tiny remnant Indian enclaves "Negro" based on the "one-drop rule" concept.[6]

However, historians recognize and even embrace constant change; change is history, history is change. Different notions of what constitutes "race" and "identity," and even "Indian" for that matter, flowed through Virginia over the course of nearly three centuries before the rise of the Jim

Crow South, with its strict ideas about the color line. To Jim Crow, all who were not entirely white were simply "colored" and it mattered little if one colored person was biologically more Indian than "Negro." However, this was not always the case.

A century before the institution of Jim Crow, Virginia's preeminent judges and the judiciary saw otherwise (from say, at least 1772 into the 1830s). Even so-called Negroes descended in their maternal line from Indian ancestors were still labeled "Indians," regardless of presumed cultural affiliation or, in some instances, even physical appearance. Virginia authorities, religious leaders, and laypersons alike recognized "black" Indians and "colored" persons "of Indian descent."[7] Slave owners themselves recognized "white" Indians, "mulatto" Indians, and "Negro" Indians as well as just plain "Indians." There were "free" Indians (essentially citizens), tribal town and reservation Indians (noncitizens), and servant Indians and slave Indians (the former could become citizens or return to noncitizens). Some noncitizen tribal and reservation Indians were "white," while others were "black" and "mulatto."[8] Despite occasional challenges to their official status, Indians—whatever their physical color—generally lived as "Indians," though this varied from place to place and over time. In one county, "Indian" status could be terminated, while in another it could persist, even receiving the protection of the governor. Indian history is far from cut and dry; it is quite complicated. One of the complicating factors is the historical existence of Indian slavery.

Years before the first documentation of Africans in the colony, Virginians could and did refer to certain Indians as slaves.[9] Even while still negotiating the status of those first Africans, Virginians took Indians captive and "made slaves of them." Indeed, during the Anglo-Powhatan war of 1622–1632, official directives mandated Indian slavery.[10] By 1626 the colonial government thought nothing of bestowing a recently captured Indian man to Captain William Claiborne so that he might test his newly invented restraining device, an apparatus designed to make "Indians more serviceable" to the colonists.[11] This practice of turning captives into slaves was already well ensconced when in 1644 another war broke out between American natives and colonists. Colonial response was unambiguous. In

1645 "many prisoners" were taken on a march into tribal towns. Most of these captives were transported out of Virginia on a ship owned by Virginia Governor William Berkeley and sold in England's West Indian colonies. Over the course of the next five years, twenty-eight Indians appear in surviving colonial deeds and inventories as either servants or slaves. Four appear to be covenant or contract servants, purchasers bought six others from an estate sale, and at least another six are unambiguously slaves, delivered and sold as merchandise and bequeathed in perpetuity to estate heirs through last wills.[12] Twenty-eight is not an overwhelming number until one realizes that this figure actually exceeds that known for Africans through the same period.

From 1610 to 1646, colonists engaged local tribes in three major wars. During this time enslavement was generally punitive retribution. In several instances, though, Virginia exported Indians, suggesting an existing external market for American slaves. Evidence quite strongly indicates that "many" local Indians were readily enslaved and exported during the course of the Third Anglo-Powhatan War (1644–1646).[13] With the existence of an external market for Indian slaves, financial incentive may have played as much a role in slavery as did colonial vengeance. One wonders how knowledge and profit related to this market informed Virginians' notions of slavery during this era, widely acknowledged as the formative period of African slavery in North America.

It is not surprising that there were importations of Indian slaves into Virginia even during times of relative peace within the colony. For instance, peace came again to Virginia in 1646 with the Treaty of Necotowance. Along with the treaty came a formalized segregated coexistence and several important provisions. The newly subjugated native tribes were required to return runaway Indians to colonial masters and colonists were obliged to treat all Indians according to the letter of the law: no native, allied, or tributary Indian could be enslaved. This says nothing of "foreign" or hostile Indians, for which prohibitive measures were not put into place until decades later.[14] So the trade in non-local, non-tributary Indian slaves continued.

In 1648, for example, Maryland rebuked Virginian William

South for having come into Maryland to purchase an Indian girl from the Wicomicco tribe. In 1650 planter Thomas Gerard of Northumberland County claimed land due through head rights on four imported Indians, and several years later another Northumberland resident brought in the Indian "Francisco." Francisco's non-Anglo name suggests origins, or perhaps captivity, in an Iberian colony.[15] In May 1650 the Northumberland Court heard a case in which six local male colonists admitted taking Indian women and ninety-three deerskins and beaver pelts from Patuxent Indian Town in Maryland. In compensation, the Virginia court awarded the Patuxent sovereign only a paltry "six Tradinge Cloath match Coats." No mention is made of the stolen women in the judgment.[16] The colonists either kept them for themselves or sold them.

In the Third Anglo-Powhatan War, during William Berkeley's first tenure as Virginia governor, countless Indians were enslaved and a good number exported, defraying the colony's expenses in prosecuting the war.[17] Berkeley himself purchased two young Indians from Lieutenant Thomas Smallcombe, one of the principals of Fort Royal on the Pamunkey River, from where were launched sorties into the main Pamunkey Indian Town. In 1646 the administrators of Smallcombe's estate enumerated six Indian slaves.[18] So Governor Berkeley, too, likely profited directly from Indian slavery. Without doubt the Pamunkeys stood to lose a lot. Certainly, the claims they made years later that the colonists were accustomed to selling their children were not baseless.[19] Combined with relentless colonial military action, slaving subdued the Powhatan tribes. Other tribal nations gambled that they could avoid enslavement by becoming tributaries of Virginia.

Despite the guarantees of freedom by the Treaty of Necotowance, Virginians persisted in the enslavement of local Indians, particularly children, which threatened to drag the colony back into war.[20] Concurrently, colonial trade with Indians exploded beyond the narrow confines of the developing plantation society along the colony's tidewater rivers. This expansion fomented an Anglo-Dutch rivalry and competition with Maryland and Indian nations to Virginia's north, leading Virginians to look elsewhere for new trade opportunities.

Under the aegis of Governor Berkeley, the 1650 Edward Bland–Abraham Wood mercantile expedition penetrated southward into northern North Carolina along the Roanoke River. Four years later an expedition led by Nathaniel Battes and Francis Yeardley solidified Virginia's ties with coastal Carolina tribes and the powerful Tuscaroras and other inland nations. That Battes and Yeardley were already selling Indian slaves may provide some insight into the motivations behind their expedition.[21] During the summer of 1656, a multiethnic group composed of disparate refugee elements — some from Virginia, Iroquoian Eries from the Great Lakes, and others ultimately from as far away as Spanish Florida — combined with the Nesson people (also called the Nahyssans or the Nassaws), and coalesced near the falls of the James River, at what is now Richmond. Alarmed colonists, fearing the sudden appearance at the colonial frontier of some 700 "strange" Indians, called for the removal of these "Rickahockans." Tributary informants assured the governor that the Rickahockans, whom they called "Richahecrian" and "Nahyssan" (Nesson), had no hostile intentions, and in fact were amassing in order to beat back a northern incursion from the "Massahocks," or Iroquoian Mohawks and Senecas. Given Virginia's recent efforts to open the southern frontier, the Rickahockans likely settled closer to Virginia in order to improve or guard their own trade interests. Or perhaps the Rickahockans were simply returning "home."

As far back as 1608, the Virginia Company's Captain John Smith visited a Chickahominy town on the lower reaches of the Chickahominy River, called "Righkahauck."[22] Another "Rickahockan" town was mentioned in 1622, when some "of the Westerly Runnagados" (i.e., western renegades) fled into Nansemond territory southeast of the colony following the discovery of their conspiracy to poison the Laughing King of Accomack.[23] The Laughing King was a staunch English ally who had recently entered into a new trade agreement with the colonists. By this arrangement, the Accomacks would supply the English with corn, thus undermining one of the principal advantages the mainland Algonkian-speaking and Powhatan tribes — such as the Chickahominies — maintained over the colonists.[24] After their plot was uncovered, the "Runnagados" made a new settlement, called "Rickahake," somewhere about the northern section of the Great

Dismal Swamp, just beyond reach of easy English reprisal. A Dutchman noted the Rickahake Town on Virginia's southern frontier on a map he made in 1640.[25]

During the Third Anglo-Powhatan War, the main body of the Chickahominy and Mattaponi tribes moved together north from the James and Pamunkey rivers to a new town on the north side of the Mattaponi River. Additional pressure and conflict with colonists led them to move again several times before finally requesting the governor and council's permission to seat again at their old town—which they called "Rickahock"—on the north bank of the Mattaponi River. The record suggests that town site was never again inhabited. For the next decade, colonial records do not report any other encounters or troubles with the Rickahockans.

Then, in 1656, the Rickahockans and Nessons massed about the falls of the James River. Virginia enlisted more than one hundred tributary Pamunkey warriors to help drive these collective Rickahockans away from the colony's frontier. With their native auxiliaries, Virginia waged two major offensives—the Rickahockans beat back the first offensive—against the native "intruders." After the second assault in 1657, the Rickahockans retreated south from the colony. Thirteen years later, Virginia explorer John Lederer made a tentative peace with at least some of them, after which they became generally recognized as the "Westos," whose principal town was called "Rickahauga"—a name strikingly evocative of Virginia's "Richahecrian" enemy/ally and the name of the Westo town that Carolinian Dr. Henry Woodward visited in late October of 1674. "Rickahauga" is virtually if not entirely synonymous with "Rickahock."

Finally, by the 1646 Treaty of Necotowance, Fort Henry was the assigned trading mart located at the falls of the Appomattox River, effectively marking Virginia's southwestern border, with Fort Royal, the trading post established north of the James River, marking the northwestern border. The natives visiting this latter place, according to historian A. J. Morrison, referred to it as "Rickahacke."[26] Upon his visit to the Westos in 1674, Henry Woodward remarked that their trade was regular, to "ye northward," set at designated points of the year and limited to specific locales.[27] Such trade practices are quite consistent with contemporary Virginia law, and reflect the tightly controlled and restricted trade characteristic of the colony in the several years before Bacon's Rebellion in 1676.[28] In this light, the Savannah River Westo settlement of Rickahauga could be viewed as a "Virginia" Indian town, at least concerning trade alliances up to that point in time. The evidence suggests that the Westos, the Rickahockans, were a conglomeration of Eries, Nessons, and Chickahominy people, linked together for paramountcy in trade.[29] For two decades or so they were paramount, inspiring awe from at least central Virginia to what is now coastal Georgia.[30]

In March 1670 John Lederer, with three tributary Chickahominy guides, Magtakunh, Hoppotoguoh, and Nannugh from treaty-ordained (reserved) Indian Neck (the peninsula between the Pamunkey and Mattaponi rivers), set out to explore the southern and western regions beyond Virginia's bounds. Heading due west from Pamunkey River into the mountains, they were forced to turn back due to cold and snow. Starting out on a second trip in May, this time with a Susquehannock named Jackzetavon, Lederer traveled more southerly and reached the "Nahyssans" (Nessons). Lederer described the Nessons as a "rich" and powerful, "warlike" nation living in three main towns, called Sapon, Nahyssan, and Pintahae, on the upper Roanoke River, in the heart of "Ahkontshuck," or what later became known as the Piedmont. At first Lederer feared approaching the Nessons because some "ten years before" they "had been in continual Hostility" with Virginia, referring at least in part to the conflicts near the falls of the James. Lederer also mentioned Nesson contact with the "Florida" Indians—hostile and otherwise—suggesting southern incursions right in line with contemporaneous Spanish reports of gun-toting northern invaders accompanied at times by a few Englishmen.[31] Lederer also noted, by way of Nesson informants, that just beyond the first crest of the Blue Ridge—in a land "of waves," as the Nessons referred to Virginia's ridge-valley region—almost due west of the Nessons, dwelt the Rickahockans proper.[32] After distributing trade goods and promising to return with more in six months, Lederer asked directions to his next destination, Occaneechee Town. Shortly after his arrival at Occaneechee, Rickahockan emissaries arrived—no doubt upon communication and direction of the Nessons—likely seeking, as native nations had already done and would continue to do for the next half century, to guard their own trade interests.

Contemporaneously, Virginians acknowledged that the Indian trade was extensive and economically important. Through several acts of Assembly from the mid-1650s into the early 1660s, the government had already recognized the value of this burgeoning trade. In April 1658, less than a year after repulsing the Rickahockans, and just about a year prior to the earliest known invasions of "northern," English-armed and -accompanied Indians into northern Florida, Virginia actually permitted an unrestricted, free, and open trade with "friendly"—and not necessarily "tributary"—Indians "for guns, powder, and shott." These statutes also acknowledged that prominent among those engaging in the Indian trade were non-commissioned, self-serving, unofficial traders who sold arms and ammunition to *any* Indians whatsoever—not simply "tributary" or "friendly" tribes—and occasionally dealt with Indian leaders in a less than affable manner. In 1659 and 1660, concurrent with the Florida incursions, Virginia authorities attempted to discourage roving packhorse traders from going out amongst the tribes, tacitly implying that this method was already the common practice.[33] However, freemen—"all the inhabitants of this country"—were permitted, under license, to repair to the special colonial forts established about the falls of the rivers and there engage with the Indians in trade.[34] This marks Virginia's first effort to regulate and control an opportunistic, increasingly valuable—and potentially danger-ous—trade. Then, in March 1661, perhaps on the authority of some now-long-lost colonial—or native—intelligence regarding Spanish concerns with Virginia traders, Governor William Berkeley formally prohibited Virginia traders from taking slaves among the Indians; that is, forbid the purchasing of Indians from Indians.[35] This move was ostensibly an effort to both appease and protect tributary tribes—at that time essential to the general trade—and to shield colonists from the fury of offended foreign tribes and nations.

Probably not coincidentally, it was between early 1659 and early 1661 that Spanish authorities in Florida were reporting on the violent incursions from their north. The Spanish referred to these raiders as

"Chichimecos," though it is apparent from other sources that these were the Rickahockans. The raiders—quite probably working with or at the behest of roving noncommissioned traders—were sweeping down through the interior and driving refugees to the coastal missions established by the Spanish friars in what is now southeastern South Carolina and northern Georgia.[36] As noted earlier, some of the invaders carried guns, and, on at least one occasion, several Englishmen reputedly accompanied them.[37] Importantly, there were also reports of slaving. Perhaps not unexpectedly, in 1660 Northumberland County, Virginian George Colclough received a head-right claim on his Indian slave "Francisco." The following year, Surry County interpreter Thomas Busby, likely a trader, sold a five-year-old Indian boy to planter William Rollinson "for ye term & time of his life."[38]

These Indians were not indentured servants. Like Rollinson's boy, Indians served masters not for four years or seven years, but until they died, no matter how many years that might be. Indisputably, and by 1661 at the latest, Indians could be—and were—lifelong servants. Judging from the deeds and wills of the 1640s through the 1660s, Indian servitude was generally something more than lifelong service. The children of Indian "servants" were also servants for life, born into that condition. Moreover, Virginia did not limit enslavement only to Indians captured from distant Spanish territory by dubious allies or disreputable traders. Virginia—after decades of struggling for survival from 1607 until the late 1640s—was stabilizing, growing increasingly more powerful and secure. Still, there were occasional threats to security. By the late 1650s and early 1660s, with trade opportunities expanding and contact with distant tribes increasing, rather than hindering or limiting slavery, armed conflict between colonists and natives provided justification for, and rationalization of, slavery.

For example, in 1660, when Northumberland resident John Powell complained of damages incurred upon his estate by unspecified Indians, the colonial legislature passed an act authorizing county commissioners to demand monetary satisfaction from all Indians living within county bounds. If any of these Indians did not or were unable to immediately comply, "then soe many off them as the court shall thinke fitt shall be apprehended and sold into a fforraigne country." Indeed, the governor and council subsequently appointed and authorized themselves "to cause some of those Indians to be apprehended and to bee accordingly disposed of."[39] This transpired some sixteen years before Bacon's Rebellion—an event cited by earlier scholars as the seminal event leading to the eventual, but temporary, enslavement of certain Indians, and, perhaps more notably, two years prior to Virginia's first legislative act recognizing the condition of "Negro" slavery.[40] Probably realizing a profit from the direct capture and sale of Indian slaves in 1660 (as in 1646) the Berkeleyan administration sought with its Indian slavery act of 1661 to circumvent the growing power and influence of independent traders.

Again, in 1666—and barely a decade before the onset of Bacon's Rebellion—Governor Berkeley issued an order against the Rappahannock River tribes. Members of these tribes allegedly murdered some colonists in that section in violation of the treaty of 1646. With the 1660/1661 retribution act in place, the General Court, Berkeley presiding, declared that "for revenge" of the alleged murders and "for the prevention of future mischiefs," the tribes would be prosecuted with war and "their women and children" taken and then "disposed of according to such instructions as shall be issued from the Right Honourable the Governor."[41]

The governor's precise instructions do not survive. However, shortly before the General Court convened, Berkeley wrote in reply to Rappahannock County justice and Colonial Council member Major General Robert Smyth. Smyth had reported to Berkeley on the activities of the local tribes and Berkeley urged their destruction, saying that such could be accomplished without charge since "the Women and Children will Defray it." If, for whatever reason, the Council could not raise enough men through the regular muster, Berkeley noted that plenty would certainly volunteer "for their Share of the Booty."[42] Drawing on at least two decades of experience, Berkeley was confident that enslavement was incentive enough for colonists to march against the Indians. Simultaneously, enslavement, coupled with the killing that certainly ensued, hastened the decline of the Rappahannock River tribes, freeing up additional land for colonial patent. These and other activities suggest that Berkeley was using his office to exert some control over the Indian trade as well to generate profit from slaving, all supposedly for Virginia's benefit.[43] But Berkeley's policies and their alleged benefits, even his authority in these matters, would face challenges.

Early in 1670, eighteen-year-old William Byrd arrived in Virginia from London for the reading of the last will of his uncle, Thomas Stegge. William Byrd would play a significant role in Virginia's development for the next three decades, culminating in one of the finest and largest estates in the land. But Byrd's rise to prominence did not follow the stereotypical trajectory of the tidewater tobacco planter. Rather, Byrd's path to glory stretched southward, into regions far beyond the ordered plantations of colonial settlement. Byrd's path was already well worn, though, intersecting with other paths reaching northward from palisaded villages surrounded by fields of corn and beans. Traffic flowed two ways over and across these intersecting paths, human porters carrying an array of goods to exchange for more exotic cargoes. Among the "goods" transported over these paths were other humans.

By November 1683, less than thirteen years after he set foot in the colony, Governor Lord Francis Howard, Baron of Effingham, and the Colonial Council appointed William Byrd commissioner to enter negotiations with Seneca raiders then warring in Virginia.[44] The Senecas were one of the tribes of the powerful Five Nations Iroquois of what is now New York.[45] In the fall of 1683, Senecas fell upon several of the Virginia tributary Indian towns, killing some people and taking a number of captives. Byrd met with the Senecas and arranged for a treaty. The treaty ceremony was held the next summer on neutral treaty ground at Albany, New York, not too distant from the Five Nations. Then late in the summer of 1685, Governor Howard sent Byrd back to Albany to engage Five Nations chiefs in negotiations for a more lasting peace. Byrd told the assembled leaders he was well aware that earlier that summer some Five Nations raiders had "seized, and Carried away one Indian girle" from an Englishman's house near the falls of the Appomattox River, where she was doing laundry, and that the previous year three Appomattox Indian boys, servants of the same Englishman, were likewise "carried away." Byrd then demanded that if the Five Nations wished to avoid a general war with Virginia, if they wished to "Renew the Covenant chain" to keep it "bright and clear," and allow the "tree of Peace" to remain "fresh and green," they must "Deliver up all Christian, Indian, or Negro Servants and Slaves, that are amongst you" that had been "Caried away" from English masters in Virginia.[46]

In their response to Byrd's forceful demand, the Five Nations speakers Carachkondie, Taggojerhos and Canondodawe took turns accusing one or the other of the nations in the kidnappings. Carachkondie, of the Onondaga nation, denied knowledge of the captive "Indian girle," yet carefully and perhaps strategically declared her a "heathen."[47] The Senecas pleaded absolute faith to the original 1684 treaty with Virginia, laying all blame on "the four [other] nations who sit here," boldly accusing them "right in their faces." Taggojerhos, speaking for the Cayugas, also denied any knowledge of the girl but said that the three Appomattox boys were in the Oneida and Mohawk towns. Probably put on the spot, the Oneidas would neither admit nor deny anything. However, they let Byrd know "that a great deal of trouble" would be "connected with this, to free [the boys] from those houses to which they have been given." Speaking last, Canondodawe, of the Mohawks, denied any involvement, and chastised the Cayugas and Oneidas for all the trouble. Singing songs of admonishment to his confederates and covenant to the Virginians, Canondodawe presented Commissioner Byrd with a belt of wampum for the governor of Virginia.[48]

William Byrd, still a relative newcomer to Virginia, was nevertheless the governor's obvious choice for commissioner of Indian affairs. Even as he blustered through negotiations with the Five Nations, Byrd knew well their military strength and power, and so carefully employed the proper language of Iroquois diplomacy.[49] Despite the discussions, of which these were neither the first nor the last, there were more incursions into Virginia from the north in 1686 and, perhaps not coincidentally, this time there were several "Indians lossed" from Colonel Byrd's own plantation.[50] The best explanation for how those "lossed" Indians came to be on Byrd's plantation in the first place can be found by returning to the paths mentioned above.

Byrd's rise to prominence was not mere happenstance. In 1670 young William inherited from his uncle a fine house at the falls of James River, as well as a rather lucrative burgeoning Indian trade enterprise. Thomas Stegge's involvement in the Indian trade stemmed from his association with, and license from, Governor William Berkeley.[51] The precise nature and extent of Stegge's trade is unknown. However, when Byrd inherited Stegge's land, house, and stocks, Mrs. Stegge, Byrd's aunt, also inherited an Indian slave.[52] By the winter of 1671, Byrd was personally leading expeditions to the southwest of Virginia along the upper Roanoke River.[53] Two years later Byrd was selling Indians to his neighbors.[54] Byrd's own son, William Byrd II, still held several Indian slaves more than a quarter of a century later.[55]

In 1680—in post–Bacon's Rebellion Virginia—Berkeley loyalist and Council President Nicholas Spencer accused William Byrd of botching negotiations with several frontier tribes then considering tributary status.[56] In this, Spencer disparagingly referred to Byrd as one of the "Indian traders." Former Berkeley patron and supporter Colonel Abraham Wood had arranged for negotiations and a treaty in Jamestown, but the frontier tribes never showed. Spencer wrote to the Lords of Trade and Plantations with his knowledge and explanation of events. Members of one of the tribes allegedly committed a murder in the settlements. Colonial agents demanded the culprits, and seven men surrendered themselves and were brought with their families to Byrd's house. There, in an allegedly not so thinly veiled attempt to "upset this arrangement of Colonel Wood" for his own gain, Byrd executed all seven men and then "took away their wives and children."[57] Better known today for establishing the settlement that would become the city of Richmond, and for being a successful merchant-planter who engaged in the African slave trade, Byrd's Indian trade and Indian slaving predated these more famous exploits.

William Byrd's contemporary and one of his primary competitors was Cadwallader Jones. Jones was based farther north on the Rappahannock River, at modern Fredericksburg, but it was not uncommon for his factors to trek 450 miles or more to trade in what is now East Tennessee and Georgia. Early in March of 1682 Jones ranked "indyan children prisoners" as the single most valuable commodity in his entire trade.[58] About the same time Jones sent out one of his agents, Thomas Owsley, to trade with the Nanticoke tribe in southeastern Maryland.[59] Colonial authorities there issued Jones a special communiqué authorizing Owsley to traffic for six months in a variety of commodities, excepting munitions, with the "Nantecoke Indians."

At this time Jones was looking to Maryland, to the Nanticoke, to acquire something of importance that he needed for his trade with the southern Indians. He wrote to Lord Baltimore begging the proprietor to grant him permission to collect (apparently by way of the local Nanticoke and other tribal peoples) "peake" or "Roanoke" shells from along the colony's eastern shore. Despite the variety of English manufactured products a Virginia trader could offer Indian customers, natives insisted that goods or products traditionally carried past the fall line from the coast were still important. "This yeere [1682] the Indyans will have Roanoake," Jones grumbled, "not with standing all other com[m]odities be p[re]sented," he having at that time "a considerable parcell of other goods amongst them unsold."[60]

Still, this trade was lucrative enough to draw Virginians great distances from their colonial settlements into foreign lands for many decades. Carolina traders established an inland trade late in 1674 with the Rickahockans or Westos, a mighty and far-ranging conglomerate nation of raiders and traders that had been trading with Virginians at least since 1659, when Spanish authorities in Florida began reporting dramatic incursions into the mission territory of coastal Georgia by English-allied gun-armed Indians.[61] In 1674 fledging Carolina had contacted most of the tribes within about one hundred miles of their settlement at Charles Town, and Indian trade, though recognized as valuable, was still somewhat limited in scope, due in part to the Westos' fierce reputation in the region. The coastal tribes reportedly quaked in fear at the very word "Westo," insisting that the Westos carried away their women and children.[62] Perhaps these were the same women and children that men like William Byrd and Cadwallader Jones were selling as slaves in Virginia.

In October 1674, Westo envoys approached Carolinian Dr. Henry Woodward offering to open a new trade. Not coincidentally, in September

1674, the Virginia Assembly prohibited the sale of arms to any Indians what-soever, and declared war on all frontier and foreign nations in retribution for several murders in the colony's outlying settlements.[63] Back in 1671, though, Henry Woodward was actually in Virginia when Abraham Wood dispatched Thomas Battes and Robert Fallam to the Cherokee country.[64] A Barbadian Carolina landgrave, colonist John Yeamans, had dispatched Woodward to Virginia in an official capacity in order to investigate the potential for Indian trade. The purpose of the mission remained covert to the Virginians.[65]

Woodward's experiences with Indians in Charles Town—mainly Chickahominy relatives, the Cusabos—and the western reaches of Caro-lina, and his associations with Spanish Florida, where he was previously imprisoned, transformed him into an interpreter and South Carolina's preeminent authority on regional Indian affairs. Late in 1673, Virginian James Needham, a former acquaintance of Woodward's, established formal trade relations between Virginia and the Cherokees, enemies of the Wes-tos.[66] So in October of 1674, would-be trader Woodward—almost certainly cognizant of Westo disaffection from Virginia and their hostility toward Spanish-allied or mission Indians—traveled with Westo envoys to their large fortified settlement on the upper Westo River, later renamed the Savannah River, after a contingent of the Shavanos, or Shawnees, moved in to dislodge the Westos. Here, at their river and town in 1674, the Westos received Woodward with a volley of small-arms fire and an offer for him to purchase Indian slaves in exchange for more guns and other goods.

Woodward noted recent trade activity between the Westos and the Virginians, the items of exchange in this trade consisting in the main of "arms, ammunition, tradeing cloth & other" items which the Westos received for "drest deare skins furrs & young Indian Slaves."[67] Such "young Indian Slaves" were perhaps the very children that coastal Cusabos reported to the Carolinians the Westos were "Carryinge awaye," or were some of the very "people, whom they either steal, or force away" as related to Virgin-ian John Lederer by the inland piedmont Catawbas several years before Woodward visited the Westos.[68]

Fifteen years earlier, the Westos or Rickahockans were making their first known incursions into the northerly sections of Spanish-claimed Florida. Then about or shortly after 1663, the Westos established a settlement on the Savannah River, building a fortified town just out of the reach of Spanish authorities, but close enough to wage swift raids for plunder into outlying Spanish mission villages.[69] Perhaps spurred on by the Virginia traders' demand for slaves, Westo presence and activity drove many hundreds of immigrants into refugee towns along the northern Georgia coast, where they collectively became the "Yamasees." The Yamasees would later play a pivotal role in South Carolina history, figuring prominently in one of the most central events of colonial southern history—the Yamasee War. The destruction and disruption of that conflict also brought about the general demise of Indian slavery as an institution.[70] However that did not happen until about 1720 or so. Prior to then, though, rather than hindering or limiting slavery, armed conflict between colonists and natives provided justification for, and rationalization of, slavery.

Timing is everything, it would seem, as in the fall of 1674 the South Carolinians were quite interested in expanding their trade while the Westos were seeking a new ally to preserve their own power and wealth. South Carolina had ulterior motives of which the Westos may not have been aware: to destroy the coastal Cusabos and eventually, after tapping into the heart of the interior, cutting off the Westos. As it happened, almost two years after Virginia Governor William Berkeley stopped selling guns to Indians and declared war on hostile tribes, Virginia rebel Nathaniel Bacon and his ragtag army of colonists assaulted the Occaneechees and a number of friendly tributary tribes. In a fine piece of shrewd manipulation, Bacon harangued the Occaneechees into setting upon their Susquehannock friends, at that very moment encamped only a few miles from Occaneechee Town. Bacon then carefully surrounded the victorious Occaneechees, trained his guns on these ostensible allies, and the ensuing battle raged for more than twelve hours. The triumphant colonists took Occaneechee prisoners—mostly women—back to their settlements. The surviving Occaneechees fled and regrouped on the Eno River, near what later became Hillsboro, North Carolina, where they lived in a small, palisaded town and remained a thorn in Virginia's side for a quarter of a century.

Eventually, Virginia authorities successfully removed several small piedmont tribes—including the Occaneechees—to a controlled settlement on the Meherrin River, called Fort Christanna. Governor Alexander Spotswood and a new company of merchants known as the Virginia Indian Company built the fort in 1714. Manned by cannoneers and mounted colonial rangers, Christanna also functioned as a trading post. The fort's resident tribes would presumably serve as a buffer to hostile foreign tribes, while simultaneously reaping the presumed benefits of close association with colonists.[71]

The roots of Occaneechee fortune—both gained and lost—are found in slavery. The Westos were trading with Virginia right up to the time they introduced themselves to Woodward in October 1674. Indian slaves were pivotal to that trade. But with Virginia's ban on the gun trade, the Westos found a new trading partner in South Carolina in 1674, and so the Virginians went looking elsewhere for Indian slaves. The Occaneechees filled the void. Interestingly, shortly after his arrival in Virginia earlier that same year (1674), Nathaniel Bacon Jr. received an Indian trade license from his kinsman—his cousin—Governor William Berkeley. Berkeley also saw to it that Bacon settled at Curles Plantation on the James River, close to trader William Byrd, with whom he was partnered in trade.[72] Berkeley introduced Bacon to the most prominent traders in the colony, and young Bacon undoubtedly reaped the benefits of those relations.

Like his new neighbors and fellow traders, Bacon was no planter. Following the collapse of his 1676 rebellion, royal commissioners investigating the tumult's causes inventoried the dead rebel leader's estate. According to the commissioners' findings, Bacon held three servants—one "Negro" woman, a cook, and housekeeper—and two whites listed with their full names as well as the remainder of their contract time. In a column separate from the servants, the commissioners listed seven Indian slaves ranging in age from as old as forty to as young as one year.[73] Bacon also held stocks of Indian trade goods. This is very important to understanding Bacon's motive for warring against "the Indians."

His own stated reason for initially going out against the undefined Indian enemy was to achieve revenge for the death of his Dutch overseer.

Bacon held no African slaves, and but two white servants. There is nothing listed in Bacon's inventories to suggest extensive landholdings or that he engaged in heavy agriculture. Who or what, then, did the overseer supervise and manage, and why? Why did the hostile Indians—presumably Susquehannocks—come to Bacon's plantation in the first place? Why was the overseer their sole victim? What became of Bacon's Indians after the itemization and valuing of his estate? Did Berkeley seize and sell Bacon's estate as he did others? No record of any such sale survives. However, the royal commissioners who later investigated the sources of Bacon's Rebellion noted that Governor Berkeley seized an Indian man from another rebel leader's estate and sold him to a friend.[74] Therefore this fate is at least plausible.

The murder of his overseer by a ranging war party threw Nathaniel Bacon into hysterics. Bacon seemed to fear tribal Indians, and for whatever reason could not, or refused to, differentiate friend from foe—or, maybe not. After all, Bacon was William Byrd's close associate, and there was not a man in the colony more knowledgeable of Indians. In response to the murder, Bacon and a few allies (names unknown) seized a number of friendly Appomattox Indians.[75] Before Berkeley could calm the situation, Bacon drummed up armed volunteers and marched on Jamestown to demand a military commission to fight "the Indians."[76] With the governor at gunpoint, Bacon received his commission. When he left Jamestown, the governor declared him and his supporters rebels. Bacon's men proceeded northwest and came upon various camps or settlements of tributary tribes. They captured several Nanzatticos, Rappahannocks, and Mattaponies. In his assault on the peaceful Pamunkey town, Bacon took forty-five captives and paraded them through Jamestown which the governor had now fled.[77]

Bacon seized control of the General Assembly and reconvened it. The Baconian Assembly passed a series of laws, the first declaring that "[a]ll plunder either Indians or otherwise" taken by his soldiers in their assaults on Indian settlements, were their spoils and booty, thus emphasizing the legality of enslaving Indians captured in war.[78] Known as "Bacon's Laws," the Assembly's resolutions encouraged the seizure of all Indians deemed hostile to the colony, and declared those Indians' towns colonial property once taken and claimed by colonists. The laws define as hostile those who fled their towns, whether or not they engaged Bacon's forces. In every documented instance Indian town inhabitants fled into the woods at the approach of Bacon's army. The benefit for colonists was twofold. Through Bacon's promotion of Indian slavery, colonists stood to gain both land and labor in one fell swoop. Hundreds—particularly recent freemen—rallied behind the cause.

This technique, such as it was, merely followed a general pattern of enslavement by warfare. Governor Berkeley—Bacon's benefactor—given his history, hardly stood on high moral ground when he criticized Bacon's treatment of Indians. Indeed, although Berkeley bemoaned Bacon's methods and railed against his insolence, he too had engaged in similar tactics for decades. At the same time, one wonders how Bacon, a newcomer, had the audacity to condemn Berkeley for *appeasing* Indians while leaving the colony "defenseless." Berkeley warred against Indians, conquered them, treated with them, traded with them and, at times, bought and sold them. Perhaps his many years of experience led the governor into the new policies he pursued at the time of Bacon's arrival. After all, Berkeley and his council had outlawed the trade in arms the same year. Moreover, it was Berkeley, not Bacon, who ordered the building and provisioning of outposts at the frontiers on the major rivers, and ordered that armed rangers patrol between the forts.

The erection and maintenance of forts and rangers cost money. Berkeley imposed taxes to protect the colony and the trade, which was increasingly regulated in an effort to prevent abuses that might lead to conflict. Thus Bacon both objected to Berkeley's ostensible policies of appeasement, while seeking a greater share in the trade and slaves for himself and his cohorts. After five months in arms, Nathaniel Bacon perished from illness in November 1676, and his so-called revolution died with him. Bacon's laws were declared null and void—all, that is, save one. Berkeley pardoned the vast majority of rebels, but permitted all to keep their Indian slaves.[79] Indeed, in 1677 and 1679 the Assembly renewed the acts setting forth the legitimacy of Indian enslavement, culminating with acts in 1681 and 1682 deregulating and opening a general and expansive Indian trade, and restating Bacon's law for enslavement.[80] Perhaps these acts merely echoed the tenor of the times. If Bacon's Rebellion succeeded at nothing else, it democratized and redirected the trade, and eased any restrictions against continued Indian slavery. Bacon and his confidant neighbor Byrd—an early supporter of the rebellion—were, before all else, Indian traders. Bacon owned Indians and Byrd sold them. Lifting trade restrictions and easing access to Indian slaves may have been the primary thrust behind the "Indian Warr" of 1676.

There may never be a way to know the exact number of Bacon's native victims. However, the fragmentary extant record—the investigative commissioners' reports, later deeds, orders, and probate records—suggest widespread enslavement. An indenture made the fourth of May 1681, between Andrew and Sarah Boyer and Robert Prid, both of Old Rappahannock County, in the area that later became Essex County, assigned over two Indians, both of whom were unnamed, from Prid to the Boyers. The Indians, belonging to Prid by "right of Conquest," were given to the Boyers in exchange for 200 acres of real estate, not for lease, but in perpetuity. Andrew and Sarah Boyer acknowledged that following their deaths the two Indians were to be returned to Prid "and his heires."[81] This is a rather unusual indenture in that the servants were the spoils of war, exchanged for real property, and inheritable. Nothing in the record suggests either the Indians' consent or any limit to their service. In June 1690 another Rappahannock County resident made complaint that his "Indian Woman and an Indian boy" absconded from him and he suspected they were "Concealed" by the local Rappahannock Indians. The county court ordered the "King of the sd Rappa Indians" to appear at the next court to answer the charge.[82] The woman, but not the boy, had been taken "in the late war." Perhaps the boy was her son, born into servitude. Vincent Cox of Northumberland County saw service in the so-called Indian War of 1676.[83] According to a record made in 1691, he was the owner of a "Nanzatiker" Indian "slave" captured during the "Indian Rebellion" in 1676.[84] In another example, at the Richmond County court of October 1694, an "Indian Woman" named "Bess," who said she belonged to "the Mattaponie Town," filed a complaint against the executors of Simon Miller's will and estate, for allegedly keep-ing her as an involuntary servant. The court was aware that Bess was taken as a "Prisoner of Warr" during the "late Indian Rebellion."[85]

In all these cases, Bacon's Rebellion is referred to as an Indian war and never as a colonists' rebellion. This speaks volumes on how con-temporary Virginians understood and interpreted the conflict. Despite the importance of the civil conflict that followed between the rebels and the government, Bacon's Rebellion remained first and foremost, in the words of eyewitnesses and in the memories of those who participated, an Indian war.[86] More than likely, for the Native Americans the "rebellion" was first and foremost a war with the colony, and the conflict between Bacon and the government may have had little meaning. The entire war, then, should be recast as a contest between rivals in trade—the Indian trade. In this instance, the Indian nations and tribal communities in alliance with Berkeley and the colony—the tributary Appomattox and Pamunkey com-munities, and the trading Occaneechees and Susquehannocks—bore the brunt of Bacon's frustrations. The war crushed or dispersed these regional tribes, and relegated many individuals to slavery.

By removing Berkeley and the Occaneechees from the trade, Ba-con placed himself and his allies and associates in a paramount position; they were carving out a niche for themselves at least as large as that of Bacon's kinsman and one-time patron, William Berkeley. Bacon, William Byrd, and a few others aspiring to greater wealth and prestige recognized that control of the lucrative Indian trade was a path to power. In essence, too, this was something of a replication of, or rather a usurpation of, the Berkeleyan policies of the past. If, as Bacon claimed after his first Indian assaults, he was the mouthpiece for the people at large, then his call to arms and enslavement reflected common ideas. The "threat" purportedly posed on the colony's periphery was that of northern aggressors such as the Susquehannocks and the Senecas or Oneidas, and southern intermediaries, like the Occaneechees, through whom filtered traders—Native American and colonial—and trade goods. The Susquehannocks controlled the route to the north, and facing pressure and competition from other Iroquoian peoples, like the Senecas and Oneidas, were pressing ever further south.

Also complicating matters were border and jurisdictional disputes with Maryland as well as increasing inter-colonial competition in the trade.

Maryland traders for the most part "controlled" the Susquehannock trade and the upper Potomac—a people and region only recently the exclusive domain of the Virginians. Just a few years earlier, Marylanders pushed some Doeg and Piscataway Indians across the Potomac into Virginia, where they disputed over trade debts with an offensive landowner and murdered him. The Doegs fled the scene, and the Virginians, following an ill-conceived law, wrongly assaulted the unsuspecting Susquehannocks since the latter happened to be the closest resident tribe to the alleged atrocities. The larger native groups were expanding their influence and power, and were capable of inflicting serious damage on the colony had they been so inclined. They were not inflicting such damage, though, even if they were probably prone to answering impudence and disagreements with colonial settlers on the frontier with the same force known by their native enemies. These are among the primary factors that brought about the general alarm of 1676.

On the other hand, the small and peaceful Pamunkey, Nanzattico, Rappahannock, and other tributary tribes who bore the brunt of Bacon's fury had little or nothing to do with the cause of the so-called rebellion. Yet Bacon was careful *not* to engage the Susquehannocks in direct assault. Rather, Bacon and his captains feigned alliance with the slightly smaller and probably weaker—but still audacious—Occaneechees. Declaring that Virginia firearms would back them, Bacon urged the Occaneechees to prove their trade alliance to Virginia through a frontal engagement with the Susquehannocks. Surprising their friends, the Occaneechees utterly routed the Susquehannocks. The Susquehannock king's head was severed and the few survivors fled northward. The Occaneechees even secured from the Susquehannocks a number of captive Monakin Indians. Bacon wanted the redeemed Monakins for himself, though, and so turned several hundred guns on the celebratory Occaneechees. In the ensuing melee, Bacon may have grabbed the Monakins, but managed to secure only ten or so Occaneechee captives.

While acquiring slaves was clearly a Baconite goal, this particular battle was not, in the immediate sense, about acquiring slaves. The Occa-neechees were more or less in amity with the colony—with Berkeley—as Virginia traders had been active among them for years. The Occaneechees had little to gain by alienating Virginia, but Bacon—by stepping into the void created by their departure—had everything to gain; he could readily usurp control of much of the lucrative southern trade. Indeed, in the decade that followed, close Bacon associates William Byrd and William Hatcher and sons were the most successful traders in the colony, and they traded in Indian slaves.[87] Yet by transforming the Occaneechees from border-patrolling brokers and intermediaries into "hostile" refugees, they also became possible future slaves, a factor seemingly carefully calculated by Bacon as revealed in the post–Occaneechee assault acts of Assembly of June 1676. That they were enslaved is borne out elsewhere in the colonial record. Regardless, without the Occaneechee chokehold on the conduit of goods flowing north and south through the expansive area they controlled, and without the potential overlapping claims or interference of the Susquehan-nocks, Bacon and his agents could readily move out and into the vacated territory, more easily acquiring buckskins and "foreign" slaves.

However, Bacon's plan did not succeed entirely. The few surviving reports of what transpired at Occaneechee Town are conflicting, at least one suggesting that Bacon and his men barely escaped with their lives. This account may be the most accurate. For while Bacon claimed an over-whelming victory, others present at the battle said quite otherwise. Further, from their new home in what is now North Carolina, the Occaneechees continued to harass Virginia and its traders for a quarter of a century. In an ironic twist, facilitated perhaps by Bacon's rashness as well as his sudden death, Virginia's access to skins and slaves was initially stifled rather than eased. Even as trade gradually rebounded, threat persisted. In 1684 six Henrico County traders working for William Byrd were murdered just thirty miles past the new Occaneechee settlement.[88] In 1698 Richard Traunter, one of Byrd's agents, wrote of the threat still posed to Virgin-ians by the "Occaneeches" who, according to other native informants "would certainly kill them all." Indeed, when several of James Moore's South Carolina traders—Robert Stevens, John Herne, and an Indian slave "of Capt.n James Moor's" who was "called Indian Jacke"—set out to open an overland trade with William Byrd for horses, then in short supply at Charleston, they met with this very fate.[89] At a small neck of land on the north side of the "Ronogue" (Roanoke) River, the party was "sett upon by the Occaneeches" who "shott Robert Stevens dead on the place, and shott the Indian through the Thigh." Herne escaped by jumping into the river and swimming across to safety, and though wounded, Indian Jack fled into "the Outsettlements" of Virginia on the Nottoway River.[90] Later encountering some Virginia traders, Herne was taken to Byrd's quarter on the Appomattox, where Traunter "lived and Merchandized with the Indians" for Byrd. Byrd soon learned the whereabouts of the slave Jack and sent a surgeon to tend to him. Shortly afterward Traunter returned to Byrd's "and acquainted him that the Indian Slave was very desirous to goe again to Carolina." Byrd replied that Jack could go "with the Traders [after] they came in, as farr on his journey as they traded, which was to a Nation of Indians called the Esaw's, there being a brother of this Indian that would conduct him safe to his master in Carolina."[91]

The Esaws would later become generally known as the Catawba nation, and in the 1690s they resided on the Catawba River in western North Carolina and northern South Carolina, some 200 miles northwest of Charleston, and about 320 miles from Byrd's Westover home.[92] It is significant that at this late date Virginians, not South Carolinians, were active among the Catawba. Traunter claimed that he, at Byrd's behest, initiated the Catawba trade to and from Charleston, as he undertook an expedition in 1698 to open a new and shorter overland trade route leading from the trading post on the Appomattox River to Charleston.[93]

Traunter makes no appearance in the published annals of Virginia history. Yet in less than a decade he affected more trade and alliance in the Indian country between Virginia and South Carolina than would British administrators and commissioners in the half century that followed. Just when and where Traunter entered the trade is unknown, but by 1698 he spoke and conversed in Tuscarora, Wateree, and Waxhaw, and quite diplomatically facilitated alliances between native groups to the advantage of both the Virginia and South Carolina traders. Traunter also commissioned—though on what authority is not certain—several native leaders in a general anti-Occaneechee alliance, ultimately setting in motion that tribe's final demise and paving the way for a generation of traders.[94] In so excluding the Occaneechees from trade and further reducing their stature, Byrd and Traunter—with the aid of the Waterees, who in retaliation for shooting Jack, captured a number of Occaneechee slaves to sell at Charleston—finally succeeded in 1698 where Bacon (and Byrd) fell short in 1676.

Still, Virginians had not fully learned—or soon forgot—all the hard lessons of the 1670s. In January 1691 several Tuscarora chiefs complained to William Duckingfield of North Carolina's Executive Council about two of their men who had gone missing, saying that they suspected Carolinians had killed them. Happening to be present at the Council, a Meherrin Indian from Virginia, said he knew that Daniel Pugh of Nansemond County, Virginia, had "[s]ent them to Barbados" as slaves. The understandably upset Tuscaroras threatened general revenge, but Duckingfield convinced them to go to Virginia and ask the governor to enquire and "do them Justice." Duckingfield later said that when he was in Nansemond County he was credibly informed that Pugh sent not two, but four Tuscaroras out of the country, two to Barbados in the *Prout*, and the others (also possibly to Barbados) in the *Swallow of Barbados*. On February 19, Thomas Tyler, master of the brigantine *Swallow of Barbados*, arrived at the General Court to give an account of how he came by the Tuscaroras he transported as slaves. Tyler produced a bill of lading signed to Daniel Pugh of Nansemond for the Indians, and shared Pugh's instructions to him for the "disposal of them." To keep the irate Tuscarora leaders at bay, the Executive Council ordered that the sheriff of Nansemond County arrest Pugh and hold him at Jamestown until the next general court.[95]

What happened next is unknown, as some of the minutes for the next general court session do not survive. Curiously, though, by 1706 Daniel Pugh had relocated adjacent to the Chowan Indians in North Carolina.[96] The Chowans were a tribe of Algonkian stock long accustomed to trading with Virginians. That relationship went back at least as far as 1646, when Virginian Edward Bass married a Christianized Chowan woman called

Mary Tucker and went to live with the Chowans, expressly for engaging in trade.[97] Within a decade other Virginia traders were coming into Chowan territory. It is quite likely that the Chowans supplied Daniel Pugh with captives that he in turn sold as slaves.[98] Interestingly enough, Daniel Pugh's own son Francis Pugh would become a trader to the Tuscarora after full cessation of the Tuscarora War in 1713.[99]

The so-called Tuscarora War erupted on September 11, 1711. Less than a month later, North Carolina Governor Edward Hyde convened with several Tuscarora emissaries at the Nottoway Town in Virginia. Through the assistance of the Virginia interpreter to the Tuscaroras, the delegates, emanating from neutral or non-hostile Tuscarora villages, claimed some measure of allegiance to the colony and in an effort to secure peace offered to bring to justice the perpetrators of the late massacre of September. In so doing, the "friendly" Tuscarora leaders requested of North Carolina six trade blankets for each "enemy" male killed, and "the usual price of slaves" for every woman and child delivered to colonial authorities. Governor Hyde agreed to the terms, with the caveat that some hostage children of the friendly villages be delivered as bond to ensure the alliance. The tribal leaders conferred, tentatively agreeing to the obligation, requesting five days to spread the message of the alliance and its terms to all the northern, or "neutral," Tuscarora towns. The requested hostages, however, were not forthcoming. Still, the negotiations strongly suggest a common understanding of the value of, or price for, Indian slaves, also implying a practice corroborated in other contemporaneous records. The Tuscaroras—at least the so-called friendly Tuscaroras—were already well accustomed to dealing with the colonists in Indian slaves.[100]

Over the next two years, more than 500 hostile Tuscaroras and their Machapungo, Coree, Bear River, and Cape Fear Indian allies were taken and sold into slavery. Several hundred other Tuscaroras fled the colony, either camping in the Virginia Blue Ridge or seeking refuge among the Five Nations Iroquois.[101] The Chowans participated in the war on the side of the colonists and were among the slave catchers.[102] The Virginia-allied and resident Saponi tribe also fought with the colonists against the hostile Tuscarora towns. After the war, only the friendly Tuscaroras remained in North Carolina. Francis Pugh traded with these towns, which were probably dependent or reliant upon Virginia trade. Francis's father Daniel possibly acquired the slaves he had sold in 1691, if not directly from the Chowans, from these same towns. Alternatively, if those towns attacking the colony had been the victims of enslavement—as they alleged in 1710, on the eve of the Tuscarora War—then slavery was a determining factor in the war.[103] By the middle of the eighteenth century, Tuscarora leadership adopted the Pugh name as their own—if indeed Daniel or Francis did not actually father children by Tuscarora women—and the nation was fully connected to English colonial interests.[104]

Prior to the outbreak of the war, Tuscaroras had hunted and traded in Virginia as far north as the James River for two decades. Occasionally they came into colonial plantations and sold their services as hunters to planters. A general familiarity grew out of such activities, and so it is not surprising that a Tuscarora man was on the King William County plantation of Colonel John Walker in the winter of 1707 and 1708. This man assisted in interpreting and translating the story of one Lamhatty, a twenty-six-year-old male Towasa tribe member who had escaped slavery among the Shawnee and fled naked into the Virginia plantations of the Mattaponi River.[105] With some difficulty at first, Lamhatty related his story by signs and drawing in the dirt, until, interestingly, "some of his Country folks" were located as slaves on other plantations in the neighborhood. Perhaps here the remaining linguistic barrier was broken, for Lamhatty was then able to relate his nine months of captivity, being sold from tribe to tribe, finally finding himself among a Shawnee hunting party on the headwaters of Virginia's Rappahannock River in the Blue Ridge Mountains.

The Towasas were a small nation of about ten villages near Mobile, on the Gulf Coast of what a century later became Alabama. Lamhatty accused Tuscaroras of initially enslaving him during a series of raids conducted by that nation in the spring of 1707. There were two raids of which Lamhatty was aware. In the first, three Towasa towns were laid waste, all the inhabitants being captured or killed. After the Tuscaroras sold their captives they returned to assault and take four more towns. This is when Lamhatty was captured. His Tuscarora captors took him into northern

Creek towns, where colonial traders were quite active. He served there for several months as an agricultural laborer. Eventually the Creeks sold him to some "Savannahs," or Shawnees, who carried him north through the mountains, final destination unknown. That Lamhatty could be dragged so far from his homeland, from Creeks to Shawnees, and end up in a plantation society where he encountered both captors—the Tuscaroras—and kinsmen—other Towasas—is remarkably revealing of the social contours of the domestic North American Indian slave trade. Further, Lamhatty's account suggests that tribes traded slaves to one another as well as to colonists, and that they could serve Indian masters in much the same capacity as they served colonial masters. Moreover, Colonel Walker, when presented with Lamhatty to determine what should be done with him, decided to just keep him, implying a commonplace colonial practice where strange or foreign Indians were concerned. Contemporary Virginian Robert Beverley wrote that Walker "ill used" Lamhatty, who, after several months in such service, ran away and was never seen again.[106]

This episode reveals that the Tuscaroras were quite willing to engage in the wholesale enslavement of other Indians. That this fate should ultimately befall them, too, suggests something about the colonial perception of Indians in general. The Towasas could be colonial slaves because they were foreigners purchased of Indians allied in trade with the colony. But that trade alliance proved no stronger or more enduring for the Tuscaroras than the Occaneechee association with Berkeley or the Westo pact with Woodward in South Carolina. As soon as they allegedly severed their bonds with the North Carolinians, the Tuscaroras too were fair game. Only those Tuscaroras who agreed to aid the colony—supplied with Virginia arms and ammunition—and who acknowledged a willingness to bring slaves to the colonists, were spared the same fate. In the end, driven by their dependence on the trade, as well as the colonists' thirst for slaves, Tuscaroras were willing to enslave Tuscaroras.

But Lamhatty and the Towasas are not anomalous. In 1701 a number of Acolapissas were exported to Barbados from Virginia. A Muskhogean-speaking people, the Acolapissas at that time lived near the populous Choctaw nation above the mouth of the Pearl River, in what has since become the state of Mississippi. The French commander of Forte de Misssissipi (and soon-to-be governor of Louisiana), Jean-Baptiste Le Moyne, Sieur de Bienville, visited the Acolapissa settlements in the winter of 1700–1701, learning that just two days before his visit they had been attacked by an estimated 200 Chickasaws led by several English slave hunters. According to a missionary accompanying Bienville, at least eighty prisoners had been carried away. These eighty captives—or some of the survivors from amongst them—are certainly the same "Colapisas" who arrived in Barbados from Virginia in 1701.[107]

Following Bienville's visit, the Acolapissas firmly attached themselves to French interests and by 1705 relocated to the north shore of Lake Pontchartrain in Louisiana. One cannot doubt but that alliance and relocation resulted directly from Virginia-Chickasaw slave raiding. Nothing of this episode is preserved in surviving Virginia records, which at first might suggest some covertness to this trade in Indian slaves. Then again, the threat of transportation (as it was called in those days) to the West Indies was used more than once by Virginia authorities against tribes under the colony's influence, in order to coerce them into cooperation and submission. So the slave trade was well enough known that such threats could be made with effect to keep wayward natives in line with colonial law. If the Towasa situation six years later is in any sense analogous, then there must have been other cases like that of the Acolapissas. It is unlikely that the Virginia-led raid—concerted, and deep in Choctaw country, nearly a thousand miles from the tidewater plantations—was an isolated incident. How did Lamhatty's kinsmen, those other Towasas, end up in central Virginia? And, though circumstances vary, there are more clear-cut examples.

In May 1705 virtually all the remaining Nanzatticos were shipped to Antigua. Holding to what by then was an old Virginia law, the colony held the entire tribe accountable for the murder of one Anglo settler family. The Nanzatticos were prosecuted in what appears to have been the largest trial in Virginia's colonial history. Yet no chronicler of Virginia's storied past has ever written on the affair. Along with the governor and Council, ordered to attend the trial were two to three "great men" from the other tributary tribes, along with their interpreters, the speaker of the House of Burgesses, senior members of the neighboring county courts of Essex, Stafford, and Westmoreland, all the justices of Richmond County, the court clerks for all four counties, and senior members of each county militia. Sixteen justices, rather than the usual twelve, heard the case, but for some reason just two members of the Council, rather than the usual four, sat in judgment before the accused. Perhaps not so incidentally, these two judges, Robert Carter and John Smith, played significant roles in the dispossession of the Wicocommicco tribe in neighboring Lancaster County.[108]

The judges found the accused guilty. Five adult males were immediately, and publicly, executed by hanging. Two other Nanzattico males had their sentences commuted, and one man, "Frank," an informant, was acquitted. Everyone else over the age of twelve was ordered transported into servitude outside of the colony. Members of the Council kept the tribe's children as servants, drawing lots to determine who would get which child. Four of the children were babies between nine months and eighteen months old.[109] One wonders if by adulthood they even knew what a Nanzattico was and why they were enslaved. Certainly, well before the outbreak of the Tuscarora War, and even before Bacon's Rebellion, Indian slavery and the Indian slave trade were ingrained, if somewhat cyclical, facets of colonial Virginia. Indeed, the record reflects continued enslavement well into the eighteenth century.

A secure assumption is that many Native Americans, from Virginia's northern and western frontiers, all the way to the lower Mississippi River valley, were shipped out of Virginia to Caribbean ports, sold into other colonies, or kept on Virginia plantations where they labored as slaves. That is the most important part of this story. Imagine the displacement and sorrow for homes and lives lost, the deculturation and reculturation that comes with being lifted out of town and country, bound by strangers and carried six, seven, or eight hundred miles to a strange country. Many Indians so displaced were packed onto strange vessels and carried across strange waters to another strange country, forced to labor in other men's fields for other men's benefit. This sort of slave traffic ran into, through, and out of the Old Dominion. And a good number of Indians remained in Virginia as slaves. Historians of slavery in Virginia can no longer tell only of the cruel importation and brutal treatment of Africans. There was a domestic traffic in humans that preceded the mass importation of Africans in the late seventeenth and early eighteenth centuries. Even concurrent with that traffic, there was another one, just as tragic, flowing just as insidiously, but often in the opposite direction. Indeed, as that venerable old Virginian Thomas Jefferson once exclaimed, "An inhuman practice once prevailed in this country of making slaves of the Indians."[110]

Notes

1. This chapter is an excerpt from C. S. Everett's dissertation, "'An Inhuman Practice Once Prevailed in this Country': Indian Slavery in Virginia," Vanderbilt University (2009). The chapter's title is taken from Act XII of the Virginia General Assembly session of October 1670, clarifying that any non-Christian servants imported by sea would be slaves. The act passed in response to the question of whether Indians were servants or slaves, and within the context of ongoing negotiations concerning the limiting and regulating of continued Indian enslavement.

2. Just a cursory search on several university library databases is rather revealing. Early in the summer of 2004, utilizing Vanderbilt University's Jean and Alexander Heard ACORN search of Vanderbilt's holdings, and tapping the system's access to numerous online databases, I executed keyword searches for publications on "Colonial Massachusetts" and "Colonial Virginia." ACORN returned 308 titles for Massachusetts and 340 for Virginia. A WorldCat search returned some 5,375 titles for Massachusetts and an astounding 8,234 for Virginia. ArticlesFirst and JournalArticles returned a combined total of just sixty-five titles for Massachusetts, but 102 for Virginia.

3. Historian April Lee Hatfield's recent *Atlantic Virginia: Intercolonial Relations in the Seventeenth Century* (Philadelphia: University of Pennsylvania Press, 2004) proves the exception to the rule, devoting more energy and thought to this subject than most. The intention here in this chapter is not to disparage anthropology as a discipline. Rather it is just to say that "history" by historians still seems reserved for other peoples, and not American Indians. Anthropologists—almost exclusively—have penned most recent histories of Virginia Indians. See Helen C. Rountree and E. Randolph Turner III, *Before and After Jamestown: Virginia's Powhatans and Their Predecessors* (Gainesville: University Press of Florida, 2002); Helen C. Rountree and Thomas E. Davidson, *Eastern Shore Indians of Virginia and Maryland* (Charlottesville: University Press of Virginia, 1997); Helen C. Rountree, ed., *Powhatan Foreign Relations, 1500–1722* (Charlottesville: University Press of Virginia, 1993); Helen C. Rountree, *Pocahontas's People: The Powhatan Indians of Virginia through Four Centuries* (Norman: University of Oklahoma Press, 1990); Frederic W. Gleach, *Powhatan's World and Colonial Virginia: A Conflict of Cultures* (Lincoln: University of Nebraska Press, 1997); and Margaret Holmes Williamson, *Powhatan Lords of Life and Death: Command and Consent in Seventeenth-Century Virginia* (Lincoln: University of Nebraska Press, 2003). Like Gleach and Rountree, Holmes is an anthropologist, a professor at Mary Washington College, in Fredericksburg, Virginia. In her introduction to *Powhatan Lords of Life and Death* (2003: 29) Holmes states that "the present book is not in any sense a history either of the Jamestown colony or of the Powhatan." There is minimal discussion in any of these books of Indian servitude and slavery. As for historians writing on Virginia Indians

or Indians in Virginia, there has been too little work for decades. Even the exceptions are often cursory treatments, limiting examination to Pocahontas, later colonial and early state policies, and the western frontier.

4. Almon Wheeler Lauber, *Indian Slavery in Colonial Times within the Present Limits of the United States*, Studies in History, Economics, and Public Law, Volume 54, No. 3 (New York: Columbia University, 1913).

5. J. Leitch Wright Jr., *The Only Land They Knew: American Indians in the Old South* (New York: Free Press, 1981).

6. This is a complex issue. There is, though, a surprisingly large—and growing—body of literature on the so-called tri-racial isolate phenomenon, mixed communities of allegedly African, European, and American ancestry. Communities labeled "tri-racial" tend to display aspersion toward the term, considering it an epithet. However, ethnic and racial identities vary widely from community to community. Sixty years ago, scholars believed there were about 200 such groups, largely in the South, and that these groups were dispersing and rapidly disappearing. Actually many persist to this day. Early in the twentieth century, anthropologist Frank Speck made a point of visiting some of these groups in Virginia, and he believed they were primarily of American Indian descent and identity, even cataloguing presumably "aboriginal" cultural traits among them. Conversely, similar groups in North Carolina tend to be culturally and racially more "black." See William S. Pollitzer, E. Boyle Jr., et al., "Physical Anthropology of the Negroes of Charleston, S. C.," *Human Biology* 42, no. 2 (1970): 265–79; William Pollitzer and R. C. Hartmann, et al., "Blood Types of the Cherokee Indians," *American Journal of Physical Anthropology* 20 (1962): 33–43; William Pollitzer and R. M. Menegaz-Bock, et al., "Factors in the Microevolution of a Triracial Isolate," *American Journal of Human Genetics* (hereafter *AJHG*) 18, no. 1 (1966): 26–38; William Pollitzer and R. M. Menegaz-Bock, et al., "Hereditary Benign Intraepithelial Dyskeratosis: A Linkage Study," *AJHG* 7 (1965): 104–8.

For an introduction to the literature, see Rhett S. Jones, "Black/Indian Relations: An Overview of the Scholarship," *Transforming Anthropology* 10 no. 1 (2001): 2–16. See also Reginald G. Daniel, "Triracial Isolates: Runaways and Refuseniks," in *More than Black? Multiracial Identity and the New Racial Order* (Philadelphia: Temple University Press, 2002), 68–75; Virginia Easley DeMarce, "'Verry Slightly Mixt': Tri-Racial Isolate Families of the Upper South: A Genealogical Study," *National Genealogical Society Quarterly* 80, no. 1 (March 1992): 5–35; Susan Greenbaum, "What's in a Label? Identity Problems of Southern Indian Tribes," *Journal of Ethnic Studies* 19, no. 2 (1991): 107–26; and C. H. Humbles, "A Visit to the Melungeons," *Home Missions Monthly* 11 (1897): 237–40. Curiously, there has been little exploration of interethnic and interracial relations between Africans and Indians in slavery, the presumption having been that tri-racial groups descend from independent tribes and not from slaves.

7. For Indians as mulattoes, see Henrico Court Minutes, 1737–1746: 86 (July 1739) and 128 (November 1740), and Prince George's County, Maryland, Court Records, 1730–32: 402. For "Black Indian," see Norfolk County, Virginia, Orders, 1766–68: 73. For others, see Surry County, Virginia, Deeds and Wills, 2: 157; Jean M. Mihalyka, *Loose Papers and Sundry Court Cases, 1628–1731* (Eastville VA: Hickory House), 239, and *Virginia Gazette* (Williamsburg VA [John] Dixon & [William] Hunter), March 11, 1775. See also the *Journal of the House of Delegates of the Commonwealth of Virginia . . . 1832–1833*: 131; Virginia, Acts of Assembly, 1832–1833: 51; Norfolk County Minute Books, 23: 180; 24: 27, 43, 44, 67; 26: 436; 29: 122; 30: 216, 226, 250, 341, 346; James Stanton Memoir, Virginia Historical Society (hereafter VHS), Richmond, Mss 5:1 St 267:1.

8. Northumberland County Orders, 1713–19, October 1713 (page numbers illegible), Library of Virginia, Richmond, mf reel 49. See also Lancaster County Tithables, 1745–1795: 1, 6, Library of Virginia, mf reel 316 (original Virginia County records microfilm are housed in the Library of Virginia, Richmond, and are hereafter cited by record or as "LVA" with reel number); Revolutionary War and Bounty Land Warrant Application of Henry Cato, New Jersey, R. 1815, March 1834.

9. William Strachey, The Historie of Travell into Virginia Britania, 2nd series, Vol. 103, Louis B. Wright and Virginia Freund, eds. (Cambridge: Hakluyt Society, 1953 [1612]), 61.

10. Letter of Richard Frethorne to his father and mother, March 20, April 2 and 3, 1623, in Susan Kingsbury, ed., The Records of the Virginia Company of London, Volume 4 (Washington DC, Government Printing Office, 1935), 61; "The Manner Howe to Bringe the Indians into Subiection," December 15, 1622, Additional Manuscripts, 12496, fos. 459–60, Caesar Papers, List of Records, No. 384; also S.R. 00037, R. 546, Miscellaneous Papers of Sir Julius Caesar, 1622–1627, f.459; "Book of Wyatt MSS compiled by Richard Wiatt in 1727," Romney Deposit, British Library Loan Collection, Alderman Library, Special Collections, Manuscripts Division, University of Virginia, Acc. No. 3182, M-284, 7v. See also, "A Letter of Advice to the Governor of Virginia, 1624," J. Frederick Fausz and John Kukla, eds., William and Mary Quarterly, 3rd series, 34, no. 1. (January 1977): 104–29 (at 127).

11. H. R. McIlwaine, compiler, Minutes of the Council and General Court of Virginia, 1622–1632, 1670–1676 (Richmond: Virginia State Library, 1979 [1924]), 111 (and hereafter cited as Minutes of the Council); Minutes of the Council, 12 Oct 1626, 118, and 13 Jan 1627, 136; see also Nathaniel Hale, Virginia Venturer: A Historical Biography of William Claiborne, 1600–1677 (Richmond VA: Dietz Press, 1951), 111–12. Claiborne does not appear in Edmund Morgan's heralded American Slavery, American Freedom: The Ordeal of Colonial Virginia (New York: W. W. Norton, 1975).

12. For many of these, see York County, Virginia, Deeds, Wills, Orders, 2, 1638–1648: 308 (December 1647); ibid., 329 (January 1647/48); ibid., 373; ibid. (10 June 1648, n.p.); York County, Virginia, Order Book, 1646–1648: 280; York Deeds, Orders, Wills 3, 1657–1662: 34; Northampton Orders, Deeds, & Wills, Book 4, Folio 9, 1650; ibid., Folio 34, June 1650; Ruth and Sam Sparacio, Deed & Will Abstracts of Northumberland County, Virginia, 1658–1662 (McLean VA: Antient Press, 1992–1994), 118; Ruth Sparacio and Sam Sparacio, Deed & Will Abstracts, 1662–1666, 25 (hereafter cited as Sparacio); Nell Marion Nugent, comp., Cavaliers and Pioneers: Abstracts of Virginia Land Patents and Grants, 1623–1800, vol. 1 (Richmond: Dietz Printing, 1934), 57, 199 (hereafter cited as Nugent, with volume number); Norfolk County, Virginia, Wills and Deeds, C, 55.

13. Clifford Lewis, "Some Recently Discovered Extracts from the Lost Minutes of the Virginia Council and General Court, 1642–1645," William and Mary Quarterly, 2nd series, 20 (1940): 63–70.

14. William Waller Hening, comp. and ed., The Statutes at Large, Being a Collection of All the Laws of Virginia, Vol. 1 (New York, 1809–1823), 323–26. The exceptions to the law appear first in 1670, in the act cited above, at note 1. Others followed.

15. See Maryland Archives, 4: 399, 392. Thomas Gerrard served as Lord Baltimore's factor in the Indian trade before his emigration to Virginia.

16. Sparacio, Deed & Will Abstracts, 1650–1655, 12.

17. Lewis, "Lost Minutes of the Virginia Council," reprinted in McIlwaine, 1979, 564, and cited in Helen C. Rountree, Pocahontas's People, 310. The General Court Minutes of June 7–August 9, 1645, report that the second major expedition against Powhatan forces, possibly

aided by the Rappahannock tribe and other Indians "not in amity with Opechancanough" (see February 1645: 159 in Lewis, op. cit.) was successful in that "many prisoners" were taken. The court ordered that "all" of the prisoners "over eleven years of age" be exported from the mainland in William Berkeley's ship to the "Western Island," most probably Bermuda (see also *Minutes of the Council*, 1979, 356).

18. York County Deeds, Orders, Wills, Etc. 2, 1645–1649: 99, and York County Orders, 1646–1648: 130–31.

19. Alexander Spotswood, *The Official Letters of Alexander Spotswood, Lieutenant-Governor of the Colony of Virginia, 1710–1722,* 2 vols. (Richmond: Virginia Historical Society, 1882), 1:125. During Spotswood's administration, the colony and the College of William and Mary attempted to have the tributary tribes send children to the Brafferton School, established by an endowment from Robert Boyle in 1691 solely to educate Indian children. The tribes refused, citing "the breach of a former Compact made long ago" by Virginia with the tribes, and the subsequent transportation "of their Children" to "other Countrys" where they were "sold as Slaves."

20. In 1649, less than three years after the Treaty of Necotowance, the General Assembly enacted a law against retaining local Indian children "for what Cause soever" and also transferring or selling to others any Indian children. For this, and the admonishments and edicts issued by the Surry County Court, see Surry County, Deeds, I: 32–33. Then see the Acts of the General Assembly for 1655, Act I: 38, especially n4, as cited in Jane Purcell Guild, *Black Laws of Virginia: A Summary of the Legislative Acts of Virginia Concerning Negroes from Earliest Time to the Present* (New York: Negro University Press, 1936).

21. See *Maryland Archives*, 41: 82, 186, 254, for the 1652 delivery of two "Indian Slaves."

22. Lyon Gardner Tyler, ed., *Narratives of Early Virginia, 1606–1625* (New York: Charles Scribner's Sons, 1907), 41; John T. Juricek, "The Westo Indians," *Ethnohistory* 11, no. 2 (1964): 152–53.

23. Tyler, *Narratives*, 355.

24. I disagree with Helen Rountree's and Thomas Davidson's assessment that the "Westerly Runnagados" simply wanted to take the Laughing King's territory. See Rountree and Davidson, *Eastern Shore Indians*, 50–51.

25. Northampton County, Virginia, Deeds, Wills, and Orders, 3: 207r; Hening, *Statutes*, 1:391. John Smith, *The Generall Historie of Virginia, New England, and the Summer Isles, 1624,* in *The Complete Works of Captain John Smith (1580–1631),* 2 vols., Philip Barbour, ed. (Chapel Hill: University of North Carolina Press, 1986), 2:264–65, 291. William P. Cumming, *The Southeast in Early Maps,* 2nd ed. (Chapel Hill: University of North Carolina Press, 1962), plate 26.

26. A. J. Morrison, "The Virginia Indian Trade to 1673," *William and Mary College Quarterly Historical Magazine*, 2nd series, no. 1 (October 1921), 227–28.

27. Henry Woodward, "A Faithfull Relation of my Westoe Voiage," in Alexander S. Salley, ed., *Narratives of Early Carolina, 1650–1708,* Original Narratives of Early American History, J. Franklin Jameson, general editor (New York: Charles Scribner's Sons, 1911), 125–34, and in *South Carolina Historical Magazine* (Charleston, South Carolina, 1857–1897), in the Collections of the South Carolina Historical Society, 100 Meeting St., Charleston, South Carolina [hereafter CSCHS, with volume number]), No. (Volume) 5: 456–62.

28. See Alden T. Vaughan, ed., *Early American Indian Documents: Treaties and Laws, 1607–1789* (Washington DC: University Publications, 1998), Volume 15, "Virginia and Maryland Laws," Virginia Doc. 65: 53 (Law Permitting Sale of Arms to Indians, 1659), Doc, 72: 56 (Law to Regulate Indian Trade, 1661), Doc. 80, Doc. 81 (1662); Hening, *Statutes*, 11:336–40.

29. The origin of the alliance lay in the documentary shadows of early Virginia. In all

likelihood the groups tied themselves together in the wake of the Third Anglo-Powhatan War, just about the same time the Five Nations Iroquois were extending their own forays farther west and south, pressing the Dutch-armed Susquehannock and Doeg (a Susquehannock and Tuscarora-affiliated people) down into the Virginia backcountry. Competition was certainly afoot. In 1650 when merchant Edward Bland and Captain Abraham Wood, of trading post Fort Henry on the Appomattox River, traveled back north on their expedition to the edge of Tuscarora country, they passed "the old fields of *Manks Nessoneicks*" just twelve miles south-westerly from the fort and post. "Manks" is a Powhatan language term for "great," "large," or even "powerful." Serving the expedition as a guide was Pyancha, a Powhatan of the Appomattox tribe. At the time, native informants of the Weynoke and Nottoway nations also informed Bland and Wood that the "Nessonicks" were living up the Roanoke River, which is where Lederer found them in 1670 with their neighbors the Rickahockans. See Edward Bland, *The Discovery of New Brittaine* (London: Printed by Thomas Harper for John Stephenson, 1651; reproduction of original in Library of Congress), 12, 16. In other words, the Nessons and Chickahominies were, probably a few years prior to 1650, in close proximity to each other as well as to the new fort and trading post. Indians coming into trade from the west or northwest were ordered to repair to Fort Royal. The Nessons and their neighbors, such as the Monakins (sometimes called Monacans and Mannskins), according to the standard interpretation concerning them, were supposedly situated at this time so as to trade to Fort Royal. The Monakins appear to have actually moved downriver closer to Virginia in order to have better access to the fort. The Nessons kept a respectable distance, but probably became accustomed to trading at the same location. Later, though, they appear to have shifted to Fort Henry, apparently following the colonial-Pamunkey assaults of 1656 and 1657, by which they retreated south and west.

30. See the Spanish accounts, cited above, as well as the Lederer account, the latter suggesting bitter Iroquois and Rickahockan enmity. See also the Chickahominy Petition to Governor Lord Howard Effingham, Colonial Papers, Folder 6, No. 24, LVA. For the joint Virginia-Pamunkey assault, see Charles City County, Virginia, Records, 1655–1656: 61, LVA Reel 1; Hening, *Statutes*, 1:402–3; John Lederer, in William P. Cumming, ed., *Discoveries of John Lederer, with Unpublished Letters by and about Lederer to Governor John Winthrop, Jr., and an Essay on the Indians of Lederer's Discoveries by Douglas L. Rights and William P. Cumming* (Charlottesville: University Press of Virginia, 1958 [1672]), 16; H. R. McIlwaine, *Minutes of the Council and General Court of Virginia, 1622–1632, 1670–1676*, 2nd ed. (Richmond, 1979 [1924]), 505. In South Carolina, Woodward—who could speak a number of local Indian languages—and other Carolinians discovered that Westo war leaders and councilors were called "Cocka-wases" and "Warawanses." These terms are more or less identical with the Virginia Powhatan "Cawcawassoughes," a term favored by the Chickahominy, and "Werowances," for a sort of appointed "mayor." See Juricek, "Westo Indians," 147–50; Robert Beverley, *History of the Present State of Virginia* (Chapel Hill: University of North Carolina Press, 1947 [1705]), 226; Robert Ferguson, *Present State of Carolina with Advice to Settlers* (London, 1682), 14.

31. John E. Worth, *The Struggle for the Georgia Coast: An Eighteenth-Century Spanish Retrospective on Guale and Mocama*, Anthropological Papers (New York: American Museum of Natural History, 1995): 15, 17, 18. In the summer of 1992 Worth discovered a long-forgotten and overlooked package of seventeenth-century documents pertaining to St. Augustine, Florida, in the Archivo General de Indias in Seville, Spain. These documents were originally sorted and bundled by Florida Governor Don Manuel Montiano in 1739 under orders from King Philip V of Spain. Worth's translations can be checked against transcripts now housed in the

American Museum of Natural History, Central Park West at 79th St., New York, New York.

32. William P. Cumming, ed., *The Discoveries of John Lederer*, 1–3, 6–9, 11–14. The Ricka-hocakan "land of waves" must have been in the modern Radford-Blacksburg-Roanoke corridor.

33. Ben C. McCary, *Indians in Seventeenth-Century Virginia* (1957; repr., Charlottesville: University Press of Virginia, 1992), 75–76; also, Douglas Summers Brown, Papers, 1963–1993, Ms. Ac. 34568, "Beyond the Blackwater," 1650: 33; Hening, *Statutes*, 1:525; 2:20, 124, 138–43. See also Morrison, "Virginia Indian Trade," 217–36, esp. 232.

34. Sources of the time state that such trading posts were at "the heads" of the rivers, but this was not in fact the case. To the colonial inhabitants of Virginia, the falls marked the westernmost extreme of settlement. The forts were not exceedingly distant from the settled plantations.

35. Berkeley's first term as governor ended in 1652. He returned to the position in March 1660, following the death of Governor Samuel Mathews Jr. Berkeley served for one year, returning to England to lobby for royal support of his plans for economic diversification. During this sojourn, Berkeley produced his *Discourse and View of Virginia*. Berkeley resumed the governorship upon his return to Virginia late in 1662. For the act see Hening, *Statutes*, as cited in note 28.

36. The Spanish in "La Florida" adapted the term "Chichimeco" from their prior experience in Mexico with hostile northern enemies. There the word applied to peoples considered barbaric and wild by the Nahuatl speakers in Mexico's Central Valley, and the Spanish merely adopted the term. They would later apply the same word to the allegedly fierce and naked inland tribes of "Indians" in the Philippines. The earliest South Carolina colonists picked up the designation "Rickahockans" from the fearful, war-ravaged coastal natives. By that time, of course, the term had already thrived in Virginia for more than a decade. The coastal South Carolina tribes quickly allied themselves with the colonial newcomers, perhaps for protection. Certainly, these Carolina "Rickahockans" of the 1670s and 1680s bear some relationship to the "Rickahockans" of Virginia and the Chichimecos of Spanish Florida in the 1650s.

37. Worth, *Struggle for the Georgia Coast*, 15, 17–18.

38. Charles City County Orders 1655–65: 374, sale dated to 1661; deed of sale proved and recorded 20 April 1663.

39. Hening, *Statutes*, 11:16 (October 1660).

40. See, for instance, Lauber, *Indian Slavery*, 26, on the connection between Bacon's Rebellion and Indian slavery.

41. *Virginia Magazine of History and Biography* (hereafter *VMHB*) 5 no. 2 (Oct. 1897): 114, "Decisions of the General Court."

42. Rappahannock County, Virginia, Records, Deeds, Wills, Orders, etc., No. 1, 1665–1677 c, unpaged index, 1–113 (Deeds, 1665); 114–224 (Wills, 1672–1677): 57, LVA Reel 10.

43. This is a rather complicated history and there is no room here for explication. However, with patience, one can trace certain developments. For instance, in Sparacio's *Deed Abstracts of Old Rappahannock County, Virginia . . . 1656–1664*, vol. 1 (McLean VA: R. & S. Sparacio, 1989), 12, a committee appointed "Col. More Fantleroy" to enter into a treaty with the Rappahannock tribes in September 1657. In Bishop William Mead's *Old Churches, Ministers, and Families of Virginia*, vol. 2 (Baltimore: Genealogical Publishing Co., 1966); 478–81) there is a sketch of the Fauntleroy family, which includes a copy of a deed, dated April 4, 1651, from the king and great men of the Rappahannock tribes to Moore Fauntleroy. The tribes conveyed to Fauntleroy a vast tract stretching from the Rappahannock north to the Potomac

River and from Rappahannock Creek east to Morattico Creek—a goodly portion of modern Richmond County. However, as Fauntleroy attempted to acquire additional tribal lands, he disputed increasingly with the Indians. Turning to the General Assembly, Fauntleroy and the tribes began arguing with that body over ownership of the land. An investigative committee concluded that "neither the deede nor the evidence appearing" proved that Fauntleroy acted in any legal capacity. See Hening, *Statutes*, 11:14, Assembly of 1660). Several months later in 1661, the Assembly formally charged Colonel Fauntleroy with "[s]eizing and binding the King and chief man of the Indians." At the same session, the Assembly fined other colonists for their offenses against the same tribes. Eventually, as tensions escalated and there were several alleged murders, the government's feeble attempts to curtail colonists' abuse of the Rappahannock Indians must have fallen short. The government's response was to attack the tribes and sell off the captives. Surely these and other episodes fueled the sentiments behind Bacon's Rebellion in 1676.

44. H. R. McIlwaine, comp., *Executive Journals of the Council of Colonial Virginia*, 5 vols. (Richmond: Library of Virginia, 1925), 1:53. Hereafter cited as *Executive Journals*.

45. On Five Nations (Haudenosaunee) league formation, power, and influence, see Francis Jennings, *The Ambiguous Iroquois Empire: The Covenant Chain Confederation of Indian Tribes with English Colonies from its Beginnings to the Lancaster Treaty of 1744* (New York: W. W. Norton, 1984); Bruce Elliott Johansen and Barbara Alice Mann, eds., *Encyclopedia of the Haudenosaunee* (Westport CT: Greenwood Press, 2000); William N. Fenton, *The Great Law and the Longhouse: A Political History of the Iroquois Confederacy* (Norman: University of Oklahoma Press, 1998); Doug George-Kanentiio, *Iroquois Culture & Commentary* (Santa Fe NM: Clear Light Publishers, 2000); Richard Aquila, *The Iroquois Restoration: Iroquois Diplomacy on the Colonial Frontier, 1701–1754* (Detroit: Wayne State University Press, 1983).

46. Lawrence H. Leder, ed., *Livingston Indian Records, 1666–1723* (Gettysburg: Pennsylvania Historical Association, 1956), 84–86. See also Francis Jennings, William N. Fenton, Mary A. Druke, and David R. Miller, eds., *The History and Culture of Iroquois Diplomacy: An Interdisciplinary Guide to the Treaties of the Six Nations and Their League* (Syracuse: Syracuse University Press, 1985), especially section one and chapters 4–6. "Covenant Chain" is an Iroquois figure of speech, in translation, for treaty. The literal translation is "arms linked together." The Tree of Peace was supported by the White Roots. The tree symbolically represented the Iroquois extension of authority and internal peace to subject peoples and tributary tribes or villages. Many of these figures of speech and the diplomatic traditions that accompany them are still used today.

47. Virginia law at that time did allow for some concessions to Christian Indians. Imported non-Christians were to be held as slaves. Perhaps the Onondagas were cognizant of this peculiarity in Virginia law. See also note 1, above.

48. Leder, *Livingston Indian Records*, 88–89.

49. See Jennings, et al., *History and Culture of Iroquois Diplomacy*, for Iroquois diplomacy.

50. *Executive Journals*, I: 78–79.

51. Stegge had served on the Colonial Council under Berkeley, and prior to his death was the secretary general for the colony. Stegge, though owner of a substantial estate consisting of "stocks and slaves," was not a planter.

52. William Byrd Title Book, 1637–1743, Mss 5:9 B9965:1, 54, VHS; Francis Earle Lutz, *Chesterfield: An Old Virginia County* (Richmond: William Byrd Press, 1954), 51–53. See also the Thomas Stegge will in *VMHB* 48: 31.

53. British Public Records Office, colonial office, Series 1, Box 1, fol. 24, 25, transcripts,

Colonial Records Project, Library of Virginia, Richmond. British Public Records from the colonial office are hereafter cited C.O., by office and box. See also John Clayton, "Transcript of the Journal of Robert Fallam," in Clarence Alvord and Lee Bidgood, eds., *The First Explorations of the Trans-Alleghany Region by Virginians, 1650–1674* (Cleveland: Arthur H. Clark Co., 1912), 192–93.

54. Henrico County Deeds, Wills, Etc., 1677–1692: 134, referencing deed of sale and transfer of 17 November 1673.

55. See Louis B. Wright and Marion Tinling, eds., *Secret Diary of William Byrd of Westover, 1709–1712* (Richmond: Dietz Press, 1941). These Indians were "Indian Peter" or "Redskin Peter," "Indian boy Ned" and "Indian Harry." See the entries of 5 and 6 July, 1709, 3 February, 11 August, 21 August, 23–26 August, 2 September, 8 September, 11 September, and 3 November, 22 November 1710, 22–23 January 1711, 10–11 January 1712, 16–19 February, 21–24 February, and 12 May 1712.

56. Spenser to Sir Henry Coventry, August 6, 1676, Coventry Papers LXXVII, fol. 170, in Papers relating to Virginia, Barbados, and other Colonies, Vol. 76–78, 1606–1705, Library of Virginia, Richmond, Archives and Manuscript Room, 36082 Miscellaneous Reel 429–31; Spenser to "your Lordships," August 7? 1676, ibid., fol. 169. In the 1660s, Nicholas Spencer served Governor Berkeley as a land agent in the Northern Neck, along the Rappahannock River.

57. Noel Sainsbury and J. W. Fortescue, eds., *Calendar of State Papers, Colonial Series, America and West Indies, 1677–1680* (London: Eyne and Spottiswoode, 1896 [originals in the British Public Record Office]), March 18, 1680; for another reference to Byrd "bringing away the women and children captives" see C.O. 1/44, no. 42, fol. 131.

58. Cadwallader Jones to Lord Baltimore, C.O., 1/48 f. 115.

59. Maryland Historical Society, *Archives of Maryland*, XVII: 88, 14 March 1681/2. An inventory of Owsley's estate in 1701 revealed that he owned a nine-year-old "Indian slave." The slave is clearly differentiated from a "servant" also listed as part of the estate. See Stafford County Record Book, 1699–1709: 114.

60. Jones to Baltimore, 115–16.

61. See Worth, *Struggle for the Georgia Coast*, note 31; see also note 39.

62. CSCHS 5: 166, 194; Juricek, "Westo Indians," 134–73, esp. 134–35, 137.

63. Hening, *Statutes*, 11:336–40, Act II, Grand Assembly, September 1674.

64. CSCHS 5: 411; Verner W. Crane, *The Southern Frontier, 1670–1732* (Westport CT: Greenwood Press, 1977 [1929 repr.]), 15.

65. Sir John Yeamans lived in Barbados for several years before moving in 1665 to the Lower Cape Fear in North Carolina and founding Clarendon, near modern Wilmington. Yeamans later served as proprietary governor of South Carolina from late 1671 through 1674, and was in office when Woodward entered into his trading arrangements with the Westos. Just before assuming the governorship, Yeamans commissioned Woodward's journey to Virginia via an overland route. Native informants or traders probably communicated the knowledge of this route. Yeamans wrote Carolina governor Joseph West concerning the trip. The nature and scope of Virginia's trading activities were of concern to Carolina, then exploring its own economic pursuits. See CSCHS 5: 338. See also Crane, *Southern Frontier*, 15, and J. W. Barnwell, "Dr. Henry Woodward," *South Carolina Historical and Genealogical Magazine*, 8: 29–41, and Morrison, "Virginia Indian Trade," 236.

66. Woodward listed the nations with which the Westos raided and who were supposed to be hostile to the Westos. These were the Cowetas and the Cussetas, two of the main Creek

tribes, the "Chorakaes," or Cherokees, and the "Checsaws," or Chickasaws. All of these could have supplied Virginia with slaves. See Woodward, "A Faithfull Relation," in Salley, Narratives: 125. For Needham, see CSCHS 5: 345, 411, 453.

67. Woodward, in CSCHS 5: 458.

68. Woodward, in CSCHS 5: 194; Cumming, Discoveries of John Lederer, 30.

69. Worth, Struggle for the Georgia Coast, 18–19, citing Anguiano certification of 1663, Campaña certification of 1663, and Governor Don Alonso de Aranguiz y Cotes order to Pacheco y Salgado, 1662.

70. On the Yamassees, see Worth, Struggle for the Georgia Coast, 18–22, 26–28, 50, 163–64; Crane, Southern Frontier, 12, 25–26, 30–33, 120, 128, 138, 144, 159, 164–65, 168–73, 178, 184–86, 190, 206, 254, 272; William Ramsey, "'Heathenish Combination': The Natives of the North American Southeast During the Era of the Yamasee War," PhD dissertation, Tulane University, 1998; Alan Gallay, The Indian Slave Trade: The Rise of the English Empire in the American South, 1670–1717 (New Haven: Yale University Press, 2002), chapter 12.

71. Executive Journals, III: 196, 375–76, 397–98; CO 5/1316, 618–25.

72. Bacon to Berkeley, Sept. 18 1675, Bath Papers, LXXVII: f. 6, Colonial Records Project, LVA; Pierre Marambaud, "William Byrd I: A Young Virginia Planter in the 1670s," VMHB 81, no. 2 (April 1973), 137.

73. C.O. 5/1371: 220 [455].

74. C.O. 5/1371: 225–27 [446].

75. For this episode, and for a concise introduction to some of the background to Bacon's Rebellion, see Wilcombe E. Washburn, The Governor and the Rebel: A History of Bacon's Rebellion in Virginia (Chapel Hill: Published for the Institute of Early American History and Culture at Williamsburg by the University of North Carolina Press, 1957). Bacon's Rebellion against the governor may have commenced in 1675, after Berkeley censured Bacon for the seizure. One of the seized Appomattox people may have been the "Indian Girl" taken by Bacon's men and confirmed to a colonist's ownership on January 22, 1676. See Henrico Deeds and Wills, 1677–1692: 33.

76. Morgan, American Slavery, 256, 258, 260, 262, 264. See also Coventry Papers, LXXVII: 93.

77. Morgan, American Slavery, 268.

78. Hening, Statutes, 11:341–55, Grand Assembly of 5 June 1676, Act I, 342, 346, 348.

79. Hening, Statutes, 11:365, 380, 401, 404.

80. Hening, Statutes, 11:346, 404, 440, Act I; and 490–92, Act I, 1682.

81. Rappahannock County, Virginia, Records (Wills, Invs., Etc., No.2) c:304–305, LVA, Reel 11.

82. Rappahannock Orders, 1686–1692: 230, court of June 4, 1690.

83. Northumberland O. B. 1675/6–1688/9: 166, 176. In October of 1679 the allotment to the soldiers at the Potomac fort was ordered to go to Mr. Vincent Cox's at Youcomoco. Cox also was ordered to supply a horse as head of his "forty" on January 28, 1680.

84. Cox was reimbursed on November 10, 1682 by the colony for a horse lost in service at the Potomac Garrison. See the Journal of the House of Burgesses, 1659/60–1693: 173, 182; for the Nanzattico slave, see Northumberland O. B. 1690–1698: 32.

85. Richmond County Orders, 1694–1697: 15.

86. Note the very title in the following source; even contemporaneously, the "rebellion" was cast as a war between "Christians"—not freemen, laborers, or servants—and "Indians"—not the oligarchy or upper class. See Strange News from Virginia: Being a Full and True

Account of the Life and Death of Nathanael Bacon, Esquire, Who Was the Only Cause and Original of All the Late Troubles in That Country: With a Full Relation of All the Accidents Which Have Happened in the Late War There between the Christians and Indians (London: Printed for William Harris ..., 1677); original at Henry E. Huntington Library.

87. For some of Byrd's trading activities, see Henrico County, Record Book 1, Deeds and Wills, 1677–1692 (transcripts), Reel 4a, 35: 21 Feb. 1677, and 134–35. Actually Berkeley pardoned William Hatcher due to his age, asking him only to ransom his freedom in pork. See Hening, *Statutes*, 11:366–72, and 549–56. These records also reveal that among the rebel leadership were seven or eight other traders and interpreters. Though William Hatcher may soon have retired, his sons picked up right where he left off. See Henrico Record Book 1, op. cit., 216, 222, and 224; Henrico Record Book 2, Orders and Wills, 1678–1693 (trans.), 84 [166]: Aug. Court, 1684; Order Book and Wills, 1678–1693, 43/136, 1 Feb. 1682/3; Order Book and Wills, 1678–1693, June 1686: 136/213.

88. Marion Tinling, ed., *The Correspondence of the Three William Byrds of Westover, Virginia, 1684–1776*, vol. 1 (Charlottesville: University Press of Virginia, for the Virginia Historical Society, 1977), 15–16; also printed in the *Virginia Historical Register* 1 (Richmond, Virginia, 1848–1853), 64–65. The original correspondence, Byrd to Thomas Grendon, n.d., circa April 29, 1684, is in the William Byrd Letterbook, VHS, Richmond, Virginia.

89. Richard Traunter Journals, 1698–1699, Mss5: 9 T6945:1 (Rec. No. 159753), VHS. Traunter's journals are unpublished. They were acquired by the Society in 2001. The journals are hereafter cited as Traunter, "Journal," followed by folio number and journal (a for 1698, and b for 1699).

90. Traunter, "Journal," 2a–3a.

91. Traunter, "Journal," 4a.

92. See James H. Merrell, *The Indians' New World: Catawbas and Their Neighbors from European Contact through the Era of Removal* (Chapel Hill: Published for the Institute of Early American History and Culture by the University of North Carolina Press, 1989), Map 1, p. 4, and also 47, 55, 94.

93. Traunter, "Journal," 1a, 5a–7a, 33a, 35a; 1b–2b, 24b–25b, appendix.

94. Traunter, Journal, 21a–24a, 33a; 4b–5b, 9b, 11b, 12b–30b.

95. *Executive Journals*, I, June 11, 1680–June 22, 1699: 146–47, and Jan. 26, 1690/91: 157–58.

96. Robert J. Cain, ed., *Records of the Executive Council, 1664–1734*, vol. 7, (Raleigh NC: Department of Cultural Resources, Division of Archives and History, 1984), 7.

97. "John Basse's Sermon Book," in possession of Chief Barry Bass of the Nansemond Tribe. A copy of the original is at LVA, Manuscripts, Acc. No. 26371: 8.

98. On Virginia traders in Chowan territory, see Thomas Birch, ed., *A Collection of the State Papers of John Thurloe*, 7 vols. (London: Printed for the Executor of the late Mr. Fletcher Gyles, 1742), 2:273–74; Elizabeth G. McPherson, "Nathaniell Batts, Landholder on Pasquotank River, 1660," *North Carolina Historical Review* (hereafter NCHR) 43 (January 1966): 73–74; and William S. Powell, "Carolana and the Incomparable Roanoke: Explorations and Attempted Settlements, 1620–1663," *NCHR* 51 (1974), 1–21. For the Chowans assisting the colonists against the Tuscaroras, and engaging in the slave trade, see Cain, ed., *Records of the Executive Council*, vol. 7, 48, 99.

99. Stephen Bradley, ed., *Early Records of North Carolina: Wills, 1723–1736*, vol. 5, no. 393, Will of Francis Pugh, 5 July 1733.

100. William L. Saunders, ed., *Colonial Records of North Carolina* (Raleigh NC: P.M. Hale [etc.] State Printer, 1886), I:815; *Executive Journals*, III: 287–88, 293–95.

101. Christine Ann Styrna, "The Winds of War and Change: The Impact of the Tuscarora War on Proprietary North Carolina, 1690–1729," PhD dissertation, College of William and Mary, 1990; William C. Sturtevant, general editor; Bruce G. Trigger, volume editor, *Handbook of North American Indians: Volume 15* (Washington DC: Smithsonian Institution, 1978), part 3, section on Iroquoian tribes of the Virginia–North Carolina coastal plain, and part 4, section on Tuscaroras among the Iroquois in New York.

102. Cain, *Records of the Executive Council*, vol. 7, 99.

103. See Gallay, *Indian Slave Trade*, chapter 10, passim; Douglas L. Rights, *The American Indian in North Carolina* (Winston-Salem: John Blair, 1957), 46; *Minutes of the Provincial Council of Pennsylvania*, vol. 3 (Philadelphia: Joseph Severns, Colonial Records of Pennsylvania, 16 vols., 1852–53), 3:511–12; Edmund B. O'Callaghan and Berthold Fernow, eds., *Documents Relative to the Colonial History of the State of New York*, vol. 5 (Albany: Weed, Parsons, 1854), 387.

104. For Tuscaroras, see Lewis Thompson Papers, 716, Subseries 1.1., folder 1, Southern Historical Collection (hereafter SHC), Manuscripts Department, Library of the University of North Carolina at Chapel Hill; Miscellaneous Papers, Indians, 1697–1758, 1764, Treaties, Petitions, Agreements, and Court Cases, North Carolina Department of Archives and History, Raleigh; American Philosophical Society ms. 3818. [1757]. D. copy 1p. [60(81)]; *Executive Journals*, III; Bertie County, North Carolina, Deed Books L and M: 31, passim.

105. Lee Family Papers, 1:L51, fol. 677, VHS.

106. David L. Bushnell Jr. "The Account of Lamhatty," *American Anthropologist* 10, no. 4 (October–December 1908): 568–74; Wilbur W. Stout, "Lamhatty's Road Map," *Southern Quarterly* 2, no. 3 (1962–1964): 247–54.

107. Patricia Penn Hilden, "Hunting North American Indians in Barbados," paper presented at the "Colloquium on the Socio-Economic Legacy of Slavery," University of California, Berkeley, May 2, 2002; Paul Du Ru, *Journal of Paul Du Ru: Missionary Priest to Louisiana*, translated by Ruth Lapham Butler (Chicago: Caxton Club, 1934), 66.

108. For Smith, see Northumberland County, Record Book, 1718–1726: 95–96 (deed of 1718, citing an earlier transaction), and William P. Palmer, ed., *Calendar of Virginia State Papers*, vol. 2 (Richmond, Virginia, 1875), 14; *Executive Journals*, II: 284. For Robert Carter, see the discussion of the Nickens family and John Carter in Everett, " 'An Inhuman practice.' "

109. Richmond County Order Book 3, 1699–1704 c, [1]: 361–64, 373–84; Richmond County Miscellaneous Records, 1699–1724 c (Bonds, Attachments, Executions and Estate Settlements): 26–29; Waverly Winfree, comp., *Laws of Virginia: Being a Supplement to Hening's Statutes at Large*, 1700–1750 (Richmond: Library of Virginia, 1971): 41–45.

110. Thomas Jefferson, *Notes on the State of Virginia*, William Peden, ed. (Chapel Hill: University of North Carolina Press, for the Institute of Early American History and Culture, 1982), 61. It is from this quote that the author of the current chapter has taken the title of his dissertation.

3. South Carolina's Entrance into the Indian Slave Trade
Alan Gallay

When the English planted a settlement at Carolina in 1670, no one could envision the extent of its impact on the South.[1] The colony was but a beachhead for an expanding English empire in the Americas. The lords proprietors who owned the colony intended to attract settlers with the promise of land on easy terms, and build an agricultural society that could provide highly valuable commodities for trade. The free migrants, some of whom brought slaves with them from Barbados, experimented with tobacco and other crops, cut lumber for export to the Caribbean, and searched for other ways to make money quickly. With their eye on the main chance, the most lucrative enterprise to present itself was trade with Indians—for animal pelts and humans.

This essay examines Carolinians' entry into the Indian slave trade—a trade that eventually provided the capital for colonists to create a highly successful plantation society built on African slaves producing rice. The Carolinians did not initiate the Indian slave trade in the American South, but they expanded it immensely, prompting a frenzy of slaving that extended from the Atlantic Coast to Texas, and from the Ohio River south to the Gulf of Mexico. Although the lords proprietors did not oppose slavery, in fact assumed that their colonists would use African slaves to develop their colony, they condemned the large-scale capture and sale of Native Americans. This forced the Carolinians to rationalize their behavior, allowing us an opportunity to see how seventeenth-century colonists faced the moral issue of engaging in the enslavement of free people.

The Carolinians entered a region in the throes of vast cultural, social, and political change. Most of the Native American chiefdoms that had dominated the southern landscape had collapsed, replaced by decentralized American Indian communities coming to terms with the introduction of new diseases, the Spanish presence in Florida, and the immigration of native peoples from the north. The most important group of migrants, who posed a threat through much of the Southeast, were the Westos. The Westos had just migrated to the Savannah River from Virginia, where they were known as the Rickahockans. One anthropologist, Marvin T. Smith, believes them to have been displaced Eries (an Iroquoian group) from New York and Pennsylvania, who had been forced south by the Iroquois wars of 1654–1656.[2] The expansion of English Virginia westward pressured the Powhatans and other Virginia Indians, which forced the Westos to migrate again, but not before having established trade relations with English Virginians. From their new home along the Savannah, they aggressively attacked southern Indians to the east, southeast, and south. Smith claims that the Virginians' arming of the Westos gave them undue advantage, forcing the technologically inferior bands to the south to confederate as the Creek Indians. The new weaponry, however, could scarcely have provided the Westos with anything more than a psychological advantage, for the firepower of seventeenth-century guns paled in comparison to the bow and arrow, which could be shot more frequently and accurately.[3] The acquisition of guns alone is insufficient to explain why the Westos terrorized their neighbors. Instead Westo aggression can be attributed to the two forced migrations in the fifteen years before they arrived on the Savannah and their desperate need to carve out living space. Just how many Westos migrated is unknown, though the Spanish reported that they had variously 500 and 2,000 gunmen, which implies a population of 1,700 to 8,000. A group of American Indians of that size required a large territory—hundreds of square miles, most of which was needed for hunting—to sustain itself.

The Westo relationship with Virginia traders also shaped the nature of their aggressiveness toward their neighbors. The Virginians offered trade goods to the Westos in exchange for captives.[4] It made more sense to the Westos to devote their energy to enslaving Indians than to hunting and processing pelts. Instead of killing their enemies or intimidating them to flee, the Westos sold them to the English, which not only removed their foes but gained them something in return. Their single-mindedness to gain land, and their organizational skills, tactics, and trade connections gave them numerous advantages over the region's other Indians. Just as the Westos set in motion the formation of the Creek Confederacy by forcing their southern neighbors to band in defense, they also mortally wounded the Spanish mission system in Guale and Mocama along the Atlantic coast of Georgia and Florida, while inducing some of Carolina's coastal Indians to welcome the English into the region as an ally.

Whatever expectations Indians had of the new Carolina colony, and they had little reason to expect its survival, as the previous Spanish attempts to colonize the area had been fleeting, the settlement was of a permanent nature, quickly transforming the Carolina low country. Although the new European immigrants and their African slaves hunted and fished like the coastal Indians, they also introduced livestock, particularly cattle, which roamed freely before shipment to the West Indies.[5] Both Indians and Europeans farmed, but the English cleared relatively large areas for lumber and commercial agriculture, consciously aping other European colonies in their search for marketable commodities for sale abroad. The African slave laborers, transferred from West Indian plantations, felled trees, erected buildings, and helped transform low country land to pasture and farm use. English settlement, although it provided coastal Indians with trade goods and a needed ally against the Westos, could not help but create resentment as it altered the landscape and drove away the wild animals so necessary for Indian existence in the region. This compelled low country indigenes to travel greater distances to hunt, while also leading many to work for the Europeans to obtain clothing, tools, and other items that they formerly produced themselves.

The eight lords proprietors were granted Carolina under patent from King Charles II in 1663. They held complete control over the disposal of Carolina land and the structure and form of its government, as long as they approved no laws repugnant to the laws of England. The proprietors had the right to direct colonial relations with local Indians, which became a constant point of contention, not just between the proprietors and the colonists, but between the proprietors and their own appointed officials. During most of the proprietary period, the struggle for control over Indian affairs defined the colony's history and shaped the fortunes of all involved. The proprietors asserted their claims within the colony through the Fundamental Constitutions, by which they established colonial government.[6] Largely the work of Proprietor Anthony Ashley Cooper, and his secretary, the philosopher John Locke, the constitutions provided penalties of forfeiture of one's entire estate, movable and unmovable property, as well as banishment, for anyone who claimed land by purchase or gift from any Indian or Indian nation.[7] The proprietors did not dismiss Indian ownership of land within their domain, but they believed that their patent gave them ownership of non-Indian land and the exclusive right to negotiate with Indians for land. This measure served as a statement of proprietary rights and precluded Indians from losing their land through settler trickery. Until they lost their patent, the proprietors clumsily but consistently tried to balance their interests with Indian rights.[8]

The proprietors explicitly ordered the local government not to disturb Indian lands. In 1669 they issued instructions that no one could take up land within two and a half miles of an Indian settlement on the same side of a river.[9] Division of the land into 12,000-square-acre parcels (baronies) reserved the village barony plus an adjacent barony for the Indians. In spite of the proprietors' expressed concerns, Indian land rights never assumed great importance in their plans. Ten years later, when the proprietors granted forty of these baronies (totaling 480,000 acres) to Sir John Cochrane and Sir George Campbell for the settlement of Scots Presbyterians in the Port Royal region, they instructed the Scots to reserve one or more squares for the Indians if they refused to leave, hardly adequate compensation for the many Indians in the area. The proprietors assured the Scots that they would "use their best endeavors to obtain the consent of the Indians concerned"[10] and to protect grantees from Indian claims. Indians possessed usufruct rights in English law over land cultivated and inhabited—the proprietors thus could not legally ride roughshod over Indian land—but these rights generally did not protect hunting land.[11]

The proprietors seem not to have realized or cared that leaving the Indians a 12,000-acre parcel in the midst of English settlement would not allow them to maintain their traditional way of life. Indians required large hunting preserves to obtain food and clothing. The proprietors were not unlike most other Englishmen in holding Indian hunting in contempt. In England hunting was a sport reserved for the elite; it rankled the wellborn in their own society.[12] Most English colonists wanted Indian men to give up the bow and arrow for the plow and to alter the gender roles that had women working the fields and men hunting. Carolina, however, was different. The colony's economy for its first fifty years revolved around the Indian trade: colonists wanted Indians to hunt to bring in the animal skins and furs they could exchange for European goods. Indians were encouraged to hunt, not near the plantations, but to the west and south. This inconvenienced the "settlement Indians," who received their name from living near and among the English colonists. The Europeans also preferred to have Indians move to the edges of European settlement because there they could provide a first line of defense against intruders.

Whereas the colonists envisioned local Indians as allies and trading partners who would remain external to Carolina, the proprietors wished to incorporate Indians who lived within their patent into their colony. "Hoping in time to draw the Indians into our government," the proprietors wanted to lure Indians through various enticements.[13] Inclusion would be on "enlightened" terms of religious tolerance. The Fundamental Constitution provided that although the "Natives . . . who will be concerned in our Plantation are utterly strangers to Christianity," their "Idolatry, Ignorance or Mistake gives us no right to expel or use them ill." The constitution tolerated all religions, in part because the proprietors wanted to attract settlers. They foresaw that people arriving from other places "will undoubtedly be of different opinions concerning Matters of Religion." The Church of England would be the only church supported by government, and the constitution expressed the hope that all would convert, but this could only occur if non-Anglicans, "having an opportunity of acquainting themselves with the true and reasonableness of its Doctrines and the peaceableness and Inoffensiveness of its profession, may by good usage and persuasion . . . be won over to embrace and unfeignedly receive the truth."[14]

In this age of religious bigotry, wherein English high church Anglicans and Dissenters had spent the previous decades at one another's throats, trying to disenfranchise, disempower, penalize, and kill one another (as well as Catholics and the new sects that proliferated), this was a remarkable statement of tolerance, though not a unique one; Maryland and Rhode Island offered religious toleration, as did Pennsylvania, founded soon after Carolina. Still, Carolina's offer was far more liberal than that of most other colonies, and the colony's policies toward Indians were as liberal as Pennsylvania's and Rhode Island's. Under the Fundamental Constitution, native religion was treated no differently than any religion other than the Church of England, though this "enlightened" approach was shared less by Carolina colonists than by Pennsylvania Quakers. It was a view held by some Europeans but few American colonists, who tended toward religious bigotry where Indians were concerned.

Of much less concern to the proprietors were the African slaves who the free colonists imported to the colony. They foresaw that some Africans would seek to convert to Christianity and that planters might prevent conversion out of fear that enslaving Christians would be illegal. The proprietors put slave owners at ease by stipulating in the Fundamental Constitution that conversion would not release slaves from their condition.[15]

Late seventeenth-century English considered African slavery a moral, legal, and socially acceptable institution. Copying the Spanish, Portuguese, and Dutch colonies, the English enslaved Africans on their plantations both in the West Indies and on the North American mainland. (Before establishing colonies, English had participated in the African slave trade, at least as early as the late sixteenth century, when John Hawkins provided Spanish colonies with slaves.)[16] Europeans were not alone in keeping slaves—many human societies of this era can be characterized by their exploitation of unfree labor—but the exploitation of non-European peoples by Europeans in the colonies was especially virulent and brutal. In England, the force of law and custom, together with the power of the state, allowed the ruling classes to rule with more ease: labor discipline was accomplished more easily at home than in foreign countries or new colonies, where the resentments of laborers combined with a weaker government to lead those who controlled labor to employ force more often and heavily than they could have at home. Sixteenth- and seventeenth-century England employed brutal force in its Irish colony, under Oliver Cromwell especially, which provided a model for the treatment of non-English peoples in its American colonies. The English readily drew parallels between the Irish, whom they characterized as dark savages beyond the pale of civilization, and Africans, whom they also considered savage and incapable of civilization.[17]

The English rationale for enslavement lay in the belief that captives taken in a "just war" could be offered enslavement as an alternative to death.[18] The narrowness of the options offered prisoners did not diminish the "voluntary" nature of the decision, for the captives had in effect forfeited their lives when they were captured. Captors considered themselves benevolent by giving captives the choice of enslavement or death.[19] By the mid-seventeenth century, the English had added another rationale for enslavement by determining that the children of a slave mother inherited her condition, so that slave status passed from one generation to the next. Two oddities characterized this rationale. First, in law, children's status devolved from the father, not the mother. The change perpetuated enslavement by making status hereditary (a condition contrary to most African slave traditions) and by not freeing the many mulattoes born from the union of free white males and slave females.[20] The second oddity lay in the original justification of enslavement as the product of capture in a just war. English planters had not captured their slaves in a just war or in any war: they had purchased them from slave traders. The English thus extended the rationale for enslavement to the purchase of slaves captured by other people in a just war. But had the Africans been captured in wars, just or otherwise? Some had, but many had not. Often African slaves were the victims of raiders whose sole intent was to capture free people to sell to slave traders.

In Europe many viewed the enslavement of Native Americans somewhat differently from the enslavement of Africans, though both were subject to incipient racialization by Europeans who considered both as savages. Africans were deemed a "brutish people" whose inherent savagery and physical nature suited them to a life of labor.[21] Having Africans judged intellectually and spiritually inferior to all other humans, the slavers devoted little thought to elevating Africans' status or incorporating them fully within European or colonial societies. Indians, however, were romanticized as noble people who could be elevated to Christian civilization or perhaps could be left alone to live in their conceived state of purity. Many Europeans thought of Indians as their biological equals, positing that only circumstances of separation by the Atlantic had led to Indians' very different social and political development. Some Europeans opposed enslavement of the New World's indigenous peoples. Spain outlawed Native American enslavement in its empire in the sixteenth century, though local governments and Spanish colonists found ways to skirt the laws and keep Indians in various states of unfree labor.[22]

In England the sentimentality of the concept of the noble savage created opposition to enslavement but never involved the state or the established church as it did in Spain. In Spain organized religion played an active role influencing, initiating, and administering government policy, and its empire's highly centralized system took a uniform approach to Indian slavery.[23] By contrast, in the English colonies jurisdiction over enslavement was a local consideration, not a matter of imperial policy. All English colonies, with the notable exception of Georgia during its first twenty years, permitted slavery.[24] Each colony created a body of laws to govern the institution, though slavery was practiced before laws defined its parameters.

In Carolina, the proprietors made distinctions between enslaving Africans and enslaving Indians. They distinguished between Africans and American Indians because Africans would arrive in the colony as slaves for private use by free people, whereas Indians were indigenous, free, and in possession of existing rights to the land. But the proprietors' concerns were also practical: they worried that enslavement of Indians would initiate wars, which might not only prove expensive but bring unwanted attention from forces within England that might wish to take away their patent. The proprietors repeatedly urged their officials and colonists to treat Indians fairly, and they tried to create a society that would institutionalize and maintain justice for them.

As early as 1680 the proprietors ordered the Carolina government to ensure Indians equal justice with European settlers. They published regulations and distributed them widely so no one could claim ignorance. They suggested steep penalties for anyone interfering with Indian embassies and instructed the governor and Council to establish a commission to meet at least every two months in Charles Town to hear all complaints.[25] Astute enough to recognize that presents would be necessary "to purchase their friendship and alliance,"[26] and that trade between settlers and natives would bind the two peoples, the proprietors also insisted that Indians receive retribution for offenses committed against them by the English, with perpetrators punished by the colony's government and forced to pay reparations. Establishing this system of justice proved nearly impossible given the views of colonists and local officials, who saw the exploitation of Indians as the easiest way to wealth. Nevertheless the proprietors persisted, and officials made several attempts to protect Indians, though these usually arose out of expediency rather than any sense of justice. The ultimate failure of proprietary idealism arose from a combination of factors. Even when structures were in place to provide justice, the propensity to commit injustice, though sometimes punished, proved too overwhelming for proprietary and local governments to overcome. It was a question of will and resources. Government rarely possessed the will to devote the resources necessary to create a tolerant and equitable society. Could colonists who exploited Africans be expected to treat Indians any differently?

The proprietors had self-interested reasons to prevent abuses and keep colonists out of the Indian trade. They had reserved most of the Indian trade for themselves and did not want to share this moneymaking enterprise. They also thought that the trade would deter colonists from developing their landholdings. The proprietors believed their plan of colonization to be a reasonable arrangement: the colonists had the use of the land and its timber and in return were expected to pay a quitrent, a tax on their land.[27] The English settlers agreed with the scenario, but only to a point. Few could see any reason to pay the quitrent—a problem faced by proprietors and the royal government in other colonies. Moreover, establishing commercial agricultural enterprises took time; land had to be cleared, crops planted, and crops and seed experimented with until colonists found what would thrive in the Carolina soil. Further, the cultivation of staples for export meant that labor had to be purchased, which in turn required capital. The more labor one commanded, the more quickly profits could be made. Some planters brought laborers, both slave and indentured servant, with them, but they always desired more and thus needed more capital. To obtain that capital, the planters looked to the Indian trade, where investment brought quicker returns. Animal pelts—hunted and processed by Indians—could be purchased by colonists with little effort of time and labor on their part. Indians who could be shipped easily to other colonies as slave laborers were even more valuable. The trade in Indians and pelts quickly tied Carolina into England's inter-colonial network, for both commodities had value throughout the empire and thus could be exchanged for other commodities: tools, seed, manufactured goods, and African slave laborers.[28]

Two economies thus grew side by side in Carolina: a frontier exchange with Indians that brought in animal pelts and Indian slaves, which were then turned into needed capital and commodities to develop a plantation system, which produced food and wood products. At the heart of both economies lay slavery—slaves as laborers and slaves as saleable commodities. The proprietors made money from neither and perceived the transformation of Indians into commodities as the gravest threat facing the colony.

The English enslavement of Native Americans in Carolina occurred at first settlement, though colonial officials felt it necessary to justify themselves to the proprietors. To show compliance with custom, in December 1675, Carolina's Grand Council carefully explained to the proprietors why they had approved of the sale of Indians into slavery. The Sewees, they reported, "and other our Neighbouring Indians" had offered to sell their "Indian prisoners" to the colonists. These captives, "Lately taken, are Enemies to the said Indians who are in Amity with the English." It did not matter that the Indians were not at war with the English, only that they were taken in war and that their captors chose to sell them. Telling the proprietors that these Indians were enemies of friends demonstrated that they were not enslaving "innocent" Indians and that they were complying with their Indian allies' wishes. The council noted, undoubtedly for the proprietors' benefit, "that the said Indian prisoners are willing to work in this Country, or to be transported from hence,"[29] thus fulfilling both the custom of enslaving no one against their wishes and the proprietors' order that "no Indian upon any occasion or pretense whatsoever is to be made a Slave, or without his own consent be carried out of Carolina."[30]

Control over the Indian slave trade lay in the hands of the proprietors' appointed officials in Carolina. These appointees, who comprised the colony's elite, tried to keep the colonists out of the trade, but only so that they themselves could reap the profits. They heeded proprietary orders only when it coincided with their interests. They held no loyalty to the proprietors who had appointed them to office and granted them land. Instead they chafed under proprietary prohibitions on the Indian trade, which aimed at keeping them from the area of opportunity that promised the quickest route to wealth.

Disregard of proprietary rules at the highest levels of colonial administration—the colony's governors and Council members—had far-reaching effects on Carolina's development. With the governor and Council typically placing their interests above those of the proprietors, there was little respect for the law. The colony's elite split into factions and jockeyed for power. Because there was so much conflict over the spoils of office, the elite could not maintain order among themselves. Local elites resorted to fighting, rioting, and illegal jailing to improve their position.[31] With almost total disdain for proprietary rules and imperial law, the colony became a haven for pirates who traded with elites,[32] probably for items the pirates would have had little difficulty trading elsewhere—pelts and Indian slaves. Abuse of office led the proprietors frequently to remove governors, periodically heightening the intense competition for office and the inevitable vying for the ear of new governors. Neither Crown nor proprietors could force the Carolina elite to accept the rule of law, though English discontent over the colony's active participation in trade with pirates ultimately led to an imperial crackdown.

The contest for power among elites effected a struggle over who would control the Indian trade. Within the colony, colonists could trade with local Indians,[33] which they did for foodstuffs, pelts, and slaves. But the proprietors reserved for their agents the potentially profitable trade with the large tribes outside the colony, which local elites eyed greedily. The proprietors claimed a monopoly on this trade for several reasons: they believed that the Indians needed the trade and that the colonists seemed incapable of participating in it without taking advantage of the Indians; they fully expected trade abuses to lead to war or the desertion of their Indian neighbors to the Spanish, and they hoped, as noted, to see some return on their investment in the colony.[34] In April 1677 the proprietors forbade for seven years all trade with the Spanish and all Indians who lived beyond Port Royal, particularly the Westos and Cussetas, "two warlike and fierce Nations . . . [with] who[m], if quarrels should arise," the colony would face grave danger.[35] Five proprietors signed an agreement to control the trade, each agreeing yearly to subscribe £100 for trade goods. Dr. Henry Woodward, who had initiated the trade and played a key role in Indian affairs in the colony's early years, agreed with the proprietors to conduct it for them in return for 20 percent of the profits. The proprietors also licensed London merchants to trade with Spanish St. Augustine and with Indians anywhere along the Carolina coast or Florida cape.[36]

As already noted, the Westos arrived in Carolina shortly before the colony's founding and brought ties to the Virginians with them. These ties did not presume that the Westos would establish friendly relations with Carolina. English colonies often negotiated with Indian groups one by one, and Indians responded in kind. Virginia and Carolina traders operated independently of one another, answerable only to their respective governments. This independence of action did not mean that the Crown would approve of one colony's traders inciting Indians to war with another colony, but conflicts and conflict of interest did occur from the decentralization of English Indian policies. The Carolinians, to secure their financial and diplomatic interests, looked to replace the Virginians as trading partners with Indians from the Cherokees southward. For the remainder of the colonial period Carolina worked to exclude Virginia from the southern trade.[37] To a large extent the Carolinians succeeded, and needed to, for at stake were not only profits but the colony's well-being. For Virginia, by contrast, trade with southern Indians was mostly an economic concern, for those Indians were too distant to threaten the Old Dominion. In spite of Carolina's steadily growing preeminence in the trade, the Virginia traders retained a share, and during wars between Carolina and its neighbors, Virginians sometimes acted as a source of supplies for the colony's enemies.

Carolina needed to establish relations with the powerful Westos and replace the Virginians as trading partners. As anthropologist Marcel Mauss pointed out in *The Gift*, two neighboring peoples who do not engage in trade must necessarily exist in a warlike state.[38] Before trade ties could be established, however, warfare with the Westos had broken out in 1673. Westo attacks against Carolina coastal Indians extended to the English, and the fledgling colony was hard put to stop them. Carolina had to rely on neighboring Indians, not just for defense, but for offensive operations as well.

Carolina turned to the Esaws, a Piedmont people, who, according to Carolina's Grand Council, "are well acquainted with the Westo habitations, and have promised all the help they can afford." Whether the Esaws offered their assistance to gain the colony's goodwill or to enlist an ally against their own enemy is unknown, but it probably combined both motives. In desperate straits, the English laid aside their arrogance—they not only accepted Esaw assistance but let the Esaws determine the best way to subdue the Westos. Illustrating the serious nature of the task, the Grand Council instructed its four-man negotiating party to the Esaws, half of whom were Council members, and thus among the most important personages in the colony, to go to the Esaws to "treat and agree with the said Indians as *they* shall find most convenient for the better carrying on of the said War, and for the discovery of those parts of this Country" where the Westos live.[39]

For reasons unknown the party did not leave for four months, but on their "safe" return, the council not only listened to their report but heard a "complaint . . . by neighbouring Indians" concerning the theft of goods by three white men, who were ordered to restore the goods and pay a fine of twenty shillings "to satisfy for their trespass." If they did not comply, a warrant of distress would be issued.[40] The need for an alliance with local Indians convinced the council to provide a modicum of justice for settlement Indians. Carolina had to prove to local Indians that their property would be secured—and speedily. At the next meeting the Council announced a system for settling property disputes that would avoid trials and allow Indians and English to settle their differences quickly. A complainant could "bring a Petition to the Secretaries Office," where a summons would be issued requiring both parties to "appear with their evidences before the Grand Councill." As long as both parties agreed to submit to the Council's judgment, the parties could avoid a court case.[41] The system apparently did not work. Indians, suspicious of the process, did not flock to the Council with cases. Even if they had, it is questionable whether European defendants would have agreed to submit to a Council decision when they would have had a much better chance of winning a case in front of a jury of their peers. And it is questionable whether many Indians would have filed court cases in the unfamiliar English legal system. Still, the Council's attempt signifies its recognition of the need to protect settlement Indians' property.

The first war with the Westos ended in December 1674, when the Westos initiated an alliance by appearing at the plantation of Dr. Henry Woodward. Already known from Florida to Carolina as the most important Englishman in Carolina's diplomacy with Indians, Woodward had arrived in Carolina in 1666 under proprietor sponsorship to learn Indian languages and pave the way for English settlement. Two years later he was captured by the Spanish and imprisoned in St. Augustine. He escaped, served as a surgeon on a privateer, and returned to Carolina in 1670. Woodward's linguistic and personal skills placed him in the key position as negotiator of trade and political relations with neighboring Indians.

Woodward's reputation had spread to the Westos, and they now made it clear to him that they desired both to end the hostilities and open trade. They escorted him to their towns on the west side of the Savannah River, above modern-day Augusta, where the Westos had arranged a reception. As Woodward entered the towns, the Westos saluted him with a volley of fifty to sixty small arms, thus displaying not only their firepower but their ability to obtain European arms. "The chief of the Indians made long speeches intimating their own strength (and as I judged their desire of friendship with us)." In a show of respect and hospitality, in the evening they "oiled my eyes and joints with bears oil," gave presents of deerskins, and feted Woodward with enough "food to satisfy at least half a dozen of their own appetites."[42] In this way the Westos showed Woodward that they wanted a new relationship with Carolina but that they made this offer from a position of strength, not weakness.

The host town featured double palisades on one side; the side that fronted the river was defended by only a single palisade. On the banks of the river "seldom lie less than one hundred fair canoes ready upon all occasions." Woodward was impressed to find the Westos well supplied with arms, ammunition, trading cloth, and other English goods they had obtained from the northward, for which they exchanged "dressed deerskins and young Indian slaves." The Westos hoped to establish a trade with Carolina, whose nearer location made the exchange of goods more convenient, hence more profitable. It also might have been much safer. Woodward learned that the Cherokees were the Westos' enemies, and if the Cherokees were obtaining goods from the Virginians, it would have been expedient for the Westos to procure goods from the Carolinians.[43]

The Westos could ill afford an alliance between the Cherokees and the Virginians. Cherokee numbers made them a grave threat. The Westos needed allies. Carolina was one possibility, but during Woodward's visit another arose. Two Savannah (Shawnee) Indians arrived from the vicinity of the Apalachicola River, near the Gulf of Mexico. The Savannahs were a unique Indian group. Most inhabited a large number of towns in the Ohio River valley. Probably as a result of the Iroquois wars that began in the 1640s, many Savannahs migrated to places as diverse as Florida, Georgia,

Pennsylvania, and Maryland.[44] It was not unusual for Indian groups to splinter and move in myriad directions, but the Savannahs found strength in diaspora and retained close ties among their towns, so that there was frequent reforming, moving, and splintering. Individuals unhappy with the living situation in one area could leave and move to another town or migrate with others and form new towns in other distant places—yet know that they could always return and join older Savannah establishments. Their diaspora and visiting from one town to another led to important ties with numerous peoples east of the Mississippi. Their language became a lingua franca, and their experiences made them particularly suited for initiating and leading the pan-Indian movement of the nineteenth century that extended from the Ohio valley to the Gulf of Mexico.[45] Woodward thus witnessed a historic occasion: the Savannahs establishing first contact with the powerful Westos and with Carolina.

The Savannahs had remained outside the Spanish orbit in Florida and were seeking allies for themselves. Although the Savannahs and the Westos could not understand each other's languages, they exchanged information by signs, and according to Woodward, the Savannahs informed the Westos that the Cussetas, Chickasaws, and Cherokees were going to attack them. It is questionable whether all three were preparing a concerted attack. In previous years the Westos had warred with the Cherokees and with Indians to the south like the Cussetas, and they had probably sold captives from both groups to the Virginians. But this is the first evidence that the Westos had attacked the Chickasaws, which meant that they might have gone as far as the Mississippi in search of land and captives. The Westos did not take the warning lightly and prepared for the invasion.

The Savannahs probably warned of the impending attack to earn Westo goodwill. They could not establish a relationship with Carolina without first opening one with the Westos, who ranged over the land between them and the English. The Savannahs understood the value of European trade. Their towns in the Ohio valley had had contacts with English traders by the 1670s, and the Spanish in Florida had provided them with trade goods, though in limited quantities. While the Westos were distracted by preparing for the invasion, the Savannahs approached

Woodward about striking up a trade, showing him beads they had obtained from the Spanish.

Woodward's visit to the Westos was a success, and it resulted in a profitable trade in Indian slaves that lasted from 1675 to 1680. The Westos preyed on Spanish-allied Indians in Guale and Mocama. They also continued to attack other groups, including the settlement Indians. Carolina's need to retain an alliance with the coastal Indians precluded any permanent rapprochement with the Westos, who for unknown reasons would not or could not end their wars with the coastal Indians.[46] The Westos also continued their wars with the Cherokees, Chickasaws, Chiscas, Cowetas, and Cussetas.[47] The Carolinians thus learned that alliance with the Westos limited their options in opening positive relations with virtually any other southern Indians, for the Westos effectively blocked the pathways west and south and there was little chance that the Westos' enemies would trade with the Westos' English allies. The Savannahs' meeting with Woodward was most unfortunate for the Westos. Once the English realized the desirability of trade with those Indians, the Westos became expendable, and the Savannahs later would help destroy the Westos before replacing them on the Savannah River as allies of the English.[48]

War with the Westos erupted again in the winter of 1679–1680. The proprietors learned of it in February from a ship's captain rather than from the Carolina government. They blamed the governor and Council for not maintaining friendship with the Westos and for not protecting the settlement Indians from them. Coupling amity with firmness, the proprietors averred, would have instilled in the Westos both love and fear of the colony. Carolina's failure to protect the coastal Indians had led to an escalation of violence that could not help but lead to war. The proprietors ordered their officials to make peace immediately with the Westos, though on safe and reasonable terms. They insisted that peace was in the planters' economic interests, not realizing that the planters preferred war to peace. Only through warfare could Carolinians obtain the slaves they desired to exchange for supplies to build their plantations. Peaceful coexistence with Indians might be fine for subsistence farmers or profit-making large plantations, but not for Carolinians hoping to amass capital quickly.

The proprietors instructed the Carolinians to make peace with the Westos on "equal terms."[49] The Westos must cease attacking the coastal Indians, but they should be supported to prevent other Indians from "daring to offend" the colony. Westo trade needs had to be met. The proprietors urged Councilor Andrew Percival to include in the "articles of peace" stipulations that the Westos would "be supplied by us with necessaries by way of Trade which will make us useful to them." And yet the Westos must not have free access to the colony. Trade would be restricted to two plantations that were "strong in numbers and well fortified."[50] The Westos "must be plainly told that if they go to any other Plantations it shall be looked upon as a breach of the peace and they must take what follows." Colonists would have viewed these restrictions with skepticism. The two plantations where trade would be conducted belonged to the Earl of Shaftesbury and Sir Peter Colleton—the earl a proprietor and Colleton the brother of one. Whatever humanitarian motives the proprietors had in calling for an end to the war, their obvious desire to protect their trade monopoly was not lost on the colonials.

The proprietors ordered Percival to keep all details of their proposals secret from everyone, including Woodward, illustrating their lack of trust in their own appointees. Maurice Mathews, who was to negotiate the peace, had to sign his instructions—agreeing to be bound by them. The proprietors urged Mathews to reestablish the beaver trade as quickly as possible with the Westos. If this was not possible, "with all your skill jointly endeavour to have the said Trade . . . restrained for as many years as you can obtain it to us" by "Act of the Parliament," meaning the Carolina legislature.[51] The proprietors worried over the legality of their monopoly, and they did not want the royal government interfering in their affairs. They hoped that the Carolinians would voluntarily preserve the proprietary monopoly over the Indian trade.

One of the more interesting recommendations conceived by the proprietors but not actually made to their officials was to have the peace treaty translated into the Westo language, with a written copy made in Westo that would be signed and given to them. Another copy would be kept in the colony to be read every time "they come amongst us." Someone must have informed the proprietors of the problems associated with transliterating such a document, but the sentiment illustrates their faith in treaties to settle differences—as long as the parties understood the terms.[52]

In his *History of South Carolina under the Proprietary Government* (1897), Edward McCrady observed how unreasonable it was for the proprietors to restrict the Indian trade, "the principal source of gain to the industrious traders, among who were the chief men in the colony."[53] McCrady chided the proprietors for attempting to control Indian affairs from England. "It was scarcely to be expected that, situated as the colonists were, with their families exposed to the tomahawk and scalping-knife, they would leave the important matter of their relations with the savages to be governed by the diplomacy of any set of men on the other side of the Atlantic." McCrady then excused the colony's resident leaders' "disregard of instructions" as the acts of responsible men.[54] McCrady's point concerning the difficulties of conducting diplomacy from afar carries much water. And yet this was always the excuse used by colonial officials and colonists in English, French, Spanish, Portuguese, and Dutch colonies when they disregarded their own imperial and proprietary laws and enslaved Indians, stole their land, and abused them in any number of ways. Imperial officials beckoned their agents and their colonists to treat aboriginal peoples with justice, giving their people a moral and ethical framework for intercultural relations, not a detailed blueprint that would compromise the settlers' safety. These officials' motivations were not entirely moral, for they wished to avoid the costly expense of sending troops to extract colonists from local wars, the purpose of which was not to aid the empire but to fulfill individuals' desire for gain at American Indian and home government expense. In Carolina, as in other English colonies, rejection of proprietary rule (and then royal rule) was made in part to gain local control over Indian affairs, so that Indians could be exploited without outside interference, much as the southern states later rejected federal government authority so that exploitation of African Americans could continue without outside meddling.

McCrady, in claiming the need for settler protection, also overlooked the fact that the Westos had become less of a threat to the colony than Carolina had become to them. McCrady's articulation of the standard shibboleths of his time depicting terrifying images of "savages" removing scalp locks just does not apply to the Westo war. The Grand Council's records include alleged Indian abuses against colonists but do not cite the Westos as a source of settler complaints.[55] No doubt the proprietors were governed by self-interests, but at least their self-interested monopoly of trade was predicated on peace, in contrast to the colonists and local officials, whose self-interests led them to promote war. Irate over the renewed outbreak of war with the Westos, the proprietors demanded from the colony "[d]epositions to prove the matter of Fact upon which this war was grounded." They wanted to know whether the war was made for "preservation of the Colony, or to serve the ends of particular men by trade." They asked for depositions from the "[i]nterpreters that they did truly interpret what was delivered by the Indians. Also a Copy of Dr. Woodward's Letter attested wherein he says if Trade were not permitted to the Westoes they would cut all your Throats. Also the Letter from the Spanish Governor of St Augustine's wherein he complains that the Doctor endeavoured to set the Chichimecas and other Indians to war upon the Spaniard."[56]

The proprietors defended their monopoly over the Indian trade as a source of peace with the Westos. They claimed to have monopolized the trade "not merely out of a design of gain: But with this further consideration, that by furnishing a bold and warlike people with Arms and Ammunition and other things useful to them, which they could not fetch from Virginia, New England, New Yorke, or Canider without great labour and hazard." By doing so, "We tied them to so strict a dependence upon us, that we thereby kept all the other Indians in awe: and by protecting our Neighbours from their Injuries would make them think our being seated near them a benefit to them; and that by them we should so terrify those Indians with whom the Spaniards have power." Unfortunately for the proprietors, this rationale would not convince the Council to accept the monopoly over trade. The colonists were uninterested in making Indians dependent on trade to further the colony's political goals; they simply wanted to make money through the Indian slave trade. Still, the proprietors persisted. Learning that the Westos were "ruined," the proprietors considered whether another nation of Indians might be set up in their place—"one whose Government is less anarchical than theirs"—probably meaning one that could be more easily subjugated to English influence. The proprietors hoped that they "could furnish them with arms and ammunition but restrict them from selling to any other nation." In other words, the new ally would police other Indians, because they would have European arms, and be a defensive buffer to keep the "Northern and Spanish Indians from daring to infest you."[57]

The colony's leadership convinced the Savannahs to move into the defeated Westos' vacated position along the Savannah River and become their chief partner in the enslaving of Indians. The proprietors were aghast that the colony had substituted the Savannahs for the Westos; they feared this move would force other Indians to unite in resisting the Savannahs and the colony. The proprietors rhetorically asked Governor Joseph Morton (September 1682–1684; October 1685–November 1686) why the colony had no wars with Indians when it was first founded and weak, and then had warred with the Westos "whilst they were in treaty with that government and so under the public faith for their Safety and [then] put to death in Cold blood and the rest Driven from their Country"? The proprietors astutely recognized the Carolina elites' program: the "Savannahs not affording that profitable trade to the Indian Dealers that was Expected in beaver etc.," the Carolinians turned them to enslaving Indians. Reprehensibly, then, the colony began a war with the Waniahs, a group of Indians who lived along the Winyaw River, "upon pretense they had cut off a boat of runaways."[58] The Savannahs then captured Waniahs and sold them to an Indian trader who shipped them to Antigua. The proprietors promised to collect depositions from both the Waniahs and the trader. In the meantime, they learned that the Savannahs were at first not going to sell the Waniahs but had been intimidated by slave traders into doing so. The proprietors received testimony that a false alarm "was Contrived by the Dealers in Indians that they might have thereby an opportunity of Showing themselves at the sevanah Towne with forces and thereby frighten those people into a sole trade with themselves." The pretense of the alarm was that the Westos were going to attack the Savannahs—but the proprietors wondered how that was possible. Not only were there no Westos near the town, but "the Indian Dealers have written us there are not 50 Westohs

left alive and those Divided. Are the Savannahs so formidable a people as
. . . you allege . . . that the whole English settlement must be alarmed and
a great charge" incurred "to send out men to defend" the Savannah from
fifty Westo?[59]

The proprietors also received word that the surviving Westos had
wanted peace with Carolina and wished the Savannahs to mediate, "but
their messengers were taken and sent away to be sold." The same fate befell
the messengers of the Waniahs. Sarcastically the proprietors rued, "but
if there be peace with the Westohs and Waniahs where shall the Sevanahs
get Indians to sell the Dealers in Indians"? The proprietors were sure that
the cause of both the Westo and Waniah wars, and the reason for their
continuance, lay in the colonists' desire to sell Indians into slavery.[60] The
governor and Council responded to these accusations with a public letter,
but the proprietors condemned their appointees' specious rationale that
they had acted with great humanity by enslaving Indians, for otherwise,
the Carolinians proclaimed, the Savannahs would have put their captives
to "[c]ruel deaths." Disingenuously the enslavers pleaded that the Savannahs had been too powerful to refuse: "having united all the tribes . . . it is
dangerous to disoblige them."[61] First the leading men had raised an army
to protect the "weak" Savannahs from the Westos, but then they had had to
buy their captives because the Savannahs were too powerful to resist.[62]

The proprietors rejected all claims that the trade in Indian slaves
was undertaken for the Indians' and the public good rather than for private gain. They received a letter from Colonel John Godfrey, one of the
Council, who along with former governor Joseph West apparently had
refused to sign the public letter, disputing the governor's and Council's
interpretation of events.[63] Even some of the "Indian dealers" who signed
the public letter wrote privately to the proprietors of the greed that had
led to the enslavement of friendly Indians. The proprietors concluded
from the evidence that the colony's leadership had induced the Savannahs
"through Covetousness of your guns, Powder and shot and other Europian
Commodities to make war upon their neighbors, to ravish the wife from
the Husband, kill the father to get the Child, and to burn and Destroy the
habitations of these poor people into whose country we are cheerfully

Received by them, Cherished and supplied when we were weak or at least never have Done us hurt." You have repaid their kindness, the proprietors wrote, by setting them "to do all these horrid wicked things, to get slaves to sell the dealers in Indians [and then] call it humanity to buy them and thereby keep them from being murdered." The proprietors questioned the morality of attacking all Waniahs for the crimes of a few who had killed the runaways, so that "poor Innocent women and children [were] Barbarously murdered, taken and sent to be sold as slaves, who in all probability had been Innocent."[64] The Waniahs should have been pressured to give up the guilty parties, for they had been too weak to resist.

The proprietors lectured the governor and Council on the value of Indians to the colony. Without them, who would catch their runaway African slaves? Moreover, they should have more concern for God's approbation. They could not "[e]xpect Gods blessing nor quiet in a Government so managed nor can we answer it to god, the King . . . Nor our own Consciences."[65] Remonstrations aside, the proprietors understood they could no longer rely on common sense, ethics, or their appointees' belief in the public good to stop them from waging war against innocents.

The proprietors tried a variety of tactics to reform the treatment of Indians. In 1680 they limited enslavement of Native Americans to those who lived more than two hundred miles from Carolina, though they left the door open to abuse by stipulating this applied only to Indians in league or friendly with the colony.[66] In their "Temporary Laws," given to the colony in 1682, articles 8, 9 and 10 specifically addressed colonial relations with Indians. Article 8 prohibited sending any Indian, "upon any pretense or Reason whatsoever . . . away from Carolina," while article 9 extended the area under which Indians were protected from within two hundred miles to within four hundred miles of Charles Town. No Indians in this area could be enslaved or injured by the inhabitants of Carolina. The proprietors hastened to add that colonists must obey these laws not as subjects of the proprietors but as subjects of the king.[67] Article 10 provided that the powers of the commission to hear Indian grievances were revoked.[68] The two-year experiment had failed,[69] since the powers of the "[c]ommission we conceiving Rather to be obtained for the oppression than protection of the Indians." Once again they implored their officials to good treatment of Indians, reminding them of the Indians' value for catching runaway slaves, "and also for fishing, fowling and hunting." They warned the colonists against encroaching on Indian land, iterating the barring of settlement within "two miles of the same Side of the River of an Indian Settlement." They called on those settling near Indian towns to "help to fence in the Indians' Cornfield so that the Cattle and hogs of the English may not Destroy the Indians' Corn and thereby disable them to subsist amongst us." Adamantly they insisted that Indians not be forced from the colony.[70]

Significantly the proprietors chose to disband the commission rather than replace it with other men; neither did they punish those who had abused their power of office. The commission had included some of the most august men in the colony—West, Percival, Mathews, and Joseph Boone. The proprietors were not shy about replacing appointees; they just found that the replacements often were worse than those they had removed.

The proprietors reproved their appointed officials for wrongheaded and immoral behavior, and they repeatedly juggled the pathways of power to prevent abuse of Indians. But they were never able or strong-willed enough to fire all disreputable appointees and replace them with honest men who shared their vision. The men who accepted appointments in Carolina had no reason to go there except to advance their estates. They were not career men serving the king out of loyalty or hope for a sinecure or a better appointment. Loyalty to one's king as might exist in a royal colony could not be equated with loyalty to a proprietor. Proprietary appointees had little or no hope of moving up the career ladder as was possible in the royal patronage system. The men who reached the pinnacle in a proprietary colony, the governor and members of the Council, wanted only riches. If Carolina had been founded for a religious or utopian reason, as had Pennsylvania, the proprietors might have found servants willing to work to fulfill a noble vision. But the offer of free land and religious toleration was noble only to the humble free colonists, not the "great" men or those who aspired to be great men, and who ruled in order to line their pockets, not serve the common good. Appointees by oath promised fealty to proprietary instructions and then disregarded directives to protect Indians, ensure justice, and preserve the proprietary monopoly over the Indian trade. For their part, the appointees and the colonists could not fathom why such profitable enterprises as the Indian trade should be restricted to men who lived three thousand miles away.

The proprietors lacked skill, funds, and will—the cornerstones of implementing a successful colonial policy. Skill was needed to rule over colonists, keep appointees on a leash, and treat with neighbors and foreign peoples incorporated into the new society. Funds were a prerequisite for defense, building an adequate economic infrastructure (a safe port to attract ships, for instance), purchasing trade goods for the conduct of peaceful relations, and giving or lending supplies to newly arrived settlers who were sick or needed help getting started. A strong will was necessary to see plans through to fruition, even in the face of strong opposition. Proprietary and royal officials lacked the firm resolve and resources to enforce compliance with the laws, though royal officials were more easily punished for their behavior.[71] Generally the Crown and its officials in Europe turned their heads while their colonists and local officials engaged in illegal trade, enslavement of free peoples, and instigating and conducting unapproved wars. This was especially so in the English mainland colonies, where despite their self-perception as law-abiding people, colonists followed only those laws that suited them and held particular disregard for royal or proprietary directives regarding trade and relations with Indians. Laws were obeyed when convenient.

Royal rule did not guarantee better results than proprietary rule. The royal colonies, such as Virginia and New York, also had trouble controlling their officials and difficulty maintaining Indian relations beneficial to colony, empire, and Indians. But the Crown developed skills—a professional class of loyal bureaucrats and other imperial servants who believed in the empire. The Crown also had the funds to implement some of its policies. Ultimately whether a colony was royal or proprietary probably mattered less than the expectations and goals of the colonists. Most sought ways to make money and improve their station. Some merely desired land to obtain independence, but others aggressively pursued wealth through any avenue available. America attracted the adventurous, the desperate, the impetuous, and the risk taker. Even where only a small portion of the colonists disregarded colonial and imperial laws in the pursuit of wealth, that group had dramatic impact because neither fellow colonists nor government officials would or could stop them. Justices of the peace refused to arrest, juries declined to convict, and officials ignored malfeasance unless it affected their personal interests or they feared the wrath of the king and his ministers.

Carolina proprietors had the foresight to see that they needed to empower more colonists in order to reduce the abuse of Indians; not that one group of colonists would be more humane than another but that cells of power could counter the strength of governor and Council. The proprietors looked to the elected assembly as a potential check on elites. In 1683 they instituted a licensing system to govern the exportation of Indians from the colony, commissioning the assembly to examine each group to be transported and obtain the names of every person and his or her nation. They would employ "sworn Interpreters" to verify "how and by whom" the enslaved were taken. Only Indians captured in a just and necessary war could be transported. The assembly would issue the license, but the governor, landgraves, and caciques all had to approve it—each providing a check on the other. If a law was broken, the proprietors promised to use all in their power to inflict the "utmost punishments the Law appoints to such offenders."[72]

Why the proprietors did not come up with another solution, such as banning the Indian slave trade, is worth asking. After all, the English colonies repatriated Spanish and French soldiers they captured in war. Granted, Waniahs and Westos could not be repatriated if their villages no longer existed. South Carolina officials argued that Indians had to be sold into slavery to satisfy their Indian captors and to prevent them from being slaughtered. Carolina officials and proprietors were probably unaware that many Indian groups incorporated captives, particularly the women and children. In fact, saving captives from murder was a specious argument. Indians did kill and torture captives, particularly males, for a variety of cultural and ritualistic reasons, and purchasing women and children who

otherwise would have been killed could be viewed as humanitarian, but by allowing "licensing," the proprietors opened the door for the same abuses that had existed before—Europeans setting Indians to capture other Indians for the purpose of obtaining captives to sell to the English.[73] Because the proprietors knew that most of those enslaved and transported were innocents, they should have closed the door right then. They could have instituted any number of alternative solutions, such as selling captives as indentured servants in other colonies or establishing new towns of settlement Indians in distant areas where they could be of service to the colony, as was later done with the Apalachees in 1704 (resettled from Florida to the Savannah River) and the Tuscaroras in 1712 and 1713 (resettled from North Carolina to South Carolina and New York).

All of this is not to say that English, or indeed European, enslavement of Indians was unusual at this time nor that we should condemn seventeenth-century slaveholders for keeping slaves. I am not trying to make a presentist argument against slavery. It is unfair to expect past peoples to consider an institution wrong that their generation viewed as legitimate and moral. But three factors must be emphasized in a discussion of European enslavement of Indians in the American South. First, the enslavement of Indians as practiced in Carolina was undertaken illegally by Carolina laws and moral standards. Enslavement of free people was a condition reserved for captives taken in a "just war" or prisoners who lost their freedom by conviction for a crime. The enslaved in Carolina were not captured in a "just war"[74] but in raids conducted for the sole purpose of turning free people into slaves. The enslavement of free people was considered morally reprehensible, so much so that no English colony or later state government of the United States permitted the enslavement of freeborn American people, including those of African descent. Slaves had to inherit their condition, arrive in America as slaves, or be war captives.

Second, nowhere in the English empire at this time was the enslavement of Indians undertaken on such a large scale as in Carolina. Puritan New England was just ending its period of large-scale enslavement of Indians, victims of the Pequot War (1636–1637) and King Philip's War (1675–1676), though they continued to enslave native peoples through a variety of means.[75] The Carolinians were neither less nor more moral in disregarding their own ethical values than English colonists living else-where. But they had the opportunity to enslave Indians on a scale not available elsewhere. New Englanders in the late seventeenth century had reduced much of the native population by enslavement and war, and were blocked from expanding northward by the French and westward by the Iroquois. New York and Pennsylvania colonists were not in a position to enslave, except through purchase of other colony's slaves, particularly those of Carolina. New York made far too much from the profitable fur trade to alienate Indians through slaving, and Pennsylvania, when it did have the opportunity of purchasing slaves, outlawed slavery because of the neighboring Indians' objections.[76] Virginia participated in the Indian slave trade but by the time of Carolina's founding had developed a profit-able plantation system and had to travel too far to organize a large-scale slave trade in the South. Yet even under difficult circumstances Virginia had established such a trade with the Westos, and the colony might have expanded it to the Mississippi were it not for Carolina's much more ad-vantageous location. Nor can we ascribe religion as a differentiation in whether colonists would enslave, for high Anglicans as well as Puritans and other Dissenters equally participated in the Indian slave trade.[77]

Last, all the European powers enslaved Indians. Only the Spanish expressly outlawed enslavement, but, as noted earlier, Spaniards found numerous ways to keep Indians in various conditions of unfree servitude to obtain their labor. The French enslaved Indians in Canada and Louisiana but did not practice slavery on the scale of the English because they were in a weak position to do so; their settlements lacked a strong population base to build a plantation society, leaving them utterly dependent on Native Americans for trade and military alliance.[78] Another difference between the English and the French and Spanish: the governments of the latter were both concerned with the ethical and religious ramifications of enslaving Indians. The Spanish outlawed it; the French even looked to incorpora-tion of Indians in colonial society through intermarriage, as long as the Indians converted beforehand.[79] There was no broad-scale debate within the English imperial system or any of the churches or in the society at large on the expediency and morality of enslaving Native American peoples. The opposition raised by the Carolina proprietors to Indian slavery never extended to other English imperial or religious institutions or to other colonies because of the private nature of their ownership of Carolina. As in other proprietary colonies, the patentees hoped to attract as little attention as possible to their colony. They had constant fear of outside interference that might undermine their authority and right to rule. The Carolina proprietors intended to solve all their problems themselves.

The new licensing system in Carolina did nothing to alter the illegal enslavement of Indians. In November 1683 two of the proprietors' appointed officials, Maurice Mathews and James Moore, "most contemptuously disobeyed our orders about sending away of Indians and have contrived most unjust wars upon the Indians in order to the getting of Slaves and were Contriving new wars for that purpose." They were removed as deputies "by desire of the major part of the Lords Proprietors," and it was hoped that the two proprietors on their way to the colony, Seth Sothell and John Archdale, would not employ them.[80] But seven months later the proprietors complained that Mathews was still serving as surveyor general and in other civil and military capacities and was continuing to ignore their instructions. The proprietors again pleaded that only Indians taken "in a Just and necessary war" be transported from the colony, and only then as "Encouragement of the soldiers" who captured them. They had adjusted their restrictions so that even purchasing slaves from Indians to save them from death was no longer a legitimate justification: "we did not thereby mean that the parliament should license the transporting of Indians bought of other Indians by way of trade, nor are you to suffer it, for that would but occasion the dealers in Indians to contrive those poor people into wars upon one another that they might have slaves to buy."[81]

In 1685 the proprietors strictly warned the new governor, Joseph West, against allowing the enslavement of Indians except under the condition that they were captured in a war that Carolina itself was involved in, and only then as a reward for the soldiers. They reaffirmed the prohibition against transporting any Indian living within four hundred miles of Charles Town, hoping that this would prevent the colonists from fomenting wars with any Indians they could reach.[82] West was also ordered not to reappoint Mathews, Moore, and Arthur Middleton to the Grand Council because they had been removed from their positions for transporting Indians.[83] These three formed an antiproprietary party that the proprietors labeled the "Indian Dealers."[84] By the 1680s Indian slavery had become the most important political issue in the colony and was representative of the division between the proprietors' and many of the colonists' vision of Carolina's purpose and future. The Indian Dealers were hell-bent on the exploitation of human resources—African and Indian—to make their wealth. Moore and Middleton became founders of two of the colony's most prominent families. Other families, too, would build their fortunes first on Indian slavery, then on African slavery. These men opposed the proprietors at every turn. When the proprietors tried to reapportion representation in the assembly, they met stern resistance from the "dealers in Indians [who] are the chief sticklers in it." The proprietors heard that these "dealers in Indians boast they can with a bowl of punch get who they would Chosen of the parliament and afterwards who they would chosen of the grand Councell." In control of Carolina's government, these men enacted laws that no one could "sell arms, etc., to the Indians upon forfeiture of all his estate and perpetual banishment . . . but brook it themselves for their private advantage and escaped the penalty." They also "made wars and peace with Indians as best suited their private advantage in trade," which cost the colony much money and resulted in the loss of lives. Who, the proprietors wondered, would want to live under a government led by such men? Who indeed but like-minded men.[85]

In spite of the proprietors' objections, Mathews and Moore were returned to the Council. The proprietors demanded their indictment but got nowhere, probably owing to the instability that occurred during the governor's illness in the summer of 1685. Deputy Governor John Godfrey handled affairs for a short while until West resigned, and Robert Quarry took over for three months, appointed by the Council. Joseph Morton then served his second term as governor. For a second time, the proprietors removed him from office. James Colleton (1686–1690), brother of one of the proprietors, was appointed. By his arrival in late 1686, piracy had temporarily replaced the trade in Indians as the proprietors' first order of business—the Crown was upset, understandably, that Carolina conducted a large trade with Caribbean pirates, some of whom operated out of the nearby Bahama Islands.[86] Colleton was given power to create deputies who would not only seize the illegal privateers and punish the guilty but also arrest those who sent "away the poor Indians."[87] Colleton tried to crush the pirates and the Indian dealers, who were about to invade Spanish Florida. Colleton prevented the invasion and arrested pirates but could not subdue the Indian dealers, who banished him.

The Carolinians and the Westos were two very different peoples. But as newcomers to the region they shared a method for carving out living space and improving their fortunes: the capture of humans for sale into an international market. Although the Westos held many advantages over the Carolinians, including greater military power and better skills for conducting slave raids, the Carolinians quickly prevailed over them. The Westos, by failing to ally to themselves with any significant group of Indians, were unable to overcome the Carolinians' ability to unite Indian peoples against them. Whereas the Westos had alienated natives throughout the region by their slaving, the Carolinians enticed Indian groups to do their bidding. The Carolinians, for all their internal divisions, succeeded because they not only offered Indian peoples valuable trade goods but could also market Indians' commodities. The English did not have to become enslavers themselves, only intermediaries between the raiders and the marketplace. To resist the Carolinians, the Westos would have had to compete against them, to form their own alliances and find someone else to supply their needs and purchase their commodities. But the Spanish were unwilling and unable, and Virginia was too distant to compete with Carolina on the Savannah River.

South Carolina's star was in ascension, and its influence quickly grew in the South. Yet in spite of the colony's favorable position for building a network of alliances that would secure and promote English interests in the region, internal divisions, ignorance, and greed kept South Carolina hovering near disaster. For the first fifty years of the colony, volatility characterized its Indian relations. The colony's leaders proved inept at maintaining stable alliances and preventing their people from exploiting allies. Native American peoples remained attracted to the Carolinians' trade goods, but to varying extents they recognized the limitations of becoming partners with the English. New groups entered the South and went about establishing their own bases of power and networks of alliances, notably the French in Louisiana. Yamasees and Scots also played a significant role, emigrating to the Savannah River, where they established permanent settlements. Both followed the Westos and the English by becoming fully engaged in the Indian slave trade and the topsy-turvy politics that increasingly defined the region.

With Carolina's proprietors unable to control the Indian dealers, the colony was firmly set on expanding the Indian slave trade through the South. In the 1690s, Carolina traders established alliances with the Yamasees, Creeks, Chickasaws, and others, who then hunted Indians to the tip of the Florida peninsula, and west all to way to Texas and Arkansas. Tens of thousands of Indians were enslaved, most exported from the South to the West Indies and the more northerly mainland colonies. Not until the end of the second decade of the eighteenth century would this massive trade in Native Americans begin to subside in the South. By then the Carolinians' African slave plantation society was on its way to becoming the dominant economic and political mode in Carolina, and would extend across the region. Its foundation lay in the enslavement of native peoples, a foundation conveniently forgotten by future generations.

Notes

Words quoted, except proper names, have modernized spelling. Commas and periods have been added to make reading easier.

1. For the economic expectations of proprietors and colonists, see S. Max Edelson, *Plantation Enterprise in Colonial South Carolina* (Cambridge: Harvard University Press, 2006).

2. Marvin T. Smith, *Archaeology of Aboriginal Cultural Change in the Interior Southeast: Depopulation During the Early Historic Period* (Gainesville: University Press of Florida, 1987), 131–32. For a recent study of the Westos, see Eric E. Bowne, *The Westo: Slave Traders of the Early Colonial South* (Tuscaloosa: University of Alabama Press, 2005).

3. For a discussion of Indian adaptation of seventeenth-century guns in New England, see Patrick M. Malone, *The Skulking Way of War: Technology and Tactics Among the New England Indians* (Lanham MD: Madison Books, 1991). Unfortunately Malone does not adequately address the question of the bow and arrow versus the gun.

4. John E. Worth, *The Struggle for the Georgia Coast: An Eighteenth-Century Retrospective on*

Guale and Mocama, Anthropological Papers of the American Museum of Natural History, 75 (Athens: University of Georgia Press, 1995), 17.

5. Peter H. Wood, *Black Majority: Negroes in Colonial South Carolina from 1670 through the Stono Rebellion* (New York: Norton, 1974), chapter 1, "The Colony of a Colony."

6. I have pluralized "constitution" because the proprietors employed several drafts, which created confusion for the colonists and themselves. M. Eugene Sirmans, *Colonial South Carolina: A Political History, 1663–1763* (Chapel Hill: University of North Carolina Press, 1966), 7–16, 37–38, 67. The best study of the proprietors is L. H. Roper, *Conceiving Carolina: Proprietors, Planters and Plots, 1662–1729* (New York: Palgrave Macmillan, 2004).

7. *Records in the British Public Record Office Relating to South Carolina, 1663–1717*, 5 vols. ([Various publishers], 1928–1947), hereafter cited as *Records*, 1:204. The proprietors ignored this restriction on occasion. For instance, in 1686 they approved a thousand-acre grant to Maurice Mathews, a notorious abuser of Indians who had managed to obtain bills of sale to a tract of land from several Indian groups: the Stonos, Ashepoos, Saint Helenas, Coosas, Wichaughs, and Wimbees. See A. S. Salley, ed., *Commissions and Instructions from the Lords Proprietors of Carolina to Public Officials of South Carolina, 1685–1715* (Columbia: Historical Commission of South Carolina, 1916), 72–73.

8. For the proprietors' loss of their patent, see Sirmans, *Colonial South Carolina*, 127–29.

9. "Coppy of Instruccons annexed to ye Comission for ye Governr Councell," July 27, 1669, in William James Rivers, *A Sketch of the History of South Carolina to the Close of the Proprietary Government by the Revolution of 1719; With an Appendix Containing Many Valuable Records Hitherto Unpublished* (Charleston SC: McCarter, 1856), hereafter cited as *Sketch*, 348.

10. *Records*, 1:217.

11. For an excellent discussion of English concepts of Indian land rights, see William Cronon, *Changes in the Land: Indians, Colonists, and the Ecology of Colonial New England* (New York: Hill and Wang, 1983), 64–81.

12. Cronon, *Changes in the Land*, 52–53; James Axtell, "The Invasion Within: The Contest of Cultures in Colonial North America," in Axtell, *The European and the Indian: Essays in the Ethnohistory of Colonial North America* (New York: Oxford University Press, 1981), 52–53.

13. "Coppy of Instruccons," 348. Unlike the proprietors, Charles II did not intend Carolina to incorporate Native Americans. See Anthony Pagden, *Lords of All the World: Ideologies of Empire in Spain, Britain and France, c. 1500–c. 1800* (New Haven: Yale University Press, 1995), 37.

14. *Records*, 1:201. They allowed any seven persons to "constitute a Church or profession to which they shall give some name to distinguish it from others," extending this right to Jews, heathens, "and other deserters" from Christianity.

15. For instance, the 1682 version of the constitution stated in article 109, "Every Freeman of Carolina shall have absolute power and authority over Negro slaves of what opinion or Religion soever." *Records*, 1:204.

16. Kenneth R. Andrews, *Trade, Plunder and Settlement: Maritime Enterprise and the Genesis of the British Empire, 1480–1630* (Cambridge: Cambridge University Press, 1984), 116–28.

17. Nicholas P. Canny, "The Ideology of English Colonization: From Ireland to America," *William and Mary Quarterly*, 3rd series, 30 (1973), 575–98. See also the anthology by K. R. Andrews, N. P. Canny, and P. E. H. Hair, eds., *The Westward Enterprise: English Activities in Ireland, the Atlantic, and America, 1480–1650* (Detroit: Wayne State University Press, 1979); and Angus Calder, *Revolutionary Empire: The Rise of the English-Speaking Empires from the Fifteenth Century to the 1780s* (1981; repr., London: Pimlico, 1998).

18. According to Dauril Aulden, the first Portuguese law to deal with Indian affairs, enacted

in 1570 in Brazil, "prohibited the enslavement of the natives of Brazil except for those taken in a just war." See "Black Robes versus White Settlers: The Struggle for 'Freedom of the Indians' in Colonial Brazil," in Howard Peckham and Charles Gibson, eds., *Attitudes of Colonial Powers Toward the American Indian* (Salt Lake City: University of Utah Press, 1969), 25.

19. Prisoners were viewed as having lost their freedom by their voluntary commitment of a crime. On the rationales employed by Europeans for justifying enslavement, see David Brion Davis, *The Problem of Slavery in Western Culture* (Ithaca NY: Cornell University Press, 1966); and Winthrop D. Jordan, *White over Black: American Attitudes toward the Negro, 1550–1812* (Chapel Hill: University of North Carolina Press, 1968).

20. Jordan, *White over Black*, 167–78; Thomas D. Morris, *Southern Slavery and the Law, 1619–1860* (Chapel Hill: University of North Carolina Press, 1996), 22–23.

21. Edmund S. Morgan, *American Slavery, American Freedom: The Ordeal of Colonial Virginia* (New York: Norton, 1975); Jordan, *White over Black*, chapter 2.

22. Lewis Hanke, *The Spanish Struggle for Justice in the Conquest of America* (Philadelphia: University of Pennsylvania Press, 1949); Edward H. Spicer, *Cycles of Conquest: The Impact of Spain, Mexico, and the United States on the Indians of the Southwest, 1533–1960* (Tucson: University of Arizona Press, 1962); Amy Bushnell, *The King's Coffer: Proprietors of the Spanish Florida Treasury, 1565–1702* (Gainesville: University Presses of Florida, 1981); Kathleen A. Deagan, "Spanish-Indian Interaction in Sixteenth-Century Florida and Hispaniola," in William W. Fitzhugh, ed., *Cultures in Contact: The European Impact on Native Cultural Institutions in Eastern North America, A.D. 1000–1800* (Washington DC: Smithsonian Institution Press, 1985), 281–318; Lolita Gutiérrez Brockington, *The Leverage of Labor: Managing the Cortés Haciendas in Tehuantepec* (Durham NC: Duke University Press, 1989). On the Portuguese experience in Brazil, see Aulden, "Black Robes," 19–46.

23. An excellent discussion of the development of Spain's imperial policies is Geoffrey Parker, *The Grand Strategy of Philip II* (New Haven: Yale University Press, 1998).

24. Betty Wood, *Slavery in Colonial Georgia, 1730–1775* (Athens: University of Georgia Press, 1984).

25. *Records*, vol. 1, 55, 97–102. The commission could neither interfere with alliances or public treaties nor establish policy—it could only rectify injustice. The Grand Council, composed of the colony's governor and Council, continued to administer proprietary rules. The Council ascertained all complaints to be heard by the commission. The governor could play a large role in this system for he alone comprised the commission if the other commissioners were unavailable. To ensure compliance with proprietary rules, the proprietors sent the commission a book to enter Indian grievances and petitions as well as other relevant information about Indian affairs. The governor and Council had to sign each entry, after which the book was to be forwarded to the proprietors yearly or earlier if circumstances warranted.

26. Quotation from "Coppy of Instruccons," 350; but also see "Instructions to Joseph West," 350–51; and "Instructions to the Governor and Council of Ashley River," May 1, 1671, in *Sketch*, 366–69.

27. Robert K. Ackerman, *South Carolina Land Policies* (Columbia: University of South Carolina Press, 1977); Sirmans, *Colonial South Carolina*, 12, 38–39, 54, 120, 123; David Duncan Wallace, *South Carolina: A Short History, 1520–1948* (Columbia: University of South Carolina Press, 1969), 25, 47, 53.

28. For the early economic development of South Carolina, see Converse D. Clowse, *Economic Beginnings in Colonial South Carolina, 1670–1730* (Columbia: University of South Carolina Press, 1971).

29. Council meeting, Dec. 10, 1675, in A. S. Salley, ed., *Journal of the Grand Council of South Carolina, August 25, 1671–June 24, 1680* (Columbia: Historical Commission of South Carolina, 1907), 80.

30. These instructions were given in 1671 and 1672. See "Temporary Laws," in *Sketch*, 353; and "Agrarian Laws or Instructions from the Lords Proprietors to the Governor and Council of Carolina," June 21, 1672, in *Sketch*, 358.

31. For examples of the intermixing of violence and politics among the elite, see "Barnwell of South Carolina," *South Carolina Historical Magazine* 2 (January 1901), 47–50, which notes John Barnwell's use of a mob against the colony's chief justice; "Letters from John Stewart to William Dunlop," Apr. 27, 1690, *South Carolina Historical Magazine* 32 (January 1931), 26–27, and June 23, 1690, *South Carolina Historical Magazine* 32 (April 1931), 105, which describes dueling and other violence among elites; and "Deposition of Samuel Everleigh," Oct. 8, 1706, Additional Manuscripts, 61647, folio 112, BL, in which Everleigh claims that Colonel William Rhett threatened to cut off the ears of political opponent Joseph Boone (when he returned from England, where he had taken Dissenter complaints against High Anglicans) and that Rhett had caned James Burt and John Toomer.

32. Shirley C. Hughson, *The Carolina Pirates and Colonial Commerce, 1670–1740* (Baltimore: Johns Hopkins University Press, 1894).

33. Two places to begin for study of Carolina's Settlement Indians are Gene Waddell, *Indians in the South Carolina Lowcountry, 1562–1751* (Spartanburg SC: Reprint Company, 1980); and J. Norman Heard, *Handbook of the American Frontier: Four Centuries of Indian-White Relationships*, vol. 1: *The Southeastern Woodlands* (Metuchen NJ: Scarecrow, 1987).

34. "The Articles and Agreemt. of ye Lds. Proprietrs. of Carolina, Betweene themselves, concerninge the trade there," in *Sketch*, 390.

35. "Order concerning the Trade with the Westoes and Cussatoes Indians," in *Sketch*, 388–89; *Records*, vol. 1, 60–61.

36. "Articles and Agreemt. of ye Lds. Proprietrs. of Carolina."

37. Carolina's efforts to remove the Virginia traders are discussed in Alan Gallay, *The Indian Slave Trade: The Rise of the English Empire in the American South, 1670–1717* (New Haven: Yale University Press, 2002), chapter 7.

38. Marcel Mauss, *The Gift: The Form and Reason for Exchange in Archaic Societies*, trans. W. D. Halls (1950; repr., New York: Norton, 1990).

39. Council meeting, Oct. 7, 1673, *Journal of the Grand Council*, 64, emphasis added. According to James Merrell, "Esaw" was a term employed by the Carolinians to refer to a variety of Piedmont peoples in the Wateree-Catawba valley. See *The Indians' New World: Catawbas and Their Neighbors from European Contact Through the Era of Removal* (Chapel Hill: University of North Carolina Press, 1989), 47.

40. *Journal of the Grand Council*, Feb. 2, 1673, 66–67.

41. *Journal of the Grand Council*, Mar. 7, 1673, 67.

42. Henry Woodward, "A Faithfull Relation of My Westoe Voyage," Dec. 31, 1674, in Alexander S. Salley Jr., *Narratives of Early Carolina, 1650–1708* (New York: Charles Scribner's Sons, 1911), 130–34.

43. For the opening of Virginia trade with the Cherokees, see Alan Vance Briceland, *Westward from Virginia: The Exploration of the Virginia-Carolina Frontier, 1670–1710* (Charlottesville: University of Virginia Press, 1987).

44. For the Iroquois wars, see Daniel K. Richter, *The Ordeal of the Longhouse: The Peoples of the Iroquois League in the Era of European Colonization* (Chapel Hill: University of North Carolina

Press, 1992); and Richter, "Iroquois Wars," in Alan Gallay, ed., *Colonial Wars of North America, 1512–1763: An Encyclopedia* (New York: Garland, 1996), 317–19.

45. For discussion of Savannah as a lingua franca, see Gallay, *Indian Slave Trade*, chapter 8. For the pan-Indian movement, see Gregory Evans Dowd, *A Spirited Resistance: The North American Indian Struggle for Unity, 1745–1815* (Baltimore: Johns Hopkins University Press, 1992).

46. Worth, *Struggle for the Georgia Coast*, 35.

47. Worth, *Struggle for the Georgia Coast*, 26–27; "Testimony of David Turner," Oct. 25, 1680, in "The Spaniards and the English Settlement in Charles Town," trans. José Miguel Gallardo, *South Carolina Historical Magazine* 37 (October 1936), 137–38.

48. Francis Le Jau would write of the Savannahs in 1708: they "settled near this province Even before the Nation of the Westos were destroyed and to this day they keep about the places where the Westos lived, but perhaps are not so numerous." Frank J. Klingberg, ed., *The Carolina Chronicles of Dr. Francis Le Jau, 1706–1717* (Berkeley: University of California Press, 1956), 68.

49. *Records*, 1:106.

50. *Records*, 1:107.

51. *Records*, 1:112.

52. *Records*, 1:107.

53. Edward McCrady, *The History of South Carolina under the Proprietary Government, 1670–1719* (1897; New York: Russell and Russell, 1969), 178.

54. McCrady, *History of South Carolina*, 178.

55. McCrady's nonsense also extended to his view of Indian land rights. A lawyer, McCrady came up with the interesting legal notion that since Indians did not understand land tenures they had "no rights" to the land. *History of South Carolina*, 179.

56. *Records*, 1:115–16.

57. *Records*, 1:116–17.

58. *Records*, 1:256. According to James Merrell, the Waniahs (or Winyaws) later moved closer to the English colonists by settling on the Santee River. In 1716, during the Yamasee War, they returned to the Winyaw River. *Indians' New World*, 100.

59. *Records*, 1:257.

60. *Records*, 1:257–58.

61. *Records*, 1:255.

62. *Records*, 1:255.

63. *Records*, 1:255.

64. *Records*, 1:259.

65. *Records*, 1:260.

66. *Records*, 1:99.

67. *Records*, 1:142.

68. *Records*, 1:142.

69. *Records*, 1:98–99.

70. *Records*, 1:174.

71. The Board of Trade and Plantations made constant complaint against proprietary governments, hoping to transform all colonies to royal rule. The board accused them of countenancing illegal trade and "other Irregular Practices, to the great prejudice of her Majesties Revenue of fair traders, and otherwise." Although these criticisms were self-interested—the board hoped to expand its power through eliminating colonial proprietorships—in the case of Carolina, the charges were true. Quotation from "Report from the Commissioners of

Trade and Plantations, of the 16th of December 1703," Manuscript Collection, University of London, Manuscript 78.

72. *Records*, 1:254, 261.

73. Both torture and incorporation of captives are discussed in Gallay, *Indian Slave Trade*, chapter 6.

74. For discussion of the concept of "just war," see John Morgan Dederer, *War in America to 1775: Before Yankee Doodle* (New York: New York University Press, 1990), 162–64, 167–69, 262n78.

75. Margaret Ellen Newell, "The Changing Nature of Indian Slavery in New England, 1670–1720," in *Reinterpreting New England Indians and the Colonial Experience*, eds., Colin G. Calloway and Neal Salisbury (Boston: Colonial Society of Massachusetts, 2004), 106–36.

76. For estimates on the extent of the Indian slave trade through the South, see Gallay, *Indian Slave Trade*, chapter 10.

77. David Hackett Fischer makes the sophistical argument that slavery "was fundamentally hostile to the Puritan ethos of New England." This view is clearly contradicted by Puritans actively engaging in slaveholding wherever slavery flourished in the Atlantic world. *Albion's Seed: Four British Folkways in America* (New York: Oxford University Press, 1989), 53. See also Joanne Pope Melish, *Disowning Slavery: Gradual Emancipation and "Race" in New England, 1780–1860* (Ithaca NY: Cornell University Press, 1998), 11–49; Michael Zuckerman, "Identity in British America: Unease in Eden," in Nicholas Canny and Anthony Pagden, eds., *Colonial Identity in the Atlantic World* (Princeton NJ: Princeton University Press, 1987), 144–45, 148–49.

78. On Indian slavery in Canada, see Marcel Trudel, *L'esclavage au Canada français: Histoire et conditions de l'Esclavage* (Quebec: Presses Universitaires Laval, 1960). See Gallay, *Indian Slave Trade*, chapter 11 for discussion of Indian slavery in Louisiana.

79. [Jean-Baptiste Le Moyne] de Bienville au Comte de Pontchartrain, Oct. 10, 1706, AC, microfilm copies, Manuscript Reading Room, LC, C13, B:1; [Nicolas] de la Salle au Comte de Pontchartrain, June 20, 1710, AC, microfilm copies, Manuscript Reading Room, LC, C13A, 2:519; le Cte de Pontchartrain á [Antoine Alexandre] de Remonville, Sept. 14, 1710, AC, microfilm copies, Manuscript Reading Room, LC, C13, B32:207; Jean Delanglez, *The French Jesuits in Lower Louisiana (1700–1763)* (Washington DC: Catholic University of America, 1935), 394; Richard White, *The Middle Ground: Indians, Empires, and Republics in the Great Lakes Region, 1650–1815* (Cambridge, England: Cambridge University Press, 1991), 69–70; Pagden, *Lords of All the World*, 149.

80. *Records*, 1:266–67.

81. *Records*, 1:290.

82. *Records*, 2:20–21, 59–60.

83. *Records*, 2:28.

84. *Records*, 2:33.

85. *Records*, 2:34.

86. For the crackdown on piracy, see Robert C. Ritchie, *Captain Kidd and the War Against the Pirates* (Cambridge MA: Harvard University Press, 1986); and Marcus Rediker, *Between the Devil and the Deep Blue Sea: Merchant Seamen, Pirates and the Anglo-American Maritime World, 1700–1750* (Cambridge, England: Cambridge University Press, 1987), 281–85.

87. *Records*, 2:181.

4. Anxious Alliances

Apalachicola Efforts to Survive the Slave Trade, 1638–1705
Joseph Hall

How valuable were the lives of five of one's own people? The Apalachicolas, who had lost five to captivity in the English colony of South Carolina, were not sure. In the summer of 1685, as they welcomed Carolinian traders into their towns on the Chattahoochee River, the question became more pressing. The last five years had been scarred by conflict as Indians allied with the colony captured and sold Apalachicolas to traders from Charles Town.[1] Despite the recent losses, perhaps this visit meant that the Apalachicolas' persecutors would become their protectors. Then again, perhaps the traders sought merely to gain what fortunes they could before resuming the wars that dragged Apalachicolas into bondage. Indeed, despite the English traders' supposed desire for peace, they had neglected to return the five captives as a sign of that desire. Ambivalence abounded: while some Apalachicolas enthusiastically welcomed the English traders to the thirteen towns along the Chattahoochee valley by "cleaning the paths as is usually done for the arrival of a governor," others expressed their discomfort less ceremoniously, preventing the foreigners from completing their trading houses.[2]

The ceremonial display of respect was prudent. For some, the English offered the best route to security in the region. Apalachicolas doubtless recognized and appreciated much of what the visitors carried. Spanish traders and their Apalachee allies were regular if infrequent visitors from the land of La Florida to the South. Like Spaniards and Apalachees, English offered an array of European beads, hoes, and cloth. Unlike these southern trading partners, only the English would provide "muskets and munitions," powerful tools in this increasingly violent region.[3] Because many Apalachicola towns were located along or near piedmont trails that followed the fall line south of the Appalachian Mountains, the towns lay within easy reach of Carolina's dangerous allies. But this fact also presented an opportunity for Anglo-Apalachicola cooperation. The same trails that made Apalachicolas so vulnerable to attack from the east also enabled them to control access to the large concentrations of potential captives of the Gulf plain and Mississippi valley to the west. Some Apalachicolas probably realized that they could turn their vulnerability into a virtue: not only might they become allies, they might become influential ones.

But if such opportunities seemed prudent to some, they could not erase the anxieties harbored by the kin and friends of the five Apalachicola slaves in Carolina. For Apalachicolas and many of their native neighbors, prisoner exchanges often formed a fundamental element of peace overtures. Freed prisoners served as evidence of one side's good intentions and they could bridge the linguistic divide between former belligerents.[4] Later English actions would raise the troubling possibility that their failure to free the five Apalachicolas was deliberate: in March 1686, seven months after the first English embassy, English traders returned with trade goods but "without giving [the Apalachicolas] hopes of recovering the . . . slaves."[5] Though the traders might have avoided such ill-considered candor during the first summer visit, the absence of the five captives signaled to many that Carolinians remained unredeemed enemies. As Apalachicolas examined the blankets, beads, and guns, they probably understood the traders' visit as a stark offer: trade with or be traded by the English.

Despite the Carolinians' failure to observe diplomatic protocols of prisoner exchange, the Apalachicolas agreed to open trade relations. Evidently the Apalachicolas believed the value of English cooperation superceded the value of their missing kin. Later events demonstrated just how much Apalachicolas and English had to gain from such an association, as both became regional powers largely due to their close association.

But Apalachicolas did not suddenly forget the painful absence of their five kin or earlier lessons from contact with Europeans. Past experience taught Apalachicolas not to enter uncertain relations with these Europeans—or, for that matter, any Europeans—alone. The alliances that enabled Apalachicolas to secure their prominence as English trading partners, to patch up their internal disagreements regarding this partnership, and to project their influence far beyond the Chattahoochee valley lay not with the English of Carolina or even the Spaniards of La Florida. Instead Apalachicolas looked to native neighbors who could become allies and mediate with Europeans and eventually secure their prominence within the English slave-trading regime.

As the mixed reception for the English suggests, the development of this diplomatic strategy was not simple, and a summary of its history includes moments of indecision and reconsideration. The new overtures began even before the arrival of the English when Apalachicolas sought an Apalachee-mediated friendship with the Spanish in the 1630s. Apalachicola relations with the Apalachees and Spaniards warmed and cooled over the rest of the century, but the ties between the people of the Chattahoochee and those of St. Augustine remained tenuous. Beginning about 1675, in the wake of intensifying slave raids on their towns, Apalachicolas began a decade of direct overtures to Spaniards and English in an effort to gain some shelter from the violence. Although the 1685 Carolinian visit suggests that the English finally secured the exclusive alliance that both colonies coveted, their mixed reception suggests that some Apalachicolas wanted to keep Europeans, or at least the English, at some distance. They accomplished this by building close ties to their Yamasee friends. Together these two peoples became Charles Town's principal partners for the slave trade south and west of the colony. The association among the three grew strong enough that in 1704 Apalachicolas drove old Apalachee friends from their homeland. In every case Apalachicolas forged alliances in the hopes of promoting security without sacrificing autonomy.

Although this brief summary suggests the confidence of a people destined for regional influence, Apalachicola diplomats could hardly afford such arrogance. As English unwillingness to return Apalachicola captives suggested, Europeans were powerful but dangerously ambiguous. Native allies, familiar with diplomatic etiquette and tied by bonds of kinship, could reduce the risks that accompanied the newcomers. Despite the importance of these intertribal relationships and the internal debates that shaped them, scholars have paid them almost no attention.[6] Apalachicolas' actions, then, fill an important gap in colonial North American history. They show how much the early colonial Southeast remained a Native American land, and they suggest some of the emotions of Indian slave raiders, people more noted for their savagery than their sensibility.[7]

More important, though, a history of Apalachicola diplomacy with other Native Americans presents an important window into the ways that American peoples shaped the courses of European empires. It is easy to forget such influence amid the violence and insecurity of the southeastern slave trade. Apalachicolas' efforts to forge (and sunder) a series of alliances with the Spaniards, English, Apalachees, Westos, and Yamasees can tell us much about the ways they and other indigenous peoples coped with Europeans' hunger for humans between 1660, when the English slave trade began, and 1704, when it reached its peak. In their alliances we gain glimpses into some of the ways that Native Americans lived with one another in a region they now shared with Europeans. In those alliances also lie clues to the ways that Natives shaped colonial development even as colonial interests radically altered their political and social worlds.

Inhabiting a New World of Violence

Despite the significance the Apalachicolas' future held for southeastern and even imperial development, the questions that most troubled them were likely the more personal ones connected to their five missing kin and townspeople. Even these questions had broad ramifications, though. Native Americans and their European allies captured as many as 50,000 southeastern natives for export to European homes and plantations from Boston to Biloxi to Barbados.[8] The English of Charles Town dominated this trade, endowing their native partners with firearms and formidable reputations. Carolina's proprietors, struggling to end the violent commerce, wrote that potential victims lived in fear that their assailants would

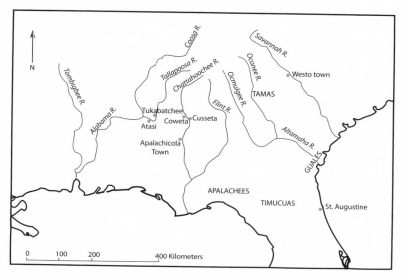

1. Apalachicolas and their neighbors, ca. 1660

"ravish the wife from the husband, and kill the father, take the child, and burn and destroy the dwellings of the poor people who received us into their country."[9]

The earliest and most infamous of these English allies in the Southeast were the Westos. Forced south from the shores of Lake Erie by Iroquois armed with muskets, Westos arrived in the region in 1659.[10] The immigrants quickly distinguished themselves with their technology and their tactics because, according to Native Americans' reports to the Spaniards, they "use many firearms and come laying waste to the land."[11] In 1675 Bishop Gabriel Díaz Vara Calderón included them in his report on Florida's missions, describing them as "such cruel and barbarous pagans that their sole purpose is to assault the towns of Christians as well as pagans, taking their lives without regard to age, sex, or state, roasting and eating them."[12] (The bishop must have appreciated the three companies of soldiers and Indians who escorted him on his tour.)[13]

Despite the vividness of his prose, Díaz did not present an entirely accurate picture. If they were like other, later slave raiders, Westos did not hunt humans indiscriminately, preferring women and children to men.[14] Although it is likely that Westos ritually consumed some of their

151

captives, many prisoners could expect to survive as slaves.[15] Lacking the protection of clan members who could provide support in times of trial and vengeance in times of injustice, a slave became, at least according to Muskhogean speakers, *este-vpuekv*, which translates literally as "domesticated animal-person." Dependent on the protection and sustenance of a stranger, slaves suffered a social death, becoming the social equivalent of domesticated animals and reduced to performing subsistence tasks like gathering wood, clearing fields, and cleaning animal skins.[16]

In other respects, Díaz may have been more accurate than he would have liked. English traders had altered the dynamics of captivity and exchange by seeking them not for subsistence purposes but for more expansive commercial ones. Instead of eating or keeping most of their prisoners, Westos exchanged them for firearms, cloth, beads, and other trade goods from the English of Virginia and then, after 1674, with the English of Carolina. Unlike Canadian traders, who reluctantly accepted Indian captives to reaffirm friendly relations with native allies, or New Mexicans, who shared with their native neighbors certain notions of slaves as symbols of male authority, Carolinians were interested almost exclusively in captives' capacity to work.[17] Living in Carolina or even in other distant colonies, Indian slaves of the English learned that shackles of iron bound them to a society that defined them not only as without kin but as property. Unlike slaves supplementing native captors' subsistence activities, Carolinian slaves labored at the endless task of amassing wealth for their owners. Perhaps English ambitions inspired the desperation that Díaz unknowingly captured: Westos and others were not eating their captives, but their English trading partners were indeed consuming them whole.[18]

With ruthless violence, Indian slave raiders and their English sponsors transformed the Southeast. But there is more to this story than savage attackers and pathetic victims. The slave trade was violent and chaotic, but even in the garbled secondhand reports of people like Bishop Díaz lies a coherence, even if a disturbing one: security for some meant joining the very sponsors of the new violence. It was a route to new kinds of power—and peril. During these uncertain times Apalachicolas built their alliances.

Foundational Alliances:
Apalachicola Origins and Political Theory

If an intertribal diplomatic history is crucial for understanding the Southeast during this turbulent period, the Apalachicolas are one of the few groups for whom adequate documentation exists for such an account. More appropriately still, they were themselves the product of alliance. In fact their very name suggests some of the strength and the ambiguity of this association. Beginning in the 1630s Spaniards referred to the thirteen towns along the Chattahoochee as the province of "Apalachicola," after the southerly and very influential town of the same name. Reflecting the vagaries of geography but also a shifting balance of power in the valley, English writers in the 1670s and 1680s referred to the collection of settlements as "Cowatoes" and "Cussetaws" in recognition of the prominent northern towns of Coweta and Cusseta, which also happened to be on the most direct path of trade (or war) to Charles Town. The town of Apalachicola, also called Pallachucula, evidently had less relevance for later English observers, even though Spaniards continued to use the collective name Apalachicola well into the eighteenth century. Thus the vagaries of time and perspective both suggest that the province I will call Apalachicola was held together by bonds both fluid and contested.[19]

Later Apalachicola stories explaining the origins of this multitown alliance confirm this impression. They also offer some insights into the diplomatic practices that brought (and kept) the towns together. The earliest such story comes from 1735, when Chekilli, the peace chief, or *mico*, of Coweta, explained the history and sacred traditions of his people to leaders of the new colony of Georgia. His two-day lesson described how the people called the Cussetas emerged from the earth and migrated eastward, learning their sacred ceremonies and eventually finding and following a white path. Knowing that white symbolized peace and strength, Cussetas followed the path eastward in search of its makers. After destroying one town whose residents rejected their peaceful overtures, the Cussetas arrived at the path's source, the town of the Pallachucula people. Although the "Bloody minded" Cussetas were still bent on war, the Pallachucula People made them Black Drink as a Token of Friendship And told them their Hearts were white And they must have White Hearts and lay down their Bodys in Token That they Shod be White. . . . [The Cussetas] strove for the Tomihawk but the Pallachacula People by fair prswasion gain'd it from them And Bury'd it under their Cabbin[.] The Pallachacula People told them their Captain Sho[ul]d all [be] one with there People and gave them White ffeathers.

Ever Since they have lived together And they Shall always live Together and bear it in remembrance.

The two peoples lived together from that point onward, with the Cussetas establishing two towns, Cusseta and Coweta, which became the head towns of the Apalachicolas.[20]

Ultimately Chekilli sought to impress his listeners with the power of his people and his own leadership, his "Strong Mouth," as he put it.[21] In making these claims, though, Chekilli also presented an Apalachicola perspective on intertribal diplomacy. Both ceremony and oratory had important roles, but even with them peace overtures defied simple predictions. Despite their professed interest in the white path, Cussetas only barely refrained from spilling their hosts' blood. On the other hand, such inauspicious beginnings did not prevent the Cussetas and Pallachuculas from forming a durable and powerful partnership.

Chekilli provided more than a metaphorical history, though.[22] He recalled events that correspond to archaeological and documentary evidence that a number of different towns, including that of Cusseta, migrated eastward from the Tallapoosa valley into the Chattahoochee valley some time in the century following 1540. These Muskhogean-speaking peoples met towns of Hitchiti speakers, including residents of the town of Apalachicola (or Pallachucula), who enjoyed the respect and tribute of their neighbors. Despite significant linguistic differences, immigrants settled their towns in the north end of the valley.[23]

Chekilli explained much during his two days, but it is nonetheless remarkable how much he (or, perhaps his English recorder) omitted. More than feathers must have changed hands at that fateful meeting between Cussetas and Pallachuculas. The leaders of the Mississippian societies that dominated the political landscape of the Southeast before the arrival of Europeans depended on the exchange of rare goods to buttress their authority. By using sacred objects made from Great Lakes copper or conch shells from the Gulf of Mexico, southeastern leaders demonstrated their connection to faraway peoples whose very distance suggested links with the supernatural. Among their many functions in southeastern political and ceremonial life, these goods also secured ties of alliance or tribute between old enemies.[24] But none of these exchanges could guarantee peace. Even when former prisoners paved the way for peace, they remained living reminders of conflict; they as well as Chekilli knew that the boundaries between amity and enmity blurred easily.[25]

In addition to omitting any discussion of the material anchors of peace, Chekilli also failed to mention the challenges facing his authority. This second oversight was probably intentional. Some of his Hitchiti compatriots exposed one piece of his omission when, shortly after he concluded his story, they promised the English listeners a different version of the past "which they say will be an Improvement to his."[26] Even among the people of his own town, Chekilli probably did not speak unopposed. In 1708 the ever-observant Thomas Nairne noted that southeastern *micos* "seldom ever use any Coercion, only harrangue."[27] Clans in particular complicated *micos'* ambitions. By calling on the allegiances of a common maternal ancestry, influential clan members could mobilize kin in defense of these extended family networks, including avenging the lives of clan members killed in combat.[28] Amid the conflicts of the late seventeenth and early eighteenth centuries, the voices of clan members carried significant weight. When Chekilli claimed to possess a "Strong Mouth" among the Apalachicolas in 1735, then, his assertion implied that many voices were competing for influence in the town squares along the Chattahoochee River.

The arrival of Europeans in Apalachicolas' lives a century before Chekilli's speech meant that there was much to debate. After 1638, the year Apalachicolas opened friendly relations with Apalachee and their Spanish allies, the peoples of the Chattahoochee River confronted deeply troubling questions. What would the new objects that Apalachees carried north from the colony mean for their possessors or the evolving networks of exchange? Two decades later, following the arrival of the Westos in the region in 1659, Apalachicolas faced new and more mortal concerns that accompanied the spread of a new form of warfare and captivity. Even a new friendship with the English in 1685 did not promise to remove Apalachicolas from this cycle of violence; it merely offered them a better chance to adapt to and shape it.

If the debates in Apalachicola villages blended insecurity and ambition, the speakers and listeners inhabited a society that knew enviable power and disconcerting vulnerability. Apalachicolas first became acquainted with the slave trade as victims; when the English refused to accede to the Apalachicola requests for their kin, Apalachicolas suffered a personal as well as diplomatic blow. No society can afford to consider any of its members expendable, but epidemics might have inflected Apalachicola pleas with greater urgency. Archaeologists have found evidence that strongly suggests that epidemics caused interior populations to consolidate their shrinking towns in the century and a half after 1550. Unfortunately certainty is elusive on this crucial matter; no documentary evidence exists before 1696 for any major epidemic beyond the coast.[29] Even if the diseases that consumed approximately three-quarters of La Florida's mission population between 1635 and 1681 did not scar Apalachicolas, they would have at least left a chilling lesson of the dangers of European contact.[30]

Fortunately for the Apalachicolas, their population was relatively large and their leaders strong. By 1674, rumors had reached Charles Town that the "Cussitaws" were a "powerful nation." One year later, Bishop Díaz referred to the "great population" that lived in the "province of Apalachicoli." Perhaps the Muskhogean migration into the Chattahoochee valley enabled the province to resist the demographic declines of other regions. Regardless, colonists' vague assessments suggest that the Apalachicolas possessed a formidable—if not overwhelming—safety in numbers.[31] Powerful leaders likely augmented this population's influence in the region. In 1682 La Florida's Governor Juan Márquez Cabrera characterized the *mico* of Coweta as "the most feared cacique in the lands bounded by the Chichimecos [Westos]."[32]

Even such imposing power did not translate into complete control.

As Chekilli knew, "a Strong Mouth" counted for much, but so too did the "fair persuasion" that prevented Apalachicola-Cusseta bloodletting. Alliances were the subject of continuous and often contentious negotiation among Apalachicolas themselves. Thus, although strong leaders would ensure a common voice, the regular participation of followers would determine the strength of any accord. In a world of slave raiding, where the traffic in captives fueled ever-widening circles of conflict, and where English traders offered the tools of security even as they refused to yield the human symbols of peace, the need for such accords became painfully clear.

Uncertain Friendship:
Apalachicola Ties with Apalachees and Spaniards

The 1685 alliance with the English marked a pivotal and perilous turn for Apalachicola diplomacy because it marked the beginning of the Apalachicolas' rise as regional power brokers but also exposed them to the violent shifts of Carolinian ambition. As they entered this new alliance, Apalachicolas employed old strategies. As Chekilli suggested, Apalachicolas' desire to follow the white path, the path of peace and power, inspired their interest in alliance. Since concluding the peace with Apalachees and their Spanish allies in 1638, that quest for peace and power increasingly involved the acquisition of European manufactures. During the seventeenth century, glass beads, woolen cloth, and metal tools came to occupy roles similar to the shell beads, dressed skins, and copper gorgets that marked elite status and served as gifts to secure alliance. But if the old strategy of alliance seemed advisable in the quest for new symbols of power, the Europeans who provided these items seemed to warrant new tactics. Despite the value of Europeans' goods, Apalachicolas initially preferred to acquire them indirectly, allying with native groups like the Apalachees. With the rise of the slave trade, Apalchicolas sought closer ties with Spaniards and English, but the liabilities of such associations, combined with the internal discord they caused, convinced Apalachicola leaders to back away from this policy.

By opening relations with Spaniards via the Apalachees, Apalachicolas were acknowledging the power of this people of the Gulf Coast.

Apalachees inhabited a dozen towns in the fertile hill country around modern Tallahassee, Florida. Spaniards had a deep, if grudging, respect for the inhabitants of this well- organized chiefdom. Apalachee warriors drove off conquistadors in 1528 and again in 1539. Although Spaniards founded a permanent outpost at St. Augustine in 1565, Apalachees did not accept their first missionaries until 1633. Leaders of both societies welcomed the new relationship. Franciscans and their gifts provided Apalachee leaders with new sources of symbolic and ceremonial power and Apalachee converts renewed Spanish evangelism and augmented St. Augustine's unpredictable food supplies.[33]

Apalachicolas had a less sanguine view of these hill-country farmers. Despite their deceptively similar names, Apalachees' war with the Apalachicolas and other peoples to the north was a constant threat to the missionaries' safety.[34] Only after the arrival of the first Spanish supply ship off the Apalachee coast in 1637 did the Apalachicolas consider peace. Gifts from the ship sparked hundreds of conversions in Apalachee, and, combined with Spanish mediation, some of these items sealed a friendship between the old belligerents in 1638.[35] The initial diplomatic exchanges among the three parties expanded over succeeding decades, with Apalachees bringing Spanish axes, hoes, large bronze bells, glass beads, blankets, and coarse woolen cloth, and returning with Apalachicola deerskins and amber.[36] Though never reaching the volume of the later English trade, the commerce was brisk. In 1688 the governor reported, perhaps with some exaggeration, that "many people regularly went to the province to trade, with the natives there being so open that they came and went to their [the colonists'] businesses and ranches."[37]

While Spaniards celebrated the development of a modest export trade with Havana, Apalachicolas welcomed the new symbols of status that complemented the decorated shell, stone, ceramic, and copper ornaments fundamental to their ceremonial, political, and material culture. These goods also promoted Apalachicolas' collective influence. During the decades following 1638, Apalachicolas became the linchpin in a trade network that distributed Spanish goods as far west as the Mississippi.[38] Peace with Apalachee cleared new paths to Apalachicola prominence.

Though pivotal, the nature of the peace defies easy characterization. Trade between people who were not kin always had the potential to devolve into the unregulated, and potentially violent, exchanges common to strangers. Consequently southeastern Indians' ties of trade also became ties of family.[39] For some these ties possessed great symbolic power. In 1716, Seepeycoffee, the son of the powerful *mico* of Coweta, claimed to one Spanish official that by virtue of his wife and mother both being Christian Apalachees, "he did not consider himself an Infidel."[40] Despite such pronouncements, Apalachees themselves probably discouraged Apalachicolas from pursuing close relations, metaphorical or otherwise, with Spaniards. From exhausted Apalachee burdeners, Apalachicolas would have heard complaints about diseases ravaging the missions, Spanish labor demands, and Franciscan intolerance regarding ceremonies sacred to Apalachees and Apalachicolas alike.[41]

Shifting Alliances:
Apalachicola Relations with the Westos and English

If familiarity with Spaniards bred contempt, Apalachicolas might have considered reaching out to the largely unknown English who founded Carolina in 1670. Pressures from the intensifying slave trade in the 1670s likely also played a role in the association that emerged after 1675. Continuing slave raids probably encouraged Apalachicolas to abandon the circumspection that had characterized their initial relationship with the Apalachees and Spanish. With the new approach came a host of new lessons.

The province's four northern Muskhogean towns spearheaded the quest for English alliance. The English were similarly interested, and in late 1674 Henry Woodward, a talented linguist and negotiator, opened trade with the Westos. By the spring of 1675, reports of English traders on the Chattahoochee River were reaching Spaniards in La Florida. By 1677 Westos and Apalachicolas together shared influential positions in Carolina's network of trade and alliance.[42]

The sudden end to Westo-Apalachicola hostilities seems improbable, especially given the Westos' reputed ferocity, but both native groups had much to gain from accommodation. Apalachicolas looked forward to trade with the English and peace with the Westos. The Westos also stood to gain, for their bloodthirsty reputation could not conceal the fact that many fathers, sons, and brothers never returned home from slave raiding. The mathematics were grim: some 500 to perhaps 2,000 Westo warriors attacked one Guale mission in 1661; twenty-two years later, English traders believed that there were "not fifty Westos left alive."[43] Perhaps in their efforts to avoid such loss of life, they attacked with a savagery that encouraged defenders to flee instead of fight; perhaps continuing deaths convinced them to cooperate with Apalachicolas after 1675.

Despite the potential advantages for both peoples, many southern Apalachicolas opposed the new alliances. The chief of Sabacola, Apalachicola's southernmost town, decided to accept Spanish missionaries just as his northern counterparts welcomed Westos and English, and in the late spring of 1675, he agreed to travel up the Chattahoochee to investigate Spanish apprehension of English activities.[44] In the next four years, others joined Sabacolas at the mission that had been established in 1675. That Spaniards and English were simultaneously making new friends among the Apalachicolas suggests that many of the natives considered close ties with Europeans important in a way that they had not before. This new sentiment also seemed to be pulling southern Hitchitis and northern Muskhogeans apart. The mico of Coweta closed the rift in 1679 by threatening to send his Westo allies against the missionaries. The Franciscans promptly left, but the threat exposed the extent to which the province's unity depended on force, and outside force at that.[45]

The crisis led to no Muskhogean-Hitchiti split, in part because one of the two sources of friction collapsed later that year. In 1680 English traders encouraged Savannah Indians to destroy the Westos. The causes of the war had less to do with the Westos than with Carolinian politics. Just as the Westos controlled the sale of slaves to Carolinians, the colony's proprietors controlled access to the Westos. Traders frustrated with the monopoly decided to destroy the more vulnerable of the two partners. Within a year, the people who had first introduced the slave trade to the Southeast succumbed to it. Perhaps because they harbored Westo refugees, Apalachicolas also entered a new period of conflict with Carolina and its allies. Within months of the end of the Westo War, Apalachicolas were confronting new raids with "firearms that they have taken from the English on some occasions."[46] Clearly the English made dangerously unreliable friends.

Despite the obvious liabilities of a close association with Spaniards, some Apalachicolas were willing to reopen the question after 1680. Between 1680 and 1685, four Apalachicola embassies visited St. Augustine to seek a new missionary. Unfortunately these efforts ran afoul of Spaniards' mistaken impression that the affirmations of friendship constituted "giving obedience" to the Spanish governor and king.[47] A missionary did return to Sabacola, but the mission languished; its small population probably included only a minority of Apalachicolas. The Spanish abandoned it in 1692.[48]

The Spaniards' failure to win Apalachicola converts, even in the midst of a new English threat, suggests some abiding concerns about the burdens of evangelization, and if Spaniards' insistence on religious and political submission discomfited Apalachicola dignitaries, it must have alarmed their followers. In the past, Spanish religious and royal officials had offered native leaders gifts and rituals that could augment chiefly authority. In exchange these leaders gave tributary submission to St. Augustine.[49] Increasingly after 1640, as Spanish soldiers and royal officials sought to profit from the trade between Apalachicola and Havana, these rare goods became available to a broader population; by the end of the century, non-elite Apalachicolas possessed the objects and symbols formerly reserved for their leaders.[50] As broader segments of the population gained greater access to the material symbols of influence, non-elite Apalachicolas would have had greater resources to resist a relationship that would promote *micos'* authority at their expense. Observant missionaries like Fray Rodrigo de Barrera, who served at Sabacola, recognized this political shift when he advised La Florida's governor in 1681 to promise Apalachicolas a different mission experience, one that would not subject commoners to the labor drafts that Apalachees and others had to serve. As would become clearer later, Father Barrera's solitary suggestion was the first official indication that the Florida missions had an uncertain future as a tool for empire. The

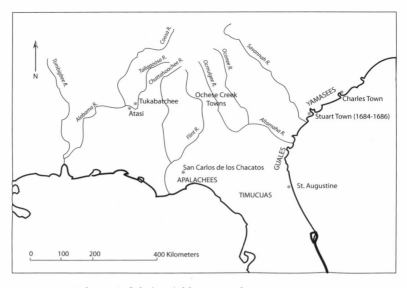

2. Ocheses and their neighbors, ca. 1690

fate of this evangelical project lay in the hands of thousands of circumspect commoners in and outside the missions.[51]

Europeans had provided Apalachicolas new foundations for regional influence, and they seemed to promise protection from the uncertainties of the age, but efforts to build close ties with either (or both) peoples seemed fraught with trouble. Spanish inflexibility and English unpredictability must have confirmed the wisdom of keeping both groups at a distance. Unfortunately this wisdom provided scant comfort. Apalachicola towns, like many others, were haunted by the memories of those who were perhaps dead, perhaps alive as human livestock. But just as clans could not leave murdered kin unavenged, so too did they refuse to abandon those who might still live. In those ambitions lay the foundations for a new kind of relationship with the English and a return to older efforts to cultivate indigenous allies.

Ambivalent Alliance:
Apalachicola Partnership with the Yamasees

In the summer of 1685 the Apalachicolas welcomed English traders for the first of three fateful visits to renew ties of trade. At the least, the English demanded less of their native allies than the Spanish. However, Carolinian political strife made them far less predictable friends. The Spanish were hardly free of internal dissention, but because every man of influence depended on royal subsidies and royal approval for his position, Spaniards conducted most of their squabbles through the slow channels of the imperial bureaucracy. Their disputes, however acrimonious, could not cause violent swings in colonial disposition toward subjects and neighbors. Carolinians, split among proprietary supporters and those seeking their own local bases of power, lacked any such formal higher authority for settling disagreements. Worse, because trade with Native Americans constituted one of the colony's most lucrative and bitterly contested activities, colonial conflicts could quickly turn native power brokers into refugees.[52] The Westos knew this all too unhappily.

Despite their unpredictability and their unwillingness to bring the five prisoners who could help build that trust, the English did come with others who could provide some reassurance. The fifty Yamasees from the Carolina coast who escorted the English included friends and former neighbors of the Apalachicolas. Not only could these neighbors, as powerful new allies of the English, reassure their ambivalent hosts, they might also become allies who could mitigate the risks of association with the English. The pressures of slave raiding and the promise of Carolinian trade doubtlessly encouraged Apalachicolas to improve their relations with the English, but they did not abandon their preference for native partners in the process.

The Yamasees were surprising new players in southeastern power politics. Many of the people Spaniards called "Yamasees" had grown up as members of various polities from central or coastal Georgia. In 1663 Westo attacks forced them to flee to the Apalachicolas and the Spanish missions of Guale and Apalachee, where Spaniards called the heterogeneous immigrant communities "Yamasis" or "Yamases."[53] Although a product of weakness, dispersal soon became a source of strength. When Spanish labor demands and political slights convinced Yamasees to abandon Guale in 1683, they moved north to Port Royal, home of some of the migrants in less troubled times.[54]

Shortly before the Yamasees' move north, Carolina's proprietors had granted the same territory to Scottish Presbyterians, who established Stuart Town near today's Port Royal. Together, Scottish and Yamasee immigrants forged a friendship born of a shared hatred of the Spanish and a desire to profit from the sale of captives from the missions. Their raids proved so successful that many Yamasee refugees left their homes among the Apalachicolas and the missions and flocked to Stuart Town's environs.[55] Between 1683 and 1703, the population mushroomed from several hundred to over 4,000.[56]

More than opportunists, the Yamasees were opportunists with impeccable timing. Proprietors in England and traders in Charles Town and Stuart Town were all looking for a well-situated population to serve as go-betweens to interior peoples, as the proprietors put it, "in the roome of ye Westoes."[57] The Yamasees, with their "siblings and relatives" among the Apalachicolas, lived along the coast just north of the Savannah River, the best route to the upland trails leading west.[58] Not surprisingly, when the Scots of Stuart Town began to discuss "a method for correspondence and treade with Cuita and Cussita nations of Indians," they undoubtedly had Yamasees in mind as crucial partners.[59]

Unfortunately for the Scots, the proprietors had plans of their own. For this sensitive mission they sent Henry Woodward.[60] When Woodward and the Yamasees arrived at Coweta, Apalachicolas must have recognized the double opportunity to improve relations not just with the Carolinians but also with the increasingly powerful refugees who had once lived among them. The problem was that Apalachicolas found themselves in the delicate position of trying to establish trading ties with the English without alienating the Spanish. They proved remarkably adept players, and much of this success depended on their Yamasee friends and kin.

When Spaniards learned of Woodward's venture in the summer of 1685, Governor Juan Márquez Cabrera dispatched his lieutenant, Antonio Matheos, with 250 Apalachees and six soldiers. Despite Matheos's imposing force and his torture of a few unfortunate Apalachicolas who had failed to flee to the woods, Apalachicolas refused to succumb to Matheos's intimidation. None but the sixty-year-old mico of Apalachicola and three companions willingly spoke with the invaders, and most of what they said misled.[61] Woodward and his party escaped, and Matheos left as he came, with threats: if Apalachicolas welcomed the traders again, they could expect fire and blood.[62] The English did return in December, and so did Matheos, but Apalachicolas again proved uniformly uncooperative. Only by chance did Spaniards and Apalachees come across one of the trading houses, concealed in the woods six miles outside Coweta.[63] Now certain of Apalachicola duplicity, Matheos plundered the trading house and threatened to burn any town whose leaders did not meet with him to reaffirm Spanish allegiance. *Micos* of the Hitchiti towns timorously appeared at the meeting, but none betrayed the English. Frustrated again, Matheos burned the unrepentantly pro-English towns of Coweta, Cusseta, Colone, and Tasquique, hoping the display would "give rise to some discord among" those towns willing to negotiate with him and those who refused.[64] He failed. Apalachicolas remained devoted to cautious neutrality with both colonial powers.[65]

The irascible Matheos was clearly ill-suited for such delicate missions, but the roots of his failure are nonetheless complex. Many Apalachicolas welcomed English trade goods, but they feared their purveyors, too. Matheos himself admitted, "they are more afraid of [the English] than us."[66] The Apalachicolas had good reason for trepidation. Woodward and his companions not only neglected to bring the five captives, but some Spanish records suggest that the visit did not halt English-sponsored slave raids on the Chattahoochee valley.[67] Even if fear played a role in the Apalachicolas' decisions, Yamasees ensured the success of the English visits, and their influence hints at the pragmatism and caution behind the Apalachicola ceremonies of welcome. Brandishing English muskets and modeling the latest in English-sponsored Indian fashion, these visitors were advertisements for alliance.[68] But in the delicate negotiations, Yamasees' mutual friendship with the principals must have helped refashion violent exchanges into peaceful ones. As Apalachicolas later explained in an effort to mend fences with the Spanish in 1690, "they wanted only the friendship of the Spaniards but that the first time [the English] had come to enter into their towns, that the Yamasee nation had brought them."[69] Whether or not the Apalachicolas acted with such guiltless passivity, they at the very least considered their friendship with the Yamasees to be a worthy excuse.

Yamasee mediation was especially important in light of the complexity and intensity of negotiations among Apalachiolas themselves. When a third trade embassy of five traders arrived in the Chattahoochee valley in the spring of 1686, a lone English trader accompanied forty-five Yamasees to speak at Apalachicola town. Inside the council house, men, women, and children from the neighboring towns and villages, including some Yamasees and other resident "new people," gathered to hear from the trader and his Yamasee companions.[70] The trader and his escort had chosen the destination with care. The Hitchiti audience, consisting of people nearest to Apalachee traders and invaders, had understandably proven less enthusiastic about the English visits than the Muskhogeans who controlled the trading path to Charles Town; they also likely wanted assurances that their towns would not suffer the conflagrations that Matheos had inflicted on the Muskhogean towns.

While the Carolinian observed a prudent silence, the Yamasees did the convincing.[71] For one, Yamasees and Hitchitis spoke similar languages, and Yamasees living in or near Apalachicola town could have served as translators, advocates, and character references. Perhaps responding to Apalachicola fears of Matheos, the leader of the visiting Yamasees boasted of recent military successes against the missions and promised an imminent invasion of St. Augustine. Through such conversations, too, Yamasees, Hitchitis, and Muskhogeans forged and reinforced ties of kinship, shared knowledge, and trust.[72] In 1688 the governor of Carolina noted to his counterpart in St. Augustine that Yamasees were outside the limits of English influence because they "were confe[derated] with a bigger Nation than themselves, which with the Yamosyes are about 1400 men."[73]

This new alliance would ultimately reorient the region. Although Spanish officials later tried to undo the heavy-handed blunders of Lieutenant Matheos and Governor Márquez, Spaniards continued to insist that Apalachicolas avoid all contact with the English. To ensure that they did so, St. Augustine's governor constructed a new fort among the Apalachicolas in 1689. These and other pressures eventually convinced most Apalachicolas that their interests were better served not with neutrality but with a closer relationship with the Yamasees and their English partners. Some time before the fall of 1691, Muskhogeans and then Hitchitis abandoned the Chattahoochee for the river bottoms of the Ocmulgee about one hundred miles to the northeast. Joined by Savannahs, Yuchis, and other groups, the relocated settlements entered English records as the "Ochese Creek towns." For the people of Apalachicola town, the Yamasee alliance meant enough that they eventually moved southeast, settling two towns on the western bank of the Savannah River, thirty miles from the Yamasees.[74] In the Apalachicolas' quest for security, a security that included access to European items and the absence of European intervention, Spanish-Apalachee friendship could not compete with what Yamasees and English could offer.

Yamasees' friendship with the Apalachicolas had opened the path of peace with Charles Town, but more important, the alliance kept it from becoming a path to submission. Yamasees controlled the inland water route to the Savannah River, which was the easiest route inland to the trading path that followed the fall line. The recently moved Apalachicolas sat astride that path as it headed to the Mississippi valley. They controlled the trade westward even as they also stood as Carolina's principal bulwarks against any invasion from that quarter.[75] As frustrated Carolinian traders noted in 1691, the Yamasees had become "[t]he onely people fitt to assist the English, in a way of trade to the Inlands."[76] Together Yamasees and Apalachicolas had joined the English trading network. Together they had become indispensable to it.

Such growing prominence may have derived in part from the Apalachicolas' own connections to other western peoples. These friends connected Apalachicolas to a trade network that extended far inland and assured Apalachicolas of continuing relevance even as English traders ventured west to the Mississippi River. Two towns along the Tallapoosa River, Atasi and the influential town of Tukabatchee, were particularly important to these western connections.[77] Both had been trading with Apalachicolas probably long before their first recorded exchanges in 1686.[78] After Apalachicolas moved east in 1691, Tukabatchees and Atasis joined them, but neither town relocated in its entirety.[79] Both may have been affirming their close ties with their eastern comrades and cousins, but by sending only segments of their populations, they may also have helped guarantee that their western towns would remain prominent within the Apalachicolas' trade network. Cowetas probably had similar intentions when some established a Tallapoosa valley settlement some time before 1700.[80] Both sets of bifurcated towns ensured continuing Apalachicola relevance in English trade with peoples to the west.

As Chekilli made clear in 1735, alliances secured the path to peace and power. This philosophy must have carried great weight, for beginning in 1638 Apalachicolas had placed alliances at the center of their efforts to obtain the benefits and reduce the risks that accompanied European goods. Before 1685 that strategy had involved minimizing contact with Europeans. Even after that year, when they decided that their power depended on direct relations with Carolinians, they remained cautious. Apalachicolas may have favored English traders, but they did not trust them. Not only did these latter turn on their supposed friends the Westos, they failed to free the captives who would reassure their new Apalachicola friends of their peaceful intentions. Ultimately Apalachicolas' friendship with the Yamasees to the east and the Tukabatchees and Atasis to the west grew out of that mistrust. Even as these ties enabled Carolina to expand its influence to the Mississippi River by 1700, they also ensured Apalachicolas' prominence in that expanding network of trade, alliance, and war.

Power and Fear: Apalachicolas, Yamasees, and the English

Direct relations with the English increased the risks to Apalachicolas, but the risks were growing regardless. In the decade following Woodward and Matheos's shadow dance along the Chattahoochee, Spaniards and English increasingly made the interior Southeast the field of their competition. Spaniards sought to counteract English diplomatic and commercial influence with a trade embassy to the Alabama and Tallapoosa valleys in 1686, three devastating raids on Stuart Town and the Yamasees in 1686 and 1687, and the construction of a fort among the Apalachicolas in 1689. Meanwhile English traders continued to venture west from Charles Town, with natives frequently welcoming them for fear that their enemies might do so instead.[81] Amid these maneuvers, natives could not avoid the challenges of living in a world not entirely of their own making.

In seeking English alliance, Apalachicolas and many other southeastern peoples had sought refuge from the terrors of slave raids. Seeking to maintain that alliance and the weapons and tools it provided, they became terrifying raiders themselves. As the English network of trade and alliance spread westward, the sources of captives most readily available from the Ocmulgee valley lay among the poorly armed Spanish mission populations to the south. The Apalachicolas' alliance with Apalachee would suffer for this fact. Although some Apalachees initially hoped they might enjoy some "fruit of the commerce that they [the Apalachicolas?] have with the English," after 1691, Apalachicolas ventured south with growing frequency to raid rather than trade. In addition to a number of small raids, Apalachicolas joined Yamasees and English in large-scale attacks against Timucua in 1691 and several against the Chacato mission of San Carlos de los Chacatos, just northwest of Apalachee, through 1694.[82] In most instances the attackers took as many captives they could find, pillaged churches of their sacred (and valuable) ornaments, and razed towns.[83] The old friendship died slowly, though. In fact, the success of a 1694 raid on the Chacatos depended in part on the continuing ambiguity of the Apalachicolas' relationship with their southern neighbors. Prior to the attack, some Apalachicolas traded in San Carlos while their comrades prepared outside the village for their later assault. As far as the raiders were concerned, this assault marked the beginning of the Apalachees' end. Returning northward, they boasted to their prisoners that their sale would purchase the firearms necessary to "finish once and for all the Spaniards and Apalachees."[84]

The Apalachicolas were formidable, but those words were probably uttered with more bravado than foresight. Administering a coup de grace to one of the region's most populous and powerful peoples required more than muskets. With a population of about 9,600 clustered into large and well-defended towns, the Apalachees were an intimidating adversary.[85] Apalachicolas had been uncomfortable witnesses of Apalachee strength when hundreds of warriors accompanied Matheos to the Chattahoochee in 1685 and 1686. Such memories might have influenced Apalachicolas to direct the large-scale slave raids of 1691–1694, not against the Apalachees but against their weaker Timucua and Chacato neighbors. Although some Apalachicolas were beginning to value the Apalachees more as captives than as partners, they could not expect to acquire them easily or without retribution. If native allies provided Apalachicolas with the best protection from meddling colonists, whose formidable power remained confined mostly to the coast, native enemies presented them with the greatest threat.[86]

This fact became starkly clear in December 1694, when Apalachees and Chacatos avenged the Apalachicolas' attack on San Carlos. Apalachicolas sought refuge in the woods, and four hundred mission Indians and seven Spaniards found only empty towns. Although the defenders lost few lives, they suffered terribly from the invaders' scorched-earth tactics. Apalachicolas suffered a year of privation, and they knew it could happen again. Their bodies stressed by seasons of shortage in 1695, the recovering population must have been especially vulnerable to the smallpox epidemic that swept westward from Charles Town in 1696.[87] For all of their power, not even Apalachicolas possessed immunity to the scourges of war, famine, and pestilence.

Although these trials did not prevent Apalachicolas from mounting their own reprisals against the Apalachees, significant numbers of both populations opposed this increasingly belligerent turn. When Chacatos under the command of Apalachee lieutenant Francisco de Florencia ambushed Apalachicola hunters in 1699, Apalachee leader Don Patricio de Hinachuba warned a trusted Spanish friend, "[I]t is certain, sir, . . . that we will have to pay for these actions."[88] Peace and conflict simultaneously bound the provinces. Apalachicolas continued to trade with Apalachees despite Spanish officials' efforts to prohibit mission Indians from trading horses, silver, or anything else that had not been part of pre-contact exchanges. Apalachee defiance of the embargo presented its own risks in the midst of uncertain relations with the Apalachicolas. In 1702 three Apalachee traders were "cruelly and inhumanly" killed when they requested Apalachicolas provide them with English muskets in exchange for the forbidden horses.[89]

The murders either comprised a small part of an ill-timed coincidence or reflected Apalachicola awareness of recent events in Europe. Disputes over the heir to the Spanish throne brought England into conflict with France and Spain in the spring of 1702. News of war reached Charles Town by late August and may have arrived among the Apalachicolas just before the unfortunate Apalachees.[90] In the late summer of 1702, Apalachicolas ambushed 800 Apalachee invaders intent on avenging the deaths of their ambassadors. The ambush routed the Apalachees, inflicting over 300 casualties.[91] Despite the expanding violence, Apalachicolas must have still entertained some friendly sentiments. When the assembly authorized a joint English-Apalachicola expedition against the mission province in 1704, they expressly instructed its commander James Moore first "to endeavour to gain by all peaceable means possible the appalaches to our interest."[92] Given Carolinians' obsessive fears of Apalachee invasions of the colony, who else but the Apalachicolas would have inspired the Carolina assembly—an assembly closely tied to slave-trading interests—to eschew the blanket enslavement of all captives?[93]

Longstanding ties of friendship and family did not prevent war from reaching Apalachee in January of 1704, when 1,500 Apalachicolas and fifty English invaded the province. In acts of violence that blended revenge, disdain for the Spanish, and calculated warnings to others who entertained resistance, the invaders burned the first town they encountered, torturing prisoners, and desecrating the mission church. Other Apalachees avoided that fate with the help of timely ransoms or unbreachable fortifications, but many other towns surrendered, joining the invading force as it withdrew northward.[94] A June invasion assisted by several dozen Apalachees convinced survivors to abandon the province before the end of August.[95]

In addition to the thousands of captives, approximately 600 Apalachees migrated north to settle lands on the Savannah River, across the river from present-day Augusta and astride the trading path between Charles Town and the Ocmulgee. Despite Carolinians' initial fears that they would turn on the colony with "barbarous cruelty," the Apalachee arrivals began new lives trading with their former partners and assailants, carrying packs for English traders heading hundreds of miles inland, and even joining them in raids on what remained of La Florida's native and colonial population.[96] Though Apalachees had suffered defeat and many had been enslaved, the 600 who continued as free people despite Carolinian misgivings doubtless owed some of that freedom to their Apalachicola captors.[97]

The removal, enslavement, and dispersal of the Apalachees erased the most immediate threat to Apalachicolas' well-being. The peoples of the Ocmulgee and their allies east and west had obtained a measure of security they probably had not enjoyed since the middle seventeenth century and a position of influence that they could not have imagined a half-century earlier. The careful leadership of micos and the disparate demands of influential followers had made this rise possible, but both groups had made their decisions in partnership with other natives who improved access to and protection from the powerful Carolinians and their violent trade.

In fact, even in that moment of triumph lay the seeds of future difficulties. The traders who sold the tools, cloth, ornaments, and weapons that conferred power were becoming increasingly volatile in their dealings with their so-called partners, especially those closest to the colony. Traders killed Yamasees' horses, stole their canoes, and burned their storehouses. One trader forced Yamasees to build him a house while another had the gall to steal two guns from a widow.[98] Parallel to these haphazard assertions of personal power was a rising sense of imperial entitlement among colonial officials more generally. In 1705 Apalachicola leaders and a number of their allies to the east and west signed an accord with the Carolinians, published in London as "The Humble Submission of the Kings, Princes, General, &c. to the Crown of England." The agreement, which made no mention of submission but did include an acknowledgement that "our Protection depends upon the English," seemed to contradict the purpose behind all of the alliances that Apalachicolas had forged with their native neighbors. In their quest for European manufactures, perhaps they had simply avoided Spaniards' callous impositions only to become trapped in a comfortable, if still confining, cage of English manufacture.

But rhetoric, as the English well knew, hardly captured reality. Say what the English would, the Apalachicolas still remained beyond the effective reach of any colony. More than that, they had the power to shape the European settlements. No one ever heeded Barrera's 1681 suggestion regarding a less-burdensome mission system, but Spanish officials could not help noticing the many Indians who continued to avoid or flee the missions before 1704. When Spaniards finally established a new fort in Apalachee in 1717, they directed their resources almost entirely to offering gifts and trade with the Apalachicolas. Evangelical considerations placed a distant second. For the English, Apalachicola anxieties about Apalachees provided Charles Town with an indispensable partner for the destruction of the missions in 1704, but no Carolinians could have imagined or desired that many Apalachees would be living freely on the doorstep of their colony. Just as they could not stop the slave trade, Apalachicolas could not stop the wider process of colonization. They did, however, shape it more than any colonist would have liked.

Perhaps more ominously for the Apalachicolas, the title of the "Humble Submission" intimated the changing nature of that colonization. Although the title may have said more about the imperial sentiment of a London publisher than the agreement's Carolinian sponsors, there is no question that the interest, if not the apparatus, for a more orderly control of the king's dominions was growing on both sides of the Atlantic.[99] In 1705, though, English ambitions probably disturbed Apalachicolas less than the haphazard way the Carolinians pursued them. As the traders visiting their towns became more indebted to creditors in Charles Town and London, they abandoned the expensive gift-giving that renewed their trading alliance with the Apalachicolas, Yamasees, and other trading partners. As Carolinian regulators proved increasingly incapable of countering this diplomatic breakdown with coherent reassurances of their own, Apalachicolas and other Indians again questioned the reliability of their violently unpredictable friends.[100]

Apalachicolas' response, not surprisingly, would be to strengthen the alliances that had made their power both possible and prudent. When native frustration with Carolinian impositions exploded into the Yamasee War in 1715, those alliances encouraged many peoples, including those along the Yamasee–Apalachicola–Tukabatchee trading path, to join in a simultaneous strike against English traders. The intensity of that war would further temper these alliances into the collection of peoples known as Creek.[101]

Notes

1. The author would like to thank Sylvia Hawks for retyping drafts and Alan Gallay, Evan Haefeli, Steven Hahn, Daniel Richter, Melissa Sundell, and the McNeill Seminar for Early American Culture for their comments. Thanks, too, to Camille Parrish, Will Ash, and the Bates College Imaging Center for producing the maps. In the interests of consistency with the naming of the time, I will refer to modern Charleston by its colonial name. Although Carolina was not divided into northern and southern pieces until 1729, the heart of the colony was around Charles Town. When I write about Carolina, I am effectively referring to South Carolina.

2. Antonio Matheos to Governor Juan Márquez Cabrera, Casista, September 21, 1685, enclosed in *Autos sobre la entrada*, enclosed in Márquez Cabrera to King, St. Augustine, March 20, 1686, Santo Domingo 839, Archivo General de Indias, Seville, Spain. (Hereafter abbreviated AGI SD, followed by the number of the *legajo* or bundle. Documents from other sections of the archive besides Santo Domingo will not be abbreviated. All cited correspondence from the AGI is dated in St. Augustine unless otherwise noted.)

3. These are the only two items identified in a Spanish list that also included "other goods that they needed." This summary category suggests that Spaniards were already familiar with—and satisfying—these other needs to some extent. Favian de Angelo to Governor Diego Quiroga y Losada, Apalachicola Fort, May 24, 1690, enclosed in Quiroga y Losada to King, June 8, 1690, AGI SD 227B, N. 68.

4. For examples, see John H. Hann, *Apalachee: The Land Between the Rivers* (Gainesville: University of Florida Press), 10–11; George Chicken, "Colonel Chicken's Journal to the Cherokees, 1725," in *Travels in the American Colonies*, ed. Newton D. Mereness (New York: Macmillan, 1916), 115–21. For a discussion of the diplomatic role of captives in the Southwest, see James F. Brooks, *Captives and Cousins: Slavery, Kinship, and Community in the Southwest Borderlands* (Chapel Hill, University of North Carolina Press, 2002), especially chapter 1.

5. Antonio Matheos to Márquez, San Luís, March 14, 1686, enclosed in *Autos sobre la entrada*, AGI SD 839. Because the records of these Anglo-Apalachicola meetings make no mention of the five captives being an issue in 1685, it is possible that slave raiders captured the five in the autumn following the Carolinians' visit. Granting this possibility, however, does not diminish the grounds for and evidence of Apalachicola ambivalence. In fact, it highlights more starkly the incompleteness of the English overtures.

6. For a corroborating opinion of the shortcomings of the scholarship, see Daniel K. Richter and James H. Merrell, "Preface to the Paperback Edition," in *Beyond the Covenant Chain: The Iroquois and Their Neighbors in Indian North America, 1600–1800*, edited by Daniel K. Richter and James H. Merrell (1987; College Park: Pennsylvania State University Press, 2003), xiv. Historians of the slave trade in the Southeast have focused much more on Europeans' motivations than those of the Indians. In an effort to organize his pathbreaking study, for instance, Alan Gallay focuses principally on English (and later British) imperial ascendancy. Others have similarly focused on Europeans as the engines of the trade and Indians as Europeans' willing allies or unwilling captives. Alan Gallay, *The Indian Slave Trade: The Rise of the English*

Empire in the American South, 1670–1717 (New Haven: Yale University Press, 2002); J. Leitch Wright, *The Only Land They Knew: The Tragic Story of the American Indians in the Old South* (New York: Free Press, 1981), 132–50; Joel Martin, "Southeastern Indians and the Trade in Skins and Slaves," in *The Forgotten Centuries: Indians and Europeans in the American South, 1521–1704*, ed. Charles Hudson and Carmen Chaves Tesser (Athens: University of Georgia Press, 1994). For one recent exception to this trend, see Wendy St. Jean, "Trading Paths: Mapping Chickasaw History in the Eighteenth Century," *American Indian Quarterly* 27, no. 3–4 (2003): 758–80.

7. The Westos exemplify the stereotypical savage slave raider, with one Carolinian noting that "of them [the coastal Indians near Charles Town] are more afraid than the little children are of the Bull beggars in England." Later scholars have followed this lead, discussing the ways that Westos "terrorized" their victims and speculating whether the Westos and other "predatory polities" were akin to the "Mongols" who invaded medieval Europe. Although no scholar has presented these portraits of the Westos (or the Mongols) with pejorative intentions, only Eric Bowne has sought to understand such savagery as a conscious strategy rather than (for lack of discussion) an apparent fault of character. My own discussion of the Apalachicolas should further enrich our understanding of the strategic considerations behind the raiders' terrifying masks. William Owen to Lord Shaftesbury, Ashley River [Charles Town], September 15, 1670, in *The Shaftesbury Papers and Other Records Relating to Carolina and the First Settlement on Ashley River prior to the Year 1676*, ed. Langdon Cheves, South Carolina Historical Society Collections 5 (1897): 200–201; David H. Corkran, *The Creek Frontier, 1540–1783* (Norman: University of Oklahoma Press, 1967), 48; Charles Hudson, "Introduction" in *The Transformation of the Southeastern Indians, 1540–1763*, edited by Robbie Ethridge and Charles Hudson (Jackson: University Press of Mississippi, 2002), xxvii, xxix; Eric E. Bowne, *The Westo Indians: Slave Traders of the Early Colonial South* (Tuscaloosa: University of Alabama Press, 2005), 18.

8. Gallay, *Indian Slave Trade*, 299.

9. Lord Proprietors of Carolina to the governor and deputies, September 30, 1683, *Calendar of State Papers, Colonial Series: America and West Indies, 1681–1685*, ed. J. W. Fortescue (London: Spottiswoodie, 1898), 509. Despite their humanitarian rhetoric, the proprietors protested because they sought to reserve for themselves the colony's most profitable venture. Verner W. Crane, *The Southern Frontier, 1670–1732* (Ann Arbor: University of Michigan Press, 1929), 117–19; Gallay, *Indian Slave Trade*, 47–48.

10. For more on the Westos, see John E. Worth, *Struggle for the Georgia Coast*, American Museum of Natural History, Anthropological Papers, no. 75 (Athens: University of Georgia Press, 1994), 15–19; and Bowne, *The Westo Indians*.

11. Governor Alonso Aranguiz y Cotes to the king, October 21, 1659, AGI SD 839.

12. Bishop Gabriel Díaz Vara Calderón to king, Havana [?], 1675, AGI SD 151.

13. Díaz to king, 1675, AGI SD 151.

14. Detailed references to slaves are rare, but a few documents offer suggestive details about later patterns of the slave trade. English frequently bought boys (Governor Quiroga y Losada to king, April 10, 1692, AGI SD 227B, N. 89); when they planned a massive attack on Apalachee in 1703, Apalachicolas intended to kill the men and take only the women prisoner (Francisco Romo de Uriza to Governor Joseph Zúñiga y Cerda, San Luis, October 22, 1703, AGI SD 858); and, in 1712, when advising prospective colonists about establishing a farm, one Carolina promoter suggested slave women fieldworkers, a suggestion likely shaped by market conditions, since English believed that men should work in fields. Jack P. Greene, ed., *Selling a New World: Two Colonial South Carolina Promotional Pamphlets* (Columbia: University of South Carolina Press, 1989), 132.

15. The Westos' Iroquoian neighbors, the Five Nations, practiced ritual cannibalism as a ceremonial way of incorporating their enemies. Westos probably brought this practice south. Daniel K. Richter, *The Ordeal of the Longhouse: The Peoples of the Iroquois League in the Era of European Colonization* (Chapel Hill: University of North Carolina Press, 1992), 35–36.

16. Jack Martin and Margaret McKane Mauldin, *A Dictionary of Creek/Muskogee with Notes on the Florida and Oklahoma Seminole Dialects of Creek* (Lincoln: University of Nebraska Press, 2000), q.v. "slave." "Este" translates as person and "vpuekv" as livestock or domesticated animal. For a similar definition from Cherokee, see Theda Perdue, *Slavery and the Evolution of Cherokee Society* (Knoxville: University of Tennessee Press, 1979), 4, 12. I borrow the term "social death" from Orlando Patterson, *Slavery and Social Death: A Comparative Study* (Cambridge: Harvard University Press, 1982). For a discussion of clans, see Charles Hudson, *The Southeastern Indians* (Athens: University of Georgia Press, 1976), 193–96; Thomas Nairne, *Nairne's Muskhogean Journals: The 1708 Expedition to the Mississippi*, edited by Alexander Moore (Jackson: University Press of Mississippi, 1988), 32–34, 60–61.

17. Brett Rushforth, "'A Little Flesh We Offer You': The Origins of Indian Slavery in New France," *William and Mary Quarterly*, 3rd series, 60, no. 4 (2003): 793–95. Rushforth and Brooks both explore some Indians' motives for trading slaves, but such considerations are much less clear for the Southeast. We should nonetheless not assume Indians' wholehearted acceptance of the Carolinian trade. The likely preponderance of female captives suggests that Indians did not respond with alacrity to English demand for men. Although no words of Westo protest entered Carolinian records, sixteenth-century Brazilian natives sometimes resisted Portuguese efforts to turn captives into commodities. John M. Monteiro, "Crises and Transformations in Invaded Societies: Coastal Brazil in the Sixteenth Century," in *The Cambridge History of the Native Peoples of the Americas*, Vol. 3, *South America*, Part 1, edited by Stuart Schwartz and Frank Salomon (New York: Cambridge University Press, 1999), 993–94.

18. For a discussion of the lives of Indian slaves in the colony, see William L. Ramsey, "All & Singular the Slaves': A Demographic Profile of Indian Slavery in Colonial South Carolina," in *Money, Trade, and Power: The Evolution of South Carolina's Plantation Society*, edited by Jack P. Greene, Rosemary Brana-Shute, and Randy J. Sparks (Columbia: University of South Carolina Press, 2001). For a detailed discussion of south-central African references to the European slave trade as a commerce that, like cannibalism, consumed people, see John Thornton, "Cannibals, Witches, and Slave Traders in the Atlantic World," *William and Mary Quarterly*, 3rd series, 60, no. 2 (2003): 273–94.

19. Because the existence of a town called "Apalachicola" in the province of the same name might cause confusion, I will use the term "Apalachicola" to refer to the province of thirteen towns and "Apalachicola town" to refer to the particular Hitchiti town. For examples of Spanish and English nomenclature, see Díaz to king, 1675, AGI SD 151; Henry Woodward, "A Faithfull Relation of my Westoe Voiage," in *Narratives of Early Carolina, 1650–1708*, ed. Alexander S. Salley Jr. (New York: Charles Scribner's Sons, 1911), 133–34

20. Edgar Legare Pennington, "Some Ancient Georgia Indian Lore," *Georgia Historical Quarterly* 15, no. 2 (1931): 192–98; quote from p. 197. For a different version, see "Talk of Creek leaders, Savannah, June 11, 1735," in Kenneth Coleman and Milton Ready, eds., *The Colonial Records for the State of Georgia*, vol. 20 (Athens: University of Georgia Press, 1982), 381–87. Many historians have referred to this account as a "Creek" origin story. Although many peoples known as Creeks appear in the story, Chekilli was clear throughout that this was the story of his people, the Cussetas, and their alliance with, and superiority over, the Pallachuculas.

21. Pennington, "Indian Lore," 197.

22. On the importance of analyzing what he calls American Indian historicity, see Peter Nabokov, *A Forest of Time: American Indian Ways of History* (New York: Cambridge, 2002). For a more extended discussion of Chekilli's story as part of a larger Creek historiography of their origins, see Joseph Hall, "Making an Indian People: Creek Formation in the Colonial Southeast," PhD diss., University of Wisconsin-Madison, 2001, 50–71.

23. John E. Worth, "The Lower Creeks: Origins and Early History," in *Indians of the Greater Southeast: Historical Archaeology and Ethnohistory*, edited by Bonnie G. McEwan (Gainesville: University Press of Florida, 1998); John H. Hann, "Late Seventeenth-Century Forebears of the Lower Creeks and Seminoles," *Southeastern Archaeology* 16, no. 1 (1996): 66–80; Steven C. Hahn, *The Invention of the Creek Nation, 1670–1763* (Lincoln: University of Nebraska Press, 2004), 26–29.

24. The literature on Mississippian hierarchies is vast. See Christopher S. Peebles and Susan M. Kus, "Some Archaeological Correlates of Ranked Societies," *American Antiquity* 42, no. 3 (1977): 421–48; Paul D. Welch, *Moundville's Economy* (Tuscaloosa: University of Alabama Press, 1991); David H. Dye, "Feasting with the Enemy: Mississippian Warfare and Prestige-Goods Circulation," in *Native American Interactions: Multiscalar Analyses and Interpretations in the Eastern Woodlands*, edited by Michael S. Nassaney and Kenneth E. Sassaman (Knoxville: University of Tennessee Press, 1995).

25. For an illuminating discussion of the blurry borders between peace and war in the North American Southwest, see Brooks, *Captives and Cousins*, chapter 1.

26. Thomas Causton to Trustees, Savannah, Georgia, June 20, 1735, *Colonial Records of Georgia* 20: 401. In 1682, the Spanish governor referred to Hitchitis and Muskhogeans as members of separate provinces along the Chattahoochee River. Governor Juan Márquez Cabrera to King, August 2, 1682, AGI SD 226, N. 76.

27. Nairne was describing the Tallapoosas, the Apalachicolas' Muskhogean neighbors to the west. Nairne, *Muskhogean Journals*, 32. For a similar assessment about the Choctaws, see Fr. Beaudouin to Fr. Salmon, Chickasawhay, November 23, 1732, in *Mississippi Provincial Archives, French Dominion*, edited and translated by Dunbar Rowland and Albert Godfrey Sanders, 3 vols. (Jackson: Mississippi Department of Archives and History, 1928–1947), 1:156.

28. Hudson, *Southeastern Indians*, 193–96. It is worth noting, too, that there exist versions of the Creek origin story that focus on the actions of clans like the Wind and Tyger (or Panther) clans instead of towns like Cusseta and Pallachucula. "Social Organization and Social Usages of the Indians of the Creek Confederacy," in *Forty-Second Annual Report of the Bureau of American Ethnology* (Washington DC: Government Printing Office, 1928), 107–114; Hall, "Making an Indian People," 59–60.

29. Worth, "Lower Creeks," 269; Marvin T. Smith, *Archaeology of Aboriginal Culture Change in the Interior Southeast: Depopulation during the Early Historic Period* (Gainesville: University Press of Florida, 1987), 84–85; Ann F. Ramenofsky, *Vectors of Death: The Archaeology of European Contact* (Albuquerque: University of New Mexico Press, 1987), 55–63; Paul Kelton, "The Great Southeastern Smallpox Epidemic, 1696–1700: The Region's First Major Epidemic?" in *Transformation*, ed. Ethridge and Hudson. For a broader reconsideration of the impact of European and African diseases on American populations, see David S. Jones, "Virgin Soils Revisited," *William and Mary Quarterly*, 3rd series, 60, no. 4 (2003): 703–42.

30. Hann, *Apalachee*, 160–65.

31. Lord Shaftesbury to Henry Woodward, May 23, 1674, in *The Shaftesbury Papers and Other Records Relating to Carolina and the First Settlement on Ashley River prior to the Year 1676*, ed. Langdon

Cheves, South Carolina Historical Society *Collections* 5 (1897): 440–41; Díaz to king, 1675, AGI SD 151. Such statements were likely not colonial hyperbole: in 1688, Carolina Governor James Colleton claimed that Yamasees and "a bigger Nation" together possessed about 4,000 men. For reasons I explain later, this nation was certainly the Apalachicolas and thus had at least 2,000 men. In 1690 an English trader reported that the "kings" of Cusseta and Coweta had 2,500 "fighting men." John Stewart to William Dunlop, April 27, 1690, *South Carolina Genealogical Society Magazine* 32, no.1 (1931): 30. By way of comparison, the undeniably populous province of Apalachee had approximately 1,920 families (and perhaps a similar number of warriors) and about 9,600 total inhabitants in 1689. Hann, *Apalachee*, 166.

32. Márquez to king, January 25, 1682, AGI SD 226, N. 73.

33. Hann, *Apalachee*, 5–13.

34. Governor Damian de Vega Castro y Pardo to king, August 22, 1639, AGI SD 225, N. 39

35. Governor Francisco de Riano y Gamboa to king, Havana, August 29, 1637, and enclosed testimony in *Quaderno de todas las cartas de los distritos de las cinco Audiencias del año de 1637*, AGI Indiferente 186; Governor Luis de Horruytiner to king, June 24, 1637, AGI SD 225, N. 35; Governor Damián de Vega Castro y Pardo to king, St. Augustine, August 22, 1639, AGI SD 225, N. 39; Order of Governor Luis Horruytiner, November 3, 1638, enclosed in Antonio de Herrera López y Mesa, April 22, 1649, AGI Indiferente 114, N. 23.

36. Royal cédula, Madrid, December 5, 1651, AGI SD 229; Díaz to king, 1675, AGI SD 151; Fred Lamar Pearson Jr., *Spanish-Indian Relations in Florida: A Study of Two Visitas, 1657–1678* (New York: Garland Publishing, 1990), 238. These exchanges then became part of a significant (and perhaps too significant, in the opinion of governors in St. Augustine) trade with Havana. Governor Damian de Vega Castro y Pardo to king, July 9, 1643, AGI SD 225, N. 41; Hann, *Apalachee*, 152; Hann and Bonnie G. McEwan, *The Apalachee Indians and Mission San Luis* (Gainesville: University Press of Florida, 1998), 104, 148–50.

37. Governor Pedro Aranda y Avellaneda to king, November 10, 1688, AGI Escribanía de Cámara 156C, pieza 25.

38. Gregory A. Waselkov, "The Macon Trading House and Early European-Indian Contact in the Colonial Southeast," in *Ocmulgee Archaeology*, edited by David J. Hally, 194; Patricia Galloway, *Choctaw Genesis, 1500–1700* (Lincoln: University of Nebraska Press, 1995), 167.

39. English and French traders adopted this practice for similar reasons. John Lawson, *Lawson's History of North Carolina* (1714; Richmond VA: Garrett and Massie, 1951), 25; Antoine Simon Le Page du Pratz, *The History of Louisiana, or of the Western Parts of Virginia and Carolina: Containing a Description of the Countries that Lie on Both Sides of the River Mississippi: With an Account of the Settlements, Inhabitants, Soil, Climate, and Products*, ed. and trans. Joseph G. Tregle Jr. (1774; Baton Rouge: Louisiana State University Press, 1975), 312.

40. Andrés González de Barcia Carballido y Zúñiga, *Barcia's Choronological History of the Continent of Florida*, trans. Anthony Kerrigan (Gainesville: University of Florida Press, 1951), 362. For another earlier example, see Fr. Juan Mercado to Antonio Matheos, Santa Cruz, "today Sunday," enclosed in Autos sobre la entrada, AGI SD 839.

41. Regarding religious persecution, Franciscan attempts to eradicate the ball game, a competition involving displays of physical and spiritual power that is a distant ancestor of modern lacrosse, were particularly intense. Hann, *Apalachee*, 22–23, 88–91, 160–80.

42. Shaftesbury to Woodward, May 23, 1674, in *Shaftesbury Papers*, ed. Cheves, 440–41; Woodward, "Faithfull relation," 130–34; Governor Pablo Hita Salazar to king, June 8, 1675, AGI SD 839; Lords Proprietors, Order concerning the Trade with the Westoes and Cussatoes

Indians, April 10, 1677, in William J. Rivers, *A Sketch of the History of South Carolina*, (1856; Spartanburg SC: Reprint Company, 1972), 388–90.

43. Worth, *Struggle for the Georgia Coast*, 17; Proprietors to governor and deputies, September 30, 1683, *Calendar of State Papers*, ed. Fortescue, 509. Diseases and the Westos' recent war with Carolina's new Indian allies certainly took their tolls, but later Chickasaw and Yamasee population figures make clear that even a decade of raiding was enough to cut raiders' male populations by as much as half. Yamasees inhabiting coastal South Carolina saw their population of 800 warriors decline by half between 1704 and 1712, and the Chickasaws lost some 800 fighting men (an estimated 40 percent of their fighting-age population, according to the French governor of Louisiana, Pierre Le Moyne d'Iberville) during the decade before 1703. Francis Le Jau, *The Carolina Chronicle of Francis Le Jau*, ed. Frank J. Klingberg (Berkeley: University of California Press, 1956), 132; George C. H. Kernion, trans., "Documents Concerning the History of the Indians of the Eastern Region of Louisiana," *Louisiana Historical Quarterly* 8 (1925): 37; Richebourg Gaillard McWilliams, ed. and trans., *Iberville's Gulf Journals* (University AL: University of Alabama Press, 1981), 171–74; Jean Baptiste Bernard de la Harpe, *Historical Journal of the Settlement of the French in Louisiana.*, trans. Virginia Koenig and Joan Cain, ed. Glenn R. Conrad (Lafayette: University of Southwestern Louisiana, 1971), 59.

44. Governor Pablo Hita Salazar to king, June 8, 1675, AGI SD 839.

45. Hahn, *Invention*, 30–39, provides an excellent summary of Apalachicolas' ambivalent relations with Spaniards in 1675–1685.

46. Bowne, *Westo Indians*, 99–100. Quote from Márquez to king, January 25, 1682, AGI SD 226, N. 73.

47. Márquez to king, March 19, 1686, AGI SD 839. Spanish governors usually interpreted visits from friendly Indian leaders as the "rendering of obedience." John E. Worth, *The Timucuan Chiefdoms of Spanish Florida*, vol. 1, *Assimilation* (Gainesville: University Press of Florida), 36.

48. Hann, *Apalachee*, 47–49; Bishop Ebelino de Compostela to king, Havana, September 28, 1689, AGI SD 151.

49. Worth, *Timucuan Chiefdoms*, 1:33–43, 135–43.

50. Perhaps the best evidence of this shift comes from the Tallapoosa valley, a region that Apalachicolas would have supplied with these same trade goods. Where only 27 percent of burial sites included burial goods during AD 1400–1550, some 65 percent of burials included goods of some kind during AD 1600–1715. Cameron B. Wesson, "Creek and Pre-Creek Revisited," in *The Archaeology of Traditions: Agency and History before Columbus*, edited by Timothy R. Pauketat (Gainesville: University Press of Florida, 2001), 103. See also Vernon James Knight Jr., *Tukabatchee: Investigations at an Historic Creek Town*, 1984, Report of Investigations, no. 45 (Moundville: University of Alabama Office of Archaeological Research, 1985), 175–77.

51. For an excerpt of Barrera's quote, see Hahn, *Invention*, 39. When Barrera suggested the governor make concessions on labor drafts, he was acknowledging the power of commoners to shape the political decisions of their micos and La Florida's governor. And Apalachicola commoners had much to lose from the arrival of missionaries since, as John Worth has noted in his study of Timucua's missions, labor demands applied only to commoners. Not surprisingly, commoners in the missions were the sources of most low-level discontent. It is worth noting, for instance, that few chiefs fled the missions even as many followers did. In 1700, one Spanish official came upon numerous scattered hamlets [*rancherías*]—communities without ceremonial grounds and thus without political and religious leaders—that had been occupied by runaways from the missions "for many years." Juan de Ayala Escobar, relación de méritos, Madrid, December 7, 1702, AGI Indiferente 136, N. 55.

52. Amy Turner Bushnell, *Situado and Sabana: Spain's Support System for the Presidio and Mission Provinces of Florida*, American Museum of Natural History Anthropological Papers, no. 74 (Athens: University of Georgia Press, 1994), 148–60, 181–89; Gallay, *Indian Slave Trade*, 48–68.

53. For overviews of Yamasee history, see William Green, Chester B. DePratter, and Bobby Southerlin, "The Yamasee in South Carolina: Native American Adaptation and Interaction along the Carolina Frontier," in *Another's Country: Archaeological and Historical Perspectives on Cultural Interactions in the Southern Colonies*, ed. by J. W. Joseph and Martha Zierden (Tuscaloosa: University of Alabama Press, 2002); Worth, "Yamasee," in *Southeast*, ed. by Raymond D. Fogelson, *Handbook of North American Indians*, vol. 14, gen. ed. William Sturtevant (Washington DC: Smithsonian Institution, 2004).

54. Worth, *Struggle for the Georgia Coast*, 21–24.

55. On the Yamasees' and Scots' attacks, see Gallay, *Indian Slave Trade*, 84–86. On the Yamasees' reunion in Port Royal, see Caleb Westbrooke to Lord Cardross[?], St. Helena, February 21, 1685, in *Records in the British Public Records Office Relating to South Carolina, 1663–1710*, transcribed by William Noel Sainsbury, 5 vols. (Columbia: Historical Commission of South Carolina, 1928–1947) 2:8 (hereafter abbreviated as *BPROSC*, followed by the volume number); Governor Diego Quiroga y Losada to king, May 8, 1691, AGI SD 227B, N. 77; Quiroga y Losada to king, April 18, 1692, AGI SD 227B, N. 93.

56. George C. H. Kernion, trans., "Documents Concerning the History of the Indians of the Eastern Region of Louisiana," *Louisiana Historical Quarterly* 8 (1925): 37. The French tally of 1,400 Yamasee men is undated, but probably comes from 1702. The total population was probably three times the number of men. I base this calculation on a 1715 English census of the Yamasees that listed 413 men, 345 women, and 462 children. Governor Robert Johnson to Board of Trade, Charlestown, January 12, 1720, Transcripts of Records in the British Public Records Office Relating to South Carolina, 36 vols., 7:237–38, South Carolina Department of Archives and History, Columbia, South Carolina.

57. Lords Proprietors to Governor and Council, Whitehall, March 7, 1681, *BPROSC* 1:117. On the Scots' sudden ambitions for an inland trade, see George Pratt Insh, ed., "Cardross and William Dunlop to Peter Colleton, March 27, 1685," *Scottish Historical Review* 25 (1928): 104.

58. Manuel Serrano y Sanz, ed., *Documentos históricos de la Florida y la Luisiana, siglos XVI al XVIII* (Madrid: Librería General Victoriano Suárez, 1913), 195.

59. Insh, ed., "Cardross and Dunlop to Colleton, March 27, 1685," 104.

60. Testimony of Nicolás, December 29, 1685, enclosed Autos sobre la entrada, AGI SD 839.

61. Antonio Matheos to Márquez, Casista, September 21, 1685, enclosed in Autos sobre la entrada, AGI SD 839. On the cacique's approximate age, see Declaration of the cacique of Apalachicola, San Luís, November 5, 1685, enclosed in Autos sobre la entrada, AGI SD 839.

62. Matheos to Márquez, San Luís, October 4, 1685, enclosed in Autos sobre la entrada, AGI SD 839.

63. Matheos to Márquez, Caveta, January 12, 1686, enclosed in Autos sobre la entrada, AGI SD 839.

64. Matheos to Márquez, San Luís, February 8, 1686, enclosed in Autos sobre la entrada, AGI SD 839.

65. Soldiers more experienced and less headstrong than Matheos believed Apalachicola

ambivalence and neutrality was part of a consistent policy. Domingo de Leturiondo to Márquez, San Pedro de Potohiriba, November 28, 1685, enclosed in Autos sobre la entrada, AGI SD 839.

66. Matheos to Márquez, San Luís, March 14, 1686, enclosed in Autos sobre la entrada, AGI SD 839.

67. There is some evidence that suggests that Apalachicola conflict with the English may have continued as late as 1688. In 1693, officials in Spain cited letters from Governor Quiroga y Losada dated February 24, and April 1, 1688, as evidence that the English and their Indian allies had "at different times and occasions made prisoners of some Christian and pagan Indians of the Guale and Yamasee languages in the province of Guale and also slaves of those of Apalachicola, taking them prisoner and carrying them to Charles Town." Given the Apalachicolas' ability to mislead the Spanish, such reports should be treated with caution, but the fact that the Apalachicolas are not included among those attacking these Christians and non-Christians is at least suggestive of their rocky relationship with the English. Council of State to King, Madrid, August 18, 1693, Estado 3968, Archivo de Simancas, Simancas, Spain.

68. Matheos to Márquez, San Luis, May 21, 1686, enclosed in Márquez to king, May 29, 1686, AGI SD 839.

69. Angelo to Governor Diego Quiroga y Losada, Apalachicola Fort, May 24, 1690, enclosed in Quiroga y Losada to king, June 8, 1690, AGI SD 227B, N. 68.

70. Matheos to Márquez, May 21, 1686, enclosed in Márquez to king, May 29, 1686, AGI SD 839.

71. John H. Hann, "St. Augustine's Fallout from the Yamasee War," *Florida Historical Quarterly* 68, no.2 (1989): 189, notes the Yamasees' Hitchiti linguistic roots. These ties may have encouraged the town of Apalachicola to move to within fifty miles of the Yamasees' coastal settlements. On the later location of Apalachicola town, see below.

72. In 1703 when Carolinians heard rumors of a Spanish and French attack against the Apalachicolas, officials in Charles Town expected that their fearful allies would seek protection among their Yamasee friends. Much later, when the two peoples began fighting each other after 1717, one Apalachicola raid was foiled by an Apalachicola warrior warning his Yamasee wife and family, who promptly spread the alarm to the remaining Apalachicolas and Yamasees in the town. A. S. Salley, ed., *Journal of the Commons House of Assembly of South Carolina for 1703* (Columbia: State Company for the Historical Commission of South Carolina, 1934), 95–97; John Barnwell to Governor Robert Johnson, n.p., n.d., BPRO 8: 1–10, South Carolina Department of Archives and History, hereafter cited as SCDAH.

73. Governor James Colleton to Governor Diego Quiroga y Losada, Charles Town, April 1, 1688, AGI SD 839.

74. Hahn has demonstrated that Coweta and Cusseta likely moved east a year ahead of the others, but there is conflicting evidence regarding the timing of the events and whether any towns remained along the Chattahoochee River. Spanish efforts to repopulate the valley make me believe that Apalachicolas abandoned it entirely. Angelo to Quiroga y Losada, May 24, 1690, enclosed in Quiroga y Losada to king, June 8, 1690, AGI SD 227B, N. 68; Auto, September 18, 1691, enclosed in Governor Diego de Quiroga y Losada to king, April 10, 1692, AGI SD 227B, N. 89; Hahn, *Invention*, 49–50; Hann, "Late Seventeenth-Century Forebears of the Lower Creeks and Seminoles," *Southeastern Archaeology* 16, no.1 (1996): 77; Worth, "Lower Creeks," 279.

Although there is no mention of the Apalachicola town's new location until 1708, they must have been neighbors for some time because in 1712 Carolinian officials considered the two peoples politically and geographically close enough to merit a single colonial trade agent. Governor Nathaniel Johnson, et al., to Board of Trade, Charlestown September 17, 1708, BPROSC 5: 203–9; William L. McDowell Jr., ed., *Journal of the Commissioners of the Indian Trade, September 20, 1710–August 29, 1718* (Columbia: South Carolina Department of Archives and History, 1955), 29; Johnson to Board of Trade, January 12, 1720, BPRO 7:237–38, SCDAH.

75. Anonymous [John Barnwell] untitled map of Southeast, [1721–1727], Map Division, Library of Congress, Washington, DC; Herman Moll, untitled map of Southeast, [1712? 1717?], Map Division, Library of Congress; Salley, ed., *Journal of the Commons House of Assembly of South Carolina for 1702* (Columbia: State Company for the Historical Commission of South Carolina, 1934), 6; Salley, ed., *Journal . . . for 1703*, 95–97.

76. Assembly to Governor Seth Sothell, Charles Town, 1691[?], in Rivers, *Sketch of the History of South Carolina*, 424.

77. Mark F. Boyd, ed. and trans., "The Expedition of Marcos Delgado from Apalache to the Upper Creek Country in 1686," *Florida Historical Quarterly* 16, no. 1 (1937): 16.

78. For mention of Atasis' and Tukabatchees' contacts with the Apalachicola towns of Coweta and Cusseta, see Matheos to Márquez, San Luís, February 8, 1686, enclosed in Márquez to king, March 20, 1686, AGI SD 839. Although he wrote centuries later, Creek writer and historian Charles Gibson suggested the depth, and potentially the age, of the connection between the town of Tukabatchee and the Apalachicola town of Coweta when he wrote, "It is taught to the young people from the cradle, as it were, to keep this friendship sacred. These two towns never oppose each other in anything." Charles Gibson, "Creek Towns: Interesting Article on Creek Customs," Eufala (Indian Territory) *Journal*, November 22, 1901, 7.

79. "Tiquipache" was one of the towns that Apalachees attacked in the fall of 1694 to avenge the Apalachicolas' sacking of San Carlos earlier that year. "Adaste" appears among the Ocmulgee River towns in an English map from the 1710s. English maps and Spanish documents also note the continuing existence of both towns on the Tallapoosa. Moll, Map of Southeast, [1712? 1717?] Maps Division, Library of Congress; Torres y Ayala to king, St. Augustine, March 11, 1695, AGI SD 840; Declaration of Pedro Manuel Cavello, November 30, 1707, enclosed in Sebastian de Moscoso to Duque de Albuquerque, Santa María de Galve, February 10, 1708, AGI Mexico 633.

80. Vernon J. Knight Jr., and Sherée L. Adams, "A Voyage to the Mobile and Tomeh in 1700, with Notes on the Interior of Alabama," *Ethnohistory* 28, no. 2 (1981): 181, 191.

81. Boyd, "Expedition of Marcos Delgado," 27; Gallay, *Indian Slave Trade*, 82–84; Hahn, *Invention*, 49–51.

82. Auto of September 18, 1691, enclosed in Governor Diego Quiroga y Losada to king, April 10, 1692, AGI SD 227B, N. 89; Governor Diego Torres y Ayala to Governor of Carolina, August 5, 1695, enclosed in Torres y Ayala to king, March 11, 1695, AGI SD 840; Torres y Ayala to Governor of Carolina, March 3, 1695, enclosed in idem.

83. In responding to the Carolina governor's complaints that the Apalachees' counterattack cost him roughly 800 pesos in trade goods, Governor Torres y Ayala responded that the losses from the two missions, including gold and silver chalices, church bells, and other ornamentation, amounted to more than 8,000 pesos in value. Torres y Ayala exaggerated his losses probably by a factor of two to four, but even with these more modest losses, Apalachicola raiders had inflicted a serious financial blow in addition to a humanitarian one. Torres y Ayala to Governor of Carolina, March 3, 1695, AGI SD 840. My estimate of the actual value of the mission materials is based on Hann, *Apalachee*, 212–17.

84. Junta de Guerra, St. Augustine, November 3, 1694, enclosed in Governor Laureano Torres y Ayala to king, March 3, 1695, AGI SD 840.

85. Of the Apalachees' thirteen towns, five had populations of 1,000 or more. Bishop Diego Ebelino de Compostela to king, Havana, September 28, 1689, AGI SD 151.

86. Apalachee power may help explain Apalachicola ferocity. Hahn points out that Apalachicola attacks following their move to the Oconee valley probably owed much to their desire for "revenge" against the Christians, as one missionary put it. I agree, but it is instructive to remember that slave raiders' reputed savagery also owed much to their fears of losing too many of their own warriors. Bloodthirsty reputations that cowed defenders could save many raiders' lives. Hahn, *Invention*, 54–55; Fr. Jacinto de Barreda to Governor Diego Quiroga y Losada, April 28, 1692, enclosed in Quiroga y Losada to king, April 30, 1692, AGI SD 227B, N. 97.

87. Kelton, "Southeastern Smallpox Epidemic."

88. Don Patricio Hinachuba to Alferez Don Antonio Ponce de León, Ivitachuco, April 10, 1699, enclosed in Ponce de León to king, Havana, January 29, 1702, AGI SD 864.

89. Don Juan de Ayala to Governor Joseph de Zúñiga y Cerda, San Luís, February 22, 1701[?],AGI SD 858; Zúñiga y Cerda to king, September 30, 1702, AGI SD 858. Hahn contends that these killings were in response to Spaniards' ill treatment of Hafuluque, an *inija* or second-in-command, of Apalachicola town, who had helped broker recent Apalachicola-Apalachee accords. The document he cites, however, describes how Hafuluque was "taken captive in a skirmish [*refriega*]" of Chacatos against Apalachicolas and Yamasees in 1701. If my reading is correct, it suggests that Hafuluque did not consider Chacatos to be part of the recent peace and/or that Apalachicolas and Apalachees knew few firm boundaries between peace and war at the turn of the eighteenth century. Hahn, *Invention*, 58–60.

90. Salley, ed., *Journal . . . for 1702*, 64.

91. Zúñiga y Cerda to king, September 30, 1702, AGI SD 840; *Testimonio de autos sobre el sitio que tenia puesto ala C[iuda]d y Presidio dela florida el Gov.or de San Jorge Ingles con los Yndios y naz.es Ynfieles*, March 27, 1703, AGI SD 840; Francisco Romo de Uriza to Zúñiga y Cerda, San Luís, October 22, 1702, AGI SD 858; Zúñiga y Cerda to Governor of Havana, September 1, 1702, AGI SD 858.

92. Salley, ed. *Journal . . . for 1703*, 121.

93. Salley, ed. *Journal . . . for 1702*, 6; *Journal . . . for 1703*, 95–97.

94. Mark F. Boyd, trans. and ed., with Hale G. Smith and John W. Griffin, *Here They Once Stood: The Tragic End of the Apalachee Missions* (Gainesville: University of Florida Press, 1951), 48–49, 92.

95. Hann, *Apalachee*, 264–83; Gallay, *Indian Slave Trade*, 144–49; Manuel Solana to Andrés de Arriola, San Marcos, June 10, 1704, AGI Mexico 618.

96. A census from 1708 listed 250 men. Seven years later, another census counted 275 men and 638 men, women, and children. Johnson, et al., to Board of Trade, September 17, 1708, BPRO 5: 208; Johnson to Board of Trade, January 12, 1720, BPRO 7: 237–38; Governor Francisco Córcoles y Martínez to king, November 30, 1706, AGI SD 841. Regarding Carolinian fears, see April 26, 1704, Transcripts of the Journal of the Commons House of Assembly, transcribed by John S. Green, 5 vols., 2:232, SCDAH.

97. Gallay believes the Apalachees relocated under duress. Given the presence of Apalachee warriors in the second Apalachicola attack on Apalachee in the summer of 1704, Apalachees and Apalachicolas likely shared a hatred of the Spanish mission system. Gallay, *Indian Slave Trade*, 148–49.

98. Salley, ed. Journal . . . for 1702, 21; October 11, 1710, Transcripts of the . . . Assembly, trans. Green, 3:475, SCDAH.

99. Eric Hinderaker, "The Four 'Indian Kings' and the Imaginative Construction of the First British Empire," William and Mary Quarterly, 3rd series, 53, no. 3 (1996): 487–526; Gallay, Indian Slave Trade, 209–10.

100. For a brief overview of the debt into which native traders sank, see Richard L. Haan, "The 'Trade Do's Not Flourish as Formerly': The Ecological Origins of the Yamasee War of 1715," Ethnohistory 28, no.4 (1982): 342–43. For a persuasive new interpretation of the origins and meaning of the war, see William L. Ramsey, "'Something Cloudy in Their Looks': The Origins of the Yamasee War Reconsidered," Journal of American History 90, no. 1 (2003): 1–68.

101. Although Hahn and I disagree somewhat on the primacy of political or cultural factors and the relationships of leaders and followers, we agree that the war was pivotal to Creeks' coalescence. Hahn, Invention, 8, 81–120; Hall, "Making an Indian People," chapters 4–6.

5. Apalachee Testimony in Florida
A View of Slavery from the Spanish Archives
Jennifer Baszile

I.

In 1675 a harrowing tale made its way into the Spanish colonial record. A Chisca woman was "taken prisoner by the Chichimecas" (the Spanish name for the much-feared Westos), "who took her and sold her for a shot gun in the English town on the coast called St. George [Charles Town]." Remarkably, the woman escaped and returned to her community, in modern-day southern Georgia, where she supplied her chief with invaluable intelligence while describing her capture and escape. She had observed "English in the village of the Chichimecas . . . teaching them to use firearms." The purported goal of the training was to attack St. Augustine and destroy "the Christian Indians of the provinces of Timucria [sic] and Apalachee."[1]

The chief of the Chiscas related the story to Lieutenant Esteban de Lua, who sent a written summary to his commander, Captain Juan Fernandez de Florencia.[2] Fernandez immediately dispatched Adjutant Andres Descuedo to St. Augustine to share the news with Florida governor Pablo de Hita y Salazar. On May 26, 1675, Descuedo took a solemn oath to tell the truth and presented the facts as he understood them to the governor. A scribe recorded his statement.[3]

Because the report passed through numerous hands, it is impossible to know how faithfully the final statement represents the impressions of the Chisca captive or her chief. As the woman's account circulated through the ascending channels of Florida's colonial bureaucracy, she and her chief faded from view. By the time Descuedo appeared in St. Augustine, the most basic identifying information about the woman and her chief, their names, village and respective ages, had been lost. Whether she was a single captive or part of a larger group taken from her community, the precise circumstances lay beyond the purview of the document. The woman's explanation of her own experience, the chief's prior interactions with the captors, and more broadly, the Chiscas' perspectives and definitions of slavery do not come through with much clarity in this document about enslavement.

In both substance and form, the account provides an emerging narrative of Indian slavery in the early South. The woman's experience confirms a raid-trade model, perfected by the Chichimecos. The final report also accords prominence to the influence of Carolina traders and the threat posed to Spanish interests. In this narrative, the voices of Indians are muted at best, and even the most astute scholars have struggled to characterize Indians as something other than casualties of slavery's overwhelming institutional force or hapless pawns of dominant European powers.[4] Historians have emphasized the role of Indian slavery in the rise and decline of imperial powers and the growth of English plantations. Drawing on a rich body of evidence offered by colonists, missionaries, and bureaucrats, scholars have examined these vital themes and gleaned many valuable insights from their exploration.[5] The primary agency accorded to market forces has left little room within which to interpret the spectrum of indigenous experiences with slavery. It also has made it difficult to explain how and why members of some groups became enslavers while others became enslaved.

Between 1670 and 1717, fifteen to thirty thousand people, or at least half of the total number of native slaves sold through Carolina hailed from the territory that the Spanish called La Florida.[6] The colony was, in fact, an intricate patchwork of indigenous villages of shifting rivalries and alliances. Many communities maintained military and economic ties to the Spanish government at St. Augustine. Most of these inhabitants, especially those north and west of St. Augustine, practiced Catholicism, or participated in at least some of its rituals. For centuries the Apalachee had been the most powerful indigenous people in this area of the South—first as a great chiefdom, then, after Spanish arrival, as allies of the Europeans. But suddenly, in the last third of the seventeenth century, Apalachee power rapidly declined.

The warriors and caciques (chiefs) charted slavery's alarming transformation in painstaking detail that endures in the colonial record. By virtue of their religious education, alliances with the Spanish, linguistic facility, and knowledge of colonial bureaucracy, Apalachee leaders were among the most sophisticated commentators in the entire written record of early Southern slavery. They appear frequently and present themselves in a far less mediated manner than most other native people in the early American literature. This exceptional cadre of leaders, and the remarkable body of sources that they generated, provides useful perspectives on slavery that are undeniably elite but far from homogenous.

A series of attacks and raids in the 1670s reveal how quickly competing practices of slavery evolved during a period of intensifying colonial and indigenous conflict. This volatile period forced the Apalachees to develop their own perspectives on slavery that differed markedly from the Spanish and the English, as well as the growing number of native communities who traded captives for guns.

The men—and less often women—of Apalachee possessed a clear set of interests that they struggled to protect amid the shifting and competing currents of slavery. This was the case in 1678, when four leaders of an Apalachee war party described their assault on communities who had enslaved their neighbors: they primarily understood slave raiding as a highly adaptable weapon of warfare. For these Apalachees, the process of enslavement rather than the eventual sale of slaves was the subject of most intense interest. They devoted particular attention to the dynamics of raids: their location and nature, tactics and timing, and the identification and affiliation of the attackers.

Apalachee leaders understood that people captured in raids could be exploited in any one of several slave systems controlled by Indian traders,

Spanish colonists, or English planters, but they focused most on the Indian attackers. The Spanish system of native bondage remained a grave concern but one that could be resolved through diplomacy. The English figured obliquely, if at all, in Apalachee descriptions; they rarely were perceived as the main architects or agents of slavery's growing threat, perhaps from ignorance of what would happen to the victims after their sale to the Carolinians. The primary goal of Apalachee chiefs was to reduce the vulnerability of their communities to attack from native raiders.

II.

Unlike the Chisca woman and her chief, who figured obliquely in the slavery records, four Apalachee men dominated the written account of raiding in their province for two decades. Juan Mendoza, Matheo Chuba, Don Bernardo Ynachuba, and Bentura ranked among the most powerful people in the province of Apalachee. They were religious leaders, administrators, and warriors who maintained close ties to Spanish officials. They helped create one of the most detailed accounts of slave raiding that exists in the annals of the early South. All four men lived in the vicinity of San Luis de Talimali, the largest Catholic Indian community in the colony, which consisted of 1,400 inhabitants. San Luis was also the site of a Spanish garrison.[7]

Even within the circles of indigenous leadership, Juan Mendoza possessed unique experiences and skills that undoubtedly shaped the tone and substance of the testimony that he and the others offered about the rise of slave raiding. He was literate, spoke Spanish, and served as the parish interpreter for San Luis. A prominent indigenous leader, Mendoza's native title has been difficult to fix precisely.[8] In the powerful and prestigious capacity as parish interpreter, Mendoza functioned as the main intermediary between the indigenous laity and Franciscan missionaries.[9] In addition to his religious prominence, Mendoza also held a Spanish military rank, captain of the infantry.

In 1675 Mendoza helped prepare a document that has become known simply as "the ball game manuscript." A full-contact sport in which village-centered teams of young men competed for honor and prestige, pelota aroused the ire of Catholic officials concerned about its immoral and idolatrous dimensions. In response, Mendoza and another interpreter interviewed community elders about its origins, detailed its rich symbolic and cultural significance in Indian life, and described the conventions of play.[10] Mendoza not only supervised the translation and recording of people's comments, he helped write the final document that became the basis of a crusade to end the game. As a result, Mendoza gained intimate knowledge of the process through which "colonial documents" were generated. He also acquired a firm grasp of the means by which the transfer of spoken words to written text could shape policy and outcomes well beyond the immediate context—for he witnessed how his own information gathering and dissemination shaped Spanish action.

The experiences, ranks, and positions of the other three leaders also had established them as vital Apalachee spokesmen and Spanish allies. Matheo Chuba was a field master (*maestro de campo*) from San Luis, who was literate and fluent in Spanish. Bentura was the *inija*, or second-highest-ranking authority in San Luis, who administered matters in daily village life.[11] Bernardo Ynachuba was the principal cacique of San Damian de Cupyaca, located one league from San Luis.[12] Thus all of the men were well versed in Spanish-Apalachee diplomacy and the conventions of testimony.

The four men had proven themselves as essential military allies to the Spanish. In mid-July 1675 they led a contingent of Apalachee warriors to suppress an uprising of new converts, in which a Franciscan priest named Rodrigo claimed insurgents attempted to kill him. The Apalachee forces, along with a handful of Spanish soldiers commanded by Captain Fernandez de Florencia, arrived at the Chacato towns of San Carlos de Yacatini and San Nicolás de Tolentino, located about twenty-five miles west-northwest of the Apalachicola River, where approximately one hundred Chacatos lived at San Nicolás, and 140 people lived in San Carlos.[13] The Apalachee warriors provided security throughout the four-month Spanish investigation of the incident and facilitated the punishment of the leaders.[14]

The investigation hinged on the volatile and sensitive questions of sexuality, faith, and honor. The mastermind of the plot, Juan Diosale, attempted the assassination of the Franciscan Barrera because the priest had berated him for his failure to attend mass and insisted that he renounce three of his four wives.[15] He also had close kin and political ties to several Chisca communities who disliked the Spanish.[16] The other leading insurgent had maintained an adulterous affair with a Catholic Apalachee woman who had abandoned her husband and resented Barrera's public rebuke as well as his insistence that the woman return to her husband.[17]

During the investigation, many conspirators explained that their participation had been coerced by the threat of Chisca retaliation and sought leniency.[18] The Apalachee warriors and Spanish investigators concluded that the Chiscas' hostility to the Spanish and their status as non-Christians made them the fomenters of the plot.[19] As punishment the Spanish banished the Chacato leader with closest ties to the Chiscas.[20] They sentenced three other leaders to one-year terms of "personal service without pay" and subsequent terms of compensated, but forced, labor.[21] With the consent of Apalachee leaders, the Spanish settled the remnants of these communities among the people of San Luis. Ynachuba, Juan Mendoza, Bentura, and Matheo Chuba soon learned just how high a price they would have to pay for helping punish the Chacato leaders through servitude.

III.

In the aftermath of the Apalachee's punishment of the Chacatos, Don Bernardo Ynachuba, Juan Mendoza, Bentura, and Matheo Chuba tracked a disturbing new trend. They noticed a spike in the frequency and nature of slave-raiding assaults on their communities. "Everyday they bothered us," the men explained "and we were without peace."[22] The incessant attacks, the constant menace, "and the jeers that they [the raiders] made while leaving" reflected the tacit state of war in which these men believed they existed. "They killed our relatives, and what is more disturbing is the slaves they carried away," they further explained. They perceived a rough equivalence between physical death by murder and social death through slavery.[23]

To encourage Spanish support, Ynachuba, Juan Mendoza, Bentura, and Matheo Chuba tied the assaults to the two most potent symbols of colonial power, commerce and conversion, which compelled Spanish officials to consider the problem. The fact that so many raids took place "on the royal roads" was a claim the men must have known would concern the officials. As the main route of travel connecting the *doctrineros* or mission villages of Apalachee to the neighboring province of Timucua and to the colonial capitol of St. Augustine, Mendoza and the other men anticipated that the Spanish would have to act to protect this artery. In a colony that teetered on the brink of insolvency, criminal activity on the roads indicated unstable and vulnerable relations with the Apalachees, the most numerous and important Spanish allies in Florida. As the bulk of the colonial workforce, moreover, the Apalachees cultivated many of the crops that sustained the Spanish soldiers and Franciscan missionaries, and so were vital to Spanish survival in Florida. As the cornerstone of the continued Spanish presence, the support of the Christian Apalachees, who were also royal subjects, obligated officials to act. The fact that the men claimed that the Chiscas "attacked Christians" and killed Apalachees could not easily be ignored.

Ynachuba, Juan Mendoza, Bentura, and Matheo Chuba also noticed the ways in which the raids departed from the prevailing conventions of Apalachee warfare. They complained that raiders "took as slaves, men women and children." Previously, noncombatant women and children, the most frequent war captives, most often were adopted by their captors or lived as bound servants.[24] Until the 1670s, captives who lived among warriors were not treated as chattel or traded to other groups, and only rarely were they ransomed. Their day-to-day productive activities differed little from those of free women and children. A captive exchange in the midst of peace negotiations could end their servitude. The capture of women, though more customary in indigenous warfare, placed the matrilineal kinship system of the Apalachees and the matrilocal nature of village organization under enormous pressure. In productive terms, the absence of women also increased the burden on the remaining members of the community for the labor mobilizations so central to Spanish-Indian relations.[25]

After 1675, the more frequent capture and bondage of men marked a departure from the conventions of indigenous warfare. Male warriors usually faced death in battle. On the rare occasions when they were taken prisoner, men were tortured and eventually killed. They could demonstrate bravery and maintain their honor in defeat by making professions of their faith, chanting, or remaining stoic. For the people of Apalachee, men consigned to bound labor existed in a particularly wretched state. They regarded a surviving male captive as the equivalent of a woman or a child. As in the Chacato case of 1675, the Apalachees viewed bound servitude as a severe punishment for non-Christian enemy leaders. A form of humiliation, they considered servitude a punishment worse than death because men lived without honor and in their toil faced a consistent reminder of their degradation and defeat. Given the increased frequency with which the raids occurred, the structures of leadership that descended from eldest maternal uncle to eldest nephew faced increasing threat.[26]

Another problem emerged in the midst of this crisis that further destabilized the Apalachees: they could not definitively identify which group perpetrated the raids. Not knowing if they were Chiscas or Chichimecos proved an impediment to action. At the council house of San Luis, a thatch-roofed structure large enough to accommodate two thousand people, prominent warriors and high-ranking men assembled to formulate a response to the attacks.[27] War councils functioned on the basis of consensus, and the assent of all participants was required before action could be taken. As they summarized the recent attacks, Mendoza, Bentura, and Matheo tried to use the fictive kinship of religion to generate consensus and cooperation, and minimize the problem of the raiders' identification.

When Mendoza, Matheo and Bentura initially "proposed a departure to look for the enemy," perhaps in 1675, they received a very chilly reception from their fellow caciques. The random nature of the raids and their elusive causes made them difficult to predict and nearly impossible to prevent. As much as their fellow leaders demonstrated concern about the attacks and solidarity with Bentura and the other men, the identification of the victims only as "Christians" struck the members of matrilineal communities as curious. The apparent failure to reference the victims' village of origin, kin group, or ethnicity, also left the other leaders with little basis on which to act and the distinct impression that the supporters of immediate retaliation had something to hide. In a world defined by kinship, the lack of specificity or speculation about the perpetrators' clan ties seemed an especially conspicuous evasion that compelled many leaders to reject all calls for immediate action. The need for a clear identification of the perpetrators was the only proposal to which all council participants granted their unanimous approval.

Far more than a matter of ethnic particularity, the caciques' insistence on the definitive identification of the raiders demonstrated a great deal about their notions of slavery. The Chiscas and the Chichimecos represented formidable, but very different opponents whose defeat would require distinct strategies. The difference between the Chiscas and the Chichimecos was the difference between an isolated and specific threat versus and an endemic and generalized one.[28]

All Apalachee leaders understood the ominous nature of the threat posed by the Chichimecos. These architects of the raid-and-trade model were at the height of their power in the South and had devastated the island and mainland communities along the Atlantic coast south beyond St. Augustine and well north of Charles Town. Alleged cannibals and fierce warriors who possessed more firearms and ammunition than nearly any other community, Chichimecos had a culture that centered on the capture and trade of slaves.[29] The most systematic and powerful slavers in the area, the Chichimecos had also formed an alliance with the English. If the Chichimecos were responsible for the attacks on the Apalachees, a coordinated, multi-province retaliation would be required to stem the tide of their assaults. If the Apalachees attacked the Chichimecos in error, they then would have provoked another cycle of raids that could have annihilated their communities. Without this vital information, the caciques refused to act.

The attacks shifted again in 1677, when the as-yet-unidentified raiders fell on three villages in the winter and spring. The people of Chachaui, a satellite settlement of Chine Indians located within the jurisdiction of San Luis, suffered the first in a series of predawn assaults. Bernardo Ynachuba and his kinsmen in San Damian de Cupayaca, located one league from San Luis, suffered the second assault. Then the raiders attacked San Lorenzo de Hiutachuco, a 1,200-person community a short distance away. Although the shocked residents of Chachaui and San Damian defended themselves as best they could, only the people of San Lorenzo gave chase to their attackers. In the process, they managed to identify the perpetrators as Chiscas.[30] Still, everyone spent the winter and part of the next spring plagued by "many alarms and surprise attacks."[31]

Once the Chiscas were identified and the particular nature of the threat came into full view, the tone of council discussions shifted. Many leading warriors concluded that the Chiscas retaliated because their Chacato kinsmen had been shamed as well as dishonored by their sentences of forced labor. The other leaders present at the council concluded that the Chiscas punished the warriors who facilitated the insurgents' shame in terms that they saw as equivalent: murder and enslavement. Slave raiding no longer seemed like an indiscriminate threat. The Chisca raids also suggested to leaders whose communities had not yet been attacked that they might make themselves more vulnerable to raids by supporting Bentura and the other advocates of military action. If they participated, then their communities would foreclose the possibility of compromise with the Chiscas to prevent their exposure to raiding.

As a result, many caciques refused to participate in the counterstrike but did not denounce the measure in any subsequent council. Rather than debate the matter further, the caciques who were dubious of retaliating articulated their ambivalence in their lack of material contribution to the expedition. Only two men from Ayubale, a town of 800 people, joined the force. Similarly, of the more than 700 people of "Tomole," only three warriors participated. Like many other skeptical leaders, neither of the village caciques participated nor offered explanations for their absence.[32]

As soon as Don Bernardo, Juan Mendoza, Bentura and Matheo Chuba obtained the council's permission for the attack, they sought the approval of Captain Juan Fernandez de Florencia. They asked him to sanction the assault and grant them a license to travel. According to Spanish custom, *doctrina* Indians had to notify Spanish officials about any extensive travel planned beyond their communities. Fernandez granted the license and promised his moral support, but he did not send any Spanish soldiers to accompany the force.[33]

The size and strength of the war party demonstrated the serious reservations that many communities had about the wisdom of the counter-raid in particular, and the most effective response to slave raiding in general. From a network of villages whose population neared 10,000 people, Bernardo and the others could rouse only 190 fighters. Eighty-five men came from San Luis along with ten Chacato men who had settled among them. Don Bernardo led seventy from San Damian. Eight Chines from another of the San Luis client villages also participated.

Most of the warriors went to battle armed with hardwood bows strung with animal skin or intestine, and arrows made of cane with points of animal teeth or wood.[34] Thirty men possessed firearms—fifteen from San Luis and fifteen from San Damian. They received a supply of ammunition from Fernandez de Florencia and a small boat.[35]

Although many leaders did not find the rhetoric of Christian family compelling, the appeal to Christian brotherhood remained powerful for the warriors who participated. Gathered at the San Luis council house on September 2, 1677 the assembled warriors were encouraged to "behave as unified brothers."[36] On the ten-day journey to the Chisca palisade, the men rallied around Catholic rituals and symbols. Two days after they left San Luis, while encamped near a river, the leaders exhorted the warriors. "They were men defending their lands, women, and children," Bentura and the others explained, and their pursuit of the Chiscas was "the will of God and his Holy Mother."[37] Praying on the trail to the Chisca village, they also marched under a banner bearing "a cross" and "Our Lady of the Rosary."[38] In addition to a military honor, the warriors understood death in combat as a form of martyrdom. One warrior claimed "a strong desire to die for God."[39]

In a predawn raid that maximized the element of surprise, the Apalachee war party employed the same strategy used by the Chiscas. They planned to demoralize the Chiscas and prevent subsequent attacks. For as much as the Apalachees decried their enslavement at the hands of the Chiscas, they also understood the practice as a useful strategy by which to express their dominance over their enemies. Although Chuba and the others did not explain whether they hoped to adopt, torture, and kill, or sell the captives into chattel slavery, members of the war party "wanted to catch them [the Chiscas] and take them alive."[40]

Bentura, Mendoza, Matheo Chuba, and the warriors claimed that their effort to punish the Chiscas received divine sanction. A fire ignited spontaneously, swept through the village, and sent "men and women with their infants on their chests" running to a nearby river. "Many were almost dead."[41] After three days at the Chisca village, the Apalachees "set fire to all that remained," and they departed with their injured and prisoners.[42] Although this group of Chiscas did not again disturb the Apalachees, slave raids remained a persistent problem and the formulation of subsequent response proved more difficult.

In 1678, nineteen years after the Chichimecos first arrived in the Southeast, slavery maintained several meanings. Although Benutra, Mendoza, Chuba, and Bernardo defined slavery as a form of persecution of Christians and rallied warriors in the name of Catholic brotherhood, many of their fellow caciques rejected their explanation for the attacks as well as the obligation for coordinated action. Slavery was neither a blunt instrument of indiscriminate religious persecution, as the war leaders argued, nor yet a tool of dependency.[43] Instead slavery was a carefully directed insult and an instrument of revenge meant to convey the outrage of an aggrieved people.

When Don Bernardo Ynachuba, Juan Mendoza, Bentura, and Matheo Chuba complained about the growing threat of slave raiding, they knew how to make their case and had the credibility to command Spanish attention. Their eyewitness testimony fills more than twenty folios and was introduced by Florida governor Pablo de Hita y Salazar and concluded by public notary and scribe Alonso Solana. The resulting report, which totals more than thirty folios, is as unusual as the four men who stood at its center. Although they appear in the report as leaders of a counterstrike designed to prevent further raids, the men brought the full scope of their experience to bear on the creation of the report.

The men spoke "in their own language" and allowed their words to be translated by an interpreter.[44] Perhaps to underscore status as commanders of a war party, influenced by their Catholicism but governed by the conventions of native warfare, they decided not to speak in Spanish, even though three men could do so. Their bilingual facility also enabled them to ensure the faithful rendition of their comments. It also gave them an advantage over Juan Fernandez de Florencia, the provincial commander to whom they presented themselves, and who only spoke Spanish. By virtue of their literacy, therefore, the three men also possessed the skill to verify the accuracy of the resulting narrative, an unusual degree of power in these circumstances that made their testimony less vulnerable to unwitting distortion or manipulation.[45]

The final report transcended the time and place of its creation. As it circulated though ascending channels of the massive Spanish bureaucracy, the four men's testimony commanded attention and shaped all subsequent discussion. The choice of their words and the tone of their account would take on greater significance with each review until it reached the Council of the Indies.

As illustrated here, direct testimony and transparent testimony were very different matters. Bernardo, Matheo, Juan, and Bentura were men with a clear point of view who wanted their narrative to become the dominant one that defined the threat of slavery and the terms in which Spanish officials in St. Augustine and Spain would understand it. These Apalachee leaders understood that the justification for their actions was as important as their ultimate success against the Chiscas. As attuned as the four men were to colonial culture, they understood that greater Spanish military support was unlikely. But their painstaking recollection of slavery would help bolster their credibility among Spanish officials and encourage the closer heeding of their advice in not just this matter, but more generally.

IV.

If slavery remained only a question of warfare and foreign relations in the aftermath of the Chisca offensive, then Apalachee leaders would have faced a daunting but clearly defined challenge: to find a military or diplomatic means by which to prevent raids on their communities. In subsequent years, changing Spanish practices that bore a striking resemblance to slavery forced the Apalachees to further expand their understanding of bondage. Letters and accounts offered during inspections, and sworn statements offered between 1678 and 1701, suggest that the Apalachees defined slavery not as a single threat perpetrated by one community, but a collection of practices deployed by a growing number of communities advanced at their expense.

Because Spanish customary and legal prohibitions against the enslavement of Indians supposedly made the condition of Indian slavery impossible within the empire, the same Apalachee leaders who chronicled the rise of native slave raiding painstakingly described their labor exploitation at the hands of the Spanish—a practice they struggled to label as slavery. Apalachee leaders averred that their physical abuse, involuntary detention, lack of input over work assignments, and uncompensated work, amounted to a condition of effective enslavement and degradation at the hands of the Spanish. The external threat of capture and enslavement, and their desperation to remain free undoubtedly sharpened Apalachee concern about any conditions that resembled slavery.

The physical coercion of Apalachees, including caciques, increased after the raids. Spanish officials placed Matheo Chuba in irons after he protested soldiers' exploitation of his people. Then Matheo Chuba and Bentura were berated in public and beaten with a walnut club. When another cacique did not present the wife of a low-ranking officer with fish on a Friday, he received "two slaps in the face."[46] A newly converted leader from La Tama was forced "to prepare skins for them without pay for his work." He abandoned the province and went to "the place of Saint George" and presumably to English alliance.[47] High-ranking men protested their dishonorable treatment, and thus publicly questioned the state of their alliances with the Spanish.

Conditions that looked even more like slavery affected other village men at the same time. The *repartimiento de indios* was a draft labor system by which indigenous men who lacked high rank or military distinction performed mandatory and compensated work in the Spanish public interest. Census information, along with input from priests and caciques, helped determine the number of men available for the draft. The laborers set out from their villages accompanied by interpreters, a military escort, and in-digenous leaders to perform the work. Spanish officials alone determined the wage, or *jornal*, which was set at one real per day. In the 1680s laborers maintained the royal roads and engaged in construction as often as they hauled goods between the provinces and served individual officers. At least in theory, village leaders and Spanish officials negotiated the terms and timing of the service, but leaders decried a system riddled with abuse.[48]

The reconstruction of the Castillo de San Marcos, the main fort in St. Augustine, exposed the men of Apalachee to a range of servile labor arrangements and enabled them to compare their assignments with those of other laborers. They served alongside Spanish workers, English pris-oners, rebellious Indians punished with forced labor, and African slaves. The nature and the extent of their compensation became a matter of close attention. *Repartimiento* laborers on the fort construction project received a ration of corn, but the allotment declined from three pounds of corn per day in 1671 to two pounds per day by 1684 and remained at that low level for the next three years.[49] Indian peons received a quarter of the pay granted to Spanish peons, who performed the same work. Usually Indians received their compensation in foodstuffs, knives, beads, blankets, and axes, but officials inflated the value of trade goods to disadvantage the laborers.[50]

The *repartimiento* often led to effective slavery. Spanish officials demanded that laborers work "without paying them a wage."[51] After Apalachee men finished their *repartimiento* service in St. Augustine, "the governor and other officials detain[ed]" grown men "in the fort so they [might] serve them."[52] Illiterate and less powerful men than Mendoza and the others, these ordinary men had few avenues by which to protest their exploitation and detention. Many Apalachee men stopped returning to St. Augustine and disappeared from their communities so as to avoid *repartimiento*. Don Patricio Hinahuba, the cacique of Ivitachuco, "the great-est of all the caciques of the Province of Apalachee," complained that this exploitation drove Indian men to "to leave their women and children and abandon the law of God."[53] Don Patricio offered the information to warn of frayed Indian community ties as well as the military and economic threat to the Spanish colonial system.[54]

The wives of these men, left behind in Apalachee, used the forum of the *visita*, or inspection, to echo Hinachuba's concern and protest the abuse of their husbands and their abandonment. The hardship created by the men's absence became so acute that it was among the top concerns expressed in the *visita* of 1694 by commoners and leaders alike.[55] By 1695 a list of twenty-nine married men missing from their home villages included thirteen men who remained at the presidio and Castillo de San Marcos in St. Augustine.[56] Tomas, for example, a native of a small village called Escaui, had toiled in the quarry for three years and had not been allowed to return home. Another four married men traveled with Spanish officials and two others served individual Spanish colonists.[57]

The *sabana* system became another route to effective enslavement. It began as a mechanism by which men and women cultivated fields for leaders and also tended a communal plot to maintain the community's reserves. The men and women who performed the work received no compensation, but it was not originally perceived as a weighty obligation. It had become another source of pressure on Catholic Indian labor. Each April, as men dug a trench, women followed behind sowing corn seeds for community use.[58] So many men remained in St. Augustine that the *sabana* system became increasingly onerous, as laborers cultivated fields "as alms for missionaries and needy widows." They also planted wheat in October and harvested it in June.[59] For some Apalachee men in St. Augustine, *sabana* labor had become a full-time occupation and a form of coerced labor. A permanent force of Indians, "who usually attend to the cultivating of the lands of the residents of the Post," worked in perpetuity and required the assignment of missionaries and translators to minister to them.[60]

Another pattern of detention also emerged in Apalachee that indigenous leaders found equally disturbing. Don Patricio complained that Spanish colonists forced male "youths" to work on the ranches of colonial officials and prevented them from returning home despite the appeals of village leaders and missionaries. Don Patricio couched his objection in moral terms and explained that this work interrupted religious education and prevented them from "learning prayers or hearing Mass."[61]

Women like Chuguta Francisca of Candelaria served Spanish

officials "against their will." Chuguta cooked meals on a Florencia ranch without ever receiving compensation of any kind.[62] Even less fortunate still were the families of three unidentified women, including one described as "old." Marcos Delgado took the women by force, without the permission of the cacique or other village leaders, gave no explanation for their detention, and kept them "under his control."[63] Don Patricio alleged that six other Apalachee women had ground corn for a Spanish woman "everyday without payment for their work."[64] Five years later, Don Patricio described a situation largely unchanged in which the detention of women on ranches was another affront that made the inhabitants of Apalachee "most unhappy."[65]

V.

Rather than a single practice whose outlines were sharply delineated and agreed upon by all involved, what scholars call Indian slavery was an amalgam of conventions and practices that southern people combined in terrifying new ways. Consensus about the nature of slavery was elusive and the term "slavery" used selectively. As a practice, slavery existed in the netherworld between institutional definition and the shifting conventions of warfare that came to incorporate more and more market considerations.

On the subject of slave raiding, Don Bernardo, Juan Mendoza, Bentura, and Matheo Chuba spoke with a voice that could not be ignored, and their frequent presence in the records reflects their unabridged familiarity with Spanish-Apalachee diplomacy and their comprehension of the nature of testimony. They presented a seamless and internally consistent narrative of recent events. Their perspective did not represent the entire leadership of Apalachee, however, and the conflicts that they tried to minimize still emerged in the documents.

During the next two decades, the people of Apalachee appeared frequently in the colonial record. They protested their subjection at the hands of Spanish officials and private citizens, and a growing number of practices that bore a striking resemblance to slavery. Their testimonies and appeals reveal an often overlooked but important process unfolding in the life and culture of these people. The leaders of Apalachee and their people developed unique definitions of slavery and servility that diverged from those of their indigenous enemies who traded with the English, as well as from their Spanish allies and the English. For Mendoza and other Apalachees, bondage was a form of punishment properly reserved for outsiders and enemies, but slaves were not commodities who could be sold. An instrument of warfare that conveyed the shame and dishonor of defeat to the captive, and triumph and victory to the captor, slavery maintained its place in Apalachee life and culture. Juan Mendoza, Matheo Chuba, Don Bernardo Ynachuba, and Bentura found themselves and their people treated by the Spanish in ways that bore a striking resemblance to slavery. Constrained by a growing number of servile relations at home, they appealed for the redress of their grievances even as they struggled to name the practices. Their experience highlights the fact that the proliferation of unfree labor forms associated with slavery generated divergent rather than shared meanings.[66]

Notes

1. Declaration included in a collection of letters sent by Pablo de Hita y Salazar to the king, St. Augustine, June 15, 1675, Archivo General de Indias (AGI) Santo Domingo (SD) 226. An English translation of the declaration has been published. Katherine Reding, ed. and trans., "Plans for the Colonization and Defense of Apalachee, 1675," *Georgia Historical Quarterly*, 9(1925): 174–75.

2. For the ethnographic description of the Chiscas and the ambiguities in the 1670s, see John R. Swanton, *Early History of the Creek Indians and Their Neighbors* (1922; repr. with a foreword by Jerald T. Milanich, Gainesville: University Press of Florida, 1998), 286–311. I disagree with Swanton that the Chiscas and the Chichimecos were the same people. See below.

3. Reding, "Plans for the Colonization and Defense," 174–75.

4. In the Florida literature, slave raiding has been understood primarily as an assault on the mission system and the strength of the Spanish presence. Paul E. Hoffman, *Florida's Frontiers* (Bloomington: University of Indiana Press, 2002), 145–49.

5. Alan Gallay, *The Indian Slave Trade: The Rise of the English Empire in the American South, 1670–1717* (New Haven: Yale University Press, 2002), 6–8; Joel Martin, "Southeastern Indians and the English Trade in Skins and Slaves," in *The Forgotten Centuries: Indians and Europeans in the American South 1521–1704*, Charles Hudson and Carmen Chaves Tesser, eds. (Athens: University of Georgia Press, 1994), 308; Theda Perdue, *Slavery and the Evolution of Cherokee Society* (Knoxville: University of Tennessee Press, 1979), xi, xii, 19–35; Kathryn Holland Braund, "The Creek Indians, Blacks, and Slavery," *Journal of Southern History* 57, no. 4 (1991), 605; Verner Crane, *The Southern Frontier, 1670–1732* (Ann Arbor: University of Michigan Press, 1929), 7–11. On the role of Indian slavery in the Spanish decline, see Mark F. Boyd, Hale G. Smith, John W. Griffin, eds. and trans., *Here They Once Stood: The Tragic End of the Apalachee Missions* (Gainesville: University of Florida Press, 1951), ix–xi, 1–20; John H. Hann, *Apalachee:*

The Land Between Two Rivers (Gainesville: University of Florida Press, 1988), 227–36, 264–83; John E. Worth, *The Struggle for the Georgia Coast: An Eighteenth-Century Spanish Retrospective on Guale and Mocama*, American Museum of Natural History, *Anthropological Papers* 75 (Athens: University of Georgia Press, 1995). For a similar interpretation to the one presented here, see Brett Rushforth, "'A Little Flesh We Offer You': The Origins of Indian Slavery in New France," *William and Mary Quarterly* 60, no. 4 (2004), 777–808.

6. Gallay, *Indian Slave Trade*, 299.

7. Lucy Wenhold, ed. and trans., "A Seventeenth-Century Letter of Gabriel Diaz Vara Calderon, Bishop of Cuba, Describing the Indians and Indian Missions of Florida," *Smithsonian Miscellaneous Collections* 95, no. 16 (1936), 8.

8. Amy Turner Bushnell and John Hann disagree about the meaning of the title "holahta" used in the ball-game manuscript and other later documents. Amy Turner Bushnell, "'That Demonic Game': The Campaign to Stop Indian Pelota Playing in Spanish Florida 1675–1684," *Americas* 35, no. 1 (1978), 9–10 and Hann, *Apalachee*, 108–10.

9. Hann, *Apalachee*, 107.

10. Bushnell, "'That Demonic Game'," 1–19.

11. At the time of the attack, he did not possess a Spanish military title, but he acquired one later.

12. Pablo de Hita y Salazar to the king, Saint Augustin, November 10, 1678, AGI SD 226 r. 3. n. 41 fol. 00013.

13. Captain Juan Fernandez de Florencia, July 15, 1675, San Luis de Apalachee, AGI SD 839, fol. 234v.

14. Captain Juan Fernandez de Florencia, July 15, 1675, San Luis de Apalachee, AGI SD 839, fols. 132–33. Father Rodrigo de la Barrera y Quintanilla was a "robust" twenty-eight-year-old Franciscan with a mole on his cheek. Barrera was born at the town of Lora, in the Archdiocese of Seville in about 1644. "*El Padre Rodrigo de la Barrera y Quintanilla sazerdote de veinte y ocho años robusto Lunar en el carillo.*" AGI *Contratacíon*, 5544 r. 1, n 3. He left his assignment at the friary of San Francisco de Constantina and arrived in Seville on June 23, 1673. Maynard Geiger, *Biographical Dictionary of the Franciscans in Spanish Florida and Cuba, 1528–1841* (Paterson NJ: St. Anthony Guild Press, 1940), 32.

15. John H. Hann, "Political Leadership among the Natives of Spanish Florida," *Florida Historical Quarterly* 71 (1992) 188–208. John Hann defines *chacal* as "[a]n Indian official, at times identical with inija, but not always, who served as a sort of overseer directing community work." Hann, *Apalachee*, 401.

16. Rodrigo de la Barrera to Andres Peres, July 1675, San Carlos, AGI Escribanía de Cámara (EC) 156A fol. 122r.

17. The trouble had begun with Luis Ubabesa, a prominent warrior from San Nicolás who, though not baptized, was receiving religious instruction. He slept with a married Apalachee woman who was a Catholic. She then left her husband to live with Ubabesa. The woman's husband, a practicing Catholic, complained to Barrera who intervened. "*Que el dho Ubabefa se acosto una noche con una Yndia casada.*" "Autos sobre el tumulto de los Chacattos, Año 1675," AGI EC, 156A, fol. 131v. Barrera publicly berated Ubabesa and his mistress in church on a feast day and promised to punish them.

18. "*Autos sobre el tumulto*" AGI EC 156A fol. 131v, 133v.

19. "*Autos sobre el tumulto*" AGI EC 156A ff. 122–23.

20. "*Autos sobre el tumulto*" AGI EC 156A fol. 132–33.

21. "*Autos sobre el tumulto*" AGI EC 156A fol. 135.

22. "Report Which the Principal Leaders Who Went to Make War on the Chiscas, Who Are Juan Mendoza, Mateo Chuba, Bernardo, the Cacique of Cupayuca, and Bentura, the Inija of San Luis, Made in the Presence of Captain Juan Fernandez de Florencia and Concerning How the War Waged against the Chiscas Originated," in Pablo de Hita y Salazar to the king, St. Augustine, November 10, 1678, SD 226 r. 3. n. 41 fol. 00010. Although not used for this essay, an English translation of the report exists in Swanton, Early History of the Creek Indians, 299–304. In the notes of the document, Swanton conceded, "There is evidently something lacking or the published version is poorly copied from the original."

23. Orlando Patterson, Slavery and Social Death: A Comparative Study (Cambridge: Harvard University Press, 1982).

24. Braund, "The Creek Indians, Blacks, and Slavery," 602.

25. For an outstanding discussion of slavery's disruptive effect on matrilineal African communities, see Patrick Manning, Slavery and African Life: Occidental, Oriental and African Slave Trades (Cambridge: Cambridge University Press, 1990), 118–19.

26. Hann, Apalachee, 70, 103–4. Nearly forty years of protest by Franciscan missionaries had not disrupted this pattern in Apalachee. For the matrilineal nature of southern Indian communities see Braund, "The Creek Indians, Blacks, and Slavery," 604.

27. For a physical description of the San Luis council houses, see Wenhold, "Seventeenth-Century Letter," and Hann, Apalachee, 38–39.

28. The Chiscas are also known as Yuchis. Some commentators have argued that the Chichimecos were related, and perhaps even the same people. The context of this document suggests that Apalachee leaders made a very clear distinction between the two groups.

29. Worth, Struggle for the Georgia Coast, 16–18.

30. Hita y Salazar to the king, AGI SD 226 r. 3 n. 41, 0009.

31. Hita y Salazar to the king, AGI SD 226 r. 3 n. 41, 00010.

32. AGI SD 839 fol. 234, and Relacion, SD 226A r, 41, n. 3 00012.

33. Relacion, AGI SD 226 A r. 41, n. 3, 00011.

34. Barbara A. Purdy, "Weapons, Strategies, and Tactics of the Europeans and the Indians in Sixteenth- and Seventeenth-Century Florida," Florida Historical Quarterly (1972), 263–64.

35. Relacion, 00011–00012

36. Relacion, 00013

37. Relacion, 00014.

38. Relacion, 00026.

39. Relacion, 00015–00016.

40. Relacion, 00025–00026.

41. Relacion, 00028

42. Relacion, 00031.

43. Richard White, The Roots of Dependency: Subsistence, Environment, and Social Change Among the Choctaws, Pawnees, and Navajos (Lincoln: University of Nebraska Press, 1988), 69–96; White first made this persuasive and subtle argument for the eighteenth-century Choctaws. On the opportunities and challenges of dependency theory for the Florida-Carolina case, see Martin, "Southeastern Indians," 304–5.

44. "Report which the Principal Leaders," November 10, 1678, SD 226 r. 3. n. 41 fol. 00033.

45. For the myriad problems with the mediated nature of indigenous testimony in the colonial record, see Nancy Shoemaker," An Alliance between Men: Gender Metaphors in Eighteenth-Century American Indian Diplomacy East of the Mississippi," Ethnohistory 46,

no. 2 (1999), 240; Daniel K. Richter, *Facing East from Indian Country: A Native History of Early America* (Cambridge: Harvard University Press, 2002), 8–15.

46. Don Patricio, Cacique of Ivitachuco to the king. February 12, 1699, in *Here They Once Stood*, 25.

47. Don Patricio, Cacique of Ivitachuco to the king. February 12, 1699, in *Here They Once Stood*, 25.

48. David J. Weber, *The Spanish Frontier in North America* (New Haven: Yale University Press, 1992), 126, 129; Hann, *Apalachee*, 116–17. Bushnell, *Situado and Sabana: Spain's Support System for the Presidio and Mission Province of Florida*, American Museum of Natural History Anthropological Papers, (Washington DC: American Museum of Natural History 1994), 121–23.

49. Bushnell, *Situado and Sabana*, 139.

50. Bushnell, *Situado and Sabana*, 121–23; 139.

51. Moral, quoted in Hann, *Apalachee*, 141.

52. Moral, quoted in Hann, *Apalachee*, 141.

53. Boyd, et al., *Here They Once Stood*, 28; Amy Bushnell, "Patricio De Hinachuba: Defender of The Word of God, The Crown of the King and the Little Children of Ivitachuco," *American Indian Culture and Research Journal* 3 no. 3 (1979), 1–21.

54. Boyd, et. al., *Here They Once Stood*, 28; Amy Bushnell, "Patricio De Hinachuba," 1–21.

55. Visita to San Pedro y San Pablo de Patali 29 November 1694 in Florencia, AGI SD 157A.

56. Besita General de Apalahcee and Timucua, Salamototo, 3 January 1695 f. 108 r-v.

57. Besita General de Apalahcee and Timucua, Salamototo, 3 January 1695, f. 108 r.

58. Wenhold, "Seventeenth-Century Letter," 13.

59. Wenhold, "Seventeenth-Century Letter," 13.

60. Vara Calderon, 8; Bushnell, *Situado and Sabana*, 111.

61. Vara Calderon, 8; Bushnell, *Situado and Sabana*, 111.

62. Besita General de Apalache and Timucua, AGI EC 157 A.

63. Besita General de Apalache and Timucua, AGI EC 157 A.

64. Besita General de Apalache and Timucua, AGI EC 157 A, 25.

65. Boyd, et al., *Here They Once Stood*, 27.

66. Although she does not discuss slavery at great length, Shoemaker does argue for the emergence of shared meanings for Native and European peoples. Nancy Shoemaker, *Strange Likeness: Becoming Red and White in Eighteenth-Century North America* (New York: Oxford University Press, 2004).

6. Indian Slavery in Southeastern Indian and British Societies, 1670–1730
Denise I. Bossy

On a stormy January day in 1707, Lamhatty stumbled into a colonial settlement on the Mattaponi River in eastern Virginia. Wrists badly swollen with
rope burns, Lamhatty wept with relief at reaching the end of his ordeal.
Captured and enslaved, Lamhatty had been traded from master to master
until making a harrowing escape that took nine days. Lamhatty was a
runaway slave. An Indian runaway slave. His sudden arrival surprised and
alarmed the local colonists and once more his wrists were bound in rope
(and later chained in iron). His captors delivered him to Colonel John
Walker who tried to reconstruct the slave's narrative through two interpreters: one a Tuscarora Indian, and later Robert Beverley, a Virginia elite
who studied and wrote about American Indians. Neither spoke Lamhatty's
language. Unfortunately for Lamhatty, salvation was not to be found on
the Walker estate. After initially allowing Lamhatty his liberty, the Colonel
kept Lamhatty as a slave in his own household.[1]

Lamhatty had run away from an Indian rather than an English
master. A Towasa Indian from La Florida, Lamhatty was taken in one of the
Lower Creek raids that ultimately destroyed his nation.[2] The Lower Creeks
enslaved Lamhatty for both political and economic reasons. Lower Creeks,
particularly Ochese Creeks, attacked Indian communities in the greater
Florida region during the late seventeenth and early eighteenth centuries,
enslaving thousands.[3] The Lower Creeks targeted Indians allied with the

Spanish (in retaliation for Spanish attacks and intrusions), encouraged by English colonists in Virginia and South Carolina who wanted to purchase Indian slaves and similarly undermine the Spanish by enslaving their allies. Lamhatty's Lower Creek captors took him eastward during his nine-month captivity, eventually trading him to Savannah Indians who regularly sold their captives at the British slave markets in Charlestown.

Though the idea of Indian slavery may strike us as remarkable, Indian slaves were in fact commonplace in southeastern Indian and colonial communities during the eighteenth century. Lamhatty was by no means the only Indian slave in the Mattaponi settlement.[4] Lower Creeks (and Walker) enslaved Lamhatty at the very height of the colonial Indian slave trade in the Southeast: an uneasy partnership between select Indian communities and colonial traders motivated by their mutual desire for economic exchange. Indians wanted English products, particularly guns, cloth, and alcohol, and English wanted Indian goods, particularly slaves and pelts.[5] Indians and English captured and sold tens of thousands of Indians to colonial slave traders. Charlestown was the center of this trade; from there Indian slaves were sold throughout the British colonies, particularly to Virginia and the West Indies but also farther north to New England and New York.[6] While the majority of Indians were exported, a significant number remained in South Carolina itself where Indians comprised an estimated tenth to a quarter of the slave population before the Yamasee War (1715–1717).[7] When Lamhatty discovered that "some of his Country folks" (other Towasa Indians) were in bondage, he sank into a depression. At springtime he again ran away, still searching for his freedom.

The Indian slave trade was founded on European traditions of purchasing bound labor and Indian traditions of taking war captives.[8] Both English and Indians profited from the sale of Indian bodies and the subsequent reduction of their enemies. Both immersed themselves in the slave trade and used it to fuel their economies and promote their geopolitical power.[9]

But the mutual accord that the English and Indians reached as slavers does not mean that they viewed slavery in identical ways. While the English and Indians shared the custom of dehumanizing their slaves, they had very different motivations for enslavement.[10] Britons viewed slaves as property and their primary reason for enslaving others was economic. Though they drew on the idea of "just war" to validate enslavement, in fact the people they enslaved were rarely enemies taken in war.[11] During the seventeenth century, Britons increasingly articulated ethnocentric ideas, an embryonic racism, to rationalize the enslavement of those non-European slaves they purchased. Southeastern Indians, on the other hand, tradition-ally viewed their enemies as potential slaves. For Indians, enslaving others was predominantly motivated by a need to avenge the death or capture of a clan member rather than a need for economic laborers. By taking captives, southeastern Indians sought to restore cosmological and social balance, maintain population levels, and undermine the strength of adversaries.

The Indian slave trade represented a brief period in which Eng-lish and Indian economic and political motives collided more than they enmeshed. The trade ballooned during the late seventeenth and early eigh-teenth centuries, and Indian communities began to form confederacies to shield themselves from slave raids and wars. But even as they responded to changing political dynamics, southeastern Indians became indebted to colonial traders. When some traders began to enslave the kin and captives of their Indian trading partners to recoup their debts, the limits of this cross-cultural trade became all too clear. Southeastern Indians responded to colonial affronts with war, bringing the Indian slave trade, but not Indian enslavement, to its end. In the wake of the war, both Indians and British continued to enslave Indians for political reasons, not economic ones. While slavery was also of cosmological and social importance for Indian clans, for the British it was simply part of their colonial strategy. Examin-ing Indian slavery before and after the Yamasee War sheds light on these two different systems of slavery and on the political importance of Indian enslavement in the colonial southeast.

Lamhatty came from an Indian world in which captivity and slavery were common experiences with precolonial antecedents. Throughout the na-tive Southeast, clans and communities had long taken captives in raids and wars. These wars often assumed a cyclical nature, as clans retaliated in kind for the killing or capture of kin. This cycle was hard to break once initiated and could lead to long years of raids and wars.

English who spent much time in native communities often remarked on the profound attachment southeastern Indians expressed for their loved ones and the extensive ritualized mourning (and preparations for vengeance when necessary) that followed death. John Lawson, who traded and traveled among the Indians of the Carolinas, and published a book about them in 1709, was struck by the emotional depth that Indian peoples openly exhibited. They did not lament the loss of things; such misfortunes generally were laughed off. However, the loss of a kin or friend was met with a "deep Mourning" that lasted a long time depending on the "Dignity" of the deceased and the number of his/her relations.[12] Trader and South Carolina Indian agent Thomas Nairne observed that the Chickasaws also had elaborate mourning rituals, particularly if death had come at the hands of an enemy. For a kin member killed in war, the mourning process was not complete until "some person of that nation who killed him, be brought to suffer in reveng [sic]."[13] Just as the Iroquois based much of their warring on revenge and kin replacement—"requickening"—southeastern Indians based many of their battles on the principle of "crying blood."[14] Lawson explained: "The Indians ground their Wars on Enmity, not on Interest, as the Europeans do; for the Loss of the meanest Person in the Nation, they will go to War and lay all at Stake."[15]

The immediate family bore the responsibility, under the lead of their matriarch, to initiate revenge, and it was the clan's duty to exact proper satisfaction for the killing of any kin, male or female.[16] In Creek communities, families who did not seek revenge were denigrated. An anonymous traveler noted: "In Cases of Murder, the next in Blood is obliged to kill the Murderer, or else he is looked on as infamous in the Nation where he lives."[17] The belief in Cherokee communities that the spirit of those killed by foes could not rest until their death was avenged obliged kin to seek crying blood.[18] Not only did the clan and town expect it, but so did the enemy. According to anthropologist Robbie Ethridge, the "law of blood revenge" was "the basic principle of international law among the southeastern Indians."[19]

Women played a considerable, often pivotal role in initiating or preventing war parties. They "determined the fate of war captives" based on the clan's psychological and social needs as well as the captives' age, gender, and personality. Women actively participated in the torture of those they judged should be sacrificed.[20] Revenge restored social and cosmological balance, but it did not always lead to the death of a captive. Clan matriarchs often decided to replace their dead kin through the incorporation of a captive who literally assumed the role of the departed.

While revenge served an essential psychological and social function for southeastern Indian communities, there were also practical and cultural reasons for taking captives. The seventeenth-century Southeast was a world of towns.[21] During the fifteenth and sixteenth centuries most of the chiefdoms that dominated the southeastern geopolitical landscape had separated into towns and villages.[22] As settlements dispersed they tended to shift from settled agriculture to a more diversified economy based on hunting and agriculture. Indian communities became smaller in size and more locally oriented, and as the importance of individuals grew, so did captive taking. Labor production became predominantly subsistence-oriented, increasing the significance of a single warrior or planter to the community's economic and social survival. The loss of a single person had huge implications for a small town, leaving not only a physical but also a social vacuum that had to be filled through either retributive murder or the incorporation of an adopted captive or a slave. When crying blood had been quenched and when the clan needed to incorporate an outsider, a captive or a slave might be adopted to "augment the size of clans decimated by famine, war, disease, or low birthrate."[23]

At the center of Native communities, social balance was achieved through the balance of opposites: "men's versus women's work, Conjurers versus women, young versus old," and slave versus kin.[24] In these kin-based societies slaves were marked by the absence of clan identities, and their presence also reinforced the centrality of clan membership to social identity. They may also have reinforced the importance of political relationships across town and clan lines. Communities at peace sent beloved men to live in each other's towns where they served as ambassadors. The

Cherokees, for example, had "beloved men appointed by . . . nations with whom they are at peace."[25] Perhaps slaves were made of enemy captives as a counterbalance. These slaves were a constant, living reminder of the enmity that existed between two communities.[26]

Communities that lost members to captivity mourned the loss as though it was death, both physically and socially. Extra-tribal murder and enslavement were in fact twinned in Indian societies. Both represented social death and required revenge to reorder society. For living captives to rejoin their families, a ritualized rebirth was necessary. After losing their social identity through captivity, a captive had to be ceremonially reintegrated into their natal community. In 1708 Thomas Nairne described the purification ceremony practiced by southeastern Indians for clan members who had been "kept Long by an enemy." Surrounded by their weeping kin, a redeemed captive was carried around a fire four times, sprinkled with ashes, and washed in the river. The redeemed ate alone, took "phisick" for four days, and then was washed and oiled again before reentering society. "All this purification is because in their Esteem, he is rison from the dead, and come to life again, for as soon as any person is taken, they Account him dead, and call killing and being taken prisoner by the same name."[27] According to Alexander Long, a trader among the Cherokees, warriors also purified their "slaves (prisoners)" before bringing them into their towns.[28]

There were three possible ends for native war captives like Lamhatty: sacrifice, adoption into a clan, or enslavement.[29] Enemy warriors were difficult to integrate and often sacrificed in emotionally purging ceremonies for the community.[30] Once Europeans proved eager to purchase male captives, many (but not all) were sold rather than sacrificed. While the majority of sacrifice victims were male, the sacrifice of a woman had a particularly powerful symbolic role in Indian societies. Among Iroquoian peoples, including the Cherokees, the murder of a woman was so powerful that a higher penalty might be exacted in revenge.[31] Killing a woman was a way to directly attack a clan—the essential unit of kinship—because southeastern Indians traced their lineage through their mothers. In 1725 Richard Hasford reported that a small Cherokee war party shot, killed, and scalped two "Coosa" women while they tended their cornfields. With these two women died a section of the clan, both the kin connection of their living descendants and their ability to give birth to future children.[32]

If a community (and the matriarch) felt revenge was achieved to satisfy crying blood, then a captive could assume the place of the dead. Most women and children captured in a war or raid were not sacrificed but became slaves or were integrated into their captor's community as kin. Adoption entailed a rebirth: captives received new names and clan identities, and had their old lives erased. They became the brother or daughter lost in a previous war or from disease.[33] By incorporating new people into their clans southeastern communities were able to weather population declines prompted by war or environmental stresses.[34]

Those captives kept as slaves occupied a dangerous and liminal place in Indian towns. Without clan membership they had no status in the social community. Among southeastern Indians, clan membership formed the core of human identity. Without clan identity slaves lived out their days not simply as outsiders but as nonhumans, lacking both individuality and social connections. In Cherokee communities this "absence of kin ties" proved a "liability" for outsiders who might be "killed almost at whim."[35] Creeks often referred to a "slave race"—the Indians among them who were slaves not because of the labor they performed but because they were outsiders lacking both clan and town identity.[36] For incorporation of slaves to occur, clan ties had to be created, transforming slaves into human beings.

In contrast to Atlantic world slavery, where slaves were given an intrinsic economic value based on their potential to earn capital for their owners through their labor, native slavery was not a labor-based system.[37] Native slaves worked, but often to support, rather than enrich, their masters. Creek captives, for example, "did exactly the same work as that performed by Creek women."[38] Native slaves were not bound laborers but social outcasts. In his travels through the Carolina Piedmont, John Lawson observed that Indians did not have anything like a European servant. The same word was used to connote human slaves and domestic animals: "So when an Indian tells you he has got a Slave for you, it may (in general Terms, as they use) be a young Eagle, a Dog, Otter, or any other thing of that Nature, which is obsequiously to depend on the Master for its Sustenance."[39]

This should not be taken to mean that Indian societies did not place great value on human labor. To the contrary, human labor was the only means of production in the native protohistoric and early historic Southeast.[40] In the large chiefdoms that dominated the South until the sixteenth century, the ability to mobilize and control human labor was essential to the maintenance or expansion of power. Slave labor supported chiefly authority through the physical production of material items essential to securing popular support.[41] Chiefs expanded their power by incorporating more people or more lands into their chiefdoms, the two often going hand in hand. It was a desire to increase the population under his control that prompted Powhatan's territorial expansion in late sixteenth-century Virginia.[42] Slavery also served a vital psychological role in chiefdoms. It was a constant reminder of chiefly control over human freedom: "demonstrating to free Indians an alternative, and undesirable, existence as an 'other'."[43]

Though native slaves were not enslaved for economic reasons, there is evidence that they worked with and for their masters and mistresses in a range of activities, some of which these slaves considered debasing. Lamhatty complained that during his months in Tallapoosa his Lower Creek master had forced him to work "in ye Ground."[44] In southeastern Indian communities the work people performed was largely determined by their gender (as well as their age, skills, and interests). Among Creeks and Cherokees, for example, women controlled agriculture. Cherokee and Creek men helped women by preparing the ground for planting and assisting in the bringing in of the harvest. But women were responsible for caring for common cornfields and their family plots.[45] As ethnohistorian Theda Perdue has explained: "A person's job was an aspect of his or her sexuality, a source of economic and political power, and an affirmation of cosmic order and balance."[46]

Lamhatty had been forced to perform "women's work" in the common cornfields of the Tallapoosa Creeks. Lamhatty might have appeared physically to be a male, but as a slave his gender would not have been recognized as a part of his identity. While free Tallapoosa and Towasa men and women performed labor according to their gender, native slaves were not granted this privilege. Working as a woman was tremendously demeaning for Lamhatty. Indian societies did not have a social hierarchy based on gender. But working as a woman violated the reality of Lamhatty's identity as a man. He may also have found agricultural work demeaning because he came from a community in which chiefs still controlled certain laboring classes, including slaves. The "modified paramount chiefdoms" of the Spanish borderlands, though subordinate to the Spanish crown, remained hierarchical communities in which chiefs mobilized labor for tribute and to produce trade goods (in this case corn). The Spanish colonial regime in La Florida reinforced rather than undermined chiefly power and control over precious resources. Both land and labor remained deeply connected to chiefly power. Among the Towasas, labor likely had not only gender connotations but also class associations. Lamhatty's distress at being forced to work in the ground could therefore have been doubly painful.

Lamhatty lived in a world where two kinds of slavery—one native and political, the other Atlantic and economic—coexisted. The Indian slave trade changed what slavery (and trade) could mean to Indian captives and to their Indian captors. Before the advent of the colonial Indian slave trade, native slaves might be adopted by their captors or even returned to their natal communities in time. But in the eighteenth-century Southeast, many Indian slaves were traded to colonial masters who practiced Atlantic world slavery from which redemption was unlikely.[47]

Initially slave trading did not radicalize Indian economies. However, Indian slavers challenged traditions of captivity and slavery by prioritizing trade over community needs. As the slave trade ballooned, an increasing number of Indian people and communities became engrossed in captive taking for trade with colonists. Some Indian communities brought their slaves to Charlestown for sale, but the bulk of the trade was carried on by colonial traders who traveled deep into Indian country to buy war captives. This extensive trade swept across the Southeast, leaving no Indian community untouched; by 1707 all southeastern Indians were either slave raiders or their targets.

Historian Philip Morgan has described South Carolina as "the one British colony in North America in which settlement and black slavery went hand in hand."[48] Unlike Virginia and Barbados where slavery developed into the predominant form of labor over time, South Carolina's proprietors and colonists thought slavery "essential" to economic success from the outset. Many of the colony's first settlers (who began arriving in 1670) were white servants, small planters, and wealthy landowners from Barbados.[49] They carried with them slaves and expectations that plantation agriculture (and slave labor) would form the basis of their wealth in South Carolina.[50] But both timing and circumstance made African slaves (and European servants) much harder to acquire in the southeastern backwaters than in the sugar islands of the Caribbean or tobacco fields of Virginia.

Carolinians' preference for Africans did not preclude their use of Indian slaves. Prospective plantation owners who read John Norris's *Profitable Advice for Rich and Poor* (1712) were advised to capitalize on the Indian slave trade in South Carolina by using a combination of African and Indian slaves. For a small farm, one Indian woman and one African man were ideal, and for a large plantation Norris recommended buying eighteen Indian women, fifteen African men, and three African women.[51] Indian women were cost effective. They were cheaper than Indian men and Africans (male or female); moreover, they were skilled laborers, being the primary agriculturalists in their native communities.[52] Norris was neither the only nor the first English colonist to take advantage of this burgeoning trade in Indian slaves. There was a parallel rise in Indian and African slavery throughout the Americas at large during the late seventeenth century.[53] For instance, in Barbados colonists used Indian as well as African slaves on their sugar plantations.[54]

Many Carolinians continued this practice, purchasing Indian slaves for their plantations; some also actively engaged in the business of buying and selling Indians, investing the profits in their plantations. This symbiotic relationship kept Carolina's economy afloat as colonists struggled to launch a viable plantation crop.[55] South Carolinians usurped the lucrative slave trade that Virginians had established with the powerful Westo Indians in the 1650s.[56] They eagerly bought up Indian slaves for their own plantations or for export.

The southeastern Indian communities who engaged in slave trading did so actively but in response to European colonization and trade. The Westos, for example, moved south from their homelands near Lake Erie in the mid-seventeenth century to escape escalating Iroquois mourning wars. But they also selected their settlement sites first in Virginia and later in South Carolina for trade advantages. The Iroquois League began to target non-League Indians around the Great Lakes in the 1640s. There were two prongs to the League's wars. They were an intensification of traditional mourning wars to replace thousands of Iroquois lost to European epidemic diseases. But they also represented a new phase of economic warfare, as the League Iroquois embarked on campaigns to insert themselves in the European gun trade by stealing beaver pelts and annexing western hunting territories (particularly those occupied by the Hurons and Mahicans).[57] The League turned against the Eries in the 1650s and some of the Eries fled south to Virginia, becoming the Westos. There the Westos rapidly entered into a trade with colonists, exchanging war captives for guns and terrorizing Indians throughout the southeast with their slave raids.[58]

In the early 1660s the Westos moved south once again, this time closer to the new colony of South Carolina, a prime location near Westo slaving territory offering a market free from intertribal competition. Transporting their war captives to Virginia markets was not only laborious but was becoming increasingly dangerous for the Westos. Other native communities had begun to compete with the Westos in the gun-slave trade, impeding Westo access to Virginia markets. In creating trade ties with the newest English colonists in Carolina, Westo slavers hoped to avoid this situation.[59] In fact the Westos had contributed to the rising involvement of southeastern Indian communities in the Indian slave trade. The trade's expansion under Westo auspices meant that fewer Indian communities had a choice about their participation. Refusal to engage in slaving meant they would become targets of the slavers.

The colonial trade transformed the value of Indian slaves and with them the meaning of war for English and Indians. South Carolina's colonists became enmeshed in a succession of slave wars, launching their own wars against select Indian communities for economic and political ends.[60] While Indian enslavement had spiritual, psychological, and cultural importance for Indian communities, enslavement was largely functional for colonists. Colonists adopted the military and political aspects of enslavement but not its social import.

As southeastern Indians increasingly participated in the colonial exchange economy and began to amass significant debts, slave warring became an essential economic activity for warriors. In 1711 when the Commissioners of the Indian Trade informed the Yamasee Indians that the General Assembly had voted to forgive all rum debts: "The Indians answered they were preparing to goe to War and a hunting to pay their debts."[61] Trepped in a seemingly endless cycle of escalating debt, the Yamasees, like most southeastern Indians, intensified their warring and hunting to procure the slaves and skins that colonists coveted. This intensification challenged traditional warring and hunting practices. "Man hunting" largely supplanted revenge warfare.[62]

Slave raiding proved so lucrative in the early eighteenth century that one of the Chickasaw peace chiefs, Fattalamee, violated a sacred and absolute prohibition. As a peace chief Fattalamee was barred from engaging in wartime activities. But "finding that the warriors had the best time of it all, that slave Catching was much more profitable . . . he then turned Warrior too." Slave trading was an innovation with the power to fundamentally change social and political traditions. Some, like Fattalamee's community, resisted the social changes that this economic revolution wrought. There were consequences to Fattalamee's actions; he lost popular support and with it his power: "for this infringing the Constitutions, the people don't regard him as king."[63] By Lamhatty's age, most southeastern Indian warriors engaged in slave warring and trading. Though clans generally still initiated war parties for blood revenge, this was no longer the primary reason for waging war in the early eighteenth century.

With this economic transformation also came a transformation in gender roles. As Indian men interacted with, and learned from, colonial societies in which patriarchy was the basis of social organization, they challenged the gender balance in their own communities. Warriors increasingly sought control over the captives—to trade with their European male partners.[64] Among the Cherokees, for example, warriors undermined women's power to determine when to wage war, as the desire for profits trumped the need for revenge. Also, "war women" and "beloved women," who had proven themselves in battle, had vested privileges to decide the fate of captives. But as male warriors devoted more time to warring, hunting, and trading, they began to wrest control of captives away from women. This led to moments of virtual pageantry in some Cherokee towns, with war women dressing as traders in an effort to lay their hands on captives before warriors.[65]

Fear of enslavement spread through the Southeast, as the desire for access to trade goods led to more and more war parties seeking captives. Not all were destined for export, as the Carolinians kept an increasing number to work alongside the growing numbers of African slaves on Carolina plantations.[66] The lethal combination of enslavement, warfare and disease dramatically reduced the southern Indian population from approximately 199,400 in 1685 to 90,100 in 1715.[67] Surviving Indian communities formed political alliances that made them less vulnerable to enslavement.

By forming or joining confederacies—large decentralized polities comprised of individual towns and groups of towns—communities better shielded themselves from enslavement.[68] Towns within these confederacies became attractive to refugees who had survived the demographic and cultural collapse of their natal societies. The English (as well as the Spanish and French) helped to create the conditions that necessitated confederation and then sponsored the growth of select confederacies, such as the Savannahs, Yamasees, and Creeks.

For Indians the process of confederation was a proactive response to colonial slave raiding and disease, and based on pre-European traditions of social reorganization. The Mississippian chiefdoms that Hernando de Soto and other Spaniards encountered during their sixteenth-century *entradas* had coped with social, political, economic, and/or ecological stresses by either centralizing their populations or scattering their people into small settlements.[69] What some scholars have read as the "decline" of Mississippian chiefdoms was not a complete social collapse but rather a social reorganization.[70] The creation of confederacies was another step in the social reorganization of southeastern communities. Some of the southeastern chiefdoms that devolved into towns and provinces later reconfigured themselves as confederacies, incorporating new peoples in the process. Coweta and Cusseta, two of the most important Lower Creek towns in the eighteenth century, likely originated from a Mississippian town on the Lower Coosa River.[71]

A significant continuity between Coweta and Cusseta and their Mississippian ancestors was that they were expansionist, incorporating and annexing people and land to advance their growth.[72] They also pursed a new economic relationship with the English of Carolina, inviting English traders into their towns in the 1680s. Between 1690 and 1691 Coweta and Cusseta led a migration of Apalachicola peoples to the Ocmulgee River region. The move was fundamental, bringing the Cusseta-Coweta-Apalachicola people closer to the English and facilitating a more regular trade alliance. It was a "patently political act made in a self-conscious attempt" to attract other Indian refugees, thereby stimulating the growth and consolidation of a large and powerful confederacy of towns. The English called them the Ochese Creeks.[73]

Shortly after their relocation to the Ocmulgee region, the Ochese Creeks also began to engage in slave wars for political and economic reasons. From their new towns they raided throughout the region, targeting Spanish mission towns (particularly Apalachee) for slaves. The Ocheses were motivated both by political vengeance and a desire for English trade goods. Their attacks on Spanish mission Indians were partly prompted by the recent Spanish intrusions into Apalachicola, the Spanish burning of four towns in 1684 as punishment for trading with the English, and the erection of a Spanish fort on the Chattahoochee near Coweta. Targeting Indians allied with the Spanish also had economic benefits. The English not only paid handsomely for Indian slaves but particularly wanted the Ochese Creeks to enslave Indians allied with the Spanish to forward their own geopolitical goals in the region.

These were not traditional revenge raids, rather the "scale and ferocity" signaled a change in Ochese Creek warfare.[74] Economics and geopolitics as much as blood revenge now seemed to prompt Creek clans and towns to war and raid. During Queen Anne's War, the English tried to direct two major assaults on St. Augustine and Spanish missions, in 1702 and 1704. In both, Ochese (and Yamasee) warriors outnumbered the British, but these Indian men fought for their own reasons.[75]

While driven by a desire to punish the Spanish and to promote their own geopolitical dominance, the Ochese Creeks also needed to fight for economic reasons. The slave trade decimated many Indian communities and tightly wrapped other communities in debt. While materially enriched by their participation in the slave trade, the Ocheses and other southeastern Indian slave raiders became deeply indebted to the English traders who exchanged cloth, guns, and alcohol for slaves and deerskins. Moreover, Indian material enrichment paled in comparison with the explosive economic expansion of Carolina. For many southeastern Indians, this growing economic discrepancy became a source of deep frustration. They produced the goods that promoted Carolinian wealth, yet it was the British who benefited while they were plunged deeper into debt to often violent and unscrupulous traders.[76]

The Ocheses were not alone in joining British-led or British-sponsored battles to acquire slaves for debt repayment.[77] In 1711 close to 500 Indians (Yamasees as well as Apalachees, Yuchis, Cusabos, and numerous Piedmont-area Indians, including Catawbas) joined John Barnwell's army of thirty colonists on South Carolina's first of two campaigns to aid North Carolina during the Tuscarora War.[78] Slaves and other booty seem to have been the primary motivation for both colonial and Indian warriors alike.[79] With their local deer population on the decline and their hunting lands swallowed up by colonial development, Yamasees fought alongside colonists during both campaigns, taking slaves and booty in a desperate attempt to climb out of debt.[80] Though their remove from colonial settlements protected the Ochese Creeks from this land pinch, their spiraling debt compelled them to join the second campaign, in 1712. Having wiped out the Florida mission Indians, they turned north in the search for new booty.[81]

The Tuscarora War was not only profitable, it also sparked a fear among many southeastern Indians that they too might soon face the same fate as the defeated Tuscaroras. Between one and two thousand Tuscaroras were enslaved during the war.[82] By the second decade of the eighteenth century the native Southeast was a powder keg of anxiety, as rumors flew that the Carolinians had plans to enslave their Indian trading partners and allies.[83] With the British publicly committed to a slave economy, the Ochese Creeks and Yamasees, among others, began to look for signs that the Carolinians intended to "make Slaves of them all."[84]

Those signs seemed to abound. The Tuscarora War offered a firsthand instructive in how the British dealt with Indians who got in their way.[85] The Indian warriors who fought alongside the Carolinians shared many of the same complaints that had prompted the Tuscaroras to act: land encroachment, trader abuses, and enslavement of kin.[86] The British settlements in South Carolina, like those to the north, were expanding, and with this came a shift from trading slaves to trading deerskins and planting rice. For the first time, land was more precious than Indian slaves.[87] Yamasees and other Indians close to colonial settlements faced the very real possibility of losing their lands and their loved ones to the British.[88] When Carolina officials intruded into native communities for a commissioned census, when a Carolina trader murdered the "usinjulo" (the "beloved son" and successor) of the powerful Coweta chief Brims in a debt dispute, when the Carolina government erected a fort in Beaufort, and when other Carolina traders made good on their threats to enslave the wives and children of those indebted to them, these signs were impossible to ignore.[89]

The Carolinians had long struggled to control their own traders, who repeatedly defied restrictions on trade and enslavement for profit. Hoping to secure Indian allies rather than acquire Indian slaves, the ineffectual lords proprietors of Carolina spent much of the late seventeenth century trying to limit or ban the enslavement of Indians.[90] But they could not prevent even their self-appointed deputies from engaging in the slave trade.[91] This problem continued well into the eighteenth century when the colonial government began to shoulder the responsibility of limiting Indian enslavement to protect the colony from retributive Indian attacks. The French and Spanish had both traders and missionaries working on their frontiers, but

South Carolina depended predominantly on traders to promote Indian alliances.[92] While traders were instrumental to Carolina, providing essential insider information on the movements of Indians and other Europeans in the frontiers and borderlands, and by serving as cultural intermediaries creating links with Indian communities through marriage, friendship, and/or sexual relationships, they could prove equally dangerous. Indians frequently appeared before the Grand Council and later the Commissioners of the Indian Trade seeking redress for crimes against person and property committed by these traders. Fearful of the potentially devastating impact of trader abuses and enslavement of Indians on their colony, the South Carolina Assembly passed an act to regulate the Indian trade in 1707.[93] They, like the lords proprietors, found that regulations had little impact.[94]

The traders were entrepreneurs living dangerously for financial gain. An Indian slave was the most lucrative local trade good in the early eighteenth century. While Nairne likely exaggerated when he said that a single slave was worth "a Gun, ammunition, horse, hatchet, and a suit of Clothes," the spirit of his claim was not far off.[95] The great value of Indian slaves motivated both Indians and colonists to enslave tens of thousands of southeastern Indians. Carolina traders often capitalized on imperial contests to engage in Indian enslavement and slave trading, sponsoring and even leading slave-raiding parties. Missionary Francis Le Jau blamed the escalation of slave wars on the traders: "[I]s it not to be feared that some white men living or trading among them do foment and increase that Bloody Inclination in order to get Slaves?"[96] Even more dangerous than fomenting intertribal wars, traders began to enslave the kin of their indebted Indian trading partners. In the first decade of the eighteenth century Indian men allied with the colony began to register formal complaints against traders for enslaving family members, particularly wives and children, and for kidnapping their own slaves. When Indian communities, including the Yamasees, proved unable to pay up in the years leading to the Yamasee War, some traders seized Indian family members and sold them at Charles Town.[97]

The enslavement and murder of clan members cried for blood vengeance. Though the economic slave trade had expanded what slavery and war meant to Indian peoples, the murder and enslavement of kin still required war to restore cosmological and political balance. The Ochese Creeks and Yamasees had very different relationships with the British in 1715. The Ocheses stood on more equal footing with the Carolinians as powerful trading partners who lived beyond the reaches of frontier settlement; the Yamasees recently had been important frontier guards to the Carolina settlements but colonial expansion made their lands more valuable than their alliance. Yet both Ochese and Yamasee Indians began to consider war to stop British abuse. They shared a potent fear of their own figurative enslavement through debt and the subsequent literal enslavement of their kin to pay off this debt.[98]

In 1715 161 native towns pledged to stop the British from making slaves of them all.[99] At a meeting of Ochese Creeks and Yamasees in the Yamasee town of Pocotaligo, leaders, including Brims of Coweta, discussed war and its alternatives. While Yamasees and other Indians who also lived close to the British settlements felt they had few options, the Ocheses hoped to renegotiate their trading relationship with the British from their more powerful position.[100] In the midst of their discussions, several British traders acting as government agents arrived at Pocotaligo Town, including Thomas Nairne, the Indian agent to the Yamasees.[101]

While the traders retired from their meeting believing things had gone well, they awoke to the sounds and sights of war.[102] Handshakes were replaced by war whoops sung by warriors painted in the unmistakable colors of war: red and black.[103] Some of the Yamasees, it seems, had not taken kindly to the sudden arrival of Carolina traders. Already suffocated by the British who increasingly encroached on their lands, livelihood, and families, they suspected that the British had spies in their midst.[104] In trying to prevent a war from breaking out, Thomas Nairne and his cohort in fact catalyzed a premature strike. On Good Friday, April 15, 1715, Yamasees at Pocotaligo killed the trader-agents who had come to talk of reconciliation (only two managed to escape). For Nairne, their Indian agent and a man whom they suspected "would cause theire Lands to be taken from them," death was not swift. He was tortured over the course of three days à petit feu before succumbing.[105]

While the "Yamasee War" was likely the decentralized responses of numerous Indian communities to a complex array of problems, it was nonetheless clearly a war against Indian traders. After the massacre at Pocotaligo, other Creek, Choctaw, and some Cherokee and Chickasaw towns followed suit, killing their British traders. The colony lost ninety of its one hundred Indian traders.[106] Yamasees and Ocheses then struck Port Royal and other settlements, as colonists huddled in Charles Town.[107] South Carolinians almost completely abandoned their settlements to the south of the Stono River and between Charles Town and the Santee River (over half of Carolina's cultivated lands).[108] Governor Craven was only able to save his colony by securing a quick peace with Cherokee towns and mobilizing a multiracial force that, tellingly, was largely colonial. While South Carolina's forces in the Tuscarora War were predominantly Indian, Craven's militia consisted of 600 white men, 400 African slaves, and only 100 free Indians.[109] The colonial forces captured Pocotaligo while Yamasees fled to St. Augustine, renewing their alliance with the Spanish.[110] The British brokered peace with most of the other Indian nations and communities by 1717, including Ochese Creeks. But Yamasees continued to wage small attacks on South Carolina from the relative safety of the Spanish borderlands.

The Yamasee War accelerated the decline of the colonial Indian slave trade. Indian communities largely stopped slave raiding for commercial trade. Indian warriors would no longer trade their captives to Carolina or conduct raids solely to procure slaves for sale to Europeans. The partnership between British traders and Indian slave raiders was irrevocably broken. South Carolina lost almost an entire generation of traders and with them the ability to promote wars or raids for Indian slaves.[111] In the wake of the war, the colonial government attempted to redress trader abuses, briefly trying to maintain state control over the Indian trade from between 1716 and 1721.

Yet the war did not put an end to Indian slavery or Indian enslavement. Despite the proven dangers, the colony did not outlaw the enslavement of Indians. During the war itself, Indian enemies taken by both colonial and Indian warriors were enslaved, sold, and exported from the colony.[112] And following the war, colonists did not liberate their Indian slaves, though the proportion of Indians in the colonial slave population declined with the diminished availability of new Indian slaves and the ballooning importation of African slaves. Still, in 1724 there were close to 2,000 Indian slaves in South Carolina.[113]

The enslavement of Indians remained of vital importance to war and diplomacy for Indian and British. Indian slavery in the postwar period was decidedly political in nature: both Indian and British continued to make slaves of their Indian enemies. In the wake of the Yamasee War, Indian communities grew in size and power as confederacies increasingly coordinated their foreign political agendas. With this growth came a renewed emphasis on "crying blood," which nurtured cycles of intertribal warfare. Once again Indian enslavement became largely political. Indians no longer enslaved enemies for economic purposes (that is, explicitly for trade) though the colonial government used economic incentives to promote the enslavement of Yamasees and other Indian enemies by colonists and Indian allies. Now Indians sacrificed their war captives or kept them in their towns as slaves or adoptees. Nonetheless, years of enslaving enemies for colonial trade had changed native slavery and warfare, increasing the intensity and scope of both.

For colonists, too, Indian slavery became a largely political system after the Yamasee War. Carolinians enslaved their Indian enemies and used this system of slavery to advance their own geopolitical goals in the region. Even as they embraced the Atlantic slave trade in Africans, Carolinians engaged in the political enslavement of southeastern Indians. But while often motivated by vengeance and a desire for psychological satisfaction, Carolinians did not incorporate the cultural construct of crying blood. They targeted Yamasees for enslavement, blaming them for the late war and ongoing frontier violence. Using trade embargoes, the British tried to force Creek warriors to address the Yamasee problem by enslaving, killing, or relocating Yamasees. For the British, Indian enslavement was not central to cosmological balance but rather to political order. For Indian communities both needs motivated enslavement in the postwar era.

One of the most important consequences of the Yamasee War was the four-decades-long cycle of revenge warfare it started between Creeks and Cherokees, in which captive-taking was central. The Cherokee-Creek War affected intertribal and international relations throughout the Southeast. Some Carolinians initially thought that this war worked to their advantage, preventing alliances which might lead to another pan-Indian war, but increasingly the war threatened British attempts at geopolitical dominance.[114]

Creek and Cherokee communities had engaged in periodic cycles of war and peace prior to the Yamasee War; Cherokee and Creek towns "alternately claimed [each other] as enemy and kin."[115] When pro-British Overhill Cherokees agreed to a peace with the Carolinians in October 1715, they did so partly because they hoped for British assistance against Creeks. In August, western Cherokees had attacked Coweta Creeks, killing fifty and taking "all their women and children slaves."[116] Anti-Creek rather than pro-Carolina sentiment was likely the prime motivator for Cherokees to side with the Carolinians during the Yamasee War.

Not all Cherokee towns shared this inclination to join the Carolinians against the Creeks. The Lower Cherokees were reluctant to formalize a war with their Upper Creek neighbors. The borderland between the Lower Cherokees and Upper Creeks was the site of most of the intertribal violence; likely the Lower Cherokees worried that the levels of bloodshed would only increase if they declared war on the Creeks.[117] While "the Conjurer" of Tugaloo, a Lower Cherokee town, agreed to aid the Carolinians, he refused to war against the Yamasees, who were kin, or the Creek confederacy at large. The Conjurer would only war with Tugaloo (not Carolina) enemies: the Savannahs, Yuchis, and Apalachees. The Savannahs bore no connection with the Creeks. The Yuchis and Apalachees were not Creeks but foreigners who recently had relocated to Lower Creek country.[118]

Despite the efforts of some Cherokees, like the Conjurer, to forestall war with the Creeks, events during the Yamasee War catalyzed a Cherokee-Creek cycle of war unprecedented in intensity and scope. After agreeing to their own peace with the Carolinians, the Cherokees opened peace talks with the Creeks (whom the Cherokees refused to fight without direct British assistance and whom the Carolinians had no interest in fighting themselves).[119] Responding to the Conjurer's invitation to come to Tugaloo, where talks between the two communities frequently were held, a delegation of thirteen Creek headmen arrived in late January 1716.[120] But while the British colonel George Chicken made his way to Tugaloo for the peace talks, anti-Creek Cherokees killed all but two of the Creek headmen. Colonel Chicken arrived too late to make a peace with the Creeks.[121] The Cherokees couched the assault under a cloak of British alliance, justifying their actions as revenge for the Creek murder of two white traders weeks earlier. The traders were under the protection of the town's chief at the time, and their murders by Creek (Abihka) warriors cried for blood revenge, the Cherokees claimed.[122]

The Creeks would not forgive the Cherokees for Tugaloo. To Brims, chief of Coweta and a man of extended influence among the Lower Creeks, the murder of the peace delegation smacked of collusion between the Cherokees and Carolinians. The murder prompted many Creek towns to follow Coweta in initiating revenge slave warring.[123] A decade later, when Tobias Fitch met with Brims in 1725 to discuss peace talks with the Cherokees, Brims replied: "we will hear nothing of a Peace, we have not forgot them Men yet that was killed there in Cold blood when the White People was there and that remain in our minds and shall do as long as one of us is alive."[124] Fitch tried to persuade Brims, telling him that the Upper Creeks had already agreed to peace talks. But this was a lie. The Upper Creeks, like Brims, had flatly refused to consider Fitch's proposal until they "had Satisfaction" for the murder of "Several of the Principal Warriors of our Nation." Fitch's lie had no effect on Brims who would not be swayed from avenging his clansmen. Brims echoed the Upper Creeks' sentiment that only revenge could end the war.[125]

Fitch's meeting with Brims and the Upper Creeks was part of an official three-year campaign launched by acting governor Arthur Middleton to end the Cherokee-Creek War. Middleton wanted an alliance with the powerful Creeks and to defeat the Yamasees. This could only be achieved by ending the Creek war with the Cherokees. Though the British often used a divide-and-conquer policy to undermine Indian power in the region, in this case they needed to forge an alliance between the Cherokees and the Creeks to offset the Spanish and their Yamasee allies.

Fearing (rightly) that Brims and other Lower Creek headmen were turning their backs on the British and allying with the Spanish, Middleton sent Fitch to speak to the headmen of the largely pro-British Upper Creeks in July 1725 to broach the subject of peace.[126] But the South Carolinians rarely possessed such neat control over Indian affairs. Fitch's mission was complicated by the decentralized nature of politics within Creek towns and the nation.[127] The British used a heavy hand in trying to force the Creeks to ally, but Creek leaders pursued a foreign policy based on neutrality, a "national" commitment to stay out of imperial rivalries between the British, French, and Spanish. Brims initiated this "Coweta Resolution" in 1718.[128] Sovereignty in a Creek sense vastly differed from the British concept: it implied no national unity and no central authority. Common fear (and hatred) of the Cherokees and a commitment to internal peace united the Creeks. Creek towns were otherwise divided in their European and Indian alliances. For example, though most Lower Creek towns initially followed Brims's lead in courting the Spanish and keeping the Carolinians at arm's length, some Lower Creeks revived their alliances with the Carolinians after they imposed trade embargoes in 1723. Superior British goods and geopolitical power persuaded Cusabos of Cusseta, who reaped not only the material but also political rewards. Other Lower and Upper Creek towns followed suit, driving a wedge between pro-British Creek factions inspired by Cusabo and pro-Spanish factions that followed Brims.[129]

When Fitch met with Brims in August of 1725, the Cowetas had just returned from a slave raid against the Cherokees. Brims drew on Indian traditions of revenge warfare when he set out to enslave and kill Cherokees. But while this war party exemplified a general continuity with Indian traditions of captivity, slavery, and war, there also were important changes. Indian revenge war parties generally had been small, involving immediate clan members who took only two or three captives. But Brims brought back thirty Cherokee slaves and fifty scalps. Perhaps Brims was so angry, so stricken with grief, that he violated the normal bounds of revenge war. This could also have been a political move to promote Creek resolve and unity against the Cherokees—peace between the two would be nearly impossible. But it is difficult to imagine that Brims would have taken thirty Cherokee slaves without the precedent of decades of Indian slaving, which had had dramatically increased the scale and scope of raids and revenge wars. As Colonel Theophilus Hastings noted, a single raid would "not Satisfye the Old Man for he is resolved to go out next Month himself and he wont want Company."[130]

The elevated level of warfare left the Lower Cherokees, who had hoped to avoid further conflict with their Creek neighbors, in the heart of the battle zone. The Cherokees expected the British to aid them against the Creeks, but found themselves on their own.[131] In disgust, they reminded the British what alliance had cost them: "a continual war . . . their wives and childrens have been killed or taken away slaves . . . if it had not been to save the white people they would have been at peace and quietness."[132] While enmity with the British could make Indians, particularly Yamasees, a target of Indian slavery, alliance could have the same affect.

In 1727 Middleton tried again to end the war between the Cherokee and Creek, inviting them to peace talks at Charleston. He still needed to subdue the Yamasees, whose continued alliance with the Spanish could only be dealt with through Creek acquiescence. Middleton spoke carefully with Chigelli and the Lower Creek headmen about his intentions: the Lower Creek shared kin and clan ties with the Yamasees.

Yamasee and Lower Creek kin ties predated English colonization.[133] British demands challenged the most sacred source of identity for southeastern Indian communities. Creek towns divided between these demands and their kin loyalties.[134] Trade embargoes helped to win some Creek towns and factions to the British cause, but Brims continued to lead Coweta and the Chattahoochee towns on a path of kinship rather than war with the Yamasees, while simultaneously making vague promises of alliance to the British.[135] Under great pressure, in 1727 the Lower Creeks consented to a peace talk with the Cherokees.

When Brims's brother Chigelli arrived in Charleston he bore two emblems of peace: a white eagle wing and a Yamasee boy. Aware that the governor wanted him to "break with" the Yamasees, Chigelli presented convincing evidence of Lower Creek intentions by turning over the Yamasee boy. He explained: "I have had the talke with my People, I have been against the Yamasees, and have brought this Boy to you for a present (points to a Yamasee Boy by him)."[136] Not until the conclusion of the meeting did Chigelli give the eagle wing to Long Warrior of Tunisee. The white color of the eagle wing represented peace in both Cherokee and Creek communities, and the talks they shared were inscribed on the wing. Before offering the wing to Long Warrior, Chigelli raised it high in his hand and made a promise of peace. Long Warrior refused to accept the wing until he was assured of Chigelli's intentions, then he too raised the wing and verbally confirmed their peace. Both men inscribed their commitment to peace on the white eagle wing through imagery and words.[137]

Each of Chigelli's gifts resonated with the recipient, filled with layers of meaning. To Middleton, the Yamasee slave represented Lower Creek alliance; in British terms, submission to their political goals. To Long Warrior the eagle wing represented a promise of peace and an end to "crying blood" wars and captive taking. While the presentation of an eagle wing was a traditional way to symbolize peace among Indian peoples, Chigelli's gift of a Yamasee boy to a British leader was probably an innovation of the middle ground. The exchange of captives was part of the intertribal peace process, but the gifting of an enemy as a slave at the outset of peace talks was something new.

Governor Middleton's attempt to break the cycle of revenge warfare between the Creeks and Cherokees was not meant to end Indian slavery, but to redirect it to other enemies of the British, namely the Yamasees allied with the Spanish and the Choctaws allied with the French. Middleton questioned Chigelli: "After this Peace is made with the Cherokees, where will you get Slaves?" Similarly, Middleton asked Long Warrior: "[H]ow doe you propose to get Slaves now; If it is Peace with you and the Creeks." Both Chigelli and Long Warrior offered contingent answers. Long Warrior was skeptical that peace with the Lower Creeks, whom he described as "rogues," would last. Responding to Middleton's suggestions that the Choctaws "make good Slaves," Long Warrior concurred: "If it is Peace with the Creeks, and they Stand to their Words, wee Shall goe against the

French Indians." Chigelli, on the other hand, did not jump at Middleton's suggestion that the Lower Creeks travel the path to Florida for their slaves. Instead he countered: "I have another thought; What's the matter with the Chickesaws?" Though Middleton preferred that Coweta wage war against the Yamasees, he was eager for peace and relented, claiming the British had no trade ties with the Chickasaws and that they "have good slaves." Middleton must have known that the Chickasaws and Cherokees had kin alliances, but probably more important to him was the alliance the Chickasaws shared with the French. In these peace talks Middleton initiated conversation on the issue of Indian slavery and he suggested that the Cherokees and Creeks enslave British enemies. But Chigelli asserted a Coweta agenda.[138]

Middleton recognized the centrality of warfare and slavery to Cherokee and Creek politics and culture. An outlet for revenge and grief, war also promoted a sense of unity within Indian clans and towns. The war with the Cherokees was arguably what kept the Creek confederacy together during the eighteenth century amidst inter-town rivalry and animosity. A culture of war was also integral to Indian men. To Long Warrior, Middleton said: "It is proper for you to Consider of Some place to employ Your Young men to goe and get Slaves, It is for their Good to looke out and take them." While acknowledging the need to keep the young men "busy," Middleton also hoped to use this tradition to forward his own imperial goals in the region.[139]

For there to be peace between Cherokees and Creeks, there had to be an end to slave taking and the return of slaves to their natal communities. The Cherokees insisted on the redemption of Cherokee slaves: "the Creeks will bring down their People which are Slaves among them, and that they Intend to do the Same in order that they may be delivered to each other, before the English Governour."[140] At the conclusion of the talks, Long Warrior warned Chigelli: "We are the Red People now mett together, Our Flesh is both alike, but we must have further Talke with you, wee Shall See when we go home, whether any of our People have been Killed, and whether You are Rogues, If soe, wee Shall Know what to do." Away from Middleton, Chigelli and Long Warrior continued their own talks. Long

Warrior demanded that the Lower Creeks bring him the same symbol of alliance they had carried to Middleton: Yamasee slaves.[141]

Brims and Chigelli did not bring more Yamasees to the Carolinians or the Cherokees; in 1728 the South Carolina Council determined to destroy the Yamasees without the Lower Creeks. The Lower Creek alliance had crumbled. Throughout the summer months, some Lower Creeks joined Yamasees in Spanish-sponsored raids against the British. The final straw came in July when a Yamasee-Creek party killed and scalped Indian trader Matthew Smallwood and six other Carolina traders at their trading post, Fort King George.[142] John and William Gray, the only two survivors, were imprisoned at St. Augustine where Indians informed them "that theire orders were to kill and destroy all the white persons they could and take what negroes they could, that the Governour of Augustine had promised 'em 30 peeces of eig'ht pr. head for every white man's scalp and 100 for every live negroe."[143]

Believing that the Lower Creeks had violated their peace treaty, but still unwilling to war with this powerful nation, the South Carolina Council focused on destroying the Yamasees. In 1728 the British launched their final assault against the Yamasees, marching into La Florida as they had in the early eighteenth century. White soldiers were encouraged with the promise of £50 pounds for every Yamasee head they brought back. A small group of Chickasaws were also encouraged to aid the Carolinians in their war on the Yamasees. They were offered "[t]wenty pounds for every Scalp with the Ears of an Enemy Indian & Thirty Pounds for every Enemy Indian they shall bring in Alive."[144] The British still wanted Indian warriors to help win their wars. But, in contrast to the imperial slave raids before the Yamasee War, the Carolinians now found little support from their Indian allies. The Cherokees and Creeks refused to help the British; instead of a thousand Indian warriors, the British could only persuade one hundred, primarily Chickasaws and Tuscaroras who had relocated to the colony where they had a semi-dependent status, to join an equal number of colonists. The Carolinians destroyed the Yamasees as a political entity, routing three of the four remaining Yamasee towns and killing or enslaving a third of the population.

The British won the war against the Yamasees. Only Coweta, under Brims's influence, persisted in maintaining ties with the Spanish. But the Lower Creeks had co-opted the victory against the Yamasees. They would not abandon their kin, and welcomed Yamasee survivors into their communities.[145] Both sides made accommodations. The Creeks agreed to an alliance with the British, but they would protect the Yamasees within their polity; the British were satisfied by Yamasee removal from Spanish influence, they would no longer fear Yamasee raids.[146]

Despite the great costs to their families, the Cherokees maintained their alliance with the British. On April 3, 1730, the Cherokees agreed to send seven of their men to England with Alexander Cuming, Scottish Baronet of Coulter.[147] Cherokee leaders had expressed an interest in seeing England for some years and the small group was accorded the honor of meeting King George II.[148] The Council of Trade and Plantations urged the king to use this opportunity to enter into a treaty with the Cherokees, confirming British sovereignty over the Cherokees and their lands: "which agreement remaining upon record in our Office, would upon future disputes with any European Nation, greatly strengthen our title in those parts, even to all the lands which these people now possess."[149]

The British used a metaphor to describe their relationship: a "chain of friendship" stretched across the Atlantic like the sun, binding Moytoy (whom Cuming had appointed "emperor") and the Cherokees to the British: "nevermore to be broken, or made loose." While based on the metaphor that the Iroquois League employed in their alliance with the English in the late seventeenth century, the British understood this version of the "Covenant Chain" in their own patriarchal terms.[150] To consecrate these articles of friendship the British gave the Cherokees cloth, guns, bullets and shot, vermilion, hatchets, flints, brass kettles, leather belts, and a wampum belt. The Cherokees confirmed the alliance through gifts of a different sort: "ye scalps of yor. Enemies and feathers of glory" were laid "at H. M. feet, in token of obedience."[151] The Council understood the significance of the Cherokees giving eagle feathers and enemy scalps. Like the eagle wing Chigelli had given Long Warrior and the Yamasee slave he

234

had given Middleton, the feathers and scalps the Cherokees gifted symbolized alliance with the British.

While the Cherokee dignitaries consented to this paper alliance, they deployed their own metaphor to describe how they viewed their relationship with the British. When responding to British demands that they return runaway slaves, the Cherokees drew a sharp contrast between their traditions of slavery and those of the British: "This small rope which we shew you, is all we have to bind our slaves with, and may be broken, but you have iron chains for yours."[152] The Cherokees clearly understood British definitions of slavery to be marked by permanence. They had, after all, sold slaves into this British system. Slaves there were bound by unbreakable iron chains. A chain was also said to now bind the Cherokees to the British. The Cherokees subtly created an analogy between their views of slavery and their views of political alliance to underscore that their own alliance with the British—their "chain" of friendship—might also prove as weak as rope.

While it is tempting to read the Indian slave trade as a neat example of the totalizing effects of colonialism on Indian communities, European slavery did not subsume native slavery. In the late seventeenth and early eighteenth centuries, economics briefly motivated Indian warriors to enslave. But both before and after the Yamasee War, Indian matriarchs sought to maintain control over war captives to quench crying blood and to restore balance and order to their families, communities, and cosmos. The Indian communities of the Southeast defined Indian slavery as much as officials in South Carolina. When colonial traders violated the implicit bounds of the trade, enslaving the very Indians with whom the colony was allied, Creeks and Yamasees, joined by warriors from nearly every southeastern Indian community, killed these British men and attacked their settlements. Given the cultural gulf, it was perhaps inevitable that the colonial slave trade would lead to war between the British and their Indian slaving allies.[153]

But even after the Yamasee War, Indians and colonists continued to enslave Indians. As the Indian slave trade rapidly declined, Indian slavery became a predominantly political system. As they had prior to

English colonization, Indian communities continued to take war captives and Indian matriarchs continued to make some of these enemies slaves in their own towns. And as they had done from the outset of colonization, British men continued to promote the enslavement of Indians they deemed enemies.

Notes

1. While Walker initially claimed that Lamhatty was "at liberty about the house" and "very desirous to stay," Robert Beverley offered a contradictory view in the postscript to his own account of Lamhatty. Gregory A. Waselkov, "Indian Maps of the Colonial Southeast," in *Powhatan's Mantle: Indians in the Colonial Southeast*, Peter H. Wood, Gregory A. Waselkov, and M. Thomas Hatley, eds. (Lincoln: University of Nebraska Press, 1989), 316. Waselkov reproduces Lamhatty's map and the two narratives of his captivity and enslavement by Colonel John Walker and Mr. Robert Beverley.

2. Though the Tuscarora interpreter claimed that Tuscaroras had captured Lamhatty, it is more likely that Creeks were responsible for the attack on the Towasas. Gregory Waselkov believes that the Tuscarora interpreter (who could not speak Lamhatty's language) intentionally misled colonists into thinking his own people had warred on the Towasas, when in fact the towns Lamhatty mentioned being taken to during his enslavement were Creek. Waselkov, "Indian Maps," 317. Alan Gallay, on the other hand, accepts the interpreter's assertion. Alan Gallay, *The Indian Slave Trade: The Rise of the English Empire in the American South, 1670–1717* (New Haven: Yale University Press, 2002), 307. According to Gregory Waselkov, the Towasas were predominantly comprised of refugees from the Apalachee and Timucuan missions. The Creeks destroyed these missions on three separate raids from 1702 to 1704. They continued to wage slave wars against the refugees in 1706 and 1707. Waselkov, "Indian Maps," 317–18. Richard Durschlag postulates that some of the victims of these raids may have in fact been Creeks who had maintained contact with the Spanish. Richard Durschlag, "The First Creek Resistance: Transformations in Creek Indian Existence and the Yamasee War, 1670–1730," (PhD diss., Duke University, 1995), 309–10.

3. Slave raids devastated the Indians in La Florida, both those living in Spanish missions and non-Christians. By Lamhatty's time, between 10,000 and 12,000 had been enslaved. Gallay, *Indian Slave Trade*, 295–96. Gallay estimates that up to 30,000 Indians from the Florida region may have been enslaved between 1670 and 1715. Gallay, *Indian Slave Trade*, 295–96, 299.

4. Beverley's statement here is interesting: "after some of his Country folks were found servants [torn] he was Sometimes ill used by Walker." Waselkov, "Indian Maps," 316.

5. Indians purchased a range of other trade goods, metal items (from knives and axes to needles and hoes) and home goods, including blankets, brass kettles, combs, and mirrors. There was also a demand for cloth, lace, shirts, hats, buttons, and beads. Peter Mancall, Joshua Rosenbloom, and Thomas Weiss, "Indians and the Economy of Eighteenth-Century Carolina" in *The Atlantic Economy during the Seventeenth and Eighteenth Centuries: Organization, Operation, Practice, and Personnel*, Peter Coclanis, ed. (Columbia: University of South Carolina Press, 2005), 297–322. On alcohol, see Peter Mancall, *Deadly Medicine: Indians and Alcohol in Early America* (Ithaca: Cornell University Press, 1977).

6. Alan Gallay has estimated that between 30,000 and 50,000 southeastern Indians were enslaved by and/or sold to the British from 1670 to 1715. Though we imagine Charlestown

as the terminus in an enormous importation trade in African slaves shipped in from the West Indies and Africa, in all likelihood more Indians were exported from Charlestown than Africans imported into it during this period. Gallay, *Indian Slave Trade*, 299.

7. According to the 1708 census Indians constituted 10 percent of the slave population in 1703 and 25 percent of the slave population in 1708. "A Report of the Governor and Council, 1708," in *The South Carolina Scene: Contemporary Views, 1697–1774*, H. Roy Merrens, ed. (Columbia: University of South Carolina Press, 1977), 32. By 1708 enslaved Africans outnumbered English colonists. Interestingly, however, it was the Indian slave population that grew most dramatically from 1703 to 1708. Peter Wood, *Black Majority: Negroes in Colonial South Carolina from 1670 through the Stono Rebellion* (New York: W. W. Norton, 1974), 143–44. Compiling accurate statistics for Indian slaves in the early colonial period is terribly problematic. The colony rarely recorded censuses, a significant proportion of the colony's early probate records were destroyed in two fires—one in 1698 and the other during the Civil War, and many Indian slaves never made it into these or other records.

8. Gallay believes that "[b]ecause of their previous history of raiding for captives, many southern Indians adapted to European slave trading practically overnight." Gallay, *Indian Slave Trade*, 29.

9. Most scholars have focused on the deerskin trade, rightly pointing out its centrality to not only Indian but also colonial economies in the Southeast, but overlooking the importance of the Indian slave trade. See, for example, Kathryn E. Holland Braund, "The Creek Indians, Blacks, and Slavery," *Journal of Southern History* (November 1991): 605–7. In her later work, Braund does briefly consider the commercial Indian slave trade. Braund, *Deerskins and Duffels: Creek Indian Trade with Anglo-America, 1685–1815* (Lincoln: University of Nebraska Press, 1993), 29, 34–35. On the deerskin trade and Indian incorporation into the Atlantic economy, see Mancall, Rosenbloom, and Weiss, "Indians and the Economy of Eighteenth-Century Carolina," 297–322. But some historians, particularly Alan Gallay and Converse Clowse, have postulated that it was in fact the Indian slave trade that initially fueled South Carolina's trade economy. Gallay, *Indian Slave Trade*, 7, 49. According to Clowse, the Indian slave trade "may have been the most important generator of profits during the first five years." Converse Clowse, *Economic Beginnings in Colonial South Carolina* (Columbia: University of South Carolina Press, 1971), 66.

10. Orlando Patterson demonstrated in his sweeping comparative study of sixty-six slaveholding societies across time and space that the universal essence of slavery was not the property ownership of slaves—"chattel" slavery, as in the American context. Rather Patterson defined slavery as "the permanent, violent domination of natally alienated and generally dishonored persons." Patterson explained that all slaves experienced social death, what he terms "natal alienation." Their enslavement made them "non-persons," social outsiders with no recognized ties to community or family. They were not only denied civil rights in the slaveholding society but also any claim to their family, ancestors, and cultural heritage. Natal alienation, violence and dishonor were all integral aspects of both European and Indian slaveries in the colonial Southeast. Orlando Patterson, *Slavery and Social Death: A Comparative Study* (Cambridge: Harvard University Press, 1982), quotation from 13.

11. On English and the "just war" concept in colonial South Carolina, see Gallay, *Indian Slave Trade*, 46–47.

12. John Lawson, *A New Voyage to Carolina*, Hugh Talmage Lefler, ed. (Chapel Hill: University of North Carolina Press, 1967), 184–85. Also see John Brickell, *The Natural History of North-Carolina* (London, 1737), 293–94. Brickell draws so heavily on Lawson that his book has been widely characterized as a plagiarism. Lefler, *A New Voyage to Carolina*, lii.

13. Alexander Moore, ed., *Nairne's Muskhogean Journals: The 1708 Expedition to the Mississippi River* (Jackson: University Press of Mississippi, 1988), 49.

14. The term comes from James Adair, an eighteenth-century trader who lived with southeastern Indians from 1735 to 1768. Adair applied use of the term to southeastern Indians at large, particularly the Creeks and Cherokees. James Adair, *The History of the American Indians*, Kathryn E. Holland Braund, ed. (Tuscaloosa: University of Alabama Press, 2005), 184–85. Also see Theda Perdue, *Cherokee Women: Gender and Culture Change, 1700–1835* (Lincoln: University of Nebraska Press, 1998), 52. For the quintessential study of the Iroquois Longhouse and the importance of requickening, see Daniel K. Richter, *The Ordeal of the Longhouse: The Peoples of the Iroquois League in the Era of European Colonization* (Chapel Hill: University of North Carolina Press, 1992).

15. Lawson, *New Voyage*, 199.

16. On this gender equity in revenge, see Perdue, *Cherokee Women*, 52. Though the most detailed evidence comes from post–Yamasee War sources, there is enough from the prewar period to confirm the prevalence of women in determining when revenge war was necessary during the seventeenth century. Through the Mississippian devolutions and the reorganization of Indian communities into villages, the ways in which families were ordered remained relatively constant. In both cases these were matrilineal societies in which family and clan identity were paramount.

17. *A New Voyage to Georgia, by a Young Gentleman: Giving an Account of His Travels to South Carolina, and Part of North Carolina, to Which is Added, a Curious Account of the Indians, etc.*, 2nd ed. (London, 1737), 57–58. (The first edition was published in 1735.) The same was also true of murderers. If the individual responsible could not be held accountable, then a family or clan member would be.

18. Perdue, *Cherokee Women*, 52.

19. Robbie Ethridge, *Creek Country: The Creek Indians and their World* (Chapel Hill: University of North Carolina Press, 2003), 231.

20. On the Cherokees, see Perdue, *Cherokee Women*, chapter 4. For the Creeks, see Braund, *Deerskins and Duffels*, 23, and Claudio Saunt, *A New Order of Things: Property, Power, and the Transformation of the Creek Indians, 1733–1816* (New York: Cambridge University Press, 1999), 25.

21. For the best study on the centrality of the town to southeastern Indian social identity and political structure, see Joshua Piker, *Okfuskee: A Creek Indian Town in Colonial America* (Cambridge: Harvard University Press, 2004). As Piker points out, even town identity was subordinate to clan identity, 9.

22. The Natchez often are described as an exception to the general devolution of Mississippian chiefdoms by the colonial period. However, Karl G. Lorenz has recently argued that the Natchez did in fact disperse as a result of colonial pressures. See Lorenz, "The Natchez of Southeast Mississippi," in *Indians of the Greater Southeast*, Bonnie McEwan, ed. (Gainesville: University Press of Florida, 2000), 142–77.

23. Perdue, *Cherokee Women*, 54.

24. Thomas Hatley, *The Dividing Paths: Cherokees and South Carolinians through the Revolutionary Era* (New York: Oxford University Press, 1995), 13. For more on the deployment of power in Native social relationships, see Hatley, xii.

25. Indian Commissioner John Stuart, quoted in Hatley, *Dividing Paths*, 15.

26. Paul Lovejoy has developed a useful concept to describe this kind of slavery: the kinship idiom. Like the African communities at the heart of Lovejoy's study, kin ties were the basis for social organization in the native Southeast. In these communities, slaves were defined as

non-kin. Lovejoy developed this concept to distinguish African kin slavery from Islamic slavery. Paul Lovejoy, *The Ideology of Slavery in Africa* (Beverly Hills: Sage Publications, 1981), 22. Native slavery usually was not hereditary, but it could be. The children of slaves were often adopted into the community, but if not they too lacked clan ties and were nonpersons/slaves.

27. *Nairne's Muskhogean Journals*, 62. Colonel George Chicken similarly described the redemption of a Cherokee woman from the Abihkas (Creeks) in 1725 as a four-day ritual. "Journal of Colonel George Chicken's Mission from Charleston, S.C., to the Cherokees," in *Travels in the American Colonies*, Newton D. Mereness, ed. (New York: Macmillan Company, 1916), August 12, 1727, 121. Hereafter, "Chicken's Journal."

28. Alexander Long, "A Small Postscript on the Ways and Manners of the Indians Called Cherokees (1725)," David Cockran, ed. *Southern Indian Studies* 21 (1969), 46.

29. The sacrifice could occur at the battle site or in the captor's community. Andrew Frank adds to this a fourth option: ransom. Though he describes ransom as more common than enslavement, his evidence for this comes from the late eighteenth century and includes European captives and African slaves. While evidence of Indian slaves being returned to or redeemed by their natal communities is extant, I have found little on ransom during the period under study. Andrew Frank, *Creeks and Southerners: Biculturalism on the Early American Frontier* (Lincoln: University of Nebraska Press, 2005), 15.

30. Perhaps, too, communities without access to external markets chose to sacrifice captives rather than feed extra mouths. The practice was still a vibrant part of many southeastern Indian cultures in the mid-eighteenth century. For an example of this tradition among the Choctaw, see "Journal of John Buckles (1753)," in *Documents Relating to Indian Affairs: May 21, 1750–August 7, 1754*, vol. 1, William L. McDowell Jr., ed. (Columbia: University of South Carolina Press, 1958), 384. In his study of Africa, Claude Meillassoux has suggested that sacrifice was a way for some societies to deal with surplus "aliens." In aristocratic African societies, elites sacrificed alien slaves once their own demands were met, to prevent lower-class individuals from gaining power through slave ownership. This was not a likely factor in the town-based communities of the indigenous Southeast. Claude Meillassoux, *The Anthropology of Slavery: The Womb of Iron and Gold*, trans. Alide Dasnois (Chicago: University of Chicago Press, 1991), 220–21.

31. Paula Gunn Allen "imagines" that this Iroquoian tradition of exacting a double penalty for a woman's murder was widespread throughout Native America. Paula Gunn Allen, *The Sacred Hoop: Recovering the Feminine in American Indian Traditions* (Boston: Beacon Press, 1992), 32.

32. "Chicken's Journal," October 4, 1725, 155. Perdue, *Cherokee Women*, 87–88.

33. According to Theda Perdue, drawing on James Adair, Cherokee captives were adopted when a family member's death did not require crying blood because it had occurred naturally or because it had been avenged. Perdue, *Cherokee Women*, 54. Also see Perdue, *Slavery and the Evolution of Cherokee Society, 1540–1866* (Knoxville: University of Tennessee Press, 1979), chapter 1. On the Creeks, see Braund, "Creek Indians, Blacks, and Slavery," 602–3.

34. Perdue, *Cherokee Women*, 54.

35. On the centrality of clans to Cherokee society, see Perdue, *Cherokee Women*, chapter 2. Theda Perdue has suggested that the Cherokee "may have regarded an individual without kin ties as something less than a person." Perdue, *Cherokee Women*, 48–49.

36. See Braund, "The Creek Indians, Blacks, and Slavery," *Journal of Southern History* 4 (1991): 601–5.

37. Saunt, *New Order*, 28–31.

38. Braund, "Creek Indians, Blacks, and Slavery," 602.

39. Lawson, *New Voyage*, 201. Eric Bowne notes that in all northern Iroquoian languages the words for "dog" and "slave" are the same. Eric Bowne, *The Westo Indians: Slave Traders of the Early Colonial South* (Tuscaloosa: University of Alabama Press, 2005), 39. As Patterson has noted, "in a great many slave-holding societies masters were not interested in what their slaves produced." Patterson, *Slavery and Social Death*, 11.

40. Southeastern Indians did not keep livestock for either labor or consumption; dogs were the only domesticated animals, and kept for companionship and hunting assistance. David G. Anderson, *The Savannah River Chiefdoms: Political Change in the Late Prehistoric Southeast* (Tuscaloosa: University of Alabama Press, 1994), 133.

41. For example, during a period of intensive decentralization in Cahokia, elites tried to reconsolidate their authority by increasing the production of symbolic and subsistence goods, mobilizing labor to do so. Timothy R. Pauketat, "The Reign and Ruin of the Lords of Cahokia: A Dialectic of Dominance," in *Lords of the Southeast: Social Inequality and the Native Elites of Southeastern North America*, Alex W. Barker and Timothy R. Pauketat, eds. (Washington DC: American Anthropological Association, 1992), 40–42.

42. Alex W. Barker, "Powhatan's Pursestrings: On the Meaning of Surplus in a Seventeenth-Century Algonkian Chiefdom," in *Lords of the Southeast*, 72.

43. Gallay, *Indian Slave Trade*, 28–30. Gallay draws a distinction between slavery in chiefdoms and slavery in bands. In the latter, slaves did not contribute significantly to the economy.

44. Both accounts of Lamhatty's enslavement assert that the Tallapoosas "made him" work the ground. Waselkov, "Indian Maps," 314–15. The only texts we have describing native slavery were penned by European colonists from communities in which the main value of slaves was that they worked, and this may have colored their interpretations of native slavery.

45. Braund, *Deerskins and Duffels*, 18; Perdue, *Cherokee Women*, 17–18. Hatley points out that "this division of labor was never perfect—men assisted and sometimes took the lead in field-clearing and planting, and women joined in on the hunt—this split, which was as much vocational as occupational, provided a measure of certainty about the conduct of Cherokee life and an economic underpinning to Cherokee authority." Hatley, *Dividing Paths*, 8. Perdue argues, however, that Cherokee labor division "was more rigidly gendered than that found among some Native peoples, including neighboring Creeks." According to Perdue, Creek men not only helped to prepare the ground and bring in the harvest but also cultivated common lands. Similarly women and children usually accompanied Creek hunting parties. Perdue, *Cherokee Women*, 71.

46. Perdue, *Cherokee Women*, 18.

47. Braund, *Deerskins and Duffels*, 31.

48. Philip D. Morgan, *Slave Counterpoint: Black Culture in the Eighteenth-Century Chesapeake and Lowcountry* (Chapel Hill: University of North Carolina Press, 1998), 1. Ira Berlin has similarly described "the South Carolina lowcountry" as a distinct region "where chattel bondage arrived with the first settlers and had little competition as the main source of labor on the great rice and indigo plantations." Ira Berlin, *Many Thousands Gone: The First Two Centuries of Slavery in North America* (Cambridge: Harvard University Press, 1998), 7.

49. As Richard Dunn has explained, the Barbadian settlers were a "medley of big and middling planters, merchants, artisans, small farmers, sailors, servants, and slaves." Dunn, *Sugar and Slaves: The Rise of the Planter Class in the English West Indies, 1624–1713* (New York: W. W. Norton, 1973), 113. Also see Wood, *Black Majority*, chapter 1.

50. South Carolina's first slave law, "An Act for the Better Ordering of Slaves," was passed in 1690 and drew heavily on Barbados's 1688 slave law. Jennifer L. Morgan, "This is 'Mines':

Slavery and Reproduction in Colonial Barbados and South Carolina," in *Money, Trade and Power: The Evolution of Colonial South Carolina's Plantation Society*, ed. Jack Greene, Rosemary Brana-Shute, and Randy J. Sparks (Columbia: University of South Carolina Press, 2001), 187–216, particularly 198–200. Eugene Sirmans has suggested that the codification of this Barbadian influence on South Carolina slaveholding may have occurred even earlier. Sir Peter Colleton, one of the lords proprietors, lived in Barbados while John Locke was writing the Fundamental Constitutions (1669), which granted masters "absolute power and authority" over their slaves, and the two corresponded. Charles Lesser, ed., *The Shaftesbury Papers* (Charleston: South Carolina Historical Society, 2000), 115. M. Eugene Sirmans, "The Legal Status of the Slave in South Carolina, 1670–1740," *Journal of Southern History* 28 (November 1962): 462–73.

51. John Norris, *Selling a New World: Two Colonial South Carolina Promotional Pamphlets*, Jack Greene, ed. (Columbia: University of South Carolina Press, 1989), 132. Norris specified the labor enslaved Indian women should perform on a large plantation, ranging from work in the fields to dairying, work with livestock, and household labor. He also recommended an additional three Indian women to cook for the slaves, and three African women to do the family chores.

52. Both Indian and African women composed a large percentage of Carolina's slave population. Jennifer L. Morgan has recently refuted the prevalent notion that African men dominated the transatlantic slave trade. Morgan points out that African women and children actually outnumbered men and that early racial construction was a product of representations of African gender practices and the appropriation of African women's reproductive capacities. Jennifer Morgan, *Laboring Women: Reproduction and Gender in New World Slavery* (Philadelphia: University of Pennsylvania Press, 2004), 50–61.

53. Russell R. Menard and Stuart B. Schwartz, "Why African Slavery? Labor Force Transitions in Brazil, Mexico, and the Carolina Lowcountry," in *Slavery in the Americas*, Wolfgang Binder, ed. (Wurzburg: Konigshausen and Neumann, 1993), 106–7.

54. English settlers imported Indian slaves from other Caribbean islands, the northern coast of South America, New England, and later from South Carolina. Shortly after settling on Barbados in 1627, the English brought over a small group of free Arawak families from Dutch Guiana to instruct them in sugar cultivation. Spanish slave raids had decimated Barbados's indigenous population in the sixteenth century. A few years later, the English enslaved their Indian instructors and began to import other Indian slaves. Jerome S. Handler, "The Amerindian Slave Population of Barbados in the Seventeenth and Eighteenth Centuries," *Caribbean Studies* 8 (1968), 39. Also see Jerome S. Handler, "Aspects of Amerindian Ethnography in 17th-Century Barbados," *Caribbean Studies* 9 (1969), 50–72.

55. Gallay, *Indian Slave Trade*, 4–7 and 49.

56. Bowne, *Westo Indians*, chapter 6.

57. Richter, *Ordeal of the Longhouse*, 50–74.

58. Bowne, *Westo Indians*, chapter 4.

59. The Westos raided for slaves in the region between the Savannah River and La Florida. Bowne, *Westo Indians*, 79–85.

60. Carolinians engaged in their own slave wars nearly from first settlement. In 1671 they launched a war against the Kussoes, alarmed by their "insolencyes" and "the evil of their intentions." A. S. Salley, ed., *Journal of the Grand Council of South Carolina*, vol. 1 (Columbia: Historical Commission of South Carolina State Company, 1907), October 2, 1671, 9. Less than four months earlier, Maurice Mathews had described the Kussoes to Lord Ashley as "our friends." "Maurice Matthews to Anthony Lord Ashley," *Calendar of State Papers, Colonial*

Series, America and West Indies, W. Noel Sainsbury, J. W. Fortescue, and Cecil Headlam, eds. (London, 1860–1939), August 30, 1671, no. 610. Hereafter, *CSP*.

61. Journals of the Commissioners of the Indian Trade, September 20, 1710–August 29, 1718 (Columbia: South Carolina Department of Archives and History, 1955) (hereafter, *JCIT*), July 27, 1711, 30.

62. Nairne used this phrase to describe Chickasaw slave raids in the Mississippi valley. Nairne's Muskhogean Journals, 48. On the beginning of this transformation among the Ochese Creeks, see Steven Hahn, The Invention of the Creek Nation, 1670–1763 (Lincoln: University of Nebraska Press, 2004), 52–58.

63. Nairne's Muskhogean Journals, 39.

64. Perdue presents a complex analysis of gender relationships in colonial Cherokee communities, arguing against a neat declination model. Cherokee women fought for their traditional power as men increasingly entered the colonial world. Most notably, the increased absence of men from Indian towns gave women more control over the internal dynamics of their communities, worlds largely invisible to European eyes. Nonetheless Perdue's work also makes it clear that women's traditional sources of power were undermined during this gender struggle. Perdue, Cherokee Women, 63–64.

65. Perdue, Cherokee Women, 38–39, 53–54, 69, 90.

66. For more on South Carolina's black majority, see Wood, Black Majority, particularly chapter 5. Steven Oatis asserts that by the beginning of the eighteenth century an increasing number of Indians were being kept in South Carolina, while Gallay emphasizes that Carolina exported more Indian slaves than it imported African slaves before 1715. Steven Oatis, A Colonial Complex: South Carolina's Frontiers in the Era of the Yamasee War, 1680–1730 (Lincoln: University of Nebraska Press, 2004), 106. Gallay, Indian Slave Trade, 299.

67. Peter H. Wood, "The Changing Population of the Colonial South: An Overview by Race and Region, 1685–1790," in Powhatan's Mantle, 90. Oatis, Colonial Complex, 117. If we apply Alan Gallay's estimates to Wood's figures, then it is likely that enslavement accounts for as much as half of this population decline. Gallay, Indian Slave Trade, 299. Paul Kelton has recently proposed that the first epidemic to sweep the entire Southeast did not occur until 1696, when the Indian slave trade created the right conditions for rapid and massive transmission of diseases. Kelton, "The Great Southeastern Smallpox Epidemic, 1696–1700: The Region's First Major Epidemic?" in Transformation of the Southeastern Indians, 21–37. Kelton's argument contradicts the work of previous scholars, such as Henry Dobyns, Ann Ramenofsky, and Marvin T. Smith. Smith, however, has begun to rethink the frequency with which epidemics struck Indian communities in the sixteenth century as well as the predominance of disease in prompting chiefdom declension. He now believes disease was only one of many factors in the movement of indigenous southeastern people. Smith, "Aboriginal Movements in the Postcontact Southeast" in Transformation of the Southeastern Indians, 3–20.

68. Gallay, Indian Slave Trade, 12. Bowne, The Westo Indians, 4–6, 19. Steven Hahn has challenged the concept and term "confederacy" to describe the associations formed by Indian towns and communities in the late seventeenth and eighteenth centuries. Instead Hahn prefers "nation" because it focuses attention on land and outsiders rather than on relations within the nation. His is the search for the origins of a Creek national consciousness. It is precisely for this reason that I chose the term "confederacy" to describe these early associations. While Hahn considers the late eighteenth century as the formative period for the Creek nation, my work examines the late-seventeenth-century confederation of the Creeks and other confederacies. The towns that joined this and other confederacies often

saw themselves as independent but willing to act together for certain purposes. These were not nations in the western sense, though colonial writers often used the term "nation" to describe them. Hahn is uncomfortable with the "looseness" and "shifting" nature that scholars have ascribed to the Creek Confederacy. This fluidity was an essential element of these associations, offering strength during a time of incredible pressure and flux. Hahn, *Invention of the Creek Nation*, 1–9.

69. Anderson defines cycling as the "recurrent process of the emergence, expansion, and fragmentation of complex chiefdoms amid a regional backdrop of simple chiefdoms." Anderson, *Savannah River Chiefdoms*, 9. See also Jay K. Johnson and Geoffrey R. Lehmann, "Sociopolitical Devolution in Northeast Mississippi and the Timing of the de Soto Entrada," in *Bioarchaeology of Native American Adaptation in the Spanish Borderlands*, Brenda Baker and Lisa Kealhofer, eds. (Gainesville: University of Florida Press, 1996), 38–55. Patricia Galloway, *Choctaw Genesis, 1500–1700* (Lincoln: University of Nebraska Press, 1996), 67–74.

70. The decline of chiefdoms in the protohistoric and historic periods was not solely a result of European disease but rather prompted by a range of factors both independent of, and a result of, European colonization and exploration efforts, such as environmental degradation, diseases, slavery, and economic restructuring. According to Cassandra Hill, chiefdom decline in protohistoric west-central Alabama was characterized by periods of pronounced nutritional stress, probably due to overreliance on maize, the appearance of new diseases, and the abandonment of mound building, craft specialization, and centralized towns. Cassandra M. Hill, "Protohistoric Aborigines in West-Central Alabama: Probable Correlations to Early European Contact," in *Bioarchaeology of Native American Adaptation*, 17–37.

71. Their reconfiguration gave both new towns decided advantages. The Coweta and Cusseta people came with alliances and connections to other indigenous communities formed during their migrations, and they settled in a pivotal borderland between the English and Spanish. These town clusters retained political and cultural heritage from their sixteenth-century antecedents while pursuing new economic and political opportunities. Hahn believes they both originated from Casiste, which likely was a "middling" town subject first to Tallassee and later to Tascalusa before the eastward migrations. Hahn, *Invention of the Creek Nation*, 26–29.

72. Hahn, *Invention of the Creek Nation*, 28–40.

73. Hahn, *Invention of the Creek Nation*, 41. By the late seventeenth century, Coweta and Cusseta were the most powerful town groupings in the Apalachicola region. Smith, *Savannah River Chiefdoms*, 139.

74. Hahn argues that these raids marked a change in Ochese-Creek warfare. Hahn, *Invention of the Creek Nation*, 52–55.

75. Hahn, *Invention of the Creek Nation*, 52–80.

76. Gallay, *Indian Slave Trade*, 333. Gallay believes that this was the prime motive for the Creeks, Cherokees, and Chickasaws who joined the Yamasee War. For a discussion of colonial economic theory and the Indian trade in the colonial southeast, see Hahn, *Invention of the Creek Nation*, 75–76.

77. According to Hahn, the Ocheses would have needed 100,000 deerskins to pay off their debts in 1711 (or 250 deerskins per adult male). Hahn, *Invention of the Creek Nation*, 76.

78. Gallay, *The Indian Slave Trade*, 267–68. Oatis believes there were as many as 800 Indians from the Piedmont who joined Barnwell. Oatis, *Colonial Complex*, 87. The figures are complicated by the high incidence of desertion both early on in the campaign and throughout the war.

79. Many of the colonial soldiers had participated in the slave wars on La Florida. Oatis, *Colonial Complex*, 87–90. North Carolina Governor Edward Hyde played to the South Carolinian

thirst for slaves when trying to recruit a second expedition from the southern colony, tempting them with the information that there were 3–4,000 Indians they could enslave. "Private Instructions to Mr. Foster," 1712, *Colonial Records of North Carolina*, I, William L. Saunders, ed. (Raleigh: P.M. Hale State Printer, 1886), 900. Gallay, *Indian Slave Trade*, 274. Barnwell and his men complained that the Indian warriors beat them to the punch in taking slaves and enslaved rather than killed captives. John Barnwell, "The Tuscarora Expedition: Letters of John Barnwell," *South Carolina Historical and Genealogical Magazine* 9 (1908), 41. This Indian focus on taking slaves seems to have been just as strong in the second expedition, led by James Moore Jr. Gallay, *Indian Slave Trade*, 285.

80. Oatis, *Colonial Complex*, 117. Gallay, *Indian Slave Trade*, 267–69.

81. Hahn, *Invention of the Creek Nation*, 74. Oatis, *Colonial Complex*, 89–90.

82. Gallay, *Indian Slave Trade*, 298–99.

83. Hahn, *Invention of the Creek Nation*, 78.

84. "Creek Traders to Governor Lyttelton," July 31, 1756, quoted in Saunt, *New Order*, 28. Saunt draws a sharp distinction between English and Creek societies, asserting that Creeks "did not use bondage as a form of social control." His analysis focuses on English enslavement of Indians and Africans and "the deep, inner fear of slavery" this engendered, without considering Indian traditions of slave taking or the prominent role Creeks played in the Indian slave trade. He describes slavery as a contaminant and captivity as foreign. "Creek Traders to Governor Lyttelton," July 31, 1756, quoted in Saunt, *New Order*, 28–31. Saunt also has an article whose title is inspired by this talk. Saunt, "'The English Has Now a Mind to Make Slaves of Them All': Creeks, Seminoles, and the Problem of Slavery," *American Indian Quarterly* 22 (Winter–Spring 1998), 157–80.

85. Gallay, *Indian Slave Trade*, 276–77.

86. The Tuscarora War was predominantly a reaction to land encroachment (both by colonists and Indian groups, particularly the Swiss Palatine settlers at New Bern, and Cherokee and Catawba hunters), trader abuses, and enslavement. It seems that the anti-English factions among the Tuscaroras and their allies capitalized on a moment of colonial weakness when Edward Hyde's appointment as governor of North Carolina tipped off a political conflict known as Cary's Rebellion (after his predecessor). Gallay, *Indian Slave Trade*, 262–66; Oatis, *Colonial Complex*, 84–91.

87. Oatis, *Colonial Complex*, 105.

88. Gallay, *Indian Slave Trade*, 329–32.

89. Oatis, *Colonial Complex*, 112, 118, 123; Gallay, *Indian Slave Trade*, 330; Hahn, *Invention of the Creek Nation*, 78, 81. For a transcript of the census, see "Governor Nathaniel Johnson to the Council of Trade and Plantations," *CSP*, January 12, 1720, no. 516. Population numbers of men, women, boys, and girls were recorded for Indian communities within 640 miles of Charles Town, including Yamasees, Creeks, Chickasaws, Catawbas, and Cherokees. Brims conducted his own census, his runners recorded the number of towns willing to join in a war against the English by knotting strips of deerskins. Hahn, *Invention of the Creek Nation*, 81–82.

90. In 1671 the lords proprietors of Carolina issued their first ban on Indian enslavement. "Temporary Laws of Carolina to be added to the former," *CSP*, [December?] 1671, no. 713. Throughout the 1670s and 1680s the proprietors waffled between issuing outright bans on all enslavement of Indians and limiting enslavement to those Indians taken in a "just war," while prohibiting the enslavement of Indians who lived near the colony. In 1685 they deemed Indians near the colony English "subjects" who therefore should not be enslaved. "Instructions

of the Lords Proprietors of Carolina to Joseph West, Governor of the Province of South and West of Cape Fear." Colonial Office Records (hereafter co) 5/288, British Public Record Office, March 11, 1685, 47–48. In 1693 the proprietors reissued their orders, prohibiting the exportation of Indians for a final time, to Governor Thomas Smith. No Indians within 400 miles were to be sent away. "Instructions of the Proprietors to Thomas Smith, Governor of Carolina from the Board of Trade." co 5/289, November 29, 1693, 4.

91. In 1684 the proprietors charged Maurice Matthews, not only a deputy but also the surveyor-general, as the "ringleader" of the illegal trade in Indian slaves. They ordered him to be dismissed "for all employment whatever." Though they fired both Matthews and James Moore as their deputies for this crime, both continued to serve. "The Lords Proprietors of Carolina to Governor Joseph," CSP, September 10, 1685, no. 363.

92. The Society for the Propagation of the Gospel, founded in 1701, joined the missionary business late in the game and did not send its first missionary, Samuel Thomas, to South Carolina until 1704. Upon his arrival Thomas refused to fulfill his assignment, choosing the comforts of the governor's home over the Yamasee Indians. While there were singular men, like Francis Le Jau, who strove to make a difference in Indian communities, even these men found themselves torn between proselytizing to Indians and working in English settlements that desperately needed a strong Christian presence. Gallay, Indian Slave Trade, 226–40.

93. "An Act for Regulating the Indian Trade and making it safe to the Publick," November 28 1707. Thomas Cooper, ed., The Statutes at Large of South Carolina: Containing the Acts from 1682–1716, vol. 2 (Columbia: A. S. Johnston, 1837), 311.

94. James Child was arrested in 1707 for leading a Cherokee slave-raiding party against other English allies. Pretending to have orders from the governor, he led several Cherokee towns in a large slave raid. They took 160 slaves; Child's cut was 30 slaves. When he tried to sell his Indian slaves in Charlestown, the Assembly seized Child and freed the Indians. They repeatedly appealed to the governor to prosecute Child and to revoke his trade license, but Governor Edward Tynte, who had likely received the customary handsome bribe from Child, did nothing. Nairne's Muskhogean Journal, 13. Thomas Nairne to [the Earl of Sunderland?], CSP, July 28, [1708], no. 662.

95. Nairne's Muskhogean Journals, 48.

96. Francis Le Jau, Carolina Chronicle, 1706–1717, Frank J. Klingberg, ed. (Berkeley: University of California Press, 1956), 39.

97. The records of the Commissioners of the Indian Trade document these complaints. For example, in 1712, "Tuskena, a Chenahaw Indian . . . sent down two of his People with a Complaint that the Head Men of the Town had taken away his Wife and a Slave for the Payment of the white Men a Debt due from the Town." The Commissioners described his wife as a "slave" in their proceedings, hinting at what may have been part of the problem. Perhaps in some cases traders seized "slaves" who had in fact intermarried or become adopted by their captors' community. There certainly were other cases where traders seized free Indians allied with South Carolina. JCIT, June 10, 1712, 26.

98. Oatis believes that fear of enslavement alone cannot explain what he describes as the Yamasees' "sudden" decision to attack English traders. He argues that it was "their diminishing confidence in the South Carolina government" that prompted the Yamasees to act. However, this assessment overlooks what the enslavement of clan members signaled to southeastern Indian communities. Oatis, Colonial Complex, 118.

99. Oatis, Colonial Complex, 112–13. Hahn, Invention of the Creek Nation, 81–82.

100. Gallay, Indian Slave Trade, 334. Hahn, Invention of the Creek Nation, 81–84. Hahn puts

Brims squarely at the center of the war, arguing that he sent runners to the 161 towns and gathered leaders at Pocotaligo. At the same time, he questions "the degree to which we may call this a war in the strict sense of the term" for the Creeks, for whom, he argues, diplomacy rather than warfare was the focus during the Yamasee War period. Hahn describes the Creeks as less eager for war than the Yamasees; the Cowetas and Tallapoosas pursued diplomatic alliances with the Spanish, and the Alabamas with the French, instead of pursuing war with the English in the early phase of the war. Hahn, *Inventing the Creek Nation*, 81–87. Oatis, on the other hand, argues that the Yamasees alone took "the drastic step of attacking the province's officials and civilians." Oatis, *Colonial Complex*, 126.

101. Governor Craven dispatched William Bray and Samuel Warner to the Yamasee at Pocotaligo Town to join Indian agent Thomas Nairne, former Indian agent John Wright, John Cochran, and a few other traders. A few days earlier the Commissioners of the Indian Trade had received two separate accounts from traders Bray and Warner that the Creeks were planning to kill their traders and then fall on the settlements. Bray's wife had been warned by a Yamasee friend named Cuffy, at their home in Port Royal. Bray was traveling to St. Augustine at the time, chasing some of his slaves who had run away. Warner had received his information from Apalachicola Indians and the Board ordered him to take messages to the Yamasees and Creeks asking them to come to Savano Town to "discuss their complaints." Cuffy was rewarded with the emancipation of his wife and daughter, and a coat. *JCIT*, April 12, 1715, 65. *South Carolina Commons House Journal*, March 9, 1716, South Carolina Department of Archives and History, 33. Cuffy's narrative is the focus of William L. Ramsey's article, "A Coat for 'Indian Cuffy': Mapping the Boundary Between Freedom and Slavery in Colonial South Carolina," *South Carolina Historical Magazine* 103 (2002), 48–66. Another Yamasee, named Sanute, reportedly informed the wife of a trader about the attack ahead of time and said that the Spanish had pledged to support the Yamasees, but the trader did not tell anyone. The only course of action he took was to remove his family to Charles Town. Gallay, *Indian Slave Trade*, 327–28.

102. "Charles Rodd to his Employer in London," *CSP*, May 8, 1715, no. 167. *JCIT*, April 12, 1715, 65.

103. Rodd explained: "The red indicates War, and the black represents the death without mercy which their enemies must expect." "Charles Rodd to his Employer in London," 167.

104. In the night, a Yamasee woman, married to an English trader, had warned them of as much. Hahn, *Invention of the Creek Nation*, 82. Oatis, *Colonial Complex*, 125–26.

105. *JCIT*, June 20, 1712, 27. Hahn, *Invention of the Creek Nation*, 82. Though Oatis claims Nairne's ritualistic torture was a sign of Yamasee respect since torture was often an emotional catharsis for vengeance, it likely was more a sign of their personal anger at Nairne for his recent attempt to annex Yamasee lands and perhaps, too, a sign of their rage at the traders and government agents more generally (as Nairne was an important man in both arenas). Oatis, *Colonial Complex*, 126.

106. "An Account of the Breaking Out of the Yamasee War, in South Carolina, Extracted from the Boston News, of the 13th of June, 1715," in *Historical Collections of South Carolina*, vol. 2, B. R. Carroll, ed. (New York: Harper & Bros., 1836), 572.

107. Hahn, *Invention of the Creek Nation*, 84.

108. Walter Edgar, *South Carolina: A History* (Columbia: University of South Carolina Press, 1998), 101–2.

109. Hatley, *Dividing Paths*, 329. Indian warriors generally made up the great majority of any colonial force before the Yamasee War. That colonial militiamen outnumbered both

Indians and Africans in this battle may reflect colonial fears of Indian and African uprising and or collusion as well as an ambivalent response by Indian warriors to the colony's
predicament.

110. Not all of the Yamasees relocated to La Florida. Up to a third, according to Oatis,
found refuge in Creek towns and continued to pursue war. Oatis, *Colonial Complex*, 177–84.

111. Edgar, *South Carolina*, 101. The Indian slave trade was already in decline by 1715. The
smaller communities in the southeast, that were most vulnerable to slave raids, had been
either wiped out or formed political alliances with European and Indian powers to survive.
And by 1707 there were few Indians left in La Florida to enslave; Lower Creek and English
slave raiders had largely depopulated the region.

112. Gallay, *Indian Slave Trade*, 338. Oatis, *Colonial Complex*, 152.

113. William S. Snell, "Indian Slavery in Colonial South Carolina" (PhD diss., University
of Alabama, 1972), 94–95. Snell argues that the war in fact created labor shortages as white
emigration stalled and African slave importation was interrupted, thereby stimulating a
brief surge in colonial demand for Indian slaves. Theda Perdue argues that the Indian slave
trade only declined after 1730 when demographics and racial ideologies led to an increased
reliance on African slaves. Even this did not signal an end to economic slave trading in Indian
communities, as warriors turned to trading white captives and African slaves rather than
Indian war captives with colonists. Perdue, *Cherokee Women*, 68–69.

114. Oatis, *Colonial Complex*, 225.

115. Hatley, *Dividing Paths*, 6. Hatley notes that by the late seventeenth century some
Cherokees "had moved down the river to colonize the old homeplaces" of Creeks. He contends that the Cherokee divisions (Overhill, Lower, Middle, and he adds a fourth: Valley)
may have reflected more than geographical designations but also cultural regions that were
distinguished by their encounters with other native communities such as the Creeks. Hahn,
on the other hand, asserts that the Cherokees were new enemies of the Creeks. He argues
that though the Creeks described the Cherokees as "ancient enemies, this antagonism was
in reality of more recent origin." Hahn believes that because the Cherokees and Creeks had
"fought together during the slave wars" and were part of the "trade network that linked the
Gulf Coast to Virginia" their enmity was likely a product of the Yamasee War. Since Creek and
Cherokee politics were still largely clan- and town- oriented, it is entirely likely that discrete
clans and towns could be at war while others were at peace. This was certainly the case with
the Lower Creeks and British after the Yamasee War, to British consternation. Moreover,
southeastern Indian relationships were complex and could consist of periods of peace and
war. Hahn, *Invention of the Creek Nation*, 87–88.

116. "Chicken's Journal," 331, italics added. Hatley identifies the Creeks as Cowetas.
See Hatley, *Dividing Paths*, 25. The Cherokee Chief Conjurer, of Tugaloo, couched the attack
in geopolitical terms the English would have approved of, explaining that they also killed
sixteen French traders and seized the goods the French intended to exchange.

117. Hatley, *Dividing Paths*, 23–25.

118. "Chicken's Journal," 331. Hatley, *Dividing Paths*, 24–25. Hahn, *Invention of the Creek
Nation*, 92.

119. Hatley, *Dividing Paths*, 26; Hahn, *Invention of the Creek Nation*, 88.

120. The Cherokees would later point out that the Creek delegation was late, and say
that they believed this implied a reluctance to come to peace terms. Hahn, *Invention of the
Creek Nation*, 89.

121. This may explain why the Cherokees kept two of the Creek delegates alive after the initial

murders, later killing one and giving the other to the Carolinians to kill. Both the Cherokees and Carolinians also claimed that the Creek peace party in fact tried to persuade the Cherokees to join them in massacring the English forces then at Tugaloo. Gallay, *Indian Slave Trade*, 338.

122. Hahn, *Invention of the Creek Nation*, 89; Hatley, *Dividing Paths*, 25–26.

123. Hahn, *Invention of the Creek Nation*, 90.

124. "Captain Tobias Fitch's Journal," South Carolina Council Journal, CO 5/428: part 2, August 2, 1725, 103. Hereafter, "Fitch's Journal."

125. "Fitch's Journal," July 20, 1725, 102.

126. Arthur Middleton was president of the Royal Council from 1721 to 1730, and acting governor from 1725 to 1729 when Nicholson returned to England to fight charges of improper conduct. Middleton had a long political career in South Carolina, where he was born and died (1681–1737). Fitch was a militia captain. In 1725 he was appointed agent to the Creeks.

127. When the newly appointed royal governor Francis Nicholson met with Brims's son, Ouletta, a month after arriving in Charles Town, he expressed his frustration with this political decentralization and independence. *South Carolina Council Journal No. 1: 1671–1721*, transcribed by John Greene (Columbia: South Carolina Department of Archives and History, 1851), June 30, 1721, 132.

128. Hahn, *Invention of the Creek Nation*, 110–20.

129. Hahn, *Invention of the Creek Nation*, 127–31. Hahn points out that despite an attack led in 1723 by Cusabos of Cusseta against a Yamasee peace delegation, in which one man was killed and another taken captive, Brims did not start a war with Cusseta, likely choosing to ignore the requirements of blood revenge in order to maintain peace within the Lower Creek confederacy.

130. "Colonel Hastings to the Governor," CO 5/428: pt. 2, July 17, 1725, 105–8. Perhaps, too, Brims felt that he was no longer bound to cultural norms because of the power he had in both British and Ochese communities. The British named him "emperor" of the Creeks before the Yamasee War, and he had extended influence among the Lower Creeks both before and after the War. Hahn, *Invention of the Creek Nation*, 71–73.

131. This had, in fact, been part of their peace agreement. The Carolinians and Cherokees had agreed to take each other's enemies as their own. Hatley, *Dividing Paths*, 27; Hahn, *Invention of the Creek Nation*, 131.

132. "Statement by John Cary," CSP, September 18, 1728, no. 396. Having lived and traded with the Cherokee for seven years, Cary described himself as an "eyewitness" to the effects of Creek slave raids and attacks on the Cherokees. Also see Hatley, *Dividing Paths*, 27–28.

133. John E. Worth, *The Struggle for the Georgia Coast: An Eighteenth-Century Spanish Retrospective on Guale and Mocama* (New York: American Museum of Natural History, 1995), 22–37.

134. The Yamasees, like the Lower Creeks, were largely Muskhogean refugees who coalesced during the second half of the seventeenth century. Under pressure from Westo slave raids, they fled just north of the Spanish missions in Guale, hoping at first to enjoy Spanish protection while maintaining their sovereignty. But the intensity of Westo slave raids forced the Yamasees to relocate once again. Some sought refuge in the Spanish missions, moving deeper into the Spanish sphere. Another group found refuge in the coalescing Creek communities along the Chattahoochee. The increasing labor demands of the Spanish, pirate attacks, and the collapse of Guale under the Westo onslaught forced the Yamasee mission Indians to flee once again; some went south to Apalachee and Apalachicola, and others went north to Port Royal. Through marriages Creeks and Yamasees became intimately connected by clan. Hahn, *Invention of the Creek Nation*, 123.

135. Hahn, *Invention of the Creek Nation*, 130–39.

136. *South Carolina Council Journal*, CO 5/387, January 25, 1727, 241.

137. On the symbolism of white eagle wings and tails as tokens of peace, see Charles Hudson, *The Southeastern Indians* (Knoxville: University of Tennessee Press, 1976), 163–64.

138. Middleton also knew that the Chickasaws and Cherokees were allies with kin ties, but seemingly overlooked this in his efforts at peace.

139. *South Carolina Council Journal*, CO 5/387, January 25, 1727, 237–48.

140. "Colonel Chicken's Journal," *South Carolina Council Journal*, July 27, 1727, BPRO CO 5/429, part 1, 6. While there is no notation in the Council records, it is likely that the Creeks and Cherokees did exchange captives as part of the peace process.

141. Hahn, *Invention of the Creek Nation*, 138.

142. "President Middleton to Governor Nicholson," *CSP*, Sept. 14, 1727, no. 698. The attack on Smallwood took place on July 23 or 24.

143. "President Middleton to the Duke of Newcastle," *CSP*, June 13, 1728, no. 281.

144. The Chickasaws were asked to relocate to the south side of the Savannah River, where they would buffer the colony from the Yamasees. In addition to the scalp money they were promised six months of provisions. The Committee for Indian Affairs also recommended that James Welch, "who is related to ye Chichesaws," live among the Chickasaws to "Excite them to put into Execucon Such Orders as the Governmt shall think fitt to give." "Report of the Committee Appointed for Indian Affairs," *South Carolina Council Journal*, September 1, 1727, 68, and February 29, 1728, 142.

145. Some Yamasee survivors remained in St. Augustine, while the rest found refuge among the Lower Creeks. Oatis, *Colonial Complex*, 278–87; Hahn, *Invention of the Creek Nation*, 138–44.

146. Hahn, *Invention of the Creek Nation*, 123.

147. "Articles of Friendship and Commerce propos'd by the Lords Commissioners for Trade and Plantations to the Deputys of the Cherokee Nation in South Carolina by H. M. Order, 7th Sept., and agreed to the 9th," *CSP*, September 9, 1730, 417.

148. In 1728 Savy reported that the Cherokees were eager to meet the king and to see England. They "have a great desire to see H.M. and the strength of our Nation that they may tell their people . . . how dangerous it would be to brake friendship with us." The Cherokees were also eager to see British manufacturing. "Statement by [John Savy?]," *CSP*, September 18, 1728, 396.

149. "Council of Trade and Plantations to the Duke of Newcastle," *CSP*, August 20, 1730, 404.

150. On the "Covenant Chain," see Daniel K. Richter, *Facing East from Indian Country: A Native History of Early America* (Cambridge: Harvard University Press, 2001), 147–50.

151. "Articles of Friendship and Commerce," 417. The Cherokees purportedly consented to the alliance. "Council of Trade and Plantations to the Duke of Newcastle," *CSP*, September 30, 1730, 464.

152. "Answer of the Indian Chiefs of the Cherokee Nation," *CSP*, September 9, 1730, 464ii.

153. The very concept of trade in itself may have been an incompatible cultural gulf between these diverse peoples. While the English used trade to promote political alliances and vice versa, historian Tom Hatley describes trade as "the moral equivalent of war" for Cherokee men. He prefaces this by explaining: "War, politics, and hunting were all expressions of power in Cherokee manhood . . . forces which could not be easily separated out into

discrete economic or political activities." Cherokee warriors engaged in trade for political and economic purposes, like the English, but for different ends. The goods Cherokee warriors acquired carried political currency in their communities, currency used to exemplify individuals' power and status—"in this way the violence of Cherokee warfare was paralleled by a form of consumption motivated by dual economic and political goals." Hatley, *Dividing Paths*, 9–10, 15.

7. The Making of a Militaristic Slaving Society
The Chickasaws and the Colonial Indian Slave Trade
Robbie Ethridge

In the winter of 1540–1541, the Spanish conquistador Hernando de Soto and what was left of his army after the battle of Mabila encamped at the town of Chicaza, in present-day northern Mississippi. Four months later, De Soto and his army awoke one morning to an attack by the warriors of Chicaza, and they quickly fled. About 140 years later, in 1682, René-Robert Cavelier, Sieur de La Salle made his famous voyage to the mouth of the Mississippi River. Near present-day Memphis the expedition met a small group of Indians whom they called "Chicachas." Although the connections have yet to be demonstrated conclusively, the people of Chicaza whom De Soto met likely were the forebears of the Chicachas whom La Salle met, and both were the forbears of the eighteenth-century Chickasaws. In the 140 years between De Soto's encounter at Chicaza and La Salle's encounter on the Mississippi River, the social and political landscape of the Chickasaws and the southern Indians had changed dramatically. Southeastern Indian life had changed as well.

Over the past twenty years, archaeologists and ethnohistorians studying the southeastern Indians have made this clear—the Indians of the sixteenth-century South were quite different from the Indians of the eighteenth-century South. The Indians of the eighteenth-century South are the ones with which we are most familiar—the Creeks, the Cherokees, the Chickasaws, the Choctaws, the Catawbas. These societies formed out of the wreckage of the pre-contact southeastern chiefdoms, such as Coosa, Mabila, Chalaque, Cofitachequi, Chicaza, and others. We still do not have an adequate vocabulary to describe the southeastern Indian societies of the eighteenth century, for convenience we now call them "coalescent" societies because they were all, in varying degrees, coalescences of people from different societies, cultures, and languages.[1] However, the diffusions, coalescences, and social transformations that led to their formations are poorly understood. Scholars have identified some of the forces for this transformation—things such as military losses at the hands of early explorers and destabilization of the chiefdoms; the introduction of Old World diseases and the subsequent population losses; and political and economic incorporation into the modern world system.[2]

In regard to the latter, I have proposed elsewhere that the inauguration of commercial trade and its attendant colonial struggles contributed to the fall of the Mississippian chiefdoms through the creation of a "shatter zone"—or a large region of instability from which shock waves radiated for hundreds of miles.[3] Furthermore, I propose that the whole of the eastern woodlands of the North American continent constituted such a shatter zone, created in the seventeenth century when the English, French, and Dutch linked indigenous peoples to the global economy through a trade in furs and Indian slaves. Out of the shatter zone arose what I have dubbed "militaristic slaving societies."[4] Militaristic Indian slaving societies were societies that gained control of the trade, and who, through their slave raiding, spread internecine warfare and created widespread dislocation, migration, amalgamation, and, in some cases, extinction of native peoples.[5] Most of these militaristic slaving societies in eastern North America were short-lived, existing for only about 100 years—from about 1620 to 1720. But during this brief window of time, these Indian slaving societies were key for the creation and expansion of the shatter zone through a relentless raiding of their Indian neighbors for slaves.[6]

Between 1620 and 1690, at least four Indian societies gained control of the European trade in the eastern woodlands by which they acquired European-manufactured guns and ammunition, giving them a military edge over bow- and-arrow Indians. The first were the Iroquois, who, by the mid-seventeenth century, were conducting slave raids as far south as the Gulf Coast and as far west as the Mississippi River.[7] Iroquois slaving had wide regional repercussions. As documented by Richard White, many northeastern groups fled Iroquois raiding and moved to the northern Great Lakes region, where, along with the French, they later formed White's famous "middle ground."[8] In some cases, northeastern people made long-distance migrations. Archaeologist Marvin Jeter suggests that the Quapaws were relatively recent arrivals to Arkansas, originating in the eastern Ohio River valley and making the long migration because of Iroquois predations.[9] Also, a group of Erie moved to present-day Georgia where they became known as the Westos. En route, the Westos themselves brokered their own deals with European slave traders, and they too became slavers and—once in Georgia—controlled the trade throughout eastern Georgia and northern Florida.[10]

Meanwhile the Occaneechees, in the southern Piedmont, engaged in the slave trade and soon controlled a five-hundred-mile radius of territory.[11] Iroquois shock waves through the Appalachians may have forced out the Chiscas, who apparently originated somewhere in southwestern Virginia and eastern Tennessee. In 1624 they suddenly appeared in Spanish Florida. Over the next fifty years the Chiscas stirred up so much trouble that in 1677 a combined Apalachee and Spanish force finally ran them out. After this the Chiscas retreat into the historical shadows. Some appeared in Illinois, and some moved to the Tallapoosa River in present-day Alabama, where they slaved the groups who were beginning to form the Creeks, particularly the Apalachicola.[12]

By about 1680 this first order of slaving societies had outlived their usefulness to English trade interests and a series of European and Indian wars ensued.[13] The Occaneeches were diminished in 1676 during Bacon's Rebellion, after which the survivors moved further south.[14] After the Occaneechees were dislodged, the Tuscaroras became the prevailing intermediaries in the southern Piedmont.[15] The Westos were destroyed in 1682 by a group of Shawnee mercenaries under the pay of Carolina traders.[16] The Chiscas on the Tallapoosa River were dispatched by the Apalachicola in 1686, who, now armed with British guns, turned on these raiders who had been terrorizing them for years.[17] The Iroquois were seriously reduced by their wars with Europeans and Indians, and by 1686 they began to retreat toward Canada.[18] The Tuscaroras, surrounded by Indian enemies because of their slaving, were defeated by a Yamasee-English army in 1713. The survivors migrated to Iroquoia where, in 1722, they joined the Great League as the Sixth Nation.[19]

Chickasaw Slaving

The Chickasaws' full-scale and direct involvement in the slave trade roughly began with the decline of the Westo involvement; however, there are some hints that they were indirectly involved and raiding in the lower Mississippi River valley before then. In 1682, when La Salle met the small group of Chickasaws near present-day Memphis, they told him they were several days travel from their towns (late seventeenth-century Chickasaw towns were near present-day Tupelo, Mississippi, about 110 miles east of Memphis). The La Salle accounts, although not containing much information on this encounter, indicate that the Chickasaws probably were not yet armed with European guns, that they ranged far and wide, and that they had free access to the Mississippi River.[20]

A few years later, in 1686, in an effort to locate the unfortunate La Salle, Henri de Tonti traveled down the Mississippi from Illinois. Tonti's accounts are much more complete, and his description of the Indian groups of the lower Mississippi valley indicates much turmoil, with many being assailed by European-armed eastern groups.[21]

Since we have no documentary evidence that English traders were among the Chickasaws until 1685, it is possible that between the time of La Salle's encounter and Tonti's journey the Chickasaws became engaged in the commercial slave trade through direct contact with Canadian, Dutch, or perhaps northeastern English slavers, through an expansive Indian trade network, and/or through the notorious *coureurs de bois*. The *coureurs de bois* (which translates literally as "woods runners," but which is commonly translated as "adventurers" or "trappers"; they were also known as "voyageurs") were independent Canadian traders who were scattered throughout the Midwest and mid-South, usually living in Indian villages, where they conducted a trade not only in skins but also in slaves.[22] These men worked through French trading houses in Quebec City and Montreal and frontier outposts such as the Quapaw trading post on the Arkansas River and Kaskaskia in present-day southwestern Illinois.[23] The full scope of their numbers and influence in the Midwest and mid-South at this time is not well known. There is every indication, however, that between 1670 and 1690 the people of the lower Mississippi River valley had access to European trade goods and that they were in great turmoil. When Jolliet and Marquette, La Salle, and Tonti traveled down the Mississippi River during this time, they encountered several groups who had European-manufactured items.[24] The *coureurs de bois* certainly could have provided these Indian groups with European-manufactured items, if only on a small scale, and, although they are historically known as fur traders, the documents clearly indicate that they also traded in slaves.

There are also some indications that the Chickasaws may have been making long-distance trade journeys to points north and northeast. As is well known, the Indians of North America had far-flung trade networks prehistorically, and Helen Tanner has documented a historic period communication and travel network that corresponds closely to the shatter zone region as depicted here.[25] There are several accounts of northern Indians in and around Chickasaw towns, and Chickasaws in and around the Ohio River valley and points northeast.[26] Chickasaw slavers may have established trade relations with English slavers in the mid-Atlantic, as they regularly traveled up the Ohio and Wabash river valleys to points northeast.[27] Conversely, by the 1670s, English traders were crossing the Appalachians and regularly trading with Shawnees and other Indians along the Ohio and Wabash rivers.[28] The Chickasaws could also have been trading with French trading houses around the Great Lakes, as the Canadian and Louisiana documents indicate southern Indians moving freely that far north.[29] Recent archaeological investigation on Chickasaw sites dating from 1650 to 1700 also indicate that they may have acquired guns at this early date, lending support to an indirect trade with Europeans.[30]

Trading with Indian middlemen is also a likely way in which the Chickasaws became engaged in the slave trade before making direct contact with Virginia or Charles Town traders. In 1913 historian Almon Wheeler Lauber documented the long-distance movement of slaves through an inter-Indian slave trade network, and more recently Alan Gallay sees the inter-Indian slave trade as one of the mechanisms by which Europeans acquired slaves in the Southern slave trade.[31] And then there is the account of Lamhatty, whose story is anecdotal evidence for a long-distance, inter-Indian, slave-trade network. In 1706 some Creek slavers raiding along the present-day Florida Gulf Coast seized Lamhatty, a Towasa Indian. The Creek slavers took him to the Tallapoosas (an Upper Creek group on the lower Tallapoosa River in present-day Alabama), where he worked for several months. His captors then took him through several Creek towns and finally sold him to some Savannahs (Shawnees) on the upper Savannah River.[32] Lamhatty escaped from the Savannah slavers, only to surrender a few days later to Colonel John Walker, a Virginia planter. Walker was very curious about Lamhatty, having never encountered a Towasa Indian before. And since Lamhatty was not threatening, Walker unbound him and let him move about freely. Walker eventually took him to Robert Beverley, the famed Virginia historian and early ethnographer, who interviewed Lamhatty through a Tuscarora interpreter, thus preserving his incredible story. A while later, when Walker realized that other Towasa Indians were enslaved in Virginia, he began to treat Lamhatty like a slave. Lamhatty then "became very melancholly often fasting & crying Several days together Sometimes using little Conjurations & when Warme weather came he went away & was never more heard of."[33] Lamhatty's tale gives some indication that slaves, and presumably goods, circulated through a chain of transactions involving groups from present-day Florida to Virginia, and perhaps beyond.

English traders made their first forays into the lower South around 1674, when the slaver Henry Woodward, while on an expedition to the Westos, also surveyed the possibility of trade alliances with the Cowetas, Cussetas, and Apalachicolas who were living on the Chattahoochee River in present-day Georgia (groups who would later form the Lower Creeks).[34] Under pressure from the Westos, however, Woodward and the Carolinians chose to abide by the Westo monopoly. They did not follow up on their contacts with the Lower Creeks until eleven years later, in 1685, after they had successfully broken Westo control of the trade. Then Woodward was commissioned to go to Apalachicola, at which time he also sent his agents further west to the Tallapoosas, Abhikas, and Alabamas in present-day central Alabama (groups that would later form the Upper Creeks) and to the Chickasaws in present-day northeastern Mississippi.[35] The Creek groups soon controlled the trade from approximately the Tombigbee River to the Atlantic Coast.

The next documented visit to the Chickasaws by a Carolina trader was in 1692, seven years after Woodward's visit. At this time the governor of Carolina enlisted John Stewart to head a trading expedition to the interior groups, and "to cross the mountains to go a trading to the Chickasaw."[36] Stewart early on had recognized that Indian trade alliances would be powerful tools in the imperial contest over North America, and he had long urged Carolina officials to pursue it. Once commissioned, Stewart spent two years among the Cussetas, and while there, in 1692, he most likely made the trip to Chickasaw country. After returning to Carolina, however, Stewart used the proceeds from this expedition to purchase land, and he afterward was only peripherally involved in the Indian trade.[37] Carolina interest in a Chickasaw trade alliance were not realized for another six years. The next documented expedition into the interior lower South occurred in 1698 when two Carolina slavers—Thomas Welch and Anthony Dodsworth—headed west to the Mississippi River.[38] By this time, Carolinian officials and entrepreneurs were beginning to realize the imperial value of the Indian trade, and the Welch and Dodsworth trip to the Chickasaws was prompted in part by business interests and in part by English political and military interest in securing a land route to the Mississippi River, thus contesting French control of the river corridor.

The Chickasaws responded positively to Welch's overtures. By 1702, when Pierre Le Moyne d'Iberville settled Fort Mobile, the Chickasaws were heavily involved in the English slave trade and raiding as far south as the Gulf of Mexico, about 150 miles west of the Mississippi River, up the Mississippi River corridor perhaps as far as present-day St. Louis and maybe further, and throughout the Midwest, perhaps as far as present-day

Detroit. The Choctaws, however, took the brunt of Chickasaw slaving. Their eastern raiding appears to have been mostly as allies of other groups, most notably the Alabamas and Abihkas.[39] In fact, two letters to Iberville from Tonti, written in 1702, establish the English-sponsored Chickasaw slaving beyond any doubt.[40] Tonti wrote these letters as a report to Iberville when he journeyed to the Chickasaws to invite them to Mobile to speak with the governor. According to Tonti, the Indian guides took him on circuitous routes to the Chickasaw towns in order to avoid two raiding parties in the area—one party, apparently scouts, consisted of about ten warriors. The other party consisted of 400 Chickasaw and Chakchiuma warriors. The Indian guides told Tonti that on raids this large group would break into smaller groups, attack a village, kill the men, and abduct the women and children. These victims were then bound and led to some sort of holding pen until enough had been accumulated to march off to Carolina. Tonti, once in the Chickasaw towns, actually met the person in charge of purchasing the slaves and providing European-made goods. The man was an English slave trader, and Tonti at first did not recognize him as a European since he was dressed like his Chickasaw companions in a breechclout, blue long shirt, and with "discs at his neck" (most likely some type of gorget).[41]

Between 1685 and 1698, then, the Abihkas, Alabamas, Tallapoosas, Apalachicolas, Cussetas, Cowetas, and Chickasaws emerged as a second generation of militaristic slaving societies in the South. With many of the interior groups now militarized slavers, raiding spiraled out of control, and internecine warfare was rife. Refugees and survivors fled in all directions, seeking safety in alliances and confederations.[42] One grim outcome of living in the shatter zone was extinction. The Indians of Spanish Florida are the most dramatic example of this, and John Worth recently documented the virtual depopulation of the whole of the Florida peninsula by 1715 from Creek slaving.[43] The results of Chickasaw slaving were equally dramatic. People abandoned the lower Mississippi valley, with some becoming extinct or absorbed into other groups, as they disappear from the documentary and archaeological record. Many coalesced into the Choctaw Confederacy.[44] Although their movements have yet to be worked out, groups such as the

Yazoos, the Chakchiumas, the Ibitoupas, the Taposas, and perhaps others joined the Chickasaws. Some, such as the Grigras, the Kororas, and Kious, may have joined the Natchez. Others may have moved west, either into Arkansas or western Louisiana, with some Caddos along the Red River taking in refugees by this time. Finally, many moved south, in and around the French Gulf colonies where they formed the "*petites nations*," the Gulf equivalent of the Atlantic "settlement Indians."[45]

In less than thirty years of slave raiding, the Chickasaws and their allies had altered the political landscape of the lower South, and survivors had to maintain a constant state of vigilance against their predatory raids.[46] In less than thirty years, the Chickasaws had secured their reputation as one of the most fierce and warlike Indian groups, comparable only to the Iroquois—a reputation that has still not diminished to this day.[47]

The Militarization of the Chickasaw Trade

As we get a higher-resolution view of the seventeenth-century Chickasaws as commercial slave traders, a question emerges as to why they became involved and how this trade became militarized. One factor was surely geographic. The seventeenth-century Chickasaw location around present-day Tupelo was the terminus of the Upper Trading Path, one of the major east-west trade routes that connected the interior southern Indians to Atlantic ports. This also placed them in a strategic location for garnering attention from the English in Carolina and in Virginia.[48] With the French gaining a toehold on the Gulf Coast, the English were keen on securing a Chickasaw trade partnership and thereby using them as a barrier between French Louisiana and French Canada as well as in helping to prevent the French from gaining complete control of the Mississippi River. For the Chickasaws, this European vying meant that they could play the French and British off one another, agree to trade alliances with both, and hence begin what became the standard business operation for interior Indians throughout the South for the next two hundred years.

Geography afforded them the opportunity, but why did the trade in Indian slaves take a militarized form? Anthropologists Brian Ferguson and Neil Whitehead note that a trade in captive labors, "of all indigenous 'products' implies a high level of force as a necessary accompaniment to trade."[49] In other words, whereas trading in, say, furs or deerskins does not necessarily involve warfare, trading in slaves does because it requires force, as captives are taken from outside groups and usually from enemies. Therefore, for the Chickasaws and other southeastern Indians, the link to commercial slaving was through their military organization. Among historic period southeastern Indians, a group's military organization was one part of a two-part civic organization structured along broad kinship lines known as moieties. "Moiety" is an anthropological term used to describe a particular kinship-based institution, wherein a whole society is divided into two unilineal kin groups, although people do not know the exact lines of descent.[50] Each moiety consists of several related clans. In the case of most southeastern Indian groups, including the Chickasaws, the unilineal descent was a matrilineal one, and the moieties were the red (or war) moiety and the white (or peace) moiety.

It is not yet firmly established, but there are some indications that in the Southeast, the red and white moieties had ancient antecedents. Vernon James Knight interprets some of the Mississippian-period iconography to represent three coexistent politico-religious institutions. Knight identifies a "communal cult" which emphasized the earth, fertility, and purification, and had as its central icon the platform mound.[51] A second is the "chiefly cult" which emphasized warfare, war, and warrior titles; this institution also served to legitimate and sanctify chiefly authority through control over the rituals and spiritual underwriting of warfare and hence leadership. The icons associated with this cult were the well-known warrior and warfare ritual objects and motifs, things such as the monolithic war clubs, the bilobed arrows, the birdman warriors, the severed heads, and so on.[52] Third is a "priestly cult" which supervised the elaborate Mississippian mortuary rituals and ancestor veneration of the elite dead. The central icons of the priestly cult were the funerary goods and temple statuary.[53] Although he identifies three cults, Knight proposes that the communal and chiefly cults were organizational opposites and that, at its center, Mississippian political/religious structure was a dyad organization. He suggests that the priestly cult may have served to mediate between the chiefly and communal cults.[54]

Knight also understands that some organizational elements of the historic period southeastern Indians may be transformations of these Mississippian cults. He suggests that the communal cult was transformed into the rites of renewal and purification of the "busk," or Green Corn Ceremony, and that the chiefly cult was transformed into the warfare institutions and warrior cult. The priestly cult, no longer functioning to supervise proper elite ancestor worship with the fall of the chiefdoms, was folded into the Green Corn ceremonialism, but the priests retained their distinct order as prophets and medicine people.[55] Although Knight does not take the step, one can easily see that his transformed Mississippian institutions reflect the war/peace or red/white moieties. In the reorganization that followed the collapse of the Mississippian world, people would have used old institutions as blueprints for rebuilding their social orders, and hence the red/white moiety system could have served as one of the structural foundations to seventeenth-century Chickasaw society.[56]

Since moieties are kinship-based institutions, one must first figure out historic period southeastern Indian kinship systems, a difficult task to say the least. Except for a few cases, colonial-era Europeans generally did not understand Indian kinship systems, nor did they fully realize their social and political importance; hence they usually remarked very little on them. I do not attempt here to reconstruct the seventeenth-century Chickasaw kinship system, but I present some lines of evidence that may aid in this future effort. The early twentieth-century anthropologist John R. Swanton compiled much on southeastern Indian kinship, although his use of the ethnographic present flaws his analysis.[57] In his Chickasaw work, Swanton combined information from contemporary Chickasaws as well as from historical sources covering about 300 years. Despite the discrepancies between such disparate sources, the moieties show up in each source, indicating that they were probably long-term elements. Still, the sources do not agree on the Chickasaw names of the moieties nor on the number and names of the clans in each.[58]

After delineating all of the variations, Swanton finally settles on the moiety names of Tcukafalaha and Tcukilissa. His twentieth-century informants said that in the past the people of Tcukafalaha, which Swanton translates as "long house," were "warlike and lived on a flat or prairie country," while the people of Tcukilissa, which he translates as "empty or abandoned house," were "peaceful people living in the timber."[59] Swanton also lists fifteen clans as the composite number. Swanton notes that the clans in each moiety were ranked and that a male from each clan was assigned a leadership position, what anthropologists would call a "clan uncle."[60] The clan uncles represented their respective clans in council. The moiety itself was represented by the clan uncle from the highest-ranked clan in that moiety. Likewise each moiety had a clan from which the prophets and medicine people were chosen.[61]

The basic structure of dual moieties, ranked clans, clan uncles, and moiety leaders as described by Swanton existed in some form in the seventeenth and early eighteenth centuries. For instance, in 1708, the South Carolina Trade Commissioners sent the Carolina slaver Thomas Nairne to the Chickasaws to reaffirm their trade alliance and to offset any influences from the French. Nairne, who recorded much about his stay with the Chickasaws, was very clear about the division of the Chickasaws into war and peace lines of kinship. He lists the clans of the peace division as the "Tygar, Muclesa, and racoon fameilys together with the Chiefs."[62] This list can be compared to a ranking of Chickasaw clans obtained by Henry Schoolcraft just after the Chickasaw removal to present-day Oklahoma in the mid-nineteenth century. Schoolcraft lists the clans, in order of rank, as the Minko or Chief clan, the Raccoon Clan, the Panther Clan, the Spanish Clan, the Fish Clan, and the Skunk Clan. The Spanish clan may be an English translation of a Chickasaw derivation of "Fani" or Squirrel clan, which, as we will see below, may have been a significant lineage in the peace moiety.[63] Schoolcraft's list includes the Skunk and Fish clans, which are not on Nairne's list. Taking these two lines of evidence, we can conclude that, at a minimum, in the early eighteenth century the Chickasaw peace moiety included the clans of Minko, Raccoon, Panther, Muclesa, and most likely Squirrel. In Swanton's discussion of Chickasaw kinship it is clear that clan ranking shifted over time, so we cannot assume that Schoolcraft's ranking existed in Nairne's time, with one exception. Nairne indicates that the Minko clan ranked the highest, but the ranking of the others for this time period is uncertain.

The clans of the seventeenth- and eighteenth-century war moiety are more difficult to discern. In another general list of clan names, Nairne lists the clans of the Turkey, Deer, Bear, Eagle, Hawk or Bird, Lyslala or Demedices, Ogilisa, Fish, and "etcetera." This list probably contains the names of some of the Chickasaw war moiety clans, although their ranking is unclear.[64]

We also know that the seventeenth- and early-eighteenth-century Chickasaws had a basic town division that fell along moiety lines. This division has been called the Small Prairie and Large Prairie, and it was first noted by the French, but the archaeological location of these sites clearly shows a geographic township division among the Chickasaws that corresponds to the one noted by the French.[65] And recent archaeological and ethnohistorical investigations also show that the Large Prairie towns were war towns, with leadership drawn from the red moiety, and the Small Prairie towns were the peace towns, with leadership drawn from the white moiety.[66] The Large Prairie towns were situated along a ridge on the northern part of Kings Creek in present-day Tupelo, Mississippi, and the Small Prairie towns were located about two miles southeast of there, near the junction of King and Town creeks.[67]

Chickasaw leadership was likewise organized along this duality.[68] The red (or war) division and the white (or peace) division each drew a war chief and a peace chief, respectively, from the top-ranking clan of each moiety. Nairne noted that the peace chief was a man named Fattalamee. The war chief at this time was Oboystabee. In addition, Nairne's observations reflect that the moieties themselves appear to have been ranked, with the peace moiety taking the higher position. Nairne called the peace town of Hallechehoe the "Mother Town." The chief of Hallechehoe was the peace chief Fattalamee, and Nairne reported that, except when under military attack, all the village chiefs were subordinate to him.[69]

In seventeenth-century Chickasaw society, each moiety had complementary social and political duties: the red moiety directed matters of war, the white moiety directed matters of peace. Exactly what constituted matters of war and peace, however, is still vague. If the red moiety was responsible for decisions made in war, did this, by extension, include decisions in slaving? The concept of a slave was not new to the Chickasaws or other North American Indians, as most native groups had an indigenous form of slavery.[70] Slaves were usually war captives who had been put into a version of slavery, although it was not chattel slavery. Therefore indigenous slavery was related to warfare, which was under the jurisdiction of the red moiety. In terms of commercial slaving, we have few descriptions of actual slave raids, but Nairne described a war event that clearly included commercial slaving. Nairne's description is quite detailed, indicating that he probably witnessed the event. Nairne described a surprise attack in which a small group of men fanned out into a half moon and stealthily approached a village. At a signal from the "Chief Officer," each warrior "gives the War Whoop, and then catch as catch can. After an exploit is done, good store of prissoners taken, and Danger a little over, they hang their bages about their prissoners necks and set them all advancing."[71] This slaving was done with all the pomp and ritual of warfare, as detailed by Nairne.

Enslaving war captives, then, was nothing new to the Chickasaws, and war captives could be easily linked to commercial slaving. Even so, some critical aspects changed dramatically. The war captives now consisted of hundreds of women and children, and they were now a commodity sold to European and Indian traders. And as commodities they were quite valuable. According to Nairne, with a single slave, a Chickasaw man could purchase a gun, ammunition, a horse, a hatchet, and a suit of clothes.[72] Nairne may have exaggerated the price in his report; still, slaving was a lucrative enterprise.[73] It should be no surprise, then, that Indian slaving expeditions were sometimes quite large, with hundreds of men. Recall Tonti's 1702 trip to the Chickasaws and the 400-warrior raiding party. Recall also that Tonti related that when the raiders returned to their towns, they locked the slaves in holding pens until the English traders were ready to export them.[74] Tonti's report, as well as other reports, clearly indicates that women and children comprised the largest number of captives and that there was usually an associated high toll of adult male deaths, both among those being raided and those doing the raiding.[75]

Since slaving was part of warfare, the Chickasaws targeted enemy groups in their slaving, and, conversely, slave raiding generated military enemies among those being raided. Because of their slaving, the Chicka-saws were despised by other Indians throughout the range of their raiding, and they had many enemies. In other words, it was not just the brutality of slave raiding that created inter-Indian hostilities, but the slave raids were acts of war and, according to the southeastern Indian code of warfare, these acts required retaliation.[76]

Slaving, then, was a matter of war, which meant that the new trade system was also a matter of war, and trade now fell within the jurisdiction of the war towns and the red moiety leadership. But where did all of this leave the white or peace moiety? Obviously the leaders of this moiety were responsible for matters of peace, but what does that mean? Again we can go to Nairne for some hints. Nairne appears to have conducted much of his business with Oboystabee, the war chief, who assured Nairne that the "military men and their wives," in other words the red moiety, were firm friends of the English and that the only pro-French chiefs among them were "two refuge people who can neither hunt nor take slaves," who had no influence in these matters.[77] In a later passage, Nairne mentioned that Chickasaw beliefs prohibited the peace chiefs and their villagers (the white moiety) from engaging in war or in slaving, and that they never deliberated in any such matters.[78] I do not take this to mean that the members of the white moiety literally could not engage in hunting, warfare, and slaving, but rather that they had no decision-making authority in matters of war and trade.

According to Nairne, the peace chief of Hallechehoe and the heads of the peace clans were charged with promoting peace and quiet, not shed-ding blood of any kind, keeping treaties of peace with their friends, and to counciling about any affairs "except those concerning Warr."[79] In a later pas-sage Nairne goes into some detail about another responsibility of the peace moiety—that of appointing a "Fane Mingo," or Squirrel King. The *fanimingo* saw to the formal linking of foreign groups through a process of adoption.[80] For instance, if the Chickasaws wanted to establish a friendly alliance with an external group, the peace moiety would "adopt" a male of the external group who would then be responsible for representing Chickasaw interests to the external council; the system worked both ways and an external group could adopt a Chickasaw *fanimingo* to represent their interests in Chickasaw councils. The *fanimingo*, then, was an international diplomatic institution based on southeastern Indian principles of kinship.[81] And it was a peace town institution, headed by the white moiety leadership. And the *fanimingos* may have been chosen from one of the peace clans—the squirrel clan.

According to Nairne, the duties of a *fanimingo* were to "keep the pipes of peace by which at first they contracted Friendship, to devert the Warriors from any designe against the people they protect, and Pacifie them by carrying them the Eagle pipe to smoak out of, and if after all, are unable to oppose the stream, are to send the people private intellegence to provide for their own safety."[82] This is of particular interest here because if the peace moiety had any legitimate affairs in slaving it would be through the obligations of the *fanimingo*—the *fanimingo* could make alliances with foreign groups so that slaving could not be conducted against them or he would be well within his right to forewarn them of impending raids. Not only this, but the *fanimingo* may have served as a mechanism for coalescence since the peace towns would have had an institution in place for wholesale adoption of groups besieged by slavers or others looking for refuge with a more organized, defensive group.[83]

The moieties were adapting old institutions to new circumstances. Since slaving and warfare offered new opportunities to access European-made guns, ammunition, and alliances, a strain developed along the lines of this dual organization. Nairne was very clear that the peace chiefs were not supposed to engage in slaving. He also was clear that by 1708 some peace chiefs had become disgruntled over their diminished role in this new kind of trade.[84] Nairne was also careful to point out that the peace chief Fattalamee had condoned slave raiding and had "turned warrior," and had thereby gotten himself in disgrace with the people and had lost his office.[85] It looks as though the political power of the peace moiety had begun to erode before Nairne's 1708 visit. Despite the fact that the peace moiety outranked the red moiety, Nairne reported that the Chickasaw warriors had little regard for civil authority, but much respect for military authority. The erosion of the white moiety's prestige and power, according to Nairne, was directly linked to the fact that they had no say in the trade.[86]

The peace moiety, feeling the effects of being excluded from the English slave trade, attempted to broker their own trade with the French. Such maneuvering by the red and white moieties became more and more pronounced over time, resulting in an internal Chickasaw factionalism that fell along red and white, or Large Prairie and Small Prairie lines.[87] The Small Prairie towns became largely French partisans and the Large Prairie towns became largely English partisans.[88] Now, instead of conducting internal and external affairs along neat moiety lines, the leadership of each moiety sought to widen their jurisdictions. The white moiety became involved in something that had theretofore been in the arena of war—they began making unilateral decisions regarding the trade and hence warfare. And the red moiety eventually intruded into white duties such as the *fanimingo*, as when the Large Prairie towns allowed Natchez refugees to join their towns after their disastrous revolt against the French in 1729. This was done over the strenuous objections of the Francophile Small Prairie towns—the white towns responsible for such foreign affairs.[89] The European trade system thus worked to transform indigenous institutions by promoting internal factionalism and, in the case of the Chickasaws, by redefining the basis of the dual moiety organization from one of complementarity to one of competition. Despite the strain it put on Chickasaw society, internal factionalism, competition, and fluid roles, as is being increasingly demonstrated, were good tools for brokering with competing European powers.[90]

The red and white moiety system served as the internal mechanism by which the Chickasaws could successfully link to the capitalist economy. It was easily linked because of the form this new economy initially took—that of a slave trade which squared well with Chickasaw rules and roles of war and peace. Certainly warfare was part and parcel of the pre-contact, Mississippian life, so much so that war, not peace, may have been the accepted state of affairs. But with European contact the incentives for warfare and violence changed. Archaeologists are not certain of all the motives for Mississippian period warfare, but once Europeans came on the scene one can see that war efforts became motivated in large part by commercial interests as they became tied to international trade in ways that would have been inconceivable prehistorically.

Notes

1. I would like to thank Alan Gallay for inviting me to contribute to this volume, and Gregory Waselkov, Jay Johnson, and Brad Lieb for generously sharing their expertise. This research was funded by a grant from the National Endowment for the Humanities, by a Mellon Sabbatical Fellowship from the American Philosophical Society, and by the University of Mississippi, Faculty Research Fellowships from the Office of Research and Sponsored Programs, and the Liberal Arts Faculty Development Fund from the College of Liberal Arts.

The term "coalescent society" was coined by Charles Hudson in Robbie Ethridge and Charles Hudson, "The Early Historic Transformations of the Southeastern Indians," in Carole E. Hill and Patricia D. Beaver, eds., *Cultural Diversity in the U.S. South: Anthropological Contributions to a Region in Transition*, Southern Anthropological Society Proceedings, No. 31 (Athens: University of Georgia Press, 1998), 38–39. Hudson also discusses the problem of terminology for these Historic Period Indian societies in "Introduction," in Robbie Ethridge and Charles Hudson, eds., *The Transformation of the Southeastern Indians, 1540–1760* (Jackson: University Presses of Mississippi, 2002), xix–xxi.

2. Hudson identifies these forces in "Introduction," xxii. For fuller treatments of the changes in native life with European contact see Patricia K. Galloway, *Choctaw Genesis, 1500–1700* (Lincoln: University of Nebraska Press, 1995); Charles Hudson and Carmen Chaves Tesser, eds., *The Forgotten Centuries: Indians and Europeans in the American South, 1521–1704* (Athens: University of Georgia Press, 1994); James H. Merrell, *The Indians' New World: Catawbas and Their Neighbors from European Contact through the Era of Removal* (Chapel Hill: University of North Carolina Press, 1989); Marvin T. Smith, *Archaeology of Aboriginal Culture Change in the Interior Southeast: Depopulation During the Early Historic Period* (Gainesville: University Press of Florida, 1987); Robbie Ethridge and Sheri M. Shuck-Hall, eds., *Mapping the Mississippian Shatter Zone: The Colonial Indian Slave Trade and Regional Instability in the American South* (Lincoln: University of Nebraska Press, 2009).

3. For a detailed explanation of the shatter zone concept, see Robbie Ethridge, "Mapping the Mississippian Shatter Zone: An Introduction," in Ethridge and Shuck-Hall, eds., *Mapping the Mississippian Shatter Zone*.

4. Robbie Ethridge, "Raiding the Remains: The Indian Slave Trade and the Collapse of the Mississippian Chiefdoms," in *Light on the Path: The Anthropology and History of the Southeastern Indians*, Thomas J. Pluckhahn and Robbie Ethridge, eds. (Tuscaloosa: University of Alabama Press, 2006), 208–9.

5. R. Brian Ferguson and Neil L. Whitehead, "The Violent Edge of Empire," in *War in the Tribal Zone: Expanding States and Indigenous Warfare*, 2nd ed., School of American Research Advanced Seminar, R. Brian Ferguson and Neil L. Whitehead, eds. (Santa Fe NM: School of American Research, 1999), also understand conflict and militarization to be a result of the interface between expanding states and indigenous peoples.

6. Ethridge, "Raiding the Remains."

7. Ethridge, "Raiding the Remains."

8. Richard White, *The Middle Ground: Indians, Empires, and Republics in the Great Lakes Region, 1650–1815*, Cambridge Studies in North American Indian History (Cambridge: Cambridge University Press, 1991), 11–13.

9. Marvin D. Jeter, "From Prehistory Through Protohistory to Ethnohistory in and Near the Northern Lower Mississippi Valley," in *Transformation of the Southeastern Indians*, Ethridge and Hudson, eds., 213–19; Jeter, "Shatter Zone Shock Waves along the Lower Mississippi," in *Mapping the Mississippian Shatter Zone*, Ethridge and Shuck-Hall, eds.

10. Eric E. Bowne, in *The Westo Indians: Slave Traders of the Early Colonial South* (Tuscaloosa: University of Alabama Press, 2005), documents the rise and fall of this small, but powerfully disruptive, slaving group.

11. R. P. Stephen, Davis Jr., "The Cultural Landscape of the North Carolina Piedmont at Contact," in *Transformation of the Southeastern Indians*, Ethridge and Hudson, eds., 142–45.

12. Ives Goddard, Patricia Galloway, Marvin D. Jeter, Gregory A. Waselkov, and John E. Worth, "Small Tribes of the Western Southeast," in *Handbook of North American Indians, Vol. 14, Southeast*, Raymond D. Fogelson, ed. (Washington DC: Smithsonian Institution, 2004), 176–77; Steven C. Hahn, "The Mother of Necessity: Carolina, the Creek Indians, and the Making of a New Order in the American Southeast, 1670–1763," in *Transformation of the Southeastern Indians*, Ethridge and Hudson, eds., 93; John H. Hann, "Florida's Terra Incognita," *Florida Anthropologist* 41 (1988), 75–79; *The Native World beyond Apalachee: West Florida and the Chattahoochee Valley* (Gainesville: University Press of Florida, 2006), 52–68.

13. Ethridge, "Raiding the Remains."

14. Davis, "Cultural Landscape," 144.

15. Merrell, *Indians' New World*, 40, 54.

16. Eric E. Bowne, "The Rise and Fall of the Westo Indians: An Evaluation of the Documentary Evidence," *Early Georgia*, 28 (2000), 71–73.

17. Hahn, "Mother of Necessity," 93.

18. Daniel K. Richter, *The Ordeal of the Longhouse: The Peoples of the Iroquois League in the Era of European Colonization* (Chapel Hill: University of North Carolina Press for the Institute of Early American History and Culture, Williamsburg, Virginia, 1992), 148–90.

19. Richter, *Ordeal of the Longhouse*, 238; Merrell, *Indian's New World*, 118.

20. John D. Stubbs, "The Chickasaw Contact with the La Salle Expedition in 1682," in *La Salle and His Legacy: Frenchmen and Indians in the Lower Mississippi Valley*, Patricia K. Galloway, ed. (Jackson: University Press of Mississippi, 1982), 42, 44, 46; this episode is recounted in several of the La Salle accounts; for a discussion and analysis of the accounts of the 1682 La Salle expedition, see Patricia Galloway, "Sources for the La Salle Expedition of 1682," in *La Salle and His Legacy*, 11–40.

21. Pierre Le Moyne d'Iberville, *Iberville's Gulf Journals (1699–1702)*, Richebourg Gaillard McWilliams, trans. (Tuscaloosa: University of Alabama Press, 1981), 89; Galloway, *Choctaw Genesis*, 175; Henri de Tonti, "Memoir by the Sieur de la Tonty: Memoir Sent in 1693, on the Discovery of the Mississippi and the Neighboring Nations by M. de la Salle, from the Year 1678 to the Time of his Death, and by the Sieur de Tonti to the Year 1691," in *Historical Collections of Louisiana*, vol. 1, B. F. French, ed. (New York: Wiley and Putnam, 1846), 52–78.

22. Almon Wheeler Lauber, *Indian Slavery in Colonial Times within the Present Limits of the United States*, reprint of 1913 edition (Honolulu HI: University Press of the Pacific, 2002), 75–78, 168; Thomas Nairne, *Nairne's Muskhogean Journals: The 1708 Expedition to the Mississippi River*, Alexander Moore, ed. (Jackson: University Press of Mississippi, 1988), 37; Dunbar Rowland and A. G. Sanders, eds., *Mississippi Provincial Archives, French Dominion, Vol II. 1701–1729* (Jackson: Mississippi Department of Archives and History, 1929), 25, 32, 81; hereafter referred to as *MPA*.

23. Lauber, *Indian Slavery in Colonial Times*, 70, 76, 78.

24. Louis Jolliet and Jacques Marquette, "The Mississippi Voyage of Jolliet and Marquette, 1673," in *Early Narratives of the Northwest, 1634–1699*, Original Narratives of Early American History Series, edited by Louise Phelps Kellogg (New York: Charles Scribner's Sons, 1917), 227–80, originally published 1673; M. de Joutel, "Joutel's Historical Journal of Monsieur de

la Salle's Last Voyage to Discover the River Mississippi," in *Historical Collections of Louisiana* 1:85–193; Henri de Tonti, "Memoir; Tonty's Account of the Route from the Illinois, by the River Mississippi to the Gulf of Mexico," in *Historical Collections of Louisiana*, 1:82–83.

25. Helen Hornbeck Tanner, "The Land and Water Communication Systems of the Southeastern Indians," in *Powhatan's Mantle: Indians in the Colonial Southeast*, Peter H. Wood, Gregory A. Waselkov, and Thomas M. Hatley, eds. (Lincoln: University of Nebraska Press, 1989), 6–20; Helen Hornbeck Tanner, "Hypothesis: Consequences of Indian Long Distance Travel," paper presented at the Annual Meeting of the American Society for Ethnohistory, Quebec City, Quebec, 2002.

26. The French documents from Canada indicate much north-south movement of Indians and Frenchmen; see Archives des Colonies, Séries C11, Correspondence l'arrivée, Canada, Centre des Archives d'Outre Mer, Aix-en-Provence; hereafter cited as CAOM.

27. Iberville gives a description of this route and reports that the Chickasaws even had a satellite settlement on the upper Wabash; Iberville, *Iberville's Gulf Journals*, 174–75.

28. Gallay, *Indian Slave Trade*, 103–4, notes that the Chickasaws most likely were dealing directly with English traders operating along the Wabash and Ohio rivers by the 1670s. See also Lauber, *Indian Slavery in Colonial Times*, 62–118; Brett Rushforth, "'A Little Flesh We Offer You': The Origins of Indian Slavery in New France," *William and Mary Quarterly* 60, no.4 (2003), 777–808.

29. Iberville, *Iberville's Gulf Journals*, 175; Archives des Colonies, Séries C13, Correspondence l'arrivée, Louisiane, CAOM; Séries C11 CAOM. The documents from Louisiana and Canada contain many references to such movements; however, the full scope of this kind of long-distance trade by the southern Indians during the colonial era has not been fully explored.

30. Jay K. Johnson, John W. O'Hear, Robbie Ethridge, Brad R. Lieb, Susan L. Scott, and H. Edwin Jackson, "Measuring Chickasaw Adaptation on the Western Frontier of the Colonial South: A Correlation of Documentary and Archaeological Data," *Southeastern Archaeology*, 27, no. 1 (2008), 1–30.

31. Lauber covers all of eastern North America in this early work, but he shows that there was much trafficking in slaves between Indian groups as well as between Indians and Europeans; see especially his chapter on inter-Indian warfare and slaving, *Indian Slavery in Colonial Times*, 118–52; Gallay does not explicitly discuss an inter-Indian trade network, but he documents instances of such; Gallay, *Indian Slave Trade*, 288–314.

32. The most up- to-date analysis of Lamhatty's origins and journey is in Gregory A. Waselkov, "Indian Maps of the Colonial Southeast," in *Powhatan's Mantle*, 292–343; Waselkov also refines earlier interpretations by David Bushnell and John Swanton; see David I. Bushnell, "The Account of Lamhatty," *American Anthropologist* 10, no. 4 (1908), 568–74 and John R. Swanton, "The Tawasa Language," *American Anthropologist* 31, no. 3 (1929), 435–53; Swanton, in "Tawasa Language," first identified the Towasa language as being Timucuan, and Waselkov, in "Indian Maps," 317–18, suggests that the Towasas were a confederation of Apalachees, Timucuans, and Chatots, who, fleeing the Creek slave raids in 1706, moved from the Spanish missions in present-day Florida to Mobile, where they petitioned the French for protection. The Lamhatty account reports that Lamhatty was captured by Tuscaroras and that he traveled through many Tuscarora towns. However, Bushnell and Swanton identified the towns as Creek towns in present-day Alabama and Georgia, and Swanton, "Tawasa Language," 439, proposed that the misinformation was due to the Tuscarora interpreter; Waselkov, in "Indian Maps," notes that some scholars accept the Lamhatty version as it is written, but he goes on to corroborate Swanton's conclusion and understands that Lamhatty was enslaved

by Creeks during the 1706–1707 Creek/Carolina campaign against the Spanish missions. See also Gregory A. Waselkov, "Lamhatty's Map: How the Indians Viewed the South 300 Years Ago," *Southern Exposure* 16, no. 2 (1988), 23–29. More recently, Gallay, *Indian Slave Trade*, 307–8, accepts the account of Tuscaroras capturing Lamhatty; John H. Hann thinks that Lamhatty's interpreter misconstrued much about the story and that Lamhatty himself was confused on his movements; see Hann, "Florida's Terra Incognita," 96. Despite the controversy, Lamhatty's story is important, as it is perhaps the only recorded firsthand account by a southeastern Indian slave of his capture.

33. This quote comes from Beverley's account of Lamhatty, published in Waselkov, "Indian Maps," 316; Gallay, in *Indian Slave Trade*, 307–8, recognizes the change in Walker's treatment of Lamhatty as due to Walker's realization that the Towasas, and hence Lamhatty, were slaves.

34. Verner W. Crane, *The Southern Frontier, 1670–1732* (Ann Arbor: University of Michigan Press, 1929), 17.

35. Bowne, *Westo Indians*, 82–85, 110–11; Galloway, *Choctaw Genesis*, 170–73; Nairne, *Nairne's Muskhogean Journals*, 50.

36. Quoted in Gallay, *Indian Slave Trade*, 162.

37. Stewart's claims to the Indian trade have often been downplayed as exaggeration, but Gallay, in an in-depth exploration of Stewart's activities, gives credence to Stewart's claims and understands him to have had an impact on the formation of the Indian slave trade in the Carolinas; Gallay, *Indian Slave Trade*, 155–64.

38. Arrell N. Gibson, *The Chickasaws* (Norman: University of Oklahoma Press, 1971), 34; James R. Atkinson, *Splendid Land, Splendid People: The Chickasaw Indians to Removal* (Tuscaloosa: University of Alabama Press, 2004), 25. This six-year interval may be due to a lack of documentation rather than to the absence of British traders venturing this far west; even the Welch and Dodsworth expedition has no known documentation, except that their route is marked on some colonial maps; see Verner W. Crane, "The Southern Frontier in Queen Anne's War," *American Historical Review* 24 (1919), 382.

39. Antoine Simon Le Page Du Pratz, *The History of Louisiana*, reprint of 1774 English translation (New Orleans: Pelican Press, 1947), 57, 291, 303–4; Patricia K. Galloway, "Henri de Tonti du Village des Chacta, 1702: The Beginning of the French Alliance," in *La Salle and His Legacy*, 157; Nairne, *Nairne's Muskhogean Journals*, 37, 47, 75; William L. McDowell Jr., ed., *Journals of the Commissioners of the Indian Trade, 1710–1718* (Columbia: South Carolina Archives Department, 1958), 123, 168, 215, 238, 249; *MPA*, 2:39, 185; *MPA* 3:22.

40. Henri de Tonti, "Extrait d'une lettre de M. de Tonty á M. d'Iberville du village des Chacta, le 23 Fev. 1702 et Extrait d'autre lettre du meme au meme, des Chacta, le 14 mars 1702," Archives National de France, Archives du Ministére de la Marine, Section Modernne, Série JJ Archives du Service Hydrographique, Sous-série 2 JJ 56, Manuscrits de M. Delisle, Amérique Septentrionale, no. 20; these letters are published in translation; see Henri de Tonti, "Extract from a Letter from M. de Tonti to M. d'Iberville, from the Village of the Chacta, February 23, 1702," and "Extract from another letter from the same to the same, From the Chacta, March 14, 1702," translated by Patricia K. Galloway in "Henri de Tonti du Village des Chacta, 1702: The Beginning of the French Alliance," in *La Salle and His Legacy*, 166–73; for a detailed analysis of Tonti's letters, see Galloway, "Henri de Tonti du Village des Chacta."

41. Tonti, "Extract, February 23, 1702," 168; Tonti does not identify this man by name, but it may have been Thomas Welch, who probably spent much time with the Chickasaws as evidenced by his métis son, James Welch, who in 1727 applied for a license in South Carolina

to trade among the Chickasaws; this document notes that James Welch was "related to the Chickasaws," which most likely meant that Welch's mother was Chickasaw; see the Report of the Joint Committee, 1727, Journal of the Council and Council in Assembly, Public Records Office, Document 18, transcribed in Troy Stephen Maxcy, "Chickasaw Ethnohistory, 1721–1740: The Journal of the Council and Council in Assembly, South Carolina Sessional Papers," unpublished MA thesis, Department of Sociology and Anthropology, University of Mississippi, Oxford, 1999, 56.

42. Archaeologists and ethnohistorians have recognized for some time that the commercial trade in Indian slaves during the seventeenth and early eighteenth centuries had a profound impact on native life in the southeast; see Bowne, *The Westos*; Ethridge and Hudson, *Transformation of the Southeastern Indians*; Gallay, *Indian Slave Trade*; Galloway, *Choctaw Genesis*; Jay K. Johnson, "The Chickasaws," in *Indians of the Greater Southeast: Historical Archaeology and Ethnohistory*, edited by Bonnie G. McEwan (Gainesville: University Press of Florida for the Society for Historical Archaeology, 2000), 85–121; Joel W. Martin, "Southeastern Indians and the English Trade in Skins and Slaves," in *The Forgotten Centuries*, 304–24; Gregory A. Waselkov and Marvin T. Smith, "Upper Creek Archaeology," in *Indians of the Greater Southeast*, Bonnie G. McEwan, ed., 242–64; Wood, Waselkov, and Hatley, *Powhatan's Mantle*; John E. Worth, "The Lower Creeks: Origins and Early History," in *Indians of the Greater Southeast*, Bonnie G. McEwan, ed., 265–98; John E. Worth, *The Timucuan Chiefdoms of Spanish Florida, Vol. 1, Assimilation* (Gainesville: University Press of Florida, 1998). The turmoil in which native peoples of the eastern woodlands found themselves during the seventeenth and early eighteenth centuries is not hard to see. For the South, Verner Crane's *The Southern Frontier* was the first to note these disruptions, and colonial historians have long discussed the various "Indian wars" of the seventeenth and eighteenth centuries. Likewise, archaeologists investigating this era and place have for at least a decade been piecing together a confusing array of movements and amalgamations of native peoples after the collapse of the chiefdoms; see the essays in Ethridge and Hudson, *Transformation of the Southeastern Indians*; Smith, *Archaeology of Aboriginal Culture Change*; and Ethridge and Shuck-Hall, *Mapping the Mississippian Shatter Zone*.

43. John E. Worth, "Razing Florida: The Indian Slave Trade and the Devastation of Spanish Florida, 1659–1715," in *Mapping the Mississippian Shatter Zone*, Ethridge and Shuck-Hall, eds.

44. Pierre Francois Xavier de Charlevoix, "Letter Thirtieth. Voyage from the Akansas to the Natchez, December 25, 1721," in *Charlevoix's Louisiana: Selections from the History and the Journal of Pierre F. X. de Charlevoix*, Charles E. O'Neill, ed. (Baton Rouge: Louisiana State University Press for the Louisiana American Revolution Bicentennial Commission, 1977), 132; Galloway, "Henri de Tonti du Village des Chacta," 155, 157; Du Pratz, *History of Louisiana*, 298; Iberville, *Iberville's Gulf Journals*, 144; *MPA* 1:167; Tonti, "Extract, March 14, 1702," 170; John R. Swanton, *Indian Tribes of the Lower Mississippi Valley and Adjacent Coast of the Gulf of Mexico*, Bureau of American Ethnology Bulletin Number 43 (Washington DC: Government Printing Office, 1911), 296–97; see also Goddard, et al., "Small Tribes'"; Timothy K. Perttula, "Social Changes among the Caddo Indians in the Sixteenth and Seventeenth Centuries," in *Transformation of the Southeastern Indians*, Ethridge and Hudson, eds., 255–69; for the coalescence of the Choctaws, see Galloway, *Choctaw Genesis*.

45. Swanton, in *Indian Tribes*, first attempted to make sense of the early historic period for this area; Marvin T. Smith, in "Aboriginal Population Movements in the Post Contact Southeast," in *Transformation of the Southeastern Indians*, 17–18, understands river valley depopulation such as that which occurred in the Mississippi valley to make good case studies

for post-contact movements; for some scholarship on the movements of these groups, see Jeter, "From Prehistory Through Protohistory;" Galloway, *Choctaw Genesis*; Goddard, et al., "Small Tribes"; and Daniel Usner Jr., *Indians, Settlers, and Slaves in a Frontier Exchange Economy: The Lower Mississippi Valley Before 1783* (Chapel Hill: University of North Carolina Press for the Institute of Early American History and Culture, Williamsburg, Virginia, 1992).

46. Du Pratz, *History of Louisiana*, 303–304; Galloway, "Henri de Tonti du Village des Chacta," 157; Nairne, *Nairne's Muskhogean Journals*, 37, 47, 74; André Pénicaut, *Fleur de Lys and Calumet, Being the Pénicaut Narrative of French Adventure in Louisiana*, Richebourg Gaillard McWilliams, ed. and trans. (Tuscaloosa: University of Alabama Press, 1953), 159.

47. Du Pratz, *History of Louisiana*, 296–97; Nairne, *Nairne's Muskhogean Journals*, 37; for the Chickasaws' reputation, also see James Adair, *The History of the American Indians*, edited and with an introduction and annotations by Kathryn E. Holland Braund (Tuscaloosa: University of Alabama Press, 2005).

48. Gallay, in *Indian Slave Trade*, 14–15, 128–34, 142–43, makes this point and understands the Chickasaws' geopolitical position to have been an important factor in their involvement in the trade.

49. Ferguson and Whitehead, "Violent Edge of Empire," 23.

50. Moieties also tend to exist in small societies of fewer than 9,000 people; see Carol R. Ember, Melvin Ember and Burton Pasternak, "On the Development of Unilineal Descent," *Journal of Anthropological Research* 30 (1974), 84–89.

51. Vernon James Knight Jr., "The Institutional Organization of Mississippian Religion," *American Antiquity* 51, no. 4 (1986), 678–79; Vernon James Knight Jr., "Symbolism of Mississippian Mounds," in *Powhatan's Mantle*, 279–91.

52. Knight, "Institutional Organization," 677–78.

53. Knight, "Institutional Organization," 679.

54. Knight, "Institutional Organization," 681.

55. Knight, "Institutional Organization," 682–84.

56. Knight also argues that the chiefdom hierarchy system of the Mississippian period may have evolved out of earlier, ranked, exogamous matriclan and moiety systems. Although he does not take his argument this far, one could argue that, if Knight is correct, then the ranked matriclans and moieties of the historic period were old institutions that survived the collapse of a chiefdom; Vernon James Knight Jr., "Social Organization and the Evolution of Hierarchy in Southeastern Chiefdoms," *Journal of Anthropological Research* 46, no. 1 (1990), 1–23. Blitz suggests that a fission-fusion process of Mississippian chiefdoms, involving horizontal institutions such as township and kinship, could have served a similar function in confederacy formation during the historic period; see John M. Blitz, "Mississippian Chiefdoms and the Fission-Fusion Process," *American Antiquity* 64, no. 4 (1999), 577–92.

57. This is not to say that what Swanton reported in the twentieth century existed in exactly that way in the seventeenth and eighteenth centuries; however, anthropologists understand kinship to be a structure of the *longue durée*, and I therefore cannot dismiss the possibility that some of the twentieth-century system retained elements from the previous 200 years.

58. John R. Swanton, *Social and Religious Beliefs and Usages of the Chickasaw Indians*, Bureau of American Ethnology Forty-fourth Annual Report (Washington DC: Government Printing Office, 1928), 190–99, 211.

59. Swanton, *Social and Religious Beliefs*, 195; Swanton also reports that his colleague Frank Speck identified two Chickasaw moieties—Imosaktca'n ("their hickory chopping") and Intcukwalpa ("their worn out place"). According to Swanton, Speck further recorded the clans

of each moiety, and he noted that the Imosaktca'n were "warriors inhabiting substantial lodges, while the latter [the Intcukwalpa] were known as inferior people who lived mostly under trees in the woods," Swanton, *Social and Religious Beliefs*, 190–95.

60. For a discussion of clan uncles among the Choctaws, see Patricia K. Galloway, "'The Chief Who Is Your Father': Choctaw and French Views of the Diplomatic Relation," in *Powhatan's Mantle*, 254–78.

61. Swanton, *Social and Religious Beliefs*, 196–98, 214, 215.

62. Nairne, *Nairne's Muskhogean Journals*, 36–43.

63. Swanton, *Social and Religious Beliefs*, 196; Schoolcraft also reported that the principle chief was always chosen from the Minko clan, and it was an inherited position through the female line; see Swanton, *Social and Religious Beliefs*, 191–92, 197.

64. Moore notes that Nairne's list probably also includes some Ochese and Tallapoosa clans, as well; see Nairne, *Nairne's Muskhogean Journals*, 60, 69n19.

65. James R. Atkinson, "The Ackia and Ogoula Tchetoka Chickasaw Village Locations in 1736 During the French-Chickasaw War," *Mississippi Archaeology* 20, no. 10 (1985), 53–72; Johnson, "The Chickasaws," 98–99; *MPA* 1:288, 304.

66. Jay K. Johnson, "Stone Tools, Politics, and the Eighteenth-Century Chickasaw in Northeast Mississippi," *American Antiquity* 62, no. 2 (1997), 215–30; Jay K. Johnson, John W. O'Hear, Robbie Ethridge, Brad Lieb, Susan L. Scott, H. Edwin Jackson, Keith Jacobi, and Donna Courney Rausch, "The Chickasaws: Economics, Politics, and Social Organization in the Early 18th Century," Final Report, National Endowment for the Humanities Grant No. RZ-20620-00, coauthored with Center for Archaeological Research, University of Mississippi, Oxford, 2004. Other southeastern Indian groups also had designated "red towns" and "white towns."

67. Johnson, "The Chickasaws," 98–99, Figure 4.3.

68. This dualism in Indian leadership may account for much confusion regarding Indian affairs among scholars. For instance, in the most recent book on the Chickasaws, Atkinson, *Splendid Land*, 26–27, fails to recognize the significance of the red and white moieties and the ranked clans. He mistakenly attributes a single chief to the Chickasaws and misidentifies the peace chief as being the "great chief," charged with keeping peace. He attributes the Chickasaws' engagement in warfare as deriving from an "incongruous attitude among the Chickasaw with regard to war and peace." For a more general discussion of the confusion in the historical documents, see Nancy Shoemaker, "How Indians Got to be Red," *American Historical Review* 102 (1997), 625–44.

69. Nairne, *Nairne's Muskhogean Journals*, 38; in the early twentieth century, Speck recorded that his Chickasaw informants retained some notion of moiety ranking—in this case the moiety associated with warfare ranked higher than the one associated with peace. Swanton merely states that moiety ranking was probably remembered from some ancient social organization; see Swanton, *Social and Religious Beliefs*, 192, 196.

70. Theda Perdue, in *Slavery and the Evolution of Cherokee Society, 1540–1866* (Knoxville: University of Tennessee Press, 1979), was one of the first scholars to take an in-depth look at Indian slave practices, both indigenous ideas and imported Euro-American ones. In more recent years, other scholars have taken a new look at Indian slave practices and how they changed with colonization. See especially Richter, *Ordeal of the Longhouse*, and James F. Brooks, *Captives and Cousins: Slavery, Kinship, and Community in the Southwest Borderlands* (Chapel Hill: University of North Carolina Press for the Omohundro Institute of Early American History and Culture, Williamsburg, Virginia, 2002).

71. Nairne, *Nairne's Muskhogean Journals*, 43.

72. Nairne, *Nairne's Muskhogean Journals*, 47.

73. The price of an Indian slave fluctuated over the years and also by country. In a careful examination of the documentary evidence, Gallay tracks the changing prices over time, and he also concludes that the English could pay the best price for Indian slaves; Gallay, *Indian Slave Trade*, 311–14.

74. Galloway, "Henri de Tonti du Village des Chacta," 159.

75. Mark F. Boyd, Hale G. Smith, and John W. Griffin, trans. and ed. *Here They Once Stood: The Tragic End of the Apalachee Missions* (Gainesville: University Presses of Florida, 1951), 49, 93–94; Du Pratz, *History of Louisiana*, 297; Galloway "Henri de Tonti du Village des Chacta," 159; Iberville, *Iberville's Gulf Journals*, 171–75; Tonti, "Extract, March 14, 1702," 169.

76. Alan Gallay (personal communication) believes that this could help account for the endemic warfare between the Choctaws and Chickasaws and why the Choctaws continually spoiled French efforts to make peace between the two. For discussions of the principles of blood revenge and retaliation, see Charles Hudson, *The Southeastern Indians* (Knoxville: University of Tennessee Press, 1976), 239–44; Theda Perdue, *Cherokee Women: Gender and Culture Change, 1700–1835* (Lincoln: University of Nebraska Press, 1998), 86–108; for a thorough discussion of the principles of blood revenge and retaliation among the Cherokees, see John Phillip Reid, *A Law of Blood: The Primitive Law of the Cherokee Nation* (New York: New York University Press, 1970).

77. Nairne, *Nairne's Muskhogean Journals*, 56–58.

78. Nairne, *Nairne's Muskhogean Journals*, 38.

79. Nairne, *Nairne's Muskhogean Journals*, 38.

80. For a discussion of the *fanimingo* institution, see Galloway, "'The Chief Who Is Your Father.'"

81. Joshua Piker, in *Okfuskee: A Creek Indian Town in Colonial America* (Cambridge, Massachusetts: Harvard University Press, 2004), offers a detailed look at how the people of the Creek white town of Okfuskee used the *fanimingo* to establish a particular kind of relationship with the English during the early eighteenth century. The red-and-white duality as a southeastern Indian institution for regulating international affairs is also documented by Frederick W. Gleach, in *Powhatan's World and Colonial Virginia: A Conflict of Cultures* (Lincoln: University of Nebraska Press, 1997), who argues that John Smith's captivity by the Powhatans was a diplomatic ritual of adoption by which the Powhatans adopted the colony into the chiefdom; he also understands this external-internal diplomacy to fall along war and peace lines. Shoemaker, in "How Indians Got to be Red," argues that the references to "red" and "white" by southeastern Indians were the language of diplomacy and international affairs, and not of racial categorization.

82. Nairne, *Nairne's Muskhogean Journals*, 40.

83. Brad Leib notes that the "minority wares" (ceramics that do not look like typical Chickasaw ceramics) on late-seventeenth- and early-eighteenth-century Chickasaw sites are mostly found in the Small Prairie sites, with the exception of Fatherland Incised, which are certainly the Natchez ceramics found in the Natchez refuge town located in the Large Prairie town. Leib believes the location and other attributes of these minority wares may indicate an absorption and/or adoption of outside groups by the Chickasaw Small Prairie towns; see Leib's chapter in Johnson, et al., "The Chickasaws," 2.1–2.59. While correlating a ceramic type with a known historic period Indian group is difficult, this line of evidence may be an archaeological signature for the *fanimingo* as a mechanism for coalescence.

84. Nairne, *Nairne's Muskhogean Journals*, 56–58.

85. Nairne, *Nairne's Muskhogean Journals*, 38.

86. Nairne, *Nairne's Muskhogean Journals*, 41.

87. Patricia K. Galloway, "Ougoula Tchetoka, Ackia, and Bienville's First Chickasaw War: Whose Strategy and Tactics?" *Journal of Chickasaw History* 2, no. 1 (1996), 3–10; Johnson, "Stone Tools"; Johnson, et al., "Measuring Chickasaw Adaptation."

88. The accepted version of Chickasaw history has been that the Chickasaws were staunch Anglophiles throughout the historic period and that the English manipulated them into this position through agreeable trade agreements. However, as early as 1971, Gibson challenged this idea when he noted the emergence of a strong pro-French Chickasaw faction just after the French established Fort Mobile, *The Chickasaws*, 37. In 1996 Galloway, through a close reading of the French documents pertaining to the Chickasaw Wars, suggested that the Chickasaws took advantage of some indigenous, internal factionalism to play the English against the French, and vice versa; see Galloway, "Ougoula Tchetoka"; this was followed by Johnson's examination of the distribution within Chickasaw villages of European trade goods and thumbnail scrapers used in processing deerskin hides. Johnson's analysis reveals a distribution of these artifacts between the Small Prairie and Large Prairie divisions. Johnson concludes that the difference in artifact distributions reflects an internal factionalism between the pro-French Small Prairie towns and the pro-English Large Prairie towns; see Johnson, "Stone Tools." Most recently, this factionalism is conclusively demonstrated in Johnson, et al., "The Chickasaws"; Johnson, et al., "Measuring Chickasaw Adaptation"; and in Wendy St. Jean, "Trading Paths: Chickasaw Diplomacy in the Greater Southeast, 1690s–1790s," unpublished PhD dissertation, University of Connecticut, Storrs, Connecticut, 2004.

89. *MPA* 1:210, 236, 256 275; *MPA* 3:635, 755, 764; *MPA* 4:47, 53, 55, 147, 149, 151; Galloway, in "Ougoula Tchetoka," 6, first noted that the Natchez question could reveal much about political lines among the Chickasaws.

90. Crane, in *Southern Frontier*, first documented the southeastern Indian strategy of playing one European power off another. For one of the most detailed analyses of how the European trade undermined indigenous lines of authority, see Greg O'Brien, *Choctaws in a Revolutionary Age, 1750–1830* (Lincoln: University of Nebraska Press, 2002). Other examinations of the use of such strategies in southeastern Indian and Euro-American relations are Katherine E. Holland Braund, *Deerskins and Duffels: The Creek Indian Trade with Anglo-America, 1685–1815* (Lincoln: University of Nebraska Press, 1993); Steven C. Hahn, *The Invention of the Creek Nation, 1670–1763* (Lincoln: University of Nebraska Press, 2004); Piker, *Okfuskee*; Gregory A. Waselkov, "The Eighteenth-Century Anglo-Indian Trade in Southeastern North America," in *New Faces of the Fur Trade: Selected Papers of the Seventh North American Fur Trade Conference, Halifax, Nova Scotia, 1995*, edited by Jo-Anne Fiske, Susan Sleeper-Smith, and William Wicken (East Lansing: Michigan State University Press, 1998), 193–222; Gregory A. Waselkov, "Historic Creek Indian Responses to European Trade and the Rise of Political Factions," in *Ethnohistory and Archaeology: Approaches to Postcontact Change in the Americas*, edited by J. Daniel Rogers and Samuel M. Wilson (New York: Plenum Press, 1993), 123–31; for the Chickasaws, see Atkinson, *Splendid Land*; Johnson, "Stone Tools"; Johnson, et al., "Measuring Chickasaw Adaptations."

8. A Spectrum of Indian Bondage in Spanish Texas
Juliana Barr

In the summer of 1535, four men on foot began a trek out of present-day Texas in search of lands claimed by the Spanish crown in northern Mexico, lands which they did not reach until the spring of 1536. One of them, Álvar Núñez Cabeza de Vaca, would become famous for his narrative about their experiences. His companions were Spaniards Andrés Dorantes and Alonso del Castillo and an enslaved Moor known only as Estevanico—and together they represented the sole survivors of an expedition led by Pánfilo de Narváez which had begun its march across North America eight years before on the gulf coast of Florida. The four men had spent six years living among Indian peoples of south-central Texas, held as captives or slaves. Eventually they had negotiated for themselves positions as traders and go-betweens among different groups, as a means of survival. Yet when the four men finally reached Mexican lands—lands which they found with joy after years of hardship and desperation—their arrival brought them new dismay and horror. As their own "sad and wretched captivity" drew to a close, the evidence mounted that their Spanish countrymen were inflicting far worse bondage on Indians.[1]

In the last months of their journey, they had been aided by Indian men, women, and children who quaked in fear at the thought, much less appearance, of the "Christians" whom Cabeza de Vaca and the three others sought to rejoin. As the four men and their native companions neared their goal via Indian trails, proximity brought terror to the Indians. As they noted increasing "signs of Christians," signs of Indian habitation disappeared. At each village came new stories and new evidence of Spanish raids in which homes had been destroyed, fields burnt, and half the men and all the women and children carried off in chains. As the party moved in one direction along the trails, they met numerous Indians fleeing in the opposite direction, spreading warnings of raiding Christians to all who would listen. Those in flight dared not stay in one place, much less remain to plant and cultivate their crops. In fact, Cabeza de Vaca lamented, the Indians "were determined let themselves die, and they considered this better than waiting to be treated with as much cruelty as they had been up to that point."[2]

When Cabeza de Vaca, his companions, and their Indian escort finally encountered a party of four Spaniards on horseback, the initial shock of recognition provoked immediate judgments. The four horsemen looked upon Cabeza de Vaca with disbelief to see him strangely dressed and traveling in the company of Indians. Meanwhile Cabeza de Vaca's Indian companions noted that the strangers shared their friend's preference for a beard, but little else. When the four horsemen asserted that Cabeza de Vaca and the two other Spaniards were "of the same people as they," the Indians simply responded that they surely lied and against all arguments could not be persuaded that their companions were the same as the other "Christians." Cabeza de Vaca explained his companions' reasoning in his later account, recording that the Indians said that "we came from where the sun rose, and they from where it set; and that we cured the sick, and that they killed those who were well; and that we came naked and barefoot, and they went about dressed and on horses and with lances; and that we did not covet anything but rather, everything they gave us we later returned and remained with nothing; and that the others had no other objective but to steal everything they found and did not give anything to anyone." Lending further substance to Indian perceptions, Cabeza de Vaca soon quarreled angrily with the Spanish horsemen because they wished to enslave the Indians who had brought him out of his own captivity. In turn, his Indian friends were reluctant to leave Cabeza de Vaca in the Christian slavers' company, even as he tried to convince them to return home. Instead they wished to continue on until they could transfer him into the safekeeping of other Indians as was their custom.[3]

Cabeza de Vaca's account of these encounters was the earliest to document the spread of Spanish enslavement of Indians toward lands that later included New Spain's province of Texas.[4] Indian bondage proved to play a key role, or more accurately, many and various roles, in the foundation of the Spanish province and in the twists and turns of its fate over the eighteenth century. Yet just as Cabeza de Vaca's captivity in sixteenth-century Texas turned on its head the mythology of fierce Spanish conquistadors and passive Indian victims, so too did the experiences of later Spanish colonists in eighteenth-century Texas prove a corrective to notions of the inexorable force of European settlement dispossessing and displacing all Indians in its path. The burgeoning systems of Spanish slavery to which Cabeza de Vaca mournfully gave witness in 1536 never spread past the Río Grande into Texas. Unlike in neighboring provinces of Nuevo León, Nueva Vizcaya, Nueva Santander, New Mexico, and Louisiana, Spaniards in Texas never adopted large-scale systems that coerced Indian or African labor.[5] Nor did the Texas province have the finances to develop an extensive trade system such as in the British Southeast, Spanish New Mexico, or French Louisiana that entailed market exchanges in Indian captives which in turn evolved into an Indian slave trade. Indeed, the absence of slavery reflected the impotence of Spaniards who found themselves outnumbered and overmatched by the Indian nations all around them.

It was thus only from the peripheries of Texas that forces of slavery exerted an influence on this Spanish colonial outpost. Though systematized Indian slavery was negligible within the Texas province, the political and economic reach of nearby European provinces often gave captivity and bondage a defining role in Spanish-Indian relations in Texas. First, seventeenth-century slave-raiding expeditions in northern Mexico sent many native refugees fleeing into the region that would later become Texas. Such flight, in turn, framed the settlement of south-central Texas by encouraging the creation of confederated Indian encampments that then attracted Spanish mission-presidio complexes into the region in the early eighteenth century. Soon thereafter, Indian groups from the Great Plains came south into Texas to raid for enemy captives (as well as horses) whom they could trade for European guns and goods in New Mexico and Louisiana. Such raids sent ripples and then waves through native alliances and enmities across Texas, drawing Spaniards into conflict with powerful groups of Comanches, Wichitas, Caddos, and Apaches through the end of the century. Those conflicts in turn led Texas Spaniards to emulate their Spanish neighbors in the punitive hostage-taking and deportation of Apaches in an attempt to defend their settlements. Desperate officials across the provinces of Coahuila, Nueva Vizcaya, New Mexico, and Sonora—all established within parts of Gran Apachería—joined in similar battles with Apaches for sovereignty. Conversely, nowhere else would this policy be as short-lived as in Texas.

One must take a broad view of "slavery"—and a multiplicity of definitions for it—in order to flesh out how Indian captivity and enslavement fundamentally influenced the history of Spanish Texas. Strikingly, no matter how varied the forms bondage took in Texas, it never constituted a system of labor. In this northern province of New Spain, captives and slaves were primarily military and diplomatic capital instead of the units of productive or reproductive labor usually associated with chattel slavery in North America.[6] Moreover, the actual numbers of those who fell victim to enslavement never matched the political significance of bondage in Spanish diplomacy with Comanches, Wichitas, and Apaches. This disjuncture between rhetoric and reality reflected the powerlessness of Spaniards in the region who found themselves subject to Native American nations with whom they had little influence and no control. Spaniards in Texas bore little resemblance to the conquistadors of earlier centuries who had sufficient force to subjugate Indian peoples. Even among contemporary neighbors like New Mexico, Texas fell far short by comparison. No *genízaro* population (enslaved Indians) emerged in Texas like that in New Mexico where Spaniards enjoyed a larger population, military strength, and an active market economy, and thus both captured their own prisoners in battle and bought those of Comanches and Navajos in trade.[7] The influence of Indian enslavement from Texas's peripheries, in fact, illuminated the weak points

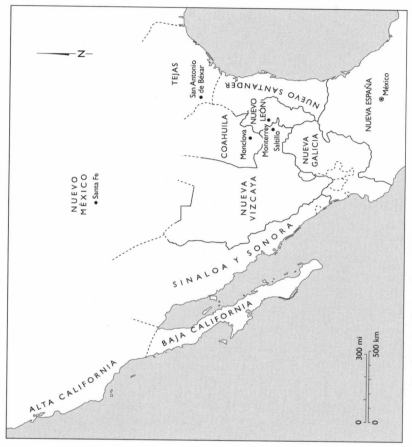

3. Northern Provinces of New Spain, ca. 1786

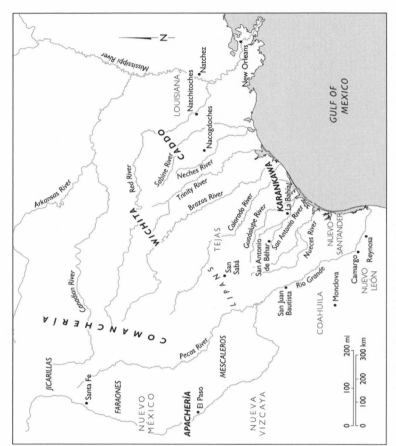

4. Native and Spanish sites, ca. 1786

of Spanish imperial claims to Texas: the province's initial dependence on Indian refugees to populate its mission-presidio complexes and its later struggle to secure those communities by holding off Apache raiders and winning over Comanche and Wichita allies.

So how did it all begin? As Cabeza de Vaca could attest, Spanish slave raiding far to the south and west of Texas made its first indelible mark on the region long before Spanish settlement materialized there. Legal prohibitions against Indian enslavement and forced labor had been put into place with the passage of the New Laws in 1542, the 1680 Recompilation of the Laws of the Indies, and periodic viceregal reiterations in the years and centuries that followed Cabeza de Vaca's trek across Texas—but the existence and the enforcement of law were two entirely different things. Widespread Spanish practices of conquest slavery in the form of *encomiendas*, *repartimientos*, *congregaciones*, and the bondage of enemy Indians taken captive in so-called just wars had long made clear the ineffectiveness of inscribed legal prohibitions in the provinces neighboring Texas. Spaniards viewed slave hunting and coerced labor as central to regional development, as their imperial reach extended northward in the sixteenth and seventeenth centuries. Across the northern provinces of New Spain, military efforts designed to "pacify" enemy Indian peoples also fed Spanish coffers through either the sale or the labor of prisoners of war and captives of raids. As they moved northward, Spaniards first exported captive and enslaved Indians to other provinces for profit, then used them instead for their own farms, ranches, mines, and households.[8] Nor surprisingly, this advance of the Spanish frontier into Nueva Vizcaya and Nuevo León in the sixteenth century and New Mexico and Coahuila in the seventeenth century put native populations into flight in multiple directions.

The spread of European diseases and the intrusion of slave-raiding expeditions each brought their own brand of annihilation.[9] Epidemics decimated native populations across the northern reaches of Mexico by 90 percent, even as royal law assigned the labor and tribute of specific Indian communities to Spaniards, a system termed "*encomiendas*." By 1600, trafficking in enslaved Indians had become an established way of life in Nuevo

León, so much so that one military officer could dispassionately record the despairing decision of an Indian father to kill his eight-year-old daughter as the only means of saving her from Spanish enslavement. Juan Bautista Chapa recorded that as the two frantically tried to reach the safety of some woods, with soldiers in pursuit, the man, already wounded himself, realized that his daughter would not escape, and so, turning, shot an arrow into her chest. Chapa concluded only that the incident was "unusual," yet one might wonder, knowing the fate awaiting anyone captured. Once Spanish policies had killed off all the nearby Indian peoples by congregating them in crowded, unsanitary work camps where death by disease or overwork devastated their numbers, local militias extended the relentless reach of their slave raids for replacement labor forces ever northward. When a 1672 royal cedula prohibited the enslavement of Indians in Nuevo León and required their Christian conversion instead, Spaniards in the region merely replaced the term "*encomiendas*" with the less materialist "*congregaciones.*" Though they purported to congregate Indian communities for acculturation and religious instruction, Spaniards continued their raids into the mid-eighteenth century in search of Indian bodies for labor, not souls for God.[10]

Spanish slave raiding out of Nuevo León and Nueva Vizcaya in the seventeenth century forced remnants of multiple, small, hunting and gathering bands to seek refuge farther and farther north, ultimately driving them across the Rio Grande into the lands of Texas. They had not gone far enough however. In the 1680s, Frenchmen with René-Robert Cavelier, Sieur de La Salle, found the remains of what appears to have been a Spanish slaving outpost along the coast of Texas—with adobe walls, towers, and a copper plate bearing the Spanish royal arms and dated 1588—that scholars speculate represented the long arm of slave raiders from Nuevo León. The establishment of the province of Coahuila in 1674 interposed a barrier between slave hunters from the two provinces and the refugees who had by that time become their prey. At the same time, however, the mission-presidio complexes used to settle and secure Coahuila created new sources of danger for Indians in the region and to the north across the Rio Grande. The threat came not from extralegal raiders seeking captives to fill the labor needs of Spanish enterprises, but from military expeditions sent to punish rebellious Indian raiders and to recruit neophytes for missions—expeditions that served both purposes with hostage taking. As cycles of epidemics emptied the missions of Indians, new expeditions repeatedly went out. The desire for new converts from the northern side of the Rio Grande became increasingly insatiable, even as the fear of disease and capture drove Indians farther away. Fray Isidro de Espinosa recorded that Indians threw thorns down behind them as they fled, hoping to impede the path of evil that, according to their beliefs, might be weakened and ultimately defeated by the sharp thorns. One wonders if the demons they envisioned took after the forms of seventeenth-century conquistadors: missionaries and presidial soldiers.[11]

Though they had originally lived in regions far different and distant from one another, a myriad of native peoples from north and south of the Rio Grande had come together in shared, mobile encampments in northeastern Coahuila and southern Texas by the late seventeenth century. There they found new strength in numbers and new consolidations of kin and alliance needed for communal shelter, subsistence, and defense. For a long time, many scholars erroneously referred to all hunting and gathering peoples of northeastern Mexico and southern Texas—those most noted for entering Spanish missions at San Juan Bautista, Coahuila, and at San Antonio, Texas—as "Coahuiltecans," conflating their regional location and periodic residence in the missions with a single, unifying linguistic and cultural identity. Part of the scholarly confusion arose because as native peoples joined together, first in confederated encampments and later in Spanish missions, they came to use Coahuilteco as a lingua franca. Recent research, however, has shown that they represented hundreds of small autonomous bands who may have shared certain general traits but whose local and regional variations made them quite distinct. Most notably, at least seven different language groups—Coahuilteco, Karankawa, Comecrudo, Cotoname, Solano, Tonkawa, and Aranama—can be distinguished among them.[12] The bands' small size and the geographical dispersion required by their socioeconomic systems limited social and political organization. Yet many groups maintained both smaller camps made up of individual ethnic groups and, at other times, larger shared settlements where two or more ethnic groups came together for purposes of hunting and defense. Archaeological evidence indicates that these dual settlement patterns existed in the pre-contact period, but the frequency of shared encampments grew during the late seventeenth and early eighteenth century in response to the upheavals caused by Spanish (and later Apache) invasions.[13]

At the beginning of the eighteenth century, south central Texas thus offered sanctuary to innumerable indigenous groups and displaced refugees. Their location there, though, put them all in the path of a new danger. Increasing numbers of mounted Apaches were also moving into the region in pursuit of migrating bison herds. As Spanish settlement expanded into Texas in the 1710s and 1720s, the presence of mission and presidial herds of cattle and horses only enhanced the region's allure to Apache raiders. Indeed, it was in response to Apache encroachments that Indians of south central Texas sought alliance with Spaniards. Past strategy of seeking safety in shared settlements may have encouraged many of these peoples to view the tiny Spanish population, like other small native bands, as potential partners in a mutual encampment. Just as they had formed real and fictive kinship ties with native bands similar to their own, they now sought to bring Spaniards into those alliances by forming joint settlements with them in the form of mission-presidio complexes. The heart of Spanish missionary settlements in Texas thus took hold at a site long used by these Indians for shared encampment, shelter, hunting, and defense—a site Indians called Yanaguana and Spaniards would come to call San Antonio de Béxar.

Once they had all been brought together, the five missions, presidio, and Spanish *villa* along the San Antonio River "form[ed] one community," as Fray Benito Fernández de Santa Ana claimed in 1740.[14] Another community of Spanish and Indian settlers developed around the missions and presidio of La Bahía closer to the coast. From the perspective of Spanish record keepers, these mission-presidio complexes might resemble familiar sites aimed at religious conversion and regimented labor, as set up throughout New Spain. But from the perspective of semi-permanent native residents, the communities looked equally familiar as sites of seasonal migration, subsistence, and communal ritual—and that perspective prevailed. Indian families integrated missions into a long list of encampments spread across southern Texas among which they moved. Missions thereby functioned as temporary seasonal bases at which individuals and family bands could meet periodically to marshal resources, reunite with lost kin, form new kinship ties, and regroup socially and culturally.

Moreover, life in these joint settlements did not mean political subjugation or social assimilation for Indians. Not only did Indians, when in residence, maintain their own subsistence and defensive labors, those native socioeconomic skills were crucial to the survival of both the Indian and Spanish populations. Franciscans would argue that Indians were "enemies of work," but, as one missionary recorded, it was "any work, *other than hunting and fishing*," that was "excessive to the Indian male." In fact, men and women labored all the time, but it was work consistent with their own communal patterns; they refused only the work demanded of them by Spaniards.[15] As Fray Benito Fernández de Santa Ana explained to his superiors, the Indians of the region who joined mission settlements "want no subjection to royalty. . . . Their first interest is in temporal comfort."[16] Moreover, civil and military officials could not compel Indian labor without risk of losing critical defensive allies. Defending mission and civil settlements against Apache horse raids became the consuming occupation of Spaniards at mid-century, and one they could not accomplish without the fighting skills of resident Indian warriors. Indian men made up the largest percentage of fighting men in San Antonio, and the Spanish government recognized their critical importance to the settlement's defense, giving them the same military provisions allocated to presidial soldiers. In 1768 a viceregal report credited the native "bow and arrow men" as the military force that put San Antonio "beyond reach of any local or outside attack."[17] Flight from slavery may have initially brought these Indians and Spaniards together, but Spanish systems of coerced labor had no role in the relations within the communities they established. Yet their concerted efforts to defend these joint settlements against the ever-expanding territorial claims of Apaches did lead Tejanos to briefly join their provincial neighbors in another form of Indian bondage.

287

The next chapter of Indian slavery in Texas—enslavement defined by punitive war—began almost immediately after Spaniards took up residence at San Antonio de Béxar. On this northern edge of Spanish settlement, the government faced serious problems attracting settlers, soldiers, and native converts with whom to populate their colonial centers. The Spanish population of the Texas province at its height reached only slightly more than three thousand.[18] More importantly, Spanish colonial development remained rigidly hemmed in by far more populous and powerful Indian nations—both indigenous to the region (such as Caddos) and newly arrived (such as Apaches in the seventeenth century and Comanches and Wichitas in the mid eighteenth century). Spaniards thus found that even in the limited areas they claimed for settlement they faced a constant struggle to hold their own with superior native rivals. The first major challenge to the Spanish presence in South Texas came at the hands of Apaches.

Though now less well known than their western relatives, at least twelve groups of Lipan Apaches lived in central Texas and represented a widespread and formidable power throughout the eighteenth century. By the 1740s, "Lipan" had become the designation used by Spaniards to refer to the easternmost Plains Apache groups known variously as Ypandes, Ysandis, Chentis, and Pelones. Like their multiple Apache relatives to the west (Chiricahuas, Mescaleros, Jicarillas, and Navajos), they spoke dialects from the southern branch of the Athapaskan language group. Their economy centered on hunting and raiding for bison and horses, which did not allow for permanent settlements, though they did practice some semi-cultivation. Social units made up of matrilocal extended families and often named after a strong leader farmed and hunted together in individual rancherías (Indian encampments) that might cluster together for defense and ceremonial ritual. Usually numbering around four hundred people, these units represented an aggregation of ten to thirty extended families related by blood or marriage that periodically united for horse raids, bison hunts, and coordinated military action. No central leadership existed, and even the leaders of individual groups made decisions in consultation with extended family headmen, but unity of language, dress, and customs maintained collective identity and internal peace.[19]

Lipans, some eastern Mescaleros, Natagés (a division of Mescaleros), and Faraones (a division of Jicarillas) had gained an early advantage among Indians in central and south Texas, with horses acquired in the seventeenth century through trading and raiding in New Mexico. They used horses to expand their control over bison territories and to better secure the mobility and protection of their settlements in times of attack, as conflicts mounted with competing Wichita and Comanche bands.[20] In fact, captive Apaches would become as valuable as Spanish horses in Comanche and Wichita trading networks into French Louisiana.[21] As horses then rose in importance for Apache defense, so too did the raiding that maintained Apache herds. In response to this growing need, Apaches mounted debilitating raids on the horse herds of newly established Spanish missions, ranches, and presidios from the 1720s to the 1740s. In their own turn, Spaniards reacted with fear and frustration when their presidial forces proved unable to stop Apache warriors' raids.[22] Reviving Spanish policies from the sixteenth century that had developed against Chichimecas who fought to keep Spanish invaders out of their lands in north central Mexico, officials across the northern provinces turned to offensive attacks on Apache villages, bent on exterminating or enslaving as many as possible in desperate bids to stem the horse raids. Technically, any Indians captured in such a "just war" were to be sentenced as criminals to a finite term of enslavement, but deportation and perpetual servitude were soon touted as the only means of "pacifying" the regions nearest Spanish settlements. The language used to describe the Apache threat bore a striking resemblance to what had been said over one hundred years earlier of Chichimecas, as Spaniards wrote from a siege mentality, rhetorically denouncing Apaches as "barbarous enemies of humankind" even as they strategized that the sale of any captives taken would be sufficient incentive to motivate civilians to take up arms for the state.[23]

In the resultant warfare, Spanish forces and their Indian allies from the missions targeted Apache women and children in daybreak raids on their villages. The scale of Spanish captive taking vastly outnumbered that of customary Indian warfare in the region, which saw only small numbers of individuals taken. Not surprisingly, hostilities mounted in proportion to Spanish raids, and in turn the situation worsened for the captive women and children held in San Antonio de Béxar. As captivities lengthened from months into years, officials distributed the Apache women and children among soldiers and civilians both in Texas and in provinces to the south. Political considerations, not labor demands, conditioned the captives' fates. Spaniards rationalized their decision to keep these captives in bondage as a necessity of defense and identified the Apache women and children as *prisioneros* (prisoners of war) rather than *cautivos*, a description reserved only for Spaniards held by Indians.[24]

The process by which captive Apache women and children became political capital in Spanish-Indian diplomacy in the middle decades of the century was a rapid one. Spanish military officials resorted to just-war enslavements within only five years of the establishment of the San Antonio de Béxar presidio and the first three missions nearby.[25] It began in 1723 when Apache warriors carried off eighty horses from the Béxar presidial herds, deftly eluding the ten soldiers guarding the gates. After a fruitless twelve-hour pursuit, the captain of the presidio, Nicolás Flores, opted for a new plan to bring the Apache men to heel—he would take hostage their wives and children. Returning to where his men had left off, Flores found signs that the Apache raiding party had divided into five groups going off in as many directions (suggesting that warriors from five bands took part in the raid), but his forces chose to follow only one. For thirty-six days they followed various trails until, more by luck than perspicacity, they reached a shared encampment of several different Apache bands gathered for a concerted bison hunt more than one hundred leagues away from San Antonio. The Spaniards attacked, a battle raged for six hours, and in the end Flores claimed to have killed thirty-four warriors, including one chief. Tellingly, however, Fray Francisco Hidalgo at Mission San Antonio de Valero wrote days later of reports that Apache men had been shot in the back, suggesting that they had been covering the retreat of their families when they were killed.[26] Flores's men plundered one hundred and twenty horses, saddles, bridles, knives, and spears, but it was clear that the twenty women and children caught in the mêlée had been the real target.[27]

Upon return to San Antonio, conflict immediately flared between military and church officials over the fate of the captives. Objecting to tactics that could only exacerbate hostilities, Fray José González, another missionary at Valero, demanded the captives be returned as a diplomatic overture to reestablish peace rather than dividing them up among the men along with the rest of the "booty" as planned.[28] After weeks of argument, Flores agreed to the missionary's plan, but in doing so he turned over only one woman to him. González quickly went to work, trying to convey to her the message of peace and promise of the captives' release to be taken back to her people. As a mark of goodwill, and perhaps as advertisement of the benefits of conversion, the missionary dressed the Apache woman "after the Spanish fashion," using beads, rosaries, as well as a petticoat, a blouse, scarlet cloth, white embroidered hose, a ribboned hat, and a green skirt all borrowed from soldiers' wives. Most importantly, to mark the peaceful spirit of her mission he presented her with "an inlaid cross, which was very beautiful and which she should wear on her neck, with an embossed ribbon which Father took with great faith, since it had served as the ribbon to the key of the depository [of the mission's sacred vessels]."[29] With a flint and rock for making fires along the way, she left for home with a group of soldiers to escort her out of town.

Twenty-two days later, the captive woman returned to San Antonio accompanying an Apache delegation led by a principal Apache man with his wife at his side and three warriors at his back. Yet with no interpreter, communication was reduced to symbolic gestures. When Flores went out to greet the arrival of the Apache party, the Apache headman showed him both a baton of command (as sign of his chief's political authority) and a bison hide painted with the image of the sun (as sign of their deities' spiritual power), perhaps in answer to the cross sent to them by González via the captive emissary.[30] The delegation stayed for three days, but their negotiations were all for naught—even as the female emissary had traveled home with González's peace commission weeks before, Flores and his soldiers had divided the remaining nineteen women and children among themselves, some of them being taken to the coastal presidio at La Bahía while others were deported to lands even more distant.[31]

The delegation at last departed carrying with them all the gifts that the Valero missionaries could find: five rosaries and five knives for Apache chiefs, two bunches of glass beads, earrings, tobacco, brown sugar candy, and ground corn. Two months later, thirty Apaches visited again, stayed at Mission Valero, and again sought to attain the return of their lost family members. Negotiations collapsed when a chief sought to end Flores's stonewalling about the captives' fate by offering four Apache men as hostages if the Spanish commander would at least free the children. Flores flatly refused. Four soldiers later testified that as Flores heatedly defended his position, the Apaches silently gathered their belongings to depart the meeting room while one chief took the hand of one of the little girls held as captive, turned her to face Flores, and sorrowfully gestured as if to say: "'This is what you want, not peace.'"[32]

The loss of their wives and children drove furious Apache warriors to expand their onslaughts against Spanish horse herds.[33] That Flores's forces had attacked multiple bands of Apaches at the shared encampment spread ire throughout a number of different groups who, until then, had not viewed Spaniards as particular enemies. Their anger found expression as Spanish traveling parties between San Antonio and the Río Grande came under increasing attack, and raids on San Antonio continued through the 1720s.[34] In the 1730s viceregal authorities instructed Texas officials to respond with more punitive expeditions to reestablish the "honor of the king's arms." As Fray Juan Domingo Arricivita interpreted the government's view, Spanish arms needed to make Apaches "feel their strength," punish their "boldness," and "impose some proper respect."[35] In October 1732 governor Bustillo y Ceballos set out to do just this with an expeditionary force made up of 175 Spaniards, 60 Indian warriors from mission settlements, 140 pack loads of supplies, and 900 horses and mules. They marched for six weeks, winding their way—and periodically losing their way—over 200 leagues through Apachería before locating four separate Lipan and Mescalero Apache *rancherías*, with an estimated population of two thousand men, women, and children, spread out for a league along the San Sabá River.

Scouting parties indicated that a majority of the Apache men, some 500 warriors, were away hunting bison, and so the prospects for victory—and more captive trophies—appeared within the Spaniards' grasp. On December 9, Spanish forces launched a daybreak attack against which a severely reduced number of Apache men held off the San Antonio forces for upwards of five hours before accepting that retreat was unavoidable. As the few Apache men sought to cover the flight of their families, Spaniards captured 700 horses, 100 mule-loads of peltry, and 30 women and children. The following morning Spanish forces awoke to see armed Apache warriors watching them from vantage points all over the surrounding hills. As they made their slow way home, marching for fifteen days back over their tracks to San Antonio, the warriors kept them under eye the entire way, insuring that the invaders left Apache lands with the loss of as many horses as opportunity allowed them to drive away from the fringes of the military expedition.[36] The women and children, however, remained under guard and beyond the reach of their husbands, brothers, and fathers.

Upon return, many Spaniards immediately began worrying about the repercussions of their violent acts. After seeing firsthand the extent of Apache bands living northwest of San Antonio, military veterans did not doubt Apache capability for revenge and, within two days of their return, petitioned Governor Bustillo to negotiate a peace, arguing, "Otherwise, this Presidio, with its town and Missions, will be exposed to total destruction by this host of enemies."[37] In the end they were far more anxious than arrogant about their deeds on the San Sabá River. Pointedly, citizen settlers, who had previously clamored for Apache slaves, now demanded that Bustillo prohibit the division and distribution of the most recent captives and instead hold them as hostages to be used to negotiate a truce. In agreement with the citizenry, Fray Gabriel Vergara promoted the "good disposition" of the captives and suggested, once again, that Apache women from among the hostages be sent as emissaries of peace.[38]

Bustillo responded to the community's widespread fears, and on January 4, 1733, two Apache women, one Mescalero and one Lipan, rode out of San Antonio with provisions for their journey, letters from the governor to their leaders, and an escort of nineteen soldiers and one missionary, all of whom traveled with the women as far as the Guadalupe River—at which point the two captives entered the security of Apachería and the Spaniards became endangered and thus turned back to San Antonio. A month after the women's departure, a delegation of three leading Apache men arrived in San Antonio in the company of one of the freed captives. While their chiefs were assembling a council that would be representative of thirty-seven Apache bands in order to consider the situation, the delegation had been sent to ascertain Spanish sincerity. After three days of being feasted and "regaled" by Spaniards, the delegation departed to find out the council's decisions, promising to return in two months. True to their word, a second delegation of three warriors and a woman returned in March to trade bison meat and pelts. Yet this time, as the party left with an escort of two soldiers, twenty-four warriors approached from the opposite direction in military formation and promptly surrounded the Spanish escort. Perhaps drawing on past experiences that indicated how slim were the chances of getting family members back from Spaniards, Apache warriors had decided on vengeance. In accounts of the event, Spaniards attested to the bodies of the dead soldiers "marked with fury and impiety," "flayed" with pikes and arrows, and "inhumanly cut to pieces."[39]

Spanish fears flared anew. The presence of captives held in San Antonio marked the Spanish town as a target at which Apache men would aim retaliatory raids for their lost wives and daughters. Spanish and Indian *vaqueros* refused to go to outlying mission ranches to guard cattle. A petition of the *cabildo* (town council) stressed the need to strengthen defenses in anticipation of an invasion by Apache warriors aimed at liberating their kinswomen. Soldiers, perhaps in mute recognition of the Apache men's grief, sought to move their own families out of harm's way—beyond the Rio Grande. In Mexico City, Juan de Oliván y Rebolledo, the auditor of war, advised the viceroy that an alliance with Caddo bands was needed if Apaches were to be "compelled to make peace." Initially, however, Apaches made no further attack.[40] Instead, for the next three years other diplomatic means were sought, as small parties of Apaches regularly came to San Antonio to trade, giving them an opportunity to check on their captive family members. Foolishly, Spanish officials let such openings pass by and gradually distributed the Apache women and children among several people both within and without the province.[41] And just as quietly but inexorably, the brief détente came to an end as everyday Spanish-Apache exchanges waned and full-scale raiding returned.[42]

In the fall of 1737, events reached an all-time low from the perspective of Spaniards, as an Apache raiding party took one hundred horses from the presidial herd stationed sixteen leagues outside of town—moved there as a safety measure—and again they did so despite the presence of presidial guards. An expedition sent in pursuit to recover the horses returned empty-handed. Presidial commander José de Urrutia doubled the guard, and Apache raiders responded by stampeding an even larger number of horses in December. A pursuit party had no more luck than the first one. Into this tense situation rode a small Apache party led by chief Cabellos Colorados and composed of eight men, seven women, and one child. They traveled to San Antonio to trade but instead found themselves surrounded and captured by twenty-eight armed soldiers. They would become public sacrificial victims of hardening Spanish policy—policy that deported them to Mexico City in a desperate bid to induce the respect of other Apache leaders.

In the months following their capture, governor Prudencio de Orobio y Basterra with great deliberation gathered testimony on the "infidelity of Apaches," implicitly deeming them all one united group, but Cabellos Colorados and his family band would stand in for all their cohort. Of the known Apache rancherías, theirs was located the closest to San Antonio, seemingly providing their raiding parties with first and best access to the town. Cabellos Colorados himself was known to be a man of standing and reputation among Apaches—in Spanish opinion, making him a leader to whom would naturally fall responsibility for leading raids against Spanish presidios as spread out as those of San Antonio, San Juan Bautista, and Sacramento.[43] Moreover his wife had been seen repeatedly among Apache trading parties in San Antonio, her presence—as the wife of such a notorious war leader—only comprehensible if she had been sent to scout troop strength and movements. By such circular logic, Spanish officials portrayed Cabellos Colorados and his band as responsible for all the horse thefts of the preceding three years.[44]

While Cabellos Colorados attempted to negotiate with his captors, one of the hostage women again emerged as a mediator (joined later by women of other bands), traveling back and forth for months between Apache *rancherías* and San Antonio in an effort to get enough horses with which to ransom the entire party's freedom. Hostile attacks from other enemies diverted Apache resources, however, which in turn limited their ability to produce enough horses to appease Spanish officials. In the meantime, the women brought bison meat with which to feed their captive kinsmen and bison hides to offer as gifts of goodwill for their Spanish captors. All to no avail. An elderly man who came with promises of peace from all the Apache bands near San Antonio found his diplomatic overture abruptly dismissed by governor Orobio. The governor refused even to hear the man's personal pleas for the emancipation of his elderly wife, one of those held hostage by Spanish forces, for whom he begged by offering up his only horse and mule.

No offers of horses or promises of truce seemed sufficient to dissuade officials that an example had to be made of the penalties that Spanish imperial force (reframed as the force of law by the proceedings of the hearing) could and would mete out. Orobio pointedly did not deign to spare the women and children from the same fate as Cabellos Colorados and his men, condemning them all to the same exile and enslavement. In his order of February 16, 1739, he declared that "the thirteen Indian men and women prisoners in the said presidio, [shall be taken] tied to each other, from jurisdiction to jurisdiction, to the prison of the capital in Mexico City, and that the two-year-old daughter of chief Cabellos Colorados, María Guadalupe, shall be treated in the same manner." Two days later, the seven men, six women, and one child marched out of San Antonio under the guard of a mixed group of soldiers and civilians.[45] They traveled for 102 days on foot—shackled each night in leg irons, stocks, manacles, or ropes—before reaching Mexico City in late May. A man and a woman died during the forced march, and seven more succumbed in the disease-ridden viceregal prison or city workhouses within six months of their incarceration. The final destiny of the other five remains unknown. Their last appearances in written records indicate that prison officials sent two men to a hospital while consigning two women, also very ill, to servitude in private homes of prominent Spaniards. The last of the five, little María Guadalupe, was separated from her mother (who was one of the two sent into servitude), and later efforts to reunite them failed when it was discovered that the woman's "employer" or "master" had made off with her, leaving the girl an orphan.[46]

The destruction of Cabellos Colorados's family band by "just war" enslavement heralded the rise of Spanish policies enacted with much more extensive reach and damage outside the borders of Texas in reaction to Spanish failure to "pacify" Apache peoples. Across the provinces of Sonora, Nueva Vizcaya, and New Mexico, Apache raids increasingly devastated struggling Spanish communities, mines, missions, farms, and ranches. Punitive enslavement spread as imperial officials sought to hold off what looked like a united onslaught from Apachería when viewed from the vantage point of Mexico City. Military regulations had first made official the legal imprisonment and deportation of Apaches to Mexico in 1729 as the only means "to restrain them and bring peace." Though later reitera-tions of such policy made claims to more humane treatment, at least for women and children, in practice the demand to eliminate any threat of Apaches' escape, return, and renewal of raids mandated the expatriation of increasing numbers of men, women, and children, not only to Mexico City but also, by the 1770s, to Veracruz and Havana. More to the point, women and children proved to be the ones destined to become convict laborers and servants in private homes. As Ana María Alonso pointedly notes, in three years alone, from 1786 to 1789, the Spanish militia in the northern provinces, excluding Coahuila and Texas, took prisoner 665 Apaches, only 55 of whom were men. Spaniards were not decimating warrior numbers—they were demoralizing them.[47]

Meanwhile back in Texas, however, Apache enslavements came to a halt almost as quickly as they had begun. The push of weakly posi-tioned military commanders to increase their political and financial gains inspired a coordinated and wrathful Apache counterpunch that proved to end Spanish slave raiding within less than a decade. As Cabellos Colo-rados's family were marched south, the military commander at the San Antonio presidio, José de Urrutia, petitioned for permission to launch new punitive campaigns against Apache rancherías—making the argument that the sale of any captives taken would pay for the soldiers, civil auxiliaries, and other assorted military costs of the undertaking. He ultimately won approval for an expedition in 1739 that captured "many" Apache women and children whose enslavement fed Spanish coffers.[48] His son, Toribio, who inherited his father's post as commander at the Béxar presidio the following year, led his own major campaign in 1745. Choosing a ranchería where the men had left on a bison hunt, Urrutia's forces attacked the Lipan and Natage families still in the camp and captured multiple women and children. The fact that fourteen of the Apache captives taken in 1745, aged one to seven years old, were immediately baptized upon the return of the campaign gave further indication that the Spaniards had no intention of using the children to barter for peace.[49] Rather, the baptisms signaled their new status as slaves of Spanish owners. In this spirit, Texas colonists, like their New Mexico neighbors, called these enslaved children criados (literally "those raised up"), to recognize the Spaniards' proclaimed role in rearing the children who in turn owed a service debt to their "guardians." In this way, they also circumvented legal prohibitions against Indian slavery.[50] The value of captives once representing diplomatic capital now appeared to rest more in an assertion of punitive power and domination.

Completely disregarding the window dressing of baptism for captive Apache children, missionaries again offered harsh criticism of the military's tactics. Fray Benito Fernández argued that nothing was to be gained by the raids except increasing Apache hatred.[51] Fray Juan Domingo Arricivita concluded that the campaigns meant to bring a "cessation of strife" had instead "enlivened the war," because "[i]n proportion as the Apache suffered harm, so did their hatred and the revenge they took increase."[52] Even Toribio de Urrutia admitted his trepidation, reporting to the viceroy that no one traveled along the roads out of fear of Apaches, that he and his forces maintained constant vigilance at all hours of the night in addition to stationed sentinels because "no moon passes without [Apache] tracks being found near the presidio," and that if things continued in this way, all respect for the presidios and settlements would be lost.[53]

Just as had the relatives of Cabellos Colorados, Apaches continued to travel each year to San Antonio and make peace overtures in hopes of seeing lost family members and obtaining their release. Yet despite the promise held out by these visits, Spanish officials in the 1740s backed the desires of military men out to prove their might. Having seemingly taken the legal distinction between *cautivos* and *prisioneros* as their carte blanche for wartime enslavements, militia groups made up of both soldiers and civilians gradually wore away at Apache family bands. When captives were never offered for exchange, Apache women and children who served as human trophies of war were parceled out among soldiers and citizens to be sold for profit to Mexican mining districts or West Indian labor camps.[54] A 1787 memorial from the San Antonio *cabildo* proudly promoted the deeds of the "flower of our ancestry" who had fought a "glorious war" in the 1730s and 1740s by seeking out Apaches in their own lands, where they "killed them, destroyed them, routed them, and drove them off." "They conquered them and formed chains of prisoners," it continued, "and spared the lives only of those captives who were likely to be converted to the faith, and the children, whom they brought back to increase the missions and the *villa*."[55]

Yet as it turned out, the 1745 slaving campaign finally ignited concerted violence by Apache warriors from numerous bands. In an unprecedented move, Apache leaders sent four women to San Antonio, first to warn missionaries at Concepción of a coming attack, notably Fray Fernández de Santa Ana, who had been one of the few in the Spanish community to respond positively to their peaceful contacts in the previous five years. Then the women notified officials at the presidio that peace was no longer an option, that only mission Concepción would be spared their vengeance.[56] Over the next three weeks, Apache raiders killed nine people and subjected presidial, mission, and civilian herds—all except Concepción—to relentless raids. Fernández de Santa Ana said later that in the attacks, Apache warriors "made war more cruelly than I have ever experienced in the province."[57] San Antonio paid in lost lives and horses for the Apache women and children they had killed and enslaved over twenty-two years.

Yet the real measure of Apache fury came in a direct attack upon the presidio itself on June 30—another unprecedented act in Apache warfare.[58] Three hundred and fifty Lipan and Natage Apaches entered San Antonio at night and began their attack. As fighting broke out, an Apache captive held at one of the missions escaped to join Apache warriors. Once identified, the escapee was asked by a Natage chief to tell him the fate of his seven-year-old daughter taken captive two months before. Upon hearing that the captives were well and in the missions, the chief consulted with other band chiefs, and they called off their men. The leaders must have believed that, like most of the captives before, their wives and children had already been sold away or deported, but the news that they were not lost to them was sufficient to stop the attack.[59] The fate of the seven-year-old daughter of the Natage chief ultimately helped to bring about the first peace accord between Spaniards and Apaches.[60]

A stream of women, both captive and free, moved back and forth between San Antonio and various Apache rancherías between 1745 and 1749 as a human line of communication, as Apache men tried one more time to regain their wives and children. The stream began in August 1745 when the captive girl's father sent a woman bearing a cross to San Antonio, accompanied only by a small boy, to offer gifts to presidial commander Urrutia as pledge of renewed Apache good will. Through the fall and spring, more than twenty visitors came to the presidio and to Mission Concepción to negotiate, each one carrying "well made" crosses.[61] In response, freed Apache women left San Antonio carrying Spanish promises to release captives from all previous campaigns in return for peace.[62] The parade of female visitors finally opened the door for Spanish and Apache men to come together in mutual truce. But the release of all the captive Apache women and children as promised proved more complicated. In March of 1749, after the last raid netted Spanish forces ninety women and forty-seven children, the captives were to be housed with missionaries but some nevertheless fell into civilian hands—and even governor Pedro del Barrio y Espriella spirited several of them off to the capital at Los Adaes before the viceroy ordered their return.[63] A month later, in April, the governor released two Apache women and one man, and sent them to their rancherías with promises of freedom for all captives. In August, Apache and Spanish leaders finally met over several days to hammer out a truce that culminated with a formal compact of peace in August of 1749.[64]

The end of Apache enslavement in Texas, then, came not from Apache capitulation to Spanish forces but rather the reverse. Indeed, shifting power relations following the growing presence of Comanches and Wichitas in the region proved to be a major impetus for both Spaniards and Apaches to suddenly look more favorably upon one another's peace overtures, seeing in the other a better ally than enemy. Bands of Wichitas and Comanches were not only expanding their territories, they were also often united in alliance—an alliance against which Apaches and Spaniards would need all the help they could muster to defend their respective territories. By the 1760s, Apaches were losing their military advantage in the region to these newcomers who were armed with European arms and ammunition from New Mexico and Louisiana. Spaniards meanwhile were overwhelmed at the notion that foes even more intimidating than Apaches were headed in their direction. Yet the newly achieved Spanish-Apache peace foundered almost immediately in the face of formidable Comanche and Wichita aggressions in the 1750s and 1760s. The complete razing of Mission San Sabá in 1758 by a united force of two thousand Comanches, Wichitas, Caddos, Tonkawas, and other allied nations—less than one year after its erection in the midst of Apachería had given institutional form to the newfound Apache-Spanish alliance—sent reverberations all the way to Mexico City.[65] Echoing worries expressed within Texas, viceregal officials feared the loss of the entire province to Comanche and Wichita conquest. "We shall have, it is undeniable, one day the Nations of the North as neighbors; they already are approaching us now," wrote the Marqués de Rubí in 1768. Not only did he concede the impossibility of further Spanish expansion northward in recognition of the "true dominions" of Comanches and Wichitas, he proposed the drawing back of Spanish borders. Rubí then designed a cordon of fifteen presidios to protect those border (which he did not identify as extending north of the Rio Grande), with presidios spread at hundred-mile intervals across the entire length of the northern provinces from the Gulf of Mexico to California. Only with great reluctance did he stop short of calling for the abandonment of San Antonio de Béxar (which would remain above the line) and the relinquishment of the entire Texas province.[66]

Beginning in the 1770s, Spanish civil and military officials tried to stave off the Comanche and Wichita nations through diplomatic overtures, and, initially, Spanish attempts to deal with the two native powers looked like they might revive Apache enslavement. Using a proposed alliance against Apaches to win them over, Spaniards sought to open up a new slave trade in Apaches. Spanish officials, they proposed, would recompense Comanche and Wichita warriors for any Apaches captured in war or raids through what they termed "ransom" and "redemption" payments. The payment for war captives would come in the form of horses and material goods. Thus, for instance, less than two months after the first peace treaty between Spaniards and Comanches had been negotiated in 1785, a Comanche party rode into San Antonio de Béxar to meet with the governor, and, on the side, "hold a sale" in which two Apache girls brought them nine horses, in addition to guns, blankets, and *piloncillos* (brown sugar candies) that they earned in exchange for deer and bison hides.[67] Yet such ransom exchanges proved rare. Unlike in New Mexico, where traffic in captives took place within the context of *ferias* (trade fairs), similar markets did not develop in Texas until after the 1790s, and there Spaniards never had sufficient goods or horses to attract Comanche exchange.[68]

Texas officials thus found they could not lure Comanches away from the better-financed and better-supplied markets and slave trade of New Mexico. Wichitas meanwhile preferred to meet their economic needs with the trade goods supplied by increasing numbers of British and later Anglo-Americans from the East, a process that similarly diminished the value of limited profits offered by Spanish diplomatic ritual in San Antonio. Their raids and captive taking thus steadily decreased in Texas, and Apaches had again made peace with Spaniards in southern Texas by the 1780s. Over the same years that Apache enslavements reached new heights in other northern provinces, Lipans found the means to refashion relations with Spaniards and, in response, officials designed a program that would provide incentives—subsidies, goods, arms and ammunition—if Apache bands agreed to settle near the watchful eye of presidios. These communities were termed

"*Apaches de paz.*" Even Comanche leaders seemed to fall in with such peace plans, declaring that they would attack Apaches only "as long as they do not find them settled in permanent towns with the Spanish." As a result, in sharp contrast to New Mexico, Nueva Vizcaya, and Sonora, where Apaches continued to be captured, enslaved, and deported to Mexico City and Cuba, the taking of Apache prisoners of war in Texas petered out.[69]

A case in 1777 hinted at the exigencies of the moment that defined Spanish relations with Apaches and the fleeting incidence of Indian slavery in the province. In a letter dated September of that year, the commandant general of the northern provinces, Teodoro de Croix, wrote to Texas governor Juan María de Ripperdá with his judgment that an Apache held at the new town of Nuestra Señora del Pilar Bucareli "should not be counted in the class of slaves." Interestingly the small town of Bucareli had been established in the midst of Caddo communities in eastern Texas near the Louisiana border—Caddo peoples who had acted as crucial intermediaries in the trade networks linking Comanche and Wichita communities to markets in the French province of Louisiana. Apache captives had traveled through this network, ending up as slaves in the French military and trading post of Natchitoches. Most likely this newly freed slave was one of those former war captives. Yet "freedom" did not mean that the Apache youth could return to his home and family. In Croix's letter (the only archival fragment reporting on the Apache's story), the commandant general went on to offer his agreement with governor Ripperdá's "providence" in granting subsistence for the Apache in order to "destroy any possible desire to incorporate back to his nation." Nevertheless, enslavement, much less deportation, was no longer deemed necessary.[70]

Almost simultaneously, conflicts in the 1770s between Texas officials and those of a new neighbor along the Gulf Coast, the province of Nuevo Santander, did more than hint at the complex shifts in Spanish attitudes regarding the enslavement of Indians in Texas. In 1772 Texas officials lodged a complaint with the viceroy, accusing Nuevo Santander residents of enslaving Indians along the lower Río Grande. The viceroy in turn ordered the governor of Texas to look into the situation, an investigation he carried out in the spring of 1773. In the *villa* of San Antonio de Béxar, governor Juan María de Ripperdá took depositions from an Indian convert from Mission Concepción as well as a presidial officer and two soldiers from the Béxar presidio. All three reported that Indian women from the area where the Rio Grande reaches the Gulf complained that Spaniards from Nuevo Santander had taken many of their children away from them by force or intimidation, offering them only *piloncillos* in consolation for the "exchange." A blacksmith from the *villa* of Camargo and a nearby rancher had confirmed the women's woeful tale, explaining further that the slavers had come from a regional salt mine and had attempted to sell children to each of them. Yet nothing appears to have been done to punish or stop the slave raiding.[71]

In fact, seven years later when the investigation was revisited by the succeeding Texas governor, Domingo Cabello, Cabello confirmed the earlier reports but concluded that this trade in Indians was justified by its benevolent ends: the victims had been "taught the Doctrine and converted to Christianity" and had "been kept in such a way that many of them are now grown up and married." The governor admitted that in some cases a "profit motive has intervened by virtue of the favorable purchase price" so that many of the children had been sold to Spaniards in other towns like Saltillo, but since the "object is always that they be Christians not that they be enslaved," the citizens could not really be found guilty of kidnapping. In other words, presumably, Christian enslavement as *criados* was preferable to heathen freedom as *indios barbáros* (independent Indians).[72]

The charges (and countercharges launched by Nuevo Santander residents against their Texas accusers) indicated that there was more here to meet the eye than just benevolent Texas Spaniards concerned for vulnerable Indian families. The case, in fact, played out against a backdrop of rivalry between the two provinces' missionaries who were vying for neophytes for their missions and had deemed the lower Rio Grande region along their shared borders a prime recruiting area. The competition revealed that the line between mission "recruiting" and slave raiding remained as blurred as it had been at the beginning of the century. Besides forgiving Indian enslavement in Nuevo Santander, the Texas investigations made clear that missionaries from Texas regularly went to the same region along the Gulf Coast to "seize" Indians for their missions—a form of capture that went entirely unquestioned by provincial authorities in the reports. Epidemics that had regularly cycled through mission populations and diminished their numbers had led Texas missionaries to deem this new form of recruitment a necessity if their missions were to survive. The Texas soldiers' testimony in 1773 about the stolen children originated from the fact that they themselves had captured the mothers who bewailed their children's loss![73]

As it turned out, Fray Francisco Durá from Mission Concepción in San Antonio, accompanied by ten Indian residents of San Antonio missions and by a detachment from the presidio, had gone to the coastal region in search of "heathen" Indians. There the party had "fallen upon" an encampment of sixty Indians but were not able to seize more than nineteen—an elderly man, three male youths, eight women, and the rest children—because their daylight attack had been seen in advance and most had escaped into nearby woods where they were saved from capture by impassable undergrowth. Nor was this a one-time event. The year before, a group from San Antonio had similarly gone out to the region in the company of Fray Asisclos Valverde but had lost their captives—whom they had surrounded and tied up—when challenged by military guards from Nuevo Santander who forced them to defer to the prior claim of the nearby royal salt mines and Mission San Joaquín del Monte in Reynosa. Thus Texas missionaries, Nuevo Santander missionaries, slave hunters, and mine representatives were all competing for the souls or labors of these Rio Grande Indians. A sordid intrigue indeed.[74]

In excusing away the capture of children by Nuevo Santander residents seven years after the initial investigation, Governor Cabello in 1780 made a point of arguing in his report that the real abuses lay in the "wretched and miserable" conditions to be found in Nuevo Santander missions, where "the poor neophytes scarcely get anything to eat; and so only a few subsist at these places, and many return to their villages or voluntarily enter some home or hacienda in the regions." The governor thus implicitly asserted that, in Nuevo Santander, missions were so bad that

Indians preferred to work as slaves rather than live as neophytes. Moreover, he made a claim for the superiority of Texas missions by proceeding to list the multiple Indian peoples from that region who could be found living in missions in San Antonio and La Bahía and, by implication, living happily since they had not chosen to run away.[75]

This was not merely provincial boosterism on the governor's part but a defense against accusations out of Nuevo Santander that Texas missions had been stealing Indians out of their jurisdiction. In a rather odd defense, Cabello went on to counter accusations of competition brewing between the two provinces' missionaries by reporting that in April 1779 another Texas missionary, Fray Manuel Gonzáles of San Juan Capistrano, had combed the entire coast near the town of Camargo, with a military escort from the San Antonio presidio, and brought back many "apostates and infidels" without any opposition from Nuevo Santander residents. In fact, his expedition had been so successful that, even as the governor sat writing his report, the missionary and soldiers were back in the coastal region patrolling for more Indians. Please note, however, that if they were capturing "apostates," then Indians *were* running away, thereby making clear that incarceration in Texas missions was no more preferable to that in the missions or mines closer to home. As late as 1784, ninety-two Borrados (which came to be the name used in the Texas missions for all Indians from the lower Rio Grande area) fled San Antonio for home five months after being brought from the coast to Mission San José.[76]

In 1785 a legal case confronted Cabello with evidence that further denied his earlier claims that Indian servitude was a benevolent institution insuring Indian children's Christian conversion, upbringing, and future marriage and civilized life in Nuevo Santander. That year, María Gertrudis de la Peña, a young Indian woman from the lower Rio Grande area, was sold as a slave to a resident of San Antonio de Béxar and then promptly went before Cabello to sue for her freedom. In unknowing contradiction of the governor's judgment that the selling of children (like herself) in Nuevo Santander was acceptable, María was convinced that with the governor of Texas "there would not be an absence of justice."[77]

Until her arrival in Texas, Maria's experience had not been an uncommon one. She explained to the governor in an initial writ, and later in a first-person deposition, that she had been passed through the hands of four owners. Her enslavement had begun at the age of four, when, according to a 1768 deed, a city official of Saltillo, named Pedro José de la Peña, had purchased María for fifty pesos in the royal salt mines of Vallecillo from a man named José Manuel de Vocanegra. Expressing no memory as to how she had come into the miner's hands, she wrote that her biological father simply had given her away—"so they tell me." That her father was laboring in the salt mines suggests that he too may have lost his freedom. María had lived with Peña until the age of sixteen. At that point, Peña had gotten her pregnant and quickly decided to sell her to a soldier at the Rio Grande presidio of San Juan Bautista. In order to avoid exposure and scandal, the city official sought to insure that she gave birth far from the town where he had risen to the level of secondary mayor. Peña, whom María referred to as her "adoptive father," told her that "this was the best way." Meanwhile, Alférez Antonio Toledo y Oquilla paid the same fifty pesos for María when Peña conferred the right he had in her "because of having brought her up," on paper marking her as a *criada*, not a slave. Though Peña added the stipulation that Toledo "see her as a daughter," one does not need to speculate too much from his own behavior to realize that these men saw little connection between what they put down on paper and how they treated her in real life.[78]

María's sexual abuse had not ended with Peña. Though she believed that she had gone to Toledo "under the name of daughter and not of slave," she eventually discovered the "fraud and deceit" perpetuated by Peña and Toledo. Her child died days after birth and, after two years with Toledo, she decided it no longer suited her to serve him and attempted to leave his house. Toledo responded that she owed him three years service as compensation for the fifty pesos and refused to count the two years already spent with him as part of that tenure. When she refused to accept his assertion of ownership, an enraged Toledo took away all her clothes, presumably her only possessions, and hired her out to a resident near the presidio in whose household María spent a month's confinement before being sold to her last owner, Angel Navarro of San Antonio de Béxar, again for the same fifty pesos. Though she did not accept her status as a slave,

María agreed to work for Navarro, on paper committing herself to three years servitude in exchange for his promise to free her—but pointedly she told governor Cabello that she had even then "hoped to appeal to the señor governor of this province (Texas)" who would give her the justice she had not found at the Presidio San Juan Bautista. Notably, she did not expect justice from her new owner, but from the province itself, and her expectations were not proven wrong.

Her contract with Navarro was made on October 24, 1784, and by January 1785, María had submitted a writ to Cabello asking that he investigate the "deed of sale of my condition of slavery, since under the name of slave I live in the house of the aforesaid don Angel, suffering many ill-treatments from all his family and especially from the referred don Angel." After taking depositions and viewing the procession of deeds of sale, Governor Cabello in March decreed that María, "being by nature free," had been the victim of transactions that were "null, fraudulent, and contrary to all the rights of man and what is stated in the royal municipal laws of these kingdoms, which are so favorable to the freedom of the Indians." He declared her free and exempt from any obligation to serve Navarro; meanwhile Navarro was also exempt from paying fifty pesos to Toledo, leaving Toledo the right against Peña to seek compensation. Happily for María, she had wisely sought emancipation in a province where outright Indian slavery might be condoned from a distance but had never taken root within its borders.[79] Cabello's decision offered further proof that the lines between bondage and freedom could be drawn quite variously at any given time given the different approaches and perspectives of soldiers, residents, missionaries, officials, and Indians themselves. María's decision to seek freedom in Texas, meanwhile, gave indication of the rather unique position the Texas province had come to hold among its neighbors.

The course of Spanish-Indian relations in Texas illuminates how amorphous the category, or categories, of slavery could be in early America. Contrasting forms of enslavement also offered a barometer of power relations among Europeans and Indians. Slave hunting based in Mexico in the sixteenth and seventeenth centuries drove the establishment of shared encampments of Indians, both native and new to Texas, who in turn fundamentally shaped the form of mission-presidio complexes that served as focal points of Spanish settlement in the eighteenth century. Apache challenges to the Spanish toehold in the region then led desperate Spaniards to fall back upon punitive strategies used in the past and in other areas of New Spain—strategies centered on the capture of prisoners of war. The raids of presidial forces at mid century for Apache captives to be deported to Mexico City represented violent efforts to hold off Apache encroachments. Later attempts to ally with Comanches and Wichitas encouraged Spaniards to try to purchase Apache captives through diplomatic ritual. Throughout all that, bondage had had little to do with labor considerations and had never developed into a system by which Spaniards could coerce labor or build the province economically.

Practices of Indian enslavement, in some sense, might be seen as odd geopolitical bookends to Spanish colonial development in Texas. At the beginning of the century, devastations wrought by the earlier slave raiding of Spaniards from other provinces first defined the limited area within which Spanish settlement would find a place in Texas. At the end of the century, the attempts of hard-pressed officials and their forces to take and enslave Apache captives measured Spanish inability to hold that place without the sanction of dominant Indian powers. By that point, Texas may have even come to represent something of a refuge for those who wished to escape enslavement elsewhere, though we must be cautious not to read too much into the rhetoric of María Gertrudis de la Peña. Thus, far removed from the higher level of politics and diplomacy, Spaniards and Indians alike questioned, challenged, and negotiated the ways in which bondage and freedom defined and redefined their everyday lives. At that level, the bookends might become the far more intimate ones measuring the life of an individual, a family, or even an entire community.

Notes

For more detailed discussions of the labor relations within the San Antonio missions and the captive and horse raids between Apaches and Spaniards, see chapters 3 and 4 of Juliana Barr, *Peace Came in the Form of a Woman: Indians and Spaniards in the Texas Borderlands* (Chapel Hill: University of North Carolina Press, 2007), from which parts of this essay have been adapted.

1. *Álvar Núñez Cabeza de Vaca: His Account, His Life, and the Expedition of Pánfilo de Narváez*, 3 vols., trans. Rolena Adorno and Patrick Charles Pautz (Lincoln: University of Nebraska Press, 1999), 1: 245; Rolena Adorno, "The Negotiation of Fear in Cabeza de Vaca's *Naufragios*," *Representations* 33 (Winter 1991), 163–99.

2. *Álvar Núñez Cabeza de Vaca*, 239–41.

3. *Álvar Núñez Cabeza de Vaca*, 249, 251.

4. Cabeza de Vaca's horror at Indian enslavement at Spanish hands highlights how the extraordinary circumstances of his own experiences among Indian peoples made him more empathetic to the plight of subjugated Indians. In later years, he proved to be a staunch proponent of better treatment for native peoples under Spanish rule in the Americas.

5. Enslaved African Americans did live in some of the settlements of Spanish Texas, but in quite limited numbers, usually as house servants. Jesús F. de la Teja, *San Antonio de Béxar: A Community on New Spain's Northern Frontier* (Albuquerque: University of New Mexico Press, 1995), 123; Alwyn Barr, *Black Texans: A History of African Americans in Texas, 1528–1995*, 2nd ed. (Norman: University of Oklahoma Press, 1996), 13–14.

6. For discussion of these categories, see Igor Kopytoff, "Slavery," *Annual Review of Anthropology* 11 (1982), 218.

7. Ramón A. Gutiérrez, *When Jesus Came the Cornmothers Went Away: Marriage, Sexuality, and Power in New Mexico, 1500–1846* (Stanford: Stanford University Press, 1991), 149–156, 171–90, 199 and James F. Brooks, *Captives and Cousins: Slavery, Kinship, and Community in the Southwest Borderlands* (Chapel Hill: University of North Carolina Press for the Omohundro Institute of Early American History and Culture, 2002), 6, 8, 121–42.

8. José Cuello, "The Persistence of Indian Slavery and Encomienda in the Northeast of Colonial Mexico, 1577–1723," *Journal of Social History* 21 (Summer 1988), 683–700; Susan M. Deeds, "Rural Work in Nueva Vizcaya: Forms of Labor Coercion on the Periphery," *Hispanic American Historical Review* 69 (August 1989), 425–49; David J. Weber, *Bárbaros: Spaniards and Their Savages in the Age of Enlightenment* (New Haven: Yale University Press, 2005), 234–41; Stafford Poole, "'War by Fire and Blood': The Church and the Chichimecas, 1585," *Americas* 22 (October 1965), 115–37; Robert S. Haskett, "'Our Suffering with the Taxco Tribute': Involuntary Mine Labor and Indigenous Society in Central New Spain," *Hispanic American Historical Review* 71 (August 1991), 447–75; Donald E. Chipman, "The Traffic in Indian Slaves in the Province of Panuco, New Spain, 1523–1533," *The Americas* 23 (October 1966), 142–55; Peter Bakewell, *Silver Mining and Society in Colonial Mexico: Zacatecas, 1546–1700* (Cambridge: Cambridge University Press, 1971); William L. Sherman, "Indian Slavery and the Cerrato Reforms," *Hispanic American Historical Review* 51 (February 1971), 25–50; Silvio Zavala, *Los Esclavos Indios en Nueva España* (Mexico City: Colegio Nacional, 1967), 179–349.

9. Daniel T. Reff, *Disease, Depopulation, and Cultural Change in Northwestern New Spain, 1518–1764* (Salt Lake City: University of Utah Press, 1991); Juan Bautista Chapa, *Texas and Northeastern Mexico, 1630–1690*, ed. William C. Foster, trans. Ned F. Brierley (Austin: University of Texas Press, 1997), 30–33, 49, 68, 141, for father-daughter story; Peter Gerhard, *The North Frontier of New Spain* (Princeton: Princeton University Press, 1982).

10. As Peter Gerhard describes, "The Indians were hunted like animals. . . . Every law concerning humane treatment of the natives was disobeyed" as they terrorized populations throughout the regions from the Gulf Coast through Coahuila, all the way north of the Rio Grande — native peoples who, once enslaved, would be termed mere *piezas* (literally "pieces" but, in this instance, synonymous with "slaves"). Gerhard, *The North Frontier of New Spain*, 328, 344–48; 345 for quote; Reff, *Disease, Depopulation, and Cultural Change in Northwestern*

New Spain, 30, 52, 126, 140; Cuello, "The Persistence of Indian Slavery and Encomienda in the Northeast of Colonial Mexico," 683–700; Vito Alessio Robles, *Coahuila y Texas en la Época Colonial*, 2nd ed. (Mexico, 1978).

11. *The Journeys of René Robert Cavelier, Sieur de La Salle*, 2 vols., ed. Isaac Joslin Cox (New York: Allerton Book Co., 1905), I: 273; Robert Weddle, *The French Thorn: Rival Explorers in the Spanish Sea, 1682–1762* (College Station: Texas A&M University Press, 1991), 29–30; Robert Weddle, *Spanish Sea: The Gulf of Mexico in North American Discovery, 1500–1685* (College Station: Texas A&M University Press, 1985), 333–49; Cuello, "The Persistence of Indian Slavery and Encomienda in the Northeast of Colonial Mexico"; Robert S. Weddle, *San Juan Bautista: Gateway to Spanish Texas* (Austin: University of Texas Press, 1968), 3–86; Fray Isidro de Espinosa, *Crónica de los colegios de propaganda fide de la Nueva España*, ed. Lino Gómez Canedo (Washington DC: Academy of American Franciscan History, 1964; Madrid, 1746), 776–77.

12. Thomas R. Hester, "Texas and Northeastern Mexico: An Overview" [for quote] and "Perspectives on the Material Culture of the Mission Indians of the Texas-Northeastern Mexico Borderlands," in *Columbian Consequences, Volume I: Archaeological and Historical Perspectives on the Spanish Borderlands West*, ed. David Hurst Thomas (Washington DC: Smithsonian Institution Press, 1989): 191–211, 213–29; T. N. Campbell, "The Coahuiltecans and their Neighbors," "Name All the Indians of the Bastrop Area," and "Indians of the San Antonio Missions," in *The Indians of Southern Texas and Northeastern Mexico* (Austin: Texas Archeological Research Laboratory), 39–59, 71–77, 79–93; *Reassessing Cultural Extinction: Change and Survival at Mission San Juan Capistrano, Texas*, ed. Alston V. Thoms, et al. (San Antonio: San Antonio Missions National Historical Park, National Park Service, and College Station: Center for Ecological Archaeology, Texas A&M University Press, 2001).

13. T. N. Campbell, *The Payaya Indians of Southern Texas* (San Antonio: Southern Texas Archaeological Association, 1975), 5.

14. Fray Benito Fernández de Santa Ana to Fray Pedro del Barco, February 20, 1740 in *The San José Papers: The Primary Sources for the History of Mission San José y San Miguel de Aguayo from its Founding in 1720 to the Present, Part I: 1719–1791*, ed. Marion A. Habig, trans. Benedict Leutenegger (San Antonio: Old Spanish Missions Historical Research Library at San José Mission, 1978), 53.

15. Mardith Keithly Schuetz, "The Indians of the San Antonio Missions, 1718-1821" (PhD diss., University of Texas at Austin, 1980), 241; Fray Benito Fernández de Santa Ana to Governor Francisco García Larios, September 9, 1748, in *Letters and Memorials of the Father Presidente Fray Benito Fernández de Santa Ana, 1736–1754: Documents on the Missions of Texas from the Archives of the College of Querétaro*, ed. Marion A. Habig, trans. Benedict Leutenegger (San Antonio: Old Spanish Missions Historical Research Library at Our Lady of the Lake University 1981), 81.

16. Fray Benito Fernández de Santa Ana to Fray Guardian Pedro del Barco, February 20, 1740, in "Two Franciscan Documents on Early San Antonio, Texas," trans. Benedict Leutenegger, *Americas* 25 (October 1968), 202.

17. Thomás Phelipe de Winthuysen to Viceroy Conde de Fuenclara, August 19, 1744, Béxar Archives, Center for American History, University of Texas at Austin; Nicolás de Lafora, *The Frontiers of New Spain: Nicolás de Lafora's Description, 1766–1768*, ed. Lawrence Kinnaird (Berkeley CA: Quivira Society, 1958), 160; Hugo O'Conor, *The Defenses of Northern New Spain: Hugo O'Conor's Report to Teodoro de Croix, July 22, 1777* (Dallas: Southern Methodist University Press for the DeGolyer Library, 1994), 57–58; Roque de Medina to Hugo O'Conor, March 8, 1774, Luis Antonio Menchaca to Hugo O'Conor, March 9, 1774, Hugo O'Conor to Rafael Martínez Pacheco, April 20, 1774, Rafael Martínez Pacheco to Hugo O'Conor, April 20, 1774, and Hugo O'Conor to Viceroy Antonio María de Bucareli y Ursúa in *Athanase de Mézières and*

the Louisiana-Texas Frontier, 1768–1780: Documents Published for the First Time, from the Original Spanish and French Manuscripts, Chiefly in the Archives of Mexico and Spain, 2 vols, ed. Herbert E. Bolton (Cleveland: Arthur H. Clark Co., 1914), 2:33, 40, 42, 43–44, 46; Viceroy Antonio María de Bucareli y Ursúa to Governor Juan María Barón de Ripperdá, February 21, 1776, Béxar Archives, Center for American History, University of Texas at Austin.

18. Donald Chipman, *Spanish Texas, 1519–1821* (Austin: University of Texas Press, 1992), 205–7, 249–50.

19. Morris Edward Opler, "The Kinship System of the Southern Athabaskan-Speaking Tribes," *American Anthropologist* 38 (1936), 620–633; Morris Edward Opler, *Lipan and Mescalero Apache in Texas* (New York: Garland, 1974); Morris E. Opler, "Lipan Apache," in *Handbook of North American Indians,* ed. William C. Sturtevant, vol. 13, *Plains,* ed. Raymond J. DeMallie (Washington DC: Smithsonian Institution Press, 1984), part 2, 941–52; Thomas F. Schilz, *Lipan Apaches in Texas,* Southwestern Studies no. 83 (El Paso: Texas Western Press, 1987); William B. Griffen, *Culture Change and Shifting Populations in Central Northern Mexico* (Tucson: University of Arizona Press, 1969); Dolores A. Gunnerson, *The Jicarilla Apaches: A Study in Survival* (DeKalb: Northern Illinois University Press, 1974); Gary Clayton Anderson, *The Indian Southwest, 1580–1830: Ethnogenesis and Reinvention* (Norman: University of Oklahoma Press, 1999), 105–44; José Cortés, *Views from the Apache Frontier: Report on the Northern Provinces of New Spain,* ed. Elizabeth A. H. John, trans. John Wheat (Norman: University of Oklahoma Press, 1989).

20. By the late seventeenth century, Wichita-speaking peoples (Wichita is one of four languages of Caddoan stock, along with Caddo, Pawnee, and Kichai) had migrated to the lower southern Great Plains and established fifteen to twenty consolidated, often palisaded, villages across the northern regions of present-day Texas. Along the Red River, they found fertile lands for extensive crop cultivation and sites ideally suited for defense against enemy raids. From these locations, Wichitas developed profitable trade relations with Frenchmen and Caddos to the east and with Comanches to the west, exchanges that supplied them with guns, horses, and military alliances critical to the security of Wichita communities. Wichita bands active in Texas included Tawakonis, Taovayas, Iscanis, Wacos, and Wichitas proper. W. W. Newcomb Jr., *The People Called Wichita* (Phoenix: Indian Tribal Series, 1977); F. Todd Smith, *The Wichita Indians: Traders of Texas and the Southern Plains, 1540–1845* (College Station: Texas A&M University Press, 2000).

Comanches, a branch of northern Shoshones of the Great Basin region, moved into the southern Great Plains during the seventeenth and eighteenth centuries and, with the acquisition of horses, rapidly evolved into a mounted, mobile military power. The territories of Apaches in Texas then attracted them further south with abundant bison herds and Spanish horses to target in raids. Comanche bands operated as independent, bison-hunting groups, but, similar to Wichitas, maintained defensive and economic alliances with one another. Eastern-dwelling bands of Kotsotekas (in contrast to western-dwelling bands of Jupes and Yamparicas) made up the primary Comanche groups active in Texas. Thomas W. Kavanagh, *Comanche Political History: An Ethnohistorical Perspective, 1706–1875* (Lincoln: University of Nebraska Press, 1996); Pekka Hämäläinen, *The Comanche Empire* (New Haven: Yale University Press, 2008).

21. For Apaches caught in the slave trade in Louisiana, see Juliana Barr, "From Captives to Slaves: Commodifying Indian Women in the Borderlands," *Journal of American History* 92 (June 2005), 19–46.

22. William E. Dunn, "Apache Relation in Texas, 1718–1750," *Quarterly of the Texas State Historical Association* 14 (January 1911), 198–274; "Notes and Reflections on the War with

the Apache Indians in the Provinces of New Spain," in Elizabeth A. H. John, "A Cautionary Exercise in Apache Historiography," *Journal of Arizona History* 25 (Autumn 1984): 304; Elizabeth A. H. John, "Bernardo de Gálvez on the Apache Frontier: A Cautionary Note for Gringo Historians," *Journal of Arizona History* 29 (Winter 1988): 427–30.

23. Poole, "'War by Fire and Blood': The Church and the Chichimecas, 1585," 119–20, 122, 126; Cuello, "The Persistence of Indian Slavery and Encomienda in the Northeast of Colonial Mexico, 1577–1723," 687. For thoroughgoing analysis of how such rhetoric and policy played out in another northern province, Chihuahua, see Ana María Alonso, *Thread of Blood: Colonialism, Revolution, and Gender on Mexico's Northern Frontier* (Tucson: University of Arizona Press, 1995).

24. Alonso, *Thread of Blood*, 37–39.

25. Letter of Marquis de Aguayo, February 1725 in *Autos Sre. Diferentes puntos Consultados por el Govr. de la Provincia de los tejas Muerte de un Correo y otras materias*, cited in Dunn, "Apache Relations in Texas, 1718–1750," 206.

26. Fray Francisco Hidalgo to Fr. Guardian Isidro de Espinosa, November 3, 1723, in Robert F. Carter, *The Tarnished Halo: The Story of Padre Francisco Hidalgo* (Chicago: Franciscan Herald Press, 1973), 153. See also Dunn, "Apache Relations in Texas, 1718–1750," 208.

27. Captain Nicolás Flores to Marqués de Aguayo, October 21, 1723, cited in Dunn, "Apache Relations in Texas, 1718–1750," 207.

28. Juan Domingo Arricivita, *Apostolic Chronicle of Juan Domingo Arricivita: The Franciscan Mission Frontier in the Eighteenth Century in Arizona, Texas, and the Californias*, 2 vols., trans. George P. Hammond and Agapito Rey, rev. trans. Vivian A. Fisher (Berkeley, CA: Academy of American Franciscan History, 1996), 2:27 (see also 1:292).

29. Hidalgo to Espinosa, November 3, 1723, in *The Tarnished Halo*, 154–55 for second quote; *Apostolic Chronicle of Juan Domingo Arricivita*, 2:27 for first quote.

30. Hidalgo to Espinosa, November 3, 1723, in *The Tarnished Halo*, 155; *Apostolic Chronicle of Juan Domingo Arricivita*, 2:28; Dunn, "Apache Relations in Texas, 1718–1750," 210.

31. Hidalgo to Espinosa, November 3, 1723, 157; *Apostolic Chronicle of Juan Domingo Arricivita*, 2:27–28; Fray José Antonio Pichardo, *Pichardo's Treatise on the Limits of Louisiana and Texas*, 4 vols., trans. and ed. Charles Wilson Hackett (Austin: University of Texas Press, 1931–1946), 1:247, 2:463, 3:411.

32. Dunn, "Apache Relations in Texas, 1718–1750," 212n1.

33. Testimony of Captain Nicolás Flores y Valdéz, *Autos Sre. Diferentes puntos Consultados por el Govr. de la Provincia de los tejas Muerte de un Correo y otras materias*, 1724, cited in Dunn, "Apache Relations in Texas, 1718–1750," 217; Fray Miguel Sevillano de Paredes, Memorial to the King, November 12, 1729, Archivo del Colegio de Santa Cruz de Querétaro, Dunn Transcripts 1716–1749, Center for American History, University of Texas at Austin.

34. *Apostolic Chronicle of Juan Domingo Arricivita*, 2:31–33; Dunn, "Apache Relations in Texas, 1718–1750," 225–30; Juan Antonio Pérez de Almazán to his Excellency the Marqués de Casafuerte, December 1, 1731, in *The San Sabá Papers: A Documentary Account of the Founding and Destruction of San Sabá Mission*, ed. Lesley Byrd, trans. Paul D. Nathan (San Francisco: J. Howell-Books, 1959), xv; Dunn, "Apache Relations in Texas, 1718–1750," 226–28.

35. *Apostolic Chronicle of Juan Domingo Arricivita*, 2:32.

36. Domingo Cabello, Informe, September 30, 1784, A. G. M. Provincias Internas, vol. 64, pt. 1, Center for American History, University of Texas at Austin; *Apostolic Chronicle of Juan Domingo Arricivita*, 2:32–33; Report of Captain Juan Antonio de Bustillo y Zevallos, January 31, 1733, *Autos sobre las providencias dadas pr. su exa. al Governador de la Provincia de Texas pa.*

la pazificazn. de los Yndios Apaches y sus aliados, cited in Dunn, "Apache Relations in Texas, 1718–1750," 232–34.

37. Petition of the garrison of San Antonio de Béjar to Governor Bustillo y Zevallos, December 24, 1732, in *The San Sabá Papers*, xvii.

38. *Apostolic Chronicle of Juan Domingo Arricivita*, 2:32.

39. Testimonies of Vicente Alvarez Travieso, Asencio del Razo, and Ignacio Lorenzo de Armas in Governor Prudenzio de Orobio Basterra's Proceedings Concerning the Infidelity of the Apaches, June 25, 1738, Béxar Archives, Center for American History, University of Texas at Austin; Antonio Bonilla, *Breve Compendio*, in "Bonilla's Brief Compendium of the History of Texas, 1772," trans. Elizabeth Howard West, *Quarterly of the Texas State Historical Association* 8 (July 1904): 42, 43; Juan Agustín Morfi, *History of Texas, 1673–1779*, 2 vols., trans. Carlos Eduardo Castañeda (Albuquerque: Quivira Society, 1935), 2:293.

40. Dunn, "Apache Relations in Texas, 1718–1750," 238; Statement of Fray Gabriel de Vergara, April 15, 1733, *Autos sobre las providencias dadas pr. su exa. al Governador de la Provincia de Texas pa. la pazificazn. de los Yndios Apaches y sus aliados*, cited in Dunn, "Apache Relations in Texas, 1718–1750," 237; Proceedings concerning the infidelity of the Apaches, June 28, 1738 and Juan de Oliván y Rebolledo to the viceroy, July 18, 1733, Béxar Archives, Center for American History, University of Texas at Austin.

41. Proceedings concerning the infidelity of the Apaches, June 28, 1738, Béxar Archives, Center for American History, University of Texas at Austin; Fray Benito Fernández de Santa Ana to Viceroy Archbishop Juan Antonio de Vizarron, June 30, 1737, in *Letters and Memorials of the Father Presidente Fray Benito Fernández de Santa Ana*, 26–27.

42. Compare José de Urrutia's letter to the viceroy, May 9, 1738 as cited in Dunn, "Apache Relations in Texas, 1718–1750," 243n4, with the testimony of San Antonio soldiers and citizens in Proceedings concerning the infidelity of the Apaches, June 28, 1738, Béxar Archives, Center for American History, University of Texas at Austin.

43. Testimony of Mateo Perez, Vicente Alvarez Travieso, and José de Urrutia, Proceedings concerning the infidelity of the Apaches, June 28, 1738, Béxar Archives, Center for American History, University of Texas at Austin; Dunn, "Apache Relations in Texas, 1718–1750," 246.

44. Testimony of Mateo Perez, Vicente Alvarez Travieso, and José de Urrutia, Proceedings concerning the infidelity of the Apaches, June 28, 1738, Béxar Archives, Center for American History, University of Texas at Austin; Dunn, "Apache Relations in Texas, 1718–1750," 246.

45. Order of Governor Don Prudencio de Orobio y Bazterra, February 16, 1739; Proceedings for the *residencia* of Prudencio de Orobio Bazterra, February 1–August 21, 1741; Proceedings concerning the infidelity of the Apaches, June 28, 1738, Béxar Archives, Center for American History, University of Texas at Austin; Benito de Fernández de Santa Ana to Viceroy Archbishop Juan Antonio de Vizarron, November 24, 1739, in *The Letters and Memorials of Father Presidente Fray Benito de Fernández de Santa Ana*, 32.

46. As Max Moorhead concluded, the "strict confinement, forced labor, family separation, and the absence of provisions for eventual release suggest an actual practice, if not a deliberate policy, of sheer genocide." Max Moorhead, "Spanish Deportation of Hostile Apaches: The Policy and the Practice," *Arizona and the West* 17 (Autumn 1975), 210–11, 215, 217, 219 for quote.

47. See, for example, articles 190–95 of the Regulations of 1729 in Thomas H. Naylor and Charles W. Polzer, eds., *Pedro de Rivera and the Military Regulations for Northern New Spain, 1724–1729: A Documentary History of His Frontier Inspection and the Reglamento de 1729* (Tucson:

University of Arizona Press, 1988), 279–80; William B. Griffen, *Apaches at War and Peace: The Janos Presidio, 1750–1858* (Albuquerque: University of New Mexico Press, 1988); Moorhead, "Spanish Deportation of Hostile Apaches," 205–20; Alonso, *Thread of Blood*, 37.

48. A unit from the San Juan Bautista presidio on the Rio Grande joined the 1739 campaign, so it is likely that Apache women and children who represented their share of the "booty" were enslaved in Coahuila. Robert S. Weddle, *San Juan Bautista, Gateway to Spanish Texas* (Austin: University of Texas Press, 1968), 220.

49. Baptisms, 12 March, 1745, San Fernando Cathedral Archives, San Antonio, Texas, cited in De la Teja, *San Antonio de Béxar*, 123, 194n18–19.

50. Unlike the *genízaro* (detribalized and enslaved Indian) population in New Mexico that constituted one-third of that province's total population, the women and children held in bondage in Texas remained few in number, reflecting the weaker military force of Spaniards in Texas and the lack of trade with Comanches who preferred to sell their Apache war captives in New Mexico markets. Gilberto M. Hinojosa and Anne A. Fox, "Indians and Their Culture in San Fernando de Béxar," in *Tejano Origins in Eighteenth-Century San Antonio*, eds. Gerald E. Poyo and Gilberto M. Hinojosa (Austin: University of Texas Press for the University of Texas Institute of Texan Cultures at San Antonio, 1991), 109–10; De la Teja, *San Antonio de Béxar*, 122–23. For New Mexico, see Gutiérrez, *When Jesus Came the Cornmothers Went Away*, 149–56, 171–90, 199 and Brooks, *Captives and Cousins*, 6, 8, 121–42.

51. Fray Benito Fernández de Santa Ana to Fray Guardian Pedro del Barco, February 20, 1740, in *The San José Papers*, 64; see also Proceedings concerning the infidelity of the Apaches, June 28, 1738, Béxar Archives, Center for American History, University of Texas at Austin; Fray Benito Fernández de Santa Ana to Viceroy Archbishop Juan Antonio de Vizarron, June 30, 1737, in *Letters and Memorials of the Father Presidente Fray Benito Fernández de Santa Ana*, 26–27.

52. *Apostolic Chronicle of Juan Domingo Arricivita*, 2:32.

53. Captain Toribio de Urrutia to the Viceroy, December 17, 1740, in *The San José Papers*, 86.

54. Moorhead, "Spanish Deportation of Hostile Apaches: The Policy and the Practice"; Christon I. Archer, "The Deportation of Barbarian Indians from the Internal Provinces of New Spain, 1789–1810," *Americas* 29 (January 1973), 376–85.

55. Memorial from the government of the *villa* of San Fernando and the Royal Presidio of San Antonio de Béxar to Governor Martínez Pacheco, regarding the people's right to the *mesteña* horses and cattle of Texas, 1787, Béxar Archives, Center for American History, University of Texas at Austin.

56. Fray Benito Fernández de Santa Ana to Viceroy Conde de Revilla Gigedo, February 23, 1750, in *The Presidio and Militia on the Northern Frontier of New Spain: A Documentary History*, Volume 2, Part 2: *The Central Corridor and the Texas Corridor, 1700–1765*, eds. Diana Hadley, Thomas H. Naylor, and Mardith K. Schuetz-Miller (Tucson: University of Arizona Press, 1997), 484.

57. Fray Benito Fernández de Santa Ana to Fray Guardian Fray Alonso Giraldo de Terreros, February 2, 1746, in *Letters and Memorials of the Father Presidente Fray Benito Fernández de Santa Ana*, 62–63.

58. Elizabeth A. H. John, *Storms Brewed in Other Men's Worlds: The Confrontation of Indians, Spanish, and French in the Southwest, 1540–1795* (College Station: Texas A&M University Press, 1975), 276.

59. Fray Benito Fernández de Santa Ana to Fray Guardian Fray Alonso Giraldo de Terreros, February 2, 1746, in *Letters and Memorials of the Father Presidente Fray Benito Fernández de Santa Ana*, 63; *Apostolic Chronicle of Juan Domingo Arricivita*, 2:35–36.

60. Fray Benito Fernández de Santa Ana to Viceroy Pedro Cebrian Conde de Fuenclara, May 16, 1745, Fray Benito Fernández de Santa Ana to Fray Guardian Fray Alonso Giraldo de Terreros, December 4, 1745, Fray Benito Fernández de Santa Ana to Captain Toribio de Urrutia, February 1, 1746, and Fray Benito Fernández de Santa Ana to Fray Guardian Fray Alonso Giraldo de Terreros, February 2, 1746, in Letters and Memorials of the Father Presidente Fray Benito Fernández de Santa Ana, 50, 54, 55–56, 58, 60.

61. Fray Benito Fernández de Santa Ana to Fray Guardian Fray Alonso Giraldo de Terreros, February 2, 1746 and Fray Benito Fernández de Santa Ana to Viceroy Conde de Revilla Gigedo, February 23, 1750, in Letters and Memorials of the Father Presidente Fray Benito Fernández de Santa Ana, 61, 66, 165; Fray Benito Fernández de Santa Ana to Viceroy Conde de Revilla Gigedo, February 23, 1750, in The Presidio and Militia on the Northern Frontier of New Spain, 483; Apostolic Chronicle of Juan Domingo Arricivita, 2:35–36, 39–40; Domingo Cabello, Informe, September 30, 1784, A. G. M. Provincias Internas, vol. 64, pt. 1, Center for American History, University of Texas at Austin.

62. Fray Benito Fernández de Santa Ana to Viceroy Conde de Revilla Gigedo, February 23, 1750, in The Presidio and Militia on the Northern Frontier of New Spain, 485.

63. Letters and Memorials of Fray Mariano de los Dolores y Viana, 1737–1762: Documents on the Missions of Texas from the Archives of the College of Querétaro, ed. Marion A. Habig, trans. Benedict Leutenegger (San Antonio: Old Spanish Missions Historical Research Library at Our Lady of the Lake University, 1985), 95–97.

64. Domingo Cabello, Informe, September 30, 1784, A. G. M. Provincias Internas, vol. 64, pt. 1, Center for American History, University of Texas at Austin; Dunn, "Apache Relations in Texas, 1718–1750," 261–62.

65. The San Sabá Papers; William Edward Dunn, "The Apache Mission on the San Sabá River: Its Founding and Failure," Southwestern Historical Quarterly 17 (April 1914); Robert S. Weddle, The San Sabá Mission: Spanish Pivot in Texas (Austin: University of Texas Press, 1964); Juliana Barr, "The Palette of Fear at San Sabá," in Presidios y Indios: Negotiating Conquest in the Spanish Borderlands, ed. James F. Brooks (Santa Fe NM: School for American Research, forthcoming).

66. Rubí Dictamen of April 10, 1768, trans. Ned. F. Brierley, in Imaginary Kingdom: Texas as Seen by the Rivera and Rubí Military Inspections, 1727 and 1767, ed. Jack Jackson (Austin: Texas State Historical Association, 1995), 182–83.

67. Governor Domingo Cabello to commandant general José Antonio Rengel, January 10, 1786; Cabello to commandant general Jacobo de Ugarte y Loyola, June 12, 1786; governor Rafael Martínez Pacheco to commandant general of the Eastern Provinces Juan de Ugalde, January 7 and February 16, 1788, Béxar Archives, Center for American History, University of Texas at Austin.

68. Elizabeth A. H. John, "Nurturing the Peace: Spanish and Comanche Cooperation in the Early Nineteenth Century," New Mexico Historical Review 59 (October 1984), 351; Jesús F. de la Teja, "St. James at the Fair: Religious Ceremony, Civic Boosterism, and Commercial Development on the Colonial Mexican Frontier," Americas 57 (January 2001), 397. For a New Mexico comparison, see Ross Frank, From Settler to Citizen: New Mexican Economic Development and the Creation of Vecino Society, 1750–1820 (Los Angeles: University of California Press, 2000), 14–21, 30–34; Brooks, Captives and Cousins, 60–68, 125, 162–64.

69. Teodoro de Croix, General Report, October 30, 1781, in Teodoro de Croix and the Northern Frontier of New Spain, 1776–1783, from the Original Documents in the Archives of the Indies, Seville, ed. Alfred Barnaby Thomas (Norman: University of Oklahoma Press, 1941), 43, 89, 97; Rafael

Martínez Pacheco to Jacobo Ugarte y Loyola, October 12, 1787, Béxar Archives, Center for American History, University of Texas at Austin; Griffen, *Apaches at War and Peace*; Bernardo de Gálvez, *Instructions for Governing the Interior Provinces of New Spain, 1786*, ed. Donald E. Worcester (Berkeley: Quivira Society, 1951); Max L. Moorhead, *The Apache Frontier: Jacobo Ugarte and Spanish-Indian Relations in Northern New Spain, 1769–1791* (Norman: University of Oklahoma Press, 1968); Alonso, *Thread of Blood*, 37–39, 44; Archer, "The Deportation of Barbarian Indians from the Internal Provinces of New Spain."

70. Teodoro de Croix to Juan María de Ripperdá, September 11, 1777, Béxar Archives, Center for American History, University of Texas at Austin.

71. Texas governor Juan María de Ripperdá carried out the investigation at the direction of viceroy Antonio Bucareli y Ursúa in January 1773 after Ripperdá had first relayed reports of the slave raiding to him in the fall of 1772. Antonio Bucareli y Ursúa to Juan María de Ripperdá, November 16, 1772; Depositions of Indian Majordomo Juan Nicolas, Lieutenant Cristóbal de Córdova, and soldiers Joseph Manuel Martínez and Juan Feliciano Cassanova, January 16, 1773, Béxar Archives, Center for American History, University of Texas at Austin.

72. Governor Domingo Cabello to commandant general Teodoro de Croix, May 28, 1780, Béxar Archives, Center for American History, University of Texas at Austin. For discussion, see also Zavala, *Los Esclavos Indios en Nueva España*, 265–79 and Omar Valerio-Jiménez, "Criados and Indios Bárbaros: Indian Slavery on the Nuevo Santander Frontier, 1749–1846," paper presented at the 2002 Annual Meeting of the American Historical Association, Seattle. See also Omar Santiago Valerio-Jiménez, "'Indios Bárbaros,' Divorcés, and Flocks of Vampires: Identity and Nation on the Rio Grande, 1749–1894" (PhD diss., University of California at Los Angeles, 2001).

73. Depositions of Indian Majordomo Juan Nicolas, Lieutenant Cristóbal de Córdova, and soldiers Joseph Manuel Martínez and Juan Feliciano Cassanova, January 16, 1773, Béxar Archives, Center for American History, University of Texas at Austin; Martín Salinas, *Indians of the Rio Grande Delta: Their Role in the History of Southern Texas and Northeastern Mexico* (Austin: University of Texas Press, 1990), 41.

74. Depositions of Indian Majordomo Juan Nicolas, Lieutenant Cristóbal de Córdova, and soldiers Joseph Manuel Martínez and Juan Feliciano Cassanova, January 16, 1773, Béxar Archives, Center for American History, University of Texas at Austin.

75. Governor Domingo Cabello to commandant general Teodoro de Croix, May 28, 1780; Daily strength report and record of daily occurrences for March 1784, Béxar Archives, Center for American History, University of Texas at Austin. Martín Salinas identifies four main groups that were brought to Texas missions in illegal "recruitments" during this period: Carrizos, Como se Llaman, Cotonames, Pauraques. Salinas, *Indians of the Rio Grande Delta*, 39, 41, 53, 56, 94.

76. Daily strength report and record of daily occurrences for March 1784, Béxar Archives, Center for American History, University of Texas at Austin; Salinas, *Indians of the Rio Grande Delta*, 53, 87–91.

77. Proceedings concerning the freedom of María Gertrudis de la Peña, February 11, 1768–May 17, 1785, Béxar Archives, Center for American History, University of Texas at Austin.

78. Proceedings concerning the freedom of María Gertrudis de la Peña.

79. Proceedings concerning the freedom of María Gertrudis de la Peña.

9. "We Betray Our Own Nation"
Indian Slavery and Multi-ethnic Communities
in the Southwest Borderlands
James F. Brooks

An unusual audience occurred in the *villa* of Santa Fe early in the summer of 1780. Bentura Bustamante, "Lieutenant of the *Genízaro* Indians," laid a bold challenge before Spain's highest-ranking representative in the province, governor and renowned Indian-fighter Juan Bautista de Anza. Unless the governor addressed this grievance, Bustamente and his thirty-three *compañeros* faced little choice but to "go in search of relief to our lands and our nation." As is too often the case in Spanish colonial legal proceedings, the exact nature of Bustamante's complaint was never explicitly mentioned, nor was it stated precisely what remedy he and his companions had in mind. But the vigor with which Bustamante asserted his community's right to make a claim displays no hesitancy. As *indios genízaros*, he claimed, their Spanish "parents and masters" had delivered his people from infidelity into the mysteries of the Holy Catholic Faith. Once in that condition, they had bought lands, built houses, and "remained obedient to the Royal Service for campaigns and war activities," even when to do so meant they had "betrayed their own Nation." For "loyal Christian Indians" to confront their governor in such a manner seems unusual. But it becomes startling when we consider that their threat to desert the colony issued from peoples who were, legally speaking, its slaves.[1]

This chapter addresses Bustamante's case and the role of *genízaros* in colonial New Mexico at some length, but these immediate details frame a guiding question: in cultural borderlands where neither indigenous nor colonial peoples could dominate the other completely, how did both free and slave assert and resist power in the interests of law, order, and justice? Scholars have long recognized that New Mexico constituted a particularly volatile "non-dominant frontier" where, despite the exceptional success of Pueblo Indian revolts between 1680 and 1696, neither colonial New Mexicans nor the numerically superior indigenous peoples proved able (or willing) to subordinate or eject the other completely.[2] Despite nearly a century of research and debate, a comprehensive picture of just how these culturally complex borderlands actually functioned remains elusive. We will see that the history of the *genízaro* slave caste opens one window on those complexities.

However unstable power seemed in the region, law provided much of its means of contestation. Legal historians have made major contributions to our understandings of the colonial legal structures underpinning Pueblo Indian and Spanish village land grants. Nominally christianized Pueblo Indians received *mercedes reales* (royal gifts) from the Spanish Crown, which cynically confirmed the "already acquired rights of indigenous peoples found in lands discovered by Spain." The conveyance of title to long-occupied lands was but one of the artifices by which Spain asserted her rights of conquest in the New World. Spanish *vecinos* (citizens) also received royal gifts in the form of *mercedes*, which contained communal lands, individual allotments for houses, and irrigated fields. In addition to community grants, individual private grants for livestock grazing were conferred upon especially favored royal subjects. Nevertheless, local Spanish administrators took some pains to protect Pueblo Indian lands against encroachment and to adjudicate *vecino* disputes in the interest of larger community harmony.[3]

The trust relationship between the Spanish Crown and its Indian subjects extended beyond issues of land tenure. Once the Crown took cognizance of Bartolomé de las Casas's argument that the natives of the New World were indeed humans, although "poor and wretched" ones, the royal conscience required that some real efforts be made to protect those who in the eyes of the law were equal to minors. In New Mexico, as elsewhere in New Spain, this concern translated into the office of the *protector de indios*, a royal appointee who acted as advocate for aggrieved Indians.[4] And, as elsewhere in Spanish America, local Indians proved quick to acquire their own legal acumen, and often drove the courts to distraction with their litigiousness.[5]

We know less about the day-to-day workings of the law among the *vecino* population, but even a cursory look through indices of the Spanish Archives of New Mexico reveals a society in which property disputes, personal assaults, and illegal trading demanded the regular attention of both the governor and local *alcaldes mayores* (district magistrates). Far from the learned jurists of Mexico and Spain, New Mexicans drew upon Castilian legal customs, *derecho indiano criollo* (law promulgated in the New World) and local traditions (including those of Indians) to initiate litigation and reach resolutions.[6]

Moreover we have also moved closer to an understanding of the military and diplomatic dance in which Spanish governors and powerful Indian groups like the Apaches, Navajos, Kiowas, and Comanches engaged for more than two centuries. Here the question was not that of land tenure or protections against everyday labor exploitation, but the complex of punitive raids, diplomatic alliances, and intercultural commerce employed by Spanish and *los indios gentiles* ("heathen" Indians) alike, to achieve some measure of stability. Although the Recopilación de Indias of 1681 (a compendium of laws governing colonial-Indian relations) made clear that "just war" doctrine applied to any "heathens" who failed to submit to Spanish authority, and thereby legalized their murder, pillage, and enslavement, actual relations in New Mexico proved much more complicated than those laws implied. Far removed from the military resources of Mexico, the presidial garrison in Sante Fe never exceeded 140 poorly armed and mounted soldiers. In a colony surrounded by highly militarized equestrian Indian groups who could field thousands of accomplished fighters at short notice, Spanish governors like Tómas Vélez de Cachupín and Juan Bautista de Anza seldom risked major military campaigns. Their diplomatic efforts drew sustenance from parallel strategies pursued by their Indian counterparts, leaders like the Comanche captain Ecueracapa who knew full well that Comanche power rested in part on their access to Spanish firearms, powder, and shot.[7]

But Bentura Bustamante's complaint hints that Spanish-Indian power relations in colonial New Mexico were even more multi-stranded than the foregoing summary suggests. Land rights, Indian rights, and intercultural diplomacy all appear at issue in his complaint. Yet we will see that the *genízaro* question draws us into a larger analysis of social inequality, ethnic identity, political economy, and customary justice in the region. When Bustamante presented himself as lieutenant of the *genízaro* Indians and "in the name of" his thirty-three companions, he did so as the representative of a slave community. When he claimed that his community had embraced Catholicism and had performed as a loyal militia in the service of the Spanish Crown, he spoke a truth designed to solicit Anza's sympathies. And when he threatened that should his community's grievances not be redressed they might desert the colony and find succor in "their lands and their Nation," he probably induced real anxiety in a seasoned diplomat and soldier, for to do so seems—paradoxically— entirely within the ability and the customary (if not doctrinal) rights of his slave community.

This chapter, then, contributes another layer of understanding to our knowledge of slavery in the colonial New Mexican borderlands, to comparisons with other Spanish borderlands, and by extension to the British colonies in North America as well. A series of cases trace the "repertoires of contention" by which the *genízaro* caste undertook to negotiate their status vis-à-vis colonial legal and economic structures between 1700 and 1821.[8] In the end, these cases suggest that as the Bourbon Reforms of 1765–1821 liberalized provincial society and economy, *genízaro* autonomy *and* vulnerability concurrently increased. As such, this study illustrates the volatile relationship between subordinate communities and those formative colonial states that exploited *and* depended upon the former for survival and growth. It also suggests that although New Mexico stood far from the political upheavals of the American Revolution, its position amid the larger transformations of the Atlantic world produced social phenomena not unlike those erupting east of the Mississippi River.

Although not rent by revolutionary upheavals, colonial New Mexico did contain moments of tangible social destabilization. This ambiguous frontier saw the creation and constant renegotiation of a "borderlands political economy," wherein Indians and Spanish colonists alike came to share some understanding of the production and distribution of wealth, as conditioned by the social relations of power.[9] So dependent were Spanish colonists and their Indian neighbors, both Pueblo and *bárbaro*, on a flexible and oft-changing network of commercial and military exchanges, that peoples like Bustamante's *genízaros*, who maintained links to all three groups, came to occupy an intermediating space simultaneously marginal and central.

There came to exist in the colony a widely shared sense that local communities had earned the right to regulate their own affairs, especially in terms of intra-group disputes and everyday economic enterprise, yet also to have their complaints heard with fairness by colonial magistrates when inter-caste conflicts arose. The *genízaros*, and some of their lower-order *vecino* neighbors, while technically "in the power of" their Spanish masters and administrative elites, served as indispensable actors in the military and commercial functioning of the colony, especially in its relations with *los indios bárbaros*. As a consequence, when able to engage in extralegal collective action, or to claim "traditional" communal (whether Indian or slave) rights, they often exerted influence well beyond what their status might imply. When subject to the law as individuals, however, their social and juridical status left them nearly defenseless. Neither Spanish, Pueblo, nor "heathen" Indian, *genízaros* dwelt in a shadow land at the interstices of law and power. This investigation of their experience shows the range of agency available to peoples who—although crucial to the political economy of the borderlands—remained socially and legally marginal until the upheavals of 1810–1821 rewrote the "modalities of rule" in effect in northern Mexico.[10]

This borderland political economy underwent considerable change over time, especially in the period between 1780 and 1821 as the

Bourbon Reforms and an incipient commerce with Americans intruded on its workings. Most evident was a gradual bifurcation in the regional economy between a "colonial" sector controlled by governors and an emerging class of merchants and sheep ranchers, and an "indigenous" sector involving customary trade with "heathen" Indians like Navajos, Utes, Comanches, and Kiowas. While the colonial sector might see *genízaros* and poor *vecinos* as prime candidates for labor dependency in farming, stock raising, and manufacturing, their central role in the indigenous economy, by which commerce some elites profited as well, set the two sectors in real tension. Within these changing and ambivalent political economies, the weak and the powerful alike developed new tactics and strategies of contention which required a constant reworking of notions of justice and the applicability of law, of free and slave. And although these dynamics encompassed all the various social and cultural groups of New Mexico, their workings may be detailed most clearly in the historical experience of Bentura Bustamante's people.

Neither "Spanish" nor "Indian," *los genízaros* have attracted significant scholarly attention in recent years. Much of the debate centers around the question of whether or not these peoples constituted a racialized and degraded social category imposed from without by Spanish authorities, or if, in time, they developed an internally generated, positive "ethnic" identity. We will see that the answer lies somewhere within this dualism, but we must first look at how the category and the people came to exist in the first place.

As noted earlier, the Recopilación of 1681, while reiterating the ban on Indian slavery first set forth in 1542, served to reinforce "just war" doctrines of enslavement. But it also encouraged Spanish subjects to redeem indigenous captives from their captors, baptize them into the Catholic faith, and acculturate them as new "detribalized" colonial subjects. These *indios de rescate* (ransomed Indians) were "saved" from slavery among their "heathen" captors, and therefore owed their Spanish redeemers loyalty and service in exchange for the cost of their ransom. Both defeated enemies and redeemed captives came to carry the appellation "*genízaro*" in New

Mexico. These servile peoples then fell under the laws governing slavery which had originated in Las Siete Partidas in AD 1265, doctrines noteworthy for their "liberal" position that "all of the laws of the world should lead towards freedom." Under these regulations slaves were conferred rights in marriage, protected against maltreatment, allowed to hold property and testify as plaintiffs or defendants, and allowed to pursue manumission. Of course, application of such principles fell far short of the ideal, for African and Indian slave alike.[11]

Enslavement of Indians under the "just war" doctrine was rampant during the seventeenth century, but tapered off after the reconquest of New Mexico between 1692 and 1696, as the Spanish sought alternative diplomatic routes to pacification of the "wild" Indians. Redemption of captives from Kiowas, Comanches, and Navajos, however, increased in scale during the eighteenth century. These occurred in roughly two forms, through formal "ransoming" at annual trade fairs (ferias or rescates), or through small-scale bartering (cambalaches) in local villages or at trading places on the Great Plains.[12] Throughout the eighteenth century, Spanish church and secular authorities vied to gain control of this trade, variously blaming each other or local alcaldes mayores for "the saddest of this commerce." In 1761 Fray Pedro Serrano chided Spanish governors, who "when the fleet was in" scrambled to gather as many horses, axes, hoes, wedges, picks, bridles and knives in order to "gorge themselves" on the "great multitude of both sexes offered for sale."[13] Fifteen years later, Fray Anatasio Domínguez reported that the Comanches brought to Taos for sale "pagan Indians, of both sexes, whom they capture from other nations." The going rate of exchange, which seems to have held quite steady until the mid-nineteenth century, was "two good horses and some trifles" for an "Indian girl twelve to twenty years old." Male captive boys brought a "she mule" or one horse and a "poor bridle . . . garnished with red rags." The general atmosphere, according to Domínguez, resembled a "second hand market in Mexico, the way people mill about."[14]

In the early nineteenth century trade fairs declined, owing to several factors—Plains Indians' determination to avoid possible exposure to Euro-American disease, attempts on the part of New Mexican villagers to escape taxation of their trade, the geographical expansion of the borderland economy—replaced with smaller, more frequent, on-the-spot bartering. Judging from extant New Mexican parochial registers, between 1700 and 1850 nearly 3,000 members of nomadic or pastoral Indian groups entered New Mexican society as *indios de rescate, indios genízaros, criados,* or *huérfanos* (slaves, servants, or orphans), primarily through the artifice of "ransom" by colonial purchasers.[15] Ostensibly the debt of ransom would be retired by ten to twenty years of service to the redeemers, after which time these individuals would become *vecinos* (tithes-paying citizens). In practice these people appear to have experienced their bondage on a continuum that ranged from near slavery to familial incorporation.

Evidence from the eighteenth-century *genízaro* community of Abiquiú on the Río Chama and Hispano settlements northward in the San Juan River system suggests that most *genízaros* achieved familial assimilation in the households of their masters through the Spanish institution of *compadrazgo,* or godparenthood. In this sense, kinship was the route by which *genízaros* gradually influenced and became a part of a larger Hispano identity group in northern New Mexico. Alternative explanations have asserted a more narrowly circumscribed "ethnic" *genízaro* identity, based on the existence of several relatively homogeneous and endogamous *genízaro* settlements in the Rio Grande valley,[16] or have emphasized exploitation, enslavement, and social alienation. Ramón Gutiérrez, for example, argues that the *genízaros* were "slaves and *criados* [servants] . . . who had no genealogical ties to the Hispano community, who were dishonored by their status as thralls, and who were deemed socially dead amid men and women of honor."[17] Gutiérrez offers numerous cases of complaints brought by *genízaros* against their Spanish masters, charging labor exploitation, cruel discipline, and sexual misuse, and buttresses these with characterizations drawn from two contemporary observers, Fray Dominguez and Fray Juan Augustin de Morfí, both of whom show contempt for the caste. Dominguez, writing in 1776, claimed that the *genízaros* were "servants among our people," unable to speak Spanish "without twisting it somewhat," and whose "weak" characters turned them into "gamblers, liars, cheats, and petty thieves."[18] Reporting on the state of the province in 1778,

Morfí (who never actually visited New Mexico, and drew his information from interviews) characterized the *genízaros* as landless "on account of their poverty, which leaves them afoot and without arms . . . they bewail their neglect and they live like animals."[19]

A deeper look into the *genízaro* experience reveals even more complexity and variation than heretofore proposed, and suggests that we must sift our analysis through a finer mesh that captures power distributions at all levels of society in colonial New Mexico. The view that beneath the level of Spanish elites, ethnic boundaries between Spanish and Indian societies eroded under the pressure of kinship and interdependency suffices only so long as we recognize that they did so within a context of unequal and often contested power. The "ethnic identity" position finds some support, but requires refinements that include those villages where *genízaros* and *vecinos* shared residence, often under the same roof. Although such cases imply easy social mixing, evidence also exists suggesting asymmetrical power relations even at the household level. Likewise, Gutiérrez's dichotomy between honorable *españoles* and dishonored *genízaros* may have been the ideal of elite Spanish ecclesiastics like Dominguez and Morfí, but probably reflects prescriptive anxieties about the existence of a *mestizo* caste neither Spanish nor Indian who were all too important to the colony's survival. Troubled by evidence of social and cultural mixing in distant villages, administrators and churchmen proved eager to find ideological devices by which *genízaros* could be subsumed within the fragile discourse of Spanish hegemony. Questions remain, therefore, especially around the origins of the category in colonial New Mexico, the quality of day-to-day relationships between *genízaros* and lower-order New Mexican *vecinos*, and the nature of their servility in terms of regional notions of customary justice.

Regarding their origins, the *genízaros* of New Mexico fit into a much larger framework of borderland conflict and accommodation available within the Spanish world than previously recognized. Between 1529 and 1830, Spain (and much of Christian Europe) suffered almost continuous harassment from the Ottoman corsairs of North Africa's Barbary Coast. In addition to plunder, these raiders seized Christian captives by the score, either as prisoners of war or in attacks on coastal settlements. Held as slaves and hostages by the Moors, these captives were pawns in a great rivalry between Islam and Christianity. Their ransom was achieved through the efforts of two orders of religious redemptionists, the Mercedarians and Trinitarians, who undertook the raising of limosnas (alms) for ransom and negotiated for captives' repatriation.[20] Thus, while Spanish colonists in New Mexico were obtaining thousands of Indian captives at the Taos and Pecos rescates (ransoms), their counterparts in Spain were rescuing thousands of Christians from the presumed horrors of captivity among the infidels. And just as the riches obtained through ransom proved crucial to the economies of North Africa, so too did the purchase of captives fuel extension of the market economy into native North America.

Many of these indios de rescate came to be known as genízaros in New Mexico, but just why they did so is unclear. The internal politics of the Barbary States yield clues to this puzzle, however. Although nominally within the Ottoman Empire, real local power lay with the Janissary Corps, the "slave armies" raised by the Ottomans through the tributary demands of the devsirme, or "levy of the boys," imposed upon their Balkan subjects. While the Balkans had few natural resources to offer, they did contain large populations from which mercenary armies could be raised. Supplementing these levies were renegade Christians from the northern Mediterranean, who found adventure and prestige in the renowned military prowess of the Janissaries. These Janissaries (from yeñi çeri, "new troops"), known as los genízaros in Spanish, had been created in the fifteenth century, as Ottoman rulers found native Turkish troops too often owed allegiance to local chiefs and aspirants to the throne, rather than the expanding Muslim state.[21] This clarifies the twin meanings ascribed to the term genízaro in Spanish, first as a subject people descending from parents of alien nations or races, and second, as prestigious military units who owed a particular loyalty to the Crown, and who ostensibly stood above the petty intrigues of court politics.[22]

These two aspects found expression in the genízaros of New Mexico as well, contributing to the trouble scholars have experienced in defining their role in the colony. Both "slaves" and "soldiers," genízaros certainly occupied a low status in the colony, yet also proved crucial in colonial defense, and ultimately acted as slave raiders themselves.[23] Colonial New Mexico, rent from within by conflicts between secular and religious authorities, between *españoles* and *mestizos*, and threatened from without by the inscrutable politics of contending *indios gentiles*, was fertile ground for the development of a "slave soldiery."[24]

The earliest reference to *genízaros* in New Mexico seems to occur when Carlos de Siguenza y Góngora stated that Diego de Vargas employed a *genízaro* guide during the *reconquista* of 1692, and that he had liberated seventy-four "*mestizos, y genízaros*" in his progress northward, who then enjoyed "the freedom to return to their brothers, relatives, and spouses."[25] This suggests that the category may have existed in the province prior to the revolt, as a way of distinguishing between a generalized *mestizo* population and those families involved in military service. Pueblo Indian auxiliaries were also occasionally termed *genízaros*, probably more descriptive of their military role than any "enslaved" status.[26] The Spanish Colonial Census of 1750 enumerated *genízaros* separately from the Pueblo Indian population, when they comprised 4 percent of the Spanish colonial population (154 of 3,809). The majority were concentrated in the Plaza de los Jarales in Belén and the Barrio de Analco in Santa Fe, but seventeen *genízaro* families resided alongside *vecino* families in Ranchos de Taos and San Juan de los Caballeros.[27]

These census data suggest a second refinement, namely the presumed "landlessness" of the caste. After an initial appeal for lands near Sandia Pueblo was refused in 1733, census reports confirm that groups of *genízaros* received land grants for settlement near Belén in 1740, at Ranchos de Taos in 1750, at Las Trampas in 1751, at Abiquíu and Ojo Caliente in 1754, at San Miguel de Carnué in 1763 and San José de Las Huertas in 1765, at Socorro near El Paso del Norte in 1773, at San Miguel del Vado in 1794, and at Anton Chico in 1822.[28] Spanish colonial authorities had a strategic objective in these settlements, namely to establish "buffers" on the frontier between nomads and villages in the Rio Grande valley.[29] Far from being landless, *genízaros* occupied key posts in the colonial defense perimeter.

But other settlements featured a mix of caste residents, which would

329

seem to have bearing on the relative legal and social autonomy of *genízaros*. The village of San Jose de Las Huertas, in the Sierra de Sandia east of Bernalillo, offers such an example. The land grant petition of 1765 contains the names of eight families, both *españole* and *genízaro*. By 1767 the village had increased to twenty-one families of mixed caste status. In its early years "there was much intermarriage with Indians of San Felipe, Santa Ana, and Sandia [Pueblos]," and villagers who died were buried in the *campo santo* at San Felipe.[30] This alliance with nearby Pueblo people suggests a range of variation in peripheral communities, and that ethnic alliances were often negotiated at the local level, whatever the desires of the elites in Santa Fe.

The Spanish Colonial Census of 1750 in Ranchos de Taos displays another blending of caste groups. Thirty-seven percent of the village families were considered Spanish, 26 percent *coyotes* (Spanish-Indian descent), and 35 percent *genízaros*. The census taker reported nine Spanish households of fifty-seven persons, six *coyote* households of fifty-five persons, and eight *genízaro* households of twenty-five persons. Even the Spanish households showed a blurring of caste relations; the house of Antonio Atiensa included his *coyota* wife María Romero, their son Domingo Romero (*castizo*), and the widow Juana with her daughter Manuela, no doubt *criadas*. Likewise the house of Juan Rosalio Villapando, an important *español*, included his wife María Valdes and their six children, all of whom are termed *coyote*, suggesting that María may have been an *india de rescate*. Pablo Francisco Villalpando's household contained three female and two male *servientes*, two of whom carry the family name. Mixing may have crossed class as well as caste lines in some village families.[31]

The fact that the census arranged households by caste category reveals a conscious concern about caste status on the part of Spanish administrators, but the data also demonstrate how informally these categories might be arranged at the village level. Census findings from a cluster of plazas at Belén show yet another pattern. In 1790 the third plaza, "Nuestra Señora de los Dolores de los Genízaros," contained thirty-three households, all designated as *genízaro*, a strong indication that in some cases homogeneous communities developed among some *indios de rescate*. But the adjacent second "Plaza de Jarales" held thirty Spanish, twelve *mestizo*, four *coyote*, and two *genízaro* households. The marriage patterns from these communities reveal little caste-anxious endogamy; of the twenty-eight unions, only one is *español-española*. Six marriages involved *genízaro-genízara*, and five *mestizo-mestiza*. The remaining sixteen show a crossing of caste lines. In most of these, hypogamy seems the rule, with women marrying men of "lower" status. Children of these unions, for example *genízaro-coyota*, seem to follow the father's status and are later enumerated as *genízaros*.[32] Thus some *genízaros* did have genealogical ties to the *vecino* community, contrary to the segregation presumed by Gutiérrez. Within households, intercultural mixing became even more complex, as *servientes* (many the illegitimate children of the *patrón*) designated "*coyotas*" or "*de color quebrado*" (of broken color) cast the purity of the family line into doubt.[33]

Whatever their residence pattern, as military slaves, *genízaros* played crucial roles in the defense of the province. From 1744 forward, when Fray Miguel del Menchero commended the *genízaros* of "Cerro de Tomé" (Belén) for the "great bravery and zeal" with which they patrolled the "country in pursuit of the enemy," these auxiliary soldiers utilized their knowledge of the geographic and cultural landscape of the borderlands to preserve the colony.[34] Their military indispensability would provide them some leverage within the social and legal constraints that governed their condition.

Genízaros did more than defend the frontiers against surrounding *indios bárbaros*. They also mobilized to protest encroachments on their communal lands by colonial *estanceros* (stockraisers). In 1746 the *genízaros* of Belén filed a complaint with Viceroy Fuenclara in Atexico (Mexico), claiming that a grant issued in 1741 to Captain Diego Torres and thirty-one others (among whom was Don Nicolás de Chávez, *alcalde* of Albuquerque) "was illegal and should be null and voided . . . since the land in question included Indian *Pueblos* [villages]." The petitioners were led by Antonio Casados and Luis Quintana, both of whom termed themselves "Apaches Caiguas" (Kiowa Apaches). Casados stated that "as a young Apache, he was sold into the household of Francisco Casados as a domestic," before settling in the Belén area in the household of Captain Torres, where he had "paid off his ransom" and joined the *genízaro* community.[35] There, he "became a war captain of the *genízaros*."

331

Fuenclara referred the complaint to Governor Codállos y Rabal in Santa Fe for investigation. For this hearing, Casados arrived in the *villa* with "seventy Indians from all the different Pueblos" in his entourage, drawing a strong rebuke from the governor, who accused him of "inciting all of the friendly Pueblos against the Spaniards." Furthermore, he was reprimanded and held in the military guardhouse for having gone outside the province "to file his charges before the Viceroy without license or permission from proper authorities."[36] Here we see the ambivalent status of *genízaros* in close focus: an important "war captain," sufficiently bold and knowledgeable to journey hundreds of miles with a community complaint, clapped in the *cuartel de guardia* for insubordination.

Governor Codállos called a series of Spanish witnesses who impugned the validity of Casados's complaint, suggesting that "since he has acquired a certain degree of high intelligence" he had become a troublemaker in the community. Don Nicolás de Chávez came forward to claim that on his authority as *alcalde* he had given "possession to the Spaniards" and to say that "there were no known obstacles or impediments to the issuance of the Grant."[37] With considerable testimony collected, the governor forwarded his findings to the viceroy. Unfortunately no final decision on this case survives, but it is significant that in 1749 the *genízaros* of Belén again brought a complaint, this time against Don Nícolas, for "allowing his livestock to foul their *acequias*." This ruling does exist, with the court instructing the Spaniard to "build bridges and protect the springs from his cattle."[38] In this case, and in all likelihood that of 1746, the ability of *genízaros* to mobilize as a community (*pueblo*) and assert their rights as wards of the Spanish Crown allowed them to gain justice in the face of local opposition.

In cases where *genízaros* acted individually, without support from a larger community, their legal and social marginality proved crippling. Some ten miles south of San Jose de las Huertas, in Tijeras Canyon, the village of San Miguel de Carnué (del Laredo) featured mixed social composition. In 1763 seventeen families received an agricultural grant from Governor Vélez de Cachupín, among whom were ten *españoles*, three *coyotes*, and those of the *genízaros* Gregorio Montoya, Francisco García, and Bartolo

Anzures. Five years later, Montoya and García stood accused of stealing eight cattle from Zia Pueblo. As the facts of the case became known, it became clear that the Spanish *teniente de alcalde* (deputy mayor), Cristobal Jaramillo, had put them up to the crime, since livestock was in short supply in the village. Although they had acted in the interests of the community, their *vecino* neighbors failed to come to their defense. The *genízaros* were put to low-paid labor until the pueblo owners were compensated, while Jaramillo went unpunished. The larcenous spirit of these socially mixed villages may have been democratically distributed, but egalitarianism did not apply when courts chose to enforce the law.[39]

But the power of extralegal collective action to shape customary justice at the local level continued despite the constraints of colonial law. A careful look at Bentura Bustamante's complaint illustrates this persistence. In 1776 Carlos III finally approved a massive reorganization of New Spain's northern frontier into the *provincias internas*, and appointed Teodoro de Croix as *comandante general*. Aimed at promoting immigration and expanding the economy in the northern provinces, the creation or relocation of presidial defenses composed one aspect of Croix's strategy. Croix selected Juan Bautista de Anza, fresh from success in establishing the presidio at San Francisco in Alta California, as governor of New Mexico. As part of his military reorganization of the province, Anza proposed to move the Santa Fe presidio from the north bank of the Río Santa Fe (where it remains today in the form of the "Governor's Palace") to higher ground on the south side, where the Barrio de Analco clustered around the Church of San Miguel. This barrio had long embraced the lands and homes of Santa Fe's *genízaro* population, which numbered in 1780 some 142 individuals in forty-two families, or 12.25 percent of the town's population.[40] Anza's plan included relocation of these *genízaros* and some "lower order" *vecino* residents to new frontier settlements, which Bustamante termed "gateway of the enemy Comanche."[41]

Although never explicitly stated, we may infer that Anza's relocation plan triggered Bustamante's complaint. His people did not wish to abandon their communal lands. Foremost among their fears stood the danger of "losing their women and children" to capture by Comanche raiders, a peril that had plagued frontier settlements since the colony's inception. The *genízaros* of Analco knew the pattern of reciprocal slave raiding all too well, for they were one consequence of the trade, and often took *cautivos* themselves during their campaigns against *los indios bárbaros*.[42] Years of military service and co-residence with colonial New Mexicans had made of them devout Catholics and loyal subjects, yet Anza's expulsion and reloca-tion plan left Bustamante's people only two alternatives—to "endure their burdens and travails" or to go in search of relief to their lands and nation. Whether this meant literal desertion and apostasy, or merely a suspension of residence and military service while Anza reconsidered his decision remains unclear. It does hint that these *genízaros* had not entirely severed their familial and cultural connections to their (presumably) Apache kin, and temporary flight remained within their tactical repertoire.

Bustamante's people may have exercised the latter option, for Anza reported to Commander-General of the Provincias Internas Teodoro de Croix that an intended expedition to Sonora had to be abandoned due to the "malicious and needless flight of the settlers of this Villa."[43] This is not certain, however. Croix later heard a complaint from twenty-four residents of the barrio at his headquarters in Arispe, Sonora, and overruled Anza's plan until such times as he could show better cause.[44] Whether the Arispe petitioners were Bustamante's *genízaros*, or poor *vecinos* who also opposed the plan, remains unfortunately obscured.[45] In either case, the people of Analco seemed willing to take extraordinary steps in their search for "mercy with justice" and to protect the interests of their community.

This case also sheds some light on a growing complex of shared interests between *genízaros* and lower-order *vecinos* occurring in parallel with expansion in the borderland economy. Anza reported to Croix in the spring of 1780 that he had been unable to persuade the citizens of the province to form a *cordón* (trading caravan) to Chihuahua that would then cooperate with his Sonoran expedition. He attributed this reluctance to the lack, that season, of "the formal trading for hides with the pagans," which occurred only every two years. He explained that these fairs "stimulate[d] and ma[d]e up the largest part of the trade of this province," without which the settlers felt a *cordón* to be fruitless.[46] As a drought and famine that began in the late 1770s persisted in the province, and with a smallpox epidemic just beginning, local economic conditions were dreadful. It is little wonder that *genízaros* and *vecinos* alike found neither relocation nor a major trade and military expedition appealing. By December 1780, the Analceños pursued their own alternative strategy. Probably guided by *genízaro* scouts like Bentura Bustamante, more than two hundred men, women, and children took to the eastern plains on a buffalo hunt, returning to their homes with some four hundred fifty loads of meat.[47]

These seasonal *viajes* would become commonplace in the nineteenth century, a phenomenon that points to the manner in which *genízaros* worked within an expanding borderland economy to elevate their status in New Mexican society. By 1800 Governor Fernando Chacón relied almost exclusively on *genízaros* or repatriated New Mexican captives as scouts and explorers onto the Plains. In June of that year, eager to get a sense of American designs on the West and to explore trade opportunities with the Cheyenne and Sioux, he dispatched the trilingual José Miguel Zenguaras, two Taos Indians, and four *genízaros* (with their wives) on a reconnaissance mission toward the Missouri.[48] In November, Comandante José Manuel Ochoa of El Paso del Norte requested from Chacón "a force of the strongest and most warlike Taos and *genízaros*," to scour the Sierras Magdalenas, San Mateos, and Piñones for Apache depredators.[49] Eight years later, following Zebulon Pike's arrest in the San Luis Valley, Comandante Salcedo formalized their rising status by creating an official Tropa de Genízaros, whom he then sent onto the Plains to monitor American solicitations of Pawnee friendship and to affirm the faith of the Spanish alliance with the Comanches.[50]

The people of eighteenth-century colonial New Mexico certainly organized their society around concepts of honor, but to argue that "Spaniards reveled in their honor only because they lived among *genízaros* who were dishonored by their enslavement," glosses over growing divisions *within* colonial society and emergent alliances between New Mexicans and neighboring *indios gentiles*.[51] The claim that *genízaros* and other conquered Indians were now "the enemy within," against which the Spanish could define their cultural integrity, overlooks the multiple roles played by this slave soldiery.[52] As culturally diverse "slaves," they did provide an example of social subordination and impurity against which *españoles* could define their *calidad* (quality). As skilled soldiers, however, they clearly received a measure of respect and occasional success within the customary justice of New Mexico. They, too, developed a sense of honor that derived from their military prowess. In 1793, for example, when Marcos Sánchez of Tomé was arrested for abusing his concubine, he protested, "I am a *genízaro*, unworthy of such base treatment!"[53] These countervailing tensions between formal caste subordination and tactical indispensability would grow, especially as the era of Bourbon reforms spurred economic growth and class divisiveness within New Mexico.

Although the *genízaros* of Nalco resisted expulsion in 1780, in the following decades relocation and resettlement would occur. Land and water shortages in the Rio Grande valley, confidence in the stability of the New Mexico–Comanche alliance negotiated between Governor Anza and Ecueracapa in 1786, and the vigorous economic exchange which followed that treaty all promoted frontier expansion. As settlers of peripheral outposts, *genízaros* and lower- order *vecinos* extended the Spanish presence in the borderlands, and elaborated their own autonomous strategies in the pursuit of wealth and security. These strategies recognized that cultural hybridization offered village society opportunities that rigid cultural differentiation did not, but such strategies also held the seeds of conflict between borderland dwellers and their colonial overlords.

In his 1794 instructions to incoming governor Chacón, Don Fernando de la Concha offered a caution about the political consequences of easy relations between *vecinos, genízaros,* and *los indios barbaros*:

The inhabitants [of this province] are indolent. They love distance which makes them independent; and if they recognize the advantages of union, they pretend not to understand them, in order to adapt the liberty and slovenliness which they see . . . in their neighbors the wild Indians.[54]

In a broad sense frontier settlement met the objectives of Spanish administrators, in that mixed *genízaro-vecino* outposts provided a skilled

336

military presence on the traditional gateways to the colony. Yet these *llan-eros* (plainsmen), as they came to be called, showed little inclination to congregate in fortified plazas and commit to a settled farming life. Instead they proved a constant irritant to their superiors. While maintaining a village-based cultural profile, borderlanders began to move freely across the Plains, traveling seasonally to hunt buffalo as *ciboleros* or trade as *coman-cheros*. In doing so they came to wear their cultural affiliation lightly, living as Spanish *labradores* (farmers) during periods of planting and harvesting, only to slip comfortably into a nomadic lifestyle when fat buffalo or barter beckoned in the autumn.

Although their "liberty and slovenliness" dismayed Spanish elites, their knowledge of the borderlands proved so valuable that the authorities had to grant allowances for both travel and settlement beyond the pale of colonial control. During this period we see the establishment of key villages east of the Sangre de Cristo Mountains: San Miguel del Vado in 1794, San José del Vado in 1803, Mora in 1818, and Anton Chico in 1822.[55] Not coincidentally, each petition for a village grant included names of men designated as *genízaros*, for these people had long served in the van-guard of intercultural negotiation.[56] In reaching out to their Comanche neighbors, New Mexican *llaneros* drew upon a century of intercultural ex-changes—whether violent or commercial—to develop new strategies for exploiting opportunities on the Plains. Looser and more flexible village organization, and cultural hybridity were among these innovations.

The fifty-two residents of Sante Fe who petitioned Governor Chacón for a grant of vacant land on the Pecos River on September 1, 1794, illustrate the blending of tradition and innovation. Led by Lorenzo Márquez and Domingo Padilla, both *vecinos*, the petitioners included thir-teen *genízaro* heads of families, all of whom claimed that although they had "some small pieces of land" in the Barrio de Analco, water shortages and overcrowding made it "impossible for all of us to enjoy its use." They had already reconnoitered (and probably farmed seasonally, given the use requirements in Spanish land law) a fertile valley twenty miles downriver from Pecos Pueblo, where there lay enough land not only for themselves, but also for "as many in the province who are destitute."[57]

Chacón confirmed the grant at San Miguel del Vado, with the understanding that at the end of two years, all able-bodied men must possess firearms (only twenty-five of the petitioners did so at the time, the others had bows and arrows), muster regularly, and build the requisite fortified plaza.[58] The settlers, however, felt less urgency. The first baptismal entry for a *vecino* of El Vado dates from 1798, when the Pecos Indian Juan de Dios Fernández married María Armijo, daughter of grantee Juan Armijo. Grantees Márquez and Padilla, however, had appeared as *padrinos* in the Pecos baptismal books in the early 1780s, suggesting that the Analceños had probably been sojourning on the Plains and farming the Pecos bottoms for some time before making their petition.[59] The effort and expense of building a fortified adobe plaza and equipping themselves with firearms was probably beyond the means of these families. Still, the risk seemed reasonable given the potential rewards of inserting themselves as intermediaries in the Plains trade.

Outgoing governor Don Fernando de la Concha had already warned Fernando Chacón to beware the emergence of easy relations between villagers and "wild Indians." Concha had grudgingly allowed the intercourse to grow, he explained, "with the idea of acquiring a complete knowledge of the waterholes and lands in which they [the Comanches] are situated." Moreover, the presidial troops needed remounts, and "the only way to acquire horses of good quality cheaply is to . . . barter with the Comanches. . . the cost of each [being] eight pesos, more or less."[60] By the beginning of the nineteenth century, Comanches had become the principal horse traders on the southern plains, and New Mexicans proved a hungry market for these mounts. The difficulty in regulating this trade, however, evoked increasing anxiety in colonial administrators.

Concha offered cautions about the general character of these villagers as well. "Under a simulated appearance of ignorance or rusticity they conceal the most refined malice. He is a rare one in whom the vices of lying and robbing do not occur together." These character traits he attributed to "the dispersion of their settlements [and] the bad upbringing resulting from this, the proximity and trade of the barbarous tribes." The governor noted that the civilian militias upon which the province depended for defense functioned virtually free from military authority, "always disturbing the Province whenever it suited them in the purpose of gaining their own ends," a chaos deriving from a "lack of obedience, willfulness, and desire to live without subjection and in complete liberty, in imitation of the wild tribes which they see nearby." With no little exasperation, he suggested that "the removal of more than two thousand *labradores* to another area" would be "very useful to the society and the state." Social stability could only be attained by "a new system of regulations and . . . a complete change in the actual system of control," especially the creation of a stable commercial agriculture and imposition of military discipline within the militias.[61]

His successor fared no better in imposing order on the borderlands. By 1803 Governor Chacón reported failure in promoting commercial agriculture in the province: "the majority of its inhabitants are little dedicated to farming, [contenting themselves] with sowing and cultivating only what is necessary for their sustenance." By implication, informal and illegal trade with Indian groups, conducted in good part by *genízaro* border men, occupied most New Mexicans. In marked contrast, Chacón praised "the Pueblo Indians who compose a third of the population, [who] develop large fields that are cultivated in common, so that they can take care of widows, orphans, the sick, [and] unemployed." Noting that only the Pueblos produced a surplus and thus "never feel the effects of hunger," he affirmed by implication their readiness for formal market participation should a more reliable trade be established between the province and the Chihuahua market centers. The governor's interest in developing an export economy was not simply a bureaucrat's endorsement of pro-market Bourbon reforms. Since Chacón had held the tithe rental contract for the province from 1796 to 1801, his personal income had probably suffered from the *vecino* population's fascination with informal commerce, an issue that would come to a head just a few years later.[62]

Chacón also complained of the "natural decadence and backwardness" of the provincial economy, where "internal commerce is in the hands of twelve or fourteen merchants . . . neither properly licensed nor versed in business matters." Ninety percent of commercial exchange was conducted "on credit . . . exacerbated by the lack of money in circulation." Even worse than this commercial core were "the rest of the citizenry [who were] so many petty merchants . . . continuously dealing and bartering with whatever products they ha[d] at hand."[63]

Ironically, "formality prevailed" only "in the trading carried on with the *Naciones gentiles* [heathen nations], that being a give-and-take business conducted in sign language." In exchange for New Mexican manufactures like saddlebags, bridles, bits, iron goods, textiles, and agricultural products both raw and processed, the "nomads give Indian captives of both sexes, mules, moccasins, colts, mustangs, all kinds of hides and buffalo meat."[64] New Mexican villagers indeed produced a local agricultural surplus, and practiced weaving, leatherworking, and blacksmithing, but were more inclined to use that surplus in exchange with Plains peoples than accept the low prices consequent to risky overland shipping and the uncertain markets of Chihuahua.

When it became clear that most local production went into the Plains trade, rather than south along the *camino real*, efforts were made in both Mexico City and Santa Fe to stem the leakage. Early in 1805 the viceroy decreed that all goods bartered by New Mexicans at the annual trade fair in the San Bartolomé valley would be free from the payment of the 6 percent *alcabala* required of other provinces. In June, Chacón's successor, Joaquín del Real Alencaster, convened a *junta* in Santa Fe to discuss methods of improving manufactures and mining, and redirect existing production toward the Mexican trade. Although a lack of capital limited any significant invigoration of the textile or nascent mining industries, Alencaster attempted first to build up local sheep flocks by prohibiting their sale to Navajos, and, second, to gain at least indirect revenue from the broader Indian trade through a licensing system. Both directives produced consequences that would confirm the worst suspicions of his predecessors.[65]

Late in the autumn of 1805, the *vecinos* of San Miguel and San José del Vado gathered near their new church, ostensibly to discuss raising alms for the upcoming Fiesta de La Señora de Guadalupe. But the *teniente de justicia*, Juan Antonio Alarí, suspected otherwise, and managed to eavesdrop on the meeting. Led by the *hermano major* of the Virgin's *cofradía* (lay

brotherhood), Don Felipe Sandoval, Alarí discovered that "all of their conversation" involved the governor's recent interference with the Comanche
trade, and that Sandoval intended to incite the settlers to reject the order
and "go to trade with the heathens as is customary." Furthermore Sandoval
claimed that the citizens of La Cañada and Río Arriba would support their
action. Fearing insurrection, Alarí broke up the meeting "with staff and
cudgels" and took Sandoval, José García of Mora, and Victor Vigil of Río
Arriba into custody.

When news of the men's arrest circulated throughout the province,
enraged bands of citizens from outlying villages converged upon the capital.
To diffuse tensions, the governor quickly convened an investigation of the
grievances beneath the scandal. Numerous respondents confirmed general
dissatisfaction with the governor's restrictions on their customary Indian
trade. It quickly became clear that limitations on commerce with Comanches
constituted only one complaint, and that Sandoval's agents had circulated
a letter throughout the province urging a general disobedience. García de
la Mora himself complained of the uncertain timing and rewards of the
Chihuahua caravan, of the governor's "lamentable decision" to prohibit
the sale of sheep to the Navajos, and the forced collection of "hundreds of
fanegas (two to three bushels)" of grain to feed the presidial soldiers in the
capital. As "many men on foot or horseback" bore down upon the capital,
Alencaster released the insurgents from jail and sent the proceedings to
Commander-General Salcedo for review. He proffered a charge of sedition
against Sandoval, but Salcedo failed to act upon his recommendation. By
1810, in fact, Sandoval found himself appointed *protector de indios* of the
Pueblo Indians of the province.[66]

At first glance, we might see this case along a continuum of successful extralegal collective actions in the interest of customary justice, from
the Belén defense of 1746 to Bustamante's action of 1780. But at San Miguel
del Vado we see asymmetries in justice reminiscent of the prosecutions of
genízaro cattle thieves at San Miguel de Carnué in 1768. Unlike Sandoval,
whose *vecino* status probably protected him, other men from San Miguel
suffered severely in the aftermath of the unrest. Even while the investigations of the *vecinos* were underway in Santa Fe, Lieutenant Alarí took four

more men into custody. "Francisco el Comanche," "Francisco Xavier de Nacion Aà" (Pawnee),[67] "José María Gurulé de Nacion Caigua," and the genízaro Antonio María were charged with seditious activities among los gentiles, especially the Comanches. Alarí claimed that the men, in disregard of the governor's licensing directives, had visited the camps of Comanche general Somicuiaio, speaking "very badly of the Spanish, and the Governor." Spreading rumors and "a thousand lies," including the accusation that customary gifts for the Indians might not be forthcoming, the men also acquired "hides, meat, and other goods" from the Indians. Alexandro Martín, a New Mexican captive returned by Comanche captain Tosapoy in 1786 at the conclusion of the Spanish-Comanche Peace Treaty, and now "interpreter to the Comanches," corroborated Alarí's testimony, claiming the men's activities resulted in "great harm to the peace." Frustrated as to what measures he could take to castigate and reprimand these "baptized and Christian Indians," Alencaster sent them by military escort to the assessor-general of the provincias internas in Guadalajara, warning of the risk that they "might flee and go to live among said Indians, and upset the Peace."[68] The resolution of this case remains unclear, but in 1807 the genízaro Antonio María was arrested for vagrancy in Chihuahua, then sent north to Santa Fe to work off his punishment in service at the presidio.[69]

The disturbances of 1805 point to the extent to which New Mexicans of several classes and castes depended upon open trade with los indios gentiles for their economic well-being, and the degree to which the borderland economy had come to function within a widely shared sense of customary justice. Borderland villagers felt that the Indian trade was their trade, and resented deeply administrative interference. They demonstrated their outrage in the same fashion that Antonio Casados, Luis Quintana, and Bentura Bustamante had in previous decades—by mobilizing their communities in extralegal public protest and coupling these with appeals to customary rights. Their actions also point to the astonishing cultural complexity and caste interdependence of borderland villagers. The "seditious" activities at San Miguel del Vado involved respectable vecinos like Felipe Sandoval, his compadres from the northern villages of the Río Arriba, genízaros like Antonio María, and mysterious transcultural social marginals like the Comanche Francisco, the Pawnee Francisco Xavier, and the Kiowa José María Gurule. Provincial grievances went beyond Alencaster's attempt to regulate the Plains trade, and included both his prohibitions against the sale of sheep to the Navajos and the responsibility of the local populace to maintain a relatively ineffective presidial troop.

Although many details remain obscure, the general condition of the province at the beginning of the century seems one of barely restrained entrepreneurial frenzy of a decidedly heterogeneous type. When Don Alberto Maynez succeeded Alencaster in 1808, he wisely relaxed his predecessor's restrictions, and this energy again expanded outward. Soon the borderland villages would be filled with seasonally nomadic *ciboleros* (bison hunters) and *comancheros* (traders and slavers) who connected with the maturing "raiding economies" of Kiowas and Comanches to lay the groundwork for the market-driven livestock economy which would emerge after 1860. In so doing they would ultimately draw the negative attention of military modernizers and capitalist developers in the 1870s.[70]

But the disturbances and resolutions at San Miguel del Vado also point to the limits of collective action to shape customary justice in the search for *equidad*, and allow for some more general observations about the functioning of power in colonial borderlands. The uprising did produce some of the desired corrections in trade policy, but the slaves who played such a central role were punished while *vecinos* were not. The four men sent to Guadalajara may have simply been *contrabandistas* caught in the act, yet they appear emblematic of a larger pattern. It may be that expanding economic opportunities on the Plains—coupled with liberal social tendencies in the Bourbon Reforms—loosened caste restraints while simultaneously scattering tightly knit (and caste-constrained) *genízaro* communities in a centrifugal fashion. Economic interdependency and shared interests failed to translate into social and legal equality. Caste may have had little salience in day-to-day relations, or may even have helped to organize, along with class interests, some aspects of community resistance, but it never lost its capacity under the law to become a tool of unequal justice when courts so wished.

Throughout the Americas, moments when changing political

economies fractured socio-legal structures of domination and allowed indigenous and/or subordinated peoples to develop new repertoires of contention occurred with growing frequency in the late eighteenth century. At the same time that Bustamante laid his challenge before Governor Anza, Bourbon military reformers in Sonora, Chihuahua, and Coahuila were settling soldier communities along Mexico's northern frontier. By the nineteenth century these would—due to their distance from colonial legal control and pivotal role in the borderland economy—become the seedbed for a staunchly independent and revolutionary "norteño" identity.[71] Far to the south, the "raiding economies" of Indian peoples in the pampas borderlands of South America were shifting from subsistence to ever-wider networks of market exchange that included many hundreds of human captives in their commerce. This socioeconomic transition would elevate Indian groups like the Araucanians and Ranqueles to the status of militarized "tribes," alternately solicited as allies or attacked as enemies by the formative Chilean and Argentine states which claimed their territory.[72] So too did American Indian groups east of the Mississippi seek new strategic space in the unstable imperial landscape, but found their options increasingly limited to tactical maneuvering within the new United States, as their former French and British allies withdrew from overtly supportive roles.[73] In most cases the fissures closed all too quickly, and renewed arts of domination and conquest asserted themselves. But for other peoples the openings of the 1780s held more lasting promise. Men and women of the white farming frontiers found power structures of the fledgling republic vulnerable, if only to a limited extent, to their political and economic demands.[74]

Despite their many and manifest differences, Indian slaveries in the Americas all involved, at some level, law and violence as instruments of domination and tools for resistance. Often built upon deep customs of capture and assimilation among indigenous groups that antedated European colonialism, the forms of Indian slavery featured in this essay, and in others of this volume, were explicitly conditioned by their colonial context. Victim and victimizer were often difficult to distinguish when procurement and enslavement unfolded in Indian country and only later reached Euro-

American markets. Occasionally victims themselves became enslavers, and even more rarely gained real political traction in early colonies. Bentura Bustamante might not have enunciated it so simply, but the meaning would have resonated with his listeners in Santa Fe that June morning.

Notes

1. Petición de Bentura Bustamante, 20 junio, 1780, *Spanish Archives of New Mexico* (hereafter *SANM*) I, no. 1138, Roll 6, Frames 323–25. I thank David H. Snow for bringing this case to my attention. The nominal definition of "*genízaros*" by which we may begin our discussion was offered by Frances Leon Swadesh in 1974, who described them as "detribalized Christian Indians living under the control of colonial authorities." According to Swadesh, "The term was primarily used to apply to Indians of various tribes not native to New Mexico who had been ransomed from captivity among the nomadic tribes and placed as servants in settler households. In practice, many *Genízaros* were Pueblo Indians who had been expelled from the home village for being overly adaptive to Hispanic culture." See *Los Primeros Pobladores: Hispanic Americans of the Ute Frontier* (South Bend: University of Notre Dame Press, 1974), xviii. The following pages will address several necessary additions to this understanding.

2. Frances Swadesh (Quintana) first proposed the "non-dominant frontier" concept in her "Structure of Hispanic-Indian Relations in New Mexico," in Paul M. Kutsche, ed., *The Survival of Spanish American Villages* (Colorado Springs: Colorado College Publications in Culture, 1979), 53–61. For a recent synthesis of the Spanish borderlands that expands this thinking, see David J. Weber, *The Spanish Frontier in North America* (New Haven: Yale University Press, 1991).

3. See G. Emlen Hall, *Four Leagues of Pecos: A Legal History of the Pecos Grant, 1800–1933* (Albuquerque: University of New Mexico Press, 1984); Victor Westphall, *Mercedes Reales: Hispanic Land Grants of the Upper Rio Grande Region* (Albuquerque: University of New Mexico Press, 1983); Charles L. Briggs and John Van Ness, eds., *Land, Water, and Culture: New Perspectives on Hispanic Land Grants* (Albuquerque: University of New Mexico Press, 1987) quoted p. 72; and Malcolm Ebright, ed., "Spanish and Mexican Land Grants in New Mexico and Colorado," *Journal of the West* (July 1980), 74–85; Malcolm Ebright, ed., "Spanish and Mexican Land Grants and the Law," *Journal of the West* (July 1988), 3–11; and Malcolm Ebright, *Land Grants and Law Suits in Northern New Mexico* (Albuquerque, University of New Mexico Press, 1994).

4. For the Las Casas–Sepulveda debate, see Lewis Hanke, *All Mankind Is One: A Study of the Disputation Between Bartolomé de Las Casas and Juan Ginés de Sepúlveda in 1550 on the Intellectual and Religious Capacity of American Indians* (DeKalb IL: Northern Illinois University Press, 1974). For the *protector de indios* in New Mexico, see Charles R. Cutter, *The Protector de Indios in Colonial New Mexico, 1659–1821* (Albuquerque: University of New Mexico Press, 1986).

5. Ross Frank's current work reveals the sophisticated and culturally specific legal tactics employed by Pueblo Indians to conceal "criminal and subversive" activities from Spanish administrators in the late eighteenth century, aspects of the cultural compartmentalization for which Pueblos became renowned in the eyes of twentieth-century American ethnographers. See "From Settler to Citizen: Economic Development and Cultural Change in Late Colonial New Mexico, 1750–1820," (PhD diss., University of California, Berkeley, 1992), 358–88; Edward H. Spicer, "Spanish-Indian Acculturation in the Southwest," *American Anthropologist* 56 (1954), 663–84; Edward P. Dozier, *The Pueblo Indians of North America* (New York: Holt, Rinehart, and Winston, 1970).

6. See Charles R. Cutter, *The Legal Culture of New Spain, 1700–1810* (Albuquerque, University of New Mexico Press, 1995) for a comprehensive treatment of *justicia real ordinaria* (ordinary royal jurisdiction) in the northern provinces of New Mexico and Texas. Angelina Veyna's work on women's *testamentos* (wills) in New Mexico illustrates the markedly superior legal status that women maintained in that colony as compared to their sisters on the eastern seaboard of North America. Angelina F. Veyna, *"Hago, dispongo, y ordeno mi testamento*: Reflections of Colonial New Mexican Women," paper presented at the Annual Meeting of the Western History Association, October 1991, Austin, Texas. David Snow's research on colonial land tenure systems suggests a shift from large-scale *estancias* and haciendas in the pre-1680 period to smaller-scale but more numerous communal *mercedes* in the eighteenth century. This seems consistent with an expanding *vecino* population and a desire to project Spanish settlement outward, both defensively and commercially, into territories ranged by indigenous nomads and pastoralists known collectively as *los indios bárbaros*. David H. Snow, "Ownership and Uses of Lands in Seventeenth-Century New Mexico," paper presented at Annual Conference of the Historical Society of New Mexico, April 1994, Taos, New Mexico; David H. Snow, "Rural Hispanic Community Organization in Northern New Mexico: An Historical Perspective," in Kutsche, ed., *Survival of Spanish American Villages*, 45–52.

7. Alfred Barnaby Thomas, *Forgotten Frontiers: A Study of the Spanish Indian Policy of Don Juan Bautista de Anza, Governor of New Mexico, 1777–1787* (Norman: University of Oklahoma Press, 1932); Alfred Barnaby Thomas, *The Plains Indians and New Mexico, 1751–1778* (Norman: University of Oklahoma Press, 1940); Charles L. Kenner, *The Comanchero Frontier: A History of New Mexican-Plains Indian Relations* (Norman: University of Oklahoma Press, 1994 [1969]); Thomas W. Kavanagh, *Comanche Political History: An Ethnohistorical Perspective, 1706–1875* (Lincoln: University of Nebraska Press, 1996).

8. See Charles Tilly, "Collective Violence in European Perspective," in Ted Robert Gurr, ed., *Violence In America: Protest, Rebellion, Reform*, vol. 2 (Newbury Park: Sage Publications, 1989 [1979]), 62–100, quote from 100.

9. For an in-depth treatment of this political·economy and its reliance upon a distinctive slave system for its integrity, see James F. Brooks, *Captives and Cousins: Slavery, Kinship, and Community in the Southwest Borderlands* (Chapel Hill: University of North Carolina Press, 2002). For recent works that deepen and refine the perspective, see Pekka Hämäläinen, *The Comanche Empire* (New Haven: Yale University Press, 2008) and Brian De Lay, *War of a Thousand Deserts: Indian Raids and the U.S.-Mexican War* (New Haven: Yale University Press, 2008).

10. Christopher Tomlins utilizes the concept of "modalities of rule" to capture both the particular autonomy of "law" in situational contexts, *and* its "constant structural relationship with the contexts in which it is located." *Law, Labor, and Ideology in the Early American Republic* (Cambridge: Cambridge University Press, 1993), chapter 1.

11. For Africans, see Colin A. Palmer, *Slaves of the White God: Blacks in Mexico, 1570–1650* (Cambridge MA: Harvard University Press, 1976) especially 84–118; for Indian slavery, see Silvio Zavala, *Los Esclavos Indios en Nueva España* (Mexico City: Edición de El Colegio Nacional Luis Gonzáles Obregón núm 23, 1967).

12. Trade fairs at Taos, Pecos, and Picuris Pueblos had long fostered the exchange of bison meat for corn, beans, and squash between Plains Indians and the Rio Grande Pueblos, and may have included some exchanges of people as well. For theoretical and empirical cases, see the essays in Katherine Spielmann, ed., *Farmers, Hunters, and Colonists: Interaction between the Southwest and the Southern Plains* (Tucson: University of Arizona Press, 1991).

13. Report of the Reverend Father Provincial, Fray Pedro Serrano . . . to the Marquis de

Cruillas . . . 1761, in Charles Wilson Hackett, trans. and ed., *Historical Documents Relating to New Mexico, Nueva Vizcaya, and Approaches Thereto, to 1773* (Washington DC: Carnegie Institution of Washington, 1937), 486–87.

14. Fray Anatasio Domínguez, *The Missions of New Mexico, 1776*, Eleanor B. Adams and Fray Angélico Chávez, eds. and trans. (Albuquerque: Museum of New Mexico Press, 1956), 252. See also Amando Represa, "Las Ferias hispano-indias del Nuevo México," in *La España Ilustrada en el Lejano Oeste* (Valladolid: Junta de Castilla y León, 1990), 119–25.

15. Since only some 75 percent of baptismal registers still exist, the actual figures are probably considerably higher. David M. Brugge, *Navajos in the Catholic Church Records of New Mexico, 1694–1875* (Tsaile: Navajo Community College Press, 1985), 2; for breakdown by tribal derivation and date, 22–23.

16. For the debate on the *genízaros*, see Frances Leon Swadesh, *Los Primeros Pobladores*; Gilberto Espinosa and Tibo Chavez, *El Río Abajo* (Pampa Print Shop, Albuquerque, date unknown), chapter 10, "The Genizaro"; Fray Angélico Chávez, "Genizaros," in *The Handbook of North American Indians*, Alfonso Ortiz, ed. (Washington DC: Smithsonian Institution, 1980), 198–200; Robert Archibald, "Acculturation and Assimilation in Colonial New Mexico," *New Mexico Historical Review*, (July 1978), 205–17; Stephen M. Horvath, "The Genizaro of Eighteenth-Century New Mexico: A Re-examination," *Discovery* [Santa Fe, School of American Research] 1977, 25–40; Russell M. Magnaghi, "Plains Indians in New Mexico: The Genizaro Experience," *Great Plains Quarterly* (Spring 1990), 86–95.

17. Ramón A. Gutiérrez, *When Jesus Came the Corn Mothers Went Away: Marriage, Sexuality, and Power in New Mexico, 1500–1846* (Stanford: Stanford University Press, 1991), 188.

18. See *The Missions of New Mexico, 1776*, 42, 126, 208, 259; quoted in Gutiérrez, *When Jesus Came*, 189.

19. For Morfí, see *Father Juan Agustín Morfi's Account of Disorders in New Mexico, 1778*, Marc Simmons, ed. and trans. (Isleta Pueblo NM: Historical Society of New Mexico, 1977) 34–35, 189.

20. For the origins of the redemptionist orders in the medieval period, see James William Brodman, *Ransoming Captives in Crusader Spain: The Order of Merced on the Christian-Islamic Frontier* (Philadelphia: University of Pennsylvania Press, 1986); for the later era, Ellen G. Friedman, *Spanish Captives in North Africa in the Early Modern Age* (Madison: University of Wisconsin Press, 1983).

21. For the origins of the Ottoman Janissaries, and their relation to slavery and servility in Middle Eastern and Muslim thought, see Cemal Kafadar, *Between Two Worlds: The Construction of the Ottoman State* (Berkeley: University of California Press, 1995), 17–18, 112; Bernard Lewis, *Race and Slavery in the Middle East: An Historical Enquiry* (Oxford: University of Oxford Press, 1990), 11–14; 62–71; for their role in the Barbary States, see Andrew C. Hess, *The Forgotten Frontier: A History of the Sixteenth-Century Ibero-African Frontier* (Chicago: University of Chicago Press, 1978); and John B. Wolf, *The Barbary Coast: Algeria under the Turks* (New York: Norton, 1979).

22. Fray Angélico Chávez, "The Genízaro," 198–99.

23. For a campaign against the Sierra Blanca Apaches by fifty-five *genízaros* in 1777, that yielded a score of captives, see letter of Cavallero de Croix, July 2, 1777, to Governor Medinuetta, SANM 2, no. 701, Roll 10, Frame 701. When viewed in comparative perspective, this ambiguity is less unique than it first seems. The enslavement of women, and the military mobilization of captive men and male children, often went hand in hand, not only in the Ottoman Empire but in Africa and Asia as well. For comparative cases, see Wendy James's treatment of Ethiopia, "Perceptions from an African Slaving Frontier"; for the Sudan, Douglas H. Johnson, "Sudanese Military Slavery from the Eighteenth to the Twentieth Century," in Leonie Archer, ed., *Slavery and Other Forms of Unfree Labour* (London: Routledge Press, 1988),

130–41; 142–56; for Asia and Africa compared, see Jack P. Goody, "Slavery across Time and Space," in J. L. Watson, ed., *Asian and African Systems of Slavery* (Oxford: University of Oxford Press, 1980), 16–42. This seems especially true in cases where complex cultural and political subdivisions threatened centralization of power, and rulers needed both concubines and soldiers who were "free" of kin and factional obligations. Claude Meillassoux terms these "symplectic [societies] . . . whose heterogeneous social components are not amalgamated but are held together by various compulsive alliances which can carry out some functions of centralizing power": "by replacing free men with slaves, the masters could protect themselves from ambitious relatives or rebellious subjects; and at the same time they could protect themselves from these henchmen, by granting them differential privileges which divided them among themselves and further attached them to their master." Claude Meillassoux, *The Anthropology of Slavery: The Womb of Iron and Gold*, trans. Alide Dasnois (Chicago: University of Chicago Press, 1991), 344, 64, 140.

24. France V. Scholes, *Church and State in New Mexico, 1610–1650*, Historical Society of New Mexico Publications in History, vol. 7 (Santa Fe: Historical Society of New Mexico, 1937).

25. Don Carlos de Siguenza y Góngora, *Mercurio Volante* (1940 [1693]) 128; Campaign Journal of Don Diego de Vargas Zapata Luján Ponce de León, January 8, 1692, in J. Manuel Espinosa, ed. and trans., *First Expedition of Vargas into New Mexico, 1692* (Albuquerque: Quivira Society, 1940), 263.

26. In his 1705 campaign into Navajo country, Captain Roque de Madrid referred to his Jemez Pueblo auxiliaries as *genízaros*. See Rick Hendrick and John P. Wilson, eds. and trans., *The Navajos in 1705: Roque Madrid's Campaign Journal* (Albuquerque: University of New Mexico Press, 1996).

27. Census of July 12, 1750, in Virginia Langham Olmstead, comp., *Spanish and Mexican Censuses of New Mexico, 1750–1830* (Albuquerque: New Mexico State Historical Society, 1981), 47–48.

28. For these dates, see "Declaration of . . . Menchero" in Hackett, *Historical Documents*, vol. 3, 401; Olmsted, comp., Spanish Colonial Censuses of 1750, 1760, and 1790, in The New Mexico State Records Center; SANM I, no. 975, "Las Trampas Grant"; Swadesh, *Primeros Pobladores*, 38; Andrew T. Smith, "The People of the San Antonio de Las Heurtas Grant," ms. in the New Mexico State Records Center; "Description of . . . the settlement at El Paso del Norte . . . in 1773," in Hackett, *Historical Documents*, vol. 3, 508; E. Boyd, "The Plaza of San Miguel Del Vado," *El Palacio* 77, no. 4 (1971), 17–28.

29. Russell M. Magnaghi, "Plains Indians in New Mexico," 88; Gutierrez, *When Jesus Came*, 305–6, also makes note of this military role, but does not attempt to integrate the paradoxical information into his earlier characterizations of "dishonored thralls." He suggests, however, that with movement to frontier outposts, *genízaros* "finally had an independent space in which to express their own identity" (305).

30. Smith, "The Peoples of the San Antonio de Las Huertas Grant, 1767–1900," ms. in the New Mexico State Records Center, 37.

31. See Olmstead, comp., *Spanish and Mexican Censuses of New Mexico, 1750–1830*, 47–48.

32. Analysis drawn from Stephen M. Horvath, "The Genízaro of Eighteenth-Century New Mexico: A Re-examination," 25–40.

33. Olmsted, comp., "The Spanish Colonial Census of 1750," 47–48.

34. See "The Declaration of Fray Miguel de Menchero, May 10, 1744," in Charles Wilson Hackett, trans. and ed., *Historical Documents*, vol. 3, 401–2.

35. Antonio Casados and Luís Quintana, *genízaros*, proceedings against Fulano Barrera,

Diego de Torres and Antonio Salazar over lands at Puesto de Belén, *SANM* 1, Roll 1, Frames 1302–1327, New Mexico State Records Center. For a discussion, see Stephen M. Horvath, "The Social and Political Organization of the *Genízaros* of the Plaza de Nuestra Senora de Los Dolores de Belen," unpublished PhD diss. (Brown University, 1979), 180–181, in New Mexico State Records Center, Santa Fe. This information suggests that, at least in some cases, unfree labor in New Mexico more closely resembled indentured servitude than chattel slavery. No documentary evidence has yet come to light describing formal indenture contracts between captives and their Spanish ransomers like that hinted at by Casados.

36. Horvath, "The Social and Political Organization of the *Genízaros*, 181.

37. Horvath, "The Social and Political Organization of the *Genízaros*, 182.

38. "Peticíon de Los Genizaros de Belèn, March 28, 1749," Archdiocesian Archives of Santa Fe (AASF), Reel 52, Frames 68–72, in the New Mexico State Records Center.

39. Diligencias criminales contra los jenízaros de Carnué, *SANM* 2, no. 636, Roll 10, Frame 400; see discussion in Frances Leon Swadesh, "Archaeology, Ethnohistory, and the First Plaza of Carnue," in *Ethnohistory* 23, no. 1 (1976), 31–44.

40. Dominguez, *The Missions of New Mexico*, Adams and Chávez, trans. and eds., 42.

41. "Geographical description of New Mexico written by . . . Fray Juan Augustin de Morfi . . . 1782," in A. B. Thomas, *Forgotten Frontiers*, 92; see also Anza to Croix, May 26, 1780, in A. B. Thomas, *Forgotten Frontiers*, p. 177; Petición de Bentura Bustamante, June 20, 1780, *SANM* 1 no. 1138, Roll 6, Frames 323–25. The fact that Bustamante described Comanches as enemies, that in campaigns the *genízaros* betrayed their own people, and that by 1780 Anza's strategy of taking war to the Sierra Blanca and Lipan Apaches was in place, suggests that the *genízaros* of Analco probably derived originally from Apache groups. Apaches represent 845 of the 1,413 non-Pueblo Indians baptized in New Mexico between 1690 and 1780; see Brugge, *Navajos in the Catholic Church Records*, 22–23.

42. For the specific role that women and children played as objects and agents of intercultural competition and negotiation, see James F. Brooks, "This Evil Extends . . . Especially to the Feminine Sex: Negotiating Captivity in the New Mexico Borderlands," *Feminist Studies* 22, no. 2 (1996), 279–309.

43. Anza to Croix, May 26, 1780, *Forgotten Frontiers*, 177.

44. "Geographical description . . . by Morfi," in Thomas, *Forgotten Frontiers*, 92, 92n28, 92n59; see also A. B. Thomas, ed. and trans., *Teodoro de Croix and the Northern Frontier of New Spain, 1776–1783* (Norman: University of Oklahoma Press, 1941), 107–8.

45. For the long and rambling complaint against Anza's plan by Manuel de Armijo and José Miguel de la Peña, "*vecinos de dicha villa*," much devoted to contesting Anza's impugnations of their character, see Document Five, the Sender Collection, New Mexico State Records Center.

46. Anza to Croix, May 26, 1780, in Thomas, *Forgotten Frontiers*, 177.

47. See note 11 on John Kessell's reproduction of the *Miera y Pacheco Map of New Mexico*, 1776–1789 (Albuquerque: University of New Mexico Press, 1975).

48. Chacón to Nava, June 10, 1800, *SANM* 2, no. 1490, Roll 14, Frames 548–49.

49. Ochoa to Chacón, November 30, 1800, *SANM* 2, no. 1519, Roll 14, Frames 658–59.

50. José Manrique, draft of a report for Nemesio Salcedo y Salcedo, Nov. 26, 1808, in the Pinart Collection, Bancroft Library, University of California, Berkeley.

51. Gutiérrez, *When Jesus Came*, 206.

52. Gutiérrez, *When Jesus Came*, 196.

53. Gutiérrez, *When Jesus Came*, 306.

54. "Don Fernando de la Concha to Lieutenant Colonel Don Fernando Chacón, Advice on Governing New Mexico, 1794," Donald E. Worcester, trans., *NMHR*, 24, no. 3 (1949), 236–54, quote from 250.

55. For these dates, see E. Boyd, "The Plaza of San Miguel del Vado," El *Palacio* 77, no. 4 (1971); Miguel Montoya, "The Preservation of a Trail-Era Community in the Mora Valley Today." Although the official grant for the village of Mora was not issued until 1835, in 1818 three hundred residents petitioned Santa Fe for a resident priest; for Anton Chico, see Michael J. Rock, "Anton Chico and its Patent," in John R. Van Ness and Christine Van Ness, eds., *Spanish and Mexican Land Grants in New Mexico and Colorado* (Santa Fe: Center for Land Grant Studies, 1980), 86–91.

56. Since by 1822 caste designations like *genízaro* were no longer used in official record keeping, for Anton Chico it is necessary to trace the *genízaro* lines by following the village's first settlers from San Miguel and San José in family chain migrations down the Pecos River.

57. San Miguel del Vado Grant, Surveyor General of New Mexico Records, no. 119, Roll 24, Frames 595–740, New Mexico State Record Center, Santa Fe; for the death blow this outpost dealt to Pecos Pueblo's role in intercultural trade, see John L. Kessell, *Kiva, Cross and Crown: The Pecos Indians and New Mexico, 1540–1840* (Albuquerque: University of New Mexico Press, 1987 [1979]), 415–21.

58. San Miguel del Vado Grant, Roll 23, Frame 599.

59. Kessell, *Kiva, Cross, and Crown*, 418.

60. "Don Fernando de la Concha to Lieutenant Colonel Don Fernando Chacón," 251.

61. "Don Fernando de la Concha to Lieutenant Colonel Don Fernando Chacón," 243–44.

62. The tithe rental contract, by which holders received a percentage of the 10 percent ecclesiastical tithe on annual increase in all agricultural products and livestock, was a much-sought-after privilege, since it was perhaps the best legal way to accrue income in addition to an administrator's wages. Governors usually won this contract, which aligned their interests with a managed, measurable economy. See Ross Frank, "From Settler to Citizen," 166–210.

63. Marc Simmons, "The Chacón Economic Report of 1803," *NMHR* 60, no. 1 (1985), 81–88, quote from 83.

64. Simmons, "The Chacón Economic Report of 1803," 87.

65. Junta report on economic development, incomplete, June 17, 1805, *SANM* 2 no. 1844, Roll 15, Frames 656–57. For the importance of reciprocal trade in sheep and captives between Navajos and New Mexicans in the pastoral borderlands west of the Rio Grande, see James F. Brooks, "Violence, Justice, and State Power in New Mexico, 1780–1880," in John M. Findlay and Richard White, eds., *Power and Place in the North American West* (Seattle: University of Washington Press, 1999).

66. For the short-lived insurrection, see "Sumaria Informacion indagatoria sobre combocatoria, commocion, y escándolo cometido entre los vecinos de las Jurisdicciones Tenencia el Pecos, y Alcaldia de la Cañada, deciembre 6–24, 1805," *SANM* 2 no. 1930, Roll 15, Frames 1043–98; Kessell, *Kiva, Cross, and Crown*, 434–35; for Sandoval's appointment, see Charles R. Cutter, *The Protector de Indios in Colonial New Mexico, 1659–1821*, 82–86.

67. Although Dolores Gunnerson argues that the Aàs were Crows in *Ethnohistory of the High Plains* (Washington DC: National Park Service, 1988), 49–50, in this case it seems probably that Elizabeth John's identification of the Aàs as the Aguages or Panismahas (Pawnee) seems most probable. See *Storms Brewed in Other Men's Worlds: The Confrontation of Indians, Spanish, and French in the Southwest, 1540–1795* (Lincoln: University of Nebraska Press, 1975), 592.

68. "Diligencias criminales contra Francisco el Comanche, Francisco Xavier, José María Gurule, y Antonio María . . . 2 diciembre 1805–28 marzo 1806," SANM 2 no. 1931, Roll 15, 1099–1117. Gurulé's Kiowa identity is questionable, in that Governor Chacón reported in 1804 that the Yamparika Comanche captain Guanicoruco claimed him as his son. Chacón countered that Gurulé was, in fact, a Skidi Pawnee genízaro, once a captive of Guanicoruco, whom Chacón had settled in 1794 as an agent for the Comanches in San Miguel del Vado. Gurulé's "unruly conduct, cheating, and horse-thieving" had led to his replacement by Alejandro Martín, the former captive of Tosapoy. See Kessell, Kiva, Cross, and Crown, 429–30.

69. Isidro Rey a Real Alencaster, 2 marzo, 1807, SANM 2 no. 2043, Roll 16, Frame 315.

70. This period is treated in chapters seven and eight of Brooks, Captives and Cousins. For the general outlines of the transition, see Thomas D. Hall, Social Change in the Southwest, 1350–1880 (Lawrence: University of Kansas Press, 1989).

71. See Ana María Alonso, Thread of Blood: Colonialism, Revolution, and Gender on Mexico's Northern Frontier (Tucson: University of Arizona Press, 1995); Daniel Nugent, "Two, Three, Many Barbarisms? The Chihuahuan Frontier in Transition from Society to Politics," in Donna J. Guy and Thomas E. Sheridan, eds. Contested Ground: Comparative Frontiers on the Northern and Southern Edges of the Spanish Empire (Tucson: University of Arizona Press, 1998), 182–200; Brooks, Captives and Cousins.

72. See Susan Socolow, "Spanish Captives in Indian Societies: Cultural Contact Along the Argentine Frontier, 1600–1835," Hispanic American Historical Review 72 no. 1 (1992), 73–99; Kristine L. Jones, "Comparative Raiding Economies: North and South," in Contested Ground, ed. Guy and Sheridan, 97–114; and Thomas D. Hall, "The Río de la Plata and the Greater Southwest: A View from World-System Theory," in Contested Ground, ed. Guy and Sheridan, 150–66; James F. Brooks, "Seductions & Betrayals: La Frontera gauchesque, Argentine Nationalism, and the Predicaments of Hybridity," in James Brooks, Chris DeCorse, and John Walton, eds., Small Worlds: Method, Meaning, and Narrative in Microhistory (Santa Fe: SAR Press, 2008).

73. Colin G. Calloway, The American Revolution in Indian Country: Crisis and Diversity in Native American Communities (Cambridge: Cambridge University Press, 1995); Andrew R. L. Cayton and Fredrika J. Teute, eds., Contact Points: American Frontiers from the Mohawk Valley to the Mississippi, 1750–1830 (Chapel Hill: Omohundro Institute for Early American History and Culture, University of North Carolina Press, 1998), Alan Taylor, The Divided Ground: Indians, Settlers, and the Northern Borderland of the American Revolution (New York: Alfred Knopf, 2006).

74. See Thomas P. Slaughter, The Whiskey Rebellion: Frontier Epilogue to the American Revolution (Oxford: Oxford University Press, 1986), Alan Taylor, Liberty Men and Great Proprietors: The Revolutionary Settlement on the Maine Frontier, 1760–1820 (Chapel Hill: University of North Carolina Press, 1990), and Alan Taylor, William Cooper's Town: Power and Persuasion on the Frontier of the Early American Republic (New York: Alfred A. Knopf, 1996).

10. "A Little Flesh We Offer You"

The Origins of Indian Slavery in New France
Brett Rushforth

It is well known the advantage this colony would gain if its inhabitants could securely purchase and import the Indians called Panis, whose country is far distant from this one. . . . The people of the Panis nation are as necessary to the inhabitants of this country for farming and other tasks as are the Negroes to the Islands. And, as these kinds of engagements are very important to this colony, it is necessary to guarantee ownership to those who have bought or will buy them. Therefore, according to his Majesty's good pleasure, we order that all the Panis and Negroes who have been bought, and who shall be purchased hereafter, shall belong in full proprietorship to those who have purchased them as their slaves.

Jacques Raudot, intendant of New France, 1709

Between 1660 and 1760, the colonists of New France pursued two seemingly contradictory policies toward their Indian neighbors. Through compromise, gift giving, and native-style diplomacy they negotiated the most far-reaching system of Indian alliances in colonial North America. At the same time, they also developed an extensive system of Indian slavery that transformed thousands of Indian men, women, and children into commodities of colonial commerce in French settlements. Although these slaves never constituted more than 5 percent of the colony's total population, they performed essential labors in the colonial economy as domestics, farmers, dock loaders, millers, and semi-skilled hands in urban trades. They also interacted regularly with French settlers at the market, in church, on village streets, and in their masters' homes. In some areas, such as Montreal's commercial district around Rue Saint-Paul and the Place du Marché, Indian slaves played an especially important role. There, fully half of all colonists who owned a home in 1725 also owned an Indian slave.[1]

While early American historians have carefully studied the nature and significance of French-Indian alliances, there has been no comparable attention given to the topic of New France's Indian slave system. The only historical work to discuss it at length is Marcel Trudel's *L'esclavage au Canada français* (1960), a general history of African and Indian slavery in early Canada. Before Trudel, the slave system was the topic of a brief conference paper by James Cleland Hamilton in 1897 and received less than one chapter in Almon Wheeler Lauber's 1913 survey of Indian slavery.[2] Still less have historians considered the relationship between the rising importance of French-Indian alliances and the origins of Indian slavery in New France. Instead there has been a tendency to take Indian slavery for granted as an inevitable consequence of colonization. "As slavery was practiced in all the European colonies," Trudel characteristically concluded, "one does not see why Canada would have escaped the international practice of reducing blacks and natives to servitude."[3]

Yet New France's Indian slave system developed for reasons unique to its time and place. In Louisiana and the Caribbean, for example, France officially forbade the enslavement of Indians.[4] In the five years preceding Jacques Raudot's ordinance legalizing Indian slavery in New France, the French crown rejected at least three petitions by Louisiana governor Jean-Baptiste Le Moyne de Bienville to authorize the trade of Indian slaves in his colony.[5] Thus, far from representing a general trend in France's American colonies, Indian slavery in New France originated in response to specific historical developments that shaped its character for the rest of the eighteenth century.

Paradoxically, the enslavement of Indians succeeded in New France because of, rather than despite, the growing importance of French-Indian alliances. Between 1660 and 1710, cultural, diplomatic, and economic forces within the growing alliance system converged to draw the French and their native allies into the Indian slave trade. First, allied Indians offered captives to French colonists as culturally powerful symbols of their emerging partnership. Although French bureaucrats initially rejected captive exchange as a legitimate token of friendship, many western traders embraced the practice as a means of strengthening trade relations and securing valuable laborers. Second, following the Great Peace of 1701, New France sought desperately to prevent warfare among its Indian neighbors and to keep its native allies from defecting to the English. French officials found that captive exchanges offered one of the most effective means of stabilizing the precarious alliance created by the new treaty. Captives therefore became increasingly available as their exchange grew more central to the maintenance of the alliance system. Finally, as Indian captives passed into New France in greater numbers—especially after 1701—a growing number of French families purchased them as laborers. To protect these investments and to put an end to disputes over the captives' legal status, colonial officials issued the 1709 ordinance legalizing Indian slavery.[6]

When the French began to colonize North America in earnest during the mid-seventeenth century, both they and the Indian societies they encountered practiced forms of human unfreedom that the French called slavery. Familiar with the plantation-based chattel slavery then developing in the European colonies, many French observers used the term "*esclave*" (slave), to describe the status of Indian war captives. Although acknowledging the practice of captive adoption, which integrated captives as members of Indian families, French colonists still considered captives to live in misery, "groaning under a bondage more grievous than death."[7] Because the lives of Indian captives differed so markedly from those of chattel slaves, however, most modern scholars have resisted the French designation, describing Indians' captive-taking as an "adoption complex" to highlight the ceremonial incorporation of captives into Indian families.[8] The defining element of French chattel slavery, as explained in the seventeenth-century *Code Noir*, was a life of persistent, coerced, and degraded labor, enforced by laws that treated slaves as property and condemned their offspring to inherit slave status.[9] Unlike the Indians of the Pacific Northwest, who did condemn their captives to a state of perpetual inherited slavery, northeastern Indians' captives often achieved a measure of social respectability and did not pass their status to their offspring.[10]

Yet if the French erred in equating Indian captives with chattel slaves, they accurately recognized the defining characteristic of Indian captivity, which was neither persistent oppression nor property in persons, but the violence and dishonor associated with capture. To shame and intimidate their enemies, all Indian peoples of the American Northeast initially treated their prisoners with great disrespect through symbolic acts of humiliation. Beginning with painful physical restraints employed on the journey home, continuing through torture and derision, and culminating in ceremonial killing or adoption, Indians designed their rituals of captivity to demonstrate their superiority over vanquished enemies and to secure the allegiance and passivity of those whom they would adopt.

Once warriors carried captives a safe distance away from a raided village, they bound them tightly with cords, usually around the hands and neck, as they walked. Pierre Boucher, who lived among the Hurons and traded extensively with nations further west, described the common events of the captive-taking process in 1664:

When [the Indians of New France] capture prisoners . . . they bind them by the arms and by the legs with cords; except when they are marching, they leave the legs free. In the evening, when they camp, they lay the prisoners with their backs against the ground, and they plant some small stakes in the earth next to the feet, the hands, the neck, and the head; then they bind the prisoner to these stakes so tightly that he cannot move, which is more painful than one can imagine.[11]

This action served the obvious practical purpose of physical restraint, but it also symbolized the victim's powerlessness before a superior enemy.

During the journey, and especially upon arrival at the warriors' village, captives were mocked and forced to sing what the French described as chansons de mort, or death songs, "to afford entertainment to their executioners." The Illinois forced captives to sing at the entrance of each cabin that had lost a family member to the captives' people.[12] Captives then passed through a gauntlet, where they experienced tortures that ranged from verbal assaults to near fatal cuts and beatings. Among the most degrading of the gauntlet's many torments was the participation of women and children, whose tauntings fell with special poignancy on captured male warriors. "This reception is very cruel," wrote Sébastien Rale of the Illinois. "Some tear out the prisoners' nails, others cut off their fingers or ears; still others load them with blows from clubs."[13] Those disfigured by the gauntlet bore permanent marks of their status as captive enemies, especially when such wounds occurred in conspicuous locations such as the face or hands. Maiming the hands also served another purpose: preventing escape or rebellion. Describing captives of the Iroquois, one Jesuit remarked that "they began by cutting off a thumb of each [captive], to make them unable to unbind themselves."[14] The resulting scarring and disfiguration were considered "marks of their captivity," which remained with living captives long after the trauma of initiation had passed.[15]

Even if captives escaped mutilation, which many did, they still bore a verbal marker that set them apart from other members of the capturing village. By the seventeenth century almost every Iroquoian and Algonkian language contained a degrading term meaning "captive" or "slave." In the Mohawk and Onondaga languages, for example, enaskwa had the dual meaning of "captive" and "domesticated animal." According to early French observers, various forms of the word could mean "domesticated," "tamed," or "enslaved."[16] Western Algonkian speakers, such as the Ottawas, Ojibwas, and Crees, used "awahkân," which had much the same meaning, designating both "captives" and "animals kept as pets."[17]

The earliest French lexicon of western Algonkian languages, recorded between 1672 and 1674 by Jesuit Father Louis Nicolas, included "aouakan," meaning "slave or prisoner of war," as one of eight essential nouns for missionaries to know to teach western Indians effectively. When Claude Allouez, Nicolas's former traveling companion and fellow student of Algonkian languages, searched for a term to describe the devil to the region's Indians, he chose "slave," or "aouakan," to indicate that the devil was "worthless" and powerless before God. Indicating the extremely negative connotation of the term, a native woman at Green Bay responded to Allouez's insult, saying, "Thou hast no sense; thou angerest the Devil too much."[18] Although some early observers described these derogatory labels as permanent markers, many others suggested that captives who survived the torturous initiation process could attain respectability, and even social prominence, within the capturing village.[19]

Once the initial tortures subsided, families who had recently suffered a death determined whether to kill or spare the surviving captives. Heads of households, according to a French officer living among the Illinois, "assemble and decide what they will do with the prisoner who has been given to them, and whether they wish to give him his life."[20] The Ottawas, Ojibwas, and Hurons did much the same, granting life to some and subjecting others to a slow and painful death. Although the particular reasons for sparing captives varied from family to family and village to village, captives could be kept alive to augment population growth, replace a dead relative, or facilitate alliances through trade. Once the captive had been granted life, he or she was washed, clothed, and given a new name, often that of the deceased he or she was intended to replace.[21]

Seventeenth-century observers consistently noted that all Indian villages spared and adopted women and children more often than men. In addition to targeting the male warriors for revenge killings, this strategy maximized the demographic benefits of captive adoption, whereas increasing the number of adult males in a village would do little to change its reproductive capacity. During times of high mortality resulting from disease or warfare, female captives often represented the best hope for rapidly restoring lost population. Especially in polygynous societies like the Illinois, female captives integrated smoothly into present social structures as second or third wives of prominent men. Children were prized because of the relative ease with which they assimilated into the capturing society, learning new languages and customs much more quickly than older captives. This selection process left a surplus of male captives, who were frequently traded outside the village.[22]

Iroquoian and Algonkian peoples often adopted captives to "requicken" or "replace" village members lost to warfare or murder.[23] Such deaths reduced both the spiritual power and the productive capacity of bereaved families, threatening the entire village with future misfortune unless the dead could be symbolically revived. Captive adoption could thus eliminate the need for future vengeance by restoring the dead to their proper place and reestablishing the possibility of peaceful relations between the antagonists. Through this process, the village appropriated the spiritual power and productive labor of the captives, forcing them to adopt the name, manners, and social responsibilities of the deceased.[24] When a raid or a murder occurred between allies, the offending village could often convince mourning relatives to accept valuable gifts in lieu of vengeance—to "cover the dead." Symbolically these gifts would absolve the killers and restore the alliance between the two groups. Because of the strong cultural demand for revenge and the need to take captives, however, covering the grave rarely proved sufficient to prevent mourning wars against an enemy.[25] Yet a gift of captives had the potential to bring enemies together by serving both purposes at once: reviving the dead and establishing an alliance through gifts to cover their graves.

Because of their symbolic power to mitigate the effects of warfare or murder, captives became an important medium of exchange in the gift giving that characterized Indian diplomacy. Captives accompanied peace delegations as gifts ceremonially offered to allies or erstwhile enemies. "Usually, they are used to replace the dead," wrote Antoine Denis Raudot of captives in the western Great Lakes, "but often some are also given to other nations to oblige these nations to become their allies."[26] In one such exchange a Fox chief received two Iroquois captives from his "neighbors [who] took them prisoners and made me a present of them."[27] A gift of captives, even more powerfully than wampum or the calumet, signified the opposite of warfare, the giving rather than the taking of life. As living witnesses to the power and ferocity of their captors, captives also offered a subtle warning of the dangers one could face as the captor's enemy. Employing the language of kinship, givers introduced captives by saying "Here is my son" or "I bring you my flesh" to represent the physical blending of familial interests between two previously disconnected groups.[28] In many cases this gift proved sufficient to erase long periods of violence between two peoples, satisfying the demands of customary justice and symbolizing the possibility of true friendship.[29]

359

At other times, a gift of captives could persuade an ally to action against a third party. In 1665, for example, while Nicolas Perrot negotiated an alliance with the tribes around Green Bay, he noted that the Potawatomis offered a captive to the Miamis to persuade them not to enter into an alliance with the French.[30] When attacked by a Sioux war party in 1672, Perrot also observed, the Ottawa chief Sinagos fell into captivity. The Sioux, on discovering a "Panys" belonging to the Ottawa chief, sent Sinagos's captive "back to his own country that he might faithfully report what he had seen and the justice that had been administered." The Sioux chief hoped that by releasing a captive of another western nation, he could convince the captive's people to join him against the Ottawas.[31]

Captives' contributions to the receiving society also made them valuable as peacetime offerings accompanying trade. Adopted captives were expected to do the work of the person whom they replaced, thereby mitigating the social costs of that person's death.[32] Those captives not fully assimilated into Indian families performed a range of tasks from which the village benefited. In 1669, for example, a Seneca woman, who had "commanded more than twenty slaves," died. Her mother expressed her hope that one of these captives might accompany her daughter into the afterlife, because the deceased "knew not what it was to go to the forest to get wood, or to the River to draw water." Without these captives in the world of spirits, the mother feared, "she could not take upon herself the care of all that has to do with domestic duties."[33] In the 1680s, Louis-Armand de Lom d'Arce, baron de Lahontan, noted that among the nations of the western Great Lakes, captives assisted in the hunt by carrying their masters' baggage, tending to sled dogs, and preparing animal skins. He also recorded that captives among the Sauks, Potawatomis, and Menominees served food at ceremonial feasts for visitors.[34] French observers found among the Illinois many "slaves in which these people are accustomed to traffic and whom they compel to labor for them."[35]

Both practically valuable and symbolically potent, captives often passed from village to village through overlapping systems of captive exchange, journeying hundreds or even thousands of miles from their birthplace. The Iroquois obtained and traded enemy Indians from the

Chesapeake to Lake Michigan.[36] The Illinois took captives from the central and southern plains and traded them into the Lake Superior region.[37] And the Ottawas joined their upper Mississippi valley allies to raid deep into the Southwest, then traded the captives far to the northeast on Lake Nipissing. In 1669 Sulpician missionary François Dollier de Casson described meeting a Nipissing chief who "had a slave the Ottawas had presented to him in the preceding year, from a very remote nation in the southwest."[38] The next year Dollier received from the Senecas a gift of two captives, one taken from the Ottawas near Michilimackinac and one from the Shawnees. They were to serve as guides and translators as Dollier and René-Robert Cavalier de La Salle traveled through the Ohio River valley.[39]

Like Dollier, many early French visitors to the West received captives from the Indian peoples they encountered. These offerings frequently signified the beginning of alliances that would endure throughout the French regime. In 1670 Jacques Marquette received an Indian captive as a token of friendship after caring for an ailing Kiskakon Ottawa man. "Saying that I had given him his life," wrote Marquette, "he gave me a present of a slave that had been brought to him from the Illinois, two or three months before." Explaining the captive's origin, Marquette wrote, "The Illinois are warriors and take a great many slaves, whom they trade with the Ottawas for muskets, powder, kettles, hatchets, and knives."[40] And four years later Marquette described the position of the Illinois in the captive and slave trade: "They are warlike, and make themselves dreaded by the Distant tribes to the south and west, whither they go to procure Slaves; these they barter, selling them at a high price to other Nations, in exchange for other Wares."[41] Marquette's experience indicates the dual nature of captive exchanges in Illinois and Ottawa society. Neither wholly economic nor exclusively symbolic, captives could signify friendship and secure valuable trade goods. Although the presence of French muskets and kettles among the Ottawas clearly had an effect on these early captive exchanges, they do not yet seem to have altered their fundamental meaning or function.

After establishing Fort St. Louis on the Illinois River in 1682, La Salle received as tokens from the Illinois two "pana slaves," an adult woman and a boy about fifteen years old, who "had been taken by the Panimaha, then by the Osages, who had given him to the Missouris, and they to the nation from which I have had him."[42] The elaborate route by which this unfortunate young man arrived in La Salle's hands indicates both the complexity and the ubiquity of captive exchanges on New France's western frontier. It also reveals the danger in assuming that "panis" slaves were primarily taken from the tribe known today as Pawnee. In the seventeenth century, names similar to "panis" actually referred to a great number of Great Plains nations, only some of which have clear modern equivalents. On a single map made in 1688, for example, French cartographer Jean-Baptiste-Louis Franquelin listed as separate nations the "Panimaha," "Panetoca," "Pana," "Paneake," and "Paneassa," any or all of whom could have suffered at the hands of Illinois raiders. Of these groups, none can be said with any certainty to be ancestors to the modern Pawnees.[43] More important, when seventeenth-century French observers noted the source of Illinois slaves, they univer-sally suggested multiple victims. Claude Charles Le Roy, Bacqueville de la Potherie, for example, recounted a captive-raiding expedition undertaken by the Illinois against "the Ozages and the Accances [Quapaw]."[44] Pierre Deliette noted that Missouri River nations "often come to trade among the Illinois," indicating that these captives may have come in trade from the various "panis" villages rather than by Illinois raids upon those groups.[45] And by analyzing the available documentation on La Salle's "pana slave," anthropologist Mildred Wedel concluded that the boy was most likely a Wichita, captured by the Skiri Pawnees, stolen by Osages, and traded to the Illinois via Missouri middlemen.[46]

Farther west, the Sioux also offered captives to French visitors as signs of friendship. In 1700 a Sioux chief held a feast to honor French trader Pierre Charles Le Sueur, offering him as gifts two powerful sym-bols of alliance: food and captives. Invoking the ceremonial language of kinship associated with captive exchanges, the Sioux chief pointed to his people and said to the French visitors, "No longer regard us as Sioux, but as Frenchmen." Le Sueur gratefully received the gift and invited the Sioux to abandon their nomadic lifestyle and settle near the French.[47]

During the 1670s, as the fur trade more thoroughly connected the St. Lawrence valley with the upper country, captive exchanges formerly confined to the West began to take place between Indians and French merchants at Montreal. In 1678, for example, Ottawa traders brought three Indian captives to Daniel Greysolon Dulhut as part of the ritual gift exchanges routinely accompanying the fur trade. "They assured me of their friendship," wrote Dulhut, "and as proof gave me three slaves."[48] Although Dulhut did not pay for the captives, they proved invaluable on his journey west to initiate friendships with the Assiniboines and the Sioux.[49]

Despite his willing participation in a ceremonial captive exchange, Dulhut rejected the cultural assumptions that motivated the Ottawas' gift. Rather than valuing these captives for their power to raise the dead or for their symbolic unification of French and Ottawa interests, Dulhut simply viewed them as "slaves" who would reduce the burdens of his pending journey to Lake Superior. The clearest example of Dulhut's rejection of Indian captive customs came in 1684 following the murder of two Frenchmen at Lake Superior. Upon learning of the death of his countrymen, Dulhut seized a group of Indian suspects and brought them to Michilimackinac for trial. According to custom, Dulhut wrote of the incident, the offending party offered a gift of "some slaves, which was only meant to patch up the assassination committed upon the French." Dulhut's emissary "perceived their intention, and therefore would not allow it, telling them that a hundred slaves . . . could not make him traffic in the blood of his brothers." When the party met with Dulhut himself, he echoed the emissary's statement: "I said the same thing here in the councils, so that they [the Ottawas] might not in future believe that they could save by presents those who might commit similar acts."[50]

Dulhut demanded and carried out the execution of two Indians for the murder rather than allowing the customary exchange of captives. By ignoring Indian captive customs, Dulhut jeopardized the already precarious alliance in the western Great Lakes at a critical time of conflict. In 1684, rumors of Iroquois preparations for a massive assault on New France rang throughout the colony and across the Atlantic. The French began to mobilize a large army and sought to induce their native allies to join them against the Iroquois. Dulhut's actions alienated key western allies crucial to New France's ability to survive another war with the more powerful Iroquois. When the French asked the Indians at Michilimackinac to arm themselves for impending battle, the Ottawas demurred, secretly warning other tribes against participation. "The French invite us to go to war against the Iroquois," one of them said. "They wish to use us in order to make us their slaves. After we have aided in destroying the enemy, the French will do with us what they do with their cattle, which they put to the plow and make them cultivate the land. Let us leave them to act alone."[51] By killing the accused murderers in violation of Indian customs, the French underscored for the Indians their unwillingness to play by the rules of alliance. Ironically Dulhut's refusal to accept a gift of slaves to raise the dead instilled the fear of enslavement in New France's Indian allies.

Having rejected the logic of Indian captive exchange, Dulhut also rejected his earlier practice of procuring captives to use as slaves.[52] He was not alone. Bureaucrats in Quebec and Paris likewise denied the viability of the Indian slave trade. They had learned that acquiring an Indian slave meant much more than the purchase of a laborer, laden as it was with such deep significance in the formation and destruction of alliances. Thus, when issuing a decree authorizing the use of slaves for New France in 1689, Louis XIV rejected the viability of Indian slavery, authorizing only the use of African slaves in the colony.[53] Yet many French colonists continued to accept captives from the Indians of the upper Mississippi and western Great Lakes, selling them extralegally as slaves into the St. Lawrence valley.

During the 1690s Indian slaves began to appear in the public records of Montreal and Quebec, indicating a small but growing acceptance of Indian slavery among New France's elite. In 1691, for example, Pierre Moreau dit Lataupine brought a young Indian slave boy to Quebec's Hôtel-Dieu, the local hospital, because of an illness. The hospital register says nothing of the boy's origins, but Moreau's background provides a likely explanation. In 1672, Moreau entered a partnership with Louis Jolliet and several others to create a fur trading company that would help fund Jolliet's exploration of the West. Through this company, and often illegally on his own, Moreau traded among the Ottawas at Michilimackinac. Moreau certainly had witnessed slave exchanges in the West, including Jolliet's receiving a slave as a gift in 1674. As they had so many times before, the Ottawas must have offered a slave to Moreau either in exchange for minor trade goods or as a gift accompanying their trade in furs.[54]

In 1700 Jean-Baptiste Bissot de Vinsenne brought an Indian slave to Montreal, where he baptized him Jean-René. The baptismal record indicates that Vinsenne acquired his slave "from the Iowa near the Arkansas [Quapaw]." Vinsenne, Jolliet's brother-in-law, spent the latter half of his life in the West as a military officer and trader. Considered the colony's foremost authority on the Miamis, he earned a post among them in 1696. While there, Vinsenne likely received his slave in negotiations with the Mascoutens or Illinois, both of whom frequently raided the Iowas.[55] In the same year René-Claude Fézeret baptized a young female slave who had served as a domestic in his home for several years as Marie-Joseph. Fézeret, Montreal's first gunsmith and a lifelong western merchant, traded firearms with the Ottawas for this slave while staying at Michilimackinac.[56] And in September 1700 the "panis" slave Jacques appeared in Montreal's baptismal register, "brought from Illinois by the Sieur Charles Lemaitre dit Auger."[57]

These examples provide a faint but clear documentary outline of the early Indian slave trade. The colony's Indian allies—especially the Ottawas and Illinois—acquired captives from their western enemies and then offered them as symbolic gifts to French merchants associated with the fur trade. Once in French hands, these captives often became slaves in Montreal and Quebec. Participating colonists understood that, like all aspects of the Indian trade, Indian slavery could serve French purposes if native customs governed their acquisition. The result was a modest but growing slave trade into Montreal and Quebec from about 1690 to 1709.

At the beginning of the eighteenth century, significant changes in the French-Indian alliance system increased the importance of captive exchanges and made Indian captives more readily available to potential French buyers. In the summer of 1701, the French successfully negotiated the Great Peace of Montreal, a treaty by which the Iroquois promised to cease warfare against the French and their allies and to remain neutral in all conflicts between the French and the English. Yet reversing decades of

French policy encouraging violence against the Iroquois proved challenging. The French strove, against barriers of their own making, to negotiate peace between their allies and the Iroquois, hoping to prevent small outbreaks of violence from erupting into general warfare. In the process, officials at Quebec would finally come to appreciate what most western traders and negotiators already understood—that the exchange of Indian captives, if conducted according to native customs, offered one of the most important available means of forging and maintaining alliances among Indian nations. This realization would inspire them to rethink their policy on Indian slavery, not only allowing but eventually promoting the trade in Indian slaves.[58]

A new test of French willingness to bend to allied captive customs came in the early stages of the treaty negotiations. For months, Governor-General Louis-Hector de Callière had been threatening the Sauks with retribution for killing a French trader among the Sioux. Speaking for his Sauk allies, the Potawatomi chief Onanguicé presented to Callière a "small slave," saying: "Here is a little flesh we offer you; we captured it in a country where people travel by horse. We wipe the mat stained with the blood of that Frenchman by consecrating it to you. Do with it as you please." Callière, eager to see the peace negotiations succeed, agreed to accept the captive, thereby pardoning the Sauks for the murder. He only demanded that the Sauks and their allies return to the Iroquois any prisoners taken from them in previous battles.[59]

Throughout the peace negotiations, nothing received more attention than the return of Iroquois captives, which was, according to one French participant, "the most essential article of the peace."[60] The Iroquois had demanded that New France's allies return all living Iroquois prisoners, and many of the western allies had made reciprocal demands of the Iroquois. At the conference, then, each delegation made an accounting of the prisoners offered. Koutaoiliboe, chief of the Kiskakon Ottawas, spoke first. "I did not want to fail, my father," he assured Governor Callière, "having learned that you were asking me for Iroquois prisoners, to bring them to you. Here are four that I present to you to do with as you please." The other delegates spoke in similar terms, but several noted that the Iroquois gave few prisoners in return. In all, French allies returned thirty-one Iroquois prisoners, a small fraction of the Iroquois captured during the previous war.[61]

In order to assuage Iroquois anger over the disappointing number of captives returned, French officials pledged to facilitate prisoner exchanges until all parties were satisfied. Accordingly Calliére and Montreal's governor Philippe de Rigaud de Vaudreuil pressed the Ottawas, especially, to return Iroquois captives. In 1705, growing impatient with the constant demands of the French, Ottawa warriors attacked a party of Iroquois who had come to trade at Fort Frontenac. As soon as the violence subsided, the French, fearing that Iroquois retaliation could escalate into full-scale war, demanded that the Ottawas and Iroquois join them to negotiate peace. At the conference, the Iroquois berated the Ottawas for attacking them and destroying the "great tree of peace" planted by the French at Montreal. Promising reprisals if no satisfaction could be made, the Iroquois nevertheless left the door open for peace. They demanded that, in addition to returning all Iroquois prisoners, the Ottawas provide them with non-Iroquois captives to replace those killed in the attack. In the interest of peace, the Ottawas agreed to "search among the Sioux" for "slaves . . . to replace their [Iroquois] dead."[62]

This new demand, familiar enough to the Ottawas as a legitimate means of restoring peace, again tested the limits of French accommodation. Up to this point, French officials had participated in something only too familiar in their own war culture: the return of an enemy's prisoners as a condition of peace. Now, however, the Iroquois were asking the French to facilitate the exchange of captives from an uninvolved third party to cover the Iroquois dead. However they felt about it, to maintain peace the French had to support the Iroquois request and oversee the acquisition of Sioux captives. Since war with England had resumed three years earlier, New France needed Iroquois neutrality more than ever to avoid costly losses on its southern frontier.

The Ottawas, however, did not deliver the captives the following summer as they had promised. Angry at this betrayal, the Iroquois approached Vaudreuil, now governor-general of the colony. "Abandon the Outaouas to us, and hold us back no longer," the Iroquois demanded. "Our warriors are all ready." They were grateful that the French had secured the return of the Iroquois prisoners, but without the promised Sioux captives to requicken their dead, they would surely attack the Ottawas and seize their captives by force. Vaudreuil assured the Iroquois that he was doing all he could to ensure Ottawa compliance. The previous spring he had sent an envoy to Michilimackinac to bring back as many captives as he could for the Iroquois. There the Ottawa chief Companissé had given the French four Sioux captives, promising "that he would bring me next year, without fail, the remainder of the slaves he had promised you." Vaudreuil then offered the captives to the Iroquois and vowed personally to deliver the balance owed them by the Ottawas. "I stay your axe as regards Michilimackinac," Vaudreuil concluded, "until they have had time to keep their word."[63]

One reason the French went to such great lengths to participate in these captive exchanges was their fear that a direct delivery from the Ottawas might draw them too close to the Iroquois. The French wanted peace between the two peoples, but they also wanted to prevent an Ottawa-Iroquois alliance. "It is not proper to have the Outaouas, Hurons, and other Indians friendly with the Iroquois," reads a margin note in Vaudreuil's 1703 report to France. "Some adroit effort must be made to prevent them becoming good friends."[64] Understanding the symbolic bonds created through captive exchange, the French intervened to prevent Iroquois-Ottawa rapprochement and to benefit from Iroquois gratitude. That way, were the Iroquois to reestablish a military alliance with the English, at least they would not take the Ottawas with them to the detriment of New France.

In addition to promoting the interests of the colony, Vaudreuil had personal incentives to deliver the captives and ensure peace. He had served in an army that had retreated from the Iroquois in 1687, and he held great respect for the strength of their warriors.[65] Moreover, writing only three months before his meeting with the Iroquois, Vaudreuil's superior at Versailles reminded him, "You have nothing so important in the present state of affairs as the maintenance of peace with the Iroquois and other Indian nations." He then warned that, in the event of failure, "I shall not guarantee to you that his Majesty would be willing to allow you to occupy for any length of time your present post."[66]

During the next two years, Vaudreuil and other colonial officials worked persistently to ensure the transfer of captives from the Ottawas to the Iroquois. In 1706 Vaudreuil again pressured the Ottawas to provide "living slaves . . . to replace the Iroquois dead."[67] In 1707 he sent strict orders to the French at Michilimackinac to ensure that the Ottawas deliver to the Iroquois "the remaining slaves that they promised to provide."[68] He even arranged for a canoe to transport the slaves, a policy explicitly sanctioned by the Crown, "it being of the utmost importance to the preservation of the Colony" to avert the pending war.[69] By 1708, when the Ottawas finally delivered the promised slaves to the French, Vaudreuil and his intendant, Jacques Raudot, had come to learn the power of Indian slavery. They concluded, in a joint letter to their superiors, that captive exchanges were the sole means of maintaining peace between their two most important Indian neighbors, the Ottawas and the Iroquois.[70] Informed with this new understanding, New France's officials grew increasingly reliant on the exchange of Indian captives in native diplomacy. When asked by Versailles in 1707 to buttress the French alliance with the Abenakis, for example, Vaudreuil promptly sent orders to Jean-Paul Legardeur de Saint-Pierre to buy "a young panis slave to be given to the Abenaki" as a token of friendship.[71]

The Abenakis also received Indian captives from the French in exchange for English prisoners. During the frontier raids of Queen Anne's War, the Abenakis and other allied Indians captured hundreds of English settlers and attempted to integrate them into their village as adoptive kin or, occasionally, as slaves. This outraged Joseph Dudley, governor of Massachusetts, who wrote to Vaudreuil, "I cannot allow that Christians should be slaves of those wretches." Dudley threatened that if the French did not secure the release of English captives among the Indians, he would turn over French prisoners at Boston to his Indian allies.[72] This threat, as well as the desire to exchange English for French prisoners, encouraged Vaudreuil and many others to purchase Indian captives from France's western allies to trade for English captives living among the Indians of the East, especially the Abenakis and the Kahnawake Iroquois.[73]

As colonial administrators increasingly relied on the exchange of Indian captives to negotiate peace, strengthen friendships, and redeem

English prisoners, they also encountered western traders, prominent merchants, and minor colonial officials who began to purchase Indian captives
to use as slaves. In 1702, at the death of François Provost, the king's lieutenant in Quebec and governor of Trois-Rivières, his Indian slave Louis passed
to his widow, Geneviève. Provost likely had obtained Louis in connection
with his fur-trading ventures, which began in 1697 when he established a
company to export furs to France.[74] In 1703, Marie-Françoise, an eighteen-
year-old Indian slave of Pierre d'Ailleboust d'Argenteuil, died in Montreal.
D'Argenteuil, a prominent military officer and seigneur, had kept her as a
domestic slave in his Montreal home for several years.[75]

In 1706, Jacques Barbel, a well-known Montreal judge who used his
office to front an illegal fur-trade operation, reclaimed a "panis" slave he had
"loaned" to a friend.[76] The same year, Jacques-Alexis Fleury d'Eschambault,
a member of Quebec's Superior Council and Jacques Raudot's closest associate, baptized his Indian slave, Charles-Alexis, in Montreal.[77] By 1706
Vaudreuil himself had obtained an Indian slave, Jacques, who appeared
that year in Quebec's hospital records. Given Vaudreuil's interest in the
illegal fur and musket trades at Montreal, he likely had obtained Jacques
there through his middleman, Pierre You de La Découverte, who acquired
his own Indian slaves from the Illinois.[78]

La Découverte's association with the upper Mississippi valley
began in the early 1680s and extended to the early eighteenth century.[79]
While in the upper country, La Découverte acquired an Indian slave he
named Pascal. Born about 1690, Pascal had been captured, traded to the
Miamis, and carried to Montreal with La Découverte by 1703. Pascal typi-
fied the slaves entering Montreal and Quebec during the first decade of the
eighteenth century; 87 percent were male, and they were, on average, aged
fourteen. These slaves experienced traumatic childhoods before entering
their permanent status as slaves in French settlements.[80]

From the Illinois country, however, Indian slaves did not always
travel to the St. Lawrence. Instead, French and Indian traders there often
sold slaves to the much more developed markets of English Carolina, where
thousands of Indian slaves either labored on plantations or embarked for
the Caribbean.[81] Between 1707 and 1708, the governors of New France and

Louisiana learned that the French settlers "living among the Kaskaskia Illinois were inciting the savage nations in the environs of this settlement to make war upon one another and that the French-Canadians themselves were participating in order to get slaves that they afterwards sold to the English."[82] French *coureurs de bois* and their Miami and Illinois partners spent much of the first decade of the eighteenth century working with Carolina traders to bring slaves and furs from the western Ohio valley to southeastern English ports.[83]

To officials at Quebec, the Carolina trade threatened not only a loss of revenues, but also a loss of military allies to a wartime enemy. One of the earliest lessons the French learned in native diplomacy was the inseparability of trade and alliance. They feared that if the Illinois and Miamis developed strong trade relationships with Carolina, the English would easily win the military alliance of these two large confederacies and overcome the French.[84] Thus in 1708 Louisiana's governor, Jean-Baptiste Le Moyne de Bienville, sent an emissary to Kaskaskia with presents for the Indians and stern words for the French meant to halt the slave trade. Bienville had built his most important alliances in Louisiana by protecting the victims of Carolina's slave raids, and he did not want to risk these alliances by allowing his own people to extend the slave market into a new quarter. In the end, however, French officials in Louisiana and Quebec understood the limits of their coercive power in the distant Illinois country.[85] The 1709 slave ordinance indicates a growing concern among Quebec officials about the potential of slave sales to weaken Illinois and Miami commitments to the French alliance. Raudot implied that it would be better for the French to sell Indian slaves in Montreal than to "trade them with the English of Carolina."[86] Once again, keeping allies in the West meant accepting Indian slaves into New France.

Yet in the 1709 ordinance legalizing Indian slavery, Raudot sought a more conventional justification for the colony's use of Indian slaves, suggesting that they were "as necessary to the inhabitants of this country for farming and other tasks as are the Negroes to the Islands." As Raudot and everyone else understood, however, Indian slavery in New France differed substantially from its African counterpart in the French Caribbean.

Aside from the fur trade, New France produced no profitable exports, and it lacked both the capital and the climate to imitate the successful plantation economies of Martinique and Saint-Domingue. Thus, while the islands organized their entire labor system around slavery, Canadians virtually ignored the institution. Despite the Crown's 1689 authorization of black slave imports into New France, only eleven appear on the records between 1689 and 1709.[87] During the same period, the plantations of the French Caribbean absorbed more than 50,000 slaves from across the Atlantic.[88]

Still, New France did need laborers. From its inception, the colony struggled to find a sufficient number of workers to meet even its basic needs. Migration to New France, never high to begin with, dropped precipitously in the 1670s, stunting the colony's population growth. Among those who did come to Canada, more than two-thirds returned to France, resulting in a deficiency of free workers.[89] Despite tireless efforts to recruit unfree labor, the importation of *engagés* virtually ended in 1666, leaving French colonists and administrators chronically anxious about labor shortages.[90] In 1689 one French official lamented that "laborers and servants are scarce and extraordinarily expensive in Canada, which ruins everyone whose enterprise depends on them."[91] A generation later, the problem persisted, leading the governor and intendant to conclude in 1716, "The small number of inhabitants in Canada causes all enterprise to fail due to the difficulty of finding workers."[92]

Labor shortages plagued the colony's agricultural regions as well. According to Gédéon de Catalogne, who surveyed the seigneuries of the St. Lawrence Valley in 1712, "In relation to the great size of the settlement, there is not one-quarter of the workmen required to clear and cultivate the land."[93] As a result, French farmers were forced to clear their land piecemeal, often hiring themselves out for part of the year to provide for their family's needs before the land could produce crops. Much of their land simply remained uncleared.[94]

Many, like intendant Michel Bégon, hoped to solve the colony's labor shortages by importing African slaves. "The majority of Englishmen and Flemings of the government of New York, adjacent to that of Montreal, never labor in agriculture," Bégon wrote in a 1716 appeal for a shipment of slaves. "It is their Negroes that do all their work," he continued, "and that colony provides the grain necessary for the subsistence of the English islands."[95] Since slaves in the colony would not produce profitable export goods, however, New France's colonists could not afford to pay the rising prices for African slaves traded on the Atlantic market. Nor did trade routes favor African slavery as a solution to New France's labor shortage, since ships traveling the well-known route of the "triangle trade" did not venture north to the St. Lawrence.[96]

The first decade of the eighteenth century witnessed New France's worst economic crisis since its founding, thus adding to the colony's inability to invest in African slave labor. Between 1700 and 1710, the glut of beaver pelts on the French market depressed prices by 75 percent, sinking to an all-time low around 1708.[97] With public finances strained beyond capacity by the war with England, official outlays to diversify the economy were out of the question. Yet precisely because of wartime expenses, colonial officials felt growing pressure from Versailles to increase self-sufficiency and to generate revenue for France. In 1707, Vaudreuil complained of the "deplorable state" of New France's economy but despaired of any solution.[98]

Individual merchants and farmers also experienced financial strain. Fur trade engagements dropped precipitously, with a corresponding decline in the quantity of trade goods merchants could profitably send west. A general monetary crisis decreased the availability of reliable currency and limited merchants' ability to extend credit. As French merchants began charging the colonists higher prices for essential textiles and manufactured goods, colonial wheat prices continued to fall, widening the gap between the income farmers earned and the expenses they incurred.[99] Because of Montreal's dependence on the fur trade and the relative immaturity of its agricultural development, its residents suffered more than most. Yet about 13 or 14 percent of Montreal's households claimed an Indian slave by 1709.[100]

Merchants' growing participation in the Indian slave trade may have been fueled, rather than hindered, by the economic crisis. Unable to profit from western trade with conventional cargoes, many merchants seem to have reduced their losses by selling Indian slaves acquired in the West during trade expeditions. Maurice Blondeau, for example, who specialized in the western trade, partnered with Alphonse Tonty at Michilimackinac. Beginning in 1696, when all but a few merchants were banned from the western fur trade, Blondeau's business began to falter. He continued to trade illegally until, in 1698, the intendant Jean Bochart de Champigny ordered his goods and effects seized. The reopening of legal trade at Detroit in 1701 promised renewed profits, but if Blondeau's fortunes mirrored that of most merchants, little materialized.[101] Possibly as a result, in 1703 he began to carry a few Indian slaves on his return journeys to Montreal. In addition to the two slaves he acquired for himself during this period, he appears to have sold at least one to his friend and business partner François Lamoureux dit Saint-Germain. This proved to be the beginning of a long connection to the slave trade for the Blondeau family, which owned twenty-four Indian slaves during the eighteenth century and traded many more to other French colonists.[102]

Thus the changing conditions of French-Indian diplomacy made captives readily available and relatively inexpensive at a time when French labor was scarce and costly. Even before their legal recognition as chattel, these slaves worked in many different capacities, contributing substantially to the wealth of slave owners and to the productivity of the colony in general. Surviving documents yield few details about slaves' work before 1709, but a few telling examples show slaves working in the fur trade, agriculture, and domestic service. Because Indian slavery originated in western trade, exploration, and diplomacy, the slaves' first tasks were often associated with these activities. Trader and explorer Louis Jolliet, for example, used "a young slave, ten years old" to aid him on a journey from the upper country to Quebec. When their canoe capsized near Montreal, the slave drowned, causing Jolliet "much regret . . . [because] he was blessed with natural goodness, quick-wittedness, diligence, and obedience." Characteristic of many similar documents, Jolliet's letter gives no details about the specific tasks assigned to the boy. Jolliet wrote to encourage Bishop François de Laval-Montigny's commitment to western missions, knowing that strong church support would help his own ambitions in the region.

Jolliet therefore emphasized the tractability of western Indians and their responsiveness to Catholic teachings. "He spoke French," Jolliet concluded, and was "beginning to read and write."[103]

At Michilimackinac, Pierre Hubert dit Lacroix purchased in 1696 an Indian slave, also named Pierre, from the voyageur Ignace Durand. After using Pierre as a slave for five years, Hubert released him from slavery and hired him as an indentured servant, promising him fifty livres, a gun, and some wheat at the completion of a two-year contract. For less than three hundred livres, then, Hubert had compelled Pierre's services for seven years. Comparable French labor could have cost up to eight times as much. One of the reasons Hubert could purchase a slave for such a relative value was that Durand, the original proprietor, had received Pierre as a gift from Ottawa traders at Michilimackinac. As a result, Durand could part with his slave for much less than the value of his labor and still earn a substantial profit.[104]

When slaves passed from the West to the rural settlements of the St. Lawrence, they primarily worked as domestic and farm laborers. Especially before 1700, these slaves' activities come to us only in fragments. René Chartier, for example, owned an Indian slave in Lachine, a developing farming village near Montreal. When the Iroquois attacked and leveled the settlement in 1689, Chartier, most of his family, and his slave were killed. The mass burial record belatedly created in 1694 contains the only evidence remaining about Chartier's slave: "pani—slave of Rene Charrier [sic], killed by the Iroquois."[105] Chartier, like most of the seventy or so families settled in Lachine, worked hard to clear enough land to subsist. His young slave likely performed routine farming chores, freeing Chartier to clear additional land and improve the family's home. Unlike the domestic servants bound to other Lachine families, however, Chartier's slave could claim no contractual protection and would be at his master's mercy for release from servitude.[106]

Among the newcomers who moved to Lachine following the Iroquois raid was Guillaume de Lorimier de la Rivière, a captain in the colonial troops, who settled there sometime before 1696. Like many of his contemporaries, Lorimier used his position as a military officer to procure Indian slaves, by 1708 acquiring an adolescent he called Joseph. Because Joseph was several years older than the average Indian slave, he worked alongside Lorimier and his sons clearing, planting, and harvesting. Given Lorimier's frequent absences during Queen Anne's War, Joseph often worked the farm alone, and by 1708 he had developed sufficient skill to farm a separate plot of land. In addition to Joseph's agricultural work, Lorimier benefited from the domestic labor of Marie-Anne dit l'Anglais, an English captive taken in 1703 and held by Lorimier as a servant. Because there were no separate slave or servant quarters, Joseph and Marie-Anne lived in close proximity, and in 1708 Marie-Anne became pregnant with Joseph's child.[107]

Shortly after discovering the pregnancy, Lorimier granted them leave to marry and settle on an adjacent plot of land. Following the marriage, Marie-Anne continued to work as a servant, but Joseph's status is more difficult to determine. He appears in the records between 1708 and his death in 1720 as many things — "*habitant*," "*pany*," "*serviteur*," "*fermier*" (tenant farmer), and "*sauvage*" — but never "*esclave*." In 1716 Marie-Anne left Joseph to live a "scandalous life" with a neighboring Frenchman. When Joseph discovered them together, he unsuccessfully attacked them with a hatchet, landing both himself and Marie-Anne in a Montreal prison. Trying to justify her actions before the court, Marie-Anne suggested that she deserved better than a "*sauvage*" for a husband. Were Joseph still a slave, she almost certainly would have pointed to that status as another reason she could not stay with him. Thus Joseph likely received his freedom from Lorimier at the time of his marriage, but he never fully recovered from his degraded status.[108]

Among the witnesses to Joseph and Marie-Anne's wedding stood André Rapin dit Skaianis, another freed Indian slave who lived nearby.[109] As with Joseph, Skaianis's childhood status survives clearly enough — he was a slave, captured by allied Indians and traded in 1686 at Montreal to André Rapin dit Lamusette. But in 1699, the year Skaianis turned eighteen, his master died, willing to Skaianis a bull and a heifer "for the services he had rendered to the family he had joined at the age of five."[110] Skaianis immediately began to cultivate his own land, and in 1706, he married a poor French widow, Anne Gourdon, a neighbor and longtime friend of his former master's family. Lachine's parish priest recorded Skaianis as the "adoptive son" of his former owner, André Rapin, an indicator of just how far Skaianis had traveled since his capture twenty years earlier. In 1723, after the death of his first wife, he contracted with Charles Nolan, a fur and slave trader, to run canoes loaded with trade goods to Michilimackinac and return with furs. After his contract expired, Skaianis returned to Lachine and settled on his farm, remarrying at the age of sixty-three to a well-established French widow.[111]

As these stories indicate, Indian slavery in New France before 1709 mirrored the fluidity and ambiguity found in the "charter generations" of many slaveholding societies.[112] Skaianis successfully integrated into French life, for example, owning livestock and a farm, taking a French wife, and freely contracting his labor. Joseph did not fare quite as well, but he still attained a measure of autonomy that slave status would have denied him. Although we do not know how typical these experiences were, the uncertain legal status of all Indian slaves mitigated the severity of their servitude and created paths to freedom. According to Jacques Raudot, many non-slaveholding colonists "inspire the slaves with ideas of liberty. Consequently, they almost always leave their masters, claiming that there are no slaves in France, which is not always true since there are colonies that depend upon slavery." No surviving documents indicate the source of these antislavery statements, but it is possible that friendships like the one between the former slave André Rapin dit Skaianis and his enslaved neighbor Joseph generated such conversations and encouraged Indian slaves to assert their freedom through flight.[113] While many slaveholders successfully recovered escaped slaves, others demanded official intervention to prevent the loss of the "considerable amounts of money" they had invested in slave property. Thus all slaves were forbidden to leave their masters, and any colonist caught encouraging or assisting their escape would face a fine of fifty livres.[114] By formalizing the legal status of Indian slaves, New France's civil officials sought to make Indian slavery in the colony more like the chattel slavery of the French Caribbean. Colonists would buy and sell slaves with enforceable contracts, and the weight of the colony's police power would fall on those seeking to interfere with slaveholders' property rights.

On June 15, 1709, Montreal notary Antoine Adhémar recorded the first Indian slave sale to occur since the legal recognition of Indian slavery two months earlier. Seigneur and military officer Pierre-Thomas Tarieu de La Pérade purchased Pascal, a nineteen-year-old Indian male, from Madeleine Just de La Découverte (the wife of Pascal's original owner) for 120 livres. The notarial record itself signified the new structures Raudot had erected to protect Indian slave property, carefully outlining the amount and method of payment and declaring the sale legally enforceable. Similar documents would be cited in court records throughout the eighteenth century to confirm the enslaved status of individual "panis" and to settle disputes over slaveholders' property.[115]

Pascal's life, too, represents both the origins of New France's Indian slave system and the transformation effected by its legalization. When he first entered the colony as the slave of Pierre You de La Découverte, Pascal had passed through a raid- and-trade network more dominated by Indian than French cultural norms. This captive exchange carried Pascal from his home on the Great Plains to a mixed French and Miami settlement in the Illinois country, where La Découverte lived with his Miami wife and métis child. As a slave of La Découverte, Pascal likely performed a combination of domestic chores and tasks associated with La Découverte's illegal fur and liquor trade on Montreal's Île-aux-Tourtes.

La Pérade's motives for acquiring Pascal, however, marked an important point of departure for Pascal and many other French-owned Indian slaves. Pascal was the first of thirteen Indian slaves that La Pérade purchased between 1709 and 1751, and their labor on his seigneurial estate largely removed them from the world of French-Indian exchange that characterized much of the early slave experience.[116] La Pérade, described by one of his subordinates as "a furious man who is out of his mind," treated free laborers so harshly that he could not find anyone willing to work for him. His reliance on slaves reflected his desire to develop his seigneury into a respectable and lucrative enterprise, much more akin to his Caribbean counterparts than to La Découverte's ambitions related to Indian trade.[117]

As French colonists demanded a growing number of Indian slaves from their allies, Native American captive customs also evolved to meet the new realities of New France's slave market. Because the slave trade rewarded brutality with valuable goods, it encouraged the colony's allies to choose warfare over peace. As Jonathan Carver noted after touring the West in the 1760s, the French demand for slaves "caused the dissensions between the Indian nations to be carried on with a greater degree of violence, and with unremitted ardor."[118] The meanings of captive taking and exchange also adjusted to the slave market, as Indian nations increasingly viewed captives as commodities of trade rather than as symbols of alliance, power, or spiritual renewal. Ironically this caused the violent rituals of humiliation and torture to decline because the resulting injuries diminished a captive's value. "Fewer of the captives are tormented and put to death," Carver continued, "since these expectations of receiving so valuable a consideration for them have been excited."[119]

Yet New France's Indian slave system never fully escaped its origins in the diplomacy and gift exchange that first brought Indian captives into French hands as slaves. The colony's native allies in the upper country remained the suppliers of Indian slaves, and they continually demanded French accommodation to their customs. Moreover, shifts in the western alliance complicated New France's slave policies, especially when the colony wished to befriend nations, such as the Fox or Sioux, whose people they held as slaves. Often slaveholders' claims on Indians as property clashed with the demands of an alliance that required a more fluid exchange of captives and slaves than French property law would allow.

By accepting "a little flesh" to stabilize their alliance with western Indians, the colonists of New France acknowledged the symbolic power of captive exchanges to build union and foster peace. Yet rather than willingly embracing their allies' captive customs, French officials only assented when natives demanded their participation. Ironically, then, Indian slavery originated as a partial defeat of New France's power over its Indian neighbors. From that defeat, however, the French built an exploitative labor system that redirected their impulse for control and domination onto distant Indian nations.

Notes

1. For the number of slaves, see Marcel Trudel, *Dictionnaire des esclaves et de leurs propriétaires au Canadafrançais* (Ville LaSalle, Québec: Hurtubise HMH, 1990). Since Trudel counts only those slaves individually confirmed in surviving records, his estimates are highly conservative. Sixty-four of the 129 people (49.6 percent) with title to a lot on Rue Saint-Paul or Place du Marché in 1725 owned at least one Indian slave. This figure includes those cases in which the property owner was married to the slaveholder, but not those cases in which other immediate family members owned slaves. It also excludes institutions, such as the Hôtel-Dieu and the Sulpician seminary, both of which employed slaves at one time or another. For those owning property, I relied on the Adhémar database of the Centre Canadien d'Architecture in Montreal, which contains data for every known lot in Montreal proper in 1725. The database is available online at http://www.cca.qc.ca/adhemar; a physical copy is available at the Centre Canadien d'Architecture in Montreal. For slaveholders, see Trudel, *Dictionnaire des esclaves*, 267–430. For a more detailed analysis of the eighteenth-century slave population, see Brett Rushforth, "Savage Bonds: Indian Slavery and Alliance in New France" (PhD diss., University of California, Davis, 2003), esp. chapter 2.

2. Almon Wheeler Lauber, *Indian Slavery in Colonial Times within the Present Limits of the United States, Studies in History, Economics, and Public Law* 54, no. 3 (New York: Columbia University Press, 1913); James Cleland Hamilton, "The Panis: An Historical Outline of Canadian Indian Slavery in the Eighteenth Century," *Proceedings of the Canadian Institute*, 1 (1897). There are references to "panis" slavery scattered throughout the New France literature, but they draw almost exclusively on these three sources. For the English-language literature, see James F. Brooks, *Captives and Cousins: Slavery, Kinship, and Community in the Southwest Borderlands* (Chapel Hill: University of North Carolina Press for the Omohundro Institute of Early American History and Culture, 2002), 15; James Axtell, *Natives and Newcomers: The Cultural Origins of North America* (New York: Oxford University Press, 2001), 154, 290; Winstanley Briggs, "Slavery in French Colonial Illinois," *Chicago History* 18 (1989–1990), 66–81; Peter N. Moogk, *La Nouvelle France: The Making of French Canada—A Cultural History* (East Lansing MI: Michigan State University Press, 2000), 109–10; Eric Hinderaker, *Elusive Empires: Constructing Colonialism in the Ohio Valley, 1673–1800* (Cambridge: Cambridge University Press, 1997), 16–17; Colin G. Calloway, *New Worlds for All: Indians, Europeans, and the Remaking of Early America* (Baltimore: Johns Hopkins University Press, 1997), 102; W. J. Eccles, *The Canadian Frontier, 1534–1760*, rev. ed. (Albuquerque: University of New Mexico Press, 1983), 149–50; Cornelius J. Jaenen, *Friend and Foe: Aspects of French-Amerindian Cultural Contact in the Sixteenth and Seventeenth Centuries* (Toronto: McClelland and Steward, 1976), 139; Mason Wade, "French Indian Policies," in Wilcomb E. Washburn, ed., *History of Indian-White Relations*, vol. 4 of William C. Sturtevant, ed., *Handbook of North American Indians* (Washington DC, 1978), 20–28; Allan Greer, *The People of New France* (Toronto: University of Toronto Press, 1997), 85–91; and Robin W. Winks, *The Blacks in Canada: A History*, 2nd ed. (Montréal: McGill-Queens University Press, 1997), 1–23.

3. Marcel Trudel, *L'esclavage au Canada Français: Histoire et Conditions de L'esclavage* (Québec: Les Presses de l'Université Laval, 1960), 315.

4. For Louisiana, see ordinance of Oct. 25, 1720, in Pierre Margry, ed., *Découvertes et Établissements des Français dans l'ouest et dans le sud de l'Amérique Septentrionale (1614–1754)*, 6 vols. (Paris: Maionneuve et Leclerc, 1876–1886), 6:316.

5. Gwendolyn Midlo Hall, *Africans in Colonial Louisiana: The Development of Afro-Creole Culture in the Eighteenth Century* (Baton Rouge: Louisiana State University Press, 1992), 57; Robert P. Wiegers, "A Proposal for Indian Slave Trading in the Mississippi Valley and Its Impact on the

Osage," *Plains Anthropologist* 33 (1988), 191. Clearly, the prohibition of the Indian slave trade, especially in Louisiana, did not prevent French colonists from acquiring and selling Indian slaves. See, for example, Hall, *Africans in Colonial Louisiana*, 97, 115, 180; Daniel H. Usner Jr., *Indians, Settlers, and Slaves in a Frontier Exchange Economy: The Lower Mississippi Valley before 1783* (Chapel Hill: University of North Carolina Press, 1992), esp. 46–51; and Richard White, *The Roots of Dependency: Subsistence, Environment, and Social Change among the Choctaws, Pawnees, and Navajos* (Lincoln: University of Nebraska Press, 1983), 35–36.

6. "Ordonnance de Raudot concernant les Panis et les négres," Apr. 13, 1709, in Archives des colonies, Série C11A, Correspondance générale, Canada, vol. 30, fols. 342–43, National Archives of Canada, Ottawa, Ontario (hereafter cited as C11A with appropriate vol. and fol.), published in *Arrêts et réglements du conseil supérieur de Québec, et ordonnances et jugements des intendants du Canada* (Québec: La Presse a Vapeur de E. R. Fréchette, 1855), 271. The published version of the document is cited as Raudot, "Ordonnance concernant les Panis." All quotations from French-language sources have been translated by the author unless otherwise noted. See also Hamilton, "The Panis:," 25. French record keepers spelled "panis" in many ways, including "pani," "pany," and "pana." Except in quotations, I adhere to the spelling given in the 1709 ordinance, which grew increasingly common until the English period, when "pani" regained favor. Where possible, persons' names are standardized according to David M. Hayne, ed., *Dictionary of Canadian Biography* (Toronto: University of Toronto Press, 1966–) (hereafter cited as *DCB*).

7. Reuben Gold Thwaites, ed., *The Jesuit Relations and Allied Documents: Travels and Explorations of the Jesuit Missionaries in New France, 1610–1791* (Cleveland: Burrows Brothers, 1896–1901), 46:207 (hereafter cited as *Jesuit Relations*).

8. For the most complete discussion of Iroquoian captivity and adoption as slavery, as well as summaries of the controversy in the historical and anthropological literature, see William A. Starna and Ralph Watkins, "Northern Iroquoian Slavery," *Ethnohistory* 38 (1991), 34–57, and Roland Viau, *Enfants du néant et mangeurs d'âmes: Guerre, culture et société en Iroquoisie ancienne* (Montréal: Boréal, 1997), esp. 137–99. To date no one has thoroughly analyzed the status of captives among the nations of the western Great Lakes and upper Mississippi valley.

9. The best annotated publication of the Code is Robert Chesnais, ed., *Le Code noir* (Paris: L'esprit frappeur, 1998), which includes both the 1685 code, intended for the Caribbean, and the 1724 version governing Louisiana.

10. For the Pacific Northwest, see Leland Donald, *Aboriginal Slavery on the Northwest Coast of North America* (Berkeley: University of California Press, 1997), esp. 69–102, 255–71.

11. Pierre Boucher, *Histoire veritable et naturelle des moeurs and productions du pays de la Nouvelle France, vulgairement dite le Canada* (Paris: Chez Florentin Lambert, 1664), 123–24. For Boucher's life, see Raymond Douville, "Pierre Boucher," *DCB*, 2:82–87. For the Iroquois, see also *Jesuit Relations*, 46:31–33, 51:79. For the Illinois, see *Jesuit Relations*, 66:273–75, and "Memoir of De Gannes [Deliette] Concerning the Illinois Country," in Theodore Calvin Pease and Raymond C. Werner, eds., *The French Foundations, 1680–1693*, vol. 23 of *Collections of the Illinois State Historical Library* (Springfield: Illinois State Historical Library, 1934), 381 (hereafter cited as Deliette, Memoir; *Collections of the Illinois State Historical Library* is cited as Ill. Hist. Coll. with identifying information about the document). Historians have generally accepted the contention, made by the editor of this volume, that the author of this memoir was Pierre Deliette, a French commander of the Illinois country in the 1720s and 1730s who lived among the Illinois in the 1680s. I follow this tradition here, although there is a strong possibility that the author was Louis de Gannes, who also spent much of his early career

among the Illinois. While the Illinois never constituted a single nation, I use the term "Illinois" throughout to signify the grouping of linguistically and culturally related villages that the French called the "Illinois confederacy." For the best summaries of divisions among the Illinois, see Charles Callender, *Social Organization of the Central Algonkian Indians*, Milwaukee Public Museum Publications in Anthropology no. 7 (Milwaukee: Milwaukee Pubic Museum, 1962); Susan Sleeper-Smith, *Indian Women and French Men: Rethinking Cultural Encounter in the Western Great Lakes* (Amherst MA: University of Massachusetts Press, 2001), 11–22; and Hinderaker, *Elusive Empires*, 10–11.

12. Deliette, Memoir, 383; and *Jesuit Relations*, 45:183.

13. *Jesuit Relations*, 67:173. Rale speculated that the Illinois adopted these cruelties only after their similar treatment as captives of the Iroquois: "It was the Iroquois who invented this frightful manner of death, and it is only by the law of retaliation that the Illinois, in their turn, treat these Iroquois prisoners with an equal cruelty." See *Jesuit Relations*, 67:173–75. This statement should be assessed cautiously, however, as the French frequently minimized the violence of their allies and exaggerated that of the Iroquois. A report of 1660 describing French-allied Indians tearing out fingernails, cutting off fingers, and burning hands and feet at Quebec, for example, was dismissed by a French observer as "merely the game and diversion of children"; *Jesuit Relations*, 46:85–101, quotation on 93.

14. *Jesuit Relations*, 50:39.

15. *Jesuit Relations*, 45:257–61. For the best description of Iroquoian disfiguration, see Viau, *Enfants du néant*, 172–86, and Starna and Watkins, "Northern Iroquoian Slavery," 43–45. For additional examples among the western Great Lakes nations, see *Jesuit Relations*, 67:171–75.

16. Viau, *Enfants du néant*, 150; Starna and Watkins, "Northern Iroquoian Slavery," 47–49.

17. Frederic Baraga, *A Dictionary of the Ojibway Language* (St. Paul MN: Minnesota Historical Society Press, 1992), 1:232, 2:56; C. Douglas Ellis, *âtalôhkâna nêsta tipâcimôwina: Cree Legends and Narratives from the West Coast of James Bay* (Winnipeg: University of Manitoba Press, 1995), 85, 159, 449. Variant spellings include "awakân" and "awahkaan."

18. Diane Daviault, ed., *L'algonquin au XVIIe siècle: Une édition critique, analysée et commentée de la grammaire algonquine du Père Louis Nicolas* (Sainte-Foy, Québec: Presses de l'Université du Québec, 1994), 5, 34, 106–7; *Jesuit Relations*, 57:269, 279, 283, 289. For a corresponding Cherokee example, see Theda Perdue, *Slavery and the Evolution of Cherokee Society, 1540–1866* (Knoxville: University of Tennessee Press, 1979), 3–18.

19. Alexander Henry, *Travels and Adventures in Canada and the Indian Territories between the Years 1760 and 1770* (New York: I. Riley, 1809), 307.

20. Deliette, Memoir, 384. For a similar process among the Iroquois, see Daniel K. Richter, *The Ordeal of the Longhouse: The Peoples of the Iroquois League in the Era of European Colonization* (Chapel Hill: University of North Carolina Press, 1992), esp. 50–74.

21. See Richter, *Ordeal of the Longhouse*, 50–74; Viau, *Enfants du néant*, 137–60; and Claude Charles Le Roy, Bacqueville de la Potherie, *History of the Savage People Who Are Allies of New France*, in Emma Helen Blair, ed. and trans., *The Indian Tribes of the Upper Mississippi Valley and Region of the Great Lakes*, vol. 2 (Lincoln: University of Nebraska Press, 1996), 36–43.

22. Richter, *Ordeal of the Longhouse*, esp. 67–68, and Gordon M. Sayre, *Les Sauvages Américains: Representations of Native Americans in French and English Literature* (Chapel Hill: University of North Carolina Press, 1997), 248–304. For Illinois social structure, see Sleeper-Smith, *Indian Women and French Men*, esp. 1–37, where she indicates the importance of women to the integration of outsiders into Illinois kin structures. For a similar captive selection process among the Indians of the Southwest, see Brooks, *Captives and Cousins*, esp. 1–40.

23. The French used two words to describe the Indian practice of raising the dead: "*ressusciter*" and "*remplacer*." *Ressusciter* meant to revive, to bring back to life, or to resurrect. French missionaries used this word to describe the resurrection of Jesus, and seventeenth-century French dictionaries indicate the latter meaning as the most common use of the word. *Dictionnaire de l'Académie Française* (Paris: Académie français, 1694), s.v. "ressus-citer." The second, *remplacer*, merely meant to replace, indicating the practice of replacing a dead relative with a live captive.

24. In general, see Sayre, *Les Sauvages Américains*, 283–96. For the Iroquois, see Richter, "War and Culture: The Iroquois Experience," *William and Mary Quarterly*, 3rd series, 40 (1983), 533–37; Richter, Ordeal of the Longhouse, 30–74; and Starna and Watkins, "Northern Iroquoian Slavery," 38–40. For the Ottawa and other western nations, see Richard White, *The Middle Ground: Indians, Empires, and Republics in the Great Lakes Region, 1650–1815* (Cambridge: Cambridge University Press, 1991), esp. 75–82. For the Illinois, see *Jesuit Relations*, 67:173, and Deliette, Memoir, 376.

25. For the most detailed discussion of the distinctions between gifts to "cover the dead" and mourning wars to "raise up the dead," see White, *Middle Ground*, 75–82, quotations on 77. For "cover the graves," see *Jesuit Relations*, 56:175, and Alan Taylor, "Covering the Grave: The Diplomacy of Murder in Upper Canada," paper presented at annual meeting, Society for Historians of the Early American Republic, Baltimore, July 2001.

26. Antoine Denis Raudot, "Memoir Concerning the Different Indian Nations of North America," in W. Vernon Kinietz, ed., *The Indians of the Western Great Lakes* (Ann Arbor: University of Michigan Press, 1965), 339–410, quotation on 360.

27. *Jesuit Relations*, 54:227.

28. For "here is my son," see *Jesuit Relations*, 59:121; for "I bring you my flesh," see Dubuisson, "Official Report . . . 1712," in Ruben Gold Thwaites, ed., *Collections of the State Historical Society of Wisconsin*, vol. 16 (1902), 282 (hereafter these collections cited as Wis. Hist. Coll. with identifying information about the document cited). For another example of captives given to forge an alliance, see Nicolas Perrot, *Mémoire sur les moeurs, coustumes et relligion des sauvages de l'Amérique Septentrionale*, in Wis. Hist. Coll., 16:30–31, and La Potherie, *Histoire de l'Amérique Septentrionale*, in Wis. Hist. Coll., 16:46.

29. White, *Middle Ground*, 75–82.

30. La Potherie, *Histoire de l'Amérique Septentrionale*, in Wis. Hist. Coll., 16:46.

31. Perrot, *Mémoire*, in Wis. Hist. Coll., 16:30–31. More than anyone else, the Sioux seem to have released captives as a strategy of ingratiating themselves to potential allies. According to Antoine Denis Raudot, "They generally send back any prisoners they make, in hope of obtaining peace; and it is only after they have lost a great many of their men and are tired of sending back prisoners without obtaining the result hoped for, that they burn them. They never torture them"; Raudot, "Memoir," 378.

32. Richter, "War and Culture," esp. 531.

33. *Jesuit Relations*, 54:93–95.

34. Louis Armand de Lom d'Arce, baron de Lahontan, *New Voyages to North America* (London: H. Bonwicke, 1703), 1:58, 62, 105, 2:51–53. Given Lahontan's stated intent to use Indians' egalitarianism as a foil to criticize European hierarchy, his description of slavery among western Algonquians is especially telling. If anything, such an admission subverted his ideological agenda. For Lahontan's ideology and motives, see Paola Basile, "Lahontan et l'évolution moderne du mythe du 'bon sauvage'" (MA thesis, McGill University, 1997). For tasks assigned to slaves, see *Jesuit Relations*, 54:93–95, and Lahontan, *New Voyages to North America*, 1:53, 2:2, 24, 37, 46.

35. "La Salle on the Illinois Country, 1680," *Ill. Hist. Coll.*, 23:10.

36. *Jesuit Relations*, 54:105, 60:185–87, 62:55–107.

37. *Jesuit Relations*, 59:127, 67:171.

38. "The Journey of Dollier and Galinée, 1669–1670," in Louise Phelps Kellogg, ed., *Early Narratives of the Northwest, 1634–1699* (New York: Charles Scribners' Sons, 1917), 167. Kellogg uses the word "tribe" instead of "nation" in her translation, but I have retained "nation" from the French original ("d'une nation fort esloignée du Sud-Ouest"). See "Récit de ce qui s'est passé de plus remarquable dans le voyage de MM. Dolleir et Gallinée (1669–1670)," in Margry, *Découvertes et établissements*, 1:112.

39. "Journey of Dollier,"181–82, 190. Although Dollier, like many other French observers, designated almost all Indian captives as "slaves," his description of these particular captives indicates that they were not destined for adoption, but given as tokens of alliance.

40. *Jesuit Relations*, 54:177, 191, translation modernized.

41. Jacques Marquette and Louis Jolliet, *Voyage et découverte de quelques pays et nations de l'Amérique septentrionale* (Paris: Chez Estienne Michaliet, 1681), 21. Translation from *Jesuit Relations*, 59:127.

42. Margry, *Découvertes et établissements*, 2:324; cited in Mildred Mott Wedel, "The Identity of La Salle's Pana Slave," *Plains Anthropologist* 18 (1973), 204.

43. Map reprinted in Kellogg, ed., *Early Narratives of the Northwest*, 342. The authoritative discussion of the etymology and historical usage of the term "Pawnee" is Douglas R. Parks, "Pawnee," in Raymond J. DeMallie, ed., *Plains*, vol. 13 of *Handbook of North American Indians* (Washington DC: Smithsonian Institution, 2001), pt. 1, 515–47, and William W. Newcomb Jr., "Wichita," in Raymond J. DeMallie, ed., *Plains*, vol. 13 of *Handbook of North American Indians* (Washington DC: Smithsonian Institution, 2001), pt. 1, 548–66. I thank Douglas Parks for providing me with advance copies of these articles.

44. La Potherie, *History*, in Blair, *Indian Tribes*, 2:36.

45. Deliette, Memoir, 387.

46. Wedel, "Identity of La Salle's Pana Slave," 204–5.

47. "Le Sueur's Voyage up the Mississippi [1700]," *Wis. Hist. Coll.*, 16:192, spelling modernized.

48. Trudel, *Dictionnaire des esclaves*, 340. For quotation, see "Mémoire du sieur Greyselon Du Lhut adresséà Monsieur le Marquis de Seignelay [c. 1682]," in Margry, *Découvertes et établissements*, 6:21.

49. See Margry, *Découvertes et établissements*, 6:21, and Yves F. Zoltvany, "Daniel Greysolon Dulhut," *DCB*, 2:262. Dulhut also purchased one captive from the Miamis to serve as a guide and translator, though no record survives indicating the origin of the slave or the price Dulhut paid for him. See "Lettre du sieur Du Lhut à M. le Comte de Frontenac, le 5 Avril 1679," in Margry, *Découvertes et établissements*, 6:29.

50. Dulhut to Minister, Apr.12, 1684, in Wis. Hist. Coll., 16:114–25, quotation on 123. For a complete discussion of the origins and outcome of this controversy, see White, *Middle Ground*, 77–80, although White underestimates the breach Dulhut's actions created within the alliance, treating the episode as an example of successful compromise on the middle ground.

51. La Potherie, *History*, in Blair, *Indian Tribes*, 2:24. The comparison between the French enslaving Indians and domesticating cattle was linguistically apt, as the Ottawa used the same word for "slave" and "domesticated animal." See discussion of "*awahkân*" above.

52. There is, at least, no record of Dulhut receiving, buying, or selling an Indian captive following the 1684 incident.

53. For the 1689 authorization, see La societé historique de Montréal, *Memoires et documents relatifs a l'histoire du Canada* (Montréal: La societé historique de Montréal, 1859), 1–3.

54. See Trudel, *Dictionnaire des esclaves*, 127, and Raymond Douville, "François Provost," *DCB*, 2:532–33.

55. For baptism, see Trudel, *Dictionnaire des esclaves*, 65. For Vinsenne, see Zoltvany, "Jean-Baptiste Bissot de Vinsenne," *DCB*, 2:68; *Jesuit Relations*, 70:316n40; "Letter of Count de Pontchartrain to Governor de Vaudreuil," June 9, 1706, *Wis. Hist. Coll.*, 16:228, text and note 2; and Edmond Mallet, *Le Sieur de Vincennes: Fondateur de l'Indiana* (Levis: Bulletin des recherches historiques, 1897), 4–6. For consistency, I have used the spelling of the *DCB*, "Vinsenne," rather than the more widely recognized "Vincennes." On the Mascoutens raiding the Iowa, see La Potherie, *History*, in Blair, *Indian Tribes*, 2:89.

56. For Fézeret's trade with the Ottawa, see "Transport à René Fezeret . . . d'un conge . . . portant permission d'aller traiter aux Sauvages outaouais et autres nations," Sept. 10, 1694, Archives Nationales, MG8, C 8, Congés et permis enregistrés à Montréal. See also Trudel, *Dictionnaire des esclaves*, 79.

57. Baptism dated Sept. 19, 1700, in Gaëtan Morin, ed., *RAB du PRDH* (CD-ROM), record no. 42253 (hereafter cited as *RAB*, with identifying information about the record in question). This CD-ROM comprises more than 700,000 entries drawn from Catholic Church and civic records of New France and early Canada before 1800. It is an improved and expanded version of an earlier printed collection, *Programme de Recherche en Démographie Historique, Répertoire des actes de bap-tême, mariage, sépulture, et des recensements du Québec ancien*, 47 vols. (Montréal: Presses de l'Université de Montréal, 1980–1990). The most efficient way to locate individual records on the CD-ROM is by "numéro," or record number, which I cite for the reader's convenience. I also cite the record type and date to facilitate location in the print version.

58. For the most comprehensive treatment of the 1701 treaty, see Gilles Havard, *The Great Peace of Montreal of 1701: French-Native Diplomacy in the Seventeenth Century*, trans. Phyllis Aronoff and Howard Scott (Montréal: McGill-Queens University Press, 2001). This is a translated and substantially revised version of Havard's earlier book, *La Grande Paix de Montréal de 1701: les voies de la diplomatie franco-amérindienne* (Montréal: Recherches amérindiennes au Québec, 1992). For other studies of the 1701 peace conference, see J. A. Brandão and William A. Starna, "The Treaties of 1701: A Triumph of Iroquois Diplomacy," *Ethnohistory* 43 (1996), 209–44; Daniel K. Richter, "Cultural Brokers and Intercultural Politics: New York-Iroquois Relations, 1664–1701," *Journal of American History* 75 (1988), 40–67; Anthony F. C. Wallace, "Origins of Iroquois Neutrality: The Grand Settlement of 1701," *Pennsylvania History* 24 (1957), 223–35; and *Recherches amérindiennes au Québec* 31 (Spring 2001), a special issue commemorating the tercentennial of the treaty. For the specific problems mentioned here, see also Richter, *Ordeal of the Longhouse*, 214–35, and Brandão, *"Your fyre shall burn no more": Iroquois Policy toward New France and its Native Allies to 1701* (Lincoln: University of Nebraska Press, 1997), 126–29.

59. La Potherie, *Histoire de l'Amérique septentrionale* (Paris: Chez Jean-Luc Nion et François Didot, 1722), 4:209–10. Portions of La Potherie's work appear in two English translations; see notes 21 and 28 above.

60. Joseph Marest to La Mothe Cadillac, Oct. 8, 1701, in *Wis. Hist. Coll.*, 16:207.

61. For an English translation of 1701 treaty text, see Havard, *Great Peace*, appendix 3, quotation on 211. For Callière demanding Iroquois prisoners of his allies, see La Potherie, *History*, in *Wis. Hist. Coll.*, 16:201.

62. "Paroles des Outaouais de Michilimackinac," Aug. 23, 1705, C11A, 22:255–55 V.

63. "Talk of Marquis de Vaudreuil with the Sonnontouans," Sept. 4, 1706, Michigan

Pioneer and Historical Society, *Historical Collections* 33 (Lansing MI: Michigan Pioneer Historical Society, 1904), 285–87, spelling modernized.

64. "Speeches of the Outaouaes of Misilimakinac," Sept. 27, 1703, *Wis. Hist. Coll.*, 16:223.

65. Zoltvany, "Philippe de Rigaud de Vaudreuil," *DCB*, 2:565–74.

66. "Letter of Count de Pontchartrain to Governor de Vaudreuil," June 9, 1706, *Wis. Hist. Coll.*, 16:228–29.

67. "Lettre de Vaudreuil et Raudot au ministre," Apr.28, 1706, CIIA, 24:3–6.

68. "Instructions de Vaudreuil à Jean-Paul Legardeur de Saint-Pierre," July 6, 1707, CIIA, 26:65–68. For quotation, "Réponse de Vaudreuil aux Onontagués," Aug.17, 1707, CIIA, 26:87–93.

69. "Louis XIV to M. de Vaudreuil," June 30, 1707, in E. B. O'Callaghan, ed., *Documents Relative to the Colonial History of the State of New York*, 15 vols. (Albany: Weed, Parsons, and Co., 1853–1887), 9:808–9.

70. "Lettre de Vaudreuil et des intendants Raudot au minister," Apr. 30, 1706, CIIA, 24:8–9. For other efforts to obtain the promised slaves, see CIIA, 24:3–6, and CIIA, 28:212–16.

71. "Letter of Count de Pontchartrain to Governor de Vaudreuil," June 9, 1706, *Wis. Hist. Coll.*, 16:229, for Versailles; "Instructions de Vaudreuil à Jean-Paul Legardeur de Saint-Pierre," July 6, 1707, CIIA, 26:65–68 for quotation.

72. For Dudley and Vaudreuil, see John Demos, *The Unredeemed Captive: A Family Story from Early America* (New York: Vintage Books, 1994), 79–99.

73. For the best explanation of "redeeming" in this period, see Emma Lewis Coleman, *New England Captives Carried to Canada between 1677 and 1760 during the French and Indian Wars* (Portland ME: Southworth Press, 1925), 1:69–129. For efforts to trade Indian for English captives, see Demos, *Unredeemed Captive*, esp. 85–86.

74. Trudel, *Dictionnaire des esclaves*, 138, 402; Douville, "Provost," *DCB*, 2:532–33.

75. Trudel, *Dictionnaire des esclaves*, 78, 267.

76. Trudel, *Dictionnaire des esclaves*, 274; André Vachon, "Jacques Barbel," *DCB*, 2:42–44.

77. Trudel, *Dictionnaire des esclaves*, 56–57, 327; "Liste apostillée des conseillers au Conseil supérieur de Québec," CIIA, 125:322–24.

78. For Vaudreuil's slave, see Trudel, *Dictionnaire des esclaves*, 407; for Vaudreuil's interest in the illegal fur trade, see "Summary of an Inspection of the Posts of Detroit and Michilimackinac, by d'Aigremont," Nov. 14, 1708, *Wis. Hist. Coll.*, 16:259. For La Découverte, see Albertine Ferland-Angers, "Pierre You de la Découverte," *DCB*, 2:672–73. For La Découverte's connection with the illegal fur trade, see trial beginning Sept. 10, 1707, Jurisdiction of Montreal, Archives Nationales du Québec-Montréal (ANQ-M), file 020–1047. The French minister of marine labeled La Découverte an "arrant trader," accusing him of trading illegally in the West and hinting that Vaudreuil had turned a blind eye to his dealings. See "Letter of Count de Pontchartrain to Governor de Vaudreuil," June 9, 1706, *Wis. Hist. Coll.*, 16:231–32.

79. D'Youville's honorary title, "de La Découverte," signified his participation in La Salle's discovery of the mouth of the Mississippi River. For his continued relationship with Tonty and La Forest, as well as his presence in the Illinois country, see "La Forest Sells Half-interest to Accault, April 19, 1693," *Ill. Hist. Coll.*, 23:264–66. In 1694, d'Youville fathered a child by a Miami woman, moving sometime before the end of the decade to Montreal; Ferland-Angers, "You de la Découverte," *DCB*, 2:672–73.

80. *RAB*, 42745, 10 May 1704. Several Illinois, Miami, and Ottawa warriors banded

together to raid the "Ozages and the Kanças" just before La Decouverte acquired Pascal, making his origin among one of those two peoples likely. See La Potherie, *History*, in *Wis. Hist. Coll.*, 16:157.

81. For the most complete treatment of the Carolina Indian slave trade, see Alan Gallay, *The Indian Slave Trade: The Rise of the English Empire in the American South, 1670–1717* (New Haven: Yale University Press, 2002), esp. 288–314. Gallay estimates that from 1670 to 1715, as many as 51,000 Indian slaves passed through South Carolina, although this number does not include those arriving from the Illinois country. See Gallay, *The Indian Slave Trade*, 299 (Table 2). See also James H. Merrell, *The Indians' New World: Catawbas and Their Neighbors from European Contact through the Era of Removal* (Chapel Hill: University of North Carolina Press for the Institute of Early American History and Culture, 1989), 36–37, and J. Leitch Wright Jr., *The Only Land They Knew: American Indians in the Old South* (Lincoln: University of Nebraska Press, 1999; orig. pub. 1981), esp. 126–50.

82. Richebourg Gaillard McWilliams, ed. and trans., *Fleur de Lys and Calumet: Being the Pénicaut Narrative of French Adventure in Louisiana* (Baton Rouge: Louisiana State University Press, 1988), 122–23, translation modernized. For similar charges a few years later, see "Letter of Ramezay and Bégon to French Minister; dated Nov. 7, 1715," *Wis. Hist. Coll.*, 16:331–32.

83. For the best treatments of French trade into Carolina between 1700 and 1710, see Hinderaker, *Elusive Empires*, 35; Verner W. Crane, "The Tennessee River as the Road to Carolina: The Beginnings of Exploration and Trade," *Mississippi Valley Historical Review* 3 (1916), 3–18; and Crane, "The Southern Frontier in Queen Anne's War," *American Historical Review* 24 (1919), 379–95.

84. "Lettre de Callière et Beauharnois au ministre," Nov. 3, 1702, C11A, 20:56–78. See also Crane, "Road to Carolina," 16–17. For broader French involvement in the Carolina trade at this time, see Galley, *Indian Slave Trade*, 308–12.

85. McWilliams, ed. and trans., *Fleur de Lys and Calumet*, 122–23.

86. "Ordonnance concernant les Panis."

87. Trudel, *Dictionnaire des esclaves*.

88. David Geggus, "The French Slave Trade: An Overview," *William and Mary Quarterly*, 3rd series, 58 (2001), 119–38, esp. Table 1 on 135.

89. Peter N. Moogk, "Reluctant Exiles: Emigrants from France in Canada before 1760," *William and Mary Quarterly*, 3rd series, 46 (1989), 463–505. See also Moogk, *La Nouvelle France*, 87–120.

90. See Gabriel Debien, "Engagés pour le Canada ou XVIIe siècle vus de La Rochelle," *Revue d'histoire de l'Amérique française* 6 (1952–1953), 177–220.

91. "Resumé des rapports du Canada avec les notes du ministre," 1689, in *Collection de manuscrits contenant lettres, mémoires, et autres documents historiques relatifs a la Nouvelle-France* (Québec: A. Coté, 1883–85), 1:476.

92. "Mémoire de Messieurs Vaudreuil et Bégon au Ministre," Oct. 14, 1716, *Collection de manuscrits contenant lettres*, 3:21.

93. "Mémoire de Gédéon de Catalogne sur le Canada," Nov. 7, 1712, C11A, 33:210–36, quoted in Zoltvany, ed., *The French Tradition in America* (New York: Harper and Row, 1969), 96.

94. Louise Dechêne, *Habitants and Merchants in Seventeenth-Century Montreal*, trans. Liana Vardi (Montréal: McGill-Queens University Press, 1992), 152–54.

95. "Vaudreuil et Bégon au Ministre," Oct. 14, 1716, in *Collection de manuscrits*, 3:21–22.

96. Robert Louis Stein, *The French Slave Trade in the Eighteenth Century: An Old Regime Business* (Madison: University of Wisconsin Press, 1979).

97. Dechêne, *Habitants and Merchants*, 67–76; for furs, see esp. Table 15.

98. See "Lettre des sieurs Vaudreuil et Raudot au ministre," Nov. 15, 1707, CⅡA, 26:9–49.

99. Dechêne, *Habitants and Merchants*, 67–89, 296, appendix D.

100. I obtained the figure on Montreal's households by comparing the number of Indian slaveholders in Montreal with the number of known households in 1704. For the number of households, I relied on the Adhémar database. The database documents between 248 and 261 households in the town in 1704. With 35 proprietors, this equals a range of 13.4–14.1 percent.

101. François Béland, "Maurice-Régis Blondeau," *DCB*, 5:89–90; "Liste de ceux qui sont montés à Michilimackinac avec Tonty," Oct. 23, 1697, CⅡA, 15:143; "Lettre de Champigny au ministre," Oct. 27, 1698, CⅡA, 16:130–38.

102. For the Blondeau slaves, see Trudel, *Dictionnaire des esclaves*, 282–83. There is no surviving documentation of a slave sale from Blondeau to Lamoureux, but Blondeau seems the most likely supplier of Lamoureux's slave based on their business connections and Blondeau's other slave sales. For Lamoureux's slaves, see Trudel, *Dictionnaire des esclaves*, 358, and trial beginning Feb. 18, 1712, ANQ-M, file 025–1328.

103. "Lettre de Jolliet à Monseigneur de Laval," Oct. 10, 1674, reproduced in Jean Delanglez, *Louis Jolliet: Vie et voyages (1645–1700)* (Montréal: Granger, 1950), 403.

104. For Pierre's life, see Greffe Adhémar, Mar. 6, 1701, ANQ-M, and Trudel, *Dictionnaire des esclaves*, 84. In the 1690s, securing the services of a French laborer in the West cost voyageurs about 350 livres per year, plus provisions. See, for example, "Engagement of Simon to Tonti and La Forest September 13, 1693," *Ill. Hist. Coll.*, 23:283–85.

105. Death of Aug. 5, 1689, *RAB*, 14543 ("extract from a note by Lachine's priest dated 28 Oct. 1694"); Trudel, *Dictionnaire des esclaves*, 23.

106. For Lachine's population, see Eccles, *Canadian Frontier*, 120. For land clearing and servants, see Dechêne, *Habitants and Merchants*, 152–68.

107. For Lorimier, see Peter N. Moogk, "Guillaume de Lorimier de La Rivière," *DCB*, 2:445–46. The most complete record of Joseph's and Marie-Anne's lives is a Montreal court case from 1716. See trial beginning Apr. 9, 1716, ANQ-M, file 033–1893. For the pregnancy and subsequent marriage, see marriage of July 31, 1708, *RAB*, 14373, and Trudel, *Dictionnaire des esclaves*, 25.

108. Trial beginning Apr. 9, 1716, ANQ-M, file 033–1893; Trudel, *Dictionnaire des esclaves*, 25.

109. Marriage of July 31, 1708, *RAB*, 14373. The name "Skaianis" appears with several variant spellings, including Kaianis, Scaianis, Scaiennis, Skaiennais, Skaiennis, Skayanis, and Skianis. I have chosen the spelling that appears most frequently.

110. Adhémar, Oct. 24, 1699, ANQ-M. Quoted in Dechêne, *Habitants and Merchants*, 327n28. See also Trudel, *Dictionnaire des esclaves*, 24.

111. Marriage of Apr. 18, 1706, Lachine, *RAB*, 14366; Trudel, *Dictionnaire des esclaves*, 24; trial beginning Sept. 19, 1715, ANQ-M, file 032–1777.

112. The term "charter generations" comes from Ira Berlin, *Many Thousands Gone: The First Two Centuries of Slavery in North America* (Cambridge MA: Harvard University Press, 1998), 15–92.

113. Skaianis and Joseph appear on many of the same documents between 1708 and 1720, witnessing the baptisms, confirmations, marriages, and burials of family members and friends.

114. Raudot, "Ordonnance concernant les Panis." For the best treatments of slavery in early modern France, see Sue Peabody, *"There Are No Slaves in France": The Political Culture of Race and Slavery in the Ancien Régime* (New York: Oxford University Press, 1996), and Pierre H. Boulle, "In Defense of Slavery: Eighteenth-Century Opposition to Abolition and the Origins of a Racist Ideology in France," in Frederick Krantz, ed., *History from Below: Studies in Popular Protest and Popular Ideology* (New York: Blackwell, 1988), 219–46.

115. Adhémar, June 15, 1709, ANQ-M.

116. Trudel, *Dictionnaire des esclaves*, 419–20.

117. André Vachon, "Marie-Madeleine Jarret de Verchères," *DCB*, 3:308–13. Large holdings like La Pérade's were not the norm, however. Most slaveholders in New France owned only one or two Indian slaves. See Trudel, *Dictionnaire des esclaves*, 265–430.

118. Jonathan Carver, *Three Years Travels through the Interior Parts of North America* (Philadelphia: Joseph Crukshank, 1789), 177. For the ramifications of the Indian slave trade for western Indians, see Rushforth, "Savage Bonds," chapter 3.

119. Carver, *Three Years Travels*, 178. For the transformation of Indians' captive-taking practices, see Rushforth, "Savage Bonds," chapter 5.

11. John Askin and Indian
Slavery at Michilimackinac
E. A. S. Demers

In 1778, Michilimackinac merchant John Askin wrote a letter to Charles Patterson, a prominent Great Lakes fur trader then at Montreal, in which he took Patterson to task for selling his own mixed-race son as a slave to the Ottawas:

Your friends in this quarter have thought themselves very happy to have a dance once a week & entertain their Company with a dish of Tea & humble Grogg during the last winter, whilst you at London [England] could have all your wants & wishes Supplied, as well as your wanton wishes.

A propos now we are on the Subject, there is a Boy here who was sold to the Ottawas, that every body but yourself says is yours, he suffered much the poor child with them. I have at length been able to get him from them on promise of giving an Indian Woman Slave in his Stead—he's at your service if you want him, if not I shall take good care of him untill he is able to earn his Bread without Assistance.[1]

This letter reveals the extent to which slavery was embedded in the domestic and economic relationships of the eighteenth-century Great Lakes. Unlike the Atlantic plantation complex, exchange, captivity, and kinship relations lay at the heart of indigenous slavery in the eighteenth-century Great Lakes. More than a labor system, Indian slavery was basically a family affair with roots in the region's network of French and native villages. These familial arrangements were often quite complex, involving country wives, métis children, legitimate French or métis wives, business associates, and the long reach of clan affiliation and personal obligation.

In the mid- to late seventeenth century, when French traders first began appearing in what they called the *pays d'en haut*, or upper country, comprising the Great Lakes, Ohio River, and upper Mississippi watersheds, they discovered a world where kinship relations dictated the terms of trade. By marrying Indian women, either according to the custom of the country or more rarely in Catholic ceremonies, Frenchmen shed the mantle of strangers and entered into a world where the exchange of gifts or presents marked obligations between individuals and cemented relationships. The furs and trade goods that made up the bulk of this exchange may have been driven by the Atlantic economy; however, the terms largely were dictated by native peoples and the local politics of the interior villages.

Captivity and slavery further complicated these relationships of people in the *pays d'en haut*. Taken as prizes in war or in retribution for the loss of family members, captives generally either faced torture and death, or adoption and potential enslavement. Adoption meant familial obligation for economic survival, and the adoptees' subjection to authority, rather than a modern, Western concept of equality and acceptance.[2] Captives adopted into their captors' families found themselves caught in the web of kinship, even if they never transcended their status as slaves in the household. Because the bulk of slaves adopted into families were women and children, families and clan groups found themselves with excess women whom they could barter to French traders as wives, for the primary purpose of binding the Frenchmen to the family and gaining access to trade goods. The traders lived with their wives' families in the interior villages, and over time, the presence of half-French and half-Indian children transformed the region. It was still an Indian world, where kinship and face-to-face negotiation dictated relations, but the mixed-race population created further opportunities for mediation between cultures, and indeed developed an interior village world of their own. Slavery remained a part of this milieu, both politically and domestically. And, in fact, the gift of a daughter, slave, or other female relation bound the trader to the village through the dual ties of giving and kinship.

By 1760 the Great Lakes borderlands were, while still an Indian world, sites of over one hundred years of culture contact and negotiation, of which slavery had been an essential element. The British, who had long encroached on French and Indian lands in the Ohio valley, viewed the fall of Quebec and loss of Canada as their passport into the established posts and routes of the Canadian and Great Lakes trade. Yet the traders faced difficult odds in establishing themselves. It is not merely because they were newcomers—indeed, they had been known adversaries for over one hundred years—but because they had as yet no entrée that would allow them to trade in the region.

There were fortunes to be made by enterprising British traders who could conduct trade on Indian terms. One of the most successful, John Askin, shrewdly utilized Indian slavery and the establishment of kin ties to forge personal trade networks. A well-connected merchant in the upper country, his activities reveal the multiple ways in which slavery intertwined with the social, commercial, agricultural, and domestic arrangements of the region. While Askin's example cannot be considered representative of every slaveholder, his business and personal records reveal the extent to which slavery permeated the upper Great Lakes, and the possibilities for slave labor within the larger context of the fur trade in the British Empire.

The British conquest of New France and the *pays d'en haut* in the Seven Years' War (1757–1763) had significant impact on the lives of the interior French and Native Americans. Suddenly the tide of English traders that the French had struggled so mightily to contain for over a century poured into the upper country's villages, posts, and towns. The trade stood at the core of the upper country's social organization over the previous century, with French and Indian families growing firmly established in its organization and maintenance.[3]

The animosity of Indians and French often led to violence against the British, who responded in kind. The interruption of trade during the Seven Years' War and the subsequent unrest caused hardship for Indians and interior French, however, and they were eager for its resumption. The British traders were handicapped in not having kin status with the fur-trading families, and not having a knowledge of local trade protocols.

When John Askin arrived in the 1760s at L'Arbre Croche, an Ottawa town and Jesuit mission adjacent to Michilimackinac, he found himself in the difficult position of unconnected outsider, but he recognized that his trading success depended on establishing kin ties with local Indians.

Since its inception, Michilimackinac's fate utterly depended on its connections to local Ottawa communities and families. The word "ottawa" (also "odawa" or "adawa") meant "trader," and the Ottawas had created a niche for themselves as such, long before contact with Europeans, particularly between Hurons and Ojibwas.[4] The French referred to the Ottawas as the people of the "raised hair," and used the term to refer to at least four related groups, the Kiskakons, Sinagos, Sables, and the Nassauaketons, who were also known as "people of the fork."[5] Individual Ottawa families owned their own hunting lands and trade routes, as well as the trading relationships along those routes, which "could be used only by the family who pioneered [the routes] and who maintained the gift exchange and kinship ties" that went with them.[6] After the arrival of the French, the Ottawas traded corn and craft pieces to the Ojibwas in exchange for furs, which they then traded to the Hurons who passed the pelts on to the French. By 1650, Ottawas began trading with the French without intermediaries, but by 1700 their prominence in the trade declined, as French middleman traders—*coureurs de bois*—poured into the west.[7] The end of the Iroquois wars in 1701 allowed for the resumption of trade in the West, while leading to the decline of the old Montreal trading fairs, where Ottawas and other traders had traveled on a seasonal basis. With the peace, French *coureurs de bois* traveled farther and farther west in search of new fur stocks and to stem British expansion into the western trade. During the mid seventeenth century, the Ottawas and Huron Petuns had moved to the Straits of Mackinac, which was "the general meeting place for all of the French traders" in the West.[8] The Indians at the Straits thus became the "provisioners for the fur brigades," and in addition to furs, supplied the French traders with agricultural produce (including corn, peas, beans, and squashes), fish, meat from hunting, and, quite crucially, birch-bark canoes.[9]

The primary Ottawa settlement at Michilimackinac had been on the north shore, near where St. Ignace is today, and comprised around 1,300 people.[10] In 1742 they relocated from the Straits to the villages and mission at L'Arbre Croche (crooked tree), about thirty miles southwest of the fort on the Lake Michigan shore.

L'Arbre Croche held anywhere between 1,500 and 3,000 people during the temperate seasons. Throughout the eighteenth century, the Ottawas raised crops and traded them with the French and British at Michilimackinac for cloth, tools, and spirits.[11] L'Arbre Croche, like other Ottawa villages, was inhabited primarily in the spring, summer, and fall. During the winter, its residents usually traveled farther south to fish and hunt along Lake Michigan's south shore. In the summers, Ottawa women grew corn, beans, squashes, and sunflowers. They made maple sugar in the spring, and visited their relatives during the summer months, throughout the Great Lakes region.[12] However, as their agricultural production became more necessary to the survival of the French posts in the West, many Ottawas took advantage of L'Arbre Croche's milder microclimate to winter-over.[13]

Gift giving, kin networks, and reciprocal exchange formed the core of Ottawa relationships. The Frenchmen who wed Ottawa women married more than merely individuals—these ceremonies ensured mutually beneficial relationships between two distinct groups of people, such as different clans. The exchange of native as well as French goods was embedded within these social networks.[14] These types of social concerns controlled all economic success in the Great Lakes, as Askin quickly perceived. In situations where native women refused to marry a British trader, or were not available, the trader had two options: he either retreated to another village or he could attempt to purchase or trade for an Indian slave, with whom he could then live in the community, begin a family, and slowly develop the necessary networks and relationships. Askin chose the latter course.

Born in what is now Northern Ireland, this son of a shopkeeper emigrated to North America in 1758 at the age of twenty-one.[15] Askin first settled in Albany, New York, where he supplied the British Army in the Seven Years' War as a sutler—a civilian provisioner.

395

With the fall of New France, Askin decided to try his luck in the western fur trade and moved to the Mackinac Straits. He formed a partnership with Robert Rogers, the famed British ranger, but mounting debts forced them into bankruptcy with their Albany creditors.[16] Rogers returned to England and left Askin to surrender all of the company's property, as well as his own, to extricate himself from bankruptcy. After escaping from this disastrous partnership in 1771, Askin was free to expand his trading activities at the Mackinac Straits where ultimately he acquired a store, a farm three miles from the fort, a house "in the suburbs," as Askin designated the village growing up outside the walls of the fort, and a farm at the nearby Ottawa village of L'Arbre Croche.

He also served as the deputy commissary and barrack master of the fort in the 1770s.[17] Askin owned several vessels above and below Sault Ste. Marie, essential to his trading and supply ventures.

A 1772 letter from Andrew Graham of the Hudson's Bay Company (HBC), master at York Fort, to the governor and committee of the company in London, mentioned Askin's trading activities in connection with competition from the nascent North West Company based at Montreal and working out of Michilimackinac. These traders, Graham wrote, "all have much influence over the Natives. Particularly Corry & Erskine [Askin], the latter formerly was a great Fur trader above Albany Town, where he became Bankrupt, & afterwards came to Canada where he carries on a large Trade, not less than 500 packs of Furrs annually, when mustered from all Parts." Graham thought that Askin hoped to lure HBC servants into his employ, "not because they want their Service, but because they draw the Natives" from trading with the HBC to their competitors at Michilimackinac. Moreover, like his British trading counterparts, Askin was not above the use of strong liquor to encourage trade, as Graham notes, "I am of the opinion [the Indians] will obey me, if Erskine's New England rum does not prevail."[18]

By attracting seasoned backcountry men into his service, Askin hoped to take advantage of their established connections with Indian families. Men who had lived a number of years in the West most likely had Indian wives and children with whom they lived and traded. These marriages were encouraged by Indians, who viewed such a binding alliance with a trader as assurance of security and prestige.[19]

HBC officers and servants kept country wives, and Askin valued the economic potential in these relationships as a way to compete with the HBC men and strengthen his own trading power, influence, and networks. Even if he proved unsuccessful in hiring HBC servants, he still had vast quantities of rum to fall back on, according to Graham. The French had long utilized brandy in trade, and the incoming British traders, with ready access to West Indian rum via Atlantic and imperial channels, were ready to step into the breach left by the French government in their surrender.

However, the British Indian Department tried to regulate the flow of spirits into the Northwest via price controls and supply restriction, a policy completely ignored by traders such as Askin who competed aggressively for command of the Northwest trade.[20] According to Charles E. Cleland, "the use of 'strong water' . . . reached unprecedented proportions during the last quarter of the eighteenth century. The traders justified its use by citing sharp competition between traders and Indian demand. In rum they found the perfect trade good: cheap, addictive, and immediately consumed."[21] The ample supply of rum incited violence and disorder both for traders and Indians, with profound and lasting consequences. Askin's liberal use of rum, referred to by Graham as a potentially disrupting influence over HBC trading relationships and Indian allies, marked him as an aggressive and ambitious trader in a dangerous era.

Rum and sex paved the way for Askin's success. Possessing valuable trade goods without the connections that sexual relations with an Indian partner provided would lead to failure. The documentary record is unclear on Askin's purchase of—and relationship with—Manette (or Monette), although there is evidence he probably bought her from René Bourassa, an influential Michilimackinac trader.[22] Records of how much Askin paid for her, or in what currency, have been lost, and very little is known about her identity, except that she seems to have been a member of the Ottawa community at L'Arbre Croche.[23] Manette bore Askin three children: John Jr., born at L'Arbre Croche in early 1762; Catherine, later the same year; and Madelaine, in 1764. In 1766 Askin manumitted Manette, at which point she disappears from the historical record.

In 1772 Askin married Archange Barthe, the daughter of prosperous Detroit merchant Charles Barthe. She brought to the union a new kin and commercial network that included Barthe, his sons, and their Indian connections as well. Throughout his life, Askin worked tirelessly to expand, strengthen, and combine these familial, business, and political ties through the marriages of his many children. His own marriage to Archange took place when his two oldest children were around ten years old, and his youngest was eight. Around the time of his marriage or before, Askin sent John Jr. to his trading associates to be educated. In 1774 the young Askin was in Schenectady, living with the Ellices of the trading firm Phyn and Ellice, and learning the business in addition to his letters. As Robert Ellice reassured the boy's father, "you many depend that all manner of Care shall be taken of your Son, and put to one of the best Schools in Schenectady, &c. &c."[24] Within six months, Askin Jr. seems to have left New York for Montreal, as Phyn and Ellice wrote his father in January 1775, "we have heard nothing from Mr. Todd respecting your Son."[25] In 1778 Askin Sr. asked James Sterling to send John Jr. back, for "I shall be very glad to see my Boy here, however I don't know if I shall send him back so soon."[26] John Jr. would have been about sixteen years old, and ready to enter business with his father, who planned to take advantage of his son's knowledge of Indian languages, his apprenticeship with the New York and Montreal merchants, and his métis connections.

That same year, Askin also noted the return of his oldest daughter to the family circle. Askin wrote to a friend, "I don't remember if I mentioned to you that I had a Daughter came up from Montreal last year, where she has been for several [years] past in the Nunnery. She was Married this Winter to Capt Robertson, a Match which pleases me well . . . [I hope] perhaps to be a grand father next year."[27] Catherine Askin, known to her family as Kitty, married first William Robertson, the captain of one of Askin's vessels, and second Robert Hamilton, the founder of Queenston, Ontario. Askin seems to have been truly excited both by his daughter's marriage and by the opportunity of being a grandfather. His letters reveal his desire to see his children, particularly his first three, establish themselves in society, and show Askin's conscious decisions to expand his network of family and commerce through fortuitous connections. Never one to miss an opportunity, Askin laid the groundwork well in advance for other advantageous connections as, still flush with Kitty's good news, Askin wrote his friend Sampson Fleming, "I sincerely wish you much joy of your Boy, perhaps he may one Day become my Son in law, I have Girls worth looking at."[28] Askin's correspondence also reveals that he furnished Kitty with a wedding dress as well as other sundries—he provided Isaac Todd and James McGill in Montreal with "an acct of some things for Kitty with directions at Bottom, please send a Seperate acct of them."[29] The youngest of Manette's three children with John Askin, Madeleine, also lived in Montreal for some time during her youth.[30]

A shrewd businessman, John Askin thus utilized several strategies for the growth and development of his affairs in the Great Lakes. He had highly valued items, especially rum to trade, and lured valuable men with experience and native connections into his employ, and he established kin relationships with an Ottawa slave, using his connections with her family and clan as well as with his own métis children to strengthen his influence and position. Manette's status as a slave would have had no impediment to the development of these ties. As part of a complex system of gift and trade exchange, female slaves represented the community's desire to establish links with the new masters of Michilimackinac.[31] Certainly the French government's lack of interest in going back to war for the reclamation of Canada, and the ultimate Indian defeat in Pontiac's War, indicated that the British were in the upper country to stay. Moreover the British government and its traders represented a buffer against American settlers who clamored for lands beyond the Proclamation Line, and who already had a well-established foothold in the Ohio valley. Interior French and Indians, with their complex trading customs and intertwined lifeways, sought to maintain the essence of their culture and ways of doing business in forging tentative ties with the British. Because Askin attempted to enter the Great Lakes trade before Pontiac's War, while many Indians sought the return of the French and the expulsion of the British, he may have been unacceptable as a potential mate, thus the necessity of taking a slave as a country wife or partner.

Askin's treatment of his own mixed-race children stands in sharp contrast to his colleague Patterson's in Montreal. Askin admonished Patterson for selling his own son, from a relationship with an Indian woman, into slavery. Askin proposed to redeem the boy by trading an "Indian Woman Slave" from his own household, reminding Patterson that "every body but yourself says [the boy] is yours." The community's acknowledgment of the child as Patterson's son indicates that the relationship was well known. If slaves could be considered as gifts in terms of reciprocal exchange between Indians and whites, then the Ottawas' offer to sell Patterson's son to Askin may have represented a shift in allegiances between the traders, or an attempt by Askin to bind not only Patterson closer to him, but also the Ottawas from whom he received the boy. The letter also illuminates at least one of the ways in which slaves may have changed hands between whites and Indians. In this case, the exchange of a male child for a female adult suggests that labor needs were not at the core of Indian slavery, but rather the bonds that could be established between both sides through the nature of the exchange.

Certainly the relationship between Patterson and his son was one of estrangement and outright denial. Askin is somewhat vague in his letter as to how the boy became enslaved in the first place. The phrase, "there is a Boy here who was sold to the Ottawas," indicates either that Patterson did not know the fate of his son or that he knew and was either directly responsible or did not care. These particular Ottawas, in fact, may have enslaved Patterson's son in order to send him a very clear and direct message about the trader's relationship with their clan group, perhaps to compensate for unpaid debts or trade goods or as an attempt to bind Patterson—an influential trader in his own right—more closely to them. This latter interpretation is supported by Askin's significant and lengthy efforts to obtain custody of the child.

Ultimately Askin's letter suggests that even among whites, as between whites and Indians, Indian slavery on the Great Lakes borderlands had to do less with chattel and labor and more with the ties of obligation that resulted through the medium of the reciprocal gift, and the resulting obligations and honors conferred when slaves became members of long-established households or clans on either side of the cultural divide.

Yet country marriages were not the only way traders obtained slaves. Garrison towns such as Detroit and Michilimackinac, which played host to the military and other administrative elements of French control as well as traders and merchants, also found in the acquisition of enslaved Indian children the cultural links to the middle ground that they needed, as well as a potential source of labor. The practice of incorporating native children into nominally European households had been interwoven in the fabric of Michilimackinac society throughout the French period. Around 1726, voyageur Pierre Parant and his wife Marianne Chaboillez became permanent, year-round residents at Fort Michilimackinac.[32] The Parant family, their children, and their two Indian slaves lived in the house until the early to mid-1760s when they sold the dwelling to English fur traders Solomon and Levy. The earliest record of the Parants as slaveholders dates from 1755, with the baptism of a twelve- or thirteen-year-old "panis" boy named Pierre-François, described by the Jesuit priest, Father Lefranc, as "an adult . . . sufficiently instructed and well disposed."[33] His godparents were local residents Pierre Monbron, whose panise Charlotte (age fourteen or fifteen and also identified as an adult) was baptized at the same time, and Marianne Chaboillez.[34] By acting as her slave's godmother, Marianne Chaboillez was acting in concert with French colonial customs in New France and the upper country and enfolding the young man into another layer of kin relationships and accountability, on both sides. As godmother, Marianne was responsible not only for Pierre-François' new name and his education, but also for his well-being. By entering this Catholic kin network, Pierre-François placed himself under the aegis not only of his godparents, but of the priests at the mission as well.[35]

The baptism record offers the only clues to Pierre-François' existence, but it suggests some intriguing possibilities. In 1755 Marianne Chaboillez may have had seven children under the age of fifteen, with four of these under the age of ten. It is not known how many of her older children had left home, were married, or still used her home as their residence when at Michilimackinac. Without the older children to help with domestic chores, Marianne may have felt that she needed additional labor in such areas as food production and household maintenance. Since fish was a primary staple at Michilimackinac, it is likely that Pierre-François spent much of his time fishing, hunting for small game, or working in the Parant's garden. He may also have been responsible for the repair of equipment related to these activities.

While it is entirely possible that Pierre-François may have been employed domestically, as was typical for enslaved Native American women and children, he may also have worked with Pierre Parant in some aspects of the voyageur trade. By 1755 the Parants may have been financially more able to procure slave labor. Certainly, "panis" did contract with traders as canoeists on trading voyages, although there is no record that Pierre-François did so. If he did paddle, he also may have been responsible for food preparation, hunting, portaging, and assisting the clerk. If he remained at the fort, repairing equipment, hauling, cleaning furs and hides, and other sundry tasks may have been his daily activities.

It is also not known how long Pierre-François lived with the Parant family, or if they sold him when they quitted their Michilimackinac house in the 1760s. He may have lived in the Parant household for a number of years before his baptism. The priest's indication that he was instructed and well disposed to baptism may be evidence for a significant sojourn with the Parants before this time, or perhaps he was raised in a native Catholic household. It also indicates that, rather than going out into the trading lands with Pierre, he had spent his time at the fort with Marianne. Since she had agreed to instruct another slave as well, then she may also have spent this time with Pierre-François as he worked with her around the house, or in the evenings.

We know even less about the other slave the Parants owned, a young native woman who was both baptized and buried in 1762 at the age of twelve. Her godparents were Sieur Michel Boyer and, again, Marianne Chaboillez, who agreed to instruct the girl before her death. As for Pierre-François, the baptism record is the only evidence of the girl's life. The date 1762 seems significant in terms of the Parant family's labor needs at this stage of the life cycle, and also in terms of the political and social situation at Michilimackinac. By this time most of Marianne's children were adults and had probably left home. Her youngest child, Angelique, was around thirteen years old. Even though her household was smaller, Marianne's domestic labor needs would have remained high, especially in terms of food preparation and laundry. Having a young woman in the house to help gather wood, cook, clean, wash, and tend the garden would have alleviated some of the labor that presumably Marianne's children had performed.[36]

The presence of these two young slaves in the Parant household suggests a master-slave relationship that went beyond mere labor. The ability to move comfortably among both Indian and European peoples was an essential component of fur trade life. In addition to the cross-cultural mixing that naturally occurred via intermarriage and the raising of métis offspring, both captivity and adoption offered opportunities for Indian and white children to gain language skills and cultural familiarity that promoted individual and community success. The presence of so many baptized "panis" children in French homes before 1763 may indicate that captivity among the French shared much in common with captivity among Indians, while smoothing the interactions of both in the frontier exchange economy. By providing "panis" slaves to the French residents of Michilimackinac, the area's Indians conducted an economic transaction, with corn, furs, and canoes, which not only led to profits for both, but fostered closer social relationships and mutual acculturation. As when the French placed young boys in Indian communities to learn native languages to become future cultural brokers, Indian families may have done the same by the sale of "panis."

The collapse of French supply lines and power structures, the "foreignness" of the new British overlords, and the collapse of Pontiac's Rebellion all contributed to the very sudden and drastic reduction in the numbers of Indian slaves baptized at the fort after 1763. Local Ottawa and Ojibwa families may have been completely unwilling to turn their children or young "panis" over to traders neither Catholic nor connected by ties of blood—people with no roots in local families, traditions, and customs. The British were strangers in their language and religion, and had yet to integrate themselves into the established French and Indian communities.

Although local Ottawas and Ojibwas sold fewer slaves to the local traders, slavery did not end in the upper country settlements. As a commodity, slaves never had the economic impact of beaver, raccoon, or deerskin, but were a profitable sideline to other businesses. In the 1730s and 1740s, French traders had sent nearly sixty slaves a year to the markets in Montreal. As W. J. Eccles notes, "most of them appear to have been Panis . . . but many were Sioux, captured by the Ottawa and Cree tribes of the north."[37] La Vérendrye, who actively advocated trading in slaves while he was commander of the far western posts, in what is now Manitoba, reminded his critics of the value of slaves to the Crown, when he asked "should no account be taken of the great number of persons to whom this enterprise means a living, of the slaves that are obtained for the country, and the furs?"[38]

Askin's records do not indicate that he carried on an extensive trade in human cargo, however. Rather slavery seems to have fit into a larger pattern of social and commercial negotiation that took into account his own labor needs as well as his relationship with local Indians and fellow traders. In May 1778, Askin wrote to one of his contacts at Green Bay, named Beausoleil, requesting, "J'aurai besoin de deux jolies Pannisses de 9 à 16 Ans. Ayez la Bonté d'en parler à ces Messieurs de m'en procurer deux" (I shall need two pretty "panis" girls of from 9 to 16 years of age. Please speak to these gentlemen to get them for me).[39] Perhaps the addition of the two young "panis" girls into his household made the older woman superfluous. Askin did not record his intentions in procuring these two girls, whether he intended to keep them as part of his own household or sell them to another trader. The specification that they be pretty suggests their sexual potential as concubines or country wives, in addition to their value as domestic servants. The following month, Askin sold an African American domestic to Philippe Dejean in Detroit, noting, "[M]y family is too numerous to keep her in my house & at present we want Bread more than Cooks."[40] The phrase "we want Bread more than Cooks" indicates

that the sale of slaves generated ready capital for supplies and other necessities. By selling the African American woman and replacing her labor with
two younger, cheaper native girls, Askin realized the economic potential
within chattel slavery by transforming labor into capital, or in this case,
most likely grain.

Askin was not the only trader to deal in slaves. In 1769 Isaac Todd,
one of the founders of the North West Company, wrote a letter to William
Edgar of the Detroit firm Rankin and Edgar, to send him a receipt for "a
Paunee girl named Mano which I purchased from Grosbeck Cuyler and
Glin, last year." Mano (probably the French Manon) had evidently lived
with the trader Groesbeck for four years. Todd hoped to sell Mano back to
Groesbeck, "but he [had] not a farthing in the world."[41] This letter suggests
that Groesbeck may have sold Mano to Todd in order to cover debts, but
wished eventually to redeem her. Indeed, even after making the purchase
Todd allowed Mano to continue to live in Groesbeck's household as a
favor to the other trader. Groesbeck's decision to go "down the country,"
or downriver to Montreal or Albany, however, necessitated Mano's sale
in Detroit. Groesbeck, in fact, had the charge of transporting Mano to
Detroit, and the receipt given was for insurance "for fear of accidents"
along the way, either drowning or escape. Todd notes in the letter that he
"could often have sold her here for the same," but did not, out of respect
for Groesbeck. Although Todd does not explicitly confirm that Mano was
a country wife or other relation, perhaps a daughter of Groesbeck's, the
fact that she continued to live in his house after being sold to Todd, and
that Todd was unwilling to sell her to anyone else other than Groesbeck,
suggests a more intimate relationship. Regardless, unable to buy her back,
Groesbeck allowed Todd to sell Mano at Detroit, and carried her there
himself. Todd's instructions to Edgar further indicate that the latter was
to "dispose of her to best advantage [as] she is a fine girl . . . [who] understands French and English."[42]

Todd's extraordinary efforts in regards to Mano's placement with
Groesbeck reveals the degree to which Indian slavery was deeply embedded in the culture and economy of the British Great Lakes trade. On one
level, Todd and Edgar certainly regarded her as chattel. Todd had assigned

a specific value—£40—to her person, indicating by his statement that he "could often have sold her for the same"; this was not merely a sentimental figure but fair market value. Nevertheless all the parties to the transaction clearly understood that Mano's relationship with Groesbeck transcended that of mere master and slave. Mano had lived with Groesbeck for four years. We do not know how he obtained her, but his extreme reluctance to part with Mano is reflected in Todd's remarkable generosity in arranging for her retention in his home. Only Groesbeck's extreme and hopeless indebtedness induced him to part with her, and by escorting her to Detroit himself, he could try to ensure her future position to the best of his abilities.

As in the French period, Indian slaves thus occupied positions in some English traders' homes, roles that may not have been privileged, but certainly were more akin to native practices of enslavement and adoption, or marriage *á la façon du pays*. Although baptism ceased to be a marker whereby Indian slaves became more integrated into their French families, Todd's letter clearly reveals the retention of interior customs regarding Indian slavery among British traders like Askin and Groesbeck, who had established relationships with Indian women. Moreover these relationships were recognized, sanctioned, and encouraged by their fellow traders who, as Todd's letter to Edgar suggests, understood the importance of such connections, as well as their emotional pull.

The practice of slavery among Europeans in the *pays d'en haut* was akin to that of the Hudson's Bay Company further north, which handed over a departing trader's native wife to an incoming trader through the early decades of the nineteenth century.[43] In both cases market forces altered an older system of enslavement defined mostly by relationships and obligations. By selling Mano to cover his debts, albeit reluctantly, Groesbeck participated in two formerly distinct slavery practices, one informed by interior culture and the other by currency and debt. For Groesbeck, Mano may have been an important and valued member of his household, but by virtue of her sale, she was a chattel slave as well.

In the postscript attached to Todd's letter concerning Mano, he further informed Edgar that "there is Some fine Slaves Expected in a few

Days . . . when I will Try and get a Good one for you & Send him in the Vessell with the . . . other things for you."[44] Slaves thus became another category of procurement. The Mano incident was not an isolated case, but part of a movement of slaves as property mostly from West to East, via traders and their firms, regardless of whether or not those slaves had been members of traders' families. The phrase "some fine slaves expected" meant that slaves were probably not an incidental occurrence in upper country trade, but eagerly sought by traders as commodities for sale.

By 1769 traders had begun to see Indian slaves through multiple facets: first, as country wives or intimate partners, as children, or as other related members of one's house or clan; and second, as chattel. Todd's insistence that he would find a good male slave for Edgar shows the dual nature of Indian slavery as well as differing expectations regarding male and female slaves. Todd's instructions to Edgar regarding Mano were to "[dispose] of her to best advantage." Yet he also promised Edgar a male slave to be sent with some "other things" in a vessel headed downriver. Clearly, the as yet unpurchased male slave and Mano had different roles in Edgar's organization, dictated most likely by gender. In contrast, the male slave seems to have been viewed by both parties primarily as chattel, unlike Mano whose status as "property" complicated her relationship with Groesbeck.

In September 1769, Todd again wrote Rankin and Edgar, "McGill and My own Canoe is Set off for Montreal 5 Days agoe, Shall Reffer you to the Bearer for News of this Metropeleus, he Takes with him 6 [Slaves] he [received] from Finley they [were] such [starved] Misarable Looking Creatures I [would] have nothing to Say to them, he [paid] Deer for them tho its to be in Corn—there has not one Slave Come in Such as you wanted being all Children."[45] Todd was thus also unable to procure for Edgar the adult male slave he requested. Again the dual nature of Great Lakes Indian slavery seems to have frustrated the traders in this instance. As children, Finley's six slaves were part of the older tradition of enslavement and adoption of youths; however, by noting that these children were not the slaves that Edgar depicted, Todd shows that expectations of slaves as chattel and as laborers were beginning to be entrenched in British traders' notions of slavery and its customs and practices. These children were not the "fine slaves expected" by Todd and his associates.

Gender or age alone did not determine whether traders regarded Indian slaves as chattel. A week after posting this letter to Edgar concerning the *panise* Mano, Isaac Todd again turned his correspondence to the slave trade, informing the firm of Dobie and Frobisher, "As Mr. Thomas Finchley is indebted to you Twenty Seven Pounds 10/ York Currency for the Balance of an [account] you will please to pay yourselves the Same out of the proceeds of a panis slave named Charlotte which we have Sent to your address under the Care of Mr. Dowe and the Remainder you will pass to our Credit on [account] of the Corn and Flour you are to deliver us here the next Spring."[46] Slavery thus performed an economic function in upper country life. The sale of Charlotte for an unspecified sum covered Finchley's debts, but also helped pay for the next season's shipment of grain.

Indeed slaves were just as likely to be sold for corn or flour as for York currency. The practice of selling slaves for grain or cash rather than furs illustrates the growing prominence of the corn and carrying trades that supported the northwestern traders, a diversification of economic resources in which John Askin would make his fortune. Slavery and grain seem inextricably linked in the upper country. The British traders saw in the interior slave trade a means to create collateral and subsidiary wealth. In this sense slaves, seemingly a sideline to the larger fur industry, became an essential element of its business model.

On June 17, 1769, Merchants Richard Dobie and Benjamin Frobisher wrote to the firm of Rankin and Edgar, "We sent the last fall to your place a panis Slave to the address of Mr. Thomas Finchley, who informs us that he Sold him to you for Forty pounds York Currency, payable this Spring in Corn or Flour, the former article at present begins to be Scarce here, and as we shall soon have a great number of men on our hands, we shall be in great need of it."[47] On August 9, 1769, Dobie and Frobisher again broached the matter to Rankin and Edgar, "[We] are surprised that Mr. Finchley should refer us to you for the payment of the panis Slave; however your information is Sufficient for Us to drop our Demand against you on that head."[48] Evidently the sale of the male slave (or exchange of debts) was to have elicited a shipment of grain from Detroit to Michilimackinac. As the middleman, Finchley seems to have specialized in brokering slaves between traders and firms, although as the above correspondence reveals, with sometimes imperfect results. The fact that Rankin and Edgar were absolved of covering the forty-pound debt may have meant the loss of a shipment of corn before the advent of winter made navigation impossible. Their inability to cover the cost of the grain through remuneration for the slave meant that Dobie and Frobisher would have needed to go into debt, in lieu of finding other slaves to sell, or other sources of income.

The sale of slaves for grain has broader connotations, as well, within the context of the trade. Voyageurs who wintered with Indians needed vast quantities of corn for their long sojourn with their native families; thus, wintering partners and voyageurs relied on the Great Lakes exchange networks that linked grain, slaves, rum, furs, and other trade goods. The sale of Indian children as slaves at Michilimackinac may have thus been a deliberate strategy on the part of Indians in the West to ensure a steady supply of grain for their voyageurs in the winter months. By selling captive children to the British traders, allied Indian peoples participated in a longstanding practice of barter that wedded gift giving, kinship, and reciprocity with the newer realities of the market.

For the British traders, the exchange or sale of Indian slaves meant not just opportunities for kinship and obligation, but new ways to capitalize or finance the supplies necessary for the maintenance and growth of the trade. Local customs thus worked in synergy with the broader economic demands of the Atlantic economy.

Upper country traders also seem to have regarded the sale of slaves as opportunities to liquidate assets. In 1770 trader William Maxwell wrote to William Edgar from Michilimackinac, "I have since sent you a fine young Pawneese to sell for me—do not sell her for less than £30 and as much more as you can; if you cannot sell her directly and you have no use for her give her to some good woman for victuals. I expect to get leave to come down next summer and I may possible take her down the country with me, but sell her if you can."[49] By sending the young "panise" to William Edgar, Maxwell hoped to take advantage of Detroit's larger community and need for household domestic labor. Yet his specification that she be sold for not less than £30 reveals not only her market value in his eyes, but his willingness to wait for the right price. Rather than have her be idle during the period of sale, Maxwell felt it better to have her employed in domestic work than to take a lower price for her. Moreover his comment that he might take her down country with him to sell her himself, shows his commitment to the price and value rather than the sale.

As with Groesbeck and Mano, Maxwell's insistence on the right price and the right placement—even temporarily—suggests a solicitude beyond the marketplace. His request that she be given to "some good woman" merely for her keep, coupled with his possible plans to take her downriver himself in the summer, indicate the trader's concern for her welfare even more perhaps than his concern for her value. Yet by insisting that she not be sold for less than £30, Maxwell may also have attempted to ensure the girl's future, reasoning perhaps that a man willing to pay the right price would take good care of her.

Regardless of any intimate relationship that may have existed between Maxwell and the young "panise," the Michilimackinac trader found himself making a similar appeal eight years later. In 1778 Maxwell again wrote Edgar, "I send you a little Pawnee wench to sell this winter she is between Charles Morrison and me we have had her a year therefore she is past danger of their first sickness, sell her for 27 or 28 pounds or a little less rather than keep her more if you can get it. You may call her by what name you please she passed by the name of Muchetyweeass."[50] The phrase, "she is between Charles Morrison and me" indicates shared ownership or investment, and it is possible that Muchetyweeass lived in either dwelling at different times. The reference to her "first sickness" indicates that captives from the interior, like captives from Africa, may have undergone a seasoning process that exposed them to European and colonial disease environments. The fact that she had survived her first year in captivity made her more attractive, in Maxwell's eyes, to potential buyers. Yet, in this letter, Maxwell holds less firmly to his price than he did with the "young Pawneese" in 1770. Instead of being willing to have Muchetyweeass live and work in someone's household until the desired price was reached, Maxwell instead suggested an approximate figure and indicated the sale was more important than the price. The phrase, "call her by what name you please" further indicates that Maxwell and Morrison viewed Muchetyweeass more as a commodity than as a valued member of the family. Moreover the retention of an Indian name shows that she was not baptized during her tenure at Michilimackinac, further evidence that the British did not follow the pre-conquest French tradition of baptizing Indian slaves. This represents an additional shift away from a French and Indian model of interior slavery in which baptism forged kinships between masters and slaves. By 1774 the British found the upper country's inclusion in the Quebec Act, which specified Catholicism as Quebec's official religion, to be a disturbing and somewhat unwelcome political trend, even though many traders had Catholic wives and families.[51]

In both 1770 and 1778, Maxwell coupled his directions for the sale of the young women with requests for livestock and new clothes, indicating a possible economic relationship between an Indian slave trade and the purchase of oxen in particular, or other supplies. Maxwell wrote "[I] was glad I did not find the Ox in my letter for that was all I would have had for him, for several people here found an ox in their letters but none in the vessel."[52] Likewise in 1778, he begged "Send me a good Ox if you can get a passage for him apply to Lieut. Archbold as I am not sure of coming down I would like to have something to eat this winter if he is poor he will not have time to mend this fall."[53] Indeed Maxwell desired not just any ox, but one possessed of good health and vigor.

The juxtaposition of the slaves with the oxen, coupled with Maxwell's insistence on a price of approximately £30 for each slave suggests a more-than-passing relationship between the use of Indian slaves as capital for supplies. The link to clothing is perhaps more tenuous, although in each letter Maxwell encloses a caribou skin to be made into breeches. In the 1778 letter he also sends his measurements, adjuring his friend to supply some new breeches — "Do not like nankeen nor stocking very well, but send me something or other." A week later he wrote Edgar again that he would "send no more carraboo skins for they all get broken to pieces."[54]

Indian slaves thus seem to have provided a means by which some traders obtained needed supplies, not through direct barter but through agreed-upon purchase. With the exception of Finley's six sickly enslaved children, however, the brokering of an Indian slave seems to have required a considerable investment in time and resources. Mano had lived with Groesbeck for over four years before unassailable debts to Todd and others forced him to sell her, albeit quite reluctantly, as Todd was reluctant in parting with his friend's property. Maxwell did not mention how long he may have owned the "panise" girl he instructed Edgar to sell in 1770, but in 1778 he noted that Muchetyweeass had lived with Charles Morrison and himself for over a year. He does not allude in his letter to what duties she may have performed or her life with him, yet archaeological investigations at Michilimackinac have suggested some possibilities beyond mere concubinage. Evidence of craft industries, including producing metal goods for the fur trade, sewing, baking, and other activities may have occupied slaves in fort households.[55]

Indian slavery at Fort Michilimackinac existed on several levels of social interaction. Before 1763, Indian slaves were common members of fort society, living in French homes, accepting baptism, having children with traders, and perhaps participating in local craft industries as the archaeological evidence suggests. With the advent of British sovereignty, Indian slavery underwent a radical transformation as significantly fewer French families sponsored their Indian slaves for baptism, indicating that Indians sent far fewer "panis" to French homes. Local native groups thus exerted considerable control over the practice of Indian slavery at the fort. With the arrival of British traders and administrators, British men still needed Indian slaves as country wives or desired them as domestic workers. Though these traders participated in older interior models of slavery, their adherence to the marketplace wrought significant change on the local institutions. By treating Indian slaves as both kin and chattel, British traders created a bridge between interior slavery and its Atlantic counterpart. The increasing use of Indian slaves in exchange for supplies of grain or livestock provided traders with yet another means to capital within the trade economy. In a few short years, Indian slavery transformed from a practice that linked disparate cultures in the borderlands through ties of exchange, obligation, and kinship, to one that served increasingly more economic than social needs. Yet Indian slavery was not completely co-opted by the marketplace. Rather, mercantile correspondence reveals that British traders like Askin and Maxwell had intimate relationships with female slaves even as they used slaves as chattel.

Enslaved Indian children and women continued to appear in traders' records for sale and as domestic servants after 1763, even as the growth of African slavery in the Atlantic economy affected such remote reaches of empire as the Great Lakes. Increasing pressure from Anglo-American land seekers and the geopolitical shifts that followed both the Revolutionary War and the War of 1812 would sound the death knell for Indian slavery in the region, albeit slowly. As the United States and British North America sought to define themselves in opposition to each other, they began to legislate slavery in the region even as they created categories of citizenship and belonging. Prohibitions against slavery in the Northwest Territory and Upper Canada suddenly legislated familial relationships that previously, as Patterson and Askin reveal, had been largely determined by individual desire. Moreover, as southern slavery tightened its grip, people in the region began to view slavery as a black-and-white issue, rather than as a local variation on longstanding interior practice.

Notes

1. John Askin to Charles Patterson at Montreal, June 17, 1778, in Milo M. Quaife, ed., *The John Askin Papers*, 2 vols. (Detroit: Detroit Library Commission, 1928), 1:135 (hereafter referred to as *AP*).

2. William A. Starna and Ralph Watkins, "Northern Iroquoian Slavery," *Ethnohistory* 31, no. 8 (Winter 1991), 34–57.

3. As Great Lakes anthropologist Charles E. Cleland observed, "Without the family connections of the French traders or knowledge of Indian customs, the English were often brutal in their dealings and especially in the use of intoxicants in the trade." Charles E. Cleland, *Rites of Conquest: The History and Culture of Michigan's Native Americans* (Ann Arbor: University of Michigan Press, 1992), 132.

4. Cleland, *Rites of Conquest*, 86.

5. W. Vernon Kinietz, *The Indians of the Western Great Lakes, 1615–1760* (Ann Arbor: University of Michigan Press, 1965), 226.

6. James A. Clifton, George L. Cornell, and James M. McClurken, *People of the Three Fires: The Ottawa, Potawatomi, and Ojibway of Michigan* (Grand Rapids: Michigan Indian Press and Grand Rapids Inter-Tribal Council, 1986), 11; Kinietz, *Indians of the Western Great Lakes*, 237.

7. Clifton, et al., *People of the Three Fires*, 13–14; James M. McClurken, *Gah-Baeh-Jhagwah-Buk (The Way It Happened): A Visual Culture History of the Little Traverse Bay Bands of Odawa* (East Lansing: Michigan State University Museum, 1991), 3.

8. Kinietz, *Indians of the Western Great Lakes*, 245; see also Cleland, *Rites of Conquest*, 96.

9. Cleland, *Rites of Conquest*, 109, 103; Kinietz, *Indians of the Western Great Lakes*, 236, 145.

10. Cleland, *Rites of Conquest*, 103.

11. McClurken, *Gah-Baeh-Jhagwah-Buk*, 4.

12. McClurken, *Gah-Baeh-Jhagwah-Buk*, 46.

13. Susan Sleeper-Smith, *Indian Women and French Men: Rethinking Cultural Encounter in the Western Great Lakes* (Amherst: University of Massachusetts Press, 2001), 75–76.

14. McClurken, *Gah-Baeh-Jhagwah-Buk*, 18–19.

15. The Askins may have been related to John Erskine, 23rd Earl of Mar, who fled to Ireland from Scotland in the early eighteenth century for his part in an unsuccessful revolt against the Crown. John Askin to John Erskine, July 1, 1793, in *AP* I, 477–78; David R. Farrell, "John Askin," *Dictionary of Canadian Biography*, vol. 5 (Toronto: University of Toronto Press, 1983), 37.

16. *AP* I: 43; see also David A. Armour, *The Merchants of Albany, New York, 1686–1760* (New York: Garland, 1986).

17. John Vattas to Askin, July 1774, *AP* I:49.

18. Andrew Graham to Governor and Committee of the Hudson's Bay Company, August 26, 1772, in *Documents Relating to the North West Company*, ed. W. Stewart Wallace (Toronto: Champlain Society, 1934), 40–41, 42.

19. Sylvia Van Kirk, *Many Tender Ties: Women in Fur-Trade Society 1670–1870* (Norman: University of Oklahoma Press, 1983), 29, 42, 47.

20. Cleland, *Rites of Conquest*, 131–32.

21. Cleland, *Rites of Conquest*, 132.

22. This was most likely René Bourassa, an influential Northwest trader whose daughter, Charlotte, married Charles Langlade, a commandant of Michilimackinac and prominent soldier during the Seven Years' War.

23. David A. Armour and Keith R. Widder, *At the Crossroads: Michilimackinac during the American Revolution* (Mackinac Island MI: Mackinac Island State Park Commission, 1978), 35.

24. R. Ellice to John Askin, August 13, 1774, Letterbooks of Phyn & Ellice, Merchants, at Schenectady, NY, 1767–1776, vol. III, 152–53. Buffalo Historical Society (hereafter BHS), Micro. Pub., No. 1, transcription in Colonial Michilimackinac Archives, Mackinaw City, Mich., Askin, John—Affairs, Detroit, card II.

25. January 3, 1775, Letterbooks of Phyn & Ellice, vol. III, 172, BHS, transcription at Colonial Michilimackinaw Archives, Askin—Business Affairs/Quebec Acts, card II.

26. Askin to James Sterling, May 8, 1778, *AP* I:80.

27. Askin to John Hay, April 27, 1778, *AP* I:67–68.

28. Askin to Sampson Fleming, April 1778, *AP* I:79.

29. Askin to Todd & McGill, May 8, 1778, *AP* I: 85.

30. Armour and Widder, *At the Crossroads*, 35–38.

31. Marcel Mauss, *The Gift: The Form and Reason for Exchange in Archaic Societies*, trans. W. D. Halls (1950; repr., New York: Norton, 1990) 73.

32. See Jill Y. Halchin, *Excavations at Fort Michilimackinac, 1983–1985: House C of the Southeast Row House, the Solomon-Levy-Parant House*, Archaeological Completion Report series, no. 11 (Mackinac Island MI: Mackinac Island State Park Commission, 1985), 36, 160; John F. M. Whitaker, *The Functions of Four Colonial Yards of the Southeast Row House, Fort Michilimackinac*,

Michigan, Archaeological Completion Report series, no. 16 (Mackinac Island MI: Mackinac State Historic Parks, 1998), 26, 117, 119.

33. Michilimackinac Baptisms, 30 March 1755, Reuben Gold Thwaites ed., *Collections of the State Historical Society of Wisconsin*, vol. 19, (Madison: State Historical Society of Wisconsin, 1910), 39–40 (hereafter *WHC*).

34. Charlotte's godparents were Louis Gervais and Ciele Cousin et Monbron, *WHC* 19:39–40.

35. For Catholic kin networks, see Sleeper-Smith, *Indian Women and French Men*, 21 and passim.

36. See Laurel Thatcher Ulrich, *A Midwife's Tale: The Life of Martha Ballard, Based on Her Diary* (New York: Vintage/Random House, 1991), on the need for additional domestic help after the children have left home.

37. W. J. Eccles, *The Canadian Frontier, 1534–1760*, rev. ed. (Albuquerque: University of New Mexico Press, 1983), 149.

38. *Journals and Letters of Pierre Gaultier de Varennes de la Vérendrye and his Sons, with Correspondences between the Governors of Canada and the French Court, Touching the Search for the Western Sea*, ed. Lawrence J. Burpee (Toronto: Champlain Society, 1927), 451–52. Indeed, slavery had the potential for tidy profits, if not the vast sums possible in furs. The average price for Indian slaves in eighteenth-century Montreal was 400 livres, and prices ranged anywhere from 120 to 750 livres. African slaves, on the other hand, had a market value of approximately twice that of a native slave. Eighteenth-century average market cost for black slaves was 900 livres, and prices ranged from 200 to 2,400 livres, with young men generally commanding higher prices. Marcel Trudel, *L'esclavage au Canada Français: Histoire et conditions de l'esclavage* (Québec: Presses universitaires Laval, 1960), 116–19. Trudel also notes that one African was roughly equivalent to two "panis," and that among the pool of Indian slaves, those designated as "panis" tended to fetch higher prices; thus, the wide-scale adoption of the term "panis" to designate any Indian slave, may have stemmed from a conscious deception in order to maximize profits from slaving. See Trudel, *L'esclavage au Canada français*, 66; Indian slaves may have commanded lower prices precisely because they were women and children. See Alan Gallay, *The Indian Slave Trade: The Rise of the English Empire in the American South* (New Haven: Yale University Press, 2002), 312–14.

39. Askin to Beausoleil, at Michilimackinac, May 18, 1778, *API*:96–98.

40. "I was favoured with yours of the 24th May last, the Mualtoe Woman shall be disposed off agreeable to your desire so soon as Monsr Cerré or Monsr Degrosolier arrives; my family is too numerous to keep her in my own house & at present we want Bread more than Cooks. I have put her at Mr. Mumforton's at present," Askin to Philippe Dejean, June 4, 1778, *API*:105–6

41. Isaac Todd to William Edgar, Michilimackinac, August 21, 1769, William Edgar Papers, 1760–1812, MG19 A1 vol. 3, T13, National Archives of Canada (hereafter NAC).

42. Isaac Todd to William Edgar, Michilimackinac, August 21, 1769, William Edgar Papers, 1760–1812, MG19 A1 vol. 3, T13, NAC.

43. Jennifer S. H. Brown, *Strangers in Blood: Fur Trade Company Families in Indian Country*, (Norman: University of Oklahoma Press, 1980), 108.

44. Postcript appears in Isaac Todd to Gentlemen, Edgar, William, Letterbook, 1760–1769, Burton Historical Collection, Detroit Public Library, Detroit, Michigan (hereafter BHC). Transcription in Michilimackinac Archives.

45. Isaac Todd to Gentlemen, Edgar, William, Letterbook, 1760–1769, September 8, 1769, 227–230, BHC. Transcription in Michilimackinac Archives.

46. Isaac Todd, Dobie & Frobisher to Rankin & Edgar, Detroit, Edgar, William, August 27, 1769, Letterbook, 1760–1769, BHC.

47. Richard Dobie and Benjamin Frobisher to Rankin and Edgar, Edgar, William, June 17, 1769, Letterbook, 1760–1769, 197–99, BHC. Transcription in Colonial Michilimackinac Archives, Trade—Michilimackinac, card II.

48. Dobie and Frobisher to Rankin and Edgar, Edgar, William, Letterbook, 1760–1769, 220–21, BHC. Transcript in Colonial Michilimackinac Archives.

49. William Maxwell to William Edgar, Michilimackinac, September 25, 1770, William Edgar Papers, 1760–1812, MG19 A1 vol. 3, M115, NAC. Punctuation added for clarity.

50. William Maxwell to William Edgar, Michilimackinac, August 24, 1778, William Edgar Papers, 1760–1812, MG19 A1 vol. 3, M119, NAC.

51. In a letter to Rankin and Edgar, Isaac Todd expressed his frustration with the Quebec Act and noted, "Among other things contained in the Act, I am sorry to tell you that English Laws is abolished and we are to have the Laws of Canada or [blank] in their stead and that the Roman Catholick Religion is the Established Religion for the Province, the English settled here are much alarmed," August 26, 1774, Record Group 36 vol. 9; MG19 A1 Vol. 3, NAC.

52. Maxwell to Edgar, 1770.

53. Maxwell to Edgar, 1778.

54. Maxwell to Edgar, August 27, 1778,

55. See Whitaker, *The Functions of Four Colonial Yards*, passim; see also Lynn L. Morand, *Craft Industries at Fort Michilimackinac, 1715–1781*, Archaeological Completion Report series, no. 15 (Mackinac Island MI: Mackinac State Historic Parks, 1994), passim.

Contributors

Juliana Barr is an associate professor of history at the University of Florida, specializing in the study of women and Indian-European interactions in the Spanish borderlands of North America. She is the author of *Peace Came in the Form of a Woman: Indians and Spaniards in the Texas Borderlands*, and "From Captives to Slaves: Commodifying Indian Women in the Borderlands," *Journal of American History* 92 (June 2005), which represents the beginning of a new book project on Indian and African women's enslavement in the French and Spanish hinterlands of the Mississippi valley.

Jennifer Baszile received her PhD in history from Princeton University in 1999. She currently is an independent scholar.

Denise I. Bossy is an assistant professor of history at the University of North Florida and a recent graduate of Yale University. Her current research project examines the cross-cultural nature of the Indian slave trade in the colonial Southeast. She lives in Atlantic Beach, Florida, with her husband and daughter.

James F. Brooks is an interdisciplinary scholar of the indigenous past, focusing primarily on colonial borderlands. He is president of the School for Advanced Research, in Santa Fe, New Mexico, which he joined in 2002, after holding faculty positions at the University of Maryland and the University of California, Santa Barbara. His books include the multiple-prize-winning *Captives & Cousins: Slavery, Kinship, and Community in the Southwest*

Borderlands (2002); Confounding the Color Line: The Indian-Black Experience in North America (2002), Women and Gender in the American West (2005), and Small Worlds: Method, Meaning, and Narrative in Microhistory (2008). His book Mesa of Sorrows: Archaeology, Prophecy, and the Ghosts of Awat'ovi Pueblo is forthcoming from W. W. Norton in 2009.

E. A. S. Demers has published articles in the Chronicle of Higher Education, Journal of Michigan History, and Southern Historian. She coedited Icons of American Cooking, forthcoming from ABC-CLIO. She is the editor of the journal French Colonial History, and is senior editor for Potomac Books, Inc. She is a PhD candidate at Michigan State University.

C. S. Everett recently finished a dissertation on Indian slavery, at Vanderbilt University. He is author or coauthor of several essays and articles. Currently an independent scholar, for the past eight years he has also served as a consultant for non-federally acknowledged tribes. He lives with his wife and two daughters in Virginia.

Robbie Ethridge, associate professor in the Department of Sociology and Anthropology at the University of Mississippi, is a cultural anthropologist and ethnohistorian specializing in the history of the Indians of the American South. She is the author of Creek Country: The Creek Indians and their World, 1796–1816 (2006) and coeditor of The Transformation of the Southeastern Indians, 1540–1760 (2002), Light on the Path: The Anthropology and History of the Southeastern Indians (2006), and the forthcoming Mapping the Mississippian Shatter Zone: The Colonial Indian Slave Trade and Regional Instability in the American South (2009).

Alan Gallay is Warner R. Woodring Chair of Atlantic World and Early American History at the Ohio State University, where he is also director of the Center for Historical Research. He is author and editor of several books, including The Indian Slave Trade: The Rise of the English Empire in the American South, 1670–1717 (2002).

Joseph Hall teaches early American history at Bates College. He is author of the forthcoming book Zamumo's Gifts: Native-European Exchange in the Colonial Southeast, to be published by the University of Pennsylvania Press.

Margaret Ellen Newell is an associate professor of early American history at the Ohio State University. She received her BA from Brown University and her MA and PhD from the University of Virginia. Her works include *From Dependency to Independence: Economic Revolution in Colonial New England* (Cornell, 1998) and a forthcoming book, tentatively titled *Race Frontiers: Indian Slavery in Colonial New England*, also with Cornell University Press. Her research has received support from the National Endowment for the Humanities, the American Council of Learned Societies, the Huntington Library, and the Massachusetts Historical Society.

Brett Rushforth is assistant professor of history at the College of William and Mary. He is coauthor, with Paul W. Mapp, of *Colonial North America and the Atlantic World: A History in Documents* (Prentice-Hall, 2008), and has published articles in the *William and Mary Quarterly*, *Pacific Northwest Quarterly*, and *Reviews in American History*. He is currently completing a book about Indian slavery in New France, forthcoming from the Omohundro Institute of Early American History and Culture.

Index

Earl of Shaftesbury, 126
Eccles, W. J., 404
Ecueracapa, 322, 336
Edgar, William, 405–11
El Dorado, 17
Eliot, John, 41, 48
Ellice, Robert, 398
Eltis, David, 35
embargoes, 229, 230
encomiendas, 18, 37, 283, 284
England: Abenaki travel to; 35–36;
    Canada and, 393; Cherokee travel
    to, 234, 249n148. *See also* Council of
    Trade and Plantations
English slaves: Africa, 11; Barbados
    and Bermuda, 39
English Civil War, 39
English colonies, 1–2, 5, 7, 12,
    207–50; Cherokees and Creeks
    and, 229; Chickasaws and, 1–2,
    267; sugar and, 18; wars against
    Westos, Yaddos, and Yamasees, 50.
    See also Barbados; Carolina; New
    England; Virginia
English-Dutch rivalry, 71
Epenow, 36
epidemics, 18, 156, 170, 242n67, 285,
    335
Eries, 72, 74, 110, 217, 253
Erskine, John, 414n15
Esaws, 91, 121–22
escaped slaves. *See* runaways
L'esclavage au Canada français (Trudel),
    354
Espinosa, Isidro de, 285
ethnicity: slavery and, 5–6
Ethridge, Robbie, 210
Europeanization. *See* assimilation
European servants, 11, 34, 57
European slaves: North Africa, 11. *See
    also* English slaves
European trade goods, 23, 25, 118,
    157, 158, 208, 219, 236n5; Ocheses
    and, 220

evangelization. *See* Christianization
exchange of Indians and African
    slaves, 43
execution and executions, 36, 45, 80,
    97, 363, 364
exhibition of Native Americans. *See*
    display of Indians
extinction, 258

Fairbanks, Jonathan, 46
Fallam, Robert, 82
fanimingo, 265–67, 275n81
Fattalamee, 218, 263, 266
Fauntleroy family, 103n43
fear of disease, 20, 285
fear of enslavement, 219, 245n98, 364
Felipe II. *See* Philip II
Ferguson, Brian, 259–60
Fernandez de Florencia, Juan, 185,
    189, 195, 197
Fernández de Santa Ana, Benito, 286,
    287, 298, 299
Fézeret, René-Claude, 365
fictive kinship, 192. *See also* godpar-
    ents and godparenthood
firearms. *See* guns
Fischer, David Hackett, 145n77
fishing, 13
Fitch, Tobias, 228, 229, 248n126
Fleming, Sampson, 399
Florencia, Francisco de, 170
Florés, Nicolás, 290–92
Florida, 22, 23, 50, 74, 75, 82;
    Apalachees and, 172; Cabeza de
    Vaca and, 277; Carolina and, 120,
    186; Creeks and, 207; depopulation,
    258; epidemics and, 156; historical
    documents, 102n31; missions, 161;
    slave population, 236n3; Westos
    and, 83. *See also* St. Augustine FL
flour: as payment for slaves, 408
forced labor, 18, 20, 23, 34, 37, 61,
    198–201

DATE DUE
